Communications
in Computer and Information Science   1528

More information about this series at https://link.springer.com/bookseries/7899

Deepak Garg · Sarangapani Jagannathan ·
Ankur Gupta · Lalit Garg ·
Suneet Gupta (Eds.)

Advanced Computing

11th International Conference, IACC 2021
Msida, Malta, December 18–19, 2021
Revised Selected Papers

 Springer

Editors
Deepak Garg
Bennett University
Greater Noida, India

Ankur Gupta
Model Institute of Engineering
and Technology
Kot Bhalwal, Jammu and Kashmir, India

Suneet Gupta
Bennett University
Greater Noida, India

Sarangapani Jagannathan
Missouri University of Science
and Technology
Rolla, CA, USA

Lalit Garg
University of Malta
Msida, Malta

ISSN 1865-0929   ISSN 1865-0937 (electronic)
Communications in Computer and Information Science
ISBN 978-3-030-95501-4   ISBN 978-3-030-95502-1 (eBook)
https://doi.org/10.1007/978-3-030-95502-1

This Springer imprint is published by the registered company Springer Nature Switzerland AG
The registered company address is: Gewerbestrasse 11, 6330 Cham, Switzerland

Preface

The 11th International Advanced Computing Conference (IACC 2021) was organized with the objective of bringing together researchers, developers, and practitioners from academia and industry working in the area of advanced computing. IACC 2021 consisted of keynote lectures, tutorials, workshops, and oral presentations on all aspects of advanced computing. It was organized specifically to help the computer industry to derive benefits from the advances of next-generation computer and communication technology. Researchers invited to speak presented the latest developments and technical solutions in the areas of advances in machine learning and deep learning, advances in applications of artificial intelligence in interdisciplinary areas, reinforcement learning, and advances in data science.

IACC promotes fundamental and applied research which can help in enhancing the quality of life. The conference was held during December 18–19, 2021, to make it an ideal platform for people to share views and experiences in futuristic research techniques in various related areas.

The conference has a track record of acceptance rates from 15% to 20%. More than 12 IEEE/ACM Fellows hold key positions on the conference committee, giving it a quality edge. In the last ten years, the conference's citation score has consistently increased. This has been possible due to adherence to quality parameters for the review process and acceptance rate, without any exception, which allows us to make some of the best research available through this platform.

December 2021

Deepak Garg
Jagannathan Sarangpani
Ankur Gupta
Lalit Garg
Suneet Gupta

Organization

Honorary Co-chairs

Sundaraja Sitharama Iyengar	Florida International University, USA
Sartaj Sahni	University of Florida, USA
Jagannathan Sarangpani	Missouri University of Science and Technology, USA

General Co-chairs

Deepak Garg	Bennett University, India
Ajay Gupta	Western Michigan University, USA
Lalit Garg	University of Malta, Malta
Ankur Gupta	MIET Jammu, India

Program Co-chairs

Kit Wong	University College London, UK
George Ghinea	Brunel University London, UK
Carol Smidts	Ohio State University, USA
Ram D. Sriram	National Institute of Standards and Technology, USA
Sanjay Madria	University of Missouri, USA
Oge Marques	Florida Atlantic University, USA
Vijay Kumar	University of Missouri-Kansas City, USA

Publication Chair

Suneet K. Gupta	Bennett University, India

Technical Program Committee/International Advisory Committee

Sumeet Dua	Louisiana Tech University, USA
Roger Zimmermann	National University of Singapore, Singapore
Shivani Goel	Bennett University, India
Seeram Ramakrishna	National University of Singapore, Singapore
B. V. R. Chowdari	Nanyang Technological University, Singapore
Hari Mohan Pandey	Edge Hill University, UK
Selwyn Piramuthu	University of Florida, USA
Bharat Bhargava	Purdue University, USA
Omer F. Rana	Cardiff University, UK
Javed I. Khan	Kent State University, USA
Harpreet Singh	Wayne State University, USA

Diganta Sengupta	Meghnad Saha Institute of Technology, India
Aarya Patel	Vitrana, India
Supriya Chakraborty	Amity University, Kolkata, India
Mamta Arora	Manav Rachna University, India
Om Prakash Jena	Ravenshaw University, India
Sandeep Singh Sengar	University of Copenhagen, Denmark
Murali Chemuturi	Chemuturi Consultants, India
Madhu Vadlamani	Cognizant, Hyderabad, India
A. N. K. Prasannanjaneyulu	Institute of Insurance and Risk Management, India
O. Obulesu	G. Narayanamma Institute of Technology and Science, India
Rajendra R. Patil	GSSS Institute of Engineering and Technology for Women, India
Ajay Kumar	Chitkara University Institute of Engineering and Technology, India
D. P. Kothari	THDC Institute of Hydropower Engineering and Technology, India
T. S. N. Murthy	JNTUK University College of Engineering, Vizianagaram, India
Nitesh Tarbani	Sipna College of Engineering & Technology, Amravati, India
Jesna Mohan	Mar Baselios College of Engineering and Technology, India
Manoj K. Patel	CSIR, Chandigarh, India
Vishnu Pendyala	San Jose State University, USA
Pravati Swain	National Institute of Technology Goa, India
Manoj Kumar	University of Petroleum and Energy Studies, India
E. S. Gopi	National Institute of Technology Tiruchirappalli, India
Benyamin Ahmadnia	Harvard University, USA
Mithun B. Patil	N. K. Orchid College of Engineering & Technology, India
Priya Saha	Lovely Professional University, India
Sahaj Saxena	Thapar Institute of Engineering and Technology, India
Dinesh G. Harkut	Prof. Ram Meghe College of Engineering and Management, India
Ninoslav Marina	University of Information Science and Technology "St. Paul the Apostle", North Macedonia
Pushpendra Singh	National Institute of Technology Hamirpur, India
Nirmala J. Saunshimath	Nitte Meenakshi Institute of Technology, India
Premanand P. Ghadekar	Vishwakarma Institute of Technology, India
Mayank Pandey	Motilal Nehru National Institute of Technology Allahabad, India
Sudeep D. Thepade	Pimpri Chinchwad College of Engineering, India
Bhupendra Singh Chauhan	GLA University, India
Pimal Khanpara	Nirma University, India
Rohit Lalwani	MIT University of Meghalaya, India

Loshma Gunisetti	Sri Vasavi Engineering College, India
Vishweshwar Kallimani	University of Nottingham Malaysia, Malaysia
Amit Kumar Mishra	DIT University, India
Pawan Whig	Vivekananda Institute of Professional Studies, India
Dhatri Pandya	Sarvajanik College of Engineering and Technology, India
Asha S. Manek	RV Institute of Technology and Management, India
Garima Jaiswal	Indira Gandhi Delhi Technical University for Women, India
Shubham Mahajan	Shri Mata Vaishno Devi University, India
Steve Dantas	CarrierDirect, Bangalore, India
Lingala Thirupathi	Methodist College of Engineering and Technology, India
P. Mahanti	University of New Brunswick, Canada
Shaikh Muhammad Allayear	Daffodil International University, India
Basanta Joshi	Tribhuvan University, Nepal
Bikram Das	National Institute of Technology Agartala, India
Satyabrata Jit	IIT (BHU), India
S. R. N. Reddy	Indira Gandhi Delhi Technical University for Women, India
John Jose	IIT Guwahati, India
Mehran Alidoost Nia	University of Tehran, Iran
Raphael de Aquino Gomes	Federal Institute of Goiás, Brazil
Ambili P. S.	Saintgits Group of Institutions, India
Abhay Kumar Singh	IIT (ISM) Dhanbad, India
M. A. Jabbar	Vardhaman College of Engineering, India
Lokendra Kumar Tiwari	Ewing Christian College, India
Abhay Saxena	Dev Sanskriti Vishwavidyalaya, India
Kanika Bansal	Chitkara University, India
Pooja M. R.	Vidyavardhaka College of Engineering, India
Pranav Dass	Bharati Vidyapeeth's College of Engineering, India
Surender Singh Samant	UPES Dehradun, India
Avani R. Vasant	Babaria Institute of Technology, India
Bhanu Prasad	Florida A&M University, USA
Barenya Bikash Hazarika	National Institute of Technology Arunachal Pradesh, India
Ipseeta Nanda	Gopal Narayan Singh University, India
Satyendra Singh	Bhartiya Skill Development University, India
Sudip Mandal	Jalpaiguri Government Engineering College, India
Naveen Kumar	IIIT Vadodara, India
Daniela López De Luise	CI2S Labs, Argentina
Parag Rughani	National Forensic Sciences University, India
K. Shirin Bhanu	Sri Vasavi Engineering College, India
R. Malmathanraj	National Institute of Technology Trichy, India
Latika Singh	Shushant University, India

Gizachew Hailegebriel Mako	Ethio Telecom, Ethiopia
Tessy Mathew	Mar Baselios College of Engineering and Technology, India
Hab. Grzegorz Chodak	Wroclaw University of Science and Technology, Poland
Neetu Verma	DCRUST Murthal, India
Sharda A. Chhabria	G H Raisoni Institute of Engineering and Technology, India
Neetesh Saxena	Cardiff University, UK
Nagaraj V. Dharwadkar	Rajarambapu Institute of Technology, India
R. Venkatesan	Ministry of Earth Sciences, Chennai, India
V. Jayaprakasan	IEEE Madras Section, India
D. Venkata Vara Prasad	SSN College of Engineering, India
Jayakumari. J.	Mar Baselios College of Engineering and Technology, India
P. A. Manoharan	IEEE Madras Section, India
S. Salivahanan	IEEE Madras Section, India
P. Santhi Thilagam	National Institute of Technology Karnataka, India
Umapada Pal	Indian Statistical Institute Kolkata, India
A. Revathi	SASTRA University Thanjavur, India
K. Prabhu	National Institute of Technology Karnataka, India
S. Suresh	National Institute of Technology Trichy, India
V. Mariappan	National Institute of Technology Trichy, India
T. Sentil Kumar	Anna University, India
S. Arul Daniel	National Institute of Technology Trichy, India
N. Sivakumaran	National Institute of Technology Trichy, India
N. Kumaresan	National Institute of Technology Trichy, India
S. Chandramohan	College of Engineering, Guindy, India
D. Devaraj	Kalasalingam Academy of Research and Education, India
S. Raghavan	National Institute of Technology Trichy, India
J. William	Agnel Institute of Technology and Design, India
R. Boopathi Rani	National Institute of Technology Puducherry, India
R. Kalidoss	SSN College of Engineering, India
R. K. Mugelan	Vellore Institute of Technology, India
V. Vinod Kumar	Government College of Engineering, Kannur, India
R. Saravanan	Vellore Institute of Technology, India
S. Sheik Aalam	iSENSE Intelligence Solutions, India
E. Srinivasan	Pondicherry Engineering College, India
B. Surendiran	National Institute of Technology Puducherry, India
M. Hariharan	National Institute of Technology Puducherry, India
Varun P. Gopi	National Institute of Technology Trichy, India
V. Vijaya Chamundeeswari	Velammal Engineering College, India
T. Prabhakar	GMRIT, India
V. Kamakoti	IIT Madras, India

D. Vaithiyanathan	National Institute of Technology Delhi, India
N. Janakiraman	KLN College of Engineering, India
S. Suresh	Hindu Banaras University, India
B. Janet	National Institute of Technology Tiruchirappalli, India
R. Sivashankar	Madanapalle Institute of Technology, India
S. Moses Santhakumar	Madanapalle Institute of Technology, India
G. Beulah Gnana Ananthi	Anna University, India
Bud Mishra	New York University, USA
S. Suresh Babu	Adhiyamaan College of Engineering, India
V. Anandakrishanan	National Institute of Technology Trichy, India
R. B. Patel	MMEC, India
Adesh Kumar Sharma	NDRI, India
Gunamani Jena	BVC Engineering College, India
Gurbinder Singh	GNDU, India
Manoj Manuja	National Institute of Technology Trichy, India
Ajay K. Sharma	Chitkara University, India
Suresh Thakur	Naval Research Board Delhi, India
Manjit Patterh	Punjabi University, India
Mayank Dave	National Institute of Technology Kurukshetra, India
A. L. Sangal	National Institute of Technology Jalandhar, India
L. M. Bhardwaj	Amity University Noida, India
Parvinder Singh	DCRUST, India
M. Syamala Devi	Panjab University, India
Rashmi B. S.	Karnataka State Open University, India
Lalit Kumar Awasthi	National Institute of Technology Jalandhar, India
Ajay Bansal	National Institute of Technology Jalandhar, India
Ravi Aggarwal	Adobe Systems, USA
Sigurd Meldal	University of San Jose, USA
M. Balakrishnan	IIT Delhi, India
V. R. Singh	National Physical Laboratory, India
Malay Pakhira	KGEC, India
Savita Gupta	Panjab University, India
B. Ramadoss	National Institute of Technology Trichy, India
Ashwani Kush	Kurukshetra University, India
Manas Ranjan Patra	Berhampur University, India
Sukhwinder Singh	Panjab University, India
Dharmendra Kumar	GJUS&T, India
Chandan Singh	Punjabi University, India
Rajinder Nath	Kurukshetra University, India
Manjaiah D. H	Mangalore University, India
Himanshu Aggarwal	Punjabi University, India
R. S. Kaler	Thapar Institute of Engineering and Technology, India
Pabitra Pal Choudhury	Indian Statistical Institute, Kolkata, India
S. K. Pal	DRDO, India
G. S. Lehal	Punjabi University, India
Rajkumar Kannan	Bishop Heber College, India

Yogesh Chaba	GJUS&T, India
Amardeep Singh	Punjabi University, India
Sriram Birudavolu	Oracle India Limited, India
Hardeep Singh	GNDU, India
Ajay Rana	Shobhit University, India
Kanwal Jeet Singh	Punjabi University, India
C. K. Bhensdadia	Dharamsinh Desai University, India
Savina Bansal	GZSCET, India
Mohammad Asger	BGSB University, India
Rajesh Bhatia	PEC University of Technology, India
Stephen John Turner	VISTEC, Thailand
Chiranjeev Kumar	IIT (ISM) Dhanbad, India
Bhim Singh	IIT Delhi, India
Anandha Gopalan	Imperial College, UK
A. K. Sharma	BSAITM Faridabad, India
Rob Reilly	MIT, USA
B. K. Murthy	CDA, Noida, India
Karmeshu	JNU, India
K. K. Biswas	IIT Delhi, India
Sandeep Sen	IIT Delhi, India
Suneeta Aggarwal	Motilal Nehru National Institute of Technology Allahabad, India
Satish Chand	NSUT, India
Savita Goel	IIT Delhi, India
Raghuraj Singh	HBTU Kanpur, India
Ajit Kumar Choudhary	Cognizant, India
D. K. Lobiyal	JNU, India
R. S. Yadav	Motilal Nehru National Institute of Technology Allahabad, India
Bulusu Anand	IIT Roorkee, India
R. K. Singh	BTKIT Dwarahat, India
Sateesh Kumar Peddoju	IIT Roorkee, India
Divakar Yadav	JIIT Noida, India
Naveen Kumar Singh	IGNOU, India
R. S. Raw	AIACTR (NSUT East Campus), India
Vidushi Sharma	GBU, India
Sumit Srivastava	Manipal University, India
Manish K. Gupta	DA-IICT, India
P. K. Saxena	DRDO, India
B. K. Das	ITM University, India
Y. Raghu Reddy	IIIT Hyderabad, India
B. Chandra	IIT Delhi, India
R. K. Agarwal	JNU, India
Basim Alhadidi	Al-Balqa' Applied University, Jordan
M. Monirujjaman Khan	North South University, Bangladesh
Emmanuel Ndashimye	University of Rwanda and CMU-Africa, Rwanda

Naveen Garg	IIT Delhi, India
K. S. Subramanian	IGNOU, India
Biplab Sikdar	NUS, Singapore
Sreeram Ramakrishna	NUS, Singapore
Vikas Mathur	Citrix, India
B. V. R. Chowdari	NUS, Singapore
Hari Krishna Garg	NUS, Singapore
Raja Dutta	IIT Kharagpur, India
Y. V. S. Lakshmi	C-DOT Bangalore, India
Vishakha Vaidya	Adobe Bangalore, India
Sudipto Shankar Dasgupta	Infosys Limited Bangalore, India
Atal Chaudhari	Jadavpur University, India
Gangaboraiah Andanaiah	KIMS Bangalore, India
Champa H. N.	UVCE Bangalore, India
Ramakanth Kumar P.	RVCE Bangalore, India
S. N. Omkar	IISC Bangalore, India
Balaji Rajendran	C-DAC Bangalore, India
Annapoorna P. Patil	MSRIT, India
K. N. Chandrashekhar	SJCIT, India
Mohammed Misbahuddin	C-DAC Bangalore, India
Saroj Meher	ISI Kolkata, India
Jharna Majumdar	NMIT, India
N. K. Cauvery	RVCE Bangalore, India
G. K. Patra	CSIR Delhi, India
Anandi	Oxford College of Engineering, India
Dinesha	IIIT Bangalore, India
K. R. Suneetha	BIT Bangalore, India
M. L. Shailaja	Dr. Ambedkar Institute of Technology, India
Andrzej Rucinski	University of New Hampshire, USA
K. R. Murali Mohan	DST Delhi, India
Ramesh Paturi	Microsoft, India
K. Chandrasekaran	National Institute of Technology Suratkal, India
S. Viswanadha Raju	JNTU Hyderabad, India
C. Krishna Mohan	IIT Hyderabad, India
R. T. Goswamy	Techno International New Town, India
B. Surekha	K S Institute of Technology, India
P. Trinatha Rao	GITAM University Visakhapatnam, India
Golla Varaprasad	BMS College of Engineering, India
M. Usha Rani	SPMVV, India
Tanmay De	National Institute of Technology Durgapur, India
P. V. Lakshmi	SPMVV, India
K. A. Selvaradjou	PEC University of Technology, India
Ch. Satyananda Reddy	Andhra University, India
Jeegar A Trivedi	Sardar Patel University, India
S. V. Rao	IIT Guwahati, India
Suresh Varma	P Adikavi Anna University, India

Y. Padma Sai	VNR Vignana Jyothi Institute of Engineering and Technology, India
T. Ranga Babu	RVR & JC College of Engineering, India
D. Venkat Rao	Narasaraopet Institute of Technology, India
N. Sudhakar Reddy	S V Engineering College, India
Dhiraj Sunehra	JNTU Hyderabad, India
Madhavi Gudavalli	JNTU, Kakinada, India
B. Hemanth Kumar	RVR & JC College of Engineering, India
A. Sri Nagesh	RVR & JC College of Engineering, India
Bipin Bihari Jaya Singh	CVR College of Engineering, India
M. Ramesh	JNTU Hyderabad, India
P. Rajarajeswari	GITAM University, India
R. Kiran Kumar	Krishna University, India
M. Dhanalakshmi	JNTU Hyderabad, India
D. Ramesh	JNTU Hyderabad, India
B. Kranthi Kiran	JNTU Hyderabad, India
K. Usha Rani	SPMVV, India
A. Nagesh	MGIT, India
P. Sammulal	JNTU Hyderabad, India
G. Narasimha	JNTU Hyderabad, India
B. V. Ram Naresh Yadav	JNTU Hyderabad, India
B. N. Bhandari	JNTU Hyderabad, India
O. B. V. Ramanaiah	JNTUH College of Engineering, India
Anil Kumar Vuppala	IIIT Hyderabad, India
Duggirala Srinivasa Rao	JNTU Hyderabad, India
Makkena Madhavi Latha	JNTU Hyderabad, India
L. Anjaneyulu	NIT Warangal, India
Anitha Sheela Kancharla	JNTU Hyderabad, India
B. Padmaja Rani	JNTUH College of Engineering, India
S. Mangai	Velalar College of Engineering and Technology, India
P. Chandra Sekhar	Osmania University, India
Chakraborty Mrityunjoy	IIT Kharagpur, India
Manish Shrivastava	IIIT Hyderabad, India
Uttam Kumar Roy	Jadavpur University, India
Kalpana Naidu	IIIT Kota, India
A. Swarnalatha	St. Joseph's College of Engineering, India
Aaditya Maheshwari	Techno India NJR Institute of Tech, India
Ajit Panda	National Institute of Science and Technology, India
Amit Kumar	Infosys, Pune, India
R. Anuradha	Sri Ramakrishna Engineering College, India
B. G. Prasad	BMS College of Engineering, India
Seung-Hwa Chung	Trinity College Dublin, Ireland
D. Murali	CMRCET, India
Deepak Padmanabhan	Queen's University Belfast, UK
Firoz Alam	RMIT University, Australia
Frederic Andres	NII, Japan

Srinath Doss	Botho University, Botswana
Munish Kumar	Maharaja Ranjit Singh Punjab Technical University, India
Norwati Mustapha	UPM, Malaysia
Hamidah Ibrahim	UPM, Malaysia
Denis Reilly	Liverpool John Moores University, UK
Ioannis Kypraios	De Montfort University, UK
Yongkang Xing	De Montfort University, UK
P. Shivakumara	University of Malaysia, Malaysia
Ravinder Kumar	TIET, Patiala, India
Ankur Gupta	Bennett University, India
Rahul Kr Verma	IIIT Lucknow, India
Gunjan Rehani	SRM-Sonipat, India
Mohit Sajwan	Bennett University, India
Vijaypal Singh Rathor	PDPM-IIITM, India
Deepak Singh	National Institute of Technology Raipur, India
Simranjit Singh	Bennett University, India
Suchi Kumari	Bennett University, India
Sridhar Swaminathan	L&T Infotech, India
Tanmay Bhowmik	Bennett University, India
Kuldeep	Bennett University, India
Indrajeet Gupta	Bennett University, India
Sanjeet Kumar Nayak	IIITM Kanchipuram, India
Shakti Sharma	Bennett University, India
Hiren Thakkar	Marwadi University, India
Mayank Swarnkar	IIT (BHU), India
Tapas Badal	Bennett University, India
Vipul Kr Mishra	Bennett University, India
Tanveer Ahmed	Bennett University, India
Madhushi Verma	Bennett University, India
Gaurav Singal	NSUT, India
Arpit Bhardwaj	Mahindra Ecole Centrale, India
Anurag Goswami	Bennett University, India
Durgesh Kumar Mishra	Sri Aurobindo Institute of Technology, India
S. Padma	Madanapalle Institute of Technology & Science, India
M. A. Jabbar	Vardhaman College of Engineering, India
Deepak Prashar	Lovely Professional University, India
Nidhi Khare	NMIMS, Mumbai, India
Sandeep Kumar	IIT Roorkee, India
Dattatraya V. Kodavade	DKTE Society's Textile and Engineering Institute, India
A. Obulesu	Anurag University, India
Abhinav Tomar	NSUT, India
Mainak Biswas	JIS University, India
Md. Dilshad Anasari	CMRCET, India
Amit Sinha	ABES Engineering College, India

K. Suvarna Vani	V R Siddhartha Engineering College, India
G. Singaravel	K.S.R. College of Engineering, India
Ajay Shiv Sharma	Melbourne Institute of Technology, Australia
Abhishek Shukla	R.D. Engineering College, India
V. K. Jain	Mody University of Science and Technology, Laxmangarh, India
B. Raveendra Babu	RVR & JC College of Engineering, India
Frederic Andres	University of Nantes, France
Edara Sreenivasa Reddy	Acharya Nagarjuna University, India
Deepak Poola	IBM India Private Limited, India
Bhadri Raju M. S. V. S.	S.R.K.R. Engineering College, India
Nishu Gupta	Vaagdevi College of Engineering, India
Yamuna Prasad	IIT Jammu, India
M. Wilscy	Saintgits College of Engineering India
Vishnu Vardhan B.	JNTUH College of Engineering Manthani, India
Virendra Kumar Bhavsar	University of New Brunswick, Canada
Koppula Vijaya Kumar	CMRCET, India
Vaibhav Anu	Montclair State University, USA
Vaibhav Gandhi	B H Gardi College of Engineering & Technology, India
V. Gomathi	National Engineering College, India
Anandakrishnan V.	National Institute of Technology Tiruchirappalli, India
Sudipta Roy	Assam University, India
Srabanti Maji	DIT University, India
Shylaja S. S.	PES University, India
Shweta Agrawal	SAGE University, India
Shreenivas Londhe	Vishwakarma Institute of Information Technology, India
Shom Das	Biju Patnaik University of Technology, India
Shirin Bhanu Koduri	Sri Vasavi Engineering College, India
Shailendra Aswale	SRIEIT, India
Shachi Natu	TSEC, India
Saurabh Kumar Garg	University of Tasmania, Australia
Sanjeevikumar Padmanaban	Aarhus University, Denmark
Santosh Saraf	Gogte Institute of Technology, India
Sanjeev Pippal	GL Bajaj Institute of Management & Technology, India
Samayveer Singh	National Institute of Technology Jalandhar, India
Sajal K. Das	Missouri University of Science and Technology, USA
Sabu M. Thampi	IIITM-K, India
Roshani Raut	Vishwakarma Institute of Information Technology, India
Rajkumar Buyya	University of Melbourne, Australia
Radhika K. R.	BMS College of Engineering, India
R. Priya Vaijayanthi	GMR Institute of Technology, India
M. Naresh Babu	National Institute of Technology Silchar, India
Krishnan Rangarajan	Dayananda Sagar College of Engineering, India
Prashant Singh Rana	Thapar Institute of Engineering and Technology, India

Pradeep Kumar	IIM-Lucknow, India
Parteek Bhatia	Thapar Institute of Engineering and Technology, India
Venkata Padmavati Metta	BIT Durg, India
Laxmi Lydia	Vignan's Institute of Information Technology, India
Nobel Xavier	Glassdoor, India
Nikunj Tahilramani	Adani Institute of Infrastructure Engineering, India
Neeraj Mittal	University of Texas at Dallas, USA
Neeraj Kumar	Thapar Institute of Engineering and Technology, India
Navanath Saharia	IIIT Manipur, India
Nagesh Vadaparthi	MVGR College of Engineering, India
Mrityunjoy Chakraborty	IIT Kharagpur, India
Milind Shah	Fr. C. Rodrigues Institute of Technology, India
Manne Suneetha	VR Siddhartha Engineering College, India
M. Mary Shanthi Rani	The Gandhigram Rural Institute, India
Luca Saba	University of Cagliari, Italy
Sumalatha Lingamgunta	JNTU Kakinada, India
K. K. Patel	Charotar University of Science and Technology, India
Kalyana Saravanan Annathurai	Kongu Engineering College, India
Kalaiarasi Sonai Muthu Anbananthen	Multimedia University, Malaysia
K. Subramanian	Indian School of Business, India
Singaraju Jyothi	SPMVV, India
Vinit Jakhetiya	IIT Jammu, India
Jagdish Chand Bansal	South Asian University, India
Yashwantsinh Jadeja	Marwadi University, India
Harsh Dev	PSIT Kanpur, India
Yashodhara V. Haribhakta	Government College of Engineering Pune, India
G. V. Padma Raju	S.R.K.R. Engineering College, India
Gurdeep Hura	University of Maryland, USA
Gopal Sakarkar	GHRCE, India
R. Gnanadass	Pondicherry Engineering College, India
K. Giri Babu	VVIT, India
Geeta Sikka	National Institute of Technology Jalandhar, India
Gaurav Varshney	IIT Jammu, India
G. L. Prajapati	Devi Ahilya Vishwavidyalaya, India
G. Kishor Kumar	RGMCET, India
Tarek Frikha	Ecole Nationale d'Ingénieurs de Sfax, Tunisia
Md. Saidur Rahman	Bangladesh University of Engineering and Technology, Bangladesh
M. Sohel Rahman	Bangladesh University of Engineering and Technology, Bangladesh
Wali Khan Mashwani	Kohat University of Science & Technology, Pakistan
Deepthi P. S.	LBS Institute of Technology for Women, India
Ramesh Suryavanshi	Fluor Corporation, UAE
Krishna Kiran Vamsi Dasu	Sri Sathya Sai Institute of Higher Learning, India

M. Sujithra	Coimbatore Institute of Technology, India
Manoj Manuja	Chitkara University, India
Jayakrushna Sahoo	IIIT Kottayam, India
Jaishankar Bharatharaj	Gnanamani College of Technology, India
Sisira Kumar Kapat	Utkal Gaurav Madhusudan Institute of Technology, India
Kuldeep Sharma	Chitkara University, Himachal Pradesh, India
Zankhana H. Shah	BVM Engineering College, India
Rekha Ramesh	Shah and Anchor Kutchhi Engineering College, India
Gopalkrishna Joshi	KLE Technological University, India
Ganga Holi	AMC Engineering College, India
Md. Ismail Jabiullah	Daffodil International University, Bangladesh
Ketan Kotecha	Symbiosis International University, India
Radhakrishna Bhat	Manipal Institute of Technology, India
J. Selvakumar	Sri Ramakrishna Engineering College, India
T. Subetha	BVRIT Hyderabad, India
Gaurav Kumar	Magma Research and Consultancy Services, India
J. Hyma	GITAM University, Visakhapatnam, India
Kuldeep Singh	Carnegie Mellon University, USA
Binod Kumar	JSPM's Rajarshi Shahu College of Engineering, India
Raju Kumar	Chandigarh University, India
Manju Vyas	JECRC University, India
Nitin S. Goje	Webster University in Tashkent, Uzbekistan
Pushpa Mala S.	Dayananda Sagar University, India
Ashish Sharma	GLA University, India
Ashwath Rao B.	Manipal Institute of Technology, India
Garima Mathur	Poornima College of Engineering, India
Sudhir Kumar Sharma	Institute of Information Technology and Management Delhi, India
Deepak Motwani	Amity University, Gwalior, India
D. N. Sujatha	BMS College of Engineering, India
V. Sowmya	Amrita School of Engineering, Coimbatore, India
Jayashri Nair	VNR VJIET, India
Parminder Kaur	Guru Nanak Dev University, India
Mini Tt	Dell Technologies Bangalore, India
Filippo Neri	University of Naples, Italy
Varun Dutt	IIT Mandi, India
Shajimon K. John	Saintgits College of Engineering, India
Sameerchand Pudaruth	University of Mauritius, Mauritius
S. Sridhar Raj	Mepco Schlenk Engineering College, India
Arya Devi P. S.	Adi Shankara Institute of Engineering & Technology, India
Rajesh C. Sanghvi	G. H. Patel College of Engineering & Technology, India
Ashwin Dobariya	Marwadi University, India
Sreejit Panicker	SSEC, India

Tapas Kumar Patra	College of Engineering and Technology Bhubaneswar, India
Sudeep Kumar Das	SAP Labs India Pvt. Ltd Banglore, India
J. Naren	Rathinam College of Arts and Science, India
D. Jeya Mala	Fatima College, India
Divya Saxena	Hong Kong Polytechnic University, Hong Kong
Rekha. K. S.	National Institute of Engineering, India
Promila Jangra	Centre of Development of Telematics Delhi, India
Mohammed Murtuza Qureshi	Storytech Private Limited, India
Larry M. Arjomandi	Monash University, Australia
Vasantha Kalyani David	Avinashilingam Institute for Home Science and Higher Education for Women, India
K. Sakthidasan	Hindustan Institute of Technology and Science, India
Manju Gupta	IMS Noida, India
Suganthi S.	Institute of Technology, India
Shreyas Rao	Sahyadri College of Engineering and Management, India
Hiranmayi Ranganathan	Lawrence Livermore National Laboratory, USA
Muhammad Aminur Rahaman	Green University of Bangladesh, Bangladesh
Rajashekhar	Oracle India Private Limited, Bangalore, India
Sanjaya Kumar Panda	National Institute of Technology Warangal, India
Puspanjali Mohapatra	IIIT Bhubaneswar, India
Manimala Mahato	Shah & Anchor Kutchhi Engineering College, India
B. Senthil Kumar	Kumaraguru College of Technology, India
Jyoti Prakash Singh	National Institute of Technology Patna, India

Contents

Application of Artificial Intelligence and Machine Learning in Healthcare

Relating Design Thinking Framework in Predicting the Spread of COVID in Tamilnadu Using ARIMA 3
    M. Shobana, S. Vaishnavi, C. Gokul Prasad, P. Poonkodi, R. Sabitha, and S. Karthik

Covid Alert System: A Smart Security System to Alert Violations of Covid Protocol Using OpenCV 11
    P. Kiran Kumar, I. Durga Sindhu, B. Vidya Yasaswini, CH. Sai Kireeti, and A. Dhana Satish

Corona Virus Detection Using EfficientNet from CT Scans 25
    D. Haritha, B. Grace Gladys Nancy, T. V. L. Vara Prasad, N. Swaroop, and B. Jaswanth

Disease Diagnosis in Grapevines – A Hybrid Resnet-Jaya Approach 39
    Piyush Mishra, Puspanjali Mohapatra, Tapas Kumar Patra, and P. Subham

Covid-19 Detection Using X-Ray Image 57
    Adarsh Sharma, Shantanu Pingale, Chanchal Mal, Sangeeta Malviya, Nikita Patil, and Shital Dongre

Alzheimer's Disease Classification Using Transfer Learning 73
    Deepanshi, Ishan Budhiraja, and Deepak Garg

A Comparative Study of Deep Learning Models for Detecting Pulmonary Embolism. 82
    Aditya Varshney, Arnav Bansal, Anshuman Agarwal, Vipul Kumar Mishra, and Tapas Badal

A Novel Compressed and Accelerated Convolution Neural Network for COVID-19 Disease Classification: A Genetic Algorithm Based Approach ... 99
    Mohit Agarwal, Suneet Kumar Gupta, Deepak Garg, and Dilbag Singh

Artificial Intelligence is Not a Foe But a Friend in the Healthcare Sector 112
    Lovleen Gupta and Srishti Jain

AI and The Cardiologist-When Mind, Heart and Machine Unite 123
    Antonio D'Costa and Aishwarya Zatale

An Analysis of the Psychological Implications of COVID-19 Pandemic on
Undergraduate Students and Efforts on Mitigation.................... 133
  Shreyas Suresh Rao, K. Pushpalatha, R. Sapna, and H. G. Monika Rani

Network-Based Identification of Module Biomarker Associated with
Hepatocellular Carcinoma 148
  Talib Hussain, Prithvi Singh, Abhinav Kumar, Nadeem Ahmad,
  Ravins Dohare, and Shweta Sankhwar

Identifying Hub Nodes and Sub-networks from Cattle Rumen Microbiome
Multilayer Networks 165
  Mengyuan Wang, Haiyang Wang, Huiru Zheng, Richard J. Dewhurst,
  and Rainer Roehe

Application of AI for Emotion and Behaviour Prediction

Machine Learning-Based Psychology: A Study to Understand Cognitive
Decision-Making... 179
  Parth Rainchwar, Soham Wattamwar, Rishikesh Mate,
  Chirag Sahasrabudhe, and Varsha Naik

Predicting Stock Market Prices Using Sentiment Analysis
of News Articles... 193
  Jayanth Narla, Sai Venkat Reddy Malreddy, Vaishnavi Bacha,
  and G. Ramesh Chandra

Sentimental Analysis on Multi-domain Sentiment Dataset Using SVM
and Naive Bayes Algorithm 201
  P. Kiran Kumar, N. Jahna Tejaswi, M. L. Vasanthi, L. L. Srihitha,
  and B. Phanindra Kumar

Artificial Intelligence in Online Stores' Processes 214
  Grzegorz Chodak and Yash Chawla

Early Warning Indicators for Financial Crisis During Covid-19........... 229
  Aakash Jignesh Modi, G. Jyothish Lal, E. A. Gopalakrishnan,
  V. Sowmya, K. P. Soman, and R. Vinayakumar

Facial Recognition Based Attendance Monitoring System.............. 244
  Amitava Choudhury, Tanmay Bhowmik, and Samya Muhuri

Transfer Learning Using Variational Quantum Circuit 254
  Rajashekharaiah Karur Mudugal Mathad, Abhishek Saurabh,
  Aditya Mishra, Sambhav Jain, Purushottam Kumar, Vardaan,
  and Satyadhyan Chickerur

Problem Solving Using Reinforcement Learning and Analysis of Data

Gait Learning Using Reinforcement Learning   271
   Bharath Raj Mahadeva Rao and Sharmila Chidaravalli

Data Science in the Business Environment: Architecture, Process
and Tools.   279
   Jing Lu

A Logarithmic Distance-Based Multi-Objective Genetic Programming
Approach for Classification of Imbalanced Data   294
   Arvind Kumar, Shivani Goel, Nishant Sinha, and Arpit Bhardwaj

Multiview Classification with Missing-Views Through Adversarial
Representation and Inductive Transfer Learning   305
   Mukhtar Opeyemi Yusuf, Divya Srivastava, Shashank Sheshar Singh,
   and Mahtab Alam

Deep Reinforcement Learning Based Throughput Maximization
Scheme for D2D Users Underlaying NOMA-Enabled Cellular Network   318
   Vineet Vishnoi, Praveen Kumar Malik, Ishan Budhiraja,
   and Ashima Yadav

An Intrusion Detection System for Blackhole Attack Detection
and Isolation in RPL Based IoT Using ANN   332
   C. Prajisha and A. R. Vasudevan

Evaluating the Efficacy of Different Neural Network Deep Reinforcement
Algorithms in Complex Search-and-Retrieve Virtual Simulations   348
   Ishita Vohra, Shashank Uttrani, Akash K. Rao, and Varun Dutt

Post-hoc Explainable Reinforcement Learning Using Probabilistic
Graphical Models   362
   Saurabh Deshpande, Rahee Walambe, Ketan Kotecha,
   and Marina Marjanović Jakovljević

Ghostbusters: How the Absence of Class Pairs in Multi-Class Multi-Label
Datasets Impacts Classifier Accuracy   377
   Sidharth Kathpal, Siddha Ganju, and Anirudh Koul

ReLearner: A Reinforcement Learning-Based Self Driving Car Model
Using Gym Environment   399
   Hiren Kumar Thakkar, Ankit Desai, Priyanka Singh,
   and Kamma Samhitha

Automating Paid Parking System Using IoT Technology   410
   Ankit Desai, Anurag Deotale, Atharva Bapat,
   and Chaitanya Khinvasara

Farmers' Survey App - An Interactive Open-Source Application for
Agricultural Survey   419
    Aditya Ghodgaonkar, Bhavya Surana, Parteek Kumar, Karun Verma,
    Balakrishna Kommanaboina, and Yosi Shacham-Diamand

Advance Uses of RNN and Regression Techniques

Improving Recognition of Handwritten Kannada Characters Using Mixup
Regularization.   433
    Chandravva Hebbi, Anirudh Maiya, and H. R. Mamatha

Research on the Detection and Recognition Algorithm of Click Chinese
Character Verification Code   448
    Duo Wang, Chongwen Wang, and Xiaotian Long

Multihead Self-attention and LSTM for Spacecraft Telemetry Anomaly
Detection   463
    Sharvari Gundawar, Nitish Kumar, Prajjwal Yash, Amit Kumar Singh,
    M. Deepan, R. Subramani, B. R. Uma, G. Krishnapriya,
    B. Shivaprakash, and D. Venkataramana

Validity and Reliability Assessment of a Smartphone Application
for Measuring Chronic Low Back Pain   480
    Jake Fenech, Vijay Prakash, Lalit Garg, Conti Carlo,
    and Anshul Sharma

Predicting Disasters from Tweets Using GloVe Embeddings and BERT
Layer Classification.   492
    Aabha Ranade, Saurav Telge, and Yash Mate

Contextual Quality Assessment of the Newspaper Articles Based
on Keyword Extraction   504
    Samya Muhuri and Susanta Chakraborty

GEDset: Automatic Dataset Builder for Machine Translation System with
Specific Reference to Gujarati-English.   519
    Margi Patel and Brijendra Kumar Joshi

Power Function Algorithm for Linear Regression Weights with Weibull
Data Analysis.   529
    Robert Ross

Special Intervention of AI

Shrub Detection in High-Resolution Imagery: A Comparative Study
of Two Deep Learning Approaches.   545
    Katherine James and Karen Bradshaw

Optimized Deep Neural Network for Tomato Leaf Diseases Identification . . .   562
    R. Sangeetha, M. Mary Shanthi Rani, and Rabin Joseph

Application of Distributed Back Propagation Neural Network for Dynamic
Real-Time Bidding   577
    Ankit Desai, Hiren Kumar Thakkar, Priyanka Singh,
    and Lakshmi Sai Bhargavi

An Efficient Minimum Spanning Tree-Based Color Image Segmentation
Approach   588
    Shahina Anwarul

Geo-ML Enabled Above Ground Biomass and Carbon Estimation
for Urban Forests   599
    Swati Uniyal, Kuldeep Chaurasia, Saurabh Purohit, S. S. Rao,
    and Vazeer Mahammood

Custom Cloud: An Efficient Model for Cloud Service Selection Based on
Neural Network   618
    Abhi Bothera, Arjun Mohnot, Neha Garg, Neeraj, and Indrajeet Gupta

A Machine Learning-Based Approach for Efficient Cloud
Service Selection.   626
    Uttam Gandhi, Abhi Bothera, Neha Garg, Neeraj, and Indrajeet Gupta

Enhancing Network Robustness Using Statistical Approach Based
Rewiring Strategy   633
    Suchi Kumari, Samya Muhuri, and Swati Chandna

A Partcle Swarm Optimization Based Approach for Filter Pruning
in Convolution Neural Network for Tomato Leaf Disease Classification.   646
    Mohit Agarwal, Suneet Kumar Gupta, Deepak Garg,
    and Mohammad Monirujjaman Khan

Data Breach in Social Networks Using Machine Learning   660
    Monalisa Mahapatra, Naman Gupta, Riti Kushwaha, and Gaurav Singal

Sentiment Analysis of Customers Review Using Hybrid Approach   671
    Jyoti Budhwar and Sukhdip Singh

Author Index   687

Editors

Dr. Deepak Garg
Dean, International and Corporate Affairs, Bennett University
Director leadingindia.ai
Chair, Computer Science and Engineering, Bennett University and Director, NVIDIA-Bennett Center of Research on Artificial Intelligence

Dr. Garg is leading the largest Development, Skilling and Research initiative in AI in India with more than 1000 institutional collaborators. He is a chief consultant for algorithmguru.in. He has done his Ph.D. in efficient algorithm design in 2006. He served as chair of IEEE Computer Society, India IEEE Education Society (2013–2015). He has handled funding of around INR 700 million including RAENG, UK on MOOCs, Machine Learning and AI. He has 110+ publications with 1400+ citations and Google h-index of 18. In his 24 years of experience, he has delivered 300+ invited talks and conducted 100+ Workshops and 15+ Conferences across the country. He has Supervised 14 Ph.D. and 35 PG students. He is a blogger in Times of India named as breaking shackles. For details please visit http://www.gdeepak.com.

Dr. Sarangapani Jagannathan is at the Missouri University of Science and Technology (former University of Missouri-Rolla) where he is a Rutledge-Emerson Distinguished Professor of Electrical and Computer Engineering and served as a Site Director for the NSF Industry/University Cooperative Research Center on Intelligent Maintenance Systems. His research interests include neural networks and learning, secure human-cyber-physical systems, prognostics, and autonomous systems/robotics. He has co-authored with his students 182 peer reviewed journal articles, 289 refereed IEEE conference articles, authored/co-edited 6 books, received 21 US patents and graduated 30 doctoral and 31 M.S thesis students. He received many awards including the 2020 best AE award from IEEE SMC Transactions, 2018 IEEE CSS Transition to Practice Award, 2007 Boeing Pride Achievement Award, 2000 NSF Career Award, 2001 Caterpillar Research Excellence Award, and many others. He is a Fellow of the IEEE, National Academy of Inventors, Institute of Measurement and Control, UK, Institution of Engineering and Technology (IET), UK and Asia-Pacific Association of Artificial Intelligence.

Dr. Ankur Gupta is the Director at the Model Institute of Engineering and Technology, Jammu, India, besides being a Professor in the Department of Computer Science and Engineering. Prior to joining academia, he worked as Technical Team Lead at Hewlett Packard India and USA, developing software in the network management and e-Commerce domains. He has 2 patents granted and 25 patents filed. He obtained his B.E, Hons. Computer Science and MS Software Systems degrees from BITS, Pilani and PhD from the National Institute of Technology, Hamirpur. He has published 75 peer-reviewed papers in reputed international journals and conferences and is a recipient of the AICTE's Career Award for Young Teachers, awarded to promising researchers under the age of 35 on a nationally competitive basis. He is the Founding Managing Editor of the International Journal of Next-Generation Computing IJNGC. He is a senior member of the ACM, senior member IEEE and a life-member of the Computer Society of India. He has received competitive grants over INR 20 million from various funding agencies besides faculty awards from IBM and EMC. He is the inventor of Performance Insight 360, a quality analytics framework for higher education, which received the Quality Council of India's D.L Shaw Platinum Award and the Startup Board Award at the India Innovation Initiative.

Lalit Garg is a Senior Lecturer in Computer Information Systems at the University of Malta, Malta, and an honorary lecturer at the University of Liverpool, UK. He has been a researcher at the Nanyang Technological University, Singapore, and Ulster University, UK. Dr. Garg has supervised 200+ Masters' dissertations, 2 DBA and 2 PhD thesis and published 120+ high impact publications in refereed journals/conferences/books, eight edited books and 21 patents. He has delivered several keynote speeches, organized/chaired international conferences, and consulted numerous public and private organizations for information systems implementation and management. His research interests are business intelligence, machine learning, data science, deep learning, cloud computing, mobile computing, Internet of Things (IoT), information systems, management science and their applications mainly in healthcare and medical domains. He participates in many EU, and local funded projects, including a one million euros Erasmus+ Capacity-Building project in Higher Education (CBHE) titled Training for Medical education via innovative eTechnology (MediTec). The University of Malta has awarded him the 2021–2022 Research Excellence Award for exploring Novel Intelligent Computing Methods for healthcare requirements forecasting, allocation and management (NICE-Healthcare).

Suneet Kumar Gupta is a Associate Professor in the Department of Computer Science Engineering at Bennett University, Gr. Noida. His current research interests are Wireless Sensor Network, Internet of Things, Natural Language Processing and Brain-Computer Interaction. Presently Dr. Gupta has completed a Wireless Sensor Network based project funded by Department of Science and Technology, Uttar Pradesh. Dr. Gupta is also part of a project funded by the Royal Academy of Science London entitled with Leadingindia.ai. He has more than 60 research articles, authored 2 books and 3 book chapters in his account.

Application of Artificial Intelligence and Machine Learning in Healthcare

Relating Design Thinking Framework in Predicting the Spread of COVID in Tamilnadu Using ARIMA

M. Shobana[1](✉), S. Vaishnavi[3], C. Gokul Prasad[2], P. Poonkodi[1], R. Sabitha[1], and S. Karthik[1]

[1] Department of CSE, SNS College of Technology, Coimbatore, India
[2] Department of ECE, SNS College of Engineering, Coimbatore, India
[3] Department of IT, Sri Ramakrishna Engineering College, Coimbatore, India

Abstract. Spread of "COVID" has taken over life of several people all around the world. In initial stages, it was gradually affecting the humans and as days goes on it started to drastically affect several people. This is because it spreads from one person to others easily. In this pandemic situation, in order to manage this pandemic situation, we must know the rate at which the infection gets spread and the analysis can be done with the pervious confirmed and death cases with the help of data sets available in web resources. ARIMA (Auto Regressive Integrated Moving Average) model can be used in forecasting the spread of COVID with the previous data sets extracted from Kaggle. Here have considered the data from March 2020 to June 2021 and predicted the COVID cases for the next one month July 2021. In specific, it has concentrated towards one particular state Tamilnadu from INDIA.

Keywords: COVID · Design thinking · ARIMA · Forecasting models

1 Introduction

COVID has become a term which is known to every individual person in the world due to its life threatening nature [1, 5–7]. The rate of deaths has been increasing in these upcoming days. The 2nd wave of covid is killing more persons than the 1st wave. The gap between these two waves was made relaxations by multiple countries and people all around took it all for well and these made the spread of disease to a more extend. It is said that there are 4waves to occur in COVID, among which we are in the 2nd stage. In the 1st stage the severity was less and it didn't affect the children's a major concern but in 2nd stage it has started to affect many kids even from their day of birth. There are many children's who get affected out of COVID and there are few who has the immunity to fight with COVID and later their immune system starts affecting their organs instead of fighting with COVID. From the Doctors community it is said as post-COVID/Multi-Inflammatory Syndrome (MIS), kids get affected by COVID if their parents or relations have been affected by COVID previously. In the 3rd wave it is said that kids may get affected by COVID since many adults by that date could have been vaccinated. In order to predict this scenario of COVID here ARIMA, a machine learning [8] forecasting algorithm is chosen to forecast the future data and take the precautions accordingly in earlier.

Design Thinking is a unique methodology that gives us a solution-based approach to solve the problem. Out of several problem solving strategies, design thinking plays a major role due to its non-linear nature of solving the problem. The five major stages of Design Thinking in incorporated here in several stages of forecasting the spread of infection in tamilnadu. The 5 stages are: empathy, define, ideate, prototype and test. When these 5 stages are done iteratively, it is not necessary to follow a sequential order and this will give us a state-of-the-art in solving the problem and giving solutions.

When there are multiple techniques to solve a problem, Design Thinking is one of the top most technique which is being used in multiple fields to solve a problem based on knowing the user needs in detail through the empathize phase. Through this phase a problem is understood in the perspectives of users and solve accordingly to their needs. The new technologies for solving problem are identified and the best is chosen from a collection of technologies and this gives us a best success to overcome the problem.

The ideate stage in design thinking is to generate multiple ideas to solve the problem and then filter one particular idea to stimulate good solutions. There are several methods in ideate such as brainstorming, brain dump, brain write, brain walk, story board, mind map, scamper and so on. Among these methods story board is used in selecting one particular state for forecasting from several states considered here. The columns for analysis each month are as follows:

- Aggregated Confirmed cases: This field helps us in knowing the number of patients getting affected day wise in each state depicted.
- Aggregated Cured cases: This field helps in knowing how is the recovery status of virus affected persons in each state
- Aggregated Death cases: This field gives the worst case scenario of the depth of virus

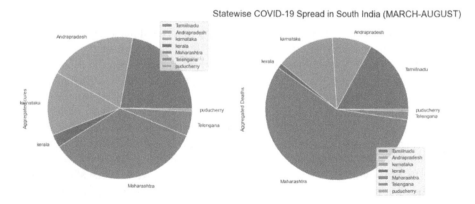

Fig. 1. State wise COVID spread in South India

With the hints given in the Fig. 1 and column analysis made it is very clear that Maharashtra and Tamilnadu are the major affected states among the 7 states considered here in South-India. So, in order to forecast the future infection rate, we have to majorly consider one of these 2 states. We can prefer a solution to a problem more accurate when it is our native than other states. In particular the Tamilnadu state is taken into account since it is the 2nd top state which has more infection rate than the other states. The future infection rate is predicted with ARIMA Model.

The empathy from COVID is that the infection spreads from one individual to another very soon; the awareness about wearing mask and social distancing is less among the humans, people doesn't seek health care at initially stages and this leads to increase in death rate, prediction about the future rate of infection will help the Government in managing the epidemic situation. In order to forecast about the future life threats of corona infection here ARIMA, a machine learning algorithm is opted and analyzed with previous month data. ARIMA (Auto Regressive Integrated Moving Average) is a popular tool used in predicting the future values with the past value as input. Here python is employed for building the ARIMA model with the past values of data which is taken from kaggle.

From the Empathy made from COVID in detail the 2nd stage of DT, Define is given as

"People all around the world need to take nutritious food and increase their immune system, maintain social distancing and get vaccinated"
"Forecasting the infection rate with ARIMA model helps people in knowing the facts about future days"

Once the define stage of the problem is done we move towards ideate, prototype and test. Where in ideate stage we analysis multiple ideas to solve a problem and pick the best one which gives more accuracy to our problem. Here have considered multiple machine learning algorithm to forecast/predict the near future with the existing data.

2 Data Depiction

The information used in forecasting future values is taken from Kaggle, an official website (https://www.kaggle.com/sudalairajkumar/covid19-in-india). In particular have taken information about covid-19 in India and extracted the data of confirmed cases, cured cases and death cases from various states of south-India. Among several states taken in South-India depending upon the number of confirmed cases have reviewed one particular state which is "Tamilnadu".

From the analysis of overall data, it shows the daily confirmed have been increasing drastically from the mid of April 2020. And also, it shows the number of cured rates is better when comparing with the confirmed cases. Here the death rate is less than the confirmed and cured cases which shows that we will be able to come out of these epidemic situations as earlier as possible with all the precautionary measures (Fig. 2).

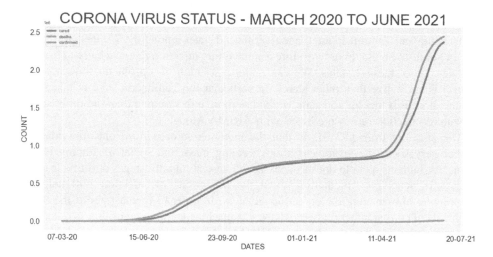

Fig. 2. Daily COVID confirmed, deaths and cured cases in Tamilnadu from the start of the epidemic

3 Forecasting Models

Forecasting is generally done in fields where the future value is of major concern to the upcoming future scenario. From [2] have ideated what are possible factors necessary for forecasting, they generally categorized into four such as Big Data, Social media/ additional communication broadcasting information, Stochastic theory/mathematical models, Data Science/Machine learning techniques.

These four factors will influence the impact of forecasting COVID in all the countries. From the first factor it is made very clear that the "data" is acting a major role in predicting the future values. If there is incorrectness in data it will lead to a wrong prediction. So, we have to take a personal care in selecting the datasets before we start our implementation process. Many of the researches have used the data from social media that is easily accessible. Mathematical models, which is an ancient technique is used by multiple researchers to evaluate the death count with the previous data. Some researchers prefer using technique which is in current trend; here comes our machine learning and Data Science Techniques. The predications made by machine learning technique are more accurate than the traditional technique, which made researchers move towards recent technologies. But when coming to ML the major concern it the amount of data and selection of appropriate parameters taken for analysis process.

Machine learning is used for forecasting [3, 4, 9] data with the time series complications. There are several machine learning methods that are used in prediction process. They are ARMA, ARIMA, SARIMA, Exponential Smoothing and VAR.

With the empathy and define stage, ideate stage is made much simpler where there are several solutions for prediction of COVID virus as mentioned earlier.

ARIMA Model was used in predicting the spread of COVID-19 in Italy by Gatano by April 2020. He has considered ARIMA [10, 11, 12] has one of the best suited model for prediction based on time series and a short-term forecasting model. The analysis was done with the data set collected and it's proven that the hike in the total number of COVID cases will be increasing in the next 40 to 50 days. It is proven that ARIMA is a good model for health monitoring applications due to its ease of use and elimination of noise in the data collected.

4 ARIMA Used for Forecasting COVID in Near Future

Among the several models in forecasting which were discussed in ideate stage, ARIMA model is a commonly used method for time series forecasting. For forecasting using the existing data, a prototype is developed using ARIMA with Python (using Anaconda platform). It is also proven that ARIMA model is used in multiple real-world scenarios such as education, health care, finance and so on. Prototype is the fourth stage of design thinking (investigation stage), where prototype is tested with a community of people and best solution is chosen for the problems discussed in the previous three stages of design thinking.

ARIMA (Auto Regressive Integrated Moving Average) is one of the models that is easy to understand and gives the forecast value depending on the past values. It mainly refers to the autocorrelation in the data. It is a combination of AR (Auto regression), I (Integration), and MA (Moving Average). AR uses the association among witnessed and some of the lagged witnessed. MA uses the dependency among the witness and residual error from a moving average model applied to lagged observations. "I" which indicates the integration represents the data value which is the difference between actual and previous values. The difference between these values is done more than once. AR is represented as follows referring from [2]: AR is represented by the Eq. (1)

$$y_t = C + \phi_1 y_{t-1} + \phi_2 y_{t-2} + \cdots \cdots + \phi_p y_{t-p} + \varepsilon_t \qquad (1)$$

MA model is represented as shown in Eq. (2)

$$y_t = C + \varepsilon_t - \theta_1 \varepsilon_{t-1} - \theta_2 \varepsilon_{t-2} - \cdots \cdots - \theta_q \varepsilon_{t-q} \qquad (2)$$

AR and MA model is combined together and we get ARIMA, Eq. (1) and (2) is combined and Eq. 3 is derived.

$$y_t = C + \phi_1 y_{t-1} + \phi_2 y_{t-2} + \cdots \cdots + \phi_p y_{t-p} + \varepsilon_t - \theta_1 \varepsilon_{t-1} - \theta_2 \varepsilon_{t-2} - \cdots \cdots - \theta_q \varepsilon_{t-q} \qquad (3)$$

Here in Eq. (1), yt is the representation of function of lags, y_{t-1} is the 1st lag if the series. In Eq. (2), yt is the representation of lagged predict errors. The errors are represented here by εt and ε_{t-1}.

Applying the fixed differentiation of data points, non-stationary data is made stationary data. There are three parameters involving in ARIMA model: p, q and d where AR model is denoted by p parameter and MA model is denoted by q parameter. Differentiation Degree is represented by parameter d.

In recent times ARIMA is used in forecasting the future infection rates of COVID in more than 15 countries and it has proven that predicted value is similar to the actual count in the current situations of those countries.

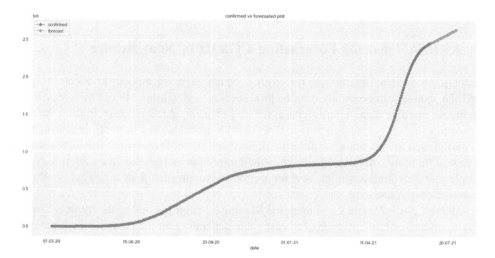

Fig. 3. Confirmed versus forecasted confirmed cases in Tamilnadu

The ARIMA model is used in forecasting the total number of confirmed cases in future with the help of data sets extracted from the previous days. The columns used in prediction are count of confirmed cases, recovered cases and death cases each day from March 2020 to June 2021. Figure 3 gives us the predicted count of confirmed cases for the month of July 2021.

If the death and recovered cases in well known in advance it could be really useful to the medical field in applying the medications to the affected persons. Figure 4 helps in knowing the recovered and death cases for the future with the previous values. It shows us 6 values which are confirmed, recovered and death count for the month of March 2020 to June 2021 and Confirmed, recovered and death count for the month of July 2021 with the help of previous values. Thus it is clearly seen from the Fig. 4 that the epidemic situation of COVID is going to continue and it has not shown any sign of decrease in count of disease. It also shows that the count of virus has increased in 2nd wave than 1st wave. So, it is necessary to take all precautions in advance to tackle this situation. One of happy entity from the Fig. 4 is that the death rate is constant and so it is a relaxation of medical field and continues their progress towards the vaccination process and make our state healthier as earlier.

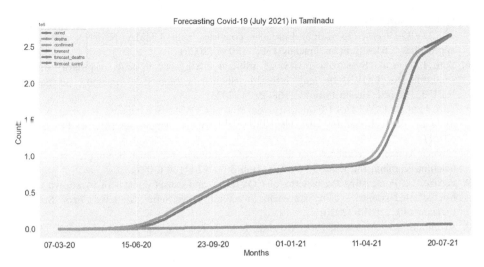

Fig. 4. Forecasting COVID in Tamilnadu for the month of July 2021

5 Conclusion

COVID which is one of the major concerns to the medical field has to be taken much care and forecasting will surely help in taking all initial measures. The parameters taken up for forecasting using ARIMA gives us the result for the next one month (July 2021) and it clearly shows the rise in the confirmed cases. Thus the precautionary measures taken by our government need to be improved and all the people need to get vaccinated. Design thinking framework helped in bringing the solution to the problem considered much simpler than other problem solving techniques. It is the responsibility of every individual to maintain social distancing, sanitize and wash their hands regularly and get out of the COVID circle and also help other people who have affected by COVID to step out of that circle as earlier as possible.

References

1. Agarwal, M., et al.: A novel block imaging technique using nine artificial intelligence models for COVID-19 disease classification, characterization and severity measurement in lung computed tomography scans on an Italian Cohort. J. Med. Syst. **45**(3), 1–30 (2021)
2. Hernandez-Matamoros, A., Fujita, H., Hayashi, T., Perez-Meana, H.: Forecasting of COVID19 per regions using ARIMA models and polynomial functions. Appl. Soft Comput. J. **96**, 106610 (2020)
3. Shinde, G.R., Kalamkar, A.B., Mahalle, P.N., Dey, N., Chaki, J., Hassanien, A.E.: Forecasting models for coronavirus disease (COVID-19): a survey of the state-of-the-art. SN Comput. Sci. **1**(4), 1–15 (2020)
4. Aijaz, I., Agarwal, P.: A study on time series forecasting using hybridization of time series models and neural networks. RACSC **13**(5), 827–832 (2020)

5. Kırbaş, İ, Sözen, A., Tuncer, A.D., Kazancıoğlu, F.Ş: Comparative analysis and forecasting of COVID-19 cases in various European countries with ARIMA, NARNN and LSTM approaches. Chaos Solitons Fractals **138**, 110015 (2020)
6. Suri, J.S., et al.: Systematic review of artificial intelligence in acute respiratory distress syndrome for COVID-19 lung infected patients: a biomedical imaging perspective. IEEE J. Biomed. Health Inform. 2168–2194 (2021)
7. Suri, J., et al.: COVLIAS 1.0: lung segmentation in COVID-19 computed tomography scans using hybrid deep learning artificial intelligence models. Diagnostics (MDPI) **11**(8), 1405 (2021)
8. Naveen Kumar, S., Kirubhakaran, R., Jeeva, G., Shobana, M.: Smart health prediction using machine learning. Int. Res. J. Adv. Sci. Hub **3**(3), 124–128 (2021)
9. Feroze, N.: Forecasting the patterns of COVID-19 and causal impacts of lockdown in top five affected countries using Bayesian Structural Time Series Models. Chaos Solitons Fractals **140**, 110196 (2020)
10. Alzahrani, S.I., Aljamaan, I.A., Al-Fakih, E.A.: Forecasting the spread of the COVID-19 pandemic in Saudi Arabia using ARIMA prediction model under current public health interventions. J. Infect. Public Health **13**(7), 914–919 (2020)
11. Roy, S., Bhunia, G.S., Shit, P.K.: Spatial prediction of COVID-19 epidemic using ARIMA technique in India. Modeling Earth Syst. Environ. **7**, 1385–1391 (2021)
12. Singh, S., et al.: Forecasting daily confirmed COVID-19 cases in Malaysia using ARIMA models. J. Infect. Dev. Ctries **14**(09), 971–976 (2020)

Covid Alert System: A Smart Security System to Alert Violations of Covid Protocol Using OpenCV

P. Kiran Kumar[✉], I. Durga Sindhu, D. Vidya Yasaswini, CH. Sai Kireeti, and A. Dhana Satish

Department of Computer Science and Engineering, Sasi Institute of Technology and Engineering (Affiliated To JNTU, Kakinada), Tadepalligudem 534101, AP, India
{kiran, durga546, vidya520, kireeti521, dhana511}@sasi.ac.in

Abstract. According to the World Health Organization, the COVID-19 pandemic is causing overall prosperity into crisis. The pandemic made all countries across the world commence lockdowns to decrease the transfer of the virus. The protection procedure is wearing a face mask in open areas. Records show that wearing face masks in crowded areas diminishes the threat of virus transfer. A novel framework is proposed in this paper to minimize the spreading of COVID-19 in crowded places like schools, malls, theaters, etc., by identifying individuals without wearing a mask. A face masks algorithm and CNN algorithm have been developed the usage of machine learning which acknowledges the faces besides masks and signals the safety system. It can detect face masks with high accuracy of 99%. The methodology proposed exhibits its high effectiveness in detecting facial masks.

Keywords: Face mask detection · Covid-19 · CNN · TensorFlow · Safety improvement · Face recognition · Deep learning technique

1 Introduction

Beginning in December 2019, a new kind of virus called COVID-19 immediately changed the world. Until July 10, 2021, more than 186 million cases had been noticed in more than 200 nations and districts throughout the planet, and over 4,037,500 patients have passed away. As of now, it is as yet proceeding to spread for a huge scope. The new kind of Covid is profoundly powerful. It is well spread through contact, drops, mist concentrates and different transporters noticeable all around, and it can make due for 5 days in the air [5].

Corona Virus primarily spreads through beads created because of hacking or wheezing by a contaminated individual. This exchanges the infection for an individual who is in close contact with the individual experiencing Covid [10]. Corona Virus is in reality an uncommon infection related to a sensibly normal group of infections with severe acute respiratory syndrome (SARS) and influenza [15]. World Health

Organization declared that symptoms of Covid are fever, running nose, sleepiness, loss of smell and taste, and dry throat [16].

During the pandemic, everybody is encouraged to wear face veils in open. As per the World Health Organization (WHO), veils can be utilized for source control (worn by a contaminated individual to restrain further transmission) or for the assurance of sound individuals. The wide-scale utilization of face veils represents a test on open face identification-based security frameworks like those present in air terminals, which can't recognize facial masks. Since the ill-advised expulsion of covers can prompt getting the infection, it has gotten fundamental to further increase facial identifiers that depend on facial parts, so identification can be performed precisely even with half-covered faces [3].

Face masks are a compelling strategy to decrease the spread of the virus. Reports show that wearing face covers is 96% viable to stop the spread of infection. The government everywhere in the world has forced exacting guidelines that everybody should wear masks while they go out. However, a couple of individuals may not wear masks and it is hard to check everyone is wearing a mask or not [10]. The utilization of face veils is exceptionally important to forestall and stop the spread of respiratory viral sicknesses, including the Coronavirus [1]. Face veil can be utilized to secure either solid individuals or forestall contamination by tainted people. In any case, wearing a face veil effectively is vital to lessen the dangers of pollution. The World Health Organization prescribes to utilize face cover at swarmed places like stations, offices, schools, and so on [14].

Face veil identification incorporates recognizing the area of the face and identifying the mask [18]. The framework used in this assessment can be executed on the surveillance CCTV to decrease the transmission of the Coronavirus by distinguishing people who are not using a cover [20]. It can be used to identify a large number of people in crowded regions, private regions, enormous scope makers, and different endeavors to guarantee wellbeing.

The proposed framework can be implemented by using CCTV to stop the spread of COVID-19. As of now, many countries have faced 2nd and 3rd waves of covid and daily new variants are being discovered throughout the world so it is necessary to wear a mask and this model will be useful. The framework is developed with deep learning and machine learning methods with OpenCV, Keras, and TensorFlow. To increase efficiency, it uses the cascaded neural network model.

2 Related Works

Snyder et al. [1] proposed Thor based framework which executes deep learning-based methods for programmed recognition of people who are not using masks in broad daylight spaces. Thor fostered an inventive methodology that coordinates various sorts of deep learning for face cover discovery. The proposed robot consists of three modules. They are ResNet-50, Multi-Task CNN model, and neural networks.

Draughon et al. [2] proposed CNN's that can perform individual identification and face cover order with high exactness. This paper presents the OPOSFM dataset, a physically curated exhibition of appearances explicitly intended to train CNN-based face mask classifiers for genuine applications, alongside a computer vision system that coordinates different modules to accomplish individual and face cover discovery and tracking.

Joshi et al. [3] methodology for identifying face covers from recordings is proposed. A profoundly compelling face detection model is utilized for acquiring facial pictures and signals. A particular facial classifier is fabricated utilizing deep learning for the assignment of deciding the presence of a face veil in the facial pictures distinguished. The subsequent methodology is strong and is assessed on a custom dataset acquired for this work.

Xue et al. [4] proposed a technique to detect and recognize people who are using masks based on Retina Face. To design an algorithm by using the principle of Retina Face algorithm is improved and detected. By Retina Face algorithm self-attention mechanism is improved and to detect face key points like eyes, mouth. B. Xue used a single-target algorithm for single capacity and high prerequisites.

Aswal et al. [5] implemented a Retina Face that beats different calculations by large execution, certainty, and exactness of the jumping box. It additionally recognizes the milestone facial highlights in instances of extreme impediments, appearances, and enlightenment. Using ResNet-50 spine, covered faces acknowledgment is accomplished with more precision and making the distinguishing proof framework appropriate for down-to-earth applications.

Bhuiyan et al. [6] implemented a YOLOv3 methodology for recognizing whether an individual is wearing a mask or not. It includes techniques like data acquisition, data annotation, and framework outline. A contribution here is an image is passed into the YOLOv3 model. This article locater is going through the image and finding the directions that are present in images. It generally partitions the contribution to a network from that it supports to analyze the features of the target things.

Negi et al. [7] proposed a facial mask detection, Haar Cascade classifier, CNN implementation, and purring model with Kera's-surgeon. The technique used is pruning, which is a deep learning approach that assists with simplifying neural networks. The framework enhancement base methodology requires wiping out undesirable weight vector esteems. It brings smoother handling of smaller neural organizations to diminish the figuring costs related to networks.

Ud Din et al. [8] proposed a novel strategy for collaboration free enormous article expulsion from facial pictures, zeroing in on cover objects. For picture finishing, GAN-based picture inpainting is used through picture-to-picture interpretation to produce a result. This paper is based on the map module and editing module which contains the editing generator, discriminators, and perceptual network.

Zung et al. [9] analyzed the developed R-CNN model to identify conditions for wearing a mask, which contains several setting highlight extractors, decoupling branches, and consideration modules. To distinguish the fine-grained states of wearing a face mask and further make commitments to the constraint of Covid-19. The first step is data construction includes data collection, data annotation, and data statistics.

Adusumalli et al. [10] used methodologies like collecting datasets, implementing, identifying the person not wearing a mask, and sending the email. Implemented machine learning classifiers are Opencv and Tensorflow. This undertaking utilizes OpenCV, Caffe-based face finder, Keras, TensorFlow, and MobileNetV2 for the location of face cover on people. The dataset used contains 3835 pictures containing 1916 pictures with masks and 1919 without masks.

Chavda et al. [11] introduced a two-way mask Detector. The primary stage utilizes a pre-prepared Retina Face model for face detection, inside the wake of differing from its performance with Dlib and MTCN. The second stage enclosed preparing three different light-weight mask classifier models on the created dataset and improving the performance. The NASNet-mobile model was chosen for grouping faces with and without masks.

Matthias et al. [12] designed a feature base approach for detecting facial masks from a video selfie. The exhibition of the planned strategy depends on the productivity of the face and its feature identifiers. To deal with face mask acknowledgment undertakings, this paper proposes two sorts of datasets, including faces without the masks (FWOM), faces with masks (FWM).

Oumina et al. [13] developed a face mask detector using deep learning features with various honor-winning pre-prepared deep learning models. The utilization of transfer learning is a decent way to deal with characterizing faces with masks and faces without masks. The method proposed is based on feature selection using pre-trained deep convolutional neural networks and classification using machine learning algorithms such as K-NN and SVM.

Vinh et al. [14] present the YOLOv3 algorithm and the Haar cascade classifier. The proposed calculation utilizes a picture upgrade strategy to work on the exactness of the framework. The proposed algorithm for face mask location comprises three stages. They are pre-processing, face discovery, mask recognition. The pre-processing step is to improve the information picture quality by utilizing auto white equilibrium, and edge upgrade utilizing an unsharp filter. The face recognition step is to distinguish the face area. Another is to recognize masks.

Negi et al. [15] developed a deep neural network for facial mask identification using the SMFD dataset. Mechanisms used are CNN and VGG16 models for finding the face mask in crowded areas. CNN model accomplished preparing, approval, and testing exactness 96.35%, 96.35%, and 97.42% individually. VGG16 model accomplished 99.47%, 98.59%, and 98.97%.

Rahman et al. [16] present a framework to reduce the widespread of Covid-19 by an automated system to find people who are not using a mask. The methodologies used are image Pre-processing, deep learning architecture. The photos obtained by the CCTV require Pre-processing. In Pre-processing step, the RGB picture is changed into a grayscale picture as it removes unwanted dreary information from the picture and resizes them.

Wang et al. [17] introduced deep neural learning and a hybrid learning system for detecting face masks. By collecting datasets to evaluate measurement and parameter setting for quantitatively analyzing. Conventional techniques utilized high-quality highlights for face location. The most utilized highlight is a Haar-like element, prepared by AdaBoost calculation for face discovery.

Das et al. [18] improved face mask detection techniques by utilizing ML devices and improved procedures. The strategy has accomplished sensibly high exactness. By importing TensorFlow, Keras, and OpenCV packages. Methods like Data Processing, Training of Model methods. CNN model has got different Computer Vision undertakings. The current technique utilizes a sequential CNN model. The convolutional layer is trained by Rectified Linear Unit (ReLU) and Max-pooling.

Sunato et al. [19] implemented the face mask discovery by utilizing the YOLOv4 algorithm. The YOLOv4 algorithm comprises a deep learning methodology. The YOLOv4 can run quicker than other deep neural network techniques to recognize objects. By mirroring outcomes, it is appropriate to execute the strategy into the constant face cover finder where high recognition precision is required to detect masks.

Samuel et al. [20] have proposed a technique that is improved with a machine learning algorithm using the image classification methods like MobileNetv2, which contains data collection, pre-processing, splitting the data, building model, and testing the model. MobileNetv2 depends on Convolutional Neural Network (CNN) model is created to develop execution and upgrade to be more proficient.

This paper is different from other papers because it is having high accuracy and is efficient.

3 Proposed Model

System Design
This task utilizes OpenCV, Kera's, MobileNetv2, and TensorFlow for the location of face masks on people. The dataset contains human faces with and without a mask and video streaming given as input. Later resizing the picture or the video outline first, trailed by identifying the mass in it. The result says whether there is a mask or not.
The system design describes how to identify people who are wearing a mask or not by using the OpenCV. The camera is completely monitoring the people in the crowded area and detects all the faces in the crowd and identifies the faces without a mask. It can be used in Schools, colleges, markets, shopping malls, and so on. It also uses DNN (deep neural networks) in the opencv2 for setting frame dimensions.

The sequence of steps used to detect are:

Data collection
From the video, it detects the faces and split them into trained data, and tested data after it is analyzed.

Model training
OpenCV model is utilized to detect faces and by preparing a Kera's model to distinguish face cover.

Identifying people who are not using the mask
An OpenCV model is prepared to identify the faces of individuals who are not wearing covers and alert the security (Figs. 1, 2, 3 and 4).

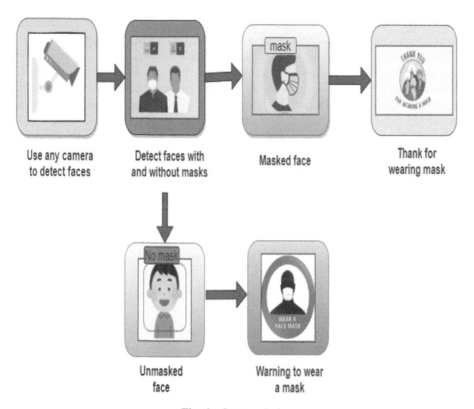

Fig. 1. System design

Proposed Model Architecture

In other cases, the dataset created contains 3833 pictures, out of which 1915 pictures have individuals with masks in them and 1918 pictures without masks. Out of this 75% is trained data and 25% is tested data.

By using the architecture, at first, it collects all the images. After that, it will clean and prepare the data/images. By using the CNN model, it will convert the pictures into gray colors and resize them. Mobilenetv2 is used for max-pooling as it is faster in process. Max-pooling is fully connected and sends as output. By using the face and mask detection model a mask is identified on the faces of the people.

Data visualization

Information perception is the way toward changing theoretical information to significant portrayals utilizing information correspondence and understanding disclosure through encodings.

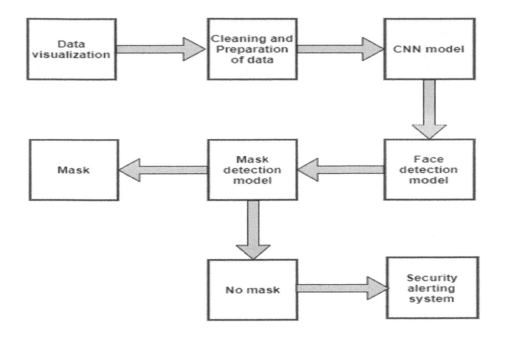

Architecture of face mask detection

Fig. 2. Architecture of face mask detection

4 Methodology

TensorFlow
TensorFlow creates spaces in software engineering, segmentation examination, voice acknowledgment, geographic data extraction, Computer Vision, text outline, and data recovery as executable Machine Learning frameworks. It is an open-source neural network. At the backend, the sequential CNN model utilizes TensorFlow. It will resize the pictures.

OpenCV
OpenCV is an Opensource Computer Vision Library. Its usage is to identify a face, objects, eye movements, identify CCTV, recognize the same picture from the dataset. OpenCV is used mainly for capturing video streaming and resizing pictures.

Keras
Keras is a very effective library for ML game plans with high speed. In the CNN model, every layer uses Kera's. In deep learning evaluation, Keras has used. It is an artificial neural network interface for running TensorFlow. Keras have been used as layers and models.

MobileNetV2
MobileNetV2 is a CNN model used mainly for cell phones. It contains an inverted residual structure that is between 19 bottleneck layers. For light in weight depth-wise convolutions, non-linear features had used in the middle layer. The design of MobileNetV2 consists of a total convolution layer with 32 filters.

CNN Model
The proposed strategy comprises a classifier and a Pre-prepared CNN model that contains two two-dimensional convolution layers associated with thick neurons layers.

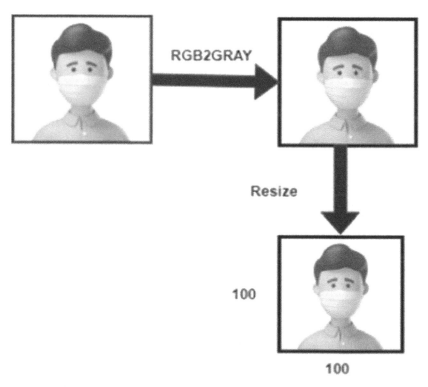

Fig. 3. Indicates the conversion from a BGR image to a grayscale image of 100 × 100 Size.

A Convolutional neural network (CNN) is a model in an artificial neural network that utilizes perceptrons, an ml unit calculation, for learning to dissect information. The CNN model applies to picture handling, language preparing, and different sorts of intellectual tasks. Pooling is used for filtering the image for high quality and to detect the person's face easily.

CNN Model Algorithm

```
 1 for each image in the dataset do
 2 |  visualize the image in two categories and label them
 3 |  convert th RGB image to ggray-scale image
 4 |  resize the gray-scale image into 100x100
 5 |  normalize the image and convert it into 4 dimensional array
 6 end
 7 for building the CNN model do
 8 |  add a convolutional layer of 200 filters
 9 |  add the second layer of 100 filters
10 |  insert a flatten layer to the network classifier
11 |  add a dense layer of 64 neurons
12 |  add the final dense layer with 2 outputs for 2 categories
13 end
14 split the data and train the model
```

Fig. 4. Algorithm of CNN model

Using a dataset that consists of 3833 images is converted into gray color. The face detection model, will identify the faces of persons in the image and resize them according to the dimensions. A face detection algorithm is executed to identify the person's face.

Face Detection Model
Using the face detection model, it is easy to identify the faces of the persons in the images or a video. In this method, the picture is converted into gray color and will detect the faces even in the crowd. After identifying the face it will draw a rectangular box around the face with the help of dimensions and display the output.

Mask Detection Model
The Mask detection model is used to identify images with and without a mask. This model will display bounding boxes for objects. Using the CNN model, it will convert the image from BGR to RGB channel ordering and resize them. These bounding boxes are added to the faces of the person by identifying whether they are wearing a mask or not.

Confusion Matrix
Table 1

Table 1. Confusion matrix

	With mask (prediction)	Without mask (prediction)
With mask (actual)	TP	FN
Without mask (actual)	FP	TN

Precision=TP / (TP + FP)
Accuracy=(TP+TN)/(TP+FN+TN+FP)
Recall=TP / (TP+FN)
F1-Score=(2*Precision*Recall) / (Precision + Recall)

5 Result

In this paper, we have developed a face mask algorithm that alerts the security system when people pass through the camera and identify who are not wearing masks and alerts the security system. Using the CNN model, Fig. 5 shows that person is wearing a mask having an accuracy of 99.91% in the green color bounding box, and Fig. 6 shows that person is not wearing a mask having an accuracy of 100% in the red color bounding box which describes without a mask. The frame size is fixed for the video streaming with a dimension of 240 × 240.

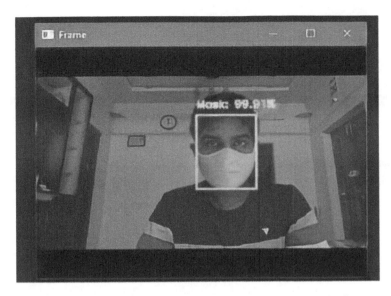

Fig. 5. When a person is using a mask. A rectangular bounding box is drawn around the person's face in green color with a label as mask and accuracy. (Color figure online)

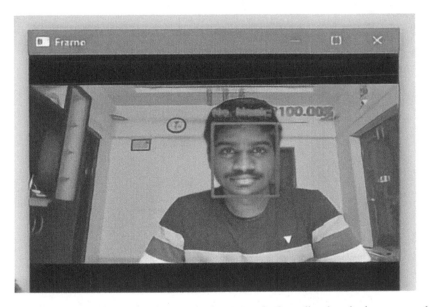

Fig. 6. When a person is not using a mask. A rectangular bounding box is drawn around the person's face in red color with a label as no mask and accuracy. (Color figure online)

When we consider a dataset with pictures of people with and without masks, the accuracy will be as shown in the below Table 2.

Table 2. Accuracy of the proposed model

	With a mask	Without a mask	Accuracy	Macro avg	Weighted avg
Precision	0.99	0.99	---	0.99	0.99
Recall	0.99	0.99	---	0.99	0.99
F1-score	0.99	0.99	0.99	0.99	0.99
Support	383	384	767	767	767

Graph

The graph describes the loss and accuracy of the training model.

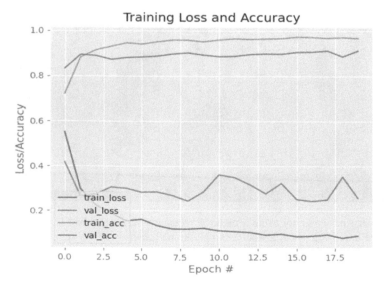

Fig. 7. Epoch vs accuracy corresponding to the dataset

Hence, this model will help find persons without masks easily with high accuracy of 99% as shown in Fig. 7, and helps in decreasing the transfer of the Coronavirus.

6 Conclusion and Future Enhancement

As COVID-19 is spreading more and more throughout the world and new variants are being discovered, it is necessary to wear a mask when we step out of the house. The proposed algorithm can be utilized, to recognize the people with and without a mask in many public areas like malls, educational institutions, offices, theatres, temples where there will be more people. Compared to other models proposed models give high accuracy. This framework detects people's faces using a camera and identifies individuals with and without masks, where humans check each person's face which is time-consuming.

So that by using this security alerting system we detect the persons who are not wearing masks easily and make them use masks properly. Finally, this framework will contribute enormously to medical care.

References

1. Snyder, S.E., Husari, G.: Thor: a deep learning approach for face mask detection to prevent the covid19 pandemic. In: Southeastcon 2021, pp. 1–8 (2021). https://doi.org/10.1109/Southeastcon45413.2021.9401874
2. Draughon, G.T.S., Sun, P., Lynch, J.P.: Implementation of a computer vision framework for tracking and visualizing face mask usage in Urban environments. In: 2020 IEEE International Smart Cities Conference (Isc2), pp. 1–8 (2020). https://doi.org/10.1109/Isc251055.2020.9239012
3. Joshi, A.S., Joshi, S.S., Kanahasabai, G., Kapil, R., Gupta, S.: Deep learning framework to detect face masks from video footage. In: 2020 12th International Conference On Computational Intelligence and Communication Networks (Cicn), pp. 435–440 (2020). https://doi.org/10.1109/Cicn49253.2020.9242625
4. Xue, B., Hu, J., Zhang, P.: Intelligent detection and recognition system for mask-wearing based on improved retinaface algorithm. In: 2020 2nd International Conference On Machine Learning, Big Data And Business Intelligence (Mlbdbi), pp. 474–479 (2020). https://doi.org/10.1109/Mlbdbi51377.2020.00100
5. Aswal, V., Tupe, O., Shaikh, S., Charniya, N.N.: Single camera masked face identification. In: 2020 19th IEEE International Conference On Machine Learning And Applications (Icmla), pp. 57–60 (2020). https://doi.org/10.1109/Icmla51294.2020.00018
6. Bhuiyan, M.R., Khushbu, S.A., Islam, M.S.: A deep learning-based assistive system to classify covid19 face mask for human safety with Yolov3. In: 2020 11th International Conference On Computing, Communication And Networking Technologies (Icccnt), pp. 1–5, (2020). https://doi.org/10.1109/Icccnt49239.2020.9225384
7. Negi, A., Chauhan, P., Kumar, K., Rajput, R.S.: Face mask detection classifier and model pruning with Kerassurgeon. In: 2020 5th IEEE International Conference On Recent Advances And Innovations In Engineering (Icraie), pp. 1–6 (2020). https://doi.org/10.1109/Icraie51050.2020.9358337

8. Din, N.U., Javed, K., Bae, S., Yi, J.: A novel GAN-based network for unmasking of masked face. IEEE Access **8**, 44276–44287 (2020). https://doi.org/10.1109/ACCESS.2020.2977386

9. Zhang, J., Han, F., Chun, Y., Chen, W.: A novel detection framework about conditions of wearing face mask for helping control the spread of covid-19. IEEE Access **9**, 42975–42984 (2021). https://doi.org/10.1109/ACCESS.2021.3066538

10. Adusumalli, H., Kalyani, D., Sri, R.K., Pratapteja, M., Rao, P.V.R.D.P.: Face mask detection using Opencv. In: 2021 Third International Conference On Intelligent Communication Technologies And Virtual Mobile Networks (Icicv), pp. 1304–1309 (2021). https://doi.org/10.1109/Icicv50876.2021.9388375

11. Amit, C., Jason, D., Sumeet, B., Ankit, D.: Multi-Stage Cnn Architecture For Face Mask Detection (2020)

12. Matthias, D., Managwu, C.: Face Mask Detection Paper (1) (2021). https://doi.org/10.13140/Rg.2.2.18493.59368

13. Oumina, A., El Makhfi, N., Hamdi, M.: Control the covid-19 pandemic: face mask detection using transfer learning. In: 2020 IEEE 2nd International Conference On Electronics, Control, Optimization And Computer Science (Icecocs), pp. 1–5 (2020). https://doi.org/10.1109/Icecocs50124.2020.9314511

14. Vinh, T.Q., Anh, N.T.N.: Real-time face mask detector using yolov3 algorithm and haar cascade classifier. In: 2020 International Conference On Advanced Computing And Applications (Acomp), pp. 146–149 (2020). https://doi.org/10.1109/Acomp50827.2020.00029

15. Negi, A., Kumar, K., Chauhan, P., Rajput, R.S.: Deep neural architecture for face mask detection on simulated masked face dataset against covid-19 pandemic. In: 2021 International Conference On Computing, Communication, And Intelligent Systems (Icccis), pp. 595–600 (2021). https://doi.org/10.1109/Icccis51004.2021.9397196

16. Rahman, M.M., Manik, M.M.H., Islam, M.M., Mahmud, S., Kim, J.-H.: An automated system to limit covid-19 using facial mask detection in smart city network. In: 2020 IEEE International IoT, Electronics, and Mechatronics Conference (Iemtronics), pp. 1–5 (2020). https://doi.org/10.1109/Iemtronics51293.2020.9216386

17. Wang, B., Zhao, Y., Chen, C.L.P.: Hybrid transfer learning and broad learning system for wearing mask detection in the covid-19 era. IEEE Trans. Instrum. Meas. **70**, 1–12 (2021). https://doi.org/10.1109/TIM.2021.3069844

18. Das, A., Wasif Ansari, M., Basak, R.: Covid-19 face mask detection using Tensorflow, Keras, and Opencv. In: 2020 IEEE 17th India Council International Conference (Indicon), pp1–5 (2020). https://doi.org/10.1109/Indicon49873.2020.9342585

19. Susanto, S., Putra, F.A., Analia, R., Suciningtyas, I.K.L.N.: The face mask detection for preventing the spread of covid-19 at Politeknik Negeri Batam. In: 2020 3rd International Conference On Applied Engineering (Icae), 2020, pp. 1–5, Doi: https://doi.org/10.1109/Icae50557.2020.9350556

20. Sanjaya, S.A., Adi Rakhmawan, S.: Face mask detection using Mobilenetv2 in the era of covid-19 pandemic. In: 2020 International Conference On Data Analytics For Business And Industry: Way Towards A Sustainable Economy (Icdabi), pp. 1–5 (2020). https://doi.org/10.1109/Icdabi51230.2020.9325631

Corona Virus Detection Using EfficientNet from CT Scans

D. Haritha$^{(\boxtimes)}$ (ID), B. Grace Gladys Nancy, T. V. L. Vara Prasad, N. Swaroop, and B. Jaswanth

SRK Institute of Technology, Vijayawada, India

Abstract. Currently, the entire world is experiencing a severe crisis. The Novel Corona Virus (COVID-19) has infected more than 18Cr and killed nearly 4L people in India. The spread rate is minimal if COVID-19 is eradicated before the epidemic spreads. By screening, isolating, and treating COVID-19 infected individuals at an early stage, the spread rate can be minimized. Deep Learning techniques can be effectively used to identify the CT scans and X-rays of COVID-19 patients at an early stage This paper focuses on identifying the CT scan images of COVID-19 patients from a mixed image set of COVID-19 and non-COVID-19 using deep learning networks that can critically impact on screening of COVID-19. The data set for this study consist of 1600 CT screenings of patients with COVID-19 as well as 1625 CT images of healthy patients that have been enhanced to create 12875 images after applying transformations. We use an EfficientNet model for Image Classification and detection that effectively utilizes higher resolution features of CT-scan input images and shows better performance than CNN models. Our results showed that the model achieves better precision and accuracy in detecting COVID-19 affected patients' CT scans.

Keywords: CNN · COVID-19 · CT scans · Deep learning networks · EfficientNet · ResNet-50

1 Introduction

The identification of disease from the outbreak of symptoms of a completely unknown infection was first identified in December 2019 in a local market in China, and a rapid action initiated by china government in understanding and curtailing the disease, drawn the attention of the entire world. In the beginning, the disease was totally unknown, but authorities pinpointed that its signs are homogeneous to those of SARS infection [4]. The distinct cause of this extensive disease was initially unknown, but after the laboratory investigation and exploration of positive phlegm by a real-time polymerase chain reaction (PCR) test, it was identified as a new viral infection, and later it was named as "COVID-19" by the (WHO) World Health Organization. The sensing of COVID-19 at an early infected stage is crucial, not only for taking care of patients but also for isolating the patients and controlling the wide-spreading to others. Due to the

D. Garg et al. (Eds.): IACC 2021, CCIS 1528, pp. 25–38, 2022.
https://doi.org/10.1007/978-3-030-95502-1_3

non-availability of the full information on the disease, the methods to prevent and combat it were not known in the initial days. But doctors and scientists observed that proper screening, quick diagnosis of the infected patients, and their isolation from the family and neighbors is a prime act to prevent the widespread.

RT-PCR is a very tedious, stagnant, expensive, and manual process which requires experienced and skilled technicians to collect the mucous from the nose and throat, and it involves a throbbing procedure. More significantly, numerous experiences indicated the slow process of the RT-PCR test and its low accuracy, affecting a decrease in the accuracy in detecting COVID-19 in various cases. The accuracy and speed of COVID-19 detection can be improved by using images, including X-ray [5, 6] and computed tomography (CT) scans. As the virus affects the lungs, medical practitioners recommended using Chest imaging as one of the rapid and simple approaches. CT scans are more efficient in diagnosing COVID-19 as compared to RT-PCR and X-rays. Hence, using CT scans will be more significant in the detection of COVID-19 [3].

1.1   Why CT Screenings?

CT imaging also called CAT (Computerized Axial Tomography) scanning is a distinctive imaging that produces cross-sectional or slice imaging. CT imaging may be more authentic, accurate, and gives a more detailed image than that of a chest X-ray. For instance, a chest X-ray may recognize irregularities whereas a chest CT scan is good enough to show the irregularities with their absolute intensity and location and are stored as electronic data files and are typically reviewed on a computer screen as a 3D image. In this paper, 1625 chest CT images of normal people and 1600 chest CT images of Covid affected patients were taken from Kaggle's chest CT images dataset [13–15]. CT scan images of COVID-19 infected and non-COVID-19 infected persons are illustrated in Figs. 1 and 2. The CT Scan image analysis is based on the following features: (a) the number of lobes (b) lesions and their spatial positioning (c) patterns of lesions like (GGO) Ground Glass Opacification with its shape and crazy-paving pattern, (d) bronchial and/or bronchiolar wall thickening, etc., signs present in the lesion and (e) any additional findings like tree-in-bud signs [10].

The whole dataset is accessible publicly for academic research basis and the data augmentation procedure was applied to avoid the overfitting problem. In our implementation, all the images are resized to 224 × 224-pixel images. Following that, we applied the transformations like horizontal and vertical flips and rotation of 10° rotation for each image in the dataset. Therefore, a total of 12857 CT images is generated from both the COVID-19 and Non-COVID class original images. After this data augmentation, the COVID-19 and the non-COVID dataset is spilt as training and testing sets in 8:2 ratio and are used for evaluating the effectiveness and accuracy of both EfficientNet and ResNet50 models. The model is to be trained on several epochs to gain perfect accuracy.

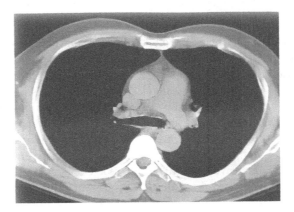

Fig. 1. Non-COVID person's CT image.

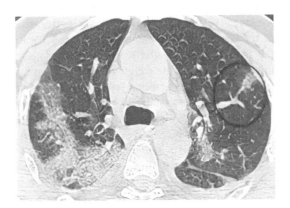

Fig. 2. COVID person's CT image.

1.2 Existing Systems

We can use the pre-trained models in numerous ways to classify images from a dataset, after image pre-processing, feature extraction, and classification. The state-of-the-art deep learning models used in classification are Visual Geometry Group(VGG-16), Residual Networks(ResNet-50), InceptionNet, ChexNet CNN [5, 8]. In our work, we analyze each of these models and especially differentiate between ResNet-50 and EfficientNet, as ResNet50 achieved significant performance and qualifies the network to preserve the information learned previously.

1.3 VGG-16

Introduced in 2014 consists of a convolution layer 1 that receives input images of 224 × 224 pixels size followed by a stack of 21 convolution layers each with 3 × 3 sized filters. These convolution layers stack is followed by 5 Max Pooling layers having size 2 × 2. Also, the convolutional layer 1 receives input images with 224 × 224-pixel dimensions, followed by a stack of 21 convolutional layers each with 3 × 3 layers. 5 Max Pooling layers have size 2 × 2 are then applied. Max Pooling layers are followed by three dense layers. It uses 64 filters in the first layer, 128 filters in the second layer, 256 filters in the third layer, and 512 filters in successive layers.

The last 3 dense layers have 4096, 4096, and 1000 channels sizes respectively. This is one of the widely used networks in diagnosing COVID-19 [27].

1.4 ResNet-50

Introduced in 2015 Fig. 5 can train many layers even several hundred and thousands and was shown to be effective that gave a significant performance with images of 224 × 224 size. But the vanishing gradient problem in back propagation makes it difficult to train many layers, i.e. when the weights are updated at a low pace, the gradient becomes infinitely small, and the weights that are updating stop after a while, resulting in network performance degradation. To overcome this problem, in ResNet-50, the residual blocks present use an identity mapping function and thus preserve the information learned previously that helps to reduce the training error though it's a deeper model [9]. This model uses global average pooling layers in place of dense layers and hence the model size is smaller than that of VGG16. The existing deep learning models for sensing COVID-19 have few limitations which require more training parameters, which not only produce a computation overload in the classification but also result in overfitting complications because of the finite availability of COVID-19 input images. To tackle these limitations, we put forward a novel deep learning model using a satisfactory layer EfficientNet b0 of the EfficientNet family can be seen in Fig. 4. ResNet50 is also one of the most used networks in detecting COVID-19 [21].

2 Literature Review

We studied a few related works available for detecting COVID-19 from different input imaging media and several deep Learning models.

Haritha. D, et al. [7] used transfer learning techniques for COVID-19 prediction from chest X-Rays. They took a balanced dataset from Kaggle consisting of chest x-rays of both COVID-19 infected and disinfected people. Their transfer learning models include VGGNet, Google Net-Inception V1, ResNet, and CheXNet. Transfer learning could be a better deep learning technique as it reduces the model training time. They obtained prediction accuracies of 99.49%, 99%, 98.63%, 99.93% respectively for the above said models. Since they used datasets of smaller sizes, their model's accuracy is to be thoroughly tested for new variants of COVID-19.

Sertan Serte, Hasan Demirel [21] proposed an artificial intelligence system to detect Covid-19 from the 3D CT volume images. Their system used ResNet50 to detect Covid-19 and showed 96% of accuracy.

Michael J. Horry et al. [16] worked on the detection of COVID-19 through transfer learning to use multi-modal imaging data like X-Rays, Ultrasound scans, and CT scans. They applied and did a comparison of all CNN models and identified that VGG19 model is suitable and optimized that model for COVID-19 prediction The results indicated that Ultrasound images provide superior prediction accuracy and gave accuracies of 86% for X-ray images, 100% for Ultrasound scans and 84% for CT Scans.

Shivani Sharma et al. [22] worked on diagnosing COVID-19 using X-Ray images and Deep learning techniques on the dataset comprising positive COVID-19, healthy images, and viral pneumonia X-ray images to reduce its computational time by using fewer layers. The model showed an accuracy of 94% on the training data set and 96% on the validation data set.

Mohammed Chachan, Younis [18] worked on CNN-based models for the classification of coronavirus species, they used LSTM model and VGG model for the detection of coronavirus, the VGG provides an accuracy of 91% as well as the LSTM model predicts 99% of accuracy.

Vruddhi Shah et al. [27] worked on diagnosing COVID-19 CT images using different deep learning algorithms. They proposed a model named as CTnet-10 that got an accuracy of 82.1%. They also examined other models like ResNet50, DenseNet-169, VGG16, Inception V3, and VGG19. Out of all VGG19 resulted with an accuracy of 94.52%. They stated that their automated diagnosis helps professionals to detect COVID-19 cases in a very quick and accurate manner.

The work done by Mohit Agarwal et al. [20], Plamen Angelov et al. [19], Luca Saba et al. [1], Suri, Jasjit et al. [24] and Di Dong et al. [2] is effective in detecting COVID-19 motivated us to do this work.

3 Deep Learning Models for Covid Detection

Deep Learning is a suitable CNN of deeper size when sufficient training data and high computational resources are available. In the pre-trained model, preceding layers contain low-level image information such as edges and color and the succeeding layers contain high-level features such as categorical features. Though many CNN models are available, the major issue to be taken care of in designing CNNs and DNNs is model scaling which helps to enlarge the model size with the aim of getting better accuracy [17]. An EfficientNet model, a new family of CNNs' model that also considers model scaling issues was released by Google in 2019. EfficientNet gives both improved accuracy and model efficiency in terms of reduced parameters and the number of floating-point operations.

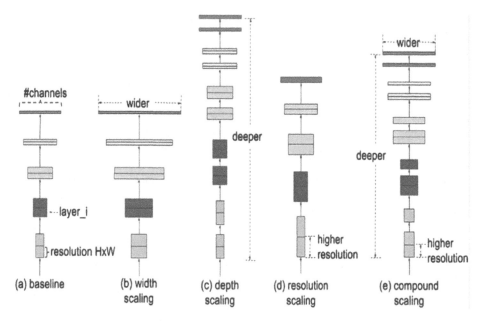

Fig. 3. Model Scaling examples. (a) baseline network, (b) width scaled network, (c) depth scaled network and (d) resolution scaled network. (e) compound scaling method that scales all width, height and resolution uniformly.

There are 8 models of EfficientNet family (B0 to B7). In EfficientNet, the authors proposed a new Scaling method called Compound Scaling as shown in Fig. 3. The Authors reviewed and studied the strategy of scaling up ConvNets [23]. Their investigation suggested EfficientNet B0 model that uses an efficient compound scaling gives higher performance and accuracy when scaling is required [17]. They also operated on ResNet-50, though it does not use compound scaling. With all the merits discussed for EfficientNet B0 model for classification, we selected this model for classifying the chest CT Scan images and distinguishing the COVID-19 screenings from the non-COVID ones and as explained in the next section.

Fig. 4. EfficientNet b0 architecture.

3.1   EfficientNet B0 Architecture

Figure 4 shows the COVID-EfficientNet B0 architecture that is used for sensing the COVID-19 virus in CT images. The authors proposed that if we scale the size by a fixed amount at an identical time and do so uniformly, we can attain far better performance. The scaling coefficients are often actually decided by the user. The main building block of this model comprises MBConv (Mobile inverted bottleneck Convolution) blocks that form a shortcut connection of the first and last, ends of convolution blocks. The parameters are added to each channel so that the network can adjust the weights of each feature map. The input activation maps use 1×1 sized convolutions to help to increase the feature maps depth and are subsequently followed by 3×3 convolutions performed depth-wise and are finally followed by point-wise convolutions to lower the size of the output feature map. This architecture helps to reduce the size of the model as well as the required number of operations.

3.2   ResNet50 Architecture

The pre-trained ResNet50 model architecture is amplified to suit the COVID-19 dataset following the process of the EfficientNet model. The training and testing dataset images are resized to 224×224. ResNet is considered to be a better deep learning model since

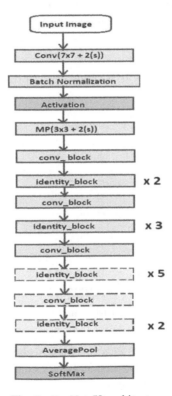

Fig. 5. ResNet 50 architecture

it is relatively easy to improve and can achieve better accuracy. ResNet50 is an altered version of the ResNet model with 48 Convolution layers, 1 Max Pooling layer, and finally, an Average Pooling layer, as shown in Fig. 5.

The methodology followed for Covid-19 detection using EfficientNet model includes the following steps:

Step 1: The dataset from the Kaggle Dataset repository is considered as input [13–15]. It consists of CT images of COVID-19 patients and non-COVID-19 persons. The sample images of both cases are shown in Figs. 1 and 2.

Step 2: Resize the input CT images of the dataset such that their sizes match that of the pre-trained model input layer dimensions.

Step 3: Transformations to the CT input images are applied to control varying rotations throughout the training, on setting rotation to 10 degrees. The image augmentation technique increases the training dataset size which helps to improve the model performance and generalization.

Step 4: The size of the training dataset is expanded artificially by generating altered versions of images in the dataset from 3225 images to 12875 images.

Step 5: Considering these new images, the data is partitioned into training and testing sets with an 8:2 ratio. Out of these, 80% of images are applied for training, and 20% are used for the testing dataset.

Step 6: The model is to be trained on several epochs to achieve better accuracy for both EfficientNet and ResNet50 networks [11, 12].

Step 7: Draw the loss versus accuracy plots for the model performance of the training and test phases.

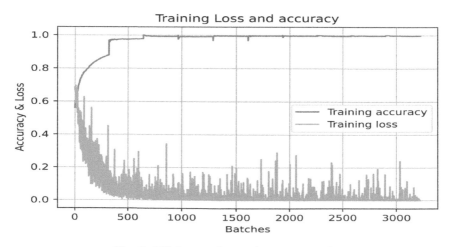

Fig. 6. Efficient net loss and accuracy graph.

The Above Figs. 6 and 7 represents the loss Accuracy of both EfficientNet and ResNet50. The x-axis in Fig. 6 is labelled as Batches and y-axis as accuracy and loss. Here the total batches of the training set are 325 since the size of each batch is 32 and when each epoch runs on every batch, we get the total number of batches as 3225.

Whereas in Fig. 7, the x-axis is labelled as Epochs and y-axis as accuracy and loss. When each epoch runs on every batch the total number of batches obtained from the training set are 3225, where each batch size is 32.The total number of batches alters with the change in number of epochs.

4   Experimental Results

The DNNs performance for the covid-19 prediction has been evaluated using two deep learning models namely ResNet50 and EfficientNet. Figures 6 and 7 shows the accuracy and the loss function respectively for EfficientNet and ResNet50. The plots show both curves during the training and validation phases. At the 10th epoch, the accuracies on the training images noted were 99% for EfficientNet and 100 for ResNet50.

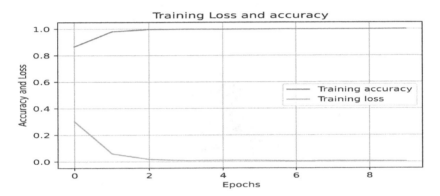

Fig. 7. ResNet 50 loss and accuracy graph.

The performance metrics used for the evaluation of model effectiveness and efficiency are Accuracy, Sensitivity, Precision, and Specificity, which are mathematically calculated. Below are the results for EfficientNet and ResNet50, as well as the Confusion Matrix without statistical significance. The results for both EfficientNet and ResNet50 were noted below along with the Confusion Matrix without normalization for true labels and predicted labels as shown in Figs. 8 and 9. The accuracy of EfficientNet was about 0.9984 and that of ResNet is 0.991 [25, 26].

$$Accuracy = \frac{TNI + TPI}{TNI + FPI + TPI + FNI}$$

$$Precision = \frac{TPI}{TPI + FPI}$$

$$Sensitivity = \frac{TPI}{TPI + FNI} = \frac{TPI}{PI}$$

$$Specificity = \frac{TNI}{TNI + FPI} = \frac{TNI}{NI}$$

Where TNI is the number of negative class images classified as negative, TPI is the number of positive class images classified as positive, FNI is the number of positive class images classified wrongly as negative and FPI is the number of negative class images wrongly classified as positive. The performance of the two models EfficientNet and ResNet50 is analyzed using the above metrics. Though ResNet50 gives an accuracy of 0.9914 with a quite good sensitivity of 0.9962, the specificity using ResNet (0.9838) as illustrated in Fig. 9 is a bit concerned as a COVID-19 affected victim is not expected to be classified as "COVID negative". Whereas, with the EfficientNet model we obtained the accuracy of COVID-19 detection as 0.9984 with quite good sensitivity of 0.9987 and specificity of 0.9978. Thus, the EfficientNet model obtained much better accuracy and efficiency over the other CNN's as shown in Fig. 10.

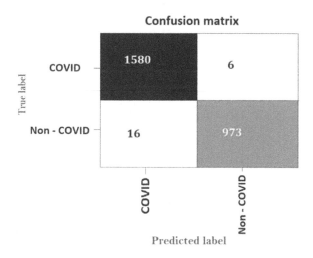

Accuracy :   0.9914563106796116
Specificity : 0.9838220424671386
Sensitivity : 0.9962168978562421
Precision :   0.9899749373433584

Fig. 8. ResNet50 confusion matrix and values of performance metrics

In this COVID-19 detection low sensitivity is a major concern and to be avoided as this virus spreads at a much faster rate than the other viruses from person to person at an exponential rate. If a victim is miss-classified as COVID positive, he/she would be unnecessary gets isolated from others. It is a bit challenging to keep the tradeoff between sensitivity and specificity in health care applications in selecting suitable Deep Learning models for prediction. However, the key benefit of such a screening approach is that besides the time required to generate a CT image, once the model networks are trained, the prediction on each task can be completed in a couple of seconds, thereby extremely reducing the testing time for the patients. Therefore, our experimentation resulted in precision and accuracy above 99% in sensing COVID-19 from CT screenings. The above algorithm is implemented and executed in Google Co-laboratory. Though we obtained a reasonably better detection accuracy, precision, and recall, this is not ready at this stage for developing a software product that can be readily usable by medical practitioners, as we implemented our model with the limited size of dataset currently available.

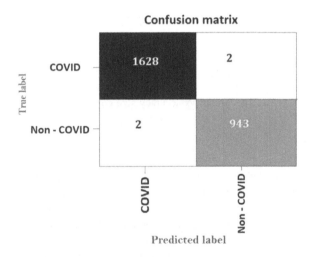

Confusion matrix, without normalization

Accuracy :	0.9984466019417476
Specificity :	0.9978835978835979
Sensitivity :	0.9987730061349693
Precision :	0.9987730061349693

Fig. 9. EfficientNet confusion matrix and values of performance metrics

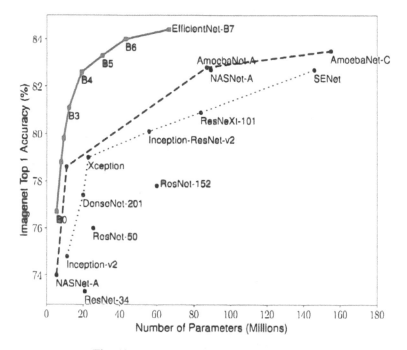

Fig. 10. Model vs accuracy size comparision

5   Conclusion

In our work, we employed EfficientNet which is a deep neural network model for sensing COVID-19 from the CT images we provided. This attained accuracy above 99% in detecting the Covid-19 virus. Our work supports the use of Artificial Intelligence, research in this direction, and in particular using Deep Neural Networks in disease prediction. Our observation throughout the experiment shows that the CNN-based approaches could be very beneficial in terms of attaining very fast and swift testing results to detect COVID-19. More precisely, the notion of using EfficientNet can enhance the performance of CNN models quite drastically achieving an accuracy of 0.9984. Our focal point of this work is to provide additional helping aid to radiologists, medical practitioners, and also the research community with a user-friendly CNN model for the early sensing of COVID-19 and hopefully, this work helps to accelerate research in this current pandemic situation.

References

1. Agarwal, M., et al.: A novel block imaging technique using nine artificial intelligence models for COVID-19 disease classification, characterization and severity measurement in lung computed tomography scans on an Italian cohort. J. Med. Syst. **45**(3), 1–30 (2021)

2. Dong, D.: The role of imaging in the detection and management of COVID-19: a review. J. IEEE Rev. Biomed. Eng. **14**, 1–1 (2020)
3. Soares, E., et al.: SARS-CoV-2 CT-scan dataset: a large dataset of real patients CT scans for SARS-CoV-2 identification. J. medRxiv (2020)
4. Quer, G., et al.: Wearable sensor data and self-reported symptoms for COVID-19 detection. J. Nat. Med. **27**, 2021 (2021)
5. Haritha, D., Pranathi, M.K., Reethika, M.: COVID detection from chest X-rays with DeepLearning:CheXNet. In: Proceedings of the 5th International Conference on Computing, Communication and Security. IEEE (2020)
6. Haritha, D., Praneeth, C., Pranathi, M.K.: Covid Prediction from X-ray Images. In: Proceedings of the 5th International Conference on Computing, Communication and Security. IEEE (2020)
7. Haritha, D., Krishna Pranathi, M.: Covid prediction from chest X-Rays using transfer learning. In: Garg, D., Wong, K., Sarangapani, J., Gupta, S.K. (eds.) Advanced Computing: 10th International Conference, IACC 2020, Panaji, Goa, India, December 5–6, 2020, Revised Selected Papers, Part I, pp. 128–138. Springer Singapore, Singapore (2021). https://doi.org/10.1007/978-981-16-0401-0_10
8. Haritha, D., Swaroop, N., Mounika, M.: Prediction of COVID-19 cases using CNN with X-rays. In: Journal of the 5th International Conference on Computing, Communication and Security (ICCCS) (2020). https://doi.org/10.1109/ICCCS49678.2020.9276753
9. He, K., Zhang, X., Ren, S., Sun, J.: Deep Residual Learning for Image Recognition, 770–778 (2016). https://doi.org/10.1109/CVPR.2016.90
10. Zuo, H.: Contribution of CT Features in the diagnosis of COVID-19. Can. Respir. J. (2020). https://doi.org/10.1155/2020/1237418
11. https://colab.research.google.com/drive/1A013l8dYa3W1bYjTs8V7lPqaUJMKfKz5?usp=sharing
12. https://colab.research.google.com/drive/1C-g1KWj8pmYb-UJcNjlundoMG6klrBtP?usp=sharing
13. https://www.kaggle.com/luisblanche/COVIDct?select=CT-COVID
14. https://www.kaggle.com/plameneduardo/sarscov2-ctscan-dataset
15. Luisblanche,et al.: COVID-19 Lung CT Scans DataSet (2020)
16. Horry, M.J.: COVID-19 detection through transfer learning using multimodal imaging data. J. IEEE Access **8**, 149808–149824 (2021)
17. Tan, M., Staff Software Engineer, Le, Q.V., Principal Scientist, Google, AI: EfficientNet: Improving Accuracy and Efficency through AutoML and Model Scaling (2020)
18. Younis, M.C.: Evaluation of deep learning approaches for identification of different corona-virus species and time series prediction. J. Sci. Direct (2021)
19. Angelov, P., Soares, E.: Towards explainable deep neural networks(xDNN). J. Neural Networks, 130 (2020)
20. Saba, L., et al.: Six artificial intelligence paradigms for tissue characterisation and classification of non-COVID-19 pneumonia against COVID-19 pneumonia in computed tomography lungs. Int. J. Comput. Assisted Radiol. Surg. **16**(3), 423–434 (2021)
21. Serte, S., Demirel, H.: Deep learning for diagnosis of COVID-19 using 3D CT scans. J. Sci. Direct (2021)
22. Sharma, S., Tiwari, S.: COVID-19 Diagnosis using X-Ray images and deep learning. In: Journal of 2021 International Conference on Artificial Intelligence and Smart Systems (ICAIS) (2021)
23. Simonyan, K., Zisserman, A.: Very Deep Convolutional Networks for Large-Scale Image Recognition. arXiv:1409.1556 (2014)

24. Suri, J.S., et al.: A narrative review on characterization of acute respiratory distress syndrome in COVID-19-infected lungs using artificial intelligence. Comput. Biol. Med. **130**, 104210 (2021)
25. Source Code of EfficientNet, Available:[12]
26. Source Code of ResNet50, Available:[11]
27. Shah, V., Keniya, R., Shridharani, A., Punjabi, M., Shah, J., Mehendale, N.: Diagnosis of COVID-19 using CT scan images and deep learning techniques. Emergency Radiol. **28**(3), 497–505 (2021)

Disease Diagnosis in Grapevines
– A Hybrid Resnet-Jaya Approach

Piyush Mishra[1], Puspanjali Mohapatra[2]([✉]), Tapas Kumar Patra[3],
and P. Subham[4]

[1] Turing Centre for Living Systems, Aix-Marseille University, Marseille, France
[2] Department of Computer Science Engineering,
International Institute of Information Technology, Bhubaneswar, India
puspanjali@iiit-bh.ac.in
[3] Department of Instrumentation and Electronics Engineering,
Odisha University of Technology and Research, Bhubaneswar, India
[4] Department of Computer Science Engineering, National Institute of Technology,
Rourkela, India

Abstract. Different diseases in grapevines have different kinds of effects on the various parts of the plant, the most drastic of such abnormalities easily seen in the leaves of the grapevines. Detection, diagnosis and prevention of diseases that could hinder the production and utilisation of the grapevine are of prime importance in viticulture. In view of the multiple hazards associated with viticulture, it is worthwhile to build on the optimisation and automation in the field. This study presents a methodology to marry the different aspects of computational mechanisms, i.e. neural network approaches along with different optimisation approaches, and apply them to diagnose the diseases that a said grapevine might suffer from. The objectives were, thus: (1) to be able to identify which disease corresponds to the effects shown in the leaves of the particular grapevine, (2) to make a robust identification mechanism by using methodologies of deep learning and soft computing, and (3) to make use of different such methodologies and infer which of those methodologies would work the best in this context. As a result, we mostly compared a 10 layer-feed forward neural network with a 34 layer-Resnet. We also employed other CNN methodologies like Densenet, VGG and Alexnet but found that they did not provide the best results in this context. Further, we hybridised these approaches with several optimisation algorithms, like the Jaya Algorithm, the Genetic Algorithm, the Particle Swarm Optimisation Algorithm, etc. We found that a hybrid Resnet-Jaya model gave the best output without overfitting, at 99.71%.

Keywords: Grape · Grapevine · Neural networks · Machine learning · Plant disease diagnosis

© Springer Nature Switzerland AG 2022
D. Garg et al. (Eds.): IACC 2021, CCIS 1528, pp. 39–56, 2022.
https://doi.org/10.1007/978-3-030-95502-1_4

1   Introduction

Grapevines are a part of the *Vitis* genus, many of the species of which have evolved throughout the world. *V. vinifera* is most commonly used for wine and table grapes. Wine accounts for a majority of the portion of usage of grapes i.e. 55% [4,24]. The grape is highly adaptable to climates in temperate, sub-tropical and tropical regions because of its high genetic plasticity. In India, 34,000 ha of land is devoted to grape cultivation: with 1 million tonnes of annual production [1,14]. Furthermore, the demand for grape related products is increasing. Thus, it becomes very essential to be able to diagnose grapevines with potential diseases in order to cater to the increasing demand for the plant, the products related to it and the complements. Early and effective diagnosis becomes especially important, since rising demand with increasing returns implies that the industry in general, has to work fast in providing the results for the market.

The principal key ideas that are elaborated in this study are as follows:

(1) Data Augmentation: It is employed to better train the model by adding certain transformative variations to the images of the plant leaves. This increases the size of the data which helps the model to learn from more variations, in turn making it highly robust [31].

(2) Transfer Learning: Pre-trained convolutional neural networks are used in the study, most notably, the Resnet34, which is already trained on the ImageNet Dataset [8,28]. It is trained for an optimum number of epochs on the training dataset to classify the diseased grapevine leaves from their more healthier counterparts. The concept of transfer learning is used because it proves to be faster and more accurate than curating a neural network from scratch [38].

(3) Effective Learning: Selection of an optimum range of learning rate becomes very essential to ensure a rising learning curve for our model [17].

(4) Handling Confident Inaccuracies: After training, the model is made to predict its results, and it is checked if the model is confused about certain labels and the confidence is measured. Here, confidence implies that the model predicts the wrong output with an objectively high loss [11].

Section 2 talks about the past research work that has already been carried out in the domain. Section 3 presents the methodology for collection of data, handling of data as well as data pre-processing. Section 4 elaborates in detail, about the contributions to the domain through this research and analysis. The results of this study are presented in Sects. 5 and 6 concludes the study and discusses the future scope of this research.

2   Related Work

There have been immense contributions in the field of viticulture in the past, and much more research is ongoing. Concern for grapevine diseases is can be found in a huge body of research. Agudelo et al. [3] study the accumulation of copper in Brazillian vineyards, which impact the plant growth. They also study the biological relationship of these grapevines with the Arbuscular mycorrhizal fungi. Arand et al. [5] study the surface of the berry in order to answer questions pertaining to maladies in grapes. This concern is also seen in [12], wherein dsRNA amplicons of different grapevines are isolated to study the effects of the Shiraz disease.

However, detecting diseases in grapevines with the help of leaf images is a newer concept. Riaz et al. have been successful in finding evidences of sexual reproduction in the grape phylloxera [33]. Yancheva et al. discuss the opportunity of in-vitro fertilisation in grapevines [41] for a faster and more efficient cultivation and management. In July 2013, Sannakki et al. published their findings on grapevine disease diagnosis [34] using feed forward convolutional neural networks. However, the computation is done in Matlab, and the size of the dataset used is very small. Moreover, the then state-of-the-art accuracies of their contributions are very low compared to the present day state-of-the-art, and will not prove to be reliable in case of production usage.

Further, resource optimisation has also been carried out in this field. Anderson et al. discuss the effects of climate change on viticulture and how that affects the current scenario [4]. Furthermore, researchers have also been using geospatial tools to navigate the management approaches of grape cultivation [29]. Instead of simple feed forward neural networks, as used by Sannakki et al. [34], this study uses a residual network with 34 neural network layers (Resnet34). It is discussed in detail in the upcoming sections.

Another significant body of work is presented by Liu et al. in [23] where they exhibit a systematic and a similar approach, as in this experimentation, towards the diagnosis of diseases in grapevines. They seek to identify diseases through leaf images, however, the experimentation is a reproduction of previously existent methodologies, i.e., the identification is only carried out using pre-trained methodologies. They propose a new convolutional model called DICNN which is influenced by several preexisting convolutional models. They achieve an accuracy of 97.22%. Instead of relying completely on neural network approach, the best parts of it are combined with the applicability of optimisation algorithms, particularly the Jaya algorithm.

3   Datasets Used

The dataset used for this research and analysis is a subset of the publicly available plantVillage dataset [27]. It contains the raw images of a number of plant leaves out of which, grape leaves have been selected for this particular research. So, the reduced dataset consists of the images of the leaves of grapevines suffering from *isariopsis leaf spot, esca, black rot* and the healthy variants; with 228, 277, 219 and 88 leaf images for the respective classes. A sample of the leaf images is shown in Fig. 1.

(a) Healthy

(b) Isariopsis Leaf Spot

(c) Esca

(d) Black Rot

Fig. 1. Variations of grape leaf types: healthy and diseased

Data augmentation [31] is carried out by generating further variations and finally, the data is normalised. Normalisation ensures that the pixel values have the same mean and standard deviation [37], which further helps the model to train fast and effectively, as well as, in a more uniform fashion.

Consider an n-dimensional greyscale image I with intensity values in the range *(Min, Max)*. The new n-dimensional image I_N with the new intensity values in the range *(newMin, newMax)* can be generated using a linear normalisation given by the following equation:

$$I_N = (I - Min)\frac{newMax - newMin}{Max - Min} + newMin \qquad (1)$$

In case of a non-linear relationship with the original and the normalised images, the relation can be given by the following equation:

$$I_N = (newMax - newMin)\frac{1}{1 + e^{-\frac{I-\beta}{\alpha}}} + newMin \qquad (2)$$

Here, α refers to the width of the input intensity range and β refers to the intensity around which the range is centred. These relationships are exploited to achieve the required normalisation in this study. Further, the images are segmented to make the model training procedure even more robust and effective. Thus, the images are made ready for training. A sample of these images is shown in Fig. 2.

(a) Healthy   (b) Isariopsis Leaf Spot

(c) Esca   (d) Black Rot

Fig. 2. Grape leaf types after segmentation: healthy and diseased

4 Proposed Methodology

4.1 Residual Networks (Resnet)

Convolution. In this study, the concept of convolutional neural networks is used because the convolution function is a highly fundamental mathematical function which can be employed in detecting and identifying features in an image. A neural network approach works better than a classical machine learning mechanism because it tends to mimic the human brain while learning to detect features [15]. The inherent function which is used for this said feature extraction, commonly known as convolutional function, is given by:

$$(f * g)(t) = \int_{-\infty}^{\infty} f(\tau)g(t - \tau)d\tau \tag{3}$$

Intuitively, a feature or filter matrix is convoluted with the image matrix to extract its features. A multitude of filters are used to get feature maps, the collection of which is widely referred to as the convolutional layer.

Rectifier Activation Function. In the pre-processing phase, one seeks to reduce the non-linearity in images with the help of normalisation, as discussed previously. In order to further reduce the non-linearity of an image, the Rectified Linear Unit activation function (ReLU) can be used [2]. The reason why other non-linear functions like the Sigmoid or the Hyperbolic tangent are not used here is because they tend to saturate easily [13]. The rectifier function is given by the following equation:

$$f(x) = x^+ = max(0, x) \tag{4}$$

Thus, in case there are any negative pixel values, they can be replaced by zeroes. This, of course, is a simple analogy but the same principles are used for activation during experiment.

The Residual Network. The Resnet34 [16] architecture of convolutional neural networks is employed for the purpose of carrying out the classification procedure. The basic architectural design of a Residual Network or Resnet is as shown in Fig. 3. Here, instead of simply moving forward, as is seen in a feed-forward based network, after every two weighted layers with an activation function in between, there is a shortcut connection. In feed-forward type neural networks, there is usually a problem of degradation as a network becomes deeper: as the network depth increases, the accuracy tends to get saturated and then declines at a fast rate [40] .

A deep residual learning framework has been introduced by Microsoft that overcomes the problem of accuracy saturation [21]. Rather than anticipating that every roughly alternating layer would directly fit an inherent mapping, they make them fit a specific mapping of residues. The conceptualisation of $F(x) + x$ can be realised by feedforward neural networks with shortcut connections [16]. Hence, this model is used for reaching conclusions.

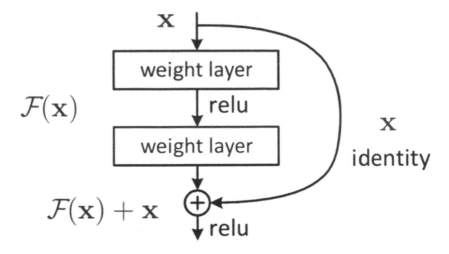

Fig. 3. The primary architecture of a resnet

4.2   Minimised Jaya Algorithm – Hybrid NN Approach

Jaya Algorithm. The Jaya Algorithm [32] is a population-based evolutionary algorithm that makes the optimisation of a specific problem extensively straightforward and intuitive. It is usually considered better than most optimisation algorithms because of the absence of hyper-parameters, like mutation probability and other such terminologies found in the literature of other optimisation algorithms, like the genetic algorithm. The heart of the algorithm says that one must move closer to the chromosome (i.e., a population candidate) with the fitness closest to the optimum fitness, and away from the chromosome with the fitness farthest away from the optimum fitness value. A similar approach is used for the structure-optimisation of wireless sensor networks which exhibits the versatility of this algorithm [26]. The general algorithm, devoid of any other problematic context, is exhibited in Algorithm 1.

Algorithm 1. A General Jaya Algorithm

---
initialise random population, X
store the best and the worst chromosomes of the population in X_{best} and X_{worst}
initialise $X' \leftarrow \phi$ as the population for the next generation
while the current generation is not the final generation **do**
    initialise $r_1, r_2 \in (0, 1]$
    $X' \leftarrow X + r_1(X_{best} - X) - r_2(X_{worst} - X)$
end while

Neural Network Approach – Hybrid with Jaya Algorithm. The principal idea is to have a neural network approach, as it is done normally. However, the error optimisation ought to be done using the minimised-jaya algorithm. This approach is explained in Fig. 4: the input that is given is the grape leaf images. This is observed by the Resnet34 mechanism which infers results from it. The error minimisation, however, is done using the Jaya algorithm. These results help reinforce the model. This goes on until a stopping criterion is reached. Some other optimisation algorithms, which are arguably the best in competing with the Jaya algorithm are also used, in order to have an unbiased comparative study: the Particle Swarm Optimisation Algorithm [19], the Genetic Algorithm [25,39] and the Ant-Colony Optimisation Algorithm [9,10]. The feed-forward aspect of the neural network is taken as is, from the residual networks discussed previously, and the back-propagation manifests itself with the usage of the respective evolutionary optimisation algorithms. Here, every error value during an epoch is taken as the population, making each data-point a chromosome in this way.

5   Experimental Results and Analysis

5.1   Computation Environment

The programming language in which the computation is carried out is Python version 3.5 with a PyTorch back-end. The computation environment has 1x single core Xeon Processor at 2.3 GHz, 46 MB cache CPU with 25.3 GB available RAM space.

5.2   Optimum Learning Rate Selection

There are a lot of techniques that can be employed to prevent a neural network based model from overfitting [7]. Conventionally, the use of dropouts [36] throughout the different neural network layers, usually proves to be an effective manoeuvre. However, while carrying out the experiment, the results offered by this method were not significantly different from those offered by not using this method.

Another technique to prevent overfitting is specifying the appropriate learning rate based on the loss-convergence of the model [17]. From Fig. 5, one can conclude the following:

(1) It is evident that increasing the learning rate beyond 10^{-4} leads to an increasing, as well as an unstable loss function.
(2) If one traces the plot from the red-dotted point to a learning rate of 10^{-4}, one can observe the loss to be mostly decreasing.

(3) Furthermore, starting from a learning rate of about 3×10^{-5} to a learning rate of 10^{-4}, the decrease in loss is much more stable: this range provides the most optimum results for the experiment.

Thus, selection of an appropriate range of learning rates is achieved.

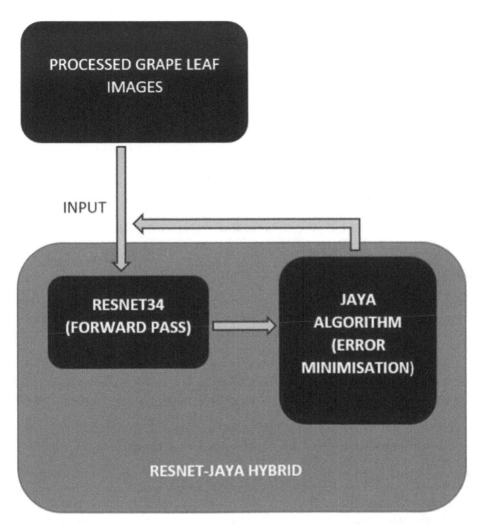

Fig. 4. The proposed methodology uses a hybrid Resnet-Jaya approach to carry out computations.

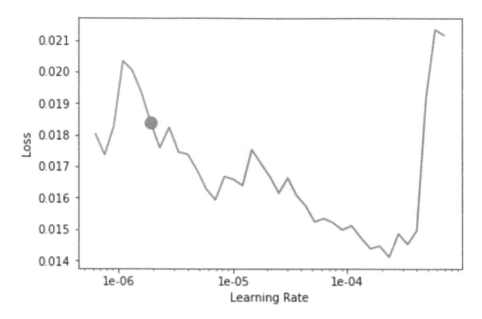

Fig. 5. Plot of progress of the learning rate and model loss

5.3   Cyclical Annealing of the Learning Rate

The loss function-convergence is an essential factor in determining the accuracy of a neural network based classification model [18]. Figure 6 shows the behaviour of the training and validation loss functions with respect to the number of batches processed. The training loss function first increases, attains a maximum value, and then decreases substantially. This is in contrast to the traditional loss function behaviour. This is because of the utilisation of a relatively novel concept of cyclical (cosine) annealing of the learning rate, a novel idea developed by Smith [35].

Traditionally, one tends to reduce the learning rates as the number of batches processed increases. However, this approach has its bottlenecks:

(1) On the one hand, a small learning rate can cause the model to optimise at only a local minimum while completely disregarding the global extreme by not exploring the loss.
(2) On the other hand, a substantially large learning rate can make the model oscillate away from the global minimum, which most certainly would be counter intuitive.

This dilemma is addressed by the utilisation of the concept of cyclical annealing of the learning rate. After a certain amounts of batches processed, it increases the learning rate to some extent so that the model has the chance to explore the entire loss function. Thus, it increments and decrements the learning rate after fixed intervals of batch processing. In this study, a single cycle annealing is used, hence only one global peak in loss is observed, as exhibited in Fig. 6.

This cyclical annealing also helps in a faster convergence of the loss function. Moreover, the optimum learning rate range ensures that the validation loss is lower than the training loss as the number of processed batches increases.

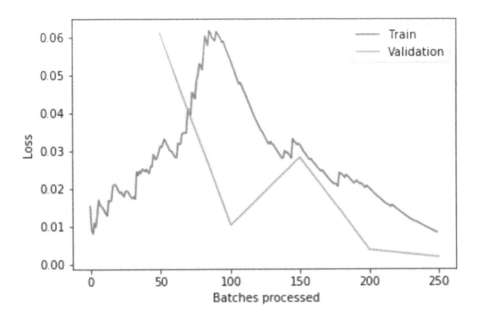

Fig. 6. Plot of the loss function with respect to the number of batches processed

5.4   Handling Confident Inaccuracies

After the initial training of the model, there were some instances wherein the model predicted the incorrect output with a large loss, i.e. the model confidently predicted the incorrect output. It was observed that the model was the most confused with *Esca* and *Black rot* in the grapevines, with 7 and 5 instances of incorrect predictions respectively Further training and manual labelling helped the model become more accurate.

5.5   Accuracy Analysis and Comparison with Previous Work

Since the dataset is nearly balanced, with no class having a significantly larger majority than the other, sub-sampling and other such techniques for dataset balancing are not employed [6]. Furthermore, the accuracy metric is kept to be the default: percentage agreement based accuracy, instead of the advanced metrics like Cohen's Kappa, which accounts for the agreement occurring by chance [22]. Hence, the model achieves a validation accuracy of 99.7%

Table 1. Proposed methodology comparison with sannaki et al.

	Methodology proposed by Sannaki et al.	Proposed methodology
Neural network architecture	Feed-forward based Cconvolutional neural network	Resnet 34
Dataset size	33 images	812 images
Number of classes	2	4
Classes	*Powdery mildew, Downy mildew*	*Isariopsis leaf spot, Esca, Black rot*, Healthy
Stages of pre-processing	Background removal, Anisotropic Ddiffusion, Segmentation	Augmentation, Segmentation, Normalisation

The results put forth by the experimentation and study in this paper have been concisely compared with those by Sannaki et al. [34] in Table 1. Some points of comparison between the proposed methodology and previous works are as followed:

(1) Sannakki et al. have performed experiments on images of grapevines suffering from *powdery mildew* and *downy mildew* whereas this experimentation uses a dataset of grape leaves suffering from *isariopsis leaf spot, esca* and *black rot.*

(2) The number of training images in the former is very less: 16 for *powdery mildew* and 17 for *downy mildew.* On the other hand, the proposed experimentation uses a much larger number of images, 228 for *isariopsis leaf spot,* 277 for *esca*, 219 for *black rot* and 88 for healthy, as previously mentioned in Section III. A larger dataset implies that the mechanism for disease diagnosis is more robust.

(3) In the former analysis, only two images, one from each class, are used for validation whereas this study uses 20% of all images as images for validation. This helps in checking whether the mechanism is moving towards overfitting or not.

(4) A smaller training set may also cause the model to learn only the features present in the images of the training set very well, i.e. the model could overfit very easily [20–30] and could possibly only identify and classify the training images; and might not be able to perform as well for testing or validation.

These limitations are done away with in this study.

Liu et al. [23] have carried out their experimentation using several approaches of pre-trained neural network concepts. They further propose a problem-specific convolutional model, through which they are able to increase the accuracy of their models to 97.22%. However, they have not tested the capability of optimisation algorithms along with neural network approaches, through which, we are able to achieve an accuracy of 98.32% without even using any problem-specific model, and 99.71% with a hybrid of Resnet34 and the Jaya algorithm, as shown in Table 2. This shows that the proposed methodology is compatible with different kinds of problems instead of catering to only one specific difficulty.

5.6 Different CNN Model Comparisons

Different models of convolutional neural networks are employed to check the efficacy of such methodologies, in an attempt to compare the best working methodology. From Fig. 7, it is evident that Resnet works the best, at least in this context. While the other algorithms are also comparable, some are quite prone to overfitting.

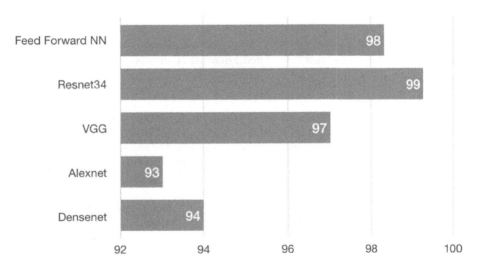

Fig. 7. Comparison of different models of CNN to carry out the task of identification of diseases in grapevines

5.7   Hybrid Jaya Algorithm Approach Compared with Other Optimisation Algorithms

Even compared to one of the most sought after optimisation algorithms, i.e., the Genetic algorithm, the Jaya algorithm fares much better because of the very fact that it has nothing to do with the algorithm-specific parameters and hyper-parameters. So it makes absolute sense that a hybrid neural-jaya approach would seemingly outperform other hybrid neural approaches too. This is something that is observed in the experimentation as well. Since there is hardly any class imbalance, we stick to the parameter of accuracy for our comparative study. This is vividly described in Table 2. Here a comparison is done with several optimisation algorithms along with a simple Feed Forward Neural Network which is 10 layers deep, denoted by FFNN followed by the number of chromosomes/candidates in one generation of a population, denoted in the parentheses.

From Table 2, one can clearly infer that the Jaya Algorithm fares the best, securing the best accuracies among all the optimisation algorithms used. While the Genetic Algorithm comes a very close second, the results don't necessarily change drastically on changing the population size, when hybridised with Resnet34. The Scatter Search algorithm fares the worst among all the optimisation algorithms, as is evident from the table. This is largely because Scatter Search is extremely problem specific and doesn't easily generalise. It even tends to overfit as the population size increases. Similarly, albeit much better in performance, the Ant Colony Optimisation Algorithm also has the tendency to overfit as the population size is increased, at least for this experimentation. This is further elaborated in Figs. 8 and 9 for Feed Forward Neural Network and Resnet34 respectively.

Table 2. Comparison of the accuracies of the hybridised models of Jaya Algorithm (JA), Genetic Algorithm (GA), Scatter Search (SS), Ant Colony Optimisation Algorithm (ACOA), Particle Swarm Optimisation Algorithm (PSOA) and Firefly Algorithm (FA) with Feed Forward Neural Networks (FFNN) and Resnet34 taking populations of 50, 100 and 150.

	FFNN(50)	FFNN(100)	FFNN(150)	Resnet34(50)	Resnet34(100)	Resnet34(150)
JA	96.35	98.12	**98.32**	97.71	99.34	**99.71**
GA	95.18	96.33	98.13	96.24	96.54	96.20
SS	89.10	82.91	83.77	90.08	89.91	90.72
ACOA	92.99	91.76	93.22	91.21	94.13	93.10
PSOA	94.08	90.79	95.89	94.18	93.70	92.91
FA	93.31	89.19	91.50	93.22	92.03	92.90

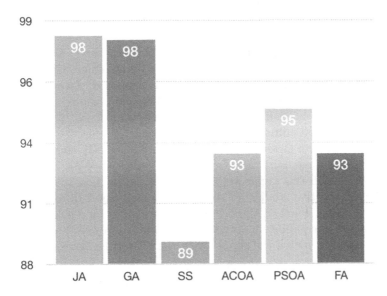

Fig. 8. Comparison of the accuracies of the hybridised models of Jaya Algorithm (JA), Genetic Algorithm (GA), Scatter Search (SS), Ant Colony Optimisation Algorithm (ACOA), Particle Swarm Optimisation Algorithm (PSOA) and Firefly Algorithm (FA) with Feed Forward Neural Networks. The accuracy values in the plot are rounded off to the nearest whole number.

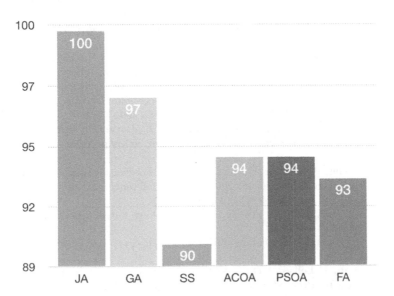

Fig. 9. Comparison of the accuracies of the hybridised models of Jaya Algorithm (JA), Genetic Algorithm (GA), Scatter Search (SS), Ant Colony Optimisation Algorithm (ACOA), Particle Swarm Optimisation Algorithm (PSOA) and Firefly Algorithm (FA) with Resnet34. The accuracy values in the plot are rounded off to the nearest whole number.

6 Conclusion

In this study, leaf images of grapevines that suffer from *isariopsis leaf spot, esca* and *black rot* are studied in order to easily detect and diagnose these diseases. A residual convolutional neural network approach is proposed to solve the problem. Notwithstanding the efforts of the domain-experts, the results from this study can facilitate a more efficient functioning of many industries that have to rely on the practices of viticulture for their sustenance. A quicker diagnosis could imply a prevention or a faster cure, which in turn, could help run the dependent firms and organisations with more vigour and efficacy. With an accuracy of 99.7%, the results in this paper are sure to help researchers and viticulturists alike in their respective studies for diagnosing plant based diseases using only the images of leaves. Further, these results can prove to be a huge leap forward towards creating an equilibrium for the demand and supply of grapes and related products: seeking to match the supply with the ever-growing rising demand.

References

1. Papademetriou, M.K., Dent, F.J.: Grape Production in the Asia-Pacific Region. Food and Agriculture Organization of the United Nations (2001)
2. Agostinelli, F., Hoffman, M., Sadowski, P., Baldi, P.: Learning activation functions to improve deep neural networks. arXiv preprint arXiv:1412.6830 (2014)
3. Agudelo, M.B., Meyer, E., Lovato, P.E.: Growth, heavy metal uptake, and photosynthesis in'paulsen 1103'(vitis berlandieri x rupestris) grapevine rootstocks inoculated with arbuscular mycorrhizal fungi from vineyard soils with high copper contents. Vitis J. Grapevine Res. **59**(4), 169–180 (2020)
4. Anderson, K., Findlay, C., Fuentes, S., Tyerman, S.: Viticulture, wine and climate change, January 2008
5. Arand, K., Bieler, E., Dürrenberger, M., Kassemeyer, H.H.: Developmental pattern of grapevine (vitis vinifera l.) berry cuticular wax: differentiation between epicuticular crystals and underlying wax. PloS one **16**(2), e0246693 (2021)
6. Chawla, N.V., Japkowicz, N., Kotcz, A.: Special issue on learning from imbalanced data sets. ACM Sigkdd Explor. Newsl. **6**(1), 1–6 (2004)
7. Cogswell, M., Ahmed, F., Girshick, R., Zitnick, L., Batra, D.: Reducing overfitting in deep networks by decorrelating representations. arXiv preprint arXiv:1511.06068 (2015)
8. Deng, J., Dong, W., Socher, R., Li, L.J., Li, K., Fei-Fei, L.: Imagenet: a large-scale hierarchical image database. In: 2009 IEEE Conference on Computer Vision and Pattern Recognition, pp. 248–255. IEEE (2009)
9. Dorigo, M., Birattari, M., Stutzle, T.: Ant colony optimization. IEEE Comput. Intell. Mag. **1**(4), 28–39 (2006)
10. Dorigo, M., Blum, C.: Ant colony optimization theory: a survey. Theoret. Comput. Sci. **344**(2–3), 243–278 (2005)
11. Fish, B., Kun, J., Lelkes, Á.D.: A confidence-based approach for balancing fairness and accuracy. In: Proceedings of the 2016 SIAM International Conference on Data Mining, pp. 144–152. SIAM (2016)
12. Goszcynski, D.: Accumulated data and results from the recent study of DSRNA isolated from grapevines used in experiments of insect and graft transmission of'shiraz'disease. Vitis: J. Grapevine Res. **59**(3), 111–116 (2020)

13. Gulcehre, C., Moczulski, M., Denil, M., Bengio, Y.: Noisy activation functions. In: International Conference on Machine Learning, pp. 3059–3068 (2016)
14. Hall, A., Lamb, D., Holzapfel, B., Louis, J.: Optical remote sensing applications in viticulture-a review. Aust. J. Grape Wine Res. **8**(1), 36–47 (2002)
15. Hall, L.O., Bensaid, A.M., Clarke, L.P., Velthuizen, R.P., Silbiger, M.S., Bezdek, J.C.: A comparison of neural network and fuzzy clustering techniques in segmenting magnetic resonance images of the brain. IEEE Trans. Neural Netw. **3**(5), 672–682 (1992)
16. He, K., Zhang, X., Ren, S., Sun, J.: Deep residual learning for image recognition. In: 2016 IEEE Conference on Computer Vision and Pattern Recognition (CVPR), pp. 770–778, June 2016. https://doi.org/10.1109/CVPR.2016.90
17. Jacobs, R.A.: Increased rates of convergence through learning rate adaptation. Neural Netw. **1**(4), 295–307 (1988)
18. Kashem, M., Jasmon, G., Mohamed, A., Moghavvemi, M.: Artificial neural network approach to network reconfiguration for loss minimization in distribution networks. Int. J. Electr. Power Energ. Syst. **20**(4), 247–258 (1998)
19. Kennedy, J., Eberhart, R.: Particle swarm optimization. In: Proceedings of ICNN 1995-International Conference on Neural Networks, vol. 4, pp. 1942–1948. IEEE (1995)
20. Kohavi, R., Sommerfield, D.: Feature subset selection using the wrapper method: overfitting and dynamic search space topology. In: KDD, pp. 192–197 (1995)
21. Kozma, R., Sakuma, M., Yokoyama, Y., Kitamura, M.: On the accuracy of mapping by neural networks trained by backpropagation with forgetting. Neurocomputing **13**(2–4), 295–311 (1996)
22. Kvålseth, T.O.: Note on cohen's kappa. Psychol. Reports **65**(1), 223–226 (1989)
23. Liu, B., Ding, Z., Tian, L., He, D., Li, S., Wang, H.: Grape leaf disease identification using improved deep convolutional neural networks. Front. Plant Sci. **11**, 1082 (2020)
24. Lutz, H.: Viticulture and Brewing in the Ancient Orient. Applewood Books, Carlisle (2007)
25. Mirjalili, S.: Genetic algorithm. In: Evolutionary Algorithms and Neural Networks. SCI, vol. 780, pp. 43–55. Springer, Cham (2019). https://doi.org/10.1007/978-3-319-93025-1_4
26. Mishra, P., Sahoo, D., Khandelwal, H., Amman, N., Sobhanayak, S.: Minimised jaya algorithm-based structure optimisation for heterogeneous wireless sensor networks. In: 2020 5th International Conference on Computing, Communication and Security (ICCCS), pp. 1–8. IEEE (2020)
27. Mohanty, S.P., Hughes, D.P., Salathé, M.: Using deep learning for image-based plant disease detection. Front. Plant Sci.**7**, 1419 (2016). https://doi.org/10.3389/fpls.2016.01419, https://www.frontiersin.org/article/10.3389/fpls.2016.01419
28. Morais, R., Fernandes, M.A., Matos, S.G., Serôdio, C., Ferreira, P., Reis, M.: A zigbee multi-powered wireless acquisition device for remote sensing applications in precision viticulture. Comput. Electron. Agric. **62**(2), 94–106 (2008)
29. Nethaji, M., Velu, E.: Grape cultivation and management approaches by geospatial tools - a review. J. Adv. Res. GeoSci. Remote Sens. **1**, 17–28 (2017)
30. Pasini, A.: Artificial neural networks for small dataset analysis. J. Thorac. Dis. **7**(5), 953 (2015)
31. Perez, L., Wang, J.: The effectiveness of data augmentation in image classification using deep learning. arXiv preprint arXiv:1712.04621 (2017)

32. Rao, R.: Jaya: a simple and new optimization algorithm for solving constrained and unconstrained optimization problems. Int. J. Ind. Eng. Comput. **7**(1), 19–34 (2016)
33. Riaz, S., Lund, K.T., Granett, J., Walker, M.A.: Population diversity of grape phylloxera in california and evidence for sexual reproduction. Am. J. Enology Viticulture **68**(2), 218–227 (2017). https://doi.org/10.5344/ajev.2016.15114, https://www.ajevonline.org/content/68/2/218
34. Sannakki, S., Rajpurohit, V., Nargund, V., Kulkarni, P.: Diagnosis and classification of grape leaf diseases using neural networks. In: 2013 4th International Conference on Computing, Communications and Networking Technologies, ICCCNT 2013, pp. 1–5, July 2013. https://doi.org/10.1109/ICCCNT.2013.6726616
35. Smith, L.N.: Cyclical learning rates for training neural networks. In: 2017 IEEE Winter Conference on Applications of Computer Vision (WACV), pp. 464–472. IEEE (2017)
36. Srivastava, N., Hinton, G., Krizhevsky, A., Sutskever, I., Salakhutdinov, R.: Dropout: a simple way to prevent neural networks from overfitting. J. Mach. Learn. Res. **15**(1), 1929–1958 (2014)
37. Torralba, A., Fergus, R., Freeman, W.T.: 80 million tiny images: a large data set for nonparametric object and scene recognition. IEEE Trans. Pattern Anal. Mach. Intell. **30**(11), 1958–1970 (2008)
38. Torrey, L., Shavlik, J.: Transfer learning. In: Handbook of Research on Machine Learning Applications and Trends: Algorithms, Methods, and Techniques, pp. 242–264. IGI Global (2010)
39. Whitley, D.: A genetic algorithm tutorial. Stat. Comput. **4**(2), 65–85 (1994)
40. Xie, S., Girshick, R., Dollár, P., Tu, Z., He, K.: Aggregated residual transformations for deep neural networks. In: Proceedings of the IEEE Conference on Computer Vision and Pattern Recognition, pp. 1492–1500 (2017)
41. Yancheva, S., Marchev, P., Yaneva, V., Roichev, V., Tsvetkov, I.: In vitro propagation of grape cultivars and rootstocks for production of pre-basic planting material. Bulgarian J. Agric. Sci. **24**, 801–806 (2018)

Covid-19 Detection Using X-Ray Image

Adarsh Sharma$^{(\boxtimes)}$, Shantanu Pingale, Chanchal Mal,
Sangeeta Malviya, Nikita Patil, and Shital Dongre

Vishwakarma Institute of Technology, Pune, India
adarsh.sharma18@vit.edu

Abstract. COVID-19 is a highly infectious viral infection with serious global health implications. The use of chest X-ray images to diagnose the severe acute respiratory syndrome coronavirus-2 (SARS CoV-2), which causes coronavirus sickness in 2019, (COVID-19), is becoming increasingly important for both patients and doctors. Furthermore, in most nations where laboratory kits for testing are unavailable, this becomes an even more important choice. The goal of this paper is to show how to combine TensorFlow, Keras, and OpenCV to diagnose COVID-19 disease using chest X-ray pictures with great accuracy. Dataset was manually collected from various publications. This dataset currently contains 1719 negative images and 538 positive images with an accuracy of 99.55%. Using several features from an X-ray image, this CNN network attained the highest accuracy. It has tested it on a total of 3257 photos to report the actual accuracy feasible in real-world situations for evaluating through the network. This computer- based tool can be used on any computer system to detect COVID-positive patients using their chest X-Ray scans and provides a result in a matter of seconds.

Keywords: Covid-19 · CNN · Detection · Web application · X-ray

1 Introduction

By infecting people with the severe acute respiratory syndrome coronavirus 2, the COVID-19 pandemic continues to have a devastating influence on the global population's health and well-being. (SARS-CoV-2). In 2020, a large number of individuals will die worldwide as a result of this disease. The virus can quickly spread through the respiratory tract and lungs. As a result of the inflammation, air sacs might be filled with fluid and expelled. The system is responsible for preventing oxygen uptake. To reduce the number of people who die as a result of this dangerous illness, doctors and health workers around the world have a tremendous challenge in detecting the infection quickly and accurately. Some people may not notice any symptoms in the early stages, although the majority of them reported fever and cough as their primary symptoms. Body aches, a sore throat, and a headache are all possible secondary symptoms caused

© Springer Nature Switzerland AG 2022
D. Garg et al. (Eds.): IACC 2021, CCIS 1528, pp. 57–72, 2022.
https://doi.org/10.1007/978-3-030-95502-1_5

by the infection. In the fight against COVID-19, effective screening of infected individuals is critical so that those who are unwell can receive timely treatment and care, as well as be isolated to prevent the virus from spreading. Because RT-PCR testing is exceedingly specific, it is the standard method, but it is a time-consuming, demanding, and complicated manual process that is in short supply. Radiological imagery, such as X-rays and computed tomography (CT) scans, is one of the most important methods for diagnosing COVID-19. The use of chest photographs is a simple and quick procedure recommended by medical and health legislation, and it has been mentioned in numerous literature as the first tool in epidemic screening. Radiography testing has been used as an alternate means of detecting COVID-19 infection. Chest radiography imaging is performed and evaluated by radiologists to see if there are any visual markers of viral infection. COVID- 19 infection has been detected using radiography testing as an alternative method. Radiologists perform and review chest radiography imaging to identify whether there are any visual signs of viral infection.

This method can detect COVID- 19 positive patients with near-perfect accuracy in a couple of seconds. As part of this research, it has also contributed a tool that may be used to discover COVID-19 positive patients. Deep learning-based solutions will always deliver an opinion without the need for human contact, even if a radiologist is not accessible or if doctor opinions differ. In terms of classification accuracy and sensitivity, the data from open sources used in this paper confirmed the efficacy of the proposed strategy. It was also compared to other benchmark studies.

2 Literature Review

Detection of COVID using chest X-ray images by Rachna Jain, Meenu Gupta, Soham Taneja & D Jude Hemanth suggested a Deep Learning model. Deep learning is the most successful machine learning technology for analysing a large number of chest x-ray pictures, which will have a significant impact on Covid-19 screening. For both covid-19 and healthy patients, PA views of chest x-ray scans were taken. Deep learning-based CNN models are employed and compared after the images have been cleaned up. [1] The accuracy was 97.97%. Deep-COVID: Using deep transfer learning, predict COVID-19 from chest X-ray pictures. Deep learning models developed by Shervin Minaee, Rahele Kafieh, Milan Sonka, Shakib Yazdani, and Ghazaleh Jamalipour Soufi to detect COVID-19 patients from chest radiography pictures. A dataset of

5000 chest X-ray scans forms the basis of the model. This model had a near-90% specificity rate [2]. T Ozturk, M Talo, E A Yildirim, U B Baloglu, O Yildirim, and U. R Acharya proposed a model for automatic COVID-19 identification using chest X-ray pictures in their paper Automated detection of COVID-19 using deep neural networks with X-ray images. For binary and multi-class classification, the suggested model gives accurate diagnostics. The accuracy of this model was 98.08% [3].

3 Methodology

3.1 Flow Chart

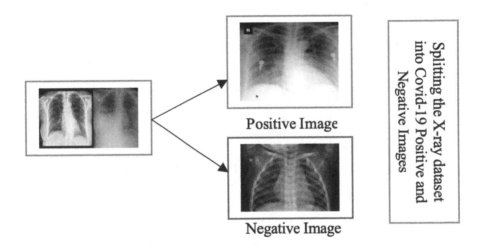

Positive Image

Negative Image

Splitting the X-ray dataset into Covid-19 Positive and Negative Images

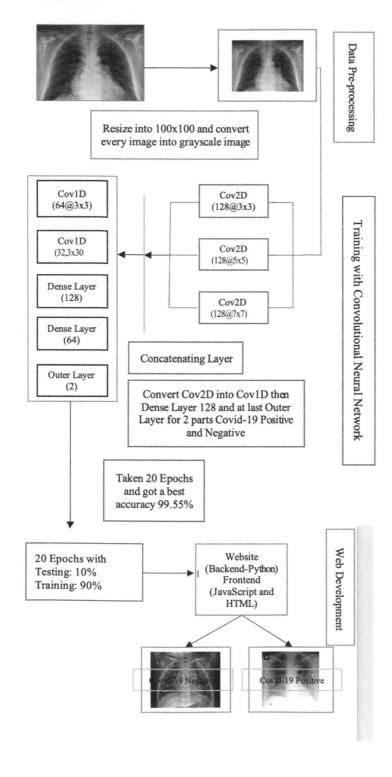

3.2   Phases of Model:

I. Creating Dataset

First and foremost, the dataset is constructed and separated into two category Covid positive and negative. The index and image are placed in positive index and positive image names, respectively, whenever the algorithm detects "COVID-19." Following that, the image names are also saved. COVID-19 negative photos are processed in the same way. If the word "Normal" is detected in this scenario, the images, names of the images, and indexes are saved in the appropriate variables.

II. 2.0 Data pre-processing

Python is used in conjunction with OpenCV, TensorFlow, and Keras in the proposed system. For data pre-processing, a sufficient amount of data is acquired. The dataset was divided into two categories: COVID positive and negative. The COVID negative category is labelled as "0" in data pre-processing, while the COVID-19 positive category is labelled as "1." To make further calculations easier, all of the collected photos are transformed to grayscale and shrunk to 100×100 pixels. The images' new data is appended to data[] and target[]. The images must be in binary format in order to conduct operations on them. The pixel is then normalised by dividing it by 255 to convert it to a binary matrix. The revised image data is returned and saved once more. The images can now be used to execute operations.

III. 3.0 Training with CNN

A CNN is a type of Neural Network that focuses on processing data using a grid-like topology, similar to an image that is primarily used to analyse a structured array of data. CNN is divided into two sections (Figs. 1, 2 and 3):

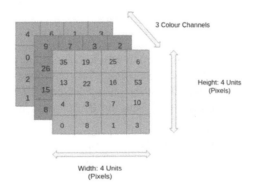

Fig. 1. RGB image $4 \times 4 \times 3$

A convolutional layer is a filter that analyses a few pixels in an image and builds a feature map that predicts which category each feature belongs.

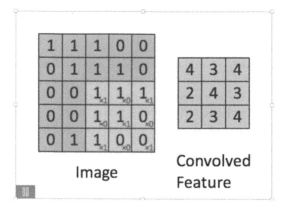

Fig. 2. Convoluting a $5 \times 5 \times 1$ picture with a $3 \times 3 \times 1$ kernel yields a $3 \times 3 \times 1$ convolved feature.

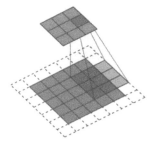

Fig. 3. Stride length = 2 convolution operation

After that, all the results are summí up to provide an output of a one-depth channel Convoluted Feature. So, finally, the conclusion of a convolutional layer is to extract high-level features from a picture that are required for prediction. X is the input to a neuron. The convoluted layer is passed from the ReLUfunction.

ReLU: ReLU is the most extensively utilised activation function. Neural networks with hidden layers are mostly used. The ReLU function, or rectified linear measure, is the same as taking the positive component of the input.

$$f(f(x) = \max(0, x))$$

Negative values are converted to positive values using the ReLU function. This is frequently done to keep the summing values from reaching zero. The pooling layer is similar to the convolutional layer in that it is responsible for lowering the dimensions of the convolved layer in question. Maximum pooling and average pooling are the two types of pooling. Because it is frequently responsible for lowering the size of activation maps, the pooling layer is also known as the down sampling layer. Because this layer ignores smaller data, picture recognition occurs during a smaller representation. Overfitting is minimised using this layer. The value is reduced since the pooling layer reduces the number of parameters. The input is split into rectangular pooling portions, and the maximum value is calculated, producing the highest result. Max pooling is a pooling procedure that selects an element from the feature map region covered by the filter. As a result, the model is more robust to changes in the input image's feature positions. The quantity of data in each feature obtained by the convolutional layer is reduced but the most relevant information is retained. Using maximal pooling, the uttermost value from the portion of the picture covered by the Kernel was pooled out. Using average pooling, the standard value was derived from the portion of the image covered by the kernel. The maximum pooling size (2,2) layers are used (Fig. 4) (Table 1).

Table 1. Convolutional layer VS pooling layer

Convolutional Layer	Pooling Layer
1. The convolutional layer is used for detecting number of patterns in different sub-regions using receptive fields.	1. The pooling layer is used for gradually reducing the spatial size of the representation
2. It is the building block of CNN. Most of the computation occurs in this layer.	2. It plays important role in reducing the number of parameters which evidently saves the amount of computation in the network.
3. Components required by convolutional layer are input data, a filter and feature map.	3. It also controls overfitting.

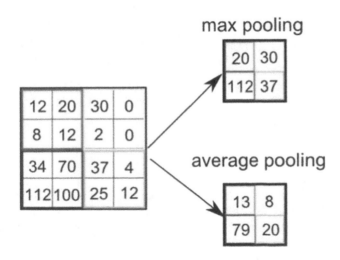

Fig. 4. Types of pooling

To stack the output convolutions from the second convolution layer, flatten the layer. To prevent the model from overfitting, use a dropout of 0.5. It turns two-dimensional matrices into a one-dimensional array or vector.

Dropout Layer: Overfitting is reduced with the help of this layer. It guarantees the network's redundancy. There is no learning during this stage. This approach is only used for training purposes. One dense layer of 50 neurons, followed by a relu activation function, and then a second dense layer of 2 neurons, followed by a softmax function, i.e. 0 for no mask and 1 for mask. This is frequently the topmost layer. The input photos are classified using the dense layer. It assigns labels to the images, and then the final layer assigns probabilities to those labels.

SoftMax: The SoftMax function is used to convert the result into a probability distribution value. Although the SoftMax function is a sigmoid function, it is useful when dealing with classification issues. It's a not-so-linear function. The SoftMax function is utilised at the classifier's output layer, where we're trying to figure out how to define each individual's class (Table 2).

Table 2. Relu vs softmax

Relu	Softmax
1. Chiefly implemented in hidden layers of Neural network.	1. The softmax function is ideally used in the output layer of the classifiers where we are actually trying to attain the probabilities to define for each input classes.
2. The activation function has the effect of adding non-linearity into the convolutional neural network.	2. A softmax function which transforms the output into a probability distribution values.
3. Relu for short is a piecewise linear function that has output where input directly is positive, otherwise, it will output zero.	3. The softmax function is a type of sigmoid function which is use to handle when we are trying to classify classification problems.

IV. Web Development

In this phase, the best and most accurate model is combined with Python on the backend and HTML and CSS on the frontend to create a web application with the least validation loss and highest accuracy among all CNN model epochs. To predict the result in real-time, the best model from the CNN model epochs will be imported to the homepage. In the backend, Python will be used with Flask to interact with a model for results, while in the frontend, JavaScript and HTML will be used to create options such as "Choose File" for browsing X-ray images as input and "Predict" for predicting the result. There are two types of Covid-19: positive and negative. Backend development is done with the Flask web framework module. The Keras and OpenCV modules are loaded in code for X-ray image operations, while the NumPy module is loaded for binary operations. Because the image should have the same size when applied to CNN, the size is predefined in python code, just as it is in the training phase. To build a web application, a flask instance is established on the backend, and the best model from all CNN model epochs is saved there. The pre-processing stage is added later. For frontend HTML file is designed. To import an image, the "Choose file" option is created in the frontend, and the button is given for getting results. JavaScript code is used to upload an image and send it to the backend. the JavaScript code will get the image and convert it into a base64image compatible with python in terms of encoding. After that once predict button is clicked, results will be fetched from backend code and will be displayed on the webpage. The frontend, which is designed in HTML, is called on the first route. The second route involves sending an image entered by the user in the frontend to the backend for encoding. Following this stage, the image will be given to the pre-processor stage, where it will be turned into a NumPy array, grayscaled, normalised, and resized. Because whatever processing is done in the training phase must be repeated in the testing phase, pre-processing is included in this stage as well. The reshaped image is applied to the best- saved model after pre-processing. Then, using the argmax function, it will calculate the maximum probability as well as the accuracy in real time.

4 Experimentation

A. Dataset: For proper data training and experimenting with the current method, our dataset contains photos of both parameters "Covid positive images" and "Covid negative images." The database has two classes: "Covid positive" with 538 images and "Covid negative" with 1719 images. TensorFlow, open cv, and keras were used to recognise preprocessing images and determine whether the person is positive or not. This data covers chest X-ray images of several individuals whose primary interest is in the lungs, which may be inspected more thoroughly with a frontal perspective than with a lateral view (Fig. 5).

66   A. Sharma et al.

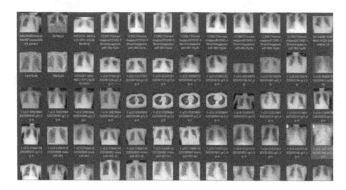

Fig. 5. Covid-19 positive X-ray

The above pictures are in the dataset and classified as Positive X-ray of person (Fig. 6).

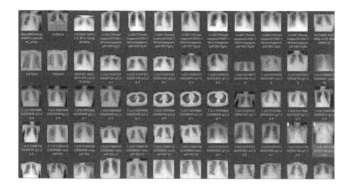

Fig. 6. Covid-19 negative X-ray

The above pictures are in the dataset and classified as with mask images of person (Table 3).

Table 3. Covid-19 "positive" and "negative" dataset

Class Name	Description	No. of Images
Covid-19 Positive	Contains Images with positive	538
Covid-19 Negative	Contains Images with negative	1719

The dataset is being collected from Kaggle online open source for deep learning datasets. Covid positive and Covid negative images are imbalanced so that negative covid-19 images can be detected properly, and it will help the model to understand about negative images very deeply so that if there is any blurriness in an input image it will directly predict tis covid-19 positive.

B. Process

Firstly, the background has been changed to grayscale image so that model can detect the images very accurately and images is resized to 100 * 100.Convert every image into binary by dividing it by 255 and later image needs to convert into 4-dimensional image as CNN needs the image in 4-dimensional format. Keras and Tenser flow is used for categorical representation because we need two neurons i.e. one for Without and other for Without Mask. Then the array list is saved in the folder with target and data in which target list is used for representation for without or without mask names and in data list the images is being stored (Figs. 7 and 8).

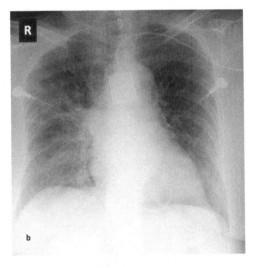

Fig. 7. Input X-ray image in the dataset

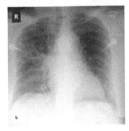

Fig. 8. Image converted into grayscale, resized to 100 * 100

In next Stage, primarily import data and the target array. Then take two Conventional Neural Network 2D layers of 128 kernels of each dimension 3 × 3, 5 × 5, 7 × 7. The input layer will have Window Size 1. After this, it will be reshaped in two Conventional Neural Network 1D layer of 64 filters of dimension 3 × 3 and another 32 filters of dimension 3 × 3. Next the layer is being Flattened and then reshaped into Dense layer with 128 kernels and then further transformed into 64 kernels dense layer. After this stage the model will result into an output layer, which consist of to two neurons i.e., Covid-19 Positive or Negative X-ray image which will help in estimating whether the person is Covid-19 Positive or Covid-19 Negative. Next step data of images will split into 90% "training part" and 10% "testing part" in which model will be run for 20 Epochs. Best epoch model will be used for predicting Covid-19 Positive and Negative.

Best model will be integrated with website for predicting X-ray of person Covid-19 "Positive" or "Negative" in which backend will be python and frontend will be JavaScript, Html.

Output of Website
Figures 9 and 10.

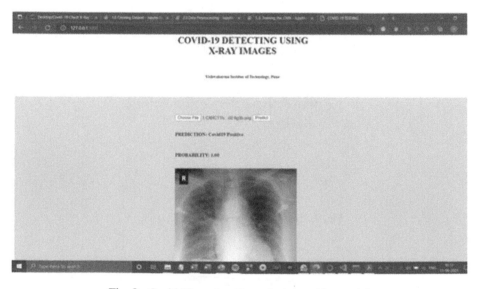

Fig. 9. Covid-19 positve X-ray is detected by model.

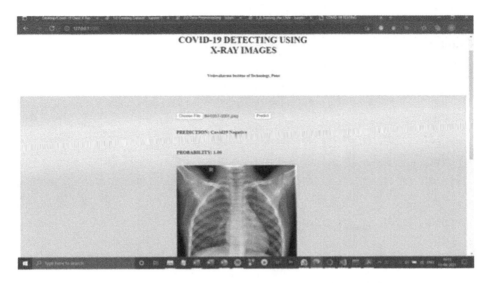

Fig. 10. Covid-19 negative X-ray is detected by model.

5   Results and Analysis

The data set is divided into 90% Training and 10% Testing sections. There are 1719 corona negative photographs and 538 c positive images in this collection. As a result, 1547 images will be utilised for training and 175 images will be used for testing. The model is trained using 20 epochs using a convolutional neural network. Epoch 18 had the best accuracy of 99.55%. Because this model has a reasonable level of accuracy, it is compared to the previous model's accuracy.

A. Accuracy Comparison
Accuracy is compared with AlexNet, NASNETMOBILE, Densenet, GoogleNet, and CNN (Table 4).

Table 4.   Model algorithm accuracy.

Model	Accuracy
DenseNet	96.66%
GoogleNet	96.84%
AlexNet	97.04%
NASNetMobile	98.72%
CNN	99.55%

Graphs:

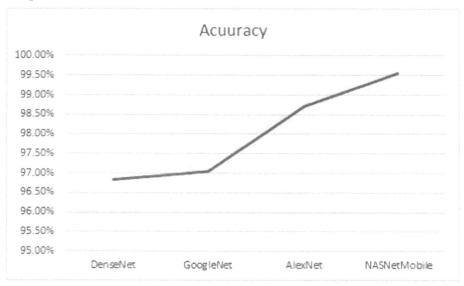

Graph 1: Comparison of Algorithm with respect to accuracy.

B. Training Loss and Validation Loss of our Proposed Model:
Figure 11.

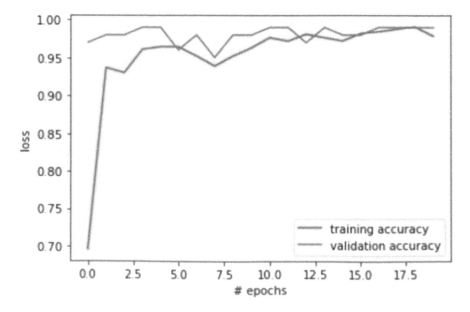

Fig. 11. The model loses during the training and testing phase.

C. Training Accuracy and Validation Accuracy for our Proposed Model:
Figure 12.

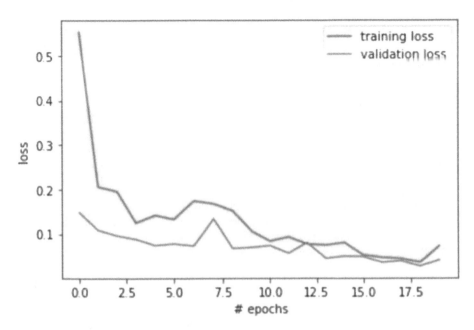

Fig. 12. Accuracy of the model for training and validation.

6 Limitations

The accuracy of the proposed model can be increased further by taking more and more precise data at the training phase. But as all know hospitals are already overwhelmed with a number of COVID-19 patients, so it becomes a bit harder to get quality data set for training.

7 Conclusion

In these times of COVID-19 pandemic, where everyone is trying to cope up with the difficulties, there are some measures listed by the doctors that are necessary to follow. One of the important measures is to wear mask. The proposed model helps in detecting whether the person is infected by Covid or not using OpenCV, TensorFlow, Keras, Flask and CNN. The accuracy of 99.55% is achieved for this model and its optimization can be done for using it in automated monitoring system. The proposed model can be used in hospitals to find out immediately whether the person is infected or not. RT-PCR tests take 1–2 days while using these X-Ray images, we will get results within a second and will help the world to end the pandemic and make Covid-free world.

References

1. Sekeroglu, B., Ozsahin, I.: Detection of COVID-19 from chest X-ray images using convolutional neural networks. SLAS Technol 25(6), 553–565 (2020). https://doi.org/10.1177/2472630320958376
2. Jain, R., Gupta, M., Taneja, S., Hemanth, D.J.: Deep learning based detection and analysis of COVID-19 on chest X-ray images. Appl. Intell. 51(3), 1690–1700 (2020). https://doi.org/10.1007/s10489-020-01902-1
3. Minaee, S., Kafieh, R., Sonka, M., Yazdani, S., Soufi, G.J.: Deep-COVID: predicting COVID-19 from chest X-ray images using deep transfer learning. Med. Image Anal. 65, 101794 (2020). https://doi.org/10.1016/j.media.2020.101794
4. Ozturk, T., Talo, M., Yildirim, E.A., Baloglu, U.B., Ozal Yildirim, U., Acharya, R.: Automated detection of COVID-19 cases using deep neural networks with X-ray images. Comput. Biol. Med. 121, 103792 (2020). https://doi.org/10.1016/j.compbiomed.2020.103792
5. Islam, S.R., Maity, S.P., Ray, A.K., Mandal, M.: Automatic detection of pneumonia on compressed sensing images using deep learning. IEEE Can. Conf. Electr. Comput. Eng. 2019, 1–4 (2019). https://doi.org/10.1109/CCECE.2019.8861969
6. Ibrahim, A.U., Ozsoz, M., Serte, S., Al-Turjman, F., Yakoi, P.S.: Pneumonia classification using deep learning from chest X-ray images during COVID-19. Cognit. Comput. (2021). https://doi.org/10.1007/s12559-020-09787-5
7. Das, A.K., Ghosh, S., Thunder, S., Dutta, R., Agarwal, S., Chakrabarti, A.: Automatic COVID-19 detection from X-ray images using ensemble learning with convolutional neural network. Pattern Anal. Appl. 24(3), 1111–1124 (2021). https://doi.org/10.1007/s10044-021-00970-4
8. Ohata, E.F., et al.: Automatic detection of COVID-19 infection using chest X-ray images through transfer learning. IEEE/CAA J. Autom. Sin. 8(1), 239–248 (2021). https://doi.org/10.1109/JAS.2020.1003393
9. Saba, L., et al.: Six artificial intelligence paradigms for tissue characterisation and classification of non-COVID-19 pneumonia against COVID-19 pneumonia in computed tomography lungs. Int. J. Comput. Assisted Radiol. Surg. 16(3), 423–434 (2021)
10. Agarwal, M., et al.: A novel block imaging technique using nine artificial intelligence models for COVID-19 disease classification, characterization and severity measurement in lung computed tomography scans on an Italian cohort. J. Med. Syst. 45(3), 1–30 (2021)
11. Suri, J.S., et al.: A narrative review on characterization of acute respiratory distress syndrome in COVID-19-infected lungs using artificial intelligence. Comput. Biol. Med. 130, 104210 (2021)
12. Suri, J., et al.: COVLIAS 1.0: lung segmentation in COVID-19 computed tomography scans using hybrid deep learning artificial intelligence models segmentation in covid19. Diagnostics 11(8), 1405 (2021)
13. Suri, J.S., et al.: Systematic review of artificial intelligence in acute respiratory distress syndrome for COVID-19 lung infected patients: a biomedical imaging perspective. IEEE J. Biomed. Health Inf. 25(11), 4128–4139 (2021)

Alzheimer's Disease Classification Using Transfer Learning

Deepanshi$^{(\boxtimes)}$, Ishan Budhiraja, and Deepak Garg

Bennett University, Greater Noida, Uttar Pradesh, India
{E20SOE819,ishan.budhiraja,deepak.garg}@bennett.edu.in

Abstract. With the rapid growth in the field of computer sciences and deep learning techniques, Alzheimer's disease classification through images has become a powerful area of research. Alzheimer's disease comes under the category of dementia in which loss of memory. Reasoning, judgment, concentration, thinking, etc. happens to prove even fatal to the patients. 60–80% of the people suffering from dementia suffer from Alzheimer's Disease only making it the most significant part to study. In the paper, we are going to compare the Deep Learning algorithms such as VGG-19, Inception-V3, Resnet-50, DenseNet-169, and CNN using Transfer Learning in which they have pre-trained weights from the ImageNet model. We are working on our model in the .jpg format of MRI images. However, the limitation in the field of Medical imaging is the limited dataset. In the paper, experimentation on the dataset, we can easily compare between the algorithm which better performance than other and show the results.

Keywords: CNN · DenseNet169 · Resnet-50 · Transfer Learning

1 Introduction

Alzheimer's Disease Classification lies under the umbrella of Dementia. People suffering from dementia have about 60 to 80% of the probability of having Alzheimer's Disease than other diseases like Vascular or Frontal Dementia or Parkinson's disease. Alzheimer's Disease has multiple symptoms like loss of memory, loss of judgment, loss of thinking, loss of proper language, loss of attention, even difficulty in movement. This neurological disorder is mostly seen in people with elderly age. It is estimated that one in 85 people will suffer from Alzheimer's by 2050. If detected in the early stages Alzheimer's is easy and fast to cure. Else it can cause permanent damage to the brain making it fatal for people [1].

Researchers are working on the detection and classification of Alzheimer's disease. Many machine learning algorithms were applied on the AD datasets which gave very good results but with the emergence of deep learning models, we have got even better results on the image dataset of MRI for Alzheimer's detection.

© Springer Nature Switzerland AG 2022
D. Garg et al. (Eds.): IACC 2021, CCIS 1528, pp. 73–81, 2022.
https://doi.org/10.1007/978-3-030-95502-1_6

Using the Deep Learning models and training them from scratch takes a lot of time and it's difficult to find tune the parameter which in return cause overfitting and underfitting in the model. Whereas using Transfer Learning in the deep Learning model we use the pre-trained weights of the ImageNet Model for making the base of the algorithm and then we fine-tune the model according to our dataset. This makes our system robust and even works well on cross-domain applications [2].

In this paper, we use the Deep Learning Algorithm such as VGG-19, Inception-V3, Resnet-50, and CNN. We show a comparative study of all the above Deep Learning Algorithm on our dataset using the Transfer Learning approach. This shows that the pre-trained parameters give very good results if we provide the training data carefully [3].

1.1 Related Work

Literature studies mostly focus on developing systems that automatically diagnose and classify Alzheimer's disease from the MRI images using traditional Machine Learning or Deep Learning methods. However, machine learning methods are computationally intense and these methods' performance depends upon the feature selection which is manually done and is difficult to obtain. Gary et al. developed a framework of multimodel classification using pairwise similarity from random forest classifier achieving classification accuracy of 89% [4]. Zhang et al. proposed a multi-view method for Alzheimer's disease diagnosis using multi-view in the first layer as input and represent the complex correlation between the features and class labels in the multilayer [5]. Lei et al. proposed a discriminative sparse learning method to predict and classify Alzheimer's disease stages using relational regularization and multimodel features.

Some of the deep learning techniques used for AD diagnosis are Islam et al. proposed a deep CNN model which is better than the existing classification approaches and outperforms them in early detection and stage detection of the disease results from three 2D DenseNet are used to find the final result which increased the accuracy of the proposed technique [6]. Liu et al. proposed a deep learning framework for classification and regression. Using a multi-task multi-channel learning system that takes into account the MRI data and personal data which collectively help in disease classification and finding regression scores [7]. Liu et al. introduced a new framework which is a combination of 2D CNN and RNNs. Decomposing 3D PET images into 2D slices and learning features for classification. The Gated Recurrent unit is used for feature extraction from the image and RNN is used for image classification. However, no segmentation method is used in it [8]. C. Feng et al. developed a novel deep learning framework using 3D-CNN for extraction of deep features from the PET and MRI images and applied FSBi-LSTM on feature map for extracting all spatial information hence providing higher efficiency for diagnosis of Alzheimer's disease [9].

1.2   Organization

The remainder of the paper is arranged in the following manner. The proposed methodology is described in Sect. 2. The suggested methodology is evaluated in Sect. 3. Section 4 contains the conclusion.

2   Proposed Methodology

In this work, we have used different Deep Learning Algorithms as the base model for our training in which we use pre-trained weights of ImageNet.

2.1   Transfer Learning

Transfer learning is a technique used widely in training Deep learning models for new tasks nowadays. In this transfer Learning, we use the knowledge and training of previously pre-trained models as the base model of the new task. Where we fine-tune the parameters according to our current model. The major reason we use transfer learning is it reduces our training time and improves our accuracy and model performance. We use transfer Learning only when we have a high start of our model or a high rate of improvement of the model [10].

2.2   Convolutional Neural Networks

Convolution Neural Network (CNN) in Neural Network is the basic network that works for image classification, Object detection, Fig. 1 shows the basic architecture of CNN model where, CNN takes input and pass it through convolution neural net then apply pooling and softmax function on classifying the image into different categories. Extraction of feature is done in the feature learning layer which is connected to the fully connected layers whose results are passed to the classification layer where we apply the softmax function on the features extracted and then classify the input. CNN is pre-trained to the back-propagation in which weights are automatically updated with each iteration in the back-propagation. While we train a CNN from scratch the weights are randomly assigned which are adjusted with each iteration as we train the model. And feed the input gain through back-propagation [11].

2.3   VGG-19

VGG-19 is a Deep Learning model we implement in using Keras. The model uses the pre-trained weights of ImageNet. VGG-19 is an advanced version of VGG 16 which is mostly used for prediction and feature extraction. It is the 19 Layer network built by the Visual Geometry Group (VGG), University of Oxford [12]. Figure 2 shows the basic architecture of VGG-19 model where, VGG uses very

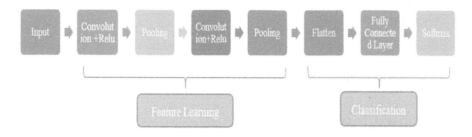

Fig. 1. Convolution Neural Network.

ConvNet Configuration					
A	A-LRN	B	C	D	E
11 weight layers	11 weight layers	13 weight layers	16 weight layers	16 weight layers	19 weight layers
input (224 × 224 RGB image)					
conv3-64	conv3-64 **LRN**	conv3-64 **conv3-64**	conv3-64 conv3-64	conv3-64 conv3-64	conv3-64 conv3-64
maxpool					
conv3-128	conv3-128	conv3-128 **conv3-128**	conv3-128 conv3-128	conv3-128 conv3-128	conv3-128 conv3-128
maxpool					
conv3-256 conv3-256	conv3-256 conv3-256	conv3-256 conv3-256	conv3-256 conv3-256 **conv1-256**	conv3-256 conv3-256 **conv3-256**	conv3-256 conv3-256 conv3-256 **conv3-256**
maxpool					
conv3-512 conv3-512	conv3-512 conv3-512	conv3-512 conv3-512	conv3-512 conv3-512 **conv1-512**	conv3-512 conv3-512 **conv3-512**	conv3-512 conv3-512 conv3-512 **conv3-512**
maxpool					
conv3-512 conv3-512	conv3-512 conv3-512	conv3-512 conv3-512	conv3-512 conv3-512 **conv1-512**	conv3-512 conv3-512 **conv3-512**	conv3-512 conv3-512 conv3-512 **conv3-512**
maxpool					
FC-4096					
FC-4096					
FC-1000					
soft-max					

Fig. 2. VGG-19

small convolution filters and having deep layers varying from 16–19 makes the architecture more robust and precise. VGG-19 has 16 Convolutional and 3 fully connected layers. VGG-19 has all the 19 layers with trainable weights, whereas the max pool layer is applied after few Convolutional layers which reduce the size of the input image and the Softmax function is used for classification.

2.4   Inception-V3

Inception V3 is a Deep Learning Model we implement in using Keras. The model uses the pre-trained weights of ImageNet. Inception V3 has 48 layers. It is a Deep learning model variant built by Google. In Inception, we apply Global average pooling in the feature learning layer which reduces the size of the feature map which is fully connected with the Softmax layer in the classification layer giving the final classification in the model. Average pooling reduces the number of parameters which results in less overfitting in inception hence, giving higher accuracy [12].

2.5   ResNet-50

ResNet-50 is a Deep Learning Model we implement in using Keras. The model uses the pre-trained weights of ImageNet. Resnet-50 has 50 layers. ResNet has resolved the problem of vanishing gradient which was not possible before that in Dense Neural networks. As the network grows large by stacking up layers the gradient starts to vanish. ResNet was able to resolve the problem of vanishing gradient by adding the concept of skip connection in ResNet we not only stacked the layers together like we did in other networks but we also added the original input to every layer making ResNet produce very good results in even bare minimum epochs. Figure 3 shows the concept how a skip connection is used between the layers [13].

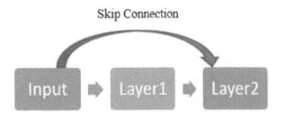

Fig. 3. Skip connection in ResNet-50

2.6   DenseNet-169

DenseNet-169 is a Deep Learning Model we implement using Keras. The model uses pre-trained weights of ImageNet. DenseNet169 is the advanced version of previous DenseNet versions it had 169 deep layers in the model. Figure 4 shows the basic architecture of DenseNet-169 model. The main feature of DenseNet is it alleviates the vanishing gradient and also decreases the parameters used [14]. In DenseNet all the layers are connected in a feed-forward fashion. In which output of all the layers is given as input to all the other layers.

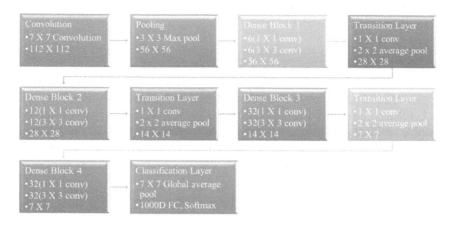

Fig. 4. DenseNet-169 architecture

3   Performance Evaluation Parameter

Studies shows that Alzheimers Disease is one of the fatal and very late detected disease. However changes in brain occur much earlier that any visual symptoms. It is divided into two sections: (i) Dataset (ii) Results and Discussion.

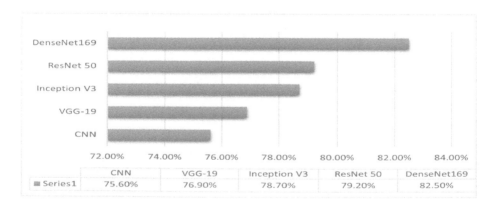

	CNN	VGG-19	Inception V3	ResNet 50	DenseNet169
■ Series1	75.60%	76.90%	78.70%	79.20%	82.50%

Fig. 5. Graphical representation of Deep Learning Algorithms

3.1   Data Set

Dataset used in the paper for Alzheimer's Disease Classification is from Kaggle. Dataset is having a total of 5121 files. MRI images of the brain in the form of .jpg format are in the dataset. All the files are having the size of 4–6 Kb.

Dataset is divided into two main category Test and Train. Where 1279 images are used for test images and the rest 3842 images are used for training. Train and Test data is further divided into four categorized 1) Mild Demented-717 files 2) Moderate Demented-52 files 3) Non-Demented- 2560 files 4) Very Mild Demented-1792 files; for test 1) Mild Demented-179 files 2) Moderate Demented-12 files 3) Non Demented- 640 files 4) Very Mild Demented-448 files. These sub category are used for Alzheimer's detection precisely at different stages

Table 1 and Fig. 5 shows the results of our dataset on the above-stated models

Table 1. Comparative analysis

S.No.	Model	Accuracy
1	CNN	75.6%
2	VGG-19	76.3%
3	Inception V3	78.7%
4	ResNet 50	79.2%
5.	DenseNet169	82.5%

we got the following accuracy from which we can state that Densenet169 gave better results on our dataset as compared to CNN, VGG-19, ResNet 50, and Inception V3

3.2 Results and Discussion

In this section, we discuss the results of the above algorithm on our dataset using Accuracy Graph which we made using Matplotlib library in python. In this paper, we explained the comparative study of the different Deep Learning Algorithms on our Dataset.

Evaluation metrics used for evaluating model performance is Accuracy. It is the ratio between the number of correctly predicted classes to the total number of prediction made by our model.

$$\text{Accuracy} = \frac{\text{True Postive} + \text{True Negative}}{\text{True Postive} + \text{True Negative} + \text{False Positive} + \text{False Negative}}$$

(1)

The accuracy measure is also measure by AUC value obtained while running the models. AUC is Area under the ROC curve. Whereas ROC is the receiver Operating Characteristics curve. ROC curve is the graph that shows the performance of the model at the classification threshold. It measures the tradeoff between the true and false positive rate. There are many evaluation metrices that can be used for evaluation like F1 Score, Recall, Precision. Here in this paper we have used Accuracy as the evaluation metrics. It is the quintessential classification metric which is easy to understand. And works best with both binary and multiclass classification problem. Figure 6 shows the accuracy on Y-axis to epochs X-axis graph of (a) CNN, (b) DenseNet 169, (c) Inception V3, (d) ResNet-50 and (e) VGG-19.

In future work, we can implement our model on other datasets and incorporate other models while optimizing the parameters for better accuracy and results. Hyper-parameter tuning or optimization is an open field for work. Choosing optimal set of hyperparameter increase the learning process of the algorithm.

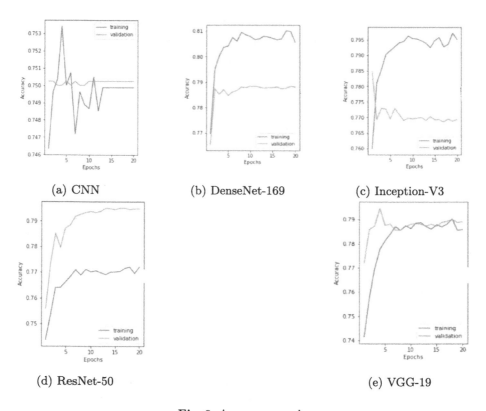

(a) CNN   (b) DenseNet-169   (c) Inception-V3

(d) ResNet-50   (e) VGG-19

Fig. 6. Accuracy graphs

4   Conclusion

This paper presents transfer learning-based Alzheimer's disease classification models from MRI images. We tested five popular models namely CNN, DenseNet 169, ResNet 50, VGG 19, Inception V3. We used the pre-trained weights of Imagenet in the base model and fine-tuned our model on the dataset to get more accurate results. We also used the concept of validation in the training of the model in which we divided 20% of our training dataset into validation which help us in parameter selection and prevent overfitting making our model more reliable. The accuracy metric is used for checking the accuracy of the model. For future extension of the work, we plan to fine-tune our model on a larger dataset and optimize feature selection and tune hyperparameters to achieve much better results Hence, reducing all the possibility of overfitting.

References

1. Lee, S., Lee, H., Kim, K.W.: Magnetic resonance imaging texture predicts progression to dementia due to Alzheimer disease earlier than hippocampal volume. J. Psychiatry Neurosci. JPN **45**(1), 7–14 (2020)
2. Liu, F., Shen, C.: Learning deep convolutional features for MRI based Alzheimer's disease classification. arXiv preprint arXiv:1404.3366 (2014)
3. Kundaram, S.S., Pathak, K.C.: Deep learning-based Alzheimer disease detection In: Nath, V., Mandal, J.K. (eds.) Proceedings of the Fourth International Conference on Microelectronics, Computing and Communication Systems. LNEE, vol. 673, pp. 587–597. Springer, Singapore (2021). https://doi.org/10.1007/978-981-15-5546-6_50
4. Gray, K.R., Aljabar, P., Heckemann, R.A., Hammers, A., Rueckert, D., The Alzheimer's Disease Neuroimaging Initiative: Random forest-based similarity measures for multi-modal classification of Alzheimer's disease. NeuroImage **65**, 167175 (2013)
5. Zhang, C., Adeli, E., Zhou, T., Chen, X., Shen, D.: Multi-layer multi-view classification for Alzheimer's disease diagnosis. In: Proceedings of the AAAI Conference on Artificial Intelligence, vol. 32, no. 1 (2018)
6. Islam, J., Zhang, Y.: Brain MRI analysis for Alzheimer's disease diagnosis using an ensemble system of deep convolutional neural networks. Brain Informat. **5**(2), 114 (2018)
7. Liu, M., Zhang, J., Adeli, E., Shen, D.: Joint classification and regression via deep multi-task multi-channel learning for Alzheimer's disease diagnosis. IEEE Trans. Biomed. Eng. (to be published)
8. Liu, M., Cheng, D., Yan, W.: The Alzheimer's disease neuroimaging initiative: classification of Alzheimer's disease by combination of convolutional and recurrent neural networks using FDG-PET images. Front. Neuroinform. **12**(35), 2 (2018)
9. Feng, C., et al.: Deep learning framework for Alzheimer's disease diagnosis via 3D-CNN and FSBi-LSTM. IEEE Access **7**, 63605–63618 (2019)
10. Plant, C., et al.: Automated detection of brain atrophy patterns based on MRI for the prediction of Alzheimer's disease. Neuroimage **50**(1), 162–174 (2010)
11. Farooq, A., Anwar, S., Awais, M., Rehman, S.: A deep CNN based multi-class classification of Alzheimer's disease using MRI. In: 2017 IEEE International Conference on Imaging systems and techniques (IST), pp. 1–6. IEEE, October 2017
12. Krishna, S.T., Kalluri, H.K.: Deep learning and transfer learning approaches for image classification. Int. J. Recent Technol. Eng. (IJRTE) **7**(5S4), 427–432 (2019)
13. Naz, S., Ashraf, A., Zaib, A.: Transfer learning using freeze features for Alzheimer neurological disorder detection using ADNI dataset. Multimedia Syst. 1–10 (2021). https://doi.org/10.1007/s00530-021-00797-3
14. Acharya, H., Mehta, R., Singh, D.K.: Alzheimer disease classification using transfer learning. In: 2021 5th International Conference on Computing Methodologies and Communication (ICCMC), pp. 1503–1508. IEEE, April 2021

A Comparative Study of Deep Learning Models for Detecting Pulmonary Embolism

Aditya Varshney, Arnav Bansal, Anshuman Agarwal, Vipul Kumar Mishra, and Tapas Badal[✉]

Bennett University, Greater Noida, Uttar Pradesh, India
{av1965,ab6573,aa6493,vipul.mishra,Tapas.badal}@bennett.edu.in

Abstract. Pulmonary Embolism (PE) is a life-threatening disease caused by the development of a clot in one of the lung arteries. While it is a common disease, it is still hard to diagnose and providing an early diagnosis can improve the odds of survival of the patient drastically.

In this paper, we aim to conduct a comparative analysis between a selection of deep learning algorithms that have been trained to detect Pulmonary Embolism(PE) and other exam level indicators which are essential for determining the severity of the disease in a patient. We consider deep learning architectures such as the MobileNet, VGG, Resnet, Xception, Inception, Unet which are extensively used for computer vision tasks and compare their performance based on evaluation metrics such as the loss, accuracy and AUC score. The results obtained during the study shows that streamlined architectures such as the MobileNet, VGG, ResNet and Unet achieve AUC scores of 0.85, 0.85, 0.82 and 0.83 respectively as compared to other models included in the study such as the inception, DenseNet and Xception which achieved an AUC score of 0.5,0.5,0.64 respectively. The links between the increasing and decreasing feature layers of the UNet provide for robust detection of features from an image. Similarly, the streamline depth-wise separable convolution layers architecture present in both the MobileNetV2 and VGG explain the feature detection in the given task. The outcomes of this research also show that there exists a significant difference of confidence between the image level and exam level features. To further support our study, we compare the performance of the selected models with models specifically proposed to detect pulmonary embolisms such as PENet [1] and Pi-PE [2]. Inferences from this methodology suggest that MobileNetV2 and VGG have similar performance as compared to PENet [1], However, Pi-PE [2] outperforms all existing architectures by achieving an AUC Score of 0.91.

Keywords: Computer Vision (CV) · Computer Aided Diagnosis (CAD) · Computed Tomography (CT) · Medical Imaging · Pulmonary Embolism (PE) · Deep Learning · Comparative Analysis

© Springer Nature Switzerland AG 2022
D. Garg et al. (Eds.): IACC 2021, CCIS 1528, pp. 82–98, 2022.
https://doi.org/10.1007/978-3-030-95502-1_7

1   Introduction

Pulmonary Embolism (PE) is a virulent and life-threatening cardiovascular disease caused by the formation of blood clots in the pulmonary arteries present in
the heart, inhibiting sufficient blood flow to the lungs. When the right ventricle
supplies oxygenated blood to the lungs, the blood clots present in pulmonary
arteries hinders its flow and can even travel into the lungs. This leads to restricted
blood flow, and hence damage to the lungs [3]. This disease, if left untreated,
could become fatal in an acute period. Prompt diagnosis and immediate medical attention are required to fight this life-threatening situation. Pulmonary
Embolisms can occur in people who have been inactive or bed-ridden for a long
period due to lack of activity. Common symptoms of PE include problems while
breathing, chest pain, persistent cough, dizziness and frequent sweat across the
body [4] (Fig. 1).

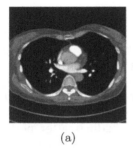

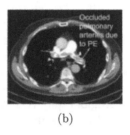

(a)

(b)

Fig. 1. CT scan of lungs (a) with no sign of PE, (b) with PE annotated using red
markers

The current practice mainly relies on a methodology called Computed
Tomography Pulmonary Angiography (CTPA), where intravenous contrast is
administered into the patient's body and a CT scan of the pulmonary blood
vessels are captured by the radiologists [5–7]. Pulmonary embolisms are classified either according to their location (Right PE i.e. PE present in the right side
of the heart, Left PE i.e. PE present in the left side of the heart and Central
PE i.e. PE present around the centre of the heart) or based on their time of
occurrence (Acute i.e. PE that has occurred in a short period or Chronic i.e. PE
that has formed over a longer duration of time) [8].

Not all pulmonary embolism show symptoms and Acute PE are said to be
more prominent and fatal because the body hasn't had sufficient time to adapt to
the changes taking place in the body. An estimated 630,000 cases and 100,000–
200,000 deaths every year are said to be caused by this life-threatening situation
[9,10]. This year the Radiological Society of North America hosted a challenge
on Kaggle which required the competitors to apply Computer Vision Methods
to accurately classify whether a patient was infected with Pulmonary Embolism,
and to also detect the location along with the type of the disease. (The dataset

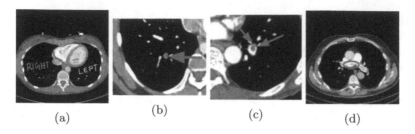

(a)   (b)   (c)   (d)

Fig. 2. CT scan of lungs (a) with all major parts of lungs labelled including right and left ventricle, (b) with Right PE, (c) with Left PE, (d) with Central PE

consisted of 9 different classes that helped describe the exact type and location of the disease in the given images) [11] (Fig. 2).

The models are trained to predict 9 classes, 1 for image-level and 8 for exam/study level. These labels include

"Negative PE", "Indeterminate", "Chronic", "Acute and Chronic", "Central PE", "Left PE", "Right PE", "RV/LV ratio $\geq$ 1", "RV/LV ratio greater $<$ 1". The only image level label is to mark the *pe_present_on_the image.*

To solve the issue of accurately detecting PE and to build computer models that can assist doctors, we aim to apply Deep Learning Methods and Techniques to automate the process of detecting PE from a Computed Tomography Pulmonary Angiography (CTPA) scan to help reduce the morbidity rate of this fatal disease. In this study, we have outlined our findings after performing a detailed comparison between some of the various commonly known deep learning models after training and inference on the provided dataset.

With the circumstances the world has recently started to face, treatment and diagnosis of health conditions has become imperative. Using deep learning techniques for the diagnosis of health conditions can help cater to areas where immediate medical attention is scarce and also reduce some amount of workload from health professionals. Since there exists limited study about the performance of various deep learning architectures on medical imaging data, by the help of this study we aim to determine the most suitable deep learning architecture for tasks related to the application of computer vision in healthcare and medical imaging.

Hence, through this study, we aim to make the following contributions:

- Compare the performance of the various recognised deep learning architectures on pulmonary CT scans.
- Provide the intuition, reasoning and an in-depth explanation of selected deep learning architectures.
- Assess the performance of the selected models with other state-of-the-art models and other existing techniques.
- Develop a pipeline for processing high resolution medical DICOM images and run multiple production Keras models on them.

2   Materials

In this study, the data has been taken from above mentioned Kaggle competition. The images are grouped by the study and further by the series. Each series then has a collection of images, uniquely identifiable by their unique identifier known as the "SOPInstanceUID". This competition requires predicting several labels at both image and study levels. The label hierarchy of the dataset is defined in Fig. 3.

The images provided in this competition are DICOM (Digital Imaging and Communications in Medicine) images, which is an internationally standardized format related to the exchange, storage and communication of digital medical images. This format eases the transfer of medical scans significantly.

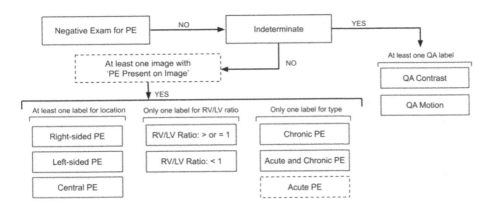

Fig. 3. Flowchart outlining the relationships between labels

CT-scan captures information about the radio density of an object or tissue exposed to x-rays. More the density of tissue, the more x-rays are absorbed. Current CT machines use 'Spiral CT', the information obtained from that is reconstructed to form a 3D volume which can be digitally sliced to obtain thinner slices as well as slices in different planes [12]. These 3D volumes are mapped to grey-level by manipulating the grey scale component of the CT image via the CT numbers, which specifically highlights particular structures hence changing the appearance of the overall image. This procedure is also known as Windowing. Windows are crucial in a radiologist's workflow [13].

Despite the major advantages of using deep learning automated PE classification on CTPA scans, major challenges arise due to large scan sizes of CTPA scans (compared to general CT scans) and PE clots representing only a small fraction of the pixel data relative to the 3D-CTPA volume. Further exacerbating the SNR (signal-to-noise ratio) problem are the inconsistencies in the subsequent CTPA scans of the same study (same patient, due to inconsistencies in patient breath-holding and IV contrast injection timings) [14,15].

While exploring the dataset, we experienced major class imbalance. As the data were essentially slices of a 3D scan, where it was scanned at the middle portion of the body (i.e. the frames where the lungs were correctly aligned to the CTPA sensor) while taking the scan that had detected the PE. This consisted of a very small percentage of scans (5%) actually consisting of PE'(Fig. 4).

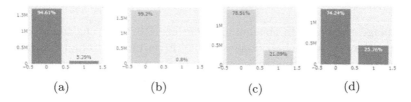

(a)   (b)   (c)   (d)

Fig. 4. Bar plots showing the class imbalance in (a) 'pe_present_on_image', (b) 'true_filling_defect_not_pe', (c) left_sided_pe, (d) 'right_sided_pe'

3   Methodology

As stated in the previous section the provided dataset was of DICOM images of the CTPA scans of various patients. The CTPA scans are 3D reconstructions of the lungs of each patient [16]. We feed these scans to our Neural Network module by converting the DICOM images into RGB images and then slicing them into a stack of 2D images. This significantly reduces computation costs due to the effective reduction of a dimension.

3.1   Preprocessing

In order to preprocess the images and make them favourable for our Neural Network module, we started by removing all metadata that was tied up to the DICOM image files as they were irrelevant for the task at hand. Additionally, we used the VTK library [17], to convert the 2D DICOM slices into NumPy arrays which are very versatile and are much easier to manipulate while being more memory efficient. Furthermore, we resized all the RGB images to a uniform 512 x 512 dimension to provide a uniform input to all our models. We then applied sampling on our train set to induce randomness in the dataset and eliminate any sort of memorization by the model. We additionally separated 20% of our train data to be used as the validation set after the completion of the model training to generate our metrics, as the ground truth for test data was not published by the competition hosts.

3.2   Neural Network Module

This module contains our complete neural network designs. As the aim of this study is to establish a comparative analysis of the performance of various deep learning models, therefore we selected well-known state of the art Deep Learning models such as MobileNet, VGG19, ResNet, InceptionNet, XceptionNet, DenseNet, Multi-UNet to extract features from the images. The Input Layer had the same dimensions as the image i.e. (512, 512, 3). Further, we experimented by freezing certain layers, adding batch normalization and dropout layers in order to boost performance. The default top layer was removed and replaced with the following set of layers: 1 Global Averaging Pooling, 1 Dropout layer with 0.25 dropout rate, 3 Dense Layers activated with the 'RoLu' activation function and then finally closed with the 9 nodes activated using the 'sigmoid' activation function, each representing the 9 output class values which are required to be predicted per image.

An image generator module was used to pick up the train set along with its ground truth and pass it into the neural network module in batches of 1000. Each of these batches was further divided into 8 mini-batches and were run for 3 epochs each in order to avoid any sort of bottleneck with the memory.

3.3 Training Parameters

The major problem we faced while taking part in the Kaggle challenge was the hardware limitation. Medical data, by nature, is an extremely detailed and heavy set of data, making it extremely hard to process with generic computational resources. Each Kaggle kernel assigned to us could run-up to a maximum of 9 h at a stretch providing each user with 12 GB RAM and only 42 h of GPU training time per week on the Nvidia K80. For a dataset like this, which consisted of approximately 1 TB of data, these specifications seemed to be rather incompetent.

In order to overcome this major constraint, the Learning rate was set to 10^{-3}. This was chosen due to the large dataset, as we didn't want our model to get stuck at a local minimum for a long time. We then divided the entire dataset ($\sim$4,00,000 images) into batches of 1000 and ran 3 epochs for each batch. Each time the validation loss decreased, we updated our model weights and saved them as a checkpoint. This way we were able to restrict our kernels from crashing when they exceeded the kernel limited memory and managed to save the best possible weights before it happened.

3.4 Models Used for Comparison

For a comparative analysis, we needed to decide which models should be chosen to achieve the best possible results. We wanted a large set of models to be included in this analysis. Hence we started by applying less complex convolution networks such as the MobileNetV2 and gradually increased our scope to models which have been designed for image classification tasks specifically for their application in the Medical Domain such as the U-Net. Further in this section, we discuss and provide reasons for the inclusion of each model in the study. Listed below are the variety of models we have used for this study (Table 1),

Table 1. Adopted model architectures

Model	Number of parameters	Number of layers
MobileNetV2	3,538,984	88
VGG-19	143,667,240	26
ResNet50	25,636,712	50
InceptionV3	23,851,784	159
Xception	22,910,480	126
DenseNet121	8,062,504	121
Multi U-Net	19,766,758	12

Now we discuss the reasons which made us select these specific models for our study.

3.4.1   MobileNetV2

Because of its less complex architecture and compact size which is obtained by using depth-wise separable convolution as efficient building blocks along with the adoption of inverted residual blocks has further improved the possibility of doing computationally tedious tasks such as Object Detection on the mobile platform. It has given exceptional results with the limited number of parameters it trains [18].

3.4.2   VGG-19

The VGG-19 was included in our analysis as the main objective behind developing this architecture was classifying images across multiple classes and hence it trains a high number of parameters. However, this architecture makes use of small convolution filters in each layer, making it computationally very expensive despite having a low number of layers compared to most other models. [19].

3.4.3   ResNet

Kaiming He et al. (2015) [20] proposed a novel architecture that was aimed at solving the degradation problem once the networks would start to converge.

The issue here is that as we start making deeper network training time is only one of the factors that prevent networks from converging. Vanishing and exploding gradients become hard to predict for different datasets trained on the very same model [19].

Accuracy saturation is another problem that is related to the degradation of networks once convergence begins and this problem is not related to overfitting. One of the ways of solving this problem is by adding spatial pyramid pooling layers between the fully connected layers.

Residual Network solved these problems by introducing residual functions between the stacked fully connected layers and merging the outputs. These functions extend the hypothesis space of the network without increasing the parameters of the network.

The result of which is a network that can be used to explore a much bigger space. The networks can also be made deeper by creating a "bottleneck" architecture without accuracy saturation as seen in traditionally fully connected networks (Fig. 5).

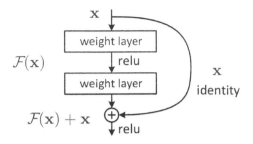

Fig. 5. Structure of a Residual Block

One of the major advantages that ResNet provided was an improved or equivalent performance to that of VGG-19(19.6 billion FLOPs) [21] as compared to that of ResNet-34(3.6 billion FLOPs) [22]. This allows for deeper networks with lower complexity.

We pre-trained our model (ResNet 50 with 25,636,712 parameters) against ImageNet Dataset [23]. Then, we transferred our model using a global average pool before targeting our labels.

3.4.4 InceptionV3

Inception was another such architecture that emerged to solve the problem of decreasing complexity of better performing neural networks [24]. It was evolved from AlexNet.

The fundamental design principle behind Inception was dimensionality reduction. It lowered the number of parameters from 60 million in AlexNet to a mere 5 million. It can be seen as an Auxiliary classifier over AlexNet (Fig. 6).

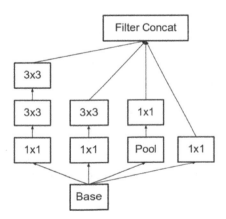

Fig. 6. Original inception block as proposed in [32]

The fundamental building block can be summed up as a split and merge architecture. This process of splitting is called spatial aggregation. A context of features is split by the inception block and without losing the translation properties of features and the filter concatenation helps in combining the output of these features in a weighted format.

The selection of kernel sizes 5×5 and 3×3 help in capturing variational concentration of features while 1×1 embedding helps in the extraction of features and reducing the dimension at the same time.

Another aspect of inception networks is the width-depth balance. As there is an involved split, if done unconditionally can result in very wide networks which would be equally hard to train and not an optimal scenario even though the quality might improve. Hyper-parameter optimization requires a measure of balance in width and depth of the network should be kept in mind to improve training error while keeping a constant step in increased cost of computation.

3.4.5 Xception

Xception net evolved from InceptionV3. It is dubbed as "Extreme Inception". It provides better performance as compared to InceptionV3 while training faster.Francois Chollet et al. [25] proposed the use of "separable convolutions"(different from spatially separable convolution) that helps to generate a similar kind of cross-channel correlations that 1×1 convolution before the spatial aggregation.

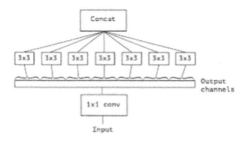

Fig. 7. Xception block

The separable convolution layer first performs a depth-wise and then a point-wise convolution (1×1).

This changes the order of layers. Another difference that Xception has is that it uses a non-linear activation after every merge rather than ReLU like in the Inception.

As it can be seen in Fig. 7, the separable convolutions reduce the complexity of computing multiple convolutions on different splits by using channels instead of splits (Fig. 8).

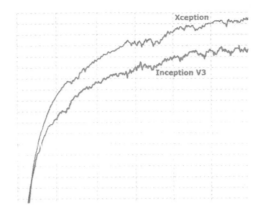

Fig. 8. Comparision between the training steps of Xception and InceptionV3

3.4.6   Dense-Net

Dense-net (Densely Connected), has emerged as another approach to Convolutional Neural Networks, which can easily surpass the 100-layer barrier [26]. The main issue with such deep neural networks; like Convolutional neural networks (CNN), is that when we go deeper into the networks, the gradient/weights "wash out"/or vanish as it reaches the terminal nodes of the network. The reason for its occurrence is that as we go deeper the gradients adjusted from the derivative become negligible and approach zero. This is due to the exponential nature of the derivative of the loss function converging to zero.

Dense-Net ensure that maximum information flow is maintained and also simplifies the connectivity pattern between the layers relative to other approaches such as Stochastic depth in ResNet [35], and FractalNets [36].

Unlike Inception Network or Xception Network, DenseNet uses the elemental reuse feature connectivity to improve performance.

The traditional convolution blocks are less likely to perform with the same invariance on data as densely connected convolutional blocks.

While densenets' have much fewer boundaries than a convolutional network, this was done on purpose. The design principle dictates that each layer must know the last layer in the block. Each layer knows its preceding feature maps and hence the term collective knowledge. So, with each new layer, some new information gets added to the feature maps of information. This unique feature mapping allows densely connected networks to converge much faster than regular networks while steps might still be slower.

Densenet also solves the gradient flow problem often associated with deep networks.

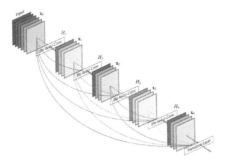

Fig. 9. DenseNet architecture

If one were to look at the network, one would observe a distribution of connections between the different convolutional blocks as shown in Fig. 9.

3.4.7   UNet

UNet was first proposed for biomedical image segmentation in [27].

The problem with segmentation tasks is the abstraction of features in both the low fidelity domain and high fidelity domain of the images.

When stacking Conv-DeConv blocks we run into the problem of diminishing features due to low-level abstraction in the middle flow of the network (Fig. 10).

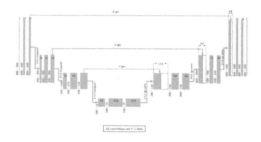

Fig. 10. U-Net architecture net block

To solve this problem, Olaf Ronneberger et al. [27] proposed connection blocks between sets of similarly padded conv-deconv blocks.

While UNet was initially targeted to solve the problem of image segmentation, its unique architecture provides us with sets of features that can be further investigated for both low level and high-level features.

3.5   Post Processing

While training the model, we saved the history of each training of the batch, this information was used to generate loss and accuracy curves for each of the labels. Once the training was complete, the generated outputs were to be post-processed, this was achieved by creating a threshold barrier of 0.5. Values that were predicted to be greater than this threshold were rounded off to 1 and those with values less than 0.5 were rounded off to 0.

The Evaluation Metric for the RSNA-STRA Pulmonary Embolism Detection Challenge was the weighted log loss, which is formulated as follows:

$$L_{ij} = -w_j * [y_{ij} * log(p_{ij}) + (1 - y_{ij}) * log(1 - (p_{ij})]$$ (1)

Once these metrics were obtained, the weighted average of each of the feature labels was taken in order to create the submission file for the competition. The weights for calculating the weighted average are as follows (Table 2):

Table 2. Weights for calculating weighted log loss function

Label	Weight
negative_for_pe	0.0736196319
indeterminate	0.09202453988
chronic	0.1042944785
acute&chronic	0.1042944785
central_pe	0.1877300613
left_pe	0.06257668712
right_pe	0.06257668712
rv_lv_ratio≥1	0.2346625767
rv_lv_ratio< 1	0.0782208589

4   Results

This section presents the main outcomes of our study. We adopt two varying approaches to determine the efficiency of algorithms under study on the given dataset. First, we evaluate the performance of MobileNetV2, VGG-19, ResNet, U-net, Xception, Inception and DenseNet on all image and exam level features Fig. 11. Furthermore, as two types of features are being predicted, namely image level and exam level, we combine the evaluation metrics for the two in order to obtain a superior understanding of the performance of the models. Secondly, we compare the performance of the above mentioned deep learning architectures with PENet [1] and Pe-PE [2], which have proposed novel architectures and have generated promising results while detecting pulmonary embolism.

Results from the first approach Fig. 11 show that the log loss for the image-level class is lower than that of exam level classes and the accuracy and AUC score for image-level class is higher than the exam level classes. The image-level feature predicted by MobileNetV2, VGG19 and ResNet achieve AUC scores of

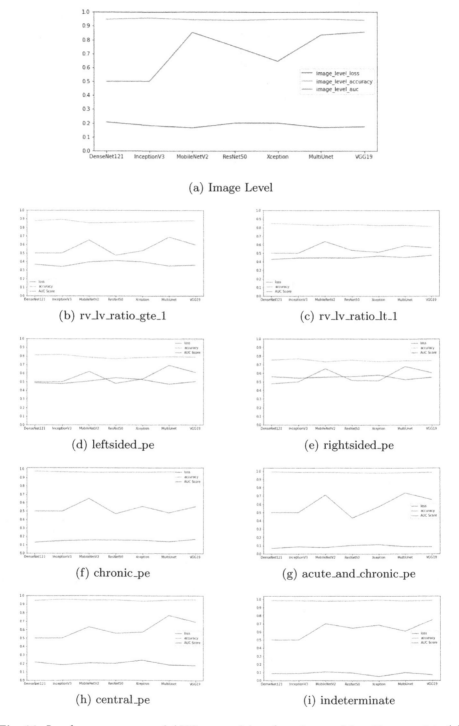

(a) Image Level

(b) rv_lv_ratio_gte_1

(c) rv_lv_ratio_lt_1

(d) leftsided_pe

(e) rightsided_pe

(f) chronic_pe

(g) acute_and_chronic_pe

(h) central_pe

(i) indeterminate

Fig. 11. Log loss, accuracy and AUC score of deep learning models with respect to (a) Image Level and (b) to (i) Exam Level classes

0.85, 0.85 and 0.82, whereas, the same models when examining study-level/exam-level features achieve 0.65 AUC score. This indicates that the models successfully determine the presence of embolism in the image, but lack in determining the exam level features such as the type of embolism, rv_lv_ratio.

Furthermore, we combined all exam level features and compared their collective performance with the image level feature. With reference to Fig. 12, we were able to support our earlier finding that the models have been able to perform better on the image level features.

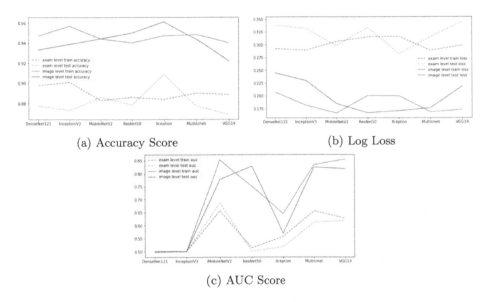

(a) Accuracy Score   (b) Log Loss

(c) AUC Score

Fig. 12. Evaluation metrics showing the difference between image level and exam level labels

Table 3 and Fig. 12 also help us draw another inference. The study suggests that the performance of models with less complex architectures, such as the MobileNet, VGG were able to classify the images with higher accuracy and AUC score as compared to complex architectures such as the DenseNet, Xception, Inception. The ResNet and Unet architectures also achieved superior metrics than that of the more complex architectures included in the study.

Table 3. A comparison between state-of-the-art models used to detect PE and other models in the study.

Name of model	AUC score
Pi-PE [2]	0.94
PENet [1]	0.84
MobileNetV2	0.85
VGG19	0.85
ResNet50	0.82
U-Net	0.82
Xception	0.56
DenseNet121	0.50
Inception	0.50

We also compared the performance of the selected architectures with other state-of-the-art models such as PENet [1] and Pi-PE [2]. PENet proposed by Huang et al. [1] is a scalable deep learning model consisting of 77 3D convolution layers consisting of a combination of Squeeze and Excitation blocks and encoders. The model was able to achieve a Validation AUC Score of 0.84 with a false positive rate standard deviation of 2 ± 0.02 on the hold out internal test-set and 0.85 AUC score along with a standard deviation of 2 ± 0.03 on external data. Rajan et al. [2] propose Pi-PE, which employs a two-stage where the first stage performs a generalization using a U-Net architecture followed by a classifier stage which uses 2D Conv-LSTM layers to further detect the embolism. Using this approach, Pi-PE [2] achieved an AUC score of 0.94 on the validation set. We compared the performance of the above mentioned state-of-the-art models to other models included models in the study as shown in Table 3.

5   Conclusion

The findings and results discussed above have led us to infer that deep learning models such as the Densenet, Inception, ResNet, Xception, MobileNet, VGG19 are more suited for tasks related to images and videos. These results have also shown that it is not necessary that a relatively denser model, such as the DenseNet or the ResNet will always perform better than relatively smaller models such as the MobileNet. We also learned the influence an imbalanced dataset has on the results of an experiment. We initially had not been doing K fold validation due to which, the models were classifying each image as a negative case for Pulmonary Embolism.

The task of working with such a huge dataset and applying various deep learning models to it has been a new experience for us. We had had issues complying with the kernel timeout that Kaggle has as some of the models required more than nine hours of training time.

6 Future Scope

Learning from the findings from this research, we aim to approach the problem with using an ensemble of models such as the MobileNetV2 or the VGG combined with models such as the LSTM which are used for text classification related tasks MobileNetV2 could be used to predict the Image level classes whereas an LSTM would be used to predict the exam level classes.

Acknowledgments. We would like to thank the organizers of the RSNA Pulmonary Embolism Detection challenge and the team at Kaggle for providing us with the resources to pursue this study.

Conflict of Interest. The authors declare that they have no conflict of interest.

References

1. Huang, S.-C., et al.: PENet-a scalable deep-learning model for automated diagnosis of pulmonary embolism using volumetric CT imaging. NPJ Digit. Med. **3**(61), 1–9 (2020)
2. Rajan, D., Beymer, D., Abedin, S., Dehghan, E.: Pi-PE: A pipeline for pulmonary embolism detection using sparsely annotated 3D CT images (2020)
3. Goldhaber, S.Z., Morrison, R.B.: Pulmonary embolism and deep vein thrombosis. Circulation **106**(12), 1436–1438 (2002)
4. Manganelli, D., Palla, A., Donnamaria, V., Giuntini, C.: Clinical features of pulmonary embolism: doubts and certainties. Chest **107**(1 suppl), 22–32 (1995)
5. Perrier, A., et al.: Diagnosis of pulmonary embolism by a decision analysis-based strategy including clinical probability, D-dimer levels, and ultrasonography: a management study. Arch. Intern. Med. **156**, 531–536 (1996)
6. Heijboer, H., Büller, H.R., Lensing, A.W., Turpie, A.G., Colly, L.P., ten Cate, J.W.: A comparison of real-time compression ultrasonography with impedance plethysmography for the diagnosis of deep-vein thrombosis in symptomatic outpatients. N. Engl. J. Med. **329**(19), 1356–1369 (1993)
7. Ozkan, H., Osman, O., Şahin, S.: Computer aided detection of pulmonary embolism in Computed Tomography Angiography images. In: 2013 International Conference on Electronics, Computer and Computation (ICECCO), pp. 355–358 (2013)
8. Lee, L.C., Shah, K.: Clinical manifestation of pulmonary embolism. Emerg. Med. Clin. N. Am. **19**(4), 925–942 (2001)
9. Anderson, F.A., Jr., et al.: A population-based perspective of the hospital incidence and case-fatality rates of deep vein thrombosis and pulmonary embolism. The Worcester DVT study. Arch. Intern. Med. **151**(5), 933–938 (1991)
10. David Prologo, J., Gilkeson, R.C., Diaz, M., Asaad, J.: CT pulmonary angiography: a comparative analysis of the utilization patterns in emergency department and hospitalized patients between 1998 and 2003. Ame. J. Roentgenol. **183**(4), 1093–1296 (2003)
11. Radiology Society of North America. RSNA STR pulmonary embolism detection—Kaggle, classify pulmonary embolism cases in chest CT scans
12. Masutani, Y., MacMahon, H., Doi, K.: Computerized detection of pulmonary embolism in spiral CT angiography based on volumetric image analysis. IEEE Trans. Med. Imaging **21**(12), 1517–1523 (2002)

13. Chan, H.-P., Hadjiiski, L., Zhou, C., Sahiner, B.: Pulmonary embolism and deep vein thrombosis. Acad. Radiol. **15**(5), 535–555 (2008)
14. Dunnmon, J.A., Yi, D., Langlotz, C.P., Ré, C., Rubin, D.L., Lungren, M.P.: Assessment of convolutional neural networks for automated classification of chest radiographs. Radiology **290**(2), 537–544 (2019)
15. Moore, A.J.E., Wachsmann, J., Chamarthy, M.R., Panjikaran, L., Tanabe, Y., Rajiah, P.: Imaging of acute pulmonary embolism: an update. Cardiovasc. Diagn. Therapy **8**(3), 225–243 (2018)
16. Rajpurkar, P., et al.: Deep learning for chest radiograph diagnosis: a retrospective comparison of the CheXNeXt algorithm to practicing radiologists. PLoS Med. **15**(11), e1002686 (2018)
17. vtk, pypi, an open-source toolkit for 3D computer graphics, image processing, and visualization
18. Sandler, M., Howard, A.G., Zhu, M., Zhmoginov, A., Chen, L.-C.: Inverted residuals and linear bottlenecks: Mobile networks for classification, detection and segmentation. CoRR, abs/1801.04381 (2018)
19. Simonyan, K., Zisserman, A.: Very deep convolutional networks for large-scale image recognition (2015)
20. He, K., Zhang, X., Ren, S., Sun, J.: Deep residual learning for image recognition. CoRR, abs/1512.03385 (2015)
21. Simonyan, K., Zisserman, A.: Very deep convolutional networks for large-scale image recognition, September 2014
22. He, K., Zhang, X., Ren, S., Sun, J.: Spatial pyramid pooling in deep convolutional networks for visual recognition. IEEE Trans. Pattern Anal. Mach. Intell. **37**(9), 1904–1916 (2015)
23. Russakovsky, O., et al.: ImageNet large scale visual recognition challenge. Int. J. Comput. Vis. **115**(3), 211–252 (2015). https://doi.org/10.1007/s11263-015-0816-y
24. Szegedy, C., Vanhoucke, V., Ioffe, S., Shlens, J., Wojna, Z.: Rethinking the inception architecture for computer vision. CoRR, abs/1512.00567 (2015)
25. Chollet, F.: Xception: Deep learning with depthwise separable convolutions. CoRR, abs/1610.02357 (2016)
26. Huang, G., Liu, Z., Weinberger, K.Q.: Densely connected convolutional networks. CoRR, abs/1608.06993 (2016)
27. Ronneberger, O., Fischer, P., Brox, T.: U-net: Convolutional networks for biomedical image segmentation. CoRR, abs/1505.04597 (2015)

A Novel Compressed and Accelerated Convolution Neural Network for COVID-19 Disease Classification: A Genetic Algorithm Based Approach

Mohit Agarwal[1][(✉)], Suneet Kumar Gupta[1], Deepak Garg[1], and Dilbag Singh[2]

[1] Bennett University, Greater Noida 201310, India
deepak.garg@bennett.edu.in
[2] Gwangju Institute of Science and Technology, Gwangju, South Korea
dilbagsingh@gist.ac.kr

Abstract. Covid 19 is an infectious disease caused by SARS-Cov-2 virus. It generally affects respiratory system of human and can be fatal if not treated early. It can be caused by coming in contact with an infected person through his/her mouth or nose due to transmission of small liquid particles by way or sneezing or coughing. Since the doctors generally depend on CT scan of suspected patients to confirm if he or she is infected. Proposed research focuses on using CT scan images for Covid-19 diagnosis. In proposed Convolution Neural Network (CNN), there are three convolution layer with 32, 16 and 8 filters in respective layers. The training accuracy of proposed model is 96.71% and testing accuracy is 84.21%. The model was also trained and tested using transfer learning and best test accuracy of 94.73% was obtained using VGG19 pre-trained network. Similarly machine learning methods were also used to classify the images and Random Forest classifier gave best accuracy of 93.33%. Since storage size of pre-trained models was very large hence they were compressed using Genetic Algorithm (GA) without much loss in performance. The VGG16 model could be compressed by 81%, AlexNet by 77.8% and VGG19 by 65.74% without drop in the F1-score. The inference time was also reduced considerably by around 79% for VGG16, 78% for VGG19 and 38% for AlexNet.

Keywords: Convolution neural network · Deep learning · Covid-19 disease · Machine learning

1 Introduction

Covid-19 virus has spread throughout the globe affecting almost every country. The statistics reveal that till Oct-2021 there has been around 235 million infections worldwide with nearly 4.8 million deaths across the globe [1].

The most common way to prevent this disease is to wear a face mask and wash hands at regular intervals. Doctors diagnose the severity of disease using

D. Garg et al. (Eds.): IACC 2021, CCIS 1528, pp. 99–111, 2022.
https://doi.org/10.1007/978-3-030-95502-1_8

X-rays or CT-scan of patients. However the opinion may vary from one physician to another and it may be very costly and painstaking. Hence to give a precise diagnosis and save time and cost of patients a deep learning based mechanism has been developed in this research.

Since the usage of tiny edge devices is increasing rapidly and there is a need for applications to run in limited memory and computing resources, an effort has been made in this direction. The pre-trained models such as AlexNet, VGG16, VGG19 which are used for image classification problems, need huge storage space and thus to compress these models Genetic Algorithm has been employed in this research.

Deep learning based methods have proved very effective in image classification problems. Several research work involving plant biology have shown wide usage of CNN for image classification [2–8]. Researchers have also shown the effectiveness of CNN based models for semantic segmentation of objects in images [9, 10]. Similarly in medical domain also several research works have been published [11–13].

Heidari et al. [14] have demonstrated that using chest X-ray images 3 class classification can be done using transfer learning with VGG16 model with accuracy of 94.5%. The 3 classes chosen were Covid-19, Non Covid pneumonia, normal cases. Khan et al. [15] have shown that using Xception based deep learning architecture a classification accuracy of 89.6% could be achieved using 4 class classification. Authors have also used X-Ray images and 4 classes of Covid-19, bacterial pneumonia, viral pneumonia and normal cases.

Aslan et al. [16] have shown that using modified AlexNet and Bidirectional Long Short-Term Memories (BiLSTM) hybrid architecture a classification accuracy of 98.7% was obtained. Authors have used chest CT-images as dataset for training and testing the model. Ismael and Sengur [17] have also employed transfer learning for classification of Covid-19 using ResNet50 pre-trained architecture and obtained accuracy of 92.6%. The dataset used by authors was of chest X-Ray images.

Agarwal et al. [12] have shown classification accuracy of 99.41% using CNN and Random Forest classifier. Authors also showed high correlation of Ground Glass opacity with Covid Severity Index calculated using block imaging. Saba et al. [13] have shown high accuracy of more than 99% with CNN and Inception V3 using transfer learning. The datasets used by the authors was different than used by us.

The main contributions of this article can be summarized as below:

– The research shows detection of Covid disease from CT scans using deep learning and machine learning.
– The paper also focuses on compression of heavy pre-trained models like VGG16, VGG19 and AlexNet using Genetic Algorithm.
– A multiobjective fitness function was also designed for Genetic Algorithm.
– Genetic Algorithm helps to search redundant filters and remove them from CNN models to compress them without loosing performance.

The rest of article is organized as follows: Sect. 2 provides a brief details of dataset and proposed simple CNN architecture. Section 3 gives results of various deep learning and machine learning models, it is followed by Sect. 4 which explains the process of CNN compression using GA. Finally paper is concluded by Sect. 5.

2   Materials and Methods

2.1   Covid Disease Image Dataset

The Covid-19 CT scan images were obtained from an internet source [18]. It consisted of 397 control images and 349 Covid-19 infected lungs images. Figure 1 shows a sample set of images from two classes.

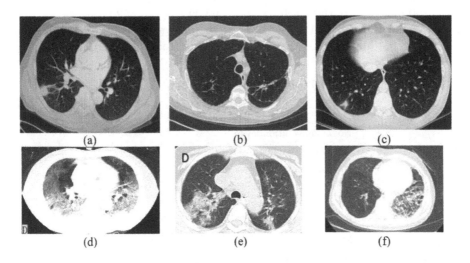

Fig. 1. a), b), c) Sample healthy images; d), e), f) Sample Covid-19 diseased images

2.2   Architecture of Convolution Neural Network for Disease Classification

The proposed CNN architecture consisted of 3 convolution layers with 64, 32, and 16 filters in each layer. Each layer is followed by a max-pool layer and at end of final max-pool layer a flatten layer is present. Next to this a Dense layer of 128 nodes is added and then final output layer has 2 nodes and softmax activation function. In other layers activation function used is ReLU. The pictorial representation of CNN architecture is shown in Fig. 2.

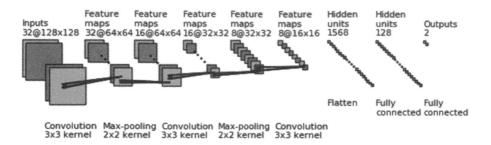

Fig. 2. CNN architecture of the proposed work.

3   Results and Discussion

A extensive simulation of proposed algorithm has been performed on NVIDIA DGX v100 machine. In the machine, 40600 CUDA cores, 5120 tensor cores, 128 GB RAM and 1000 TFLOPS speed. The hyper parameters for the experiment is searched randomly and given in following table (refer Table 1).

Table 1. Hyper parameters

Hyper-parameter	Description
No. of convolution layer	3
No. of max pooling layer	3
Drop out rate	0.5
Network weight initialization	glorot_uniform
Activation function	RELU
Learning rate	0.001
Momentum	0.999
Number of epoch	2000
Batch size	64

The comparison of performance of proposed CNN and 4 transfer learning based models is given in Fig. 3. As seen the best performance was obtained using VGG19 model.

The activation images of 1st and 2nd convolution layers is shown in Fig. 4 and 5. The figure clearly shows that how various image features such as edges and texture is passed through hidden layers to give correct prediction at output layer.

3.1   Performance of ML Classifiers

Four ML classifiers i.e. k-nearest neighbour (k-NN), Logistic Regression (LR), Decision Tree (DT) and Random Forest (RF) were also used to classify the

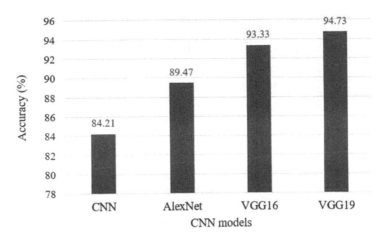

Fig. 3. Comparison of performance of different CNN models.

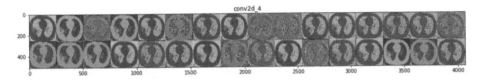

Fig. 4. Activation images of a sample Covid image from 1st convolution layer.

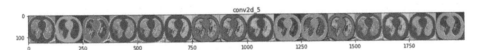

Fig. 5. Activation images of a sample Covid image from 2nd convolution layer.

images by dividing into train and test randomly in 90:10 ratio. The feature set were created by a combination of following three features:

- Local Binary Pattern [19]: These are texture features and based on 8 neighboring pixel values of any pixel in a circular manner.
- Haralick Features [20]: These are also texture-based features and obtained using Gray Level Co-occurrence matrix (GLCM).
- Hu-moments [21]: These moments of objects in an image and are invariant to translation or rotation.

The performance comparison with different combination of features is given in Table 2. The performance comparison can also be seen in ROC curves as shown in Figs. 6, 7 and 8.

Table 2. Accuracy comparison of ML models.

Features	Model	Accuracy (%)
Haralick	k-NN	65.33
Hu-moments	LR	68.00
	DT	69.33
	RF	81.33
Haralick	k-NN	65.33
LBP	LR	69.33
	DT	74.66
	RF	86.66
Haralick	k-NN	60.00
LBP	LR	74.66
Hu-moments	DT	73.33
	RF	93.33

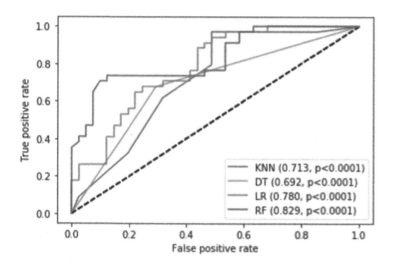

Fig. 6. ROC curve for ML classifiers using Haralick and Hu moments as features.

4   CNN Compression

Size of weight files of pre-trained models: AlexNet, VGG16 and VGG19 were 281,157 KB, 192,724 KB and 211,417 KB respectively. Their deployment on tiny edge devices will be very difficult due to constraint in memory and computational power. Hence the models were compressed using Genetic Algorithm in such a way that accuracy of the model does not deteriorate by more than 2%.

Genetic algorithm is a process guided by human evolution in which initial population set of chromosomes were created and they undergo crossover and mutation to create children chromosomes. Crossover operation helps to exchange

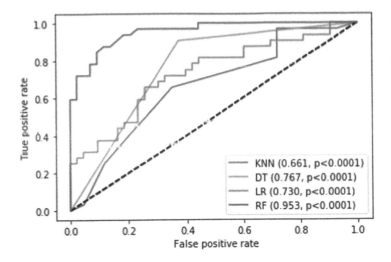

Fig. 7. ROC curve for ML classifiers using Haralick and LBP features.

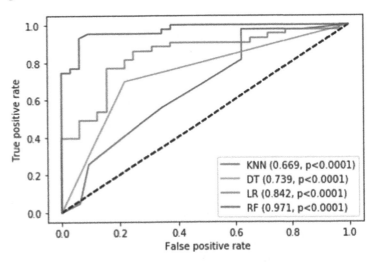

Fig. 8. ROC curve for ML classifiers using Haralick, Hu moments and LBP as features.

gene information between 2 parent chromosomes. Hence, in this process some genes of child chromosome are taken from 1st parent and remaining genes from 2nd parent. Mutation process helps in creating entirely new type of chromosomes in each iteration by randomly flipping some bits from 1 to 0 in child chromosome. Based on objective fitness criterion the chromosomes are retained or discarded. This process continues in a loop until fitness value of chromosomes saturates (change in fitness values < 0.00001). The graphical representation of GA flowchart is given in Fig. 9.

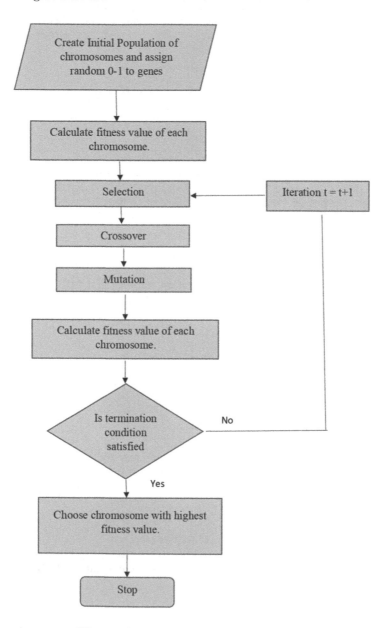

Fig. 9. Flow chart for Genetic Algorithm.

The fitness function for minimizing convolution layer filters and dense layer filters is multiobjective and based on F1-score of model on test set and nodes compression ratio. The chromosomes are created with random gene values of 0–1, where 1 denotes a particular filter/node will be retained in compressed network and 0 denotes it will discarded. A sample chromosome for VGG16 is shown in Fig. 10. For clarity of hidden filters, the architecture of VGG16 is given in Fig. 11. Thus applying GA process the best set of genes are found which can give best fitness value based on 2 objectives. The fitness criterion is given by Eqs. (1) and (2).

$$Maximize(X) = \gamma_1 \times F_1 + \gamma_2 \times \left(\frac{original\ nodes}{compressed\ nodes} \right) \tag{1}$$

$$\gamma_1 + \gamma_2 = 1 \tag{2}$$

The equation for F1-score is given in Eq. (3).

$$F_1 = \frac{TP}{TP + \frac{1}{2}(FP + FN)} \tag{3}$$

Here TP means true positive, FP means false positive and FN means false negative.

Fig. 10. A chromosome for VGG16 where different color represents hidden units of different hidden layers being pruned.

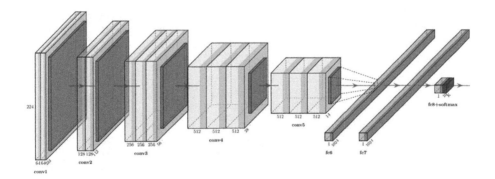

Fig. 11. VGG16 architecture.

Here F_1 is the F1-score of the compressed model on test dataset. Different combinations of γ_1 and γ_2 were taken such as 0.25 and 0.75 for more emphasis on compression ratio or 0.75 and 0.25 for more emphasis on performance of compressed model.

The comparison of original and final model size and F1-score is given in Table 3. Similarly, comparison of inference time before and after compression is given in Table 4.

Table 3. Comparison of compressed size and model F1-score using Genetic Algorithm.

Model	Original size (KB)	Compressed size (KB)	Original F1-score	Final F1-score
VGG19	211,417	72,414	0.9456	0.9318
AlexNet	281,157	62,398	0.8931	0.8728
VGG16	192,724	36,551	0.9328	0.9231
Proposed model	1,634	886	0.8419	0.8532

Table 4. Comparison of inference time of compressed model using Genetic Algorithm.

Model	Original inference time (s)	Final inference time (s)
VGG19	116.23	25.34
AlexNet	35.23	21.64
VGG16	114.23	23.87
Proposed model	10.23	8.32

The original and compressed nodes in various hidden layers of pre-trained models could be analysed pictorially as shown in Figs. 12, 13 and 14.

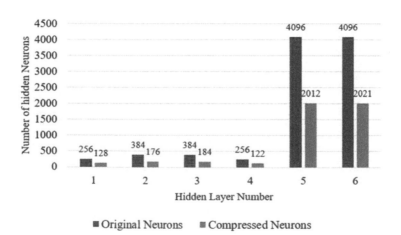

Fig. 12. Comparison of original and compressed nodes in AlexNet.

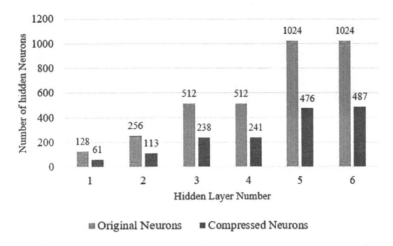

Fig. 13. Comparison of original and compressed nodes in VGG16.

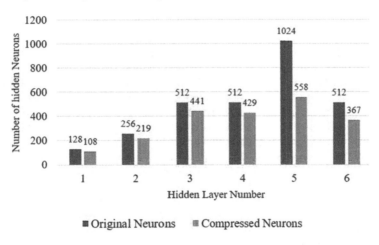

Fig. 14. Comparison of original and compressed nodes in VGG19.

5   Conclusion

Covid-19 being a fatal disease its timely diagnosis is very important. Therefore we have implemented deep learning and machine learning models for classification of Covid-19 using lung CT-scan images. It was found that best testing accuracy of 94.7% was obtained using VGG19 and best accuracy obtained using Random Forest ML classifier was 93.33% using combination of Haralick, Hu-moments and LBP features. The results of compression were showing that pre-trained models could be compressed by significant amount without loss in performance for easy deployment on tiny edge devices. The maximum reduction in size for VGG16 was around 81% and in inference time was 79%. Thus, it could help to deploy these models on mobile edge devices for real time usage.

References

1. Covid live update (2021). https://www.worldometers.info/coronavirus/
2. Agarwal, M., Singh, A., Arjaria, S., Sinha, A., Gupta, S.: ToLeD: tomato leaf disease detection using convolution neural network. Procedia Comput. Sci. **167**, 293–301 (2020)
3. Agarwal, M., Kr Gupta, S.K., Biswas, K.K.: Grape disease identification using convolution neural network. In: 2019 23rd International Computer Science and Engineering Conference (ICSEC), pp. 224–229. IEEE (2019)
4. Agarwal, M., Kaliyar, R.K., Singal, G., Gupta, S.K.: FCNN-LDA: a faster convolution neural network model for leaf disease identification on apple's leaf dataset. In: 2019 12th International Conference on Information and Communication Technology and System (ICTS), pp. 246–251. IEEE (2019)
5. Agarwal, M., Sinha, A., Gupta, S.K., Mishra, D., Mishra, R.: Potato crop disease classification using convolutional neural network. In: Somani, A.K., Shekhawat, R.S., Mundra, A., Srivastava, S., Verma, V.K. (eds.) Smart Systems and IoT: Innovations in Computing. SIST, vol. 141, pp. 391–400. Springer, Singapore (2020). https://doi.org/10.1007/978-981-13-8406-6_37
6. Agarwal, M., Bohat, V.K., Ansari, M.D., Sinha, A., Gupta, S.K., Garg, D.: A convolution neural network based approach to detect the disease in corn crop. In: 2019 IEEE 9th international conference on advanced computing (IACC), pp. 176–181. IEEE (2019)
7. Agarwal, M., Gupta, S.K., Biswas, K.K.: Development of efficient CNN model for tomato crop disease identification. Sustain. Comput. Inf. Syst. **28**, 100407 (2020)
8. Agarwal, M., Gupta, S., Biswas, K.K.: A new Conv2D model with modified ReLU activation function for identification of disease type and severity in cucumber plant. Sustain. Comput. Inf. Syst. **30**, 100473 (2021)
9. Agarwal, M., Gupta, S.K., Biswas, K.K.: A compressed and accelerated SegNet for plant leaf disease segmentation: a differential evolution based approach. In: Karlapalem, K., et al. (eds.) PAKDD 2021, Part III. LNCS (LNAI), vol. 12714, pp. 272–284. Springer, Cham (2021). https://doi.org/10.1007/978-3-030-75768-7_22
10. Agarwal, M., Gupta, S.K., Biswas, K.K.: Plant leaf disease segmentation using compressed UNet architecture. In: Gupta, M., Ramakrishnan, G. (eds.) PAKDD 2021. LNCS (LNAI), vol. 12705, pp. 9–14. Springer, Cham (2021). https://doi.org/10.1007/978-3-030-75015-2_2
11. Agarwal, M., et al.: Wilson disease tissue classification and characterization using seven artificial intelligence models embedded with 3D optimization paradigm on a weak training brain magnetic resonance imaging datasets: a supercomputer application. Med. Biol. Eng. Comput. **59**(3), 511–533 (2021). https://doi.org/10.1007/s11517-021-02322-0
12. Agarwal, M., et al.: A novel block imaging technique using nine artificial intelligence models for COVID-19 disease classification, characterization and severity measurement in lung computed tomography scans on an Italian cohort. J. Med. Syst. **45**(3), 1–30 (2021)
13. Saba, L., et al.: Six artificial intelligence paradigms for tissue characterisation and classification of non-COVID-19 pneumonia against COVID-19 pneumonia in computed tomography lungs. Int. J. Comput. Assist. Radiol. Surg. **16**(3), 423–434 (2021)

14. Heidari, M., Mirniaharikandehei, S., Khuzani, A.Z., Danala, G., Qiu, Y., Zheng, B.: Improving the performance of CNN to predict the likelihood of COVID-19 using chest x-ray images with preprocessing algorithms. Int. J. Med. Inf. **144**, 104284 (2020)
15. Khan, A.I., Shah, J.L., Bhat, M.M.: CoroNet: a deep neural network for detection and diagnosis of COVID-19 from chest X-ray images. Comput. Methods Programs Biomed. **196**, 105581 (2020)
16. Aslan, M.F., Unlersen, M.F., Sabancı, K., Durdu, A.: CNN based transfer learning-BiLSTM network: a novel approach for COVID 19 infection detection. Appl. Soft Comput. **98**, 106912 (2021)
17. Ismael, A.M., Şengür, A.: Deep learning approaches for COVID-19 detection based on chest x-ray images. Expert Syst. Appl. **164**, 114054 (2021)
18. Zhao, J., Zhang, Y., He, X., Xie, P.: COVID-CT-dataset: a CT scan dataset about covid-19. arXiv preprint arXiv:2003.13865 (2020)
19. Guo, Z., Zhang, L., Zhang, D.: A completed modeling of local binary pattern operator for texture classification. IEEE Trans. Image Process. **19**(6), 1657–1663 (2010)
20. Pathak, B., Barooah, D.: Texture analysis based on the gray-level co-occurrence matrix considering possible orientations. Int. J. Adv. Res. Electr. Electron. Instrum. Eng. **2**(9), 4206–4212 (2013)
21. Zhang, L., Xiang, F., Pu, J., Zhang, Z.: Application of improved HU moments in object recognition. In 2012 IEEE International Conference on Automation and Logistics, pp. 554–558. IEEE (2012)

Artificial Intelligence is Not a Foe But a Friend in the Healthcare Sector

Lovleen Gupta[1] and Srishti Jain[2(✉)]

[1] Hindu College, University of Delhi, New Delhi, India
lgupta@hinducollege.du.ac.in
[2] Delhi School of Economics, University of Delhi, New Delhi, India
srishtijain2708@gmail.com

Abstract. Mental health is a sensitive and a pressing issue which engulfs a large number of people. Today's scenario is worrisome as the experts' treating patients with mental illness are less in number than the rapidly increasing cases. In the backdrop of the potential mental health crisis, the present paper talks about the role of artificial intelligence in the healthcare sector specifically for diagnosing and treating mental illnesses. A structured questionnaire has been floated across people belonging to different professional backgrounds. The survey focused about the awareness and the attitude perceived by people towards artificial intelligence and mental health. Structured equation modelling has been employed for analyzing the responses from 225 respondents in an efficient manner. For a obtaining a robust result, bootstrapping has been applied in the model. The results suggest that awareness about artificial intelligence, awareness about mental health and attitude towards mental health significantly impact the role of artificial intelligence in future. Therefore, it is concluded that artificial intelligence is a way to lessen the burden on the shoulders of professional experts. In other words, artificial intelligence is a useful technique in assisting the experts.

Keywords: Artificial intelligence · Mental health · Healthcare sector

1 Introduction

Different organs make up a complete functioning body. People share the problems they experience with regard to different body parts but not mind. Social, psychological and emotional disturbance comes like a turmoil and ruins a healthy mental life of an individual. Mental health is a growing concern particularly after COVID-19. A lot of people suffered financially and emotionally during the pandemic which pushed them towards anxiety and depression. In some cases, people themselves do not know that they have become the victim of depression. Its only after formal diagnosis that they become aware about the problems they are suffering. Problems related to mind are not openly discussed in the society due to the fear of judgement and social stigma. However, this is not the right practice of dealing with such sensitive issues and hence, the problems related to mental health must be normalized.

The cases of mental illnesses have rose to an alarming level and this might result in a mental health crisis. There is a shortfall of the number of psychologists and psychiatrists

© Springer Nature Switzerland AG 2022
D. Garg et al. (Eds.): IACC 2021, CCIS 1528, pp. 112–122, 2022.
https://doi.org/10.1007/978-3-030-95502-1_9

compared to the mental health cases therefore, this further aggravate the crisis. In such a situation, AI in the field of diagnosing and treating patients with mental illness is a boon. Further, there is a high chance of accuracy and predictability of a disturbed mental health while detecting it through AI. Artificial intelligence (AI) is not a new entrant in health sector as it is extensively used in comprehending various clinical documentations. It has gained popularity post advances in various methods of data collection, machine learning and computational capacity. AI is proving its beneficial commitment in various domains like banking, security and surveillance, manufacturing, etc.

A report finds that the use of AI can diagnose depression at least three months before the formal diagnosis of the patient. In other words, AI is acting as a supportive tool to the mental health professionals. Also, a large number of people feel ashamed about them suffering with mental illness and thus, AI can overcome this obstacle as well. Generally, talking to a bot is free from prejudice and this overcomes the problem of being harshly scrutinized by the society. There are a lot of voice assistant apps like Siri and google assistant which provide unbiased opinions to the people. The upcoming latest gadgets involve the feature of diagnosing anxiety and depression which proves to be beneficial for an oblivious person.

This study attempts to understand the perception of people belonging to different age groups regarding the role of artificial intelligence in the treatment of mental illness. A structured questionnaire has been floated among the general people belonging to different professional background. This research attempts to analyze the future of AI in the healthcare sectors with respect to the assistance contributed by AI in treating mental illness by considering four independent variables – awareness about AI, attitude towards AI, awareness about mental health and attitude towards mental health. This study is unique as a survey has been conducted to observe the perception of heterogeneous community on the role of AI in treating mental illness. The remaining paper has been divided as – review of literature, research methodology, analysis and interpretation, conclusion and recommendation and limitations and scope for future study.

2 Review of Literature

The reports from World Health Organization (2018) finds that mental health affects the population severely leading to increase in morbidity and mortality. Also, there is a mismatch between the number of psychiatrists in third world countries when compared to high income countries. The same finding has been supported by a report released by World Economic Forum Global Future Council on Neurotechnologies (2019). In such a scenario, it is found that the technology in the form of wearable sensors, smartphones etc. opens up an opportunity for self-monitoring by the people (Steinhubl et al. 2013; Hinton 2018; Darcy et al. 2016).

Castagno and Khalifa (2020) conducted a study wherein the objective is to analyze the perception of the people working in healthcare sector towards the importance of AI in the future. It is reported that a lot of healthcare workers are unaware and unsure about the use of AI in the clinical practices. Another study by Doraiswamy et al. (2020) concluded that the whole community of psychiatrists in 22 countries believe that AI will soon dominate the healthcare sector leading to job losses. There is a fear of replacing the psychiatrists by the advanced technologies which pose hinder in fully accepting the machine learning ways of self-monitoring (Naylor 2018; Verghese et al. 2018). Further, a study by Graham et al. (2019) attempts to find the application of AI in the healthcare sector. They reviewed various studies using electronic health records, brain imaging data, monitoring systems, sensors used in smartphones and tried to classify them in different groups based upon the mental illness. The findings suggest that AI is excellent and accurate in predicting the mental illness of the people. The same has been reported by Bzdok and Meyer-Lindenberg (2018).

On the contrary, it has also been reported that AI can never fully replace the role of psychiatrists and it can only serve as a supporting system to the clinic-based detection and treatment of mental illness (Jiang et al. 2017; Topol 2019; Janssen et al. 2018). Some studies report that it is very difficult for a human to fully understand the social, psychological and biological data of a person suffering from mental illness and hence, AI is an important tool to assist the clinical documentation and detection of mental illness at an early stage. Lastly, a report by Marr (2019) reveals that AI helps in diagnosing the mental illness earlier than the formal diagnosing by using various AI algorithms on different words and markers which the people write on their social media posts.

It is thus, noted that majority of studies have been focused upon comprehending the perception of healthcare workers. Therefore, this study taps on the unresearched areas and attempts to study the perceptions of general public and not the healthcare workers regarding the role of artificial intelligence in diagnosing and treatment of mental illness.

3 Research Methodology

The present research paper aims to observe the future of artificial intelligence in the healthcare sector by analyzing awareness and attitude of general people towards artificial intelligence and mental health. The underlying factors capturing the essence of awareness and attitude towards AI and mental health acts as the independent variables measured by three or more statements. The structured questionnaire has been adopted in the present work to collect the responses from the heterogeneous community. In other words, convenience sampling was adopted in the current study. A total of 225 responses have been collected from different professional backgrounds like educational sector, IT sector, healthcare sector, financial sector etc. Different type of questions was asked so as to understand the level of awareness and attitude towards AI and mental health from a vast diversified pool of people. Though the sample size is adequate as per the results obtained from KMO and Bartlett's test. However, to maintain the diversity across a larger number of people, bootstrapping has been applied in the model. It is a technique to simulate a larger number of responses from a given dataset and is helpful to obtain a large sample size without any biasedness.

A large proportion of the respondents belong to 18–30 and 31–40 age group. Majority of the people believe that humans are surrounded by AI in one way or other. In other words, respondents are aware about the upcoming technologies to improvise the existing one. Respondents also believe that AI can assist psychologists and psychiatrists in treating mental illness. However, it is also observed that people are under apprehension of job losses with the introduction of AI. Therefore, they have perceived a negative attitude about AI with regard to job losses and security issues.

Further, respondents are aware about the mental health and believe that it is a serious concern which requires immediate attention. Most of them assume that family and friends alone are able to treat a person with mental illness with no care of professionals. Respondents have developed such an attitude towards mental health that they think that a person once a victim of mental illness will never be the same again. Also, there perception differs when asked about the treatment by psychologists and psychiatrists for their friends and for themselves. In other words, every person is not willing to visit a psychologist for themselves for formal diagnosis of mental illness. However, that same person will suggest his/her friends to take an appointment with professional experts of mental health. The possible reason could be the fear of judgement for oneself. It is easier to advice than to implement. Not only this, people believe that the victims of mental illness can never be the same and lose their capability of working in a society.

This study is unique when compared to the prior studies in context of the factors used to measure latent variables and target respondents. The sole objective of this paper is to investigate the knowledge base and perception of people about the role of artificial intelligence in assisting the psychiatrists and psychologists in treating people suffering from mental illness. Five latent variables have been employed out of which four variables are independent in nature while one variable is dependent in nature. Different coding has been assigned to every statement contributing in measuring the latent variable. Awareness about artificial intelligence (AW_AI) is measured by four statements coded as AW_AI1, AW_AI2, AW_AI3 and AW_AI4; attitude towards artificial intelligence (ATT_AI) is measured by three statements coded as ATT_AI1, ATT_AI2 and ATT_AI3; awareness about mental health (AW_MH) is measured by four statements coded as AW_MH1, AW_MH2, AW_MH3 and AW_MH4; attitude towards mental health (ATT_MH) is measured by four statements coded as ATT_MH1, ATT_MH2, ATT_MH3 and ATT_MH4.

For the framework to be statistically viable, we checked the sample adequacy using KMO and Bartlett's test which is shown in Table 1. The value was above the threshold limit of 0.5 and thus, it can be concluded that the sample adequacy has been matched.

Table 1. KMO and Bartlett's test

Kaiser-Meyer-Olkin measure of sampling adequacy		.823
Bartlett's test of sphericity	Approx. Chi-square	1495.369
	df	190
	Sig.	.000

Source: Author's calculation

4 Analysis and Interpretation

The objective of the current work has been analyzed through structured equation modelling (SEM) using AMOS version 23. For establishing a sound model, confirmatory factor analysis (CFA) and measurement model has been checked. CFA is used to confirm the relationship between observed variables and latent variables. Hence, validity and reliability have been computed using IBM SPSS. The results have been produced in Table 2.

Table 2. Validity and reliability of latent variables

Latent variables	AVE	Square root of AVE	Cronbach's α
Awareness about AI	0.595	0.771	0.747
Attitude towards AI	0.710	0.843	0.715
Awareness about mental health	0.800	0.894	0.775
Attitude towards mental health	0.585	0.765	0.697
Future of AI in healthcare sector	0.652	0.807	0.735

Source: Author's compilation

To check the construct validity, average variance extracted (AVE) must be greater than 0.5 and for ensuring discriminant validity, square root of average variance extracted must be greater than the correlation values obtained between the latent variables. Thus, as can be seen in Table 2, both the construct validity and discriminant validity hold true. For checking the reliability, Cronbach's α must be around 0.7, preferable greater than 0.7. Hence, as can be seen, the obtained values of Cronbach's α is above the threshold limit for all the latent variables except ATT_MH. However, it is very near to 0.7 and hence, is acceptable. Also, the communalities of each factor have been checked using IBM SPSS and all the values were above 0.5 which ensures that every statement is capable in explaining its respective latent variable.

Further, the model fit has to be checked for ascertaining the true result of the formulated objective. Table 3 produces the value of the model fit for the hypothesized model. Three model fits, i.e., absolute, incremental and parsimonious model fits have been. The values of GFI, AGFI and NFI are around 0.9 and thus, it is acceptable. Therefore, it can be concluded that the hypothesized model is fit according to the values obtained for different indicators.

Table 3. Model fit

Absolute model fit	Incremental model fit	Parsimonious model fit
Chi Square is significant at 0.05	AGFI = 0.878	CMIN/DF = 2.691
RMSEA = 0.088	CFI = 0.976	
GFI = 0.847	TLI = 0.862	
	NFI = 0.751	

Source: Author's compilation

Note: GFI (goodness of fit index); AGFI (adjusted goodness of fit index); RMSEA (root mean square error of approximation); CFI (comparative fit index); TLI (Tucker-Lewis's index); NFI (normed fit index); CMIN/DF (minimum discrepancy per degree of freedom).

4.1   Discussion of the Model

The method of maximum likelihood estimation has been employed for procuring the results. The result of the model in Table 4 suggests that all the factors are capable and efficient in explaining their respective latent variables. Further, it can be noted that awareness about artificial intelligence and awareness about mental health significantly impact the role of AI in future specifically in treating mental illness at 5% level of significance. Awareness means the knowledge obtained about a subject over a course of time. Therefore, respondents must have gathered information about AI and mental health which statistically indicates that AI can assist psychologists and psychiatrists in treating the patients suffering from mental illness in the near future.

Further, people generally think that with the widespread AI comes the widespread unemployment. In other words, people are under apprehension that AI will lead to job losses and expose private data because of its complete automation. One startling observation is that majority of the people are aware that AI will help the mental health professionals to make the process of diagnosing the mental illness quicker. However, despite of the benefit of AI which people are aware about, the thought of job losses and neglection of privacy and security induces them to develop a negative attitude towards AI. Therefore, attitude towards AI does not significantly impact the role of AI in healthcare sector in future.

Lastly, attitude towards mental health significantly impacts the role of AI in healthcare sector in future at 10% level of significance. Respondents believe that mental health is a serious concern which requires urgent treatment before it get worsens. People feel that the victims of mental illness do not report to mental health experts due to the fear of judgement. Also, it is observed that majority of the people think that people suffering from anxiety, depression, eating and behavior disorders etc. should not be treated in the same hospital as the people with physical illnesses. This ratifies the observation of fear of judgement among the people. Thus, the people have developed such an attitude where they have not learnt to normalize the problems associated with mental health. Therefore, the people believe that advancement in technology in the form of AI will resolve the problem of identity revelation and hence, the attitude formed towards mental health significantly impacts the role of AI in healthcare sector in future. In order to ensure generalizability and robustness of the model, the results were checked for the actual number of obtained responses i.e., 225 responses and post-application of bootstrapping. It was startling to observe that the results remain unchanged in both the scenarios.

Table 4. Standardized regression weights for the obtained model

			Estimate	P-value
FUT_AI	←	ATT_AI	−0.137	0.732
FUT_AI	←	AW_AI	0.47	0.045
FUT_AI	←	AW_MH	0.262	0.039
FUT_AI	←	ATT_MH	0.06	0.079
ATT_AI3	←	ATT_AI	0.452	0.001
ATT_AI2	←	ATT_AI	0.501	0.001
ATT_AI1	←	ATT_AI	0.582	0.001
AW_AI4	←	AW_AI	0.627	0.001
AW_AI3	←	AW_AI	0.549	0.001
AW_AI2	←	AW_AI	0.565	0.001
AW_AI1	←	AW_AI	0.781	0.001
AW_MH4	←	AW_MH	0.578	0.001
AW_MH3	←	AW_MH	0.823	0.001
AW_MH2	←	AW_MH	0.615	0.001
AW_MH1	←	AW_MH	0.755	0.001
ATT_MH4	←	ATT_MH	0.21	0.001
ATT_MH3	←	ATT_MH	1.995	0.001
ATT_MH2	←	ATT_MH	0.154	0.001
ATT_MH1	←	ATT_MH	−0.047	0.001
FUT_AI1	←	FUT_AI	0.555	0.001
FUT_AI2	←	FUT_AI	0.732	0.001
FUT_AI3	←	FUT_AI	0.72	0.001
FUT_AI4	←	FUT_AI	0.744	0.001
FUT_AI5	←	FUT_AI	0.319	0.001

Source: Author's compilation

Figure 1 reports the structured equation model established for analyzing the relationship between various independent latent variables and dependent latent variable. The standardized regression weights have also been outlined in the figure below.

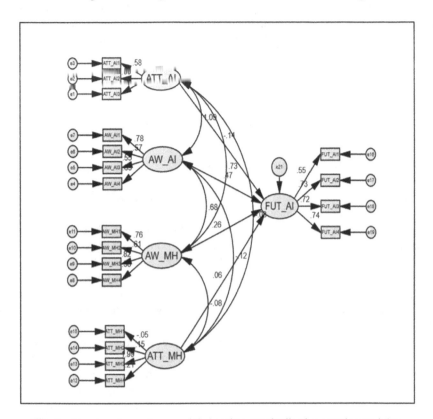

Fig. 1. Structured equation model showing standardized regression weights

An excerpt has been extracted from Table 4 to understand the impact of various latent variables on the future of artificial intelligence in the healthcare sector. Table 5 provides the concerned section for a comparative view.

Table 5. A comparative analysis of the obtained results for latent variables

Independent variable	Impact on	Estimate	Probability
Attitude towards mental health	Future of AI	0.06	0.079**
Awareness about mental health	Future of AI	0.262	0.039*
Attitude towards artificial intelligence	Future of AI	−0.137	0.732
Awareness about artificial intelligence	Future of AI	0.47	0.045*

Source: Author's creation
Note: '*' and '**' indicates significance at 5% level of significance and 10% level of significance respectively.

After applying bootstrapping, the results can be generalized for a larger number of people. The table describes the relation of independent variables with the dependent variable. It is clearly visible that the people need to change their attitude towards artificial intelligence so as to accept the new era of modern technology in future. Further, people are well aware about the rising cases of mental health problems and to a large extent believe that artificial intelligence assist the mental health experts and professionals for treating the victims of mental illness. The only concern that bothers a wide set of respondents is the identity revelation while undergoing a treatment for mental health which induces them to significantly accept the role of artificial intelligence in the healthcare sector. The reason behind the acceptance of AI is not justifiable and hence, must undergo a transition for betterment of the society.

5 Conclusion and Recommendation

Mental health is a sensitive issue which needs to be normalized. The rigid boundaries within which the people fear about getting judged has to undergo transition. It is quite absurd that people hesitate to talk about mental illness and not physical illness. There must be a complete inclusion of mind in the list of body parts. It is frustrating to live with a mental disorder without speaking about it openly. There should be open communication and sharing of experiences among diversified group without the fear of being judged. The present paper correctly captures the awareness and attitude towards AI and mental health developed among people belonging to different age groups and professional backgrounds.

The use of artificial intelligence is certainly not restricted to healthcare sector. The drastic changes in technology have both pros and cons. Even a device as small as a smartphone is efficient in transmitting worldwide upgraded technology to its users. Behind the feature of voice recognition and identifying the pattern of past searches of a user is a well-developed algorithm which is nothing but artificial intelligence. The reports concluded that these new-fashioned mechanizations and automations have assisted psychiatrists and psychologists in early detection of mental illnesses than the formal clinical diagnosis. For instance, sensors present in smartwatches is a blessing in disguise for people who may become a victim of anxiety and depression. The sensor present therein measures the level of anxiety, heartrate and blood pressure. The technologically driven devices are an instant savior as they help in early detection of chronic diseases. In other words, devices using latest technology helps in self-monitoring by the people.

Table 6. Summarization of the results

Variables related to awareness	Interpretation
Awareness about AI	People have gathered information about AI over a certain period of time which let them rationally decide the importance of AI in healthcare sector
Attitude towards AI	People are unhappy and built a negative attitude towards the emergence of AI because of the thought of large-scale unemployment and thus, their attitude does not allow to accept AI in the healthcare sector
Awareness about MH	People are well aware about the serious threat caused by the largely ignored problems related to mind. After knowing about this sensitive topic, people willingly accept AI in the healthcare sector
Attitude towards MH	People generally prefer to keep the problems related to mind in disguise and thus, they are comfortable in treating mental illness with AI due to identity concealment

Source: Author's creation

Table 6 shows the essence of the results obtained in the current study using structured equation modelling. The results suggest that respondents have acquired adequate information about AI and mental health which induces them to rationally think in a certain way. In other words, the awareness of the people about artificial intelligence and mental health significantly impacts the role of AI in healthcare sector particularly for assisting psychiatrists and psychologists in treating mental illness. Also, the attitude adapted towards mental health significantly impacts the future of AI in healthcare sector. People perceive AI as a means which keeps mental health in disguise. It needs to be focused that people tend to accept AI in the field of treating mental health because they perceive mental health as something abnormal and which is needed to be hidden by the peers. But this attitude needs to be changed and mental health problems need to be normalized. Further, a negative attitude has been developed with regard to artificial intelligence due to a mainstream thought of job losses and neglection of privacy. The role of AI is not to replace the human experts rather it is just to assist them in order to make the process of detection and treatment quicker.

6   Limitations and Scope for Future Study

Despite of a sincere effort in carrying out the research, a vast array of opportunities lies ahead of the future researchers.

- The people of different countries have different set of beliefs which influence their thought processing skills. Thus, the present study can be conducted in various countries to propound a generalized idea about the role of AI in future.
- For reporting a better result, the list of latent variables used as independent variables may be increased so as to capture the perception of the people more efficiently.

- Although the sample size was adequate in the present study but the results can be generalized and justified with a larger sample size than the one used in the current work.

It is concluded that the treatment of mental health can be faster when AI assists professional experts in the area of mental health. The only criteria which the people need to rethink about is the attitude towards AI. AI is not a foe but a friend of a human. Also, the cases of disturbed mental health have increased manifold due to various reasons after COVID-19. Artificial intelligence acts like a supporting system in making the process speedier.

References

Bzdok, D., Meyer-Lindenberg, A.: Machine learning for precision psychiatry: opportunities and challenges. Biol. Psychiatry Cognit. Neurosci. Neuroimaging 3(3), 223–230 (2018)

Castagno, S., Khalifa, M.: Perceptions of artificial intelligence among healthcare staff: a qualitative survey study. Front. Artif. Intell. 3, 1–7 (2020)

Darcy, A.M., Louie, A.K., Roberts, L.W.: Machine learning and the profession of medicine. JAMA Netw. 315(6), 551–552 (2016)

Doraiswamy, P.M., Blease, C., Bodner, K.: Artificial intelligence and the future of psychiatry: insights from a global physician survey. Artif. Intell. Med. 102, 1–7 (2020)

Graham, S., et al.: Artificial intelligence for mental health and mental illness: An overview. Psychiatry Digit. Age 21(11), 1–18 (2019)

Hinton, G.: Deep learning – a technology with the potential to transform health care. JAMA Netw. 320(11), 1101–1102 (2018)

Janssen, R.J., Mourão-Miranda, J., Schnack, H.G.: Making individual prognoses in psychiatry using neuroimaging and machine learning. Biol. Psychiatry Cognit. Neurosci. Neuroimaging 3(9), 798–808 (2018)

Jiang, F., et al.: Artificial intelligence in healthcare: past, present and future. Stroke Vasc. Neurol. 2(4), 230–243 (2017)

Naylor, C.D.: On the prospects for a deep learning health care system. JAMA Netw. 320(11), 1099–1100 (2018)

Steinhubl, S., Muse, E., Topol, E.: Can mobile health technologies transform health care? JAMA Netw. 310(22), 2395–2396 (2013)

Topol, E.J.: High-performance medicine: the convergence of human and artificial intelligence. Nat. Med. 25(1), 44–56 (2019)

Verghese, A., Shah, N.H., Harrington, R.A.: What this computer needs is a physician: humanism and AI. JAMA Netw. 2, 319–321 (2018)

Marr, B.: The incredible ways artificial intelligence is now used in mental health. Retrieved from the Forbes, Dated: 3 May 2019 (2019). Available at: https://www.forbes.com/sites/bernardmarr/2019/05/03/the-incredible-ways-artificial-intelligence-is-now-used-in-mental-health/?sh=71845065d02e

World Health Organization. Mental Health Atlas, pp. 1–68 (2018). Available at: https://www.who.int/mental_health/evidence/atlas/mental_health_atlas_2017/en/

World Economic Forum Global Future Council on Neurotechnologies. Empowering 8 Billion Minds: Enabling Better Mental Health for All via the Ethical Adoption of Technologies, pp. 1–27 (2019). Available at: https://www.weforum.org/whitepapers/empowering-8-billion-minds-enabling-better-mental-health-for-all-via-the-ethical-adoption-of-technologies

AI and The Cardiologist-When Mind, Heart and Machine Unite

Antonio D'Costa$^{(\boxtimes)}$ ⓘ and Aishwarya Zatale

BJ Wadia Hospital for Children, Parel, Mumbai, India

Abstract. Artificial Intelligence (AI) and Deep Learning have made much headway in the consumer and advertising sector, not only affecting how and what people purchase these days, but also affecting behaviour and cultural attitudes. It is poised to influence nearly every aspect of our being, and the field of cardiology is not an exception. This paper aims to brief the clinician on the advances in AI and machine learning in the field of Cardiology, it's applications, while also recognising the potential for future development in these two mammoth fields. With the advent of big data, new opportunities are emerging to build AI tools, with better accuracy, that will directly aid not only the clinician but also allow nations to provide better healthcare to its citizens.

Keywords: Artificial Intelligence · Cardiology · Machine learning · Deep Learning · Echocardiography · ECG

1 Introduction

Despite significant advances in diagnosis and treatment, cardiovascular disease (CVD) remains the most common cause of morbidity and mortality worldwide, accounting for approximately one third of annual deaths [1, 2]. Early and accurate diagnosis is key to improving CVD outcomes. A core of these can be tackled through regular screenings. Although screening programs at present can be cost inefficient for niche diseases, AI has most definitely broken the rules of what our present cardiovascular health monitoring tools can be capable of; From using ECG's for detection of left ventricular systolic dysfunction, to cardiovascular risk prediction with accuracies higher than a mammogram. In this paper, we wish to briefly touch upon the recent advancements in the field, and how AI could not only bring the birth of new technology, but also expand the capabilities of current tools available to us.

2 A Brief Introduction to AI Principles for the Clinician

2.1 Machine Learning and Deep Learning

Artificial intelligence has under it a few major subsets, two of them being Machine learning (ML) and Deep Learning (DL) [3]. Machine learning (ML) is an application of

© Springer Nature Switzerland AG 2022
D. Garg et al. (Eds.): IACC 2021, CCIS 1528, pp. 123–132, 2022.
https://doi.org/10.1007/978-3-030-95502-1_10

AI that includes algorithms that parse data, learn from that data, and then go on to make informed decisions based on what they've interpreted from it. In the music streaming industry, this would help to analyse the bulk of songs a user listens to, compare it for similarities with a bunch of other users using the same service and then provide suggestions from listeners with similar musical taste.

A subfield of ML is what is known as Deep Learning. DL is more akin to how we as humans "think", working through what is known as a "neural network". Unlike an ML algorithm, a deep learning neural network will have multiple layers, each layer consisting of an algorithm that in most simplistic terms takes an input, runs it through a mathematical function, and provides a relevant "insightful" output. This output can then be passed on as input to another layer to get another feature detail, so on and so forth, each layer honing in and picking out the most relevant details with respect to the task at hand.

In DL, one can stack multiple such layers to create a neural network of 'n' size, limited only by the amount of computing ability and processing time available at hand (Figs. 1 and 2).

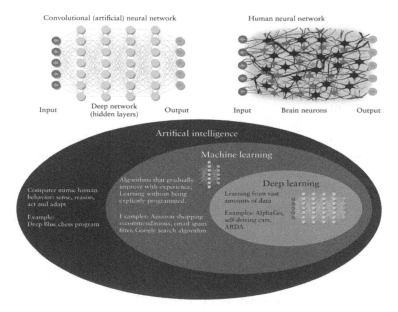

Fig. 1. The Brain, AI, ML and DL – The relationship [4]

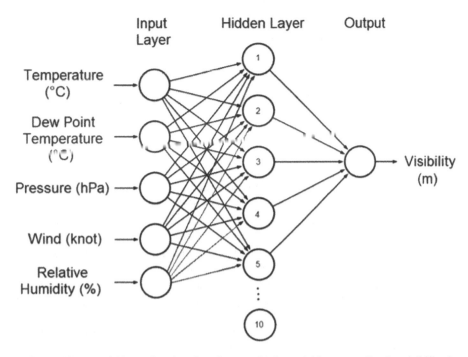

Fig. 2. A DL Neural Network using data from multiple variables to predict the visibility in a foggy situation at an airport [5]

Deep learning, with its ability to learn by itself, has significantly created newer avenues in AI research. In the field of cardiology, this technology is being used to detect and classify arrhythmias and murmurs using ECG tracings and stethoscope recordings respectively. In Echocardiography, AI image processing can help in automation of multiple parameter detection like Ejection fraction, as well as in quick screening exams.

2.2 Natural Language Processing

While most of the fields applying AI rely on data that can be easily accessed by a computer, medicine isn't one of them. Clinical narratives comprise more than 80% of data in electronic health records (EHRs) [6]. Much of this data is free-text and unstructured whose summarisation would be time and labor-intensive. For it to be made computer-manageable, tools for automatic identification and extraction of relevant data would be hence needed.

Fortunately, recent advances in technology, especially Natural language processing (NLP), have enabled this automatic information extraction from narrative text. NLP is another AI method that converts unstructured text into a structured, machine readable form. Presently, NLP has been used to extract information from clinical notes, radiology reports and pathology reports.

The advancements in NLP have been tied to advancements in AI and DL which rely on "big data" for their accuracy, making possible it's venture into the field of medicine.

3 Artificial Intelligence in Cardiology

3.1 Electrophysiology

An electrocardiogram (ECG) records the electrical signals produced by the heart through sensors placed on the skin. One of the most common tests used to quickly detect a variety of heart diseases, it's utility was thus far limited though, in comparison to more advanced imaging techniques such as 2D-Echocardiography (ECHO).

Asymptomatic left ventricular dysfunction (ALVD), a treatable condition, is present in 3–6% of the general population, and associated with reduced quality of life and longevity. Classified as stage B heart failure, it is defined as depressed left ventricular systolic function in the absence of clinical heart failure. Early detection and initiation of therapy in patients with presumed ALVD has shown to lead to better outcomes [7]. Presently 2D-Echocardiography is the only way to diagnose this condition, but AI seems to be on the verge of changing that.

Zachi et al. trained a convolutional neural network to identify patients with ventricular dysfunction using ECG data alone [8]. In their study, of the patients without ventricular dysfunction on presentation, those with a positive AI screen were at 4 times the risk of developing future ventricular dysfunction compared with those with a negative screen. This makes the study one of the pivotal one's in the field, owing to the use of a cheaper and more widely accessible modality such as ECG providing a functionality once exclusive to an ECHO.

While long-term cardiac monitoring, such as a Holter exam, provides information mostly about cardiac rhythm and repolarization, the standard, short duration, 12-lead ECG can detect a wider range of cardiac electrical activity. These include arrhythmias, conduction disturbances, acute coronary syndromes, chamber hypertrophy and enlargement, effects of drugs and electrolyte disturbances. Thus, a deep learning approach that allows for accurate interpretation of the 12 lead ECG would have the greatest impact.

A majority of physicians, including cardiologists calculate QTc incorrectly, potentially missing a Long QT syndrome, which could be deadly [9]. Although present ECG Machines can provide automated estimation of various intervals, AI based automatic ECG interpretation could aid in decreasing physician mishaps by allowing better accuracies (4% error rate) and offer more functionalities such as detecting ischaemic cardiac beats [10]. Furthermore, with the development of newer architectures and faster chips, smaller mobile devices capable of interpreting an ECG may well be an effective screening tool for both acquired and congenital long QT syndrome in a variety of clinical settings, especially where a standalone 12-lead electrocardiography is not accessible or cost-effective [11].

AI has also been used to detect arrhythmias such as atrial fibrillation and conduction blocks. Lyon et al. have been able to identify and classify ECG phenotypes associated with arrhythmic risk markers in hypertrophic cardiomyopathy [12].

The accuracy of these predictions is based on the large datasets, which are now increasingly and easily available thanks to digitisation, paving the way for future advances in this modality.

3.2 Echocardiography

Echocardiography remains the principal imaging modality in cardiology for the evaluation of cardiac structure and function. Unfortunately, being an ultrasonography based imaging modality, the acquisition and interpretation of echocardiograms remains highly dependent on operator experience and hence open to human errors. This allows an opportunity for AI which could be used to minimise such errors, and open up the possibility of standardisation.

A recent study conducted by Narang et al., concluded that AI can indeed be used to assist untrained personnel, to acquire echocardiographic studies with diagnostic potential [13]. In this study, 8 untrained nurses in ultrasonography used AI guidance to scan 30 patients with a 10-view echocardiography protocol. 5 expert echocardiographers, did a blind review of these scans and felt they were of diagnostic quality for left ventricular size and function in 98.8% of patients, right ventricular size in 92.5%, and presence of pericardial effusion in 98.8%. Their AI guidance algorithm represents a step forward in the interaction of medical imaging, and novice cardiologists, as also opening up the possibility of ultrasonography into settings that ordinarily would not have access due to lack of trained personnel.

Compared to a human, machine learning models have also been shown to provide an almost instantaneous assessment of an echocardiogram. In a study by Knackstedt et al., left ventricular ejection fraction could be analysed in approximately 8 s [14], which is far quicker than what a trained cardiologist with years of experience would be able to achieve. This quick measurement would allow cardiologists to save time, allowing for an increase in the number of scans, decreasing the reporting time, and providing a cost-benefit advantage (Table 1).

Table 1. Findings in the field of echocardiography and machine learning.

Reference	Study year	Application	Machine learning model used	Sensitivity/Specificity/Accuracy
[15]	2018	Recognise 15 echocardiography views	Convolutional neural network	–/–/91.7%
[16]	2018	Quantification of wall motion abnormalities	Double density-dual tree discrete wavelet transform	96.12%/96%/96.05%
[17]	2016	Classification/discrimination of pathological patterns (HCM vs ATH)	Support vector machine, random forest, artificial neural network	96%/77%/–
[18]	2016	Quantification of MR	Support vector machine	99.38%/99.63%/99.45%
[14]	2015	Calculation of EF and LS	AutoEF Software	–
[19]	2013	Automated detection of LV border	Random forest classifier with an active shape model	–/–/90.09%

ATH, athletes' heart; EF, ejection fraction; HCM, hypertrophic cardiomyopathy; LS, longitudinal strain; LV, left ventricle; MR, mitral regurgitation.

Further work has shown that AI models used to identify borders can provide an accurate identification of left and right ventricular cavities so as to derive their respective volumes, comparable to those measured by cardiac magnetic resonance imaging [20–24] (Fig. 3).

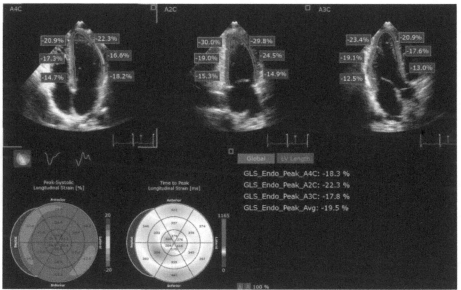

Journal of the American Society of Echocardiography 2020 331061-1066DOI: (10.1016/j.echo.2020.04.025)
Copyright © 2020 American Society of Echocardiography Terms and Conditions

Fig. 3. Automatic border detection and strain analysis from the three standard apical views calculating regional and global longitudinal strain.

3.2.1   Stress Echocardiography

Stress echocardiography is one of the most commonly used functional imaging tests for coronary artery disease. A meta-analysis of 62 published stress echocardiography studies demonstrated a wide variation in reported sensitivities and specificities for dobutamine stress echocardiography. Sensitivity ranged from 33 to 98%, whilst the specificity ranged from 38 to 97% resulting in average sensitivity and specificity for dobutamine stress echocardiography of 81 and 82%, respectively. In essence, one in every 5 patients could be potentially misdiagnosed [25].

Quantitative assessment of changes in regional wall motion is important in stress echocardiography to identify patients with prognostically significant coronary disease. It is also used in assessment of systolic heart failure. A study by Omat et al. [26] found that using a DL technique of convolutional neural networks provided a sensitivity of 81.1% compared to an expert operator interpretation, although most studies till date have been on relatively small datasets. Nevertheless, they show promise that ML models may be able to support decision making in stress echocardiography, reducing the incidence of a patient being misdiagnosed.

3.3 Clinical Decision Support and Preventive Cardiology

In clinical practice, the main goals are the right diagnosis and effective treatment of the patient.

Yan et al. propose an interesting concept- they propose that wherein the traditional model involved a clinician analysing and giving "instructions" to a patient directly, a novel approach would rather be the clinician giving instructions to an AI solution acting as a liason [27]. The AI program would then search for flaws in the clinician's interpretation and if any such were found, would then request help from a senior clinician before finally passing the corrected advice on to the patient. This approach would most definitely help in decreasing errors in medical practice, acting as a redundancy tool.

Take for example, Google has been able to determine cardiovascular risk factors from retinal fundus photographs, such as age, gender, smoking status, blood pressure and major adverse events [28]. This work allowed the scientists to use this data to predict the patient's risk of cardiovascular disease, with an accuracy as high as 70%.

It gives hope that the future clinician may be able to ascertain a much better depth of a patient's past history using devices that incorporate this tech, and hence better guide them in their medications and lifestyle.

When it comes to predicting prognosis, studies also showed that echocardiographic data and clinical factors can be used by AI tools to facilitate heart failure diagnosis, classification, severity estimation, and prediction of adverse events [29–31].

3.4 Wearable Sensors

FDA recently approved an ECG acquisition technology designed by Apple, for use in their Apple watch devices [32]. In a standard ECG limb lead, lead 1 is the potential difference between the right arm and the left arm. For the apple watch to detect an ECG, the user has to touch the digital crown of the watch. The watch also contains electrodes on the back of the device which are in continuous contact with the user's wrist. The watch then acquires the electrical potential between the electrodes and digital crown (essentially the potential differences between the two arms) to display a waveform. Software in the watch can then use this data to detect a sinus rhythm or an abnormality such as atrial fibrillation (Afib).

Wearable plethysmographs available today in most digital watches too can provide AFib detection. AI has been shown to improve the sensitivity and specificity of atrial fibrillation detection in wearable devices dramatically compared to conventional methods [33]. WATCH-AF trial is one such study that showed that the photo-plethysmographic algorithm had very high specificity and diagnostic accuracy compared to ECG data measured by cardiologists, but was limited by a high dropout rate owing to insufficient signal quality [34].

4 Moving Forward: Future Prospects

"Cultural lags", as proposed by William Ogbur, is the idea that as technological changes leap forward, they create a cultural lag in society, which then need to adapt to the new realities introduced by innovations (Ogburn, 1922). The day when AI replaces a cardiologist is not yet in sight, nor may ever be. Although not mainstream yet, we are definitely in the era where AI is assisting cardiologists across the world daily in faster and better diagnosis and image interpretations. The future lies in utilising this technology in areas not yet ventured into due to cost constraints. Furthermore, integration of automatic diagnosis and cardiovascular risk assessment systems into existing electronic medical record software would not only improve holistic treatment, but also aid in counselling of patients on modifiable risk factors, improving morbidity and mortality.

References

1. Wilkins, E., Wilson, L., Wickramasinghe, K., Bhatnagar, P., Leal, J., Luengo-Fernandez, R., et al.: European Cardiovascular Disease Statistics 2017. European Heart Network, Brussels (2017)
2. Ritchie, H., Roser, M.: Our world in data. In: Causes of Death (2018). Retrieved from: https://ourworldindata.org/causes-of-death
3. https://towardsdatascience.com/understanding-the-difference-between-ai-ml-and-dl-cceb63252a6c
4. Drukker, L., Noble, J.A., Papageorghiou, A.T.: Introduction to artificial intelligence in ultrasound imaging in obstetrics and gynecology. Ultrasound Obst. Gynecol. **56**(4), 498–505 (2020). https://doi.org/10.1002/uog.22122
5. Oğuz, K., Pekin, M.A.: Predictability of fog visibility with artificial neural network for Esenboga Airport. Avrupa Bilim ve Teknoloji Dergisi 542–551 (2019). https://dergipark.org.tr/en/pub/ejosat/issue/43603/452598
6. Jensen, P.B., Jensen, L.J., Brunak, S.: Mining electronic health records: towards better research applications and clinical care. Nat. Rev. Genet. **13**(6), 395–405 (2012)
7. Sara, J.D., Toya, T., Taher, R., Lerman, A., Gersh, B., Anavekar, N.S.: Asymptomatic left ventricle systolic dysfunction. Eur. Cardiol. Rev. **15**, e13 (2020). https://doi.org/10.15420/ecr.2019.14
8. Attia, Z.I., Kapa, S., Lopez-Jimenez, F., et al.: Screening for cardiac contractile dysfunction using an artificial intelligence-enabled electrocardiogram. Nat. Med. **25**(1), 70–74 (2019)
9. Viskin, S., et al.: Inaccurate electrocardiographic interpretation of long QT: the majority of physicians cannot recognize a long QT when they see one. Heart Rhythm **2**(6), 569–574 (2005). https://doi.org/10.1016/j.hrthm.2005.02.011. PMID: 15922261
10. Ronzhina, M., Potocnak, T., Janousek, O., Kolarova, J., Novakova, M., Provaznik, I.: Spectral and higher-order statistical analysis of the ECG: application to the study of ischemia in rabbit isolated hearts. Comput. Cardiol. **2012**, 645–648 (2012)
11. Artificial Intelligence-Enabled Assessment of the Heart Rate Corrected QT Interval Using a Mobile Electrocardiogram Device
12. Giudicessi, J.R., et al.: Artificial intelligence-enabled assessment of the heart rate corrected QT interval using a mobile electrocardiogram device. Circulation **143**(13), 1274–1286 (2021). https://doi.org/10.1161/CIRCULATIONAHA.120.050231

13. Lyon, A., Mincholé, A., Martínez, J.P., Laguna, P., Rodriguez, B.: Computational techniques for ECG analysis and interpretation in light of their contribution to medical advances. J. R. Soc. Interface **15**, 138 (2018)
14. Narang, A., Bae, R., Hong, H., et al.: Utility of a deep-learning algorithm to guide novices to acquire echocardiograms for limited diagnostic use. JAMA Cardiol. **6**(6), 624–632 (2021). https://doi.org/10.1001/jamacardio.2021.0185
15. Knackstedt, C., et al.: Fully automated versus standard tracking of left ventricular ejection fraction and longitudinal strain. J. Am. Coll. Cardiol. **66**(13), 1456–1466 (2015). https://doi. org/10.1016/j.jacc.2015.07.052
16. Madani, A., Arnaout, R., Mofrad, M., Arnaout, R.: Fast and accurate view classification of echocardiograms using deep learning. npj Digit. Med. **1**, 6 (2018). https://doi.org/10.1038/s41746-017-0013-1
17. Raghavendra, U., et al.: Automated technique for coronary artery disease characterization and classification using DD-DTDWT in ultrasound images. Biomed. Signal Process. Control **40**, 324–334 (2018). https://doi.org/10.1016/j.bspc.2017.09.030
18. Narula, S., Shameer, K., Omar, A.M.S., Dudley, J.T., Sengupta, P.P.: Machine-learning algorithms to automate morphological and functional assessments in 2D echocardiography. J. Am. Coll. Cardiol. **68**(21), 2287–2295 (2016). https://doi.org/10.1016/j.jacc.2016.08.062
19. Moghaddasi, H., Nourian, S.: Automatic assessment of mitral regurgitation severity based on extensive textural features on 2D echocardiography videos. Comput. Biol. Med. **73**, 47–55 (2016). https://doi.org/10.1016/j.compbiomed.2016.03.026
20. Gregg Belous, A.B., Rowlands, D.: Segmentation of the left ventricle from ultrasound using random forest with active shape model. In: Artificial Intelligence, Modelling and Simulation (AIMS). IEEE, Kota Kinabalu, Malaysia (2013). https://doi.org/10.1109/AIMS.2013.58
21. Performance of new automated transthoracic three-dimensional echocardiographic software for left ventricular volumes and function assessment in routine clinical practice: Comparison with 3 Tesla cardiac magnetic resonance
22. Levy, F., et al.: Arch. Cardiovasc. Dis. **110**(11), 580–589 (2017)
23. Domingos, J.S., Stebbing, R.V., Paul Leeson, J., Noble, A.: Structured random forests for myocardium delineation in 3D echocardiography. In: Wu, G., Zhang, D., Zhou, L. (eds.) MLMI 2014. LNCS, vol. 8679, pp. 215–222. Springer, Cham (2014). https://doi.org/10. 1007/978-3-319-10581-9_27
24. Stebbing, R.V., Namburete, A.I.L., Upton, R., Paul Leeson, J., Noble, A.: Data-driven shape parameterization for segmentation of the right ventricle from 3D+t echocardiography. Med. Image Anal. **21**(1), 29–39 (2015). https://doi.org/10.1016/j.media.2014.12.002
25. Transthoracic 3D Echocardiographic Left Heart Chamber Quantification Using an Automated Adaptive Analytics Algorithm
26. Tsang, W., et al.: JACC Cardiovasc. Imaging **9**(7), 769–782 (2016)
27. Three-Dimensional Echocardiographic Assessment of Left Heart Chamber Size and Function with Fully Automated Quantification Software in Patients with Atrial Fibrillation
28. Otani, K., Nakazono, A., Salgo, I.S., Lang, R.M.: J. Am. Soc. Echocardiogr. **29**(10), 955–965 (2016)
29. Factors affecting sensitivity and specificity of diagnostic testing: dobutamine stress echocardiography
30. Geleijnse, M.L., et al.
31. Omar, H.A., Domingos, J.S., Patra, A., Upton, R., Leeson, P., Noble, J.A.: Quantification of cardiac bull's-eye map based on principal strain analysis for myocardial wall motion assessment in stress echocardiography. In: 2018 IEEE 15th International Symposium on Biomedical Imaging (ISBI 2018) (2018)

32. Mei, X., et al.: Artificial intelligence–enabled rapid diagnosis of patients with COVID-19. Nat. Med. **26**(8), 1224–1228 (2020). https://doi.org/10.1038/s41591-020-0931-3
33. Poplin, R., Varadarajan, A.V., Blumer, K., et al.: Prediction of cardiovascular risk factors from retinal fundus photographs via deep learning. Nat. Biomed. Eng. **2**, 158–164 (2018). https://doi.org/10.1038/s41551-018-0195-0
34. Al'Aaref, S.J., et al.: Clinical applications of machine learning in cardiovascular disease and its relevance to cardiac imaging. Eur. Heart J. **40**(24), 1975–1986 (2019)
35. Cikes, M., Sanchez-Martinez, S., Claggett, B., et al.: Machine learning-based phenogrouping in heart failure to identify responders to cardiac resynchronization therapy. Eur. J. Heart Fail. **21**(1), 74–85 (2019)
36. Horiuchi, Y., Tanimoto, S., Latif, A.H.M.M., et al.: Identifying novel phenotypes of acute heart failure using cluster analysis of clinical variables. Int. J. Cardiol. **262**, 57–63 (2018)
37. https://www.accessdata.fda.gov/cdrh_docs/reviews/DEN180044.pdf
38. Torres-Soto, J., Ashley, E.A.: Multi-task deep learning for cardiac rhythm detection in wearable devices. npj Digit. Med. **3**, 116 (2020). https://doi.org/10.1038/s41746-020-00320-4
39. Dörr, M., et al.: The WATCH AF trial: SmartWATCHes for detection of atrial fibrillation. JACC Clin. Electrophysiol. **5**, 199–208 (2019)

An Analysis of the Psychological Implications of COVID-19 Pandemic on Undergraduate Students and Efforts on Mitigation

Shreyas Surosh Rao[1]([✉])(ⓘ), K. Pushpalatha[1](ⓘ), R. Sapna[2](ⓘ), and H. G. Monika Rani[3](ⓘ)

[1] Department of CSE, Sahyadri College of Engineering and Management, Mangalore, India
`shreyasrao.cs@sahyadri.edu.in`
[2] Department of CSE, Presidency University, Bangalore, India
[3] Department of CSE, Sir M. Visvesvaraya Institute of Technology, Bangalore, India

Abstract. The whole world is combating the COVID-19 pandemic, which has affected mankind in enormous ways. To limit its pervasive expansion, many measures were taken up by the Indian government, as a result of which colleges were closed, and education was imparted through the online mode. The pandemic has induced psychological strain in the minds of students. The present study analyses the psychological impact of the COVID-19 pandemic on engineering undergraduates in south India, who are in the age group of 19 to 22. A survey from 365 students was analyzed during the second wave of COVID-19. Data revealed that although there is an overall increased awareness about the outbreak, there is a considerable inclination towards depression, anxiety, and stress in students. Amongst the participants, 116 (31.78%) screened positive for depression, 79 (21.64%) for anxiety, and 53 (14.52%) for stress. Besides, 46 (12.60%) participants had comorbid conditions, with moderate, severe, or extremely severe levels of stress, anxiety, and depression. The Center of Excellence in AI&ML at the study center implemented a multilingual chatbot to provide mental health support during the pandemic and deployed the bot in Facebook and Web modes.

Keywords: Mental health · COVID-19 · DASS-21 · Depression · Stress. · Chatbot

1 Introduction

Coronavirus Disease 2019 (COVID-19) is an extremely infectious and spreading disease with common indications of fever, dry cough, dyspnea, fatigue and myalgia [1]. It was first discovered in Wuhan city of China on December 31st, 2019 [2]. India reported its first case in Kerala state on January 30th, 2020 with

D. Garg et al. (Eds.): IACC 2021, CCIS 1528, pp. 133–147, 2022.
https://doi.org/10.1007/978-3-030-95502-1_11

the person having a travel history to Wuhan. During this situation, the World Health Organization (WHO) demanded all the nations to combat COVID-19 [3], and subsequently stated COVID-19 as a global pandemic on March 11th, 2020. Contemporarily, the spreading rate was slightly increasing in our country, India and our country's initial case of COVID-19 death was stated on March 12th 2020. As per the WHO dashboard, the total positive cases are 238,521,855, with India alone having 34,001,743 infections, which includes 451,189 deaths [4].

COVID-19 spreads through droplets produced through coughing, sneezing, and spitting in public. Considering the threat of the contagious spread, efforts are made continually to bring awareness among the people in order to avoid spitting in public [5]. There are many challenges to the combat against the current pandemic [6,7]. During any pandemic, it is normal for people to get disturbed and distressed while handling the pandemic situation. Especially frontline Health Care Workers (HCW) tend to suffer more compared to general population [8]. A number of research have been undertaken to analyze the psychological implications of current pandemic on HCW [9], general population [10,11], youth [12,13] and students [14,15].

Since HCW face more depression, anxiety, and stress situations owing to this pandemic [16], the Indian Psychiatric Society made an effort to make Medical Council of India (MCI) aware about the critical necessity to incorporate psychological health during the pandemic management module for undergraduates (UG) [17].

Students are social beings and habituated to college routine. Several studies indicate that social isolation, fear of catching COVID-19, spread of the infection to their families or friends, future uncertainty of career life, makes students a more vulnerable group, which consequently may result in stress, anxiety, and depression [18–20].

Social isolation, rapid changes in academics caused by enforcement of online learning mode, abandonment of daily routine, active involvement in social media and online games necessitates the teaching community to monitor the mental health of their students during this global pandemic. Furthermore, the uncertainty caused due to COVID-19 along with speculative news, instills anxiety and fear into their minds, which may lead to disappointment and irritability [20].

The contribution of this study is four-fold: (a) Measures the COVID-19 related awareness among the students; (b) Analyzes the psychological implications of COVID-19 on engineering students by specifically measuring their anxiety, depression, stress, and comorbid levels; (c) Presents the features of 'Dhriti', a mental health resource chatbot developed at the study center; and (d) Recommends the best practices followed at the study center towards improving the mental health of students.

The remaining portions in the paper are planned as follows: Sect. 2 discusses the literature on psychological influence of COVID-19 on the general & student population, Sect. 3 provides the study methodology, Sect. 4 discusses the results of the case study, compares our work to contemporary literature, and provides recommendations, Sect. 5 concludes the paper and mentions future work.

2   Literature Review

In this section, we briefly give an outline on the psychological impact caused by earlier epidemics like SARS, EBOLA, and psychological consequence of COVID-19 on common people and youth.

2.1   SARS and Ebola Epidemics

The Severe Acute Respiratory Syndrome (SARS) epidemic in 2003 [21] and Ebola outbreak in 2014 [22] caused severe physical and psychological distress among the infected. A study conducted to observe the psychological stress caused due to SARS, implemented the Perceived Stress Scale (PSS) to document the responses from the SARS patients. The study concluded that the infected had higher stress and anxiety levels as compared to normal population.

At the time of Ebola outbreak, for assessing the symptoms of Post-Traumatic Stress Disorder (PTSD), anxiety, and depression, a cross-sectional survey was steered [22]. The study concluded that these symptoms persisted in people even after one year after the Ebola outbreak and suggested infected people to take psychological support to deal with the distress.

The lessons learned from these epidemics is that mental health is as serious a problem as physical health and needs to be battled on war footing [23].

2.2   Psychological Effect of COVID-19 on General Population

The paper [24] summarizes the current literature on the psychological symptoms and interferences caused due to COVID-19 pandemic. It involved a PubMed electronic database search with the usage of search items such as "novel coronavirus", "COVID-19", "nCoV", "mental health", "psychiatry", "psychology", "anxiety", "depression", "stress" in numerous arrangements and combinations. Printed articles were carefully categorized and scrutinized based on their presented evidence and collated. The author has concluded that the common responses to the COVID-19 pandemic are the subsyndromal psychological indications like anxiety, stress and depression disorders.

Fernandez et al. [9] presented a systematic analysis of nurse's experiences working in acute care hospitals during pandemics. The study recognizes the physical and emotional impact caused by the pandemic on the wellbeing of the HCW; and provides some recommendations to engage them actively to prevent their stress and burnout. Hospitals like NIMHANS provided counselling for COVID-19 patients through psychologists [25].

A survey was piloted to inspect the psychological effect of current pandemic on police professionals, which concluded that they are also battling against the disease [26]. Since most are not trained to handle such pandemic situations, it is natural to get distressed and afraid about the COVID-19 spread.

A study conducted to review the degree of psychological effect of the prevalent pandemic on common population in Saudi Arabia, used the Impact of Event Scale-Revised (IES-R) scale, in addition to the Depression, Anxiety, and Stress

Scale (DASS-21) [35] survey to gather user responses. The study concluded that people experience moderate to severe psychological stress during early pandemic, as compared with later stages of the pandemic [27].

The paper [36] investigated the depression, anxiety and stress levels on front line health care workers - nurses. The participants reported high rates of depression (55%), anxiety (56%) and stress (42%). Also, 12% of the nurses experienced comorbid conditions. DASS-21 questionnaire was used for the purpose, since it is found effective for measuring the anxiety, stress and depression levels among adult population both in terms of quantity as well as quality.

The paper [10] investigated the degrees of anxiety, stress, and depression amongst the people in the course of lockdown in India. The survey was conducted by circulating a Google form among the participants and collected the responses to analyze the psychological distress. The authors concluded that the students, healthcare professionals, and the people, who do not have enough resources to survive during lockdowns, are the most affected due to their higher psychological distress.

2.3   Psychological Effect of COVID-19 on Student Population

The study [12] evaluated the awareness, approach, anxiety, and perceived psychological healthcare among the Indian youth. The survey was conducted online through semi-structured questionnaires employing non-probability snowball sampling technique. The study showed that the participants have an average understanding of COVID-19 and satisfactory knowledge on its prevention. The study concluded that 80% of the participants had high anxiety levels due to the psychological burden of the current pandemic [12].

A study on the mental fitness of youths conducted in China in the initial months of the pandemic, indicated that 40% of the students was vulnerable to PTSD, as an immediate effect of the pandemic [13]. Furthermore, the study established that 14% of the students were more likely to get PTSD if they continued exposure to the pandemic situation.

A survey was conducted using the Generalized Anxiety Scale (GAD-7) questionnaire to analyze the anxiety levels of students in China affected by the pandemic [14]. College students experienced heightened levels of anxiety due to college/school closures, career uncertainty, economic instability, job losses, and curtailed entrepreneurship opportunities. The study concluded that the students who are staying with their parents in urban areas having stable family income fared better when compared with the students staying in rural areas facing economic instability.

The purpose of the study [28] was to examine the mental health implications of COVID-19 on students and staff in the University of Spain. They used the DASS-21 questionnaire to analyze the highnesses of anxiety, stress, and depression among the university community. They observed that these factors were less in staff, when compared to the students in the university. Hence the mental condition of students must be taken care seriously throughout this pandemic.

The authors [15] studied the psychological influence of the pandemic on undergraduate scholars in New Jersey, USA. Colleges are closed due to COVID-19 lockdowns and sudden disruptions in academic activities, along with enforced online learning formats, provide undue stress to the students. The authors conclude that the outbreak gives students' psychological health with a noteworthy negative impact, hence needs immediate addressing.

2.4 Technology

On the technical front, the application of Artificial Intelligence and Machine Learning have helped in COVID-19 disease classification [29], tissue characterisation and classification of non-COVID-19 pneumonia [30] and study on COVID-19 lung infected patients [31–33].

The above studies discussed the psychological implications of current pandemic on the mankind of affected countries. The current literature demands more focus on youth population. There are fewer assessments on the awareness aspects of COVID-19, along with the assessment of mental fitness of engineering students (aged between 18 to 22) affected by the current pandemic. India has 6300+ Engineering Institutions and Universities offering technical education programs [34]. On an average, 2.9 million students enroll for technical education; hence it is imperative to understand the need to evaluate the psychological consequence caused by COVID-19 on the engineering students. Furthermore, this process helps in directing policies and intrusions to sustain the mental health welfare of the next generation citizens.

3   Methods

3.1   Study Design and Participants

An online, cross-sectional, web-based survey was undertaken in May 2021 (during the second wave of COVID-19) to analyze the psychological influence of COVID-19 on the students. The study participants were second, third, and final year students at an engineering college in south India. A Google form was circulated to 500 students of the college via WhatsApp and Email media. The form was prepared in the English language and contained three sequentially appearing sections, i.e., (a) demographic data; (b) COVID-19 awareness quiz; and (c) mental health assessment using the DASS-21 e-questionnaire set.

Survey details such as the purpose of the study, who could participate, willingness of participation, anonymity of their identity, and other related instructions were communicated to the students prior to taking up the study. A total of 365 students participated in the survey. Once the participants filled the form, they had an option to revisit the survey and edit their responses, but were limited from submitting multiple responses. Upon completion of the survey, the score obtained in the COVID-19 awareness quiz was displayed to the participants.

DASS-21 is a self-report instrument to compute the severity levels of depression, anxiety, and stress. The scale has 3 sets with 7 scales each that offer independent measures of depression, anxiety, and stress through severity thresholds. These thresholds with cut-off scores being greater than 9, greater than 7, and greater than 14, specify a positive screening of mental health with depression, anxiety, and stress, respectively. Participants were given statements related with depression, anxiety and stress. For e.g., 'I felt I was close to panic'. The respondent had to choose one among these. The response was recorded by a 4-point Likert-type scale varying from 0 which implies 'Did not apply to me at all' to 3 which implies 'Applied to me very much or most of the time'.

The calculation of depression, anxiety and stress scores includes adding together all associated scores for each relevant item, and then, multiplied by a factor of 2 to compute the final score. Then depending on the score thus obtained, it is classified as normal, mild, moderate, severe, and extremely severe. Also, if a person has a combination of factors viz., stress & anxiety, or anxiety & depression, or stress and & depression, or all three factors, the person is said to suffer from *comorbidity*.

4   Results and Discussion

Our study considered students of age group 19 to 22, who were studying engineering in the branch of computer science. We assumed the maturity of the individual students to understand the questions sent in English language and expected them to have smart phones with internet access. As shown in Table 1, the demographic variables given to the participants included gender, family type, addiction to gaming, anxiety level after watching news, time spent online, form of media used to know about the COVID-19 information.

The mental health assessment was done with a corroborated Depression, Anxiety, and Stress Scales (DASS-21) tool as tabulated in Table 2. The COVID-19 awareness quiz contained preliminary questions on the basics of current pandemic like where it originated, how to prevent, what is PPE kit, and many others, as shown in Table 3.

Among the 365 survey participants, 192 (52.60%) were female and 173 (47.40%) male. A total of 116 (31.78%) students screened positive for depression, 79 (21.64%) for anxiety, and 53 (14.52%) for stress, as depicted in Table 4. It is observed that 139 (38.08%) students are exposed to some form of psychological disorder. However, 10 (2.74%), 10 (2.74%) and 0 (0.00%) participants screened positive for 'extremely severe' levels of depression, anxiety, and stress respectively, as shown in Table 5.

The awareness quiz has an average score of 8.8 on a scale of 10, where each question carries one mark as shown in Table 3.

The study revealed that 46 (12.60%) participants had comorbid conditions, with moderate, severe or extremely severe levels of stress, anxiety, and depression, as depicted in Fig. 1.a. Out of the comorbid cases, 30 (65.22%) were female and 16 (34.78%) were male; hence female participants suffered more comorbid issues related to male participants.

Table 1. Demographics of the survey participants

Characteristics		Count of participants N = 365 (%)
Gender	Male	173 (47.40%)
	Female	192 (52.60%)
Location	Rural	171 (46.84%)
	Urban	194 (53.15%)
Pre-existing mental condition	Yes	29 (7.95%)
	No	336 (92.05%)
Time spent online	<1 h	22 (6.02%)
	2–3 h	129 (35.34%)
	>5 h	214 (58.63%)
Media form most used	TV	105 (28.77%)
	Newspaper	6 (1.64%)
	Social media	182 (49.86%)
	News websites	72 (19.73%)
Anxious feel after watching news	Yes	89 (24.38%)
	No	68 (18.63%)
	Sometimes	208 (56.99%)
Game addiction	Yes	20 (5.48%)
	No	259 (70.96%)
	Sometimes	86 (23.56%)
Family type	Nuclear family	307 (84.11%)
	Joint family	49 (13.42%)
	Stay away from home	9 (2.47%)

It is clear that participants from nuclear families had more comorbid cases than those from joint families, as depicted in Fig. 1.b. A total of 37 (80.43%) cases belonged to nuclear family type, while 7 (15.22%) belonged to joint family type, proving that joint families give a better support system to the students during tough times.

When we analyze the location of the study subjects with comorbidity, 27 (58.7%) students were from rural and 19 (41.30%) were from urban areas as shown in Fig. 1.c, depicting rural students suffered more from comorbid conditions relatively. Also, among the 46 comorbid cases, 8 (17.39%) stated that they had pre-existing mental health conditions as shown in Fig. 1.d.

It is alarming that 39 (84.78%) students with comorbidity felt anxious after watching news about COVID-19, as shown in Fig. 1.e. The study also revealed an insight that the most used form of media by the students with comorbidity was social media, and least was the newspaper, as seen in Fig. 1.f. Adding to these, most of the students having comorbid conditions spent more than 5 h online.

On the evaluation of the hypothesis: 'whether the addiction of gaming had any effect on the comorbidity', we obtained Spearman Rho coefficient value to be

Table 2. Responses of participants to DASS-21 questionnaire

Question no	0	1	2	3
1 (s)	169 (46.30%)	156 (42.74%)	31 (8.49%)	9 (2.47%)
2 (a)	261 (71.51%)	79 (21.64%)	17 (4.66%)	8 (2.19%)
3 (d)	218 (59.73%)	111 (30.41%)	25 (6.85%)	11 (3.01%)
4 (a)	322 (88.22%)	36 (9.86%)	6 (1.64%)	1 (0.27%)
5 (d)	193 (52.88%)	138 (37.81%)	25 (6.85%)	9 (2.47%)
6 (s)	223 (61.10%)	103 (28.22%)	30 (8.22%)	9 (2.47%)
7 (a)	307 (84.11%)	45 (12.33%)	10 (2.74%)	3 (0.82%)
8 (s)	263 (72.05%)	78 (21.37%)	16 (4.38%)	8 (2.19%)
9 (a)	213 (58.36%)	115 (31.51%)	26 (7.12%)	11 (3.01%)
10 (d)	243 (66.58%)	96 (26.30%)	18 (4.93%)	8 (2.19%)
11 (s)	227 (62.19%)	108 (29.59%)	23 (6.30%)	7 (1.92%)
12 (s)	224 (61.37%)	108 (29.59%)	26 (7.12%)	7 (1.92%)
13 (d)	220 (60.27%)	113 (30.96%)	23 (6.30%)	9 (2.47%)
14 (s)	247 (67.67%)	87 (23.84%)	26 (7.12%)	5 (1.37%)
15 (a)	282 (77.26%)	72 (19.73%)	11 (3.01%)	0 (0.00%)
16 (d)	232 (63.56%)	106 (29.04%)	22 (6.03%)	5 (1.37%)
17 (d)	257 (70.41%)	74 (20.27%)	24 (6.58%)	10 (2.74%)
18 (s)	230 (63.01%)	100 (27.40%)	26 (7.12%)	9 (2.47%)
19 (a)	295 (80.82%)	54 (14.79%)	14 (3.84%)	2 (0.55%)
20 (a)	267 (73.15%)	78 (21.37%)	14 (3.84%)	6 (1.64%)
21 (d)	264 (72.33%)	71 (19.45%)	16 (4.38%)	14 (3.84%)

(d), (a) and (s) - questions on depression, anxiety and stress, respectively

Table 3. Questions used in COVID-19 awareness quiz

Q No	Questions	Correct answers N (%)
Q1	What is the full form of COVID-19?	346 (94.79%)
Q2	What are the preventive measures to fight against COVID-19?	350 (95.89%)
Q3	What is social distancing?	360 (98.63%)
Q4	The authentic sources for the latest information on the COVID- 19 outbreak are?	282 (77.26%)
Q5	Which age groups are affected by COVID- 19?	335 (91.78%)
Q6	From which Corona Virus got its name?	258 (70.68%)
Q7	Where was the initial case of COVID-19 identified?	355 (97.26%)
Q8	Where was the initial case of COVID-19 identified in India?	292 (80.00%)
Q9	The full form of "PPE" dress used by doctors is?	293 (80.27%)
Q10	Which App is launched regarding COVID-19 by the Govt. of India?	342 (93.70%)

−0.026, which is greater than 0.05. This indicates the correlation to be negative and weak. So we accept the null hypothesis and conclude that the addiction of gaming had no implication on comorbidity.

Table 4. Prevalence of depression, anxiety and stress, in students (N = 365)

Prevalence condition	Frequency
Depression	116 (31.78%)
Anxiety	79 (21.64%)
Stress	53 (14.52%)
Comorbid	46 (12.60%)

Table 5. Severity levels for depression, anxiety and stress in students

Severity level	Depression score	Anxiety score	Stress score
Normal	249 (68.22%)	286 (78.36%)	278 (76.16%)
Mild	56 (15.34%)	17 (4.66%)	56 (15.34%)
Moderate	40 (10.96%)	47 (12.88%)	22 (6.03%)
Severe	10 (2.74%)	5 (1.37%)	9 (2.47%)
Extremely severe	10 (2.74%)	10 (2.74%)	0 (0.00%)
Positive screening	116 (31.78%)	79 (21.64%)	53 (14.52%)

4.1   Dhriti - Multilingual Chatbot for Mental Health Support

In order to provide a support system for faculty and students of the Institute under study, a chatbot named 'Dhriti' was developed at the Center for Artificial Intelligence and Machine Learning within the Institute. The bot provides resources to mental health which can help people cope with the pandemic issues. It is multi-lingual and supports English, Kannada and Hindi languages currently. Features of the bot include:

- Helpline (Suicide, Alcohol De-addiction etc.)
- Directory of Mental Health Therapists (List of Counsellors, Psychologists and Psychiatrists) in Dakshina Kannada and Bangalore regions.
- Grief Counselling Support.
- List of Mental Health Apps (for Anxiety, Depression, OCD, Addictions etc.)
- Techniques for Mental Wellbeing (includes Yoga, Meditation, Pranayama)
- Social Wellbeing (includes Recreational Apps & Support Groups)
- General Covid Information (includes Symptoms, Prevention, Vaccination, Social Distance etc.)

The bot is deployed in Web and Facebook channels and has currently provided mental health support to over 2400 people in Dakshina Kannada and Bangalore regions.

4.2   Discussion

In this section, we compare the results of our study with contemporary literature and present the best practices & limitations of the study.

In general, the psychological reaction of participants to the current pandemic can be ascribed to one or more of the following factors: (a) fear of family getting infected due to virus spread; (b) being away from college campus; (c) missing peers; (d) not being comfortable with online mode of studying; (e) fear of missing career and higher studies opportunities, which is in-line with the findings presented in [22, 24]. Our study concludes that there is a considerable inclination of student population towards mental ill health, which correlates with the findings

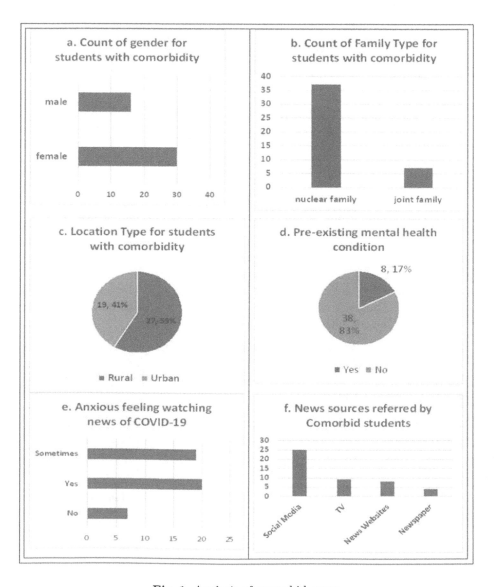

Fig. 1. Analysis of comorbid cases

made with PubMed electronic database relating to COVID-19 [27]. Female participants reported more stress than their male counterparts. One reason could be the fluctuations in hormonal levels during stressful circumstances, which makes women more prone to stress than men [37]. Second reason could be the customary beliefs that make women express more emotions during the prevalent pandemic times, compared to men [38].

Rural participants suffered more from comorbid factors ~~compared to the~~ urban ~~participants in our study~~. This observation is in tune with the study conducted in China [14], where they observed that economic instability of rural students, coupled with limited access to online media, resulted in more anxiety compared to urban students.

There is a huge amount of COVID-19 related data accessible to the people, which brings challenges in demarcating accurate from inaccurate information [39]. Also, the news regarding COVID-19 mostly concerns death and morbidity. This might be the reason for our study participants to feel anxious after watching news related to COVID-19. Positive and optimistic family environments elevate the psychological condition of the students [40], which is probably the reason why students staying in joint family environments suffered less comorbid conditions, compared to nuclear family.

The current pandemic has completely jeopardized the future studies and career plans of undergraduates [41]. The shutdown of colleges was intended for the safety of students but added additional burden of mental illness in them. Tele-mental health systems have been highly effective, resulting in cost reduction and easy accessibility [42,43]. Similar to our study, online assessment of mental well-being and self-directed psychological fitness interventions have been taken up in India and other countries in the World [44].

4.3   Best Practices and Limitations of the Study

Some best practices adopted at the Institute (under study) to improve the mental health of students include:

1. Development and deployment of Dhriti chatbot to provide mental health support to students.
2. Readjusting the teaching-learning process towards online mode of delivery.
3. Relaxing the time for the payment of fees, also giving installment facility for fee payment.
4. The college regularly sent relevant materials about COVID-19 to create awareness about the current pandemic.
5. Created COVID-19 task force involving the stakeholders like students, faculty and parents to uplift the mental health.
6. Recommended students and faculty to involve in research for creation of innovative products needed to combat the current scenario.
7. Yoga and meditation sessions were conducted regularly through online mode.

Some limitations of the study are listed in the following.

- The survey data obtained from self-reported form was never confirmed with any of those student's medical records. Further, the study accepted the data filled by participants by not being judgmental about their ethics of being honest and truthful.
- The study did not consider the socioeconomic status, which might have been useful to conclude our results.
- Since the survey was online, it unintentionally excluded students who do not have access to the internet and those students who are uncomfortable with the internet. As a result, the study was limited to willing participants who had smartphones with internet.
- The survey never asked if the participants or their families were affected by COVID-19, and if they have medical insurance or not, which could have been possible reasons for their mental ill health. The authors [37] conclude that people with private health insurance coverage sense safer in this pandemic.
- The study used the generic DASS-21 questionnaire for data collection and analysis of stress, anxiety, and depression levels; and not explicit tool such as Coronavirus Anxiety Scale (CAS), which screens dysfunctional anxiety associated with COVID-19 crisis.

5 Conclusion and Future Work

The paper discusses a study undertaken to measure the psychological health and awareness about the COVID-19 pandemic among the engineering undergraduates in south India. A DASS-21 questionnaire was circulated to the participating students for data collection. The results clearly point that there is overall improved awareness about COVID-19 amid students. The study suggests that proper mental support from family and college management, along with social awareness, is the need of the hour for achieving good health among the college students. Students need to be recommended to take up psychiatric screening when they face any problems to preserve their mental health.

Since the study was cross-sectional in nature, in the future, a longitudinal analysis is recommended for keeping track of the mental health aspects of the participants as the pandemic progresses. Further, the study can be strengthened by focusing on a representative sample.

References

1. Chen, N., Zhou, M., et al.: Epidemiological and clinical characteristics of 99 cases of 2019 novel coronavirus pneumonia in Wuhan, China: a descriptive study. lancet **395**(10223), 507–513 (2020)
2. Munster, V.J., Koopmans, M., et al.: A novel coronavirus emerging in China-key questions for impact assessment. N. Engl. J. Med. **382**(8), 692–694 (2020)
3. Drone Emprit, COVID-19 Disease. https://pers.droneemprit.id/covid19/. Accessed 10 Oct 2021

4. WHO COVID-19 Dashboard. https://covid19.who.int/. Accessed 10 Oct 2021
5. Kar, S.K., Pandey, P., Singh, N.: Understanding the psychological underpinning of spitting: relevance in the context of COVID-19. Indian J. Psychol. Med. **42**(6), 577–578 (2020)
6. Ajmera, P., Majeed, J., Goyal, R.K., Yadav, S., Mukhopadhyay, D.: Overcoming the pandemic: analysing the ongoing challenges in the prevention of COVID-19 in India. J. Health Manage. (2021). https://doi.org/10.1177/0972063420983076
7. Das, S.: Mental health and psychosocial aspects of COVID-19 in India: the challenges and responses. J. Health Manage. 22(2), 197–205 (2020)
8. CDC, Centers for Disease Control and Prevention. https://www.cdc.gov/coronavirus/2019-ncov/hcp/guidance-risk-assesment-hcp.html. Accessed 4 Oct 2021
9. Fernandez, R.: Implications for COVID-19: a systematic review of nurses' experiences of working in acute care hospital settings during a respiratory pandemic. Int. J. Nurs. Stud. **111**, 103637 (2020)
10. Rehman, U., et al.: Depression, anxiety and stress among Indians in times of COVID-19 lockdown. Community Ment. Health J. **57**(1), 42–48 (2021). https://doi.org/10.1007/s10597-020-00664-x
11. Pandey, D., et al.: Psychological impact of mass quarantine on population during pandemics-The COVID-19 Lock-Down (COLD) study. Plos one **15**(10), e0240501 (2020)
12. Roy, D., Tripathy, S., Kar, S.K., Sharma, N., Verma, S.K., Kaushal, V.: Study of knowledge, attitude, anxiety and perceived mental healthcare need in Indian population during COVID-19 pandemic. Asian J. Psychiatry **51**, 102083 (2020)
13. Liang, L., et al.: The effect of COVID-19 on youth mental health. Psychiatric Q. **91**(3), 841–852 (2020). https://doi.org/10.1007/s11126-020-09744-3
14. Cao, W., et al.: The psychological impact of the COVID-19 epidemic on college students in China. Psychiatry Res. **287**, 112934 (2020)
15. Kecojevic, A., Basch, C.H., Sullivan, M., Davi, N.K.: The impact of the COVID-19 epidemic on mental health of undergraduate students in New Jersey, cross-sectional study. PloS one **15**(9), e0239696 (2020)
16. Adiukwu, F., et al.: Global perspective and ways to combat stigma associated with COVID-19. Indian J. Psychol. Med. **42**(6), 569–574 (2020)
17. Chatterjee, S.S., Shoib, S.: Mental health: neglected domain in the pandemic management training module for undergraduates by the medical council of India. Indian J. Psychol. Med. **42**(6), 585–586 (2020)
18. Mahmoud, J.S.R., Staten, R.T., Hall, L.A., Lennie, T.A.: The relationship among young adult college students' depression, anxiety, stress, demographics, life satisfaction, and coping styles. Issues Mental Health Nurs. **33**(3), 149–156 (2012)
19. Bostan, S., Erdem, R., Öztürk, Y.E., Kılıç, T., Yılmaz, A.: The effect of COVID-19 pandemic on the Turkish society. Electron. J. Gen. Med. **17**(6), em237 (2020)
20. Matthews, T., et al.: Lonely young adults in modern Britain: findings from an epidemiological cohort study. Psychol. Med. **49**(2), 268–277 (2019)
21. Chua, S.E., et al.: Stress and psychological impact on SARS patients during the outbreak. Can. J. Psychiatry **49**(6), 385–390 (2004)
22. Jalloh, M.F., et al.: Impact of Ebola experiences and risk perceptions on mental health in Sierra Leone. BMJ Global Health **3**(2), e000471 (2018)
23. Gupta, S.D.: Coronavirus pandemic: a serious threat to humanity. J. Health Manage. **22**(1), 1–2 (2020)
24. Rajkumar, R.P.: COVID-19 and mental health: a review of the existing literature. Asian J. Psychiatry **52**, 102066 (2020)

25. Rajalu, B.M., et al.: Adopted COVID care centre model with mental health promotion at a non-COVID hospital: NIMHANS experience. Indian J. Psychol. Med. **42**(6), 584–585 (2020)
26. Khadse, P.A., Gowda, G.S., Ganjekar, S., Desai, G., Murthy, P.: Mental health impact of COVID-19 on police personnel in India. Indian J. Psychol. Med. **42**(6), 580–582 (2020)
27. Alkhamees, A.A., Alrashed, S.A., Alzunaydi, A.A., Almohimeed, A.S., Aljohani, M.S.: The psychological impact of COVID-19 pandemic on the general population of Saudi Arabia. Compr. Psychiatry **102**, 152192 (2020)
28. Odriozola-González, P., Planchuelo-Gómez, Á., Irurtia, M.J., de Luis-Garcıa, R.: Psychological effects of the COVID-19 outbreak and lockdown among students and workers of a Spanish university. Psychiatry Res. **290**, 113108 (2020)
29. Agarwal, M., Saba, L., Gupta, S.K., et al.: A novel block imaging technique using nine artificial intelligence models for COVID-19 disease classification, characterization and severity measurement in lung computed tomography scans on an Italian cohort. J. Med. Syst. **45**(3), 1–30 (2021). https://doi.org/10.1007/s10916-021-01707-w
30. Saba, L., Agarwal, M., et al.: Six artificial intelligence paradigms for tissue characterisation and classification of non-COVID-19 pneumonia against COVID-19 pneumonia in computed tomography lungs. Int. J. Comput. Assist. Radiol. Surg. **16**(3), 423–434 (2021). https://doi.org/10.1007/s11548-021-02317-0
31. Suri, J.S., Agarwal, S., Gupta, S.K., et al.: A narrative review on characterization of acute respiratory distress syndrome in COVID-19-infected lungs using artificial intelligence. Comput. Biol. Med. **130**, 104210 (2021)
32. Suri, J.S., Agarwal, S., Pathak, R., et al.: COVLIAS 1.0: lung segmentation in COVID-19 computed tomography scans using hybrid deep learning artificial intelligence models. Diagnostics **11**(8), 1405 (2021)
33. Suri J.S., et al.: Systematic review of artificial intelligence in acute respiratory distress syndrome for COVID-19 lung patients: a biomedical imaging perspective. IEEE J. Biomed. Health Inform. **25**(11), 4128–4139 (2021). https://doi.org/10.1109/JBHI.2021.3103839. Epub 2021 Nov 5. PMID: 34379599
34. MHRD website. https://www.education.gov.in/. Accessed 5 Sept 2021
35. Lovibond, S.H., Lovibond, P.F.: Manual for the Depression Anxiety Stress Scales. Psychology Foundation of Australia (1996)
36. Wang, S., Xu, H., Kotian, R.R.P., D'souza, B., Rao, S.S.: A study on psychological implications of COVID-19 on nursing professionals. Int. J. Healthcare Manage. **14**(1), 300–305 (2021). https://doi.org/10.1080/20479700.2020.1870357
37. Handa, R.J., Chung, W.C.J.: Chapter 14-Gender and Stress. Stress: Physiology, Biochemistry, and Pathology, pp. 165–176. Elsevier, Amsterdam (2019)
38. Gibson, P.A., Baker, E.H., Milner, A.N.: The role of sex, gender, and education on depressive symptoms among young adults in the United States. J. Affect. Disord. **189**(306), 13 (2016)
39. Mitchell, A.: Distinguishing between factual and opinion statements in the news. Pew Research Center. https://www.journalism.org/2018/06/18/distinguishing-between-factual-and-opinion-statements-in-the-news/. Accessed 15 Sept 2021
40. Van Harmelen, A.L., et al.: Friendships and family support reduce subsequent depressive symptoms in at-risk adolescents. PloS one **11**(5), e0153715 (2016)
41. Sahu, P.: Closure of universities due to coronavirus disease 2019 (COVID-19): impact on education and mental health of students and academic staff. Cureus **12**(4), e7541 (2020). https://doi.org/10.7759/cureus.7541

42. Langarizadeh, M., Tabatabaei, M.S., Tavakol, K., Naghipour, M., Rostami, A., Moghbeli, F.: Telemental health care, an effective alternative to conventional mental care: a systematic review. Acta Informatica Medica **25**(4), 240 (2017)
43. D'Souza, B., et al.: Healthcare delivery through telemedicine during the COVID-19 pandemic: case study from a tertiary care center in South India. Hosp. Top.1–10 (2021)
44. Mental Health in the Times of COVID-19 Pandemic. https://www.mohfw.gov.in/pdf/COVID19Final2020ForOnline9July2020.pdf. Accessed 10 Sept 2021

Network-Based Identification of Module Biomarker Associated with Hepatocellular Carcinoma

Talib Hussain[1], Prithvi Singh[2], Abhinav Kumar[2], Nadeem Ahmad[1], Ravins Dohare[2(✉)], and Shweta Sankhwar[3(✉)]

[1] Department of Biosciences, Jamia Millia Islamia, New Delhi 110025, India
[2] Centre for Interdisciplinary Research in Basic Sciences, Jamia Millia Islamia, New Delhi 110025, India
ravins@jmi.ac.in
[3] Department of Computer Science, Maitreyi College (University of Delhi), New Delhi 110021, India
ssankhwar@maitreyi.du.ac.in

Abstract. Hepatocellular carcinoma (HCC) remains a second major cause of cancer-related death worldwide due to late diagnosis at the metastatic stage, therefore there is an urgency to develop non-invasive biomarkers to unravel the molecular mechanism behind the progression of disease. MicroRNAs (miRNAs) and messenger RNA (mRNA) has been reported to be differentially expressed in HCC, and hence can play an important role of biomarkers. This work focuses on the identification of miRNA modules associated with the disease by a network-based survival-associated approach. First, a set of 10,00 miRNA datasets has been extracted from the cancer genome atlas program (TGCA) repository. Next, miRNA datasets with available expression and clinical data were identified. In total, 700–750 differentially expressed miRNA were identified to create a weighted mRNA co-expression network. By network analysis, miR302/367 clusters were identified to be differentially expressed. Later, mir302d was identified to be the potential biomarker for the disease.

Keywords: Differential expression · Co-expression network · Overall survival

1 Introduction

Liver cancer has become one of the most serious malignancies worldwide [1]. In the past few years, its prevalence has been increased to more than 80% worldwide [2]. It has become the fourth major cause of incidence and a second major cause of cancer-related death worldwide [2, 3]. Growing evidence suggests that more than one million cases will be recorded by liver cancer in 2025. Around 90% of cases of liver cancer can be attributed to Hepatocellular carcinoma (HCC) [4]. HCC has been known to be caused by Hepatitis B infection in ∼50% of reported cases. Other risk factors involve Non-alcoholic steatohepatitis (NASH), metabolic syndrome such as diabetes, and mutations by exposure to tobacco. Genetic alterations and modifications in molecular pathways get accompanied by increased reactive oxygen species (ROS) and reactive

© Springer Nature Switzerland AG 2022
D. Garg et al. (Eds.): IACC 2021, CCIS 1528, pp. 148–164, 2022.
https://doi.org/10.1007/978-3-030-95502-1_12

nitrogen species (RNS), inflammatory cytokines and fibrosis [5]. HCC initiation, progression, resistance to therapy and hierarchical organization of tumor cells can be attributed to Liver Cancer Stem Cells (LCSCs) located in tumor bulk and display the self-renewal and differentiation [6]. The molecular mechanism behind the self-renewal capability of LCSCs still needs to be elucidated.

1.1 Epidemiology

In 2016, 1.0 million incident cases and 829,000 deaths were reported (95% UI 8.8–9.1 million). In 2016, 213.2 million (95% UI) Disability-adjusted life years (DALYs) was caused by cancer. There was a 4.6% increase in absolute years of life lost that can be attributed to aging and population growth. The high prevalence of Hepatitis C virus (HCV) infection and an increase in obesity-related disorders are having a significant effect on the liver and are the major cause for high incidence in the USA. HCC shows an incidence of 1.6% per year with a 1:4 male: female ratio in India. Figure 1 represents the incidence and major aetiological factors progression of HCC.

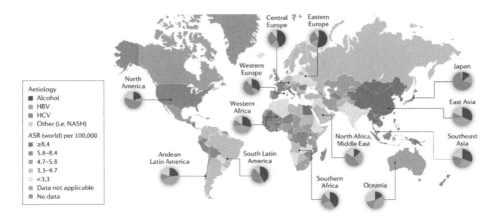

Fig. 1. Depiction of incidence and major aetiological factors. Data from refs [7]. Reprinted from Global Cancer Observatory, World Health Organization, Estimated age-standardized incidence rates (World) in 2020, liver, both sexes, all ages, Copyright (2020).

1.2 Risk Factors

Risk factors have been classified as chronic viral hepatitis, non-viral hepatitis. Certain metabolic diseases such as obesity and diabetes, alcohol consumption, and consumption of toxic substances [5].

Viral Hepatitis. Viral infection by HBV and HCV give rise to cirrhosis and HCC. HBV is responsible for ∼60% of HCC cases in Asia and Africa while 20% of cases in the western countries. In contrast to HBV, HCV is the most common cause of HCC in North America and Europe. Since HCV is an RNA virus it cannot incorporate its DNA into the host genome, therefore it is limited to infect the patient having cirrhosis. HDV causes more severe cases of liver cancer and affects 20–40 million worldwide. This is supported by a study that among the other two forms of Hepatitis virus, HDV is known to cause HCC to a much higher extent.

Non-Viral Hepatitis. Alcohol consumption is the major cause of non-viral HCC. It leads to inflammation which consequently gives rise to the secretion of cytokines. After a while epithelial-mesenchymal transition (EMT) occurs accompanied by fibrosis, leading to progression of HCC. Some metabolic factors such as Diabetes mellitus, obesity, non-alcoholic fatty liver tissue, cardiovascular diseases and inflammation leads to the progression of HCC [8]. All the above viral and non-viral factors have been summarized in Fig. 2.

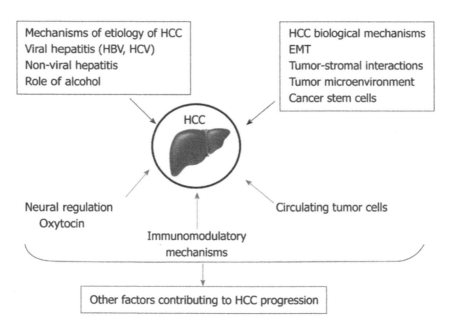

Fig. 2. Risk factors associated with Hepatocellular carcinoma (picture courtesy)

1.3 Pathophysiology of HCC

HCC development and transformation to malignancy is achieved by various factors. This is the review of all mechanisms behind the progression of HCC.

Early Molecular Changes During HCC. After liver cirrhosis, HCC initiation starts with the development of pre-cancerous cirrhotic nodules showing low-grade dysplasia. These nodules are called Low-grade dysplastic nodules (LGDNs). LGDNs further develops into High-grade dysplastic nodules (HGDNs). The advanced stage can become malignant when it originates from stem cells, or mature hepatocytes [9]. Early-stage development has shown in Fig. 3.

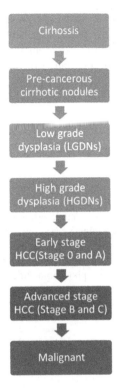

Fig. 3. Early-stage development of HCC from cirrhosis

Some of the pathways involved in early stages of HCC progression are discussed below:

TERT Promoter Mutation. A research study in mice has reported short telomeres are developed as a result of deficiency of catalytic unit of telomerase complex encoded by telomerase RNA component [10]. Mutational inactivation of TERT leads to the development of HCC suggesting these mutations to be oncogenic in nature [11, 12].

EMT and WNT-β-Catenin Pathway. EMT is a natural cellular phenomenon, occurs during wound healing. Normally epithelium cells are normally attached to the basal membrane but during EMT these cells detach from the basement membrane and attach each 5 to other. During this process, adhesive properties are lost, and migratory properties are gained by them [13, 14]. Studies suggest that RNAs and regulatory proteins involved in this process are seen to be associated with HCC. All the above factors suggest progression of HCC occurs by the EMT pathway. WNT inside the extracellular matrix binds to Frizzled family-receptor. This binding leads to the destruction of β-catenin complex leads to accumulation of β catenin in cytoplasm. B-catenin activates TCF/Lef1 complex after translocating to cytoplasm [15, 16]. Activation of WNT pathway is shown to be involved in non-viral related HCC [17].

MAP Kinase Pathway and Oxidative Stress. MAP kinase pathway is activated in the progression of advanced HCC. Many reasons are attributed to it such as amplification of region FGF3, and FGF19. One of the mutations in ribosomal protein S6 kinase leads to activation of the pathway [18, 19]. Oxidative stress leads to activation of mutation in nuclear factors erythroid 2 related factor 2 (NFE2L2). NFE2L2 is generally induced to protect the cell from HCC progression but its continuous activation helps in the progression of HCC [11, 20]. Table 1 summarizes all the biomarkers associated with progression of hepatocellular carcinoma. The factors that lead to progression of early and late progression based on molecular pathways has been shown in Fig. 4.

Table 1. Major molecular seen in HCC. ARID, AT rich interaction domain; AXIN1, axin 1; CCND1, cyclin D1; CDKN2A, cyclin-dependent kinase inhibitor 2A; CTNNB1, β-catenin; FGF, fibroblast growth factor; HCC, hepatocellular carcinoma; KEAP1, kelch like ECH associated protein 1; KMT, lysine (K)-specific methyltransferase; MAPK, MAP kinase; MLL, myeloid/lymphoid or mixed-lineage leukaemia (trithorax homologue, Drosophila); NFE2L2, nuclear factor, erythroid 2 like 2; PI3K, phosphoinositide 3 kinase; PTEN, phosphatase and tensin homologue; RB1, retinoblastoma 1; RPS6KA3, ribosomal protein S6 kinase, 90kDa, polypeptide 3; TERT, telomerase reverse transcriptase; TP53, cellular tumour antigen p53; TSC, tuberous sclerosis; Data courtesy [45].

Pathway(s)	Gene(s)	Alteration	Frequency
Telomere maintenance	TERT	Promoter mutation or amplification	54–60% 5–6%
Cell cycle control	TP53	Mutation or deletion Mutation or deletion	12–48%
	RB1	Amplification Mutation or deletion	3–8%
	CCND1 CDKN2A		7% 2–12%
WNT-β-catenin signaling	CTNNB1 AXIN1	Mutation Mutation or deletion	11–37% 5–15%
Oxidative stress	NFE2L2 KEAP1	Mutation Mutation	3–6% 2–8%
Epigenetic and chromatin remodeling	ARID1A ARID2 KMT2A (MLL1), KMT2B	Mutation	2–6%
AKT-mTOR-MAPK signaling	RPS6KA3 TSC1 and TSC2 PTEN FGF3, FGF4 and GFF19	Mutation Mutation or deletion Mutation or deletion	2–9% 3–8% 1–3%

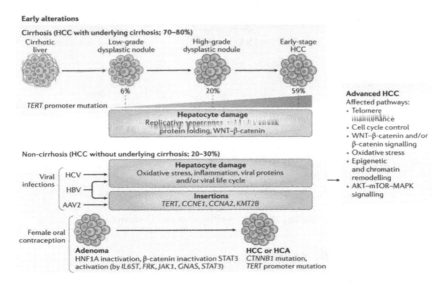

Fig. 4. Figure representing the early and advanced stage changes in the progression of HCC. Picture courtesy [45].

1.4   MicroRNA (miRNA) Biomarkers

In the diagnosis of HCC, microRNAs (miRNAs) are considered to be potential biomarkers. miRNAs are evolutionary conserved, small non-coding RNA consisting of 20–24 nucleotides, regulates the gene expression through post-transcriptional modification by binding to complementary sequences in 3′-untranslated regions of target mRNA and induce their degradation [21]. Also, the role of miRNAs is linked with many important cellular pathways such as cell proliferation, cell differentiation, and apoptosis. Therefore, for the development of cancer, miRNAs are postulated to function as oncogenes as well as tumor suppressor genes. Diverse functional roles and remarkable stability of miRNAs make them the best diagnostic tool for the detection of cancer in the early stages of cancer. Some miRNAs such as miR-532, miR-618, and miR-650 has already been detected in patients and were used to screen patients for early detection of HCC [22]. With all the above biomarkers, due to low sensitivity in some or low specificity in others, HCC can only be diagnosed in later stages of cancer. So far 163 miRNAs are associated with clinical trials as shown in Fig. 5.

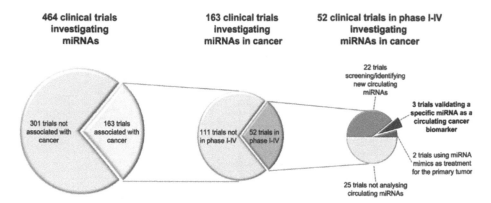

Fig. 5. Circulating miRNA in clinical trials. Data from [23].

1.5 Systems Biology for Identification

Gene expression experiments by the researchers are limited to a very small sample size which makes them uncertain [24]. These experiments are mainly individualistic approaches in which available literature is evaluated; literature review itself is a rigorous task, time-consuming. Also, quantitative data from previous reviews are rare. Therefore, tools should be used to analyze large expression data from several studies of a particular topic using statistical tools in minimum time. Meta-analysis is such an analytical and statistical tool that merges data from several primary studies to reach appropriate conclusions [25]. It is well known that a single gene is not responsible for developing a complex disorder but the genes which have similar expressions interact with each other and forms disease modules [26]. Hence the collaborative function of genes is necessary to be exploited to identify the paths for the progression of any disorder. This function is served by system biology which identifies highly expressed and co-expressed genes together and derives a relationship among them.

Systems biology provides systematic and comprehensive roles of miRNA in the regulatory network. It combines data-driven modelling and model-driven experiment to drive the map [27–29]. Systems biology approach follows four necessary steps:

(i)   **Network construction:** Network construction is being done by reviewing literature and databases. A network map is created to derive the relationship among the macromolecules such as DNA, RNA, or proteins. This map will provide the link among all the genes.

(ii)   **Model construction:** A model is constructed to convert the biological problem and available data to a mechanistic model. After the construction of this model, values are assigned to it. These values can be obtained from literature review, databases or can be assigned from experimental data. Computational experiment: After the establishment of the mechanistic model, the model is analyzed using a computational approach through any available software.

(iii) **Experimental validation:** Predictions from the model is put together with a biological explanation and are used to justify the biological hypothesis. After justification, either the model predictions are in agreement with the experiment, or they deny it. If they are in the agreement of experimental approach network are further analyzed to understand the complex behaviour of the experiment. If the agreement does not justify, a new mathematical model is generated to suggest new experiments.

In this way, a network is generated to derive the relationship from the experimental data to have more insight. Most importantly, the network biology approach helps us to investigate the correlation among the multiple complementary targets in the pathway as shown in Fig. 6.

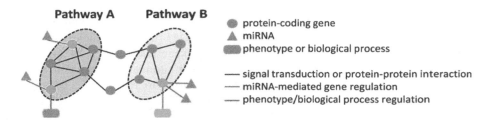

Fig. 6. Implementation of miRNA cooperativity through targeting of a shared pathway or of a shared protein-coding gene. Targeting of several interlinked protein-coding genes by multiple miRNAs leads to the regulation of a pathway and thereby modulation of the phenotypic outcome (pathway A). Concerted targeting of a protein-coding gene by two miRNAs can induce efficient regulation of a biological process that is controlled by the gene (pathway B). miRNA targets are highlighted in red. Picture courtesy [30].

Network biology represents biological structure through a theoretical framework in the form of graphical model which shows the functional flow of information through the structure [31]. The understanding network may lead to the revelation of functional behaviour, evolutionary history, and dynamic aspects of genes in its personal environment. The biological network is made scale-free, in which network hubs helps in identification of disease progression, cellular dysfunction and many other, making network hub most essential part of the biological network. A biological network is made of nodes and edges where nodes represent the genes while edges represent the correlation among them. A cluster of network nodes forms a network module to exert its biological function. It can easily be understood that the biomarker must be involved in the processes such as regulation of cell cycle, apoptosis, and cellular development that eventually leads to tumor formation [32]. Therefore, it is necessary to decipher the crosstalk between the genes to identify the cause of HCC progression and hence the potential biomarkers involved.

In this chapter, it is achieved by the construction of an unweighted miRNA co-expression network based on the Pearson correlation coefficient to identify groups of differentially expressed miRNA associated with HCC.

2 Materials and Methods

2.1 TCGA miRNA-Seq Data Extraction and Differential Expression Analysis

miRNA-Seq counts data of HCC [based on IlluminaHiSeq platform] were retrieved from the UCSC Xena browser (https://xenabrowser.net/) [33]. As the count data were $\log_2(x + 1)$ transformed, therefore they were back log-transformed using R to acquire raw integer counts. The Xena dataset samples were then verified with respect to miRNA-Seq HCC samples present in TCGA GDC [34] data portal to maintain an overall uniformity. Only primary solid tumor and solid tissue normal samples were retained in our datasets. The edgeR package [35] in R was applied on miRNA raw count data for acquiring log_2 transformed and normalized (upper quartile) expression values. ARSyNseq function within the NOISeq package was applied on the $\log_2$ normalized values for batch correction. Since the batch information was unknown in our case, the ARSyN method used the ANOVA errors to return batch-corrected miRNA expression values. Limma package [36] in R was used for the detection of Differentially Expressed miRNAs (DEMs).

2.2 miRNA Co-expression Network Construction and Module Detection

The miRNA co-expression network was constructed using DEMs with a significant level of correlation coefficient ($p - value \leq 0.05$) and visualized in Cytoscape v 3.9.0 [37] from the edge file followed by overlapping module detection.

The tendency of nodes in a graph to form clusters is called the clustering coefficient. Dense connections will have a high clustering coefficient. In a network, local clustering coefficient is given by: $Ci = \frac{2e}{k(k-1)}$.

Where i = vertex with degree deg (i) = k in undirected graph e = edges between k neighbors of i. So basically, the clustering coefficient is just the ratio of a number of edges between neighbors of i to the total number of edges. Possible values are $0 \leq Ci \leq 1$. Similarly, Average clustering coefficient C average $= \frac{1}{N}\sum_{i=1}^{N} \frac{Ei}{ki(ki-1)}$ where N = |V| i.e., the number of vertices. Networks are more likely to form when the clustering coefficient value is closer to 1.

2.3 Overall Survival (OS) Analysis

OS plots of highest degree miRNAs in denser modules/communities were retrieved from KM plotter database using default settings. miRNAs possessing only significant (p-value < 0.05) KM curves were reported.

3   Results and Discussion

3.1   TCGA miRNA-Seq Data Extraction and Differential Expression Analysis

In consideration with the dataset search criteria specified, the HCC-associated miRNA dataset comprised a total of 404 samples (354 tumor and 50 healthy normal samples. After the removal of low count miRBase IDs, we were left with 1239 miRBase IDs. The uncorrected miRNA dataset was further subjected to batch correction. Using limma, we identified a total of 196 DEMs.

3.2   miRNA Co-expression Network Construction and Module Detection

The miRNA co-expression network visualized in Cytoscape consisted of 196 nodes and 858 edges as shown in Fig. 7. From the main co-expression network, we obtained two denser modules/communities [Fig. 8(A, B)]. Both miR-519d and miR-517c had the highest degrees (i.e., 39) in module 1, whereas all the miRNAs in module 2 had equal degrees (i.e., 7).

3.3   OS Analysis

Significant miRNAs in HCC samples were retrieved from KM plotter database which revealed that lower miRNA expressions of miR-517c and miR-302c had poor median survival in HCC patient samples [Fig. 9(A, B)].

HCC is a complex disease that is characterized by dysregulation of various cellular functions in a complex cellular environment. Furthermore, genetic interaction inside a cell is more like a complex network. Therefore, to underlie the orchestration of biological process, it is necessary to perform network-based analysis for the biomarker discovery instead of traditional analysis which usually ignores the correlations between the gene expressions. We tried to decipher the roles of miRNAs in the progression of HCC from miRNA co-expression network. We tried to decipher the roles of miRNAs in the progression of HCC by constructing miRNA co-expression network. It can easily be established that the miRNAs which are forming the center of the cluster are somehow involved in the progression of HCC. To decipher the roles of miRNA in HCC progression, individual miRNA from various clusters have been identified from the miRNA network, where miR-517c, miR-519d, and miR-302c had highest degrees among all.

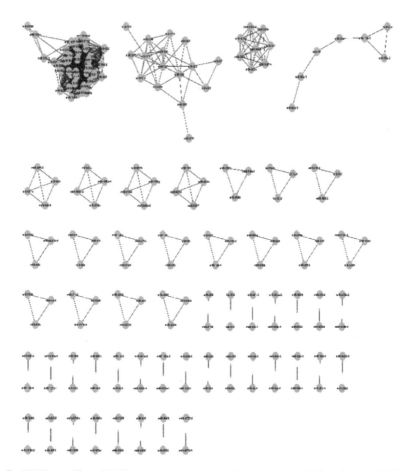

Fig. 7. HCC specific miRNA co-expression network comprising 196 nodes and 858 edges.

Considering the involvement of miR-517c in the cluster lead to the hypothesis that it must be involved somehow in HCC progression. To support the hypothesis, literature review was conducted which concluded that downregulation of miR-517c lead to development of HCC by targeting Protein tyrosine kinase 2 (Pyk2) [38]. Clustering coefficient and degree of miR-519d was found to be similar to miR 517c as identified by network identification, giving rising its possibility to be involved in one or more important pathways for HCC progression. Recent research showed the involvement of miR-517d in activation of AMPK (AMP-activated protein kinase) signaling pathway. This induces autophagy and apoptosis in HCC cells. Hence establishing the role of miR in HCC as predicted by network identification tool [39].

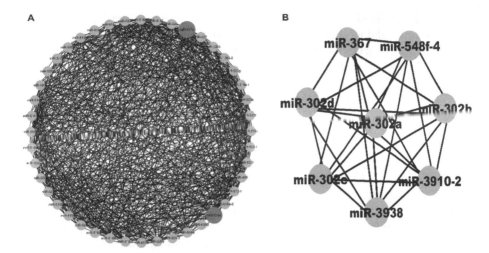

Fig. 8. (A) Module 1, and (B) Module 2 from HCC miRNA co-expression network. Red colored nodes represent highest degree miRNAs. Module 1 consisted of 44 nodes and 682 edges. Module 2 consisted of 8 nodes and 28 edges (Color figure online).

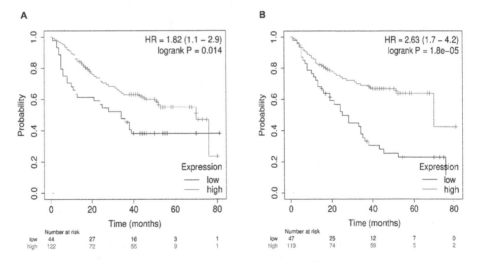

Fig. 9. KM plots showing significant OS for (A) miR-517c and (B) miR-302c.

miR-302/367 is one such cluster that has been discovered to be differentially expressed in HCC. Later, it was investigated in various cancer types, and induced pluripotent stem cells [40–42]. miR-302d, a member of miR-302 family, participates in the development and progression of various cancer types. Studies also have shown the implications of miR-302d in onset and development of HCC [43]. Therefore, identification of the molecular targets of miR-302d can help in unravelling the mechanism behind the HCC progression.

miR-302a is already shown to act as tumor suppressor in glioma cell and colon cancer cell proliferation [44, 45]. miR-302a/b/c are shown to be involved in suppression of tumor angiogenesis in HCC by targeting MACC1 [46]. All the above research concludes the role of miR-302 family in tumor suppression and inhibition of cellular proliferation.

In contrast to other family members, miR-302d is shown to act as an oncogene instead of tumor suppressor. Evidently, in human mammary epithelial cells, miR-302d is shown to rescue Ras-induced senescence by inhibition of p21 [47]. By targeting LATS2 in the Hippo pathway miR-302d promotes the proliferation of human pluripotent stem cell-derived cardiomyocytes (hESC-CM) [48]. The microarray expression profile of HCC shows the elevated level of miR-302d [49] but its role in HCC progression still remains unclear.

Apart from other members in the family, miR-302d is reported to have the oncogenic potential. miR-302d is also shown to influence the relative expression of cell cycle genes and controlling important pathways. A very few studies were conducted to find out the molecular target of miR-302d in HCC proliferation, migration, and tumorigenesis. Also, molecular pathways especially in the case of HCC affected by miR-302d are still a part of ongoing research. By fully elucidating the target genes in cell cycle, apoptosis, and migration and by deriving the relationship between expression of miR-302d and target genes, molecular pathways can be established which can help to determine the potential therapeutic target. Since miR-302d is differentially expressed miRNA in HCC therefore, it can serve as a biomarker for the diagnosis of disease.

The involvement of miR-302d in HCC progression shows the oncogenic potential and therefore, it becomes the necessity to conduct the experimental research to find molecular mechanism behind the progression of the disease.

The involvement of various miR in HCC progression as identified by network-based identification approach shows the oncogenic potential. It can be summarized that firstly, network-based identification module approach could be the promising tool to identify miRNA involved in complex pathways. Secondly, it can be utilized to identify the biomarkers of the several other complex diseases as it did in HCC progression. The above-mentioned biomarker approach can replace the traditional biomarker identification approach. As it can be clearly understood that traditional methods focus only on the target molecules and requires rigorous literature review to find the suitable biomarker which itself is a time-consuming process, while our technique involves interaction of molecules at the same time. Network based module approach can reduce the time, effort and labor by several folds, and hence it can be employed for biomarker identification.

4   Conclusion

MiRNA302d will be differentially expressed in HCC and control cells in various cancer types, there are probable chances that it will be upregulated in HCC. The predicted target gene can show direct or inverse relation with miR302d. As already stated above miR302d serve as an oncogene in various cells, and if our result also shows its oncogenic potential. In that case, if target gene is found to be upregulated in cells treated by miR302d inhibitor shows negative relation with miR302d, cell may be going towards apoptosis. This gene will surely be involved in apoptotic or inhibition of cellular migration and tumorigenesis. Hence it could serve as potential therapeutic target for HCC. While if the target gene level is increased in presence of miR302d mimic then it is positively correlated, it may serve role in inhibition of apoptosis and enhancing role in cellular proliferation, migration and invasion of HCC. Therefore, it can be served as the potential target for therapy i.e., by downregulating that gene could serve the purpose. The gene will surely be involved in cell proliferation, invasion, migration and apoptosis. One of the genes such as CDK1, SMD, AKT which are shown in cell proliferation other than HCC can be hypnotized to be targeted by miR302d. It can also be expected that miR302d can target genes in apoptotic process to prevent apoptosis of LCSCs. So, either miR302d or its potential target gene can serve as biomarker for prognosis in early stages and also can serve as a potential therapeutic target for the therapy.

Further research should be focused to find the pathways affected by miR 302 cluster. Furthermore, Network based identification approach can be employed in development of relations among molecules in complex pathways and identification of biomarkers.

References

1. Llovet, J.M., et al.: Hepatocellular carcinoma. Nat. Rev. Dis. Primers **2**, 16018 (2016). https://doi.org/10.1038/nrdp.2016.18
2. El-Serag, H.B.: Epidemiology of viral hepatitis and hepatocellular carcinoma. Gastroenterology **142**, 1264-1273.e1 (2012). https://doi.org/10.1053/j.gastro.2011.12.061
3. Tang, A., Hallouch, O., Chernyak, V., Kamaya, A., Sirlin, C.B.: Epidemiology of hepatocellular carcinoma: target population for surveillance and diagnosis. Abdom. Radiol. **43**(1), 13–25 (2017). https://doi.org/10.1007/s00261-017-1209-1
4. Kanwal, F., Kramer, J., Asch, S.M., Chayanupatkul, M., Cao, Y., El-Serag, H.B.: Risk of hepatocellular cancer in HCV patients treated with direct-acting antiviral agents. Gastroenterology **153**, 996-1005.e1 (2017). https://doi.org/10.1053/j.gastro.2017.06.012
5. Dhanasekaran, R., Bandoh, S., Roberts, L.R.: Molecular pathogenesis of hepatocellular carcinoma and impact of therapeutic advances. F1000Res **5**, 879 (2016). https://doi.org/10.12688/f1000research.6946.1
6. Liu, L.-L., Fu, D., Ma, Y., Shen, X.-Z.: The power and the promise of liver cancer stem cell markers. Stem Cells Dev. **20**, 2023–2030 (2011). https://doi.org/10.1089/scd.2011.0012
7. Singal, A.G., Lampertico, P., Nahon, P.: Epidemiology and surveillance for hepatocellular carcinoma: new trends. J. Hepatol. **72**, 250–261 (2020). https://doi.org/10.1016/j.jhep.2019.08.025
8. Alzahrani, B., Iseli, T.J., Hebbard, L.W.: Non-viral causes of liver cancer: does obesity led inflammation play a role? Cancer Lett. **345**, 223–229 (2014). https://doi.org/10.1016/j.canlet.2013.08.036
9. Marquardt, J.U., Andersen, J.B., Thorgeirsson, S.S.: Functional and genetic deconstruction of the cellular origin in liver cancer. Nat. Rev. Cancer **15**, 653–667 (2015). https://doi.org/10.1038/nrc4017

10. Brabletz, T., Kalluri, R., Nieto, M.A., Weinberg, R.A.: EMT in cancer. Nat. Rev. Cancer **18**, 128–134 (2018). https://doi.org/10.1038/nrc.2017.118

11. Nault, J.C., et al.: High frequency of telomerase reverse-transcriptase promoter somatic mutations in hepatocellular carcinoma and preneoplastic lesions. Nat. Commun. **4**, 2218 (2013). https://doi.org/10.1038/ncomms3218

12. Pilati, C., et al.: Genomic profiling of hepatocellular adenomas reveals recurrent FRK-activating mutations and the mechanisms of malignant transformation. Cancer Cell **25**, 428–441 (2014). https://doi.org/10.1016/j.ccr.2014.03.005

13. Kalluri, R., Weinberg, R.A.: The basics of epithelial–mesenchymal transition. J. Clin. Invest. **119**, 1420–1428 (2009). https://doi.org/10.1172/JCI39104

14. Lamouille, S., Xu, J., Derynck, R.: Molecular mechanisms of epithelial–mesenchymal transition. Nat. Rev. Mol. Cell Biol. **15**, 178–196 (2014). https://doi.org/10.1038/nrm3758

15. Behrens, J., et al.: Functional interaction of an axin homolog, conductin, with β-catenin, APC, and GSK3β. Science **280**, 596–599 (1998). https://doi.org/10.1126/science.280.5363.596

16. Huber, O., Korn, R., McLaughlin, J., Ohsugi, M., Herrmann, B.G., Kemler, R.: Nuclear localization of β-catenin by interaction with transcription factor LEF-1. Mech. Dev. **59**, 3 (1996). https://doi.org/10.1016/0925-4773(96)00597-7

17. Laurent-Puig, P., et al.: Genetic alterations associated with hepatocellular carcinomas define distinct pathways of hepatocarcinogenesis. Gastroenterology **120**, 1763–1773 (2001). https://doi.org/10.1053/gast.2001.24798

18. Schulze, K., et al.: Exome sequencing of hepatocellular carcinomas identifies new mutational signatures and potential therapeutic targets. Nat. Genet. **47**, 505–511 (2015). https://doi.org/10.1038/ng.3252

19. Guichard, C., et al.: Integrated analysis of somatic mutations and focal copy-number changes identifies key genes and pathways in hepatocellular carcinoma. Nat. Genet. **44**, 694–698 (2012). https://doi.org/10.1038/ng.2256

20. Sporn, M.B., Liby, K.T.: NRF2 and cancer: the good, the bad and the importance of context. Nat. Rev. Cancer **12**, 564–571 (2012). https://doi.org/10.1038/nrc3278

21. Calin, G.A., Croce, C.M.: MicroRNA signatures in human cancers. Nat. Rev. Cancer **6**, 857–866 (2006). https://doi.org/10.1038/nrc1997

22. Andersen, G.B., Tost, J.: Circulating miRNAs as biomarker in cancer. In: Schaffner, F., Merlin, J.-L., von Bubnoff, N. (eds.) Tumor Liquid Biopsies. RRCR, vol. 215, pp. 277–298. Springer, Cham (2020). https://doi.org/10.1007/978-3-030-26439-0_15

23. Ramasamy, A., Mondry, A., Holmes, C.C., Altman, D.G.: Key issues in conducting a meta-analysis of gene expression microarray datasets. PLoS Med. **5**, e184 (2008). https://doi.org/10.1371/journal.pmed.0050184

24. Glass, G.V.: Primary, secondary, and meta-analysis of research. Educ. Res. **5**, 3–8 (1976). https://doi.org/10.3102/0013189X005010003

25. Barabási, A.-L., Gulbahce, N., Loscalzo, J.: Network medicine: a network-based approach to human disease. Nat. Rev. Genet. **12**, 56–68 (2011). https://doi.org/10.1038/nrg2918

26. Lai, X., Bhattacharya, A., Schmitz, U., Kunz, M., Vera, J., Wolkenhauer, O.: A systems' biology approach to study microRNA-mediated gene regulatory networks. Biomed. Res. Int. **2013**, 1–15 (2013). https://doi.org/10.1155/2013/703849

27. Lai, X., et al.: Computational analysis of target hub gene repression regulated by multiple and cooperative miRNAs. Nucleic Acids Res. **40**, 8818–8834 (2012). https://doi.org/10.1093/nar/gks657

28. Lai, X., Wolkenhauer, O., Vera, J.: Modeling miRNA regulation in cancer signaling systems: miR-34a regulation of the p53/Sirt1 signaling module. In: Liu, X., Betterton, M.D. (eds.) Computational Modeling of Signaling Networks, pp. 87–108. Humana Press, Totowa, NJ (2012). https://doi.org/10.1007/978-1-61779-833-7_6

29. Lai, X., Eberhardt, M., Schmitz, U., Vera, J.: Systems biology-based investigation of cooperating microRNAs as monotherapy or adjuvant therapy in cancer. Nucleic Acids Res. **47**, 7753–7766 (2019). https://doi.org/10.1093/nar/gkz638

30. Zhang, S., Ng, M.K.: Gene-microRNA network module analysis for ovarian cancer. BMC Syst. Biol. **10**, 117 (2016). https://doi.org/10.1186/s12918-016-0357-1

31. Bonnefond, M.-L., et al.: Calcium signals inhibition sensitizes ovarian carcinoma cells to anti-Bcl-xL strategies through Mcl-1 down-regulation. Apoptosis **20**(4), 535–550 (2015). https://doi.org/10.1007/s10495-015-1095-3

32. Chandler, R.L., et al.: Coexistent ARID1A–PIK3CA mutations promote ovarian clear-cell tumorigenesis through pro-tumorigenic inflammatory cytokine signalling. Nat. Commun. **6**, 6118 (2015). https://doi.org/10.1038/ncomms7118

33. Grossman, R.L., et al.: Toward a shared vision for cancer genomic data. N. Engl. J. Med. **375**, 1109–1112 (2016). https://doi.org/10.1056/NEJMp1607591

34. McCarthy, D.J., Chen, Y., Smyth, G.K.: Differential expression analysis of multifactor RNA-Seq experiments with respect to biological variation. Nucleic Acids Res. **40**, 4288–4297 (2012). https://doi.org/10.1093/nar/gks042

35. Tarazona, S., et al.: Data quality aware analysis of differential expression in RNA-seq with NOISeq R/Bioc package. Nucleic Acids Res. **43**, e140 (2015). https://doi.org/10.1093/nar/gkv711

36. Ritchie, M.E., et al.: limma powers differential expression analyses for RNA-sequencing and microarray studies. Nucleic Acids Res. **43**, e47 (2015). https://doi.org/10.1093/nar/gkv007

37. Shannon, P.: Cytoscape: a software environment for integrated models of biomolecular interaction networks. Genome Res. **13**, 2498–2504 (2003). https://doi.org/10.1101/gr.1239303

38. Liu, R.-F., et al.: Down-regulation of miR-517a and miR-517c promotes proliferation of hepatocellular carcinoma cells via targeting Pyk2. Cancer Lett. **329**, 164–173 (2013). https://doi.org/10.1016/j.canlet.2012.10.027

39. Zhang, Y.-J., Pan, Q., Yu, Y., Zhong, X.-P.: microRNA-519d induces autophagy and apoptosis of human hepatocellular carcinoma cells through activation of the AMPK signaling pathway via Rab10. CMAR **12**, 2589–2602 (2020). https://doi.org/10.2147/CMAR.S207548

40. Cai, N., Wang, Y.-D., Zheng, P.-S.: The microRNA-302-367 cluster suppresses the proliferation of cervical carcinoma cells through the novel target AKT1. RNA **19**, 85–95 (2013). https://doi.org/10.1261/rna.035295.112

41. Lin, S.-L., Chang, D.C., Ying, S.-Y., Leu, D., Wu, D.T.S.: MicroRNA miR-302 inhibits the tumorigenecity of human pluripotent stem cells by coordinate suppression of the CDK2 and CDK4/6 cell cycle pathways. Cancer Res. **70**, 9473–9482 (2010). https://doi.org/10.1158/0008-5472.CAN-10-2746

42. Fareh, M., et al.: The miR 302–367 cluster drastically affects self-renewal and infiltration properties of glioma-initiating cells through CXCR4 repression and consequent disruption of the SHH-GLI-NANOG network. Cell Death Differ. **19**, 232–244 (2012). https://doi.org/10.1038/cdd.2011.89

43. Lin, S.-L., et al.: Mir-302 reprograms human skin cancer cells into a pluripotent ES-cell-like state. RNA **14**, 2115–2124 (2008). https://doi.org/10.1261/rna.1162708

44. Ma, J., et al.: MicroRNA-302a targets GAB2 to suppress cell proliferation, migration and invasion of glioma. Oncol. Rep. **37**, 1159–1167 (2017). https://doi.org/10.3892/or.2016.5320

45. Bobowicz, M., et al.: Prognostic value of 5-microRNA based signature in T2-T3N0 colon cancer. Clin. Exp. Metas. **33**(8), 765–773 (2016). https://doi.org/10.1007/s10585-016-9810-1

46. Cao, Y.P., et al.: MiR-302 a/b/c suppresses tumor angiogenesis in hepatocellular carcinoma by targeting MACC1. Eur. Rev. Med. Pharmacol. Sci. **23**, 7863–7873 (2019). https://doi.org/10.26355/eurrev_201909_18996

47. Borgdorff, V., et al.: Multiple microRNAs rescue from Ras-induced senescence by inhibiting p21Waf1/Cip1. Oncogene **29**, 2262–2271 (2010). https://doi.org/10.1038/onc.2009.497

48. Xu, F., et al.: MicroRNA-302d promotes the proliferation of human pluripotent stem cell-derived cardiomyocytes by inhibiting LATS2 in the Hippo pathway. Clin. Sci. **133**, 1387–1399 (2019). https://doi.org/10.1042/CS20190099

49. Chen, Y.-L., Xu, Q.-P., Guo, F., Guan, W.-H.: MicroRNA-302d downregulates TGFBR2 expression and promotes hepatocellular carcinoma growth and invasion. Exp. Ther. Med. **13**, 681–687 (2017). https://doi.org/10.3892/etm.2016.3970

Identifying Hub Nodes and Sub-networks from Cattle Rumen Microbiome Multilayer Networks

Mengyuan Wang[1,2], Haiyang Wang[1], Huiru Zheng[1(✉)],
Richard J. Dewhurst[2], and Rainer Roehe[2]

[1] School of Computing, Ulster University, Belfast, UK
h.zheng@ulster.ac.uk
[2] Scotland's Rural College, Edinburgh, UK

Abstract. Purpose: The purpose of this research is to represent the complex system of the rumen microbiome through a multi-layer network, to explore the main biological functions related to methane metabolism.

Methods: A three-layer heterogeneous network has been constructed based on rumen metabolites, rumen microbial genes and rumen microbial communities. Node association is calculated based on linear and non-linear association p-value voting combined with the permutation test. This research proposed a method to generate key hubs based on the topological properties of nodes in a multilayer network.

Results: 1) A total of 59 individuals (including metabolites, microbial genera, and microbial genes) were found in the topological hubs. Among them, 23 individuals appeared in more than one topologically ranked hub. 2) The metabolite with the highest topological centrality is methane, which is the top one in the 9 topological property rankings. Among the top 10 topologically central 35 microbial genes, based on the reconstruction of the metabolic network, the most involved metabolic pathway is methane metabolism which included 14 microbial genes. 3) There are 3 genera of microbes (including *Aeropyrum*, *Desulfurococcus* and *Thermosphaera*) from the same family and are ranked top 10 in at least 2 topological characteristics. In the topological hub of the Bottleneck, we found that from *Aeropyrum* and *Desulfurococcus* of the same family, their indirect paths are associated with methane. And SufD (K09015), a protein related to the family in the same hub, was also found to be positively associated with methane.

Conclusion: The nodes with important topological properties at the metabolite level and the microbial level are associated with methane functions, indicating the consistency of the biological functions of the topological properties between the layers. This method provided a solution for extracting related hubs of highly central nodes and shows potential in the understanding of biological functions. The topological property-Bottleneck showed the most potential by identified hub nodes were found as exhibiting the consistent sulfur reduction functions throughout multilayer networks.

Keywords: Rumen microbe · Metabolites · Metagenomics · Multilayer network · Topological properties

© Springer Nature Switzerland AG 2022
D. Garg et al. (Eds.): IACC 2021, CCIS 1528, pp. 165–175, 2022.
https://doi.org/10.1007/978-3-030-95502-1_13

1 Introduction

Dairy and beef cattle are responsible for 9.5% of all anthropogenic greenhouse gas emissions, with ruminal microbial fermentation accounting for 40–50% of this total [1]. The rumen microbiome is a complex system closely related to the host and regulated by multiple factors [2]. The exploration of the mechanism of microbial methane metabolism in the rumen is key to reducing the greenhouse effect and improving animal nutrition. There have been some network studies of the rumen microbiome, including the identification of biomarkers of methane emission and diet digestibility based on the correlation network of microbial gene abundance [3–5]. Other studies have used microbial taxonomy abundance correlated network community niche exploration and analysis [6], metabolite-related diffusion analysis based on a multi-layer network [7] or network analysis related to hosting phenotype and genetic characteristics of rumen methane emission [8]. However, most of the current research is based on single-layer networks.

Research in this field has urgent to find a way which can integrate comprehensive information to represent the complex host-microbial metabolic system. The multilayer network is through the embedded representation of the interaction structure of the complex system, to provide a research approach to understand the nature and function of the complex system. A complex system is composed of individuals which interact nonlinearly in static or dynamic ways. These interactions make it produce various forms of association structure and represent the system's multi-scale characteristics [9]. The identification and prediction of the influence of nodes in complex networks is a hot research area in complex networks [9], which helps us understand the internal structural characteristics of biological complex systems. Studies have shown that the topological properties and functions of proteins in protein networks the degree of importance are significantly related. However, the identification and prediction of node influence are limited to specific network topology. Once the method is not significant in the corresponding topology, then the accuracy of the recognition and prediction of the method is questionable [10]. Moreover, the topological properties and the biological significance of multi-layer network embedding for the rumen complex system are also unknown.

This research mainly develops a method for identifying and analyzing key hubs based on multi-layer network topology ranking. The main innovations and contributions of this research are: 1) The results of the study found important topological nodes with consistent biological functions between the metabolite layer/microbial community layer and the microbial gene layer (e.g., methane and its microbial functional genes). Further verified the multi-layer network method is practical to represent the complex system of rumen microbiome, which is of great significance for the exploration and understanding of the correlation pattern of the rumen microbiome. 2) In this research, the unknown and uncertainty about the characteristics of the multi-layer network structure and the driving biological mechanism, as well as the huge dense connections of the target node, make the mining of key modules more challenging. The methodology applied in the study showed huge potential to conquer the challenge by extracting the key hubs consisting of the heterogeneous nodes involved in the same biological metabolism.

2   Method

In this research, a framework for extracting key topological hubs based on the ruminal metabolome and microbiome multilayer network was developed.

Dataset: The 30 beef cattle rumen fluid samples used in this study were carried out at Scotland's Rural College's Beef and Sheep Research Centre (SRUC) [6]. The SRUC Animal Experiment Committee permitted the experiment, which was conducted in compliance with the Animals (Scientific Procedures) Act of 1986 in the United Kingdom. The rumen fluids come from samples of cattle breeds, diets, additives, and feed efficiency that is balanced, and have been analyzed by metabolomics and metagenomics. Refer to the following papers [7, 8] for the experimental process and steps.

- Metabolite dataset: A total of 119 rumen metabolites were identified and quantified in the NMR-based targeted metabolomics experiment.
- Metagenomics dataset: The relative concentration of 119 rumen metabolites, the relative abundance of 1461 microbial genes (>0.01%), and the relative abundance of 1178 microbial genera (excluding zero samples) were selected.

Construction of multilayer network: The study constructed a multi-layer network consisting of microbial genera, rumen metabolites, and microbial genes. First, nodes of the same type are connected by a linear or non-linear combination of correlations with each other to form a single-layer network. Secondly, the metabolite-microbial gene, metabolite-microbial genera linear or non-linear combination of correlation is used to connect each layer separately. The measurements and procedure of edges can refer to the following article [10, 11]. The calculation and visualization are processed by Cytoscape and the plug-in CoNet [11].

The metabolite layer was used to reflect the results of rumen microbes involved in host digestion and metabolism. The interaction layer between metabolites and microbial genes is expected to represent the metabolic results of microbial function mapping. The interaction between metabolites and the microbial community layer is expected to reflect the composition and interaction of the microbial community.

Hub collection based on topological properties: We selected the top 10 nodes of each topological property and generated the shortest connection path between them to get the sub-networks. The topological properties used to filter the key nodes are listed in Table 1. The calculation process is completed by Cytoscape plug-in cytoHubba [12]. The subsequent metabolite and microbial gene biological function analysis was completed using the tools of the KEGG mapper (Fig. 1).

Table 1. List of topological properties.

Topological properties
Degree
Edge Percolated Component (EPC)
Maximum Neighbourhood Component (MNC)
Density of Maximum Neighbourhood Component (DMNC)
Maximal Clique Centrality (MCC)
Bottleneck
Radiality
Betweenness
Stress
Closeness

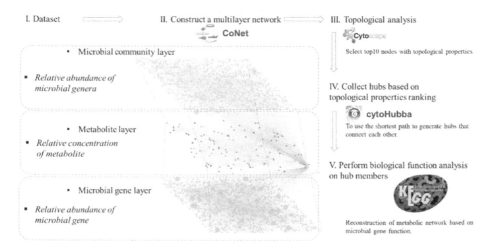

Fig. 1. Research pipeline.

3   Results

In this session, the hub composed of the top 10 nodes of each topological property was extracted from the constructed multilayer network, and the members in the hub were analyzed with biological functions. Among them, Degree, MNC, DMNC and MCC are local-based measures, that is, only the direct neighborhood of a node is considered. Closeness, Radiality, Bottleneck, Stress, Betweenness are based on the shortest path, while EPC is based on the theory of percolation.

3.1   Multilayer Network

The final multi-layer network (see Fig. 2) contains 2092 nodes and 9770 edges. Topological information is summarized in Table 2. The network finally contains 981 microbial genera, 994 microbial genes and 117 metabolites.

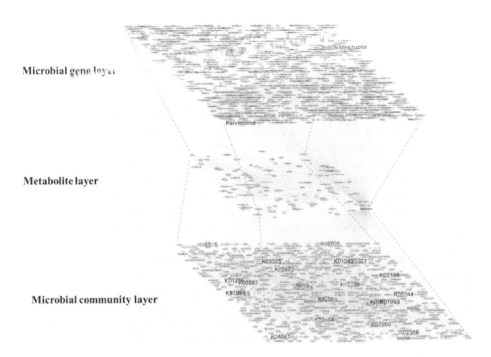

Fig. 2. Multilayer network (The orange nodes represent microbial genes. The purple nodes represent metabolites. The blue node represents the microbial community. The green edges indicate positive associations, and the red edges indicate negative associations). (Color figure online)

Table 2. Topological properties of multilayer networks.

Item	Value
Number of nodes	2092
Number of edges	9770
Average number of neighbours	9.453
Network diameter	15
Network radius	8
Characteristic path length	3.279
Clustering coefficient	0.306
Network density	0.005
Network heterogeneity	3.426
Network centralization	0.639
Connected components	14

3.2   Node Hub Ranked Based on Topological Properties

This research selects the topological properties of 10 nodes (Table 2) to analyze the network. A total of 59 individuals were obtained from the top 10 topological rankings of each feature, of which 23 individuals appeared more than once in the top 10 topological rankings. All the hubs include 35 microbial genes, 6 metabolites and 18 microbial genera.

The members of the Betweenness, Degree, MNC and Stress modules are not completely directly connected. The relationship between them is shown in Fig. 3. through indirect edges. Bottleneck, Closeness, EPC and Radiality are all methane-centric hubs. In these hubs, methane is only positively associated with other nodes. As the highest node in the network, methane connects 1327 nodes.

It is worth noting that except for DMNC, methane ranks top in nine topological rankings (Fig. 3). Methane becomes the most important node in the multilayer network. The microbial gene K01810 is in the top 5 of the rankings of five topological properties, including Closeness, Degree, EPC, Radiality and MNC. There are two microbial genera *Aeropyrum* and *Desulfurococcus*, which are ranked top 5 in the rankings of Betweenness, Bottleneck, Degree and Stress (Fig. 3). They are two genera belonging to the *Desulfurococcaceae* family. *Thermosphaera* is also a member of the *Desulfurococcaceae* family, which is included of the top 5 in Betweenness and Stress, respectively.

There are only microbial genes in the hub extracted by DMNC, and these microbial genes only appear in this topological hub. The hubs extracted by EPC and MCC are only methane and microbial genes, and they have three common members. There are four common members in the hubs of Betweenness, Stress and Bottleneck. The hub of Betweenness and Bottleneck includes three types of nodes. The stress hub does not contain microbial genes. There are eight common members in the hub of Radiality and Closeness. Degree and MNC have eight members in common.

3.3   Biological Function Analysis

We reconstructed the metabolic network in the KEGG database using 35 microbial genes from the topological hub. The metabolite pathways designed include Carbohydrate metabolism, Energy metabolism, Lipid metabolism, Amino acid metabolism and Genetic Information Processing. Among them, 14 microbial genes are enriched in the methane metabolism network (Fig. 4), followed by the Genetic Translation Ribosome, which contains 7 microbial genes (Fig. 5). Oxidative phosphorylation contains 4 microbial genes (Fig. 5). The hub members of the five metabolites are involved in amino acid metabolism, such as ornithine, which is the central part of the urea cycle to discharge excess nitrogen.

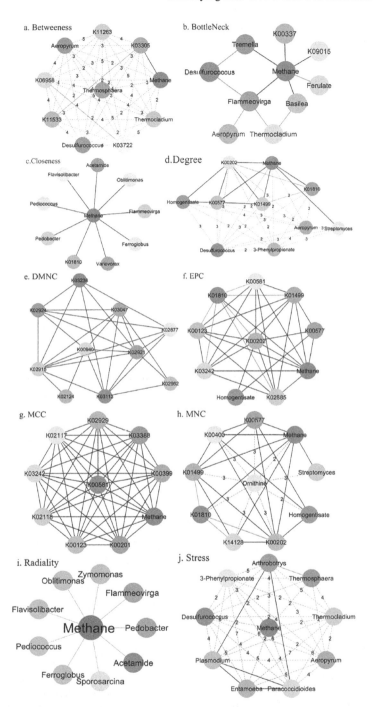

Fig. 3. Hub based on topological properties (The color of the node closer to red indicates the higher the topological property ranking. The color of the node closer to yellow indicates the lower the topological property ranking. The black line represents the direct connection, the solid line represents the positive connection, and the dotted line represents the negative connection. The red line represents the indirect connection, and the number on the line represents the number of steps between two nodes). (Color figure online)

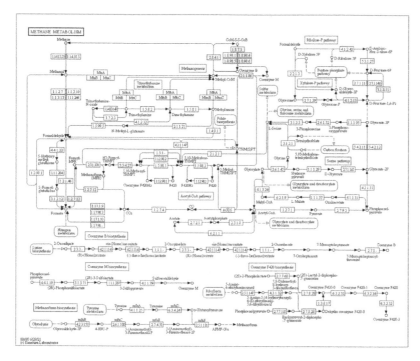

Fig. 4. Reconstructed methane metabolism (The green box represents the location of microbial functional genes). (Color figure online)

Fig. 5. Reconstructed genetic translation processing and oxidative phosphorylation (The green box represents the location of microbial functional genes). (Color figure online)

4 Discussion

Research on multi-layer networks has begun to develop from simply extending the concepts and methods of single-layer networks to defining corresponding topological properties and dynamic behaviors for multi-layer network structures and practical problems. A lot of work can be done in the research of multi-layer network topology. The potential geometric properties of complex networks have attracted much attention in recent years [13]. Exploring the internal relationship between the geometric properties and topological structure of multi-layer networks will help promote the progress of related research, such as community structure, link prediction, etc. [13].

In this study, the main analysis is based on a multi-layer heterogeneous network containing rumen metabolites, rumen microbial genes and rumen microbes. Both methane and methane-related microbial genes are in the topological center of the network, indicating that the multi-layer network representation has potential biological consistency. The finding indicated the reliability of the multi-layer network representing the complex system of the rumen microbiome. And other key topological nodes are highly possible to be importantly related to the same biological function.

In the multilayer network, methane connected 1,327 nodes. The denseness of the associated attributes in the first stage makes it very difficult to analyze the network in methods, such as module detection or diffusion analysis. Only considering the analysis of the nodes directly related to methane is already very complicated. There is an urgent need to find a way to collect the most important individuals among all the close contacts. In this study, the topological attribute rankings of nodes are calculated, and sub-networks are generated according to the rankings. Most of these topological indicators have overlapping results. DMNC, MCC and EPC are topological measurements based on direct field and percolation theory, respectively. The results show that there are dense components in the microbial gene layer. But the core members of these three components are different. Betweenness, Stress and Bottleneck are all based on the shortest path to consider the extent to which a node is passed in the network. According to previous research on protein networks. In the protein signal network, high-stress proteins indicate that their functions may be relevant to the protein in linking regulatory molecules. But it may also mean that the protein is involved in a large number of cellular processes. The higher the betweenness centrality indicates that in higher the relevance of the protein as a tissue regulator. High betweenness may be required to keep the signal mechanism functioning. Proteins with higher radiality have a higher chance to become the core of other proteins in the network. Signal networks with higher average radiality are more likely to include functional units and modules. But this needs to be accompanied by evidence of eccentricity and Closeness. The overlap of the hub members of Radiality and Closeness can show that these nodes all have a central regulatory role. The high degree of coincidence between Degree and MNC points out central nodes that are highly connected to other nodes, and dense subgraphs are likely to be generated near them.

Among these topological attributes, we have still extracted valuable hubs. The hub members of the five metabolites are involved in amino acid metabolism, such as ornithine, which is the central part of the urea cycle to discharge excess nitrogen [14]. Acetamide is a substrate that produces Acetate [15]. The associations between microbial communities seem to be more complicated, but the common associations of the same family of microbial genera seem to point to the close connection between methane and this function. *Aeropyrum*, *Desulfurococcus* and *Thermosphaera* are three genera in the *Desulfurococcaceae* family. In the bottleneck hub, *Aeropyrum* and *Desulfurococcus* are negatively related to two nodes that are positively related to methane, and the K09015 gene (SufD) appears in the same hub. Because of the crucial importance of SufD in Fe-S cluster biogenesis [16]. SufBCD stimulates SufS's cysteine desulfurase activity by working in tandem with SufE [17]. The anaerobic oxidation of methane appears to be linked to the sulfur reduction process [18].

5 Conclusion

The highly central nodes are interconnected, making the entire network super dense. It is very challenging to extract the most critical information from these dense associations. The research developed a multi-layer network hub identification based on topological property rankings to explore individuals associated with methane functions in the complex rumen microbial system. The results found the consistency of the biological functions and topological properties of the multi-layer network. The Bottleneck was identified as one of the most promising topological properties in the study by finding the sulfur-reducing family *Desulfurococcaceae* and related protein across the multi-layer of the network. The results also provided clues to understanding the relationship between the topological structure of the multilayer network and the biological meaning of the complex system. The future direction of research will be dedicated to verification on larger data sets, combined with knowledge-driven networks.

References

1. Huws, S.A., et al.: Addressing global ruminant agricultural challenges through understanding the rumen microbiome: past, present, and future. Front. Microbiol. **9**, 2161 (2018)
2. Chaucheyras-Durand, F., Ossa, F.: Review: the rumen microbiome: Composition, abundance, diversity, and new investigative tools. Prof. Anim. Sci. **30**, 1–12 (2014)
3. Lima, J., et al.: Identification of rumen microbial genes involved in pathways linked to appetite, growth, and feed conversion efficiency in cattle. Front. Genet. **10**, 701 (2019)
4. Auffret, M.D., et al.: Identification of microbial genetic capacities and potential mechanisms within the rumen microbiome explaining differences in beef cattle feed efficiency. Front. Microbiol. **11**, 1229 (2020)
5. Martínez-Álvaro, M., et al.: Identification of complex rumen microbiome interaction within diverse functional niches as mechanisms affecting the variation of methane emissions in bovine. Front. Microbiol. **11**, 659 (2020)
6. Wang, M., Wang, H., Zheng, H., Dewhurst, R.J., Roehe, R.: A heat diffusion multilayer network approach for the identification of functional biomarkers in rumen methane emissions. Methods **192**, 57–66 (2021)
7. Mengyuan, W., Wang, H., Zheng, H., Dewhurst, R., Roehe, R.: A multilayer co-occurrence network reveals the systemic difference of diet-based rumen microbiome associated with methane yield phenotype. p. 2860 (2020)
8. Faust, K., Raes, J.: CoNet app: inference of biological association networks using Cytoscape. F1000Res **5**, 1519 (2016)
9. Chin, C.-H., et al.: cytoHubba: identifying hub objects and sub-networks from complex interactome. BMC Syst. Biol. **8**, S11 (2014)
10. Lee, B., Zhang, S., Poleksic, A., Xie, L.: Heterogeneous multi-layered network model for omics data integration and analysis. Front. Genet. **10**, 1381 (2020)
11. Kivelä, M., et al.: Multilayer networks. J. Complex Netw. **2**, 203–271 (2014)

12. Pilosof, S., Porter, M.A., Pascual, M., Kéfi, S.: The multilayer nature of ecological networks. Nat. Ecol. Evol. **1**, 1–9 (2017)
13. Network approaches to systems biology analysis of complex disease: integrative methods for multi-omics data. In: Briefings in Bioinformatics, Oxford Academic
14. Barmore, W., Azad, F., Stone, W.L.: Physiology, Urea Cycle. StatPearls Publishing (2021)
15. KEGG REACTION: R00321. https://www.genome.jp/entry/R00321
16. Yuda, E., et al.: Mapping the key residues of SufB and SufD essential for biosynthesis of iron-sulfur clusters. Sci. Rep. **7**, 9387 (2017)
17. sufD – FeS cluster assembly protein SufD – *Bacillus subtilis* (strain 168) – sufD gene and protein. https://www.uniprot.org/uniprot/O32165
18. Timmers, P.H., et al.: Anaerobic oxidation of methane associated with sulfate reduction in a natural freshwater gas source. ISME J. **10**, 1400–1412 (2016)

Application of AI for Emotion and Behaviour Prediction

Machine Learning-Based Psychology: A Study to Understand Cognitive Decision-Making

Parth Rainchwar, Soham Wattamwar, Rishikesh Mate,
Chirag Sahasrabudhe, and Varsha Naik[✉]

Dr. Vishwanath Karad MIT World Peace University, Pune, India
varsha.powar@mitwpu.edu.in

Abstract. With the rise in the adaptability of emotions and technology in humans; we as humans have seen a lot of transformation in our individual thought process, social media has played a vital role in creating a fractured personality of ours where we unknowingly imbibe some or more psychological disorders. Machine learning as a field has revolutionized the way we see and interpret knowledge from Raw data. With the help of machine learning algorithms, we aim at understanding how a certain user responds to questions asked him from different categories which can help us understand his/her behavior. Behavior is a crucial entity when it comes to understanding a person and the way to interpret the sentiments behind the user's preference on a particular situation. Start-ups treat the behavioral psychology of the customers they target as an essential block to test our service upon. Since the data obtained is of structured type, various classification algorithms are implemented to determine the mindset and point-of-view of an individual. Hence, the ideology behind this research is crystal clear in determining the psychological state of the audience from varied age groups categorized as youths, adults, and millennials.

Keywords: Behavior psychology · Machine learning · Classification ·
Decision theory · Cognitive explanation theory

1 Introduction

The scientific study of the human mind and its functions, particularly those that influence behavior in a certain situation, the mental traits or attitude of a person or group are coined as Psychology. It even includes the investigation of both conscious and unconscious occurrences, as well as feelings and thoughts; a vast academic field with several possibilities. A professional practitioner or researcher who imbibes these disciplines is called a psychologist. Moreover, they engage themselves in exploring the physiological processes that underlie cognitive functions and behaviors. Incoming thoughts in our mind that are unstoppable with due reasons have a significant impact on our subconscious mind resulting in the tendency that an individual is passing through. They are specialized in either social, behavioral, or cognitive sciences background. Our research discusses the behavioral aspect of psychology, often known as "Behavioral Psychology". Some psychologists try to figure out what role mental functions play in personal and societal behavior

© Springer Nature Switzerland AG 2022
D. Garg et al. (Eds.): IACC 2021, CCIS 1528, pp. 179–192, 2022.
https://doi.org/10.1007/978-3-030-95502-1_14

Behavioral psychology has an adverse impact on the personality traits of a person. Based upon the personality traits identified by the five-factor model [1], the most important predictors of health behavior are conscientiousness and neuroticism [2, 3]. Individuals with greater levels of conscientiousness, for example, are more likely to exercise [4], adhere better to medication [5], likely to obtain preventive cancer screenings [2]. Figure 1 shows a five-factor model. Those with higher neuroticism, undergo mental trauma since it is characterized by emotional deregulation or high emotional reactivity.

We provide a psychological-behavioral model and an experiment based on it in this paper. We also go through the behavioral modification techniques that are based on this paradigm. Machine learning classification algorithms mainly Decision Tree Classifier, Random Forest Classifier [6], Gaussian Naive Bayes classifier, and Support Vector Machine [7] are applied on obtained preprocessed data to gain meaningful insights based on the target variable and feature set considered. Results obtained after training these models on the preprocessed data clearly state the psychology of an individual and behavior as a whole. The next chapters of this research brief about the related work done in this domain, followed by Methodologies, Results and discussions. Conclusion and Future Scope end our research.

2   Related Work

Yang Huanhuan [8] aim at understanding the behavioral habits of college students and cultivate good behavioral habits in them. The paper raises the issue of how nowadays people not just aim for food and clothes but also desire for a happy life and this is where positive psychology comes into the picture to understand the developmental behavior of the person with respect to its societal presence and modernization. This the paper thoroughly talks about behavior and psychology as a good developmental base for college students. While talking about the importance of developing good developing habits in college students, this paper talks about how moral habits can help in personal accomplishment for an individual college student and it directly or indirectly helps national and social development. While discussing problems existing in college students it discusses how lack of moral behavior is present in those students who tend to be influenced by the internet which results in a bad moral attitude of an individual. It also raises the issue of students facing problems in learning behavior where it talks about how weak self-control can develop bad habits which develop bad life behavior which consists of improper scheduling, lack of moral values, becoming constantly angry and jealous of anything. The main reasons for this highlighted by the paper areas lack proper upbringing, school neglecting students' behavior. For improvement in positive psychology in college students, the paper talks about how families and schools working together can help in the proper behavior development of the students.

Gomez Lopez et al. [9] discuss how love and relationships are either playing a key role in developing well-being or are becoming a negative outcome. According to the findings, romantic relationships can provide a source of happiness for teenagers and emerging adults. Study shows that relationships can improve social integration and can create a positive self-concept. The studies included in the qualitative synthesis were around 112 and SPSS from IBM was used to carry out coding and process results. From the complete study of more than 100 researchers previously done a finding which came to existence is that a relationship which is beneficial for well-being, have high-quality levels, partners developing their personal and shared goals maintain a secured attachment over some time. Personal well-being is the only key to happy and satisfied relationships of a person's life and people with disappointing or broken relationships state to face failure or depressed phase of their life or ending up they blame their previous relationships.

Astatke et al. [10] aimed to identify the correlation of emotional intelligence, academic help to seek behavior, and psychological phenomena among the 283 students of first-year regular diploma. For correlation, SPSS was used and while creating questionnaires 3 major parameters of emotional intelligence, help-seeking behavior, and attitudes towards professionals were checked. Data gathering permission from the college authorities was taken and researchers administered the questionnaire before permitting to gather data. The results showed that emotional intelligence had a significant positive correlation with students having academic achievement, it also came to a conclusion that students' emotional intelligence increases with their better academic performance.

W J Chopik [11] explored findings done by two studies about relationships in which the first involves more than 270000 people in nearly 100 countries. It is identified that family and friend relationships are associated with a healthy and happy lifestyle. From the second study done on 7500 aged people in us, it was identified that not just having friends but the quality of friends also mattered and it has played a major role in creating a behavioral personality. The findings showed that for aged people across the time prioritize friendship more than family relationship, the people who claim to be self-prioritized are the one who has been part of temporal friendships or had lost faith in the family, people generally tend to stay with friends and family at most, and they are somewhat sharing a powerful friendship with their family members as well. Concluding the result, we can say that friendship and family are not distinct at all.

Valkenburg, Patti [12] investigates how social media can influence the self-effects of the message creator(involuntarily). Self-effects can be defined as effects on cognition (knowledge or beliefs), emotions, and attitudes by some external factors. This can be seen from an experimental study where an individual is told to write a blog about something, this creation of messages not only affects the qualities (such as cognition, emotions) of readers but, it can also affect the qualities) and traits of the message sender/creator. The author concludes by saying that self-effects are stronger in online settings rather than in offline settings.

3   Methodology

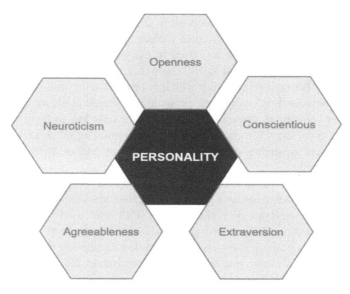

Fig. 1. Five-factor model

3.1   Sample and Data Collection

The study population is made for all over India. The people were aged between 15 and 71 where we classified them into three age groups Youth, Adults, Millennials. The majority of the respondent were between the age group from 19 to 24 falling in classes of adult and youth. While rest response was gathered from Company employees and Family members which fall in a range between 40 and 60. A total of 19 questions were asked to 200 respondents out of valid data set of 175 responses were used for data analysis.

In this study, the majority of questionnaires were Binary be- tween, yes and no, couple of them were questions based upon single choice with multiple options. And the last part consists of the multiple-choice question where the respondent is supposed to choose all the possible options on a given scale which is applied to them. Questions majorly include personality and behavioral type too. Figure 2. includes questions asked in the survey.

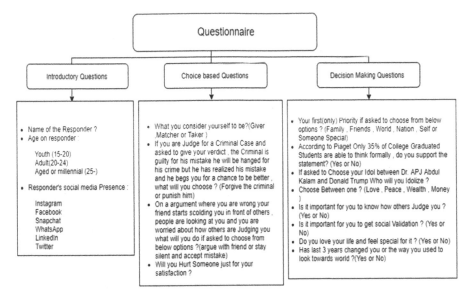

Fig. 2. Survey taxonomy

3.2   Data Analytics

The main propaganda of this research is to analyze the responses obtained from the known youth of the university and professionals(faculties). The survey was conducted from May 4, 2021, till 10th May 2021. A sufficient number of responses were obtained with satisfactory answers and no manipulations. The purpose of approaching known personnel was thereby met, and we were pretty sure that what type of answers he/she might give to the respective questionnaire.

The complete survey taxonomy was divided into 2 categories as:

- Social Media Influence of the subject and its adverse impact on behavioral psychology, his decision over social media validation as well.
- General choice-based questions answering its psychology. Figure 3. is the process flow we followed. From the data received, 17.91% were youth, 72.83% as adults, and 9.26% as millennial.

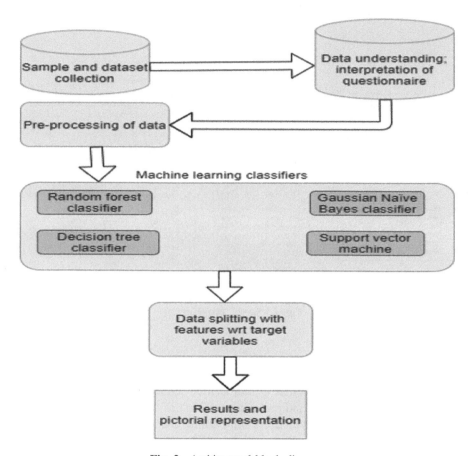

Fig. 3. Architectural block diagram

3.3 Technology Stack

Following is the technology which we worked on:

- Pre-processing – Before entering the data into our model we need to conduct some pre-processing over data with the help of cross tab, label encoding, and one hot-coding. First, over the data, we applied the cross tab to point out the relations among multiple conditions and determine the important factor which is more prominent in our data set. Secondly, we applied the label encoding to the columns of an object type to int which will be further required for the Machine algorithm model. Lastly, we applied one hot coding for the specific columns.

- Gaussian Bayes – Gaussian Bayesian classification is used for normal distribution for continuous valued features with no co variance in them, with help of Gaussian classification we are successfully able to identify relationships among various feature values. Label encoding for binary vales and one-hot encoding for categorized value is done, after encoding a target variable is selected and based upon its relationship with other variables features selection is done, after selection train, test, split method is implemented on the data set and Gaussian classifier is called for fit in training and testing data. Using sclkit-learn metrics function accuracy is identified.
- Random Forest regression – We utilized Random Forest Regression, a machine learning model that can be used for both regression and classification, to assess the significance of characteristics within the subset and apply it to the data set. We used random forest regression to predict the BMI value in relation to the specific field, and we got a lot of different outcomes with an accuracy of above 95%.
- Decision Tree – A very specific probability tree that allows you to create a decision about the process flow given. After applying label encoding and one hot-encoding we applied the decision tree on our data set where we selected the infection lingered as our target field and classified successfully with an accuracy of 86%.
- Adaboost Algorithm – A primitive classification technique also known as adaptive boosting algorithm is an Ensemble method in machine-learning which is gradually used to improve the model's accuracy.
- XGBoost Algorithm – Another preemptive ensemble method is XGBoost. It is a decision-tree based algorithm which is designed for speed and performance by implementing gradient-boosted decision trees.

4 Results

4.1 Case Studies

Case-1: - Responses received from the youth state that, we belong to such generation where social validation matters a lot. Table 1. Consists of the results and the feature set as well the target variable considered. On the other hand; adults do feel the same as youths when social validation is considered.

Table 1. Behavior of youth, adults and millennials regarding social validation.

feature set	Target variable	Algorithm	Criterion (kernel)	Results
Social media presence i.e., on "Facebook, WhatsApp, LinkedIn, Twitter, Instagram, Snapchat", Do you like people judging you, Age category – 'Youths' = 'A', 'Adults' = 'B', 'Above 25' = 'C', All Age group = 'D	Social validation	Decision Tree Classifier	Entropy	A = 69.23%
				B = 69.23%
				C = 71.15%
				D = 65.38%
		Gaussian Naïve Bayes Classifier (GNB)	–	A = 71.15%
				B = 71.15%
				C = 65.38%
				D = 65.384%
		Random Forest Classifier (RFC)	Entropy & Gini	A = 69.77%
				B = 69.23%
				C = 69.23%
				D = 69.23%
		Support Vector Machine (SVM)	Linear	A = 75.00%
				B = 75.00%
				C = 75.00%
				D = 75.00%
			Polynomial	A = 67.30%
				B = 67.30%
				C = 63.46%
				D = 63.46%
			Radial Basis Function	A = 69.23%
				B = 69.23%
				C = 73.07%
				D = 73.07%
			Sigmoid	A = 69.23%
				B = 71.15%
				C = 69.23%
				D = 71.15%
		Ada-boost	Cross validation (CV) = 0.68	A = 61.53%
				B = 65.38%
				C = 65.38%
				D = 65.38%
		XG-Boost	Cross validation (CV) = 0.67	A = 61.53%
				B = 61.53%
				C = 65.38%
				D = 65.38%

Case-2: - In this we considered, 4 questions to predict the behavior of members of respective age category i.e., youth, adults, and millennials. "Verdict to be hanged", "Whom will you choose APJ Abdul Kalam or Donald Trump", "What do you prefer as your ultimate choice from Success, wealth, love, peace" and "Argumentative situation-based decision" are those questions used. Our model proposes that people who follow APJ Abdul Kalam; Are in favor of that "verdict should be hanged" which ultimately shows a sign of positive correlation and people with this mindset have an inclination towards good psychology. On the contrary, people who follow Dr. APJ Abdul Kalam sir as their role model; answered the argumentative question as "Will Remain Silent; accept and will try to evaluate our mistake" which symbolizes the characteristics of that ideal person. Table 2 showcases the results generated by classification algorithms for this case.

Table 2. People responding to such situations by the influence of role model

Feature set	Target variable	Algorithm	Criterion (kernel)	Results
"Your role model-Dr. APJ Abdul Kalam or Donald Trump", "Verdict to be hanged", "What is your superior choice", "Age category – 'Youths' ='A', 'Adults' = 'B', 'Above 25' = 'C', All Age group = 'D	Argumentative situation- based question	Decision Tree Classifier	Entropy	A = 80.76%
				B = 76.92%
				C = 78.84%
				D = 80.76%
		GNB	–	A = 78.84%
				B = 78.84%
				C = 78.84%
				D = 78.84%
		RFC	Entropy & Gini	A = 82.69%
				B = 75.00%
				C = 78.84%
				D = 80.76%
		SVM	Linear	A = 73.07%
				B = 71.15%
				C = 73.07%
				D = 71.15%
			Polynomial	A = 71.15%
				B = 71.15%
				C = 73.07%
				D = 73.07%
			Radial Basis Function	A = 73.07%
				B = 73.07%
				C = 73.07%
				D = 73.07%
			Sigmoid	A = 73.07%
				B = 73.07%
				C = 75.00%
				D = 73.07%
		Ada-boost	Cross validation (CV) = 0.72	A = 73.07%
				B = 73.07%
				C = 73.07%
				D = 78.84%
		XG-Boost	Cross validation (CV) = 0.73	A = 73.07%
				B = 71.15%
				C = 73.07%
				D = 78.84%

Case 3: - Another stack of questionnaires considered is "Verdict to be hanged or released", "Argumentative situation- the based question", "Priority" and your nature "Are you a Giver, Matcher or Taker" [13] as feature set and "Do you feel satisfied after hurting someone" as the target variable. Table 3 includes the results of classification machine learning algorithms on these attributes. Our model can now predict the solution an individual will propose to the target variable based question on the results obtained for the feature set's questionnaire.

Table 3. Individual's aggressive behavior based on a scenario

Feature set	Target variable	Algorithm	Criterion (kernel)	Results
"Verdict to be hanged or released", "Argumentative situation- based question", "Priority" and your nature "Are you a Giver, Matcher or Taker"	Do you feel satisfied after hurting someone	Decision Tree Classifier	Entropy	A = 92.30%
				B = 92.30%
				C = 92.30%
		GNB	–	A = 84.61%
				B = 84.61%
				C = 88.46%
		RFC	Entropy & Gini	A = 92.31%
				B = 92.31%
				C = 92.30%
		SVM	Linear	A = 92.30%
				B = 92.30%
				C = 92.30%
			Polynomial	A = 84.61%
				B = 92.30%
				C = 92.30%
			Radial Basis Function	A = 92.30%
				B = 92.30%
				C = 92.30%
			Sigmoid	A = 88.46%
				B = 88.46%
				C = 92.30%
		Ada-boost	Cross validation (CV) = 0.83	A = 53.84%
				B = 88.46%
				C = 50.32%
		XG-Boost	Cross validation (CV) = 0.86	A = 53.84%
				B = 88.46%
				C = 50.32%

4.2 Findings

Extensive features of WhatsApp make it most in-demand social-media platform. Table 4. includes presence of respondents and their personal preferences while social media is considered. Instagram followed by snapchat is what our results state. Table 5 includes insights gathered by concatenation of choices gathered from multiple questions.

Table 4. Social media presence of people responded

Social media platform	Count (in percentage'%')
WhatsApp	90.75
Facebook	47.97
Instagram	78.61
Twitter	28.90
LinkedIn	47.97
Snapchat	50.28

Table 5. Meaningful insights from the obtained data

S No.	Qualities	Count Of people (%)
1	People with the merciful mindset People who feel special about their life People who remain silent in an argument-based situation	41.04%
2	People who chose peace People who tend to remain silent on the argumentative-based situation People tend to forgive others for mistakes	31.79%
3	People who Prioritize family over the rest. People who remain silent in an argument-based situation	31.21%
4	People who chose success over love, wealth, and peace People who will remain silent on an argument	6.21%
5	People who feel special in life People who are "Taker" rather than "Giver"	4.01%

4.3 Visualiations

Visualizations are a way of showing the data into a pictorial form which is the best way to visualize the data and allows us to get clear insight withing the data. It allows us to explicitly interact the data and see data through the visualization tool named as Tableau. This helps us to create an interactive dashboard with the visualization created on it. The visualization given below are created on the survey of the data which we generated.

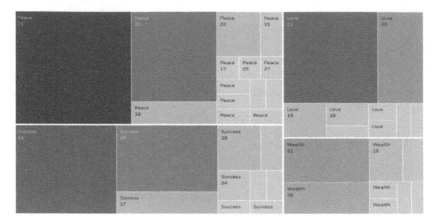

Fig. 4. Classification of choices with respect to age

In Fig. 4. we plotted a tree map depicting the relation of priority-based response of "What will you choose from Success, Wealth, Love, Peace" and all the subjects with age categories they fall into. To our surprise, we found that; Age group 20–22 want peace in their life. Age group between 15–19 prefer the rest over peace.

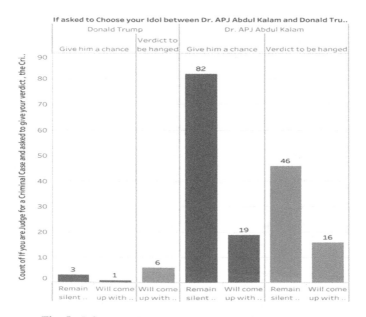

Fig. 5. Influence of ideal person on issue-based scenarios

In Fig. 5. we got the graph between the ideal person i.e. "The person you follow"; the orange block is indicated with the responses of the question "Verdict to be hanged" and blue indicates whether to "Give him a chance" where we were able to justify that people chose such responses that truly resemble the characteristics of the role model they follow. Almost all who chose Donald Trump as an ideal person, responded that Verdict should be hanged which depicts aggressive mindset of an individual.

5 Implication and Limitation

After Pandemic and change in work culture, majority of the crowd is finding the change in their behavior and thinking patter which we believe is a major concern of the society. People's mindsets have changed even their pattern of thinking after moulding to the latter lifestyle.

However, this study has many limitations. First unique finding of this study is that it has identified the relation between the behavior and thinking patter over a specific group of crowd and age specifically. Although there are some limitations in this research, though the results we obtained through the survey are specific and need to be judged when we meet these individuals in personal through which we can obtain more precise responses and can clearly see their traits of personality and behavior over the year. Second the majority of the crowd volunteered belongs to age group of 19 to 24 while we received very few responses for the category of Youth's and Millennials, hence we aren't that fortunate to talk upon these age groups.

6 Conclusion and Future Scope

This extensive study of juveniles, adults and millennials thereby claimed that irrespective of age, evaluating the psychological behavior is not a cakewalk and consequential as a whole. The survey of 16 questions proposed meaningful insights and subsequent relation of questions, showcased high quality preciseness. The received responses of the subjects indirectly state the personality trait; hence following the five-factor model. Results are obtained using machine learning algorithms specifically classification algorithms such as Decision Tree Classifier, Gaussian Naive Bayes Algorithm, Random Forest Classifier and Support Vector Machine. We achieved a considerable accuracy of 92.30% i.e., our model can now predict the choice of 92 people in 100 individuals whether they will remain silent or react forcefully on an argumentative situation. Gaussian Naive Bayes classifier gives commendable results.

Since the entire data obtained is of textual type, analyzing the sentiments behind the responses will allow us to understand the psychology of the individual by using the Natural language processing-based algorithms and we thereby aim to extend our research to that extent which eventually will provide more accurate and precise results.

References

1. Mccrae, R.R., John, O.P.: An introduction to the five-factor model and its applications. J. Pers. **60**, 175–215 (1992)

2. Aschwanden, D., Gerend, M.A., Luchetti, M., Stephan, Y., Sutin, A.R., Terracciano, A.: Personality traits and preventive cancer screenings in the health retirement study. Prev. Med. **126** (2019)
3. Emilsson, M., Gustafsson, P., Öhnström, G. et al.: Impact of personality on adherence to and beliefs about ADHD medication, and perceptions of ADHD in adolescents. BMC Psychiatry **20**, 139 (2020). https://doi.org/10.1186/s12888-020-02543-x
4. Sutin, A.R., Stephan, Y., Luchetti, M., Artese, A., Oshio, A., Terracciano, A.: The five-factor model of personality and physical inactivity: A meta-analysis of 16 samples. J. Res. Pers. **63**, 22–28 (2016)
5. Molloy, G.J., Carroll, R.E., Ferguson, E.: Conscientiousness and medication adherence: a metaanalysis. Ann. Behav. Med. **47**, 92–101 (2014)
6. Ali, J., Khan, R., Ahmad, N., Maqsood, I.: Random Forests and Decision Trees. Int. J. Comput. Sci. Issues. (9) (2012)
7. Huang, J.L., Ling, C.X.: Comparing naive Bayes, decision trees, and SVM with AUC and accuracy. In: Third IEEE International Conference on Data Mining (2003)
8. Huanhuan, Y.: Research on the Formation of College Students' Behavior Habits from the Perspective of Positive Psychology (2019)
9. Gómez-López, M., et al.: Well-being and romantic relationships: a systematic review in adolescence and emerging adulthood. Int. J. Environ. Res. Public Health **16**(13) 2415 (2019) https://doi.org/10.3390/ijerph16132415
10. Astatke, M.: First-year college students' emotional intelligence and help-seeking behaviours as correlates of their academic achieve–ment. JSAA (2019)
11. Chopik, W.J.: Associations among relational values, support, health, and well-being across the adult lifespan. Pers. Relat. **24**(2), 408–422 (2017)
12. Valkenburg, P.: Understanding self-effects in social media. Hum. Commun. Res. (2017)
13. Mäthner, E., Lanwehr, R.: Givers, takers and matchers—reciprocity styles and their contribution to organizational behaviour. Gr. Interakt. Org. Zeitschrift für Angewandte Organisationspsychologie (GIO) **48**(1), 5–13 (2017). https://doi.org/10.1007/s11612-017-0358-6

Predicting Stock Market Prices Using Sentiment Analysis of News Articles

Jayanth Narla$^{(\boxtimes)}$, Sai Venkat Reddy Malreddy ,
Vaishnavi Bacha , and G. Ramesh Chandra

Department of CSE, VNR Vignana Jyothi Institute of Engineering
and Technology, Hyderabad 500090, India
rameshchandra_g@vnrvjiet.in

Abstract. Prediction and analysis of stock markets have played an important role in today's economy. The main goal of stock prediction is to determine the future value of that stock belongs to a company and decide if it is possible to make a profitable stock trading scheme. Hence the successful stock prediction has the ability to maximize the investor gains. In this paper, Long Short Term Memory (LSTM) is applied, an improvised Recurrent Neural Network model, to predict the stock market. Both stock prices and news feed data of a company were used to predict its stock fluctuations. The goal of this project is to predict the stock price based on both technical analysis as well as fundamental analysis. Technical analysis is implemented by Deep Learning, whereas fundamental analysis is carried out by sentiment analysis.

To validate the proposed methodology, the training and testing was done on the 'Apple' dataset possessing 2517 records. A highly accurate model was obtained during our study using this approach with the RMSE of 0.064.

Keywords: Long Short Term Memory · Recurrent Neural Network · Deep Learning · Sentiment Analysis

1 Introduction

A stock is an equity investment that enables a person to be a part of the company's earnings and assets. A stock market, also called an equity market, is an aggregation of buyers and sellers of different stocks on a day-to-day basis. A stock market is an important source where companies raise money. The primary goal of a stock market is to govern stock exchanges in order to provide a fair environment for both investors and companies whose stocks are traded on the market. The technique of determining the future value of a company's shares is characterized as a stock market prediction. It is based on a supply and demand approach.

A successful forecast always results in a substantial profit. Stock prices, according to the efficient market theory, reflect all already available information, making any price movements that are not based on newly released information fundamentally unexpected. But others disagree with this and suggest that stock values are dependent on different factors such as previous stock values, decisions taken in the corporation,

© Springer Nature Switzerland AG 2022
D. Garg et al. (Eds.): IACC 2021, CCIS 1528, pp. 193–200, 2022.
https://doi.org/10.1007/978-3-030-95502-1_15

demand, and need of the products, other stocks which act as competitors to the former stock, and many more.

Stock prediction involves two important methods, which are technical and fundamental analysis. Technical analysis deals with prediction based on price and volume of stock, whereas fundamental analysis deals with prediction based on economic factors that influence the stock prices. The factors affecting the stock prices are numerous, and hence they seem to be unpredictable. In the recent years, applying artificial intelligence based methods in predicting the stock prices with high accuracy has gained momentum. In this regard, this paper focuses on studying various existing methodologies or models in predicting the stock prices. But research in this domain to predict stock prices has been prevalent for years long and is still going on at a fast pace to build more accurate and efficient stock forecasting models.

This paper focuses on implementing deep learning models for predicting the stock prices. Section 2 discusses about past work done in the area of stock market predictions using various Artificial Intelligence techniques. Section 3 focuses on the proposed methodology, where it discusses about using sentiment analysis in predicting the stock prices. In Sect. 4, description of the data sets, its pre-processing steps and deep learning model used. Section 5 elaborates about results from the study. Finally, Sect. 6, concludes the study.

2 Related Work

There is a strong association between financial news items and stock price movements. Economists believe in the Efficient Market Hypothesis (EMH) and the Random Walk Theory (RWT), which both help to explain why financial markets are unpredictable [1–3]. Research from throughout the world has shown that the stock market is unpredictable. However, present prediction methods are insufficient, making stock forecasting one of the most difficult challenges in this subject as well as one of the most attractive research topics.

Neural networks have been utilized in numerous research to estimate market values. A Neural Network learns the events that affect the stock market in a specific environment and stores the data in the network. This information is then used to forecast the future. The findings revealed that employing NN can accurately anticipate the trend of testing data with a 95% accuracy rate [4].

R. Ren et al. [5] using look-ahead bias with a rolling window with SVM, there is a significant decrease in accuracy (10%). They have employed sentiment analysis variables in SVM, which had risen 18.6% accuracy. L. Yu et al. [6] revolves around optimizing the SVM predictive model by using the least squares support vector machine [LSSVM]. Significant and consistent increase inaccuracy [72.61 standard SVM – 82.66 Evolving LSSVM] is evident as LSSVM is coupled with reducing data dimensionality with GA, which not only reduced the dimensionality but also produced an accurate model compared to PCA. Input features contained only stock data, no sentiment or other attributes considered in creating model, which represents the purpose of the model is to fit according to market trend rather than analyzing or forecasting. They did not consider various outside causes of market volatility. D. Zhang et al. [7] proposed a hybrid model which combines the power of ARMA model and SVM, but they did not consider the sentiment analysis in predicting the stock prices.

M. Doğan et al. [8] developed a model for identifying the speculators (or) influencers in the stock mark from social media data, but they are not predicting the stock prices. V. S. Pagolu et al. [9] analysed the public sentiment gleaned from tweets, which has used N-gram and Word2Vec. Random forest was the most accurate of all the machine learning algorithms used. However, the approach is slower than other algorithms due to the high number of trees. Hence it is not an optimal implementation in the real world. A. Kanavos et al. [10] proposed a entropy based model for predicting the stock prices using sentiment analysis from twitter data. M. V. D. H. P. Malawana et al. [11] proposed a logistic regression and Naïve Bayes based model, where they were considering social media data, public opinions on market and news articles. Furthermore, the social media information may not be accurate, as it is primarily opinion and does not include factual information about the company.

S. Mohan et al. [12] used 265000 financial news articles that gave a massive space in extracting features for sentiment polarity. Although the method employed in recognizing relevant data in articles based on a company name is not unequivocal, usage of the ntlk library had undermined the faultlessness of polarity extraction. As high inaccuracy during periods of low demand will have a strong impact on MAPE. The results are not consistent in featuring sentiment as the deciding factor in increasing/reducing MAPE value. C.Lee et.al proposed BERT based model, but the accuracy is 87.3%.

T. Damrongsakmethee [13] examined historical stock pricing data from Yahoo Finance over the past ten years, selecting two indexes: the Dow Jones Industrial Average and the S&P 500. Then, they created an 11 layers deep LSTM model that forecasts the price of a stock using the ADAM optimization tools. G. Li et al. [14] and R. Kumar et al. [15] employed deep learning model such as LSTM for forecasting the stock market value. Even though they have high accuracy, this isn't ideal because the price of a stock is heavily influenced by market sentiment in the real world.

According to the recent studies discussed till now, very less work was done in integrating sentiment analysis models with deep learning model such as LSTM. So, this paper proposes a methodology in integrating NLP based sentiment models with LSTM model and results were elaborated in Sect. 5.

3   Proposed Method

The main objectives of the proposed method are:

1. To perform Natural Language Processing on news feed to calculate the sentiment scores.
2. To predict the stock values based on stock price data and the sentiment scores using Long Short Term Memory (LSTM) model.

Stock prediction is a difficult undertaking for analysts to complete in a short period of time. By just viewing the recent prices of a stock we can not make predictions about the 'bull market' or the 'bear market'. There are some algorithms that can predict the stock prices and can give accurate results. A few among these include regression methods, random forest model and neural network model. Based on our examination of the literature, we have determined that deep learning is the optimal approach for solving this problem. Stock prices can be predicted using a Recurrent Neural Network model with Long Short Term Memory (LSTM) and other processing techniques. Firstly we have taken Apple (IBM) dataset for our prediction. The dataset has different attributes which include date, open, high, low, close, adjusted close, volume, index, and the news. The open, high, low, close contain the respective stock prices and the news contains different news articles regarding the company on the reported dates. So initially we apply natural language processing on the news records to analyse their sentiment scores. Then we implement the LSTM model using the price fields of the company along with the sentiment scores. Later this data is separated as training and testing data. We train the model using the training dataset and then make predictions using the test dataset.

To achieve this, we presented a prediction process to study stock variations in order to attain the above goals. Figure 1 depicts the prediction procedure.

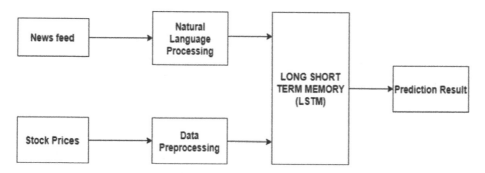

Fig. 1. The macro button chooses the correct format automatically.

The following is the proposed prediction process.

- **Step 1**: Collected Apple dataset and analyzed the data to select only useful attributes for prediction. Adjusted close prices and the news feeds are used in the prediction process. Date, Index and Volume are not used for the prediction.
- **Step 2**: Stock data is preprocessed and then normalised using MinMaxScaler function. News feed data is preprocesed and sentiment scores that is positive, negative, nuetral sentiment scores are calculated using the VADER Sentiment Analysis tool.
- **Step 3**: Later the preprocessed stock data and the sentiment scores calculated from the news feeds are sent to the Long Short Term Memory Model as input and the model architecture is designed.
- **Step 4**: From the total records available in the dataset, training and testing datasets are obtained by splitting it in 80:20 ratio. The model is then trained on the training dataset.
- **Step 5**: Using the model the test data is predicted. Finally, the prediction is plotted and the accuracy of the model is measured.

4 Description of Data Set and Its Pre-processing

4.1 Data Collection

Collected Apple (IBM) dataset which has 2517 records that is almost 10 years data from the year 2006 to 2016. It has 9 attributes which include date, open, high, low, close, volume, index, adjusted close and the news. The prices of the stock are used for the technical analysis where as the news records are used for the fundamental analysis. For the sake of consistency throughout the project, we used the Adjusted Close price as the stock price. We gathered this information from major news sources such as google news, reauters, kaggle and yahoo finance.

4.2 Data Processing

We will discuss about pre-processing in this section. Various packages were employed during the procedure. Predicting the values from the raw data is a difficult task. So, before we send our input to the model we preprocessed the data using some algorithms. The stock data preprocessing requires packages like numpy and pandas. The news data pre-processing requires tool called as VADER Sentiment Analyzer which performs the natural language processing. After the data is processed, it is divided for training and testing. Training constitutes 80% of the data whereas testing uses 20% of the total data.

Pre-processing the Stock Prices
Here we mainly use packages like Pandas and Numpy. Firstly the missing values are treated, then unecessary data is omitted like the date and index values. Finally the pre-processsing is completed by normalising the data using MinMax normalisation.

Natural Language Processing
Here the News feeds are pre-processed using the VADER Sentiment Analysis tool. This tool serves the purpose with an inbuild package called Sentiment Intensity Analyzer. By implementing this we can get the positive, negative, nuetral and compound sentiment scores of the news which is used in the prediction.

4.3 Stock Prediction

The models we applied in the prediction are discussed in this section. Recurrent Neural Network (RNN) is a deep learning methodology which predicts the stock prices by analyzing all the previous data. Its only drawback is that it gives equal importance to all of the previous data. The problem of vanishing gradients plagues RNN. Long Short Term Memory (LSTM) provides a solution to this problem by prioritizing the past data. Hence we implemented this LSTM model to make the predictions. This process mainly focuses on the pre-processed stock prices and the sentiment scores obtained after natural language processing. We tuned the LSTM model's various parameters, the number of LSTM layers, the number of units in each layer, the batch size, and the number of epochs using these as input are all variables to consider. The model's accuracy was then tested after we made predictions based on the testing data.

5 Results

The results obtained utilizing our proposed model are discussed in this section. We used Windows 10, Python 3.7, and an Intel® CoreTM i7-10710U @4.70 GHz @1.10 GHz to develop this proposed prediction process. Figure 2 shows the stock price prediction of Apple using the LSTM model. This is graph depicting the actual prices and the predictions made on the testing data. Table 1 depicts the MSE value, which is used to assess the predicted model's accuracy. To sum up, the model's RMSE is 0.064.

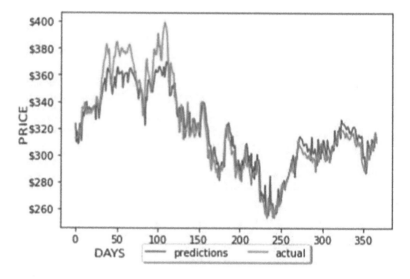

Fig. 2. Apple Stock prediction

Figure 2 depicts the actual values according to the testing data set and predicted values. So, one can see that the LSTM model is predicting almost precisely to the actual values. The error in the actual and predicted is calculated using MSE and RMSE. So, RMSE value of the test data set is 0.0664, which is very low error rate.

Table 1. Error rate of the proposed model

Sentiment analysis model using LSTM	
Train MSE	0.0012
Train RMSE	0.0355
Test MSE	0.0044
Test RMSE	0.0664

6 Conclusion

In this work, we used a combination of neural networks and financial news items to predict stock values. The findings imply that stock prices and financial news stories have a strong association. With our recurrent neural network, we were able to obtain a very low error rate of 0.064, leading us to believe that there is a direct connection between textual information and stock price direction.

This can further be improved in the coming days by taking into consideration two scenarios:-

- The detrimental consequences on a company's stock price caused by news about other related firms in the sector
- Taking a broader look at industry and global events, could indicate general market direction or consequences on a particular company.

References

1. Bollen, J., Mao, H., Zeng, X.: Twitter mood predicts the stock market. J. Comput. Sci. 2(1), 1–8 (2011)
2. Patel, J., Shah, S., Thakkar, P., Kotecha, K.: Predicting stock and stock price index movement using trend deterministic data preparation and machine learning techniques. Expert Syst. Appl. 42(1), 259–268 (2015)
3. Dutta, S., Rohit, R.: Stock market prediction using data mining 1379 techniques with R. Int. J. Eng. Sci. Comput. 7(3), 5436–5441 (2017)
4. Naeini, M.P., Taremian, H., Hashemi, H.B.: Stock market value prediction using neural networks. In: Comput. Inf. Syst. Ind. Manag. Appl. (CISIM), 2010 Int. Conf., pp. 132–136 (2010)
5. Ren, R., Wu, D.D., Liu, T.: Forecasting stock market movement direction using sentiment analysis and support vector machine. IEEE Syst. J. 13(1), 760–770 (2019)
6. Yu, L., Chen, H., Wang, S., Lai, K.K.: Evolving least squares support vector machines for stock market trend mining. IEEE Trans. Evol. Comput. 13(1), 87–102 (2009)
7. Zhang, D., Song, H., Chen, P.: Stock market forecasting model based on a hybrid ARMA and support vector machines. In: 2008 International Conference on Management Science and Engineering 15th Annual Conference Proceedings, pp. 1312–1317 (2008)
8. Doğan, M., Metin, Ö., Tek, E., Yumuşak, S., Öztoprak, K.: Speculator and influencer evaluation in stock market by using social media. IEEE Int. Conf. Big Data (Big Data) 2020, 4559–4566 (2020)
9. Pagolu, V.S., Reddy, K.N., Panda, G., Majhi, B.: Sentiment analysis of Twitter data for predicting stock market movements. In: 2016 International Conference on Signal Processing, Communication, Power and Embedded System (SCOPES), pp. 1345–1350 (2016)
10. Kanavos, A., Vonitsanos, G., Mohasseb, A., Mylonas, P.: An entropy-based evaluation for sentiment analysis of stock market prices using twitter data. In: 2020 15th International Workshop on Semantic and Social Media Adaptation and Personalization (SMA), pp. 1–7 (2020)
11. Malawana, M.V.D.H.P., Rathnayaka, R.M.K.T.: The public sentiment analysis within big data distributed system for stock market prediction– a case study on Colombo stock exchange. In: 2020 5th International Conference on Information Technology Research (ICITR), pp. 1–6 (2020)

12. Mohan, S., Mullapudi, S., Sammeta, S., Vijayvergia, P., Anastasiu, D.C.: Stock price prediction using news sentiment analysis. IEEE Fifth International Conference on Big Data Computing Service and Applications (BigDataService) **2019**, 205–208 (2019)
13. Damrongsakmethee, T., Neagoe, V.-E.: Stock market prediction using a deep learning approach. In: 2020 12th International Conference on Electronics, Computers and Artificial Intelligence (ECAI), pp. 1–6 (2020)
14. Li, G., Xiao, M., Guo, Y.: Application of deep learning in stock market valuation index forecasting. In: 2019 IEEE 10th International Conference on Software Engineering and Service Science (ICSESS), pp. 551–554 (2019)
15. Kumar, R., Kumar, P., Kumar, Y.: Analysis of financial time series forecasting using deep learning model. In: 2021 11th International Conference on Cloud Computing, Data Science & Engineering (Confluence), pp. 877–881 (2021)
16. Lee, C.-C., Gao, Z., Tsai, C.-L.: BERT-based stock market sentiment analysis. In: 2020 IEEE International Conference on Consumer Electronics – Taiwan (ICCE-Taiwan), pp. 1–2 (2020)

Sentimental Analysis on Multi-domain Sentiment Dataset Using SVM and Naive Bayes Algorithm

P. Kiran Kumar[✉], N. Jahna Tejaswi, M. L. Vasanthi, L. L. Srihitha, and B. Phanindra Kumar

Department of Computer Science and Engineering, SASI Institute of Technology and Engineering (Affiliated To JNTU, Kakinada), Tadepalligudem, India
{kiran, tejaswi5a2, vasanthi588, srihitha576, phanindra509}@sasi.ac.in

Abstract. With the advent of the significant data era, people are confronted with the vast amount of information they receive each day. The quantity of information accrued and processed by Facebook, Twitter, and other significant social networks (such as Instagram) is vast. The Twitter platform encourages users to use 280 characters each to tweet their thoughts. Because tweets can use a limited number of characters, sentiment analysis becomes more accurate. Sentiment analysis is a technique for determining whether a text is positively, negatively, or neutral. Some experiments are conducted using Natural Language Processing Toolkit (NLTK) to determine whether a tweet has a neutral, positive, or negative polarity with accuracy. Moreover, by using Naïve Bayes and SVM, the accuracy of the tweets is compared. Finally, the ROC curve will decide the efficiency of both algorithms.

Keywords: Twitter · Social networks · Sentiment analysis · Machine Learning · Natural Language Processing Toolkit (NLTK) · Naïve Bayes · SVM

1 Introduction

Research on sentiment analysis has become an interesting topic in the current world. It is the study of people's emotions, feelings and opinions with in written documents. Many businesses and organizations rely on the idea of their customers to make better decisions regarding their products, services. Platforms, such as Twitter, Facebook Etc. Allow users to take and analyze the opinions and reviews they make. The abundance of this data makes it difficult for users to interpret it correctly. As a result, sentiment analysis methods would prove helpful.

By analyzing Twitter data, we can obtain helpful information in many different fields. An example of the new information we can receive is people's sentiments on a topic. This information can be valuable in evaluating a project for improvement. By observing tweets, public sentiment information can be obtained. However, it may not be feasible to collect and analyze millions of tweets. Therefore, the existence of an application that automatically crawls and analyzes tweet sentiment will be beneficial.

D. Garg et al. (Eds.): IACC 2021, CCIS 1528, pp. 201–213, 2022.
https://doi.org/10.1007/978-3-030-95502-1_16

Several social networks and microblogging platforms allow users to express their opinions on many features of their lives in as little as 280 characters. Twitter is the most famous microblogging and social media platforms. Many of these tweets are challenging to analyze because of misspellings, emojis, and slang words. They all should go through some preprocessing steps before they are used for polarity detection (positive, negative, neutral).This is where sentimental analysis raised.

The following are the steps used in sentimental analysis.

Step1: Tokenization.

It is nothing but dividing a paragraph into a set of statements or dividing a comment into different words.

Step2: cleaning the data.

It is to remove all the special characters or any other word that does not add value to the analytics part.

Step3: removing the stop words.

Stop phrases do now no longer upload tons cost to the analytics part.

Step4: classification.

Our primary task is to classify them as positive words, negative words, or neutral words.

This paper aims to examine and understand the people sentiments using different machine learning techniques like Naïve Bayes and SVM. In this section accuracy and precision of both algorithms were compared to determine the best outcome of the two. All the above mentioned techniques are supervised learning techniques, which means that the desired data must first be trained in all of these instances. Finally, roc curve decides the best efficient algorithm from above mentioned techniques.

2 Related Works

A. Pak et al. developed a sentiment classifier using machine learning techniques to determine the polarity of tweets. The experimental assessment of the proposed strategies suggests development over the preceding methods. The collected corpus was used to train a sentiment classifier capable of detecting positive, negative, and neutral texts. The classifier is based on a multinomial Nave Bayes classifier using N-grams and POS-tags as features [1].

Sahar A. El Rahman et al. proposed a field of study known as sentiment analysis studies' opinions on several social media sites. The proposed model used several algorithms to increase the accuracy of identifying positive and negative tweets. We used an unsupervised machine learning algorithm where previously labelled data did not exist as a first step. Then the lexicon-based algorithm was used to feed the data into several supervised models [2].

Amrita Shelar et al. conducted an exploratory analysis of data from Twitter. We applied techniques in sentiment analysis and discovered people's sentiments in the form of polarity. As a future roadmap, we plan to gather more information about the users and businesses to research potential donors for non-profits [3].

Ritu S. Karan et al. proposed a slang improvement system to improve product popularity on Twitter by scaling the location of tweets. As a result, system performance is enhanced. An additional feature like location recognition of tweets helps in the product, marketing, political issue and event decision making. Thus, the performance of the system is improved. An additional feature such as location recognition of tweets is helpful when making decisions regarding events, campaigns, and political events [4].

Ike Pertiwi Windasari et al. described those thousands of Twitter users who post their opinions on their tweets every day. Businesses can take advantage of this information, but it takes a long time to do so. This is why there has to be a continuous analysis to predict tweet sentiment. In this study, we focused our search on keywords related to online transportation, particularly GoJek [5].

Huma Parveen et al. discussed how to preprocess tweeting data to remove noise. These different types of tweeting data cannot be used directly; they need to be converted first before being used. The analysis of Twitter data is done from various perspectives such as Positive, Negative and Neutral sentiments on tweets. This type of analysis will surely help any organization to improve its business productivity [6].

Using three manually annotated datasets collected from Twitter, this study analyzes the sentiment of tweets [7].

A. Agarwal et al. was proposed that a unigram model be used as a baseline, with a gain of 4% in binary classification and 3-way classification. Then, it was examined the tree kernel model and feature-based models, which surpassed the unigram model [8].

Lokesh Mandloi et al. presented these different machine learning techniques of data analysis of tweets, including Naive Bayes, SVM, and the Maximum Entropy Method. Twitter data is analyzed from various viewpoints to learn more about the sentiment analysis of Twitter. It is essential to know that sentiment analysis involves opinions that are classified into positive, negative, and neutral. Most studies have shown that Naive Bayes is the best machine learning method for predicting emotions [9].

Sanjeev Dhawan et al. proposed a sentiment polarity model for sentiments analysis in online social networks using tweet datasets. In the proposed methodology, tweet datasets are obtained from Twitter APIs to analyze sentiments emotions from different users. In this section, we check the polarity of sentiment within every tweet. Polarity is defined as the emotions of users like joy, happiness, sadness, and anger. If the polarity is equal to zero, then the tweet is neutral, and the polarity is more significant than zero, then the tweet is positive. Otherwise, the tweet is negative. By identifying tweets based on their sentiment polarity, the proposed algorithm can identify tweets of various users in this manner [10].

Hao Wang et al. examined a real-time political sentiment analysis problem, using nave Bayes to classify tweets into four categories (positive, negative, neutral, or unsure) and assess whether the system applied to the analysis of tweets during elections. Several other domains could be accessed by using this method, including movie events [11].

Neetu M et al. studied the sentiment analysis problem of tweets related to the domain of the electronic product. The machine learning approach performs better than symbolic techniques that are based on sentiments identification. The performance of the proposed enhanced vector feature was evaluated using several classifiers, including the nave Bayes, Maximum Entropy, SVMs, and Ensembles, and the results were almost similar. In the domain of electronic products opinion, the proposed feature vector showed improved performance [12].

Mohd Naim Mohd Ibrahim et al. proposed the Twitter Sentiment Classification Using Naïve Bayes Based on Trainer Perception. In this paper, researchers identified 50 tweets containing the keywords 'Malaysia' and 'Maybank' from Twitter to train perception processes on feedback from trainers. Using Naive Bayes techniques, 36 tweets were classified as positive, 42 as unfavourable or 57 as neutral. The study involved 27 trainers who were asked to analyze 25 tweets at random for their sentiment and then apply Nave Bayes training to the remaining 25 tweets based on their performance. According to the study, accuracy was 90% * 14% based on the total number of correct tweets [13].

Anis Zarrad et al. proposed that a demo of real-time Twitter sentiment analysis was developed for Bing maps as part of Microsoft Azure. The demo displayed opinions as positive, negative, or neutral tweets, and the statuses were displayed as different colours on the map [14].

The study by ParisaLak et al. showed that sentiment analysis does better at capturing general sentiment in star ratings (negative, neutral, or positive) [15].

Geeta R et al. provides a method by which people's opinions from different locations can be found regarding a particular product. The number of tweets needs to be significant to arrive at accurate results. As a result, even if a device or product does not collect an astronomically enormous amount of data, we can still collect tweets for several months from the data centres. Future work is expected to produce sentiment resources that were not available at this time [16].

Srinidhi Bhat et al. described that With the rapid increase of microblogging sites, there are many opportunities for extracting public opinion and analyzing it in a predictive manner, like sentiment analysis. The experimental assessment of the proposed strategies suggests development over the preceding methods. Rather than adding the value of these adverbs with the whole tweet sentiment, the proposed model calculated the score by multiplying its deal with the adverb like very and much [17].

Ahdi Ramadani et al. classified a relationship between the amount of training data and the classification performance. The more training data used, the more accurate and reliable the classification. Following preprocessing of 8000 raw datasets, 4845 training data points were selected for the study. As the collection of data is improved, the amount of gathered data should also be increased so that classification performance can improve [18].

Abhijit Janardan Patankar et al. have attempted to investigate the performance of states using big data Hadoop to retrieve the online tweets and assign scores for particular tweets that can be used for analyzing the performance of various communities on a large scale. Sentiment analysis has been implemented successfully with Twitter. We also studied NLP and machine learning approaches to sentiment analysis. We have learned many applications for sentimental analysis, and it is an important one to check [19].

In this paper, an algorithm to analyze Twitter sentiments based on sentiment polarity is proposed in an online social network. Twitter datasets are obtained from Twitter API for analysis of Twitter sentiments emotions of different users. Using the sentiment polarity of each tweet, we determine whether it is positive or negative. If comments are equal to zero, then the tweet is neutral; otherwise, notifications are negative [10].

3 Proposed Methodolgy

Sentiment Analysis
As one of the maxima extensively used strategies in text mining, sentiment analysis refers to analyzing how the text (here, Twitter tweets) is framed in positive, negative, and neutral sentiments. This method investigates tweets, conversations, opinions, and views (to decide business strategy, political analysis, and assess public action).

Twitter
Twitter is an American microblogging and social media platforms that permits it's users to post, like, and retweet tweets.

Flow Diagram

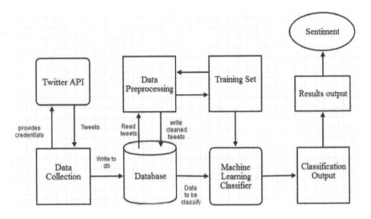

Data Collection
Data extracted from Twitter API can be used to generate large datasets of tweets that are not publicly available. To access Twitter data, one needs credentials from the developer site, so one may enter a search query to gain access to it.

Data Processing

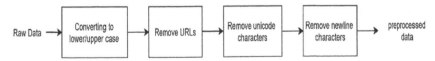

NLTK
By using NLTK, we can employ the process of sentiment analysis to analyze linguistic data to gain insights from linguistic data using powerful built-in machine learning operations.

These are the steps involved in NLTK.

- It is generating the listing of phrases withinside the tweet.
- Removing stopwords and words with unusual symbols
- Normalizing the comments in tweets (Fig. 1).

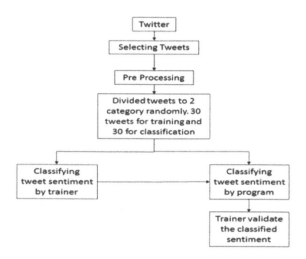

Fig. 1. Overall process

3.1 Naive Bayes Approach

1. Naive Bayes Approach
In Natural Language Processing, Naive Bayes analyses text data and therefore gives us a good result. This classification algorithm is the result of applying the Bayes Theorem to classification algorithms. The Naive Bayes algorithm uses mixture models to determine the probability of the results of the data analysis. The classifier used the concepts in mixture models to determine the effects. Combining a mixture model with the Bayes theorem can perform as a probabilistic classifier. Naive Bayes is likewise called simple Bayes or independence Bayes.

$$P(a/b) = P(b/a)P(a)/P(b)$$

Above, P(a) is the probability of class. P (b) is the prior probability of predictor. P (a/b) is the probability of class m. Where m is the target and predictory is the attribute. P (b/a) is the probability of predictor of the given type.

Input:

        Training dataset T,

        F= $(f_1, f_2, f_3,.., f_n)$ // value of the predictor variable in testing dataset.

Output:

        A class of testing dataset.

Step:

    1.   Read the training dataset T;

    2.   Calculate the mean and standard deviation of the predictor variables in each class;

    3.   Repeat

        Calculate the probability of f_i using the gauss density equation in each class;

        Until the probability of all predictor variables $(f_1, f_2, f_3,.., f_n)$ has been calculated.

    4.   Calculate the likelihood for each class;

    5.   Get the greatest likelihood;

3.2 SVM

SVM stands for Support Vector Machine which attempts to learn universally. Support Vector Machine has equal input and output, offering output to be positive or negative and information in vector space. Text documents are not helpful as input to Support Vector Machine. Texts are transformed into structured file formats, which can be employed as inputs for machine learning algorithms. The text scores are calculated and then used as inputs for Support Vector Machines. Text categorizations are compared to finalize the best one between texts. The performance estimation is used to determine which one is the most powerful. For text categorization SVM has been proven as the most important learning algorithms (Fig. 2).

Inputs:Determine the various training and test data.
Outputs:Determine the calculated accuracy.
Select the optimal value of cost and gamma for SVM.
while (stopping condition is not met) **do**
    Implement SVM train step for each data point.
    Implement SVM classify for testing data points.
end while
Return *accuracy*

Fig. 2. Algorithm for SVM

4 Results and Discussion

4.1 Accuracy Classification

Accuracy refers to how close something is to a known value. It is defined as the number of successful recognized entities by total number of entities in the data.

$$\text{Accuracy} = (\text{TP} + \text{TN})/(\text{TP} + \text{TN} + \text{FP} + \text{FN}) \qquad (1)$$

where TP denotes True Positive (case prediction of correct positive), TN denotes True Negative (case prediction of correct negative), FP denotes False Positive (case prediction of incorrect positive), and FN is False Negative(case prediction of incorrect negative).

When compared to NLTK method, Stanford NER Tagger method is more accurate [10]. The accuracy between Stanford NER Tagger and NLTK method can be plotted:

4.2 Confusion Matrix

Although the confusion matrix is not a performance indicator in and of itself, its components are critical for algorithm evaluation. It gives a matrix-like output with TP, TN, FP, and FN values, just like the accuracy metric.

Confusion Matrix

	Actually Positive (1)	Actually Negative (0)
Predicted Positive (1)	True Positives (TPs)	False Positives (FPs)
Predicted Negative (0)	False Negatives (FNs)	True Negatives (TNs)

a. Precision

Precision metric is computed by dividing the true positives by the sum of predicated positives, the accurate a classifier out of the predicated positives. Precision is known as the number case predictions of correct positive (True Positive) by the total number of case predictions of correct positive (True Positive) and case predictions of incorrect positive(False Postive). As a result, a high precision value represents that the algorithm produced a relevant result.

$$\text{Precision} = TP/(FP + TP) \tag{2}$$

b. Recall

Recall is known as the number case predictions of correct positive (True Positive) by the total number of case predictions of correct positive (True Positive) and case predictions of incorrect negative(False Negative). This means that when a model predicts a favorable outcome, the precision assures that the objects are classified as such. As a result, a high precision value indicates that the algorithm produced a meaningful result.

$$\text{Recall} = TP/(TP + FN) \tag{3}$$

c. F1 Score

It is computed by using the following formula.

$$\text{F1 Score} = TP/(TP + 1/2(FP + FN)) \tag{4}$$

From the above formulas and discussion we have calculated the precision, recall and f1 value and Accuracy.

Here for result prediction, we use SVM and Naïve Bayes Algorithms. For Naïve Bayes, we use multinomial Naive Bayes, and for SVM, we use SVC linear kernel. Finally, the result of SVM is more accurate compared to the development of Naïve Bayes.

In the end, we test both algorithms by reviewing Twitter to see which is the best performer. The results are shown in Table.

	SVM	Naïve Bayes
Accuracy	96.27	93.69
Precision	98	99
Recall	96	94
F1 Measure	97	96

The above Table shows the comparison of SVM and Naïve Bayes algorithms. The accuracy, precision and recall of SVM are 96.27, 98 and 96 respectively, where as the accuracy, precision and recall of Naïve Bayes are 93.69, 99 and 94 respectively.

The below bar charts displays the accuracy, precision, recall and F1 score of above discussed algorithms.

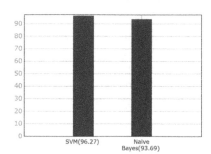

Fig. 3. Comparison of Accuracy on Both Algorithms.

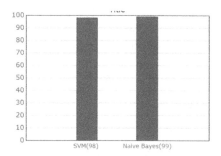

Fig. 4. Comparison of Precision on Both Algorithms

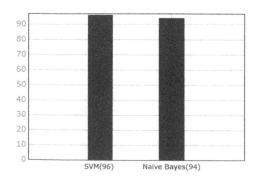

Fig. 5. Comparison of Recall on Both Algorithms.

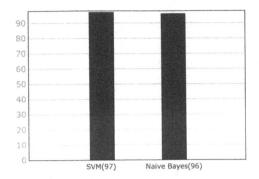

Fig. 6. Comparison of F1 Score on Both Algorithms.

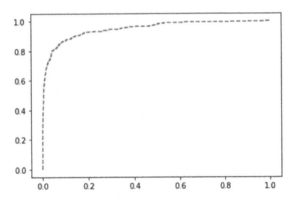

Fig. 7. ROC curve of SVM

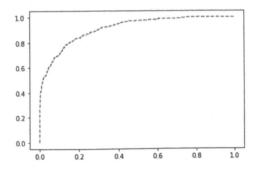

Fig. 8. ROC curve of Naïve Bayes

The area under the Fig. 3 curve is more than the area under the Fig. 4 curve from the above two ROC curves. Figure 3 is discussed about SVM, whereas Fig. 4 is discussed about Naïve Bayes. Finally, SVM is more efficient than Naïve Bayes for sentiment analysis (Figs. 5, 6, 7 and 8).

5 Conclusion

Some Machine Learning Algorithms like Naïve Bayes and SVM algorithms are used in Twitter Sentimental Analysis. Machine Learning techniques are more straightforward and efficient than Symbolic techniques. These two techniques are used in finding the accuracy, F1 measure, Precision, Recall. By comparing the accuracy of both the algorithms, SVM is more accurate than Naïve Bayes. By using the ROC curve, SVM is more efficient when compared to Naïve Bayes.

References

1. Pak, A., Paroubek, P.: Twitter as a corpus for sentiment analysis and opinion mining. Universit´e de Paris-Sud, Laboratoire LIMSI-CNRS, Batiment 508, F-91405 Orsay Cedex, France
2. Sentiment Analysis of Twitter Data by Sahar A. El_Rahman Computer and Information Sciences College Princess Nourah Bint Abdulrahman University R
3. Shelar, A., Huang, C.: Sentiment analysis of twitter data. School of Computer Science, Kean University
4. Karan, R.S.: Sentiment analysis on twitter data: a new approach. Computer Engineering, Viva Institute of Technology, Mumbai, India
5. Windasari, I.P., Uzzi, F.N., Satoto, K.I.: Sentiment analysis on twitter posts: an analysis of positive or negative opinion. Department of Computer Engineering Faculty of Engineering – Diponegoro University Semarang, Indonesia
6. Parveen, H.: Sentiment analysis on twitter dataset using Naive Bayes algorithm. Department of Computer Science and Engineering Rungta College of Engineering and Technology Bhilai, India
7. Çeliktuğ, M.F.: Twitter sentiment analysis, 3-way classification: positive, negative or neutral? Computer Engineering Bilkent University, Gazi University Ankara, Turkey
8. Agarwal, A., Xie, B., Vovsha, I., Rambow, O., Passonneau, R.: Sentiment analysis of Twitter data. In: Workshop on Languages in social media, Portland, Oregon, pp. 30–38 (2011)
9. Mandloi, L.: Twitter sentiments analysis using machine learning methods. Tech Computer Science and Engineering Meidcaps University
10. Dhawan, S.: Sentiment analysis of twitter data in online social network. Department of Computer Science and Engineering University Institute of Engineering and Technology (UIET), Kurukshetra University, Kurukshetra-136119 Kurukshetra, India
11. Wang, H., Can, D., Kazemzadeh, A., Bar, F., Narayanan, S.: A system for real-time Twitter sentiment analysis of 2012 U.S. presidential election cycle. In: ACL 2012 System Demonstrations, Jeju Island, Korea, pp. 115–120 (2012)

12. Neethu, M., Rajasree, R.: Sentiment analysis in Twitter using machine learning techniques. In: 2013 Fourth International Conference on Computing, Communications and Networking Technologies (ICCCNT) (2013)
13. Ibrahim, M.N.M.: Twitter sentiment classification using Naïve Bayes based on trainer perception. College of Information Technology University Tenaga Nasional Putrajaya, Malaysia
14. Analyze real-time Twitter sentiment with HBase. Docs.microsoft.com (2017). https://docs.microsoft.com/enus/azure/hdinsight/hdinsight-hbaseanalyze-twitter-sentiment. Accessed 20 Jan 2018
15. Lak, P., Turetken, O.: Star ratings versus sentiment analysis - a comparison of explicit and implicit measures of opinions. In: 7th Hawaii International Conference on System Science, ParisaLak (2014)
16. Geetha, R., Rekha, P., Karthika, S.: Twitter opinion mining and boosting using sentiment analysis. Department of Information Technology, SSN College of Engineering, Kalavakkam, Chennai
17. Bhat, S., Garg, S., Poornalatha, G.: Assigning sentiment score for twitter tweets. Department of Information and Communication Technology Manipal Institute of Technology, Manipal Academy of Higher Education Manipal, Karnataka
18. Comparison of Naive Bayes Smoothing Methods for Twitter Sentiment Analysis. Faculty of Mathematics and Natural Science Universitas Lambung Mangkurat Banjarbaru, Indonesia
19. Patankar, A.J.: Emotweet: a sentiment analysis tool for Twitter. Computer Sci. and Eng. Visvesvaraya Technological University, Belagavi, Karnataka

Artificial Intelligence in Online Stores' Processes

Grzegorz Chodak and Yash Chawla

Department of Operations Research and Business Intelligence,
Wrocław University of Science and Technology, Wrocław, Poland
{grzegorz.chodak,yash.chawla}@pwr.edu.pl
https://kbo.pwr.edu.pl/en/

Abstract. The global e-commerce market has been growing rapidly, even more so due to the COVID–19 pandemic which caused a number of stationery stores to close down. At the same time, Artificial Intelligence (AI) has also gained prominence. In this article, we review and describe the practical applications of AI which is helping e-commerce businesses. In particular, we have concentrated on AI in some key areas of e-commerces such as online marketing, operations in fulfillment centers, barcode identification, and autonomous delivery methods. The findings and conclusions in this article would be useful for researchers as well as businesses to get an overview of the landscape of AI applications in e-commerces.

Keywords: e-Commerce · Post pandemic era · Artificial intelligence · Online marketing · Logistics

1 Introduction

The development of e-commerce over the last two and a half decades has changed the way of doing trade. In particular, during the pandemic the popularity and turnover of online stores have increased greatly. The share of e-commerce has grown year after year, and the during last two years the Covid-19 pandemic has accelerated this process. The year 2020 was a breakthrough with regard to the increase in the share of e-commerce in total retail trade. In 2019 this increase was less than a percentage point of the total share, while in 2020 it was 4.8%, from 13.5% in 2019 to 18.3% in 2020 [1]. For instance, in Poland alone, during 2020, twelve thousand new on-line shops were registered. In the same year, Polish entrepreneurs suspended the activities of nearly 19 thousand enterprises related to retail sales in walk-in stores, which is over 7 per cent of all brick-and-mortar stores on the market [2]. These statistics show the scale of changes in patterns of trade.

Meanwhile investment in Artificial Intelligence (AI) applications has been growing rapidly as well. It is projected that about 70% of businesses will use AI by 2030 [3]. Combining these two trends, it is very likely that AI will become more and more present in many areas of e-commerce. Some of the positive implications of AI application in e-commerce oriented towards customers are advances in the following: marketing, discovery, automated purchase handling systems,

D. Garg et al. (Eds.): IACC 2021, CCIS 1528, pp. 214–228, 2022.
https://doi.org/10.1007/978-3-030-95502-1_17

automated product recommendation systems, artificial assistants, degree of personalization, effective visual immersiveness, and automated data tracking [4,5]. However, there are also negative implications, such as invasion of privacy, data theft, ethical breaches and the need for regulations on digital trade [4].

It has been emphasized in the literature that further research is required with regard to the application of AI to marketing and business operations [6]. Hence, taking this gap into consideration and concentrating on the e-commerce sector, the main aim of this paper is to present different aspects of e-commerce which are witnessing the application of AI techniques. This is a brief review bringing together various sources to provide an overview of the current use of AI in different dimensions of e-commerce.

The structure of the paper is as follows: After giving a brief introduction in Sect. 1, the application of AI in online marketing, using e.g. Facebook, Amazon and Google, are discussed in Sect. 2. Afterwards, the applications of AI in an e-commerce fulfillment centre are discussed in Sect. 3, the applications of AI in barcode identification are described in Sect. 4, and new AI-driven methods of delivery in e-commerce are discussed in Sect. 5. Finally, in Sect. 6, final remarks and conclusions are made, followed by references.

2   AI in Online Marketing

AI is changing the landscape of marketing rapidly. Using the analogy of the human nervous system, which automatically makes organs such as the heart, lungs and digestive system work, Sterne [7] empahsized that AI is taking marketing along the same path of automation. All forms of online marketing such as one to one, one to many, as well as the four P's, will be affected. Experts, such as Chandra Kumar (CEO - WiselyWise), have highlighted that AI is now ready for mass adoption in marketing for generating content, automating communication, improving relevance, and increasing sales [8]. Additionally, AI can help in identifying appropriate trendsetters and influencers, improve the return on investments, and make better decisions much faster [17]. To achieve harmony in this integration of AI into marketing, data scientists and marketeers need to be able to understand each other well and be able to speak each other's language. This is where potential obstacles, such as: Wear on IT infrastructure, not enough high-quality data, the need for privacy and regulations, users who are not willing to accept AI, budgetary constraints, and most importantly the skills gap, have been observed [17]. Online marketing giants, such as Facebook, Google, and Amazon, as well as others, have engaged in a race to provide solutions to their customers that leverage the power of AI.

Facebook and Google have been at the forefront of global digital advertising. Statistics indicate that these two companies have dominated the online digital marketing arena over the past decade [9]. However, Amazon is now catching up with Facebook and Google rapidly, with the global shift in privacy policies making it difficult to implement previously used advertising practices, for instance due to the Apple privacy update [10]. Additionally, it has been noted that these three companies have excelled in applying AI and have a distinct advantage in this area [11]. Hence, in this publication we concentrate on the these three technological giants and their use of AI to provide better marketing prospects for their customers.

2.1 Facebook Advertising

Facebook has been on the centre stage for e-commerce marketing, as the first to be able to obtain first hand feedback from their customers, as well as raising awareness about their products [16]. In July 2021, it was noted that the audience of Facebook online advertising amounted to 2.25 billion, with an average age of 31 years [12]. From an e-commerce perspective, Facebook is the most important social network for generating business. 85% of the orders through social networks came from Faceboook, on average 4.55 posts per day were published by e-commerce sites on Facebook, over $95 billion dollars were spent on Facebook marketing by e-commerce businesses, the average value of an order by a customer via Facebook was $55 [13]. There are several studies that state the importance of consumer engagement [14] and influencing consumers' intent to purchase [15].

Facebook implemented machine learning technology in its news feed for the first time in 2006 [18]. Since then, they have invested heavily in AI research. Currently, Facebook Artificial Intelligence Researchers (FAIR) lead AI development at Facebook, not only developing the company's products, but also providing open source tools and materials to support developers and researchers [19]. From an advertising point of view, Facebook uses AI and machine learning to decide which advertisments to show to people. This is a herculean task that cannot be carried out manually, due to the massive scale at which these operations are carried out, as illustrated in the above paragraph. The two main criteria used by Facebook to determine which advertisments to show to whom are audience targeting, whose parameters are selected by the advertiser, and the results of the advertisment auction [20]. At any given time, there are multiple advertisers seeking to show advertisments to the same or similar audiences. This is where the Facebook advertisment auction comes in. It takes into consideration the value of the advertiser and the quality of the advertisment, and determines the highest total score. This process is facilitated by machine learning models (MLM), to achieve the highest probability of the result desired by the advertiser, for instance installing an application or visiting a website. MLMs are also used to determine the quality of an advertisment, a factor in the auctioning process. To determine this, MLMs take into account the feedback of people viewing or hiding the advertisment, as well as assessments of other indicators of low quality, such as the presence of too much text in an image, sensationalized language or engagement bait [20].

Facebook also provides a developer platform for businesses to connect more effectively with customers and improve efficiency on Messenger, Facebook itself, Instagram and WhatsApp [21]. This provides an e-commerce business with more flexibility to integrate other tools with Facebook to improve the results of advertising. For instance, e-commerce businesses can provide Facebook with information on the Off-Facebook activities of their customers, and Facebook's AI can integrate that into their campaign [20]. Facebook has open-source tools, such as the recently released Ax and BoTorch applications, to help businesses adopt adaptive experimentation [22]. Using these tools, businesses can incorporate their machine learning tools or A/B testing via Facebook. This helps to improve the quality of advertisments, as well as making marketing campaigns more effective.

Some of the other application of AI on Facebook are: Deep Text, translations, photo image search, talking pictures, Facebook's bot API for Messenger, Caffe2go, automatic image recognition, Suicide Watch, deepfake detection, video detection, hand-on Virtual Reality and so on [23,24].

2.2 Amazon Advertising

In recent years, Amazon has made great strides forward in terms of providing options for advertising to customers, which have led them to rapidly close the gap to the big two, Google and Facebook [10]. Amazon Advertising provides solutions, such as Amazon Demand Side Platform, Amazon Live, Amazon Attributions (beta), Audio Advertisements, Personalized Advertising Solutions, Content sharing/Posts (beta), Sizmek Ad Suite, Brand sponsoring, Promoted Displays, Featured Products or Sponsored Items, Stores, and Video Ads [25]. Amazon also provides web services (Amazon Web Services - AWS) and controls 33% of the marketshare in cloud services, which is far ahead of Microsoft (18%) and Google (9%) [26]. As shown in Fig. 1, Amazon provides its services to major businesses across the world, and is said to quietly power (dominate) the Internet.

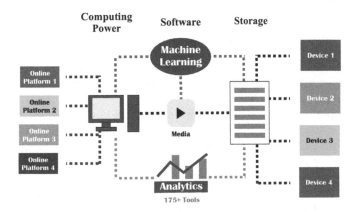

Fig. 1. How Amazon quietly powers the internet. Adapted from source [26]

Since years, Amazon has invested in pioneering machine learning and AI applications to provide advanced business solutions, and continues to do so with AWS AI services. These services include advanced textual analytics, automated system for reviewing code, configurable chatbots, demand forecasting, document analysis, business search, fraud prevention, analysis graphics and video analysis, targeted recommendations, real-time translations, text-to-speech, and transcription [27,28]. Each of these services is vital for e-commerce businesses. Hence, Amazon not only provides an online platform for sellers, but also provides AI services to other e-commerce businesses. In fact, Amazon now enables both businesses who sell via Amazon and those who do not to advertise on its platform.

Amazon's recommender system is one of the best, and has stayed the test of time [29]. It now uses data from customer activities both on and off the Amazon platform to recommend products, as well as present advertisments [25]. Businesses have an option to buy programmatic advertising, an automated system for buying and selling digital advertising, which ensures the optimal and efficient delivery of advertisments to customers. Leveraging the power of AI, Amazon's recent "Amazon Attribution", allows businesses to measure, optimize and plan advertising for non-Amazon marketing (for instance on other social media or search engines).

2.3   Google - Smart Ads

Google Smart Display is an example of the use of AI techniques in online store marketing. This is a solution to manage the complex task of displaying advertisments in online stores (and not only stores). Advertising campaigns using Smart Display combine 3 optimization technologies to help in the process of targeting customers, bidding, and creating advertisments. Using a target CPA (cost per action) as a basis, Smart Display optimizes bids according to the probability of successful conversion in auctions, in order to get the best possible value. Advanced targeting techniques optimize Google Ads campaigns, to make that advertisments are displayed increasingly often where they are expected to get the best results. Smart Display Google campaigns apply dynamic prospecting in order to display Ads to these customers who are most likely to make the conversion. All advertisment boxes are automatically generated using resources provided by the advertisers to fit into, if it is possible, all advertisment spaces across the Google Display Network [30].

Smart Display uses the following automated bidding strategies: target CPA, maximize conversions, and target ROAS (return on advertising spending), that focus on conversions. After a learning period of time, a Google campaign begins optimizing either after generating 50 conversions or in 2 weeks. Smart Display campaigns combine two different targeting techniques: remarketing to these people who visited a webpage as well as automatic targeting, that tries catch customers much earlier in the buying process [30].

Dynamic prospecting technique is the method to enhance the strength of feed-based dynamic remarketing method to reach some new customers. Unlike classical dynamic remarketing, that focuses on obtaining the greatest income/value from current customers, dynamic prospecting is applied to get new customers. Dynamic prospecting technique applies machine learning to make a prediction which feed items prospective buyers are interested in. Applying user behavior as well as historical feed performance, dynamic prospecting prepares predictions which new customers are most probably going to order products. If the system discovers relationships which are statistically significant between user's intentions and feed items, it links these intentions with demographic-based data, such as gender and age, to match the customer's intent with appropriate products. These products are then evaluated and selected considering the performance, relevance as well as other factors to set which products are most probably to be ordered [30]

3   AI in an e-Commerce Fulfillment Center

A fulfillment center in e-commerce is a type of warehouse where orders from online stores or platforms are received, processed, and fulfilled. Warehouse management is a very important component of logistics and supply chain management, due to its high influence on overall time and labor costs [31]. The problems which are most important in area of warehouse management concern: space constraints, workforce shortages (especially in developed countries), poor layouts, as well as outdated information systems (ISs) [32] as well as inappropriate levels of stock (inventory errors), problems due to expired goods or goods with a short expiry date and problems with the identification of stock keeping units (SKUs). Such problems are even more important in e-commerce fulfillment centers, which have to process a large number of, often, small packages and a large assortment and number of SKUs, while facing quick delivery schedules, such as next-day or even same-day delivery, and also highly volatile demand due to seasonal demand, Black Friday promotions, etc. Many AI-driven solutions are being developed to address these problems, including autonomous mobile robots (AMRs), assisted picking, shelf-moving robots, mixed-shelf storage, [33] as well as automated storage and retrieval systems.

Artificial Intelligence techniques and methods has the great potential to change manual tasks as well as processes in which people are limited by their physical abilities [34]. Autonomous mobile robots (AMRs) are an AI-driven successor of automated guided vehicles (AGVs). In e-commerce warehouses, AMRs collaborate with operators in order picking. There are various methods of using AMRs in warehouses. For example, an AMR can transport a number of containers from picking areas and leave them at a location where the operator can collect them. Next, the AMR moves independently to the next location. When all of the items in a specific order were collected, the autonomous mobile robot travels directly to the packing and consolidation area. There AMR is emptied and then reassigned to the next orders [35]. This method of picking enables a zone-picking strategy which improves the picking and traveling efficiency of operators and AMRs [36].

The main AI application for storing inventoried goods is an Automated Storage and Retrieval System (AS/RS). Such systems are composed from the following elements: (I) storage, retrieval, and transportation devices, (II) a rack system, (III) a control system [38]. Introducing such solutions in a warehouse saves inventory space and reduces the need for labor. AI applications in the Alibaba warehouse have helped to reduce manpower by more than 70% and also increased the accuracy of order picking [39]. AI can also be used to predict sales trends to aid storage planning and replenishment management [31]. Software based on AI methods like genetic algorithms can be used in forecasting demand for online products [40] which enables the optimization of inventory.

4   AI in Barcode Identification

One of the important achievements of artificial intelligence (AI) is the development of image processing techniques (IPTs), in which mathematical operations are applied to input images to produce output that is exported as enriched matrices and specially defined images [41, 42].

There are many areas in which AI applications can be used for image recognition and processing, such as healthcare (diagnosis, patient care, medical imaging), industrial (operation control, quality control), biometric (authentication, financial security), navigation (auto-driving, tracking, sign board assistance), sports (broadcast/reply, player location, game analysis), agriculture and environmental protection (weather forecasting, plant growth) [43]. Here, we concentrate on AI applications in barcode detection, which is a very important component of trade processes, especially in e-commerce. There are many different techniques that can be used in image recognition and classification. In the following paragraphs, some examples of techniques and methods in image recognition and processing will be presented.

Image processing as well as a fuzzy K-means clustering algorithm can be used on raw optical images in order to uncover the features of exclusive classes of given objects. Next the backpropagation algorithm (BPA) can be applied in classification process [44]. Binary features may be used in different ways to encode the content of images. Tizhoosh et al. [45] proposed "radon barcodes" that apply binarized radon projections in order to tag selected medical images with content-based binary vectors, which are named barcodes. Neural networks (NNs) are used very often for image recognition and classification processes. However, we should mention that there are many different varieties of NNs that adopt various topologies and learning algorithms [46].

Application of AI in barcode identification results from the characteristics of the codes and scanning processes. Unlike traditional camera-based image reading, the distance between the laser barcode reader (sensor) and the target object (e.g. product) is usually close to zero when the reader is applied. This is inconvenient for automating inspection, because the operator has to manipulate either the sensor or the objects being scanned. For the purpose of automating in-store inspection, the operator should be excluded from this process. Because of the effects of lens distortion as well as a noise, the barcode image sometimes, more or less, differs from the ideal one. Nevertheless if only the deviation is not significant, the system which recognizes the barcode is supposed to be able to correctly recognize it [47].

Youssef & Salem [47], proposed a smart barcode detection and recognition system based on a fast hierarchical Hough transform [48]. A backpropagation neural network was selected as a tool to perform the recognition process. Such an approach is common and not new in the literature, e.g. Liao et al. [49] proposed a camera-based bar-code recognition system using backpropagation neural networks.

Wang et al. [50] used a combination of decision trees and the AdaBoost algorithm as a method for barcode image recognition. Combining characteristics of a barcode image, a 5-dimensional method of feature extraction is applied to define the barcode image. Results indicate that this method can properly identify a barcode from any angle or distance within the line of sight and can also effectively identify dirty barcodes [50].

Zamberletti et al. [51] proposed an angle invariant method, based on the properties of the Hough Transform, for barcode detection using camera captured images. An advanced machine learning model, which is calibrated using supervised training, first detects the rotation angle of a barcode in real images using Hough transforms and then identifies the boxes surrounding the barcode [51].

In the near future, rapid development of methods improving barcode identification based on AI techniques can be expected, especially methods designed for mobile devices, not only for mobile scanners and data collectors, but also for standard smartphones, which are more commonly used in small and medium-sized companies in e-commerce logistic processes.

5 New AI-Driven Delivery Methods in E-Commerce

In this section we present three innovative methods of delivery which have already been implemented in e-commerce, but are still undergoing development. In the future, we expect that autonomous delivery robots, AI-driven drones and 3D printing will become commonly used methods of delivery in online stores.

5.1 Autonomous Delivery Robots

Other forms of delivery that are still being tested are drone or robot delivery, e.g. Amazon Scout (AS) [52]. Deliveries by drones are still subject to some legal difficulties. Hence, it is difficult to expect dissemination of goods by this mode of transport in the near future, despite the fact that the currently available technology enables implementation of this type of delivery. AS robots seem to have a better chance of becoming widespread than drones in the next decade. Amazon is one of the pioneers in developing innovative methods of delivery and is continually investing in new technologies to improve it. One recent invention is the fully electric delivery system, Amazon Scout, which is an Autonomous Delivery Robot (ADR) - designed to deliver packages to customers (Fig. 1). These robots, created by Amazon, are the size of a small cooler, and roll along sidewalks at walking pace. The devices autonomously follow their delivery route. Amazon

Scout was developed at a research and development laboratory in Seattle. It can navigate around different objects, pedestrians as well as anything what can be met in usual route in the city [52].

The purpose of designing Amazon Scout is close to autonomous cars, however with the important dissimilarity that AS generally travels at a slow pace on sidewalks. Thanks to lower speed, AS can more easily identify its environment. On the other hand, the task of moving on sidewalks is more complicated, because sidewalks are used in different ways leading to a different obstacles, from garden tools and street lamps, to street benches and many other predictable and unpredictable objects. What enables such walking robots possible nowadays is huge progress in computer vision, including object recognition and machine learning, which has been achieved in the last decade. To train a robot, simulations including digital scenery are applied. For example, engineers can add leaves to a sidewalk, thus AS can learn that an environment can change. In some cases, the AS developers use real photos in order to train robot, with human-advisors who outline and identify important features to improve the robot's decisions. Such slow, but precise, training combined with digital simulations, can give precise view of the environment to an AS [53].

Another example of an autonomous delivery robot is Yandex.Rover, tested on the Yandex campus in Moscow, which can transport small packages. While moving, the robot recognizes and safely navigates around pedestrians, pets, and any other obstacles [56].

5.2   Deliveries by Aerial Drones

One of most innovative delivery systems using AI is Prime Air from Amazon designed to get packages to customers within 30 min using autonomous aerial vehicles (drones). Prime Air has the potential to provide rapid parcel delivery that will increase the efficiency of the transportation system [54]. Such innovation would not be possible without computer vision, which is a very important component of AI-based drones. Such advanced technology allows drones to identify different objects during flyight and enables the analysis, as well as recording the image of the surroundings. Onboard image processing use a neural network, which enables drones to detect, classify, and track objects. Such data are combined in real time to help drones to avoid the collision and locate and track targets. Other very important elements for AI-based drones are environmental data and sensors, which are used to collect the data that are processed by drones for positioning. These data are used as input to machine learning models, determining how a drone should operate in the current environmental conditions, what objects it should avoid, and where it should fly to [55].

Another innovative solution in the area of deliveries by drone is being developed in collaboration by UPS (an American logistics leader) and a German drone maker, Wingcopter. This cooperation could greatly expand the use of drones for delivering products, because these drones can fly autonomously at up to 240 km/h, have a range of 120 km and can stay on course in winds up to 70 km/h. These electric drones can take off and land vertically taking advantage of a advanced tilt-rotor mechanism. This innovative mechanism allows drones to make a smooth transition between multi-copter mode, which enables hovering, and fixed-wing mode which is used for forward-flight. Intelligent flying mode change enables drones to move steadily [57].

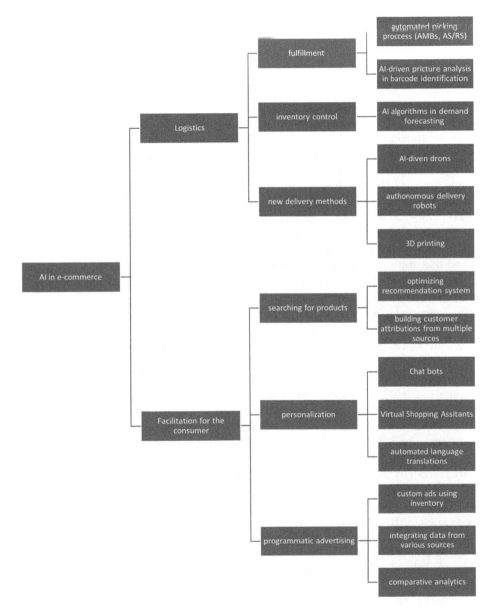

Fig. 2. Schematic diagram of AI application in e-commerce. Source: authors' own elaboration

5.3   Deliveries Using 3D Printing

The vast majority of types of product available in e-commerce are shipped in physical form. In the nearest future, the development of 3D printers will make it possible to send more and more products online in digital form to be then printed by the customer. At present, this option applies mainly to products with a rather monolithic structure made of plastic or metal. Industries such as fashion, jewelry, and toys may be greatly impacted by 3D printing technology [58]. AI can expand the opportunities for 3D printing and optimize this process, including time and the amount of materials used [59].

6   Conclusions and Discussion

Artificial intelligence is becoming more and more popular in various areas of e-commerce. In this paper, we have analysed selected solutions that use AI methods to improve the level of customer service and profitability of e-commerce platforms. Some of these solutions are still in the early stages of development and are not yet widespread in the market, others are often used by companies. The future will show which of them will stand the test of time. However, we can say for sure that AI will be increasingly used in various areas of online stores and other e-commerce platforms. While there are a number of publications found in the literature regarding the technical applications of AI, there is a void with regard to studies that compile practical applications of AI for businesses in general and for e-commerce in particular. Using the existing literature and various online sources, in this paper we have described practical applications of AI in e-commerce. Based on these observations, we have created a schematic diagram, shown in Fig. 2, that illustrates how AI is changing the landscape of business and has been integrated into various sectors of e-commerce.

In terms of Logistics for e-commerce, AI has been extensively used to for automating delivery methods, making inventory management more efficient, and managing the orders at the fulfillments centres. On the other hand AI applications in facilitation of the consumer mainly dealt with personalizing the shopping experience through chatbots or virtual assistants, optimizing the product search and display, and targetted advertising.

It is evident that there are currently only a few major players, such as Amazon, Google, Facebook, and Microsoft, who dominate the global AI market, worth $93.53 billion USD, which is forecasted to grow exponentially in the coming years [60]. In the past couple of years, the COVID-19 pandemic has caused a surge in e-commerce transactions, and AI has proved to be an efficient and effective means by which the upscaling of e-commerce has become possible. It is forecasted that in the coming years new players will enter the global AI market, which would then become more competitive, affordable and accessible. Already, companies such as Amazon are providing AI solutions through their AWS, which does not require sellers to have any technical knowledge. Such services do not just enable use on the platform owned by the parent company, but also on other platforms. Experts and researchers believe that AI will substantially impact retailing, especially e-commerce in the future, as its impact is already being felt [61]. However, they also suggest that, even though substantial impact is expected, it might not be as pronounced as the popular media are suggesting. It is thought that adoption of AI will depend on a number of factors, such as the extent to which AI applications can become customer-orientated, its contribution in value creation, technical expertise, IT infrastructure and ethical concerns, as well as environmental concerns. One thing is sure, as we move towards Industry 5.0, AI will be a driving force towards changing business practices, as well as the purchasing behaviour of customers.

Acknowledgements. This work was partially supported by the National Science Centre (NCN) in Poland under grant number: 2018/29/B/HS4/02857 (Logistics, Trade and Consumer Decisions in the Age of the Internet). We would like to express our gratitude to Prof. David Ramsey (Associate Professor, Wrocław University of Science and Technology, Poland) for his kind support in language proofing and editing.

References

1. Total retail sales worldwide from 2018 to 2022 - Statista. Accessed 10 Sept 2021
2. Bisnode & Bradstreet Report. https://www.bisnode.pl/wiedza/newsy-artykuly/ecommerce-szansa-na-przetrwanie/. Accessed 14 Apr 2021
3. Bughin, J., Seong, J., Manyika, J., Chui, M., Joshi, R.: Modeling the global economic impact of AI. McKinsey Global Institute. https://www.mckinsey.com/featured-insights/artificial-intelligence/notes-from-the-ai-frontier-modeling-the-impact-of-ai-on-the-world-economy. Accessed 19 Sept 2021
4. Singh, R.: A study of artificial intelligence and e-commerce ecosystem-a customer's perspective. Int. J. Res. Eng. Sci. Manag. 4(2), 78–87 (2021)
5. Kalia, P.: Artificial intelligence in e-commerce: a business process analysis. In: Artificial Intelligence, pp. 9–19. CRC Press, Boca Raton (2021)
6. Davenport, T., Guha, A., Grewal, D., Bressgott, T.: How artificial intelligence will change the future of marketing. J. Acad. Mark. Sci. 48(1), 24–42 (2019). https://doi.org/10.1007/s11747-019-00696-0
7. Sterne, J.: Artificial Intelligence for Marketing: Practical Applications. Wiley, Hoboken (2017)
8. How AI marketing can help brands right now. http://ai4marketing.com/2018/02/02/ai-marketing-can-help-brands-right-now/. Accessed 19 Sept 2021
9. Selected online companies ranked by total digital advertising revenue from 2012 to 2020. https://www.statista.com/statistics/205352/digital-advertising-revenue-of-leading-online-companies/. Accessed 19 Sept 2021
10. Amazon lures advertisers from Facebook after Apple privacy shift. https://www.bloomberg.com/news/articles/2021-08-09/amazon-lures-advertisers-from-facebook-after-apple-privacy-shift. Accessed 19 Sept 2021
11. The AI advantage of the tech giants: Amazon, Facebook, and Google. https://emerj.com/ai-executive-guides/ai-advantage-tech-giants-amazon-facebook-google/. Accessed 19 Sept 2021
12. Facebook stats and trends. https://datareportal.com/essential-facebook-stats. Accessed 19 Sept 2021
13. Useful eCommerce statistics you must know in 2021. https://wpforms.com/ecommerce-statistics/. Accessed 19 Sept 2021

14. Harris, L., Dennis, C.: Engaging customers on Facebook: challenges for e-retailers. J. Consum. Behav. **10**(6), 338–346 (2011)
15. Bhattacharyya, S., Bose, I.: S-commerce: influence of Facebook likes on purchases and recommendations on a linked e-commerce site. Decis. Support Syst. **138**, 113383 (2020)
16. Evolving e-commerce market dynamics. https://www.capgemini.com/wp-content/uploads/2017/07/evolving_e-commerce_market_dynamics.pdf. Accessed 15 Sept 2021
17. AI in advertising: everything you need to know. https://www.ibm.com/watson-advertising/thought-leadership/ai-in-advertising. Accessed 19 Sept 2021
18. Inside Facebook's biggest artificial intelligence project ever. https://fortune.com/longform/facebook-machine-learning/. Accessed 18 Sept 2021
19. Facebook AI research. https://ai.facebook.com/research/. Accessed 18 Sept 2021
20. Good questions, real answers: how does Facebook use machine learning to deliver ads? https://www.facebook.com/business/news/good-questions-real-answers-how-does-facebook-use-machine-learning-to-deliver-ads. Accessed 18 Sept 2021
21. Build with Facebook. https://developers.facebook.com/. Accessed 19 Sept 2021
22. Open-sourcing Ax and BoTorch: new AI tools for adaptive experimentation. https://ai.facebook.com/blog/open-sourcing-ax-and-botorch-new-ai-tools-for-adaptive-experimentation/. Accessed 19 Sept 2021
23. AI applications @ Facebook [2021 update]. https://research.aimultiple.com/introducing-facebook-ai-no-magic-just-code/. Accessed 19 Sept 2021
24. Revealing secrets - how Facebook is using artificial intelligence. https://itchronicles.com/artificial-intelligence/7-revealing-secrets-how-facebook-is-using-artificial-intelligence/. Accessed 19 Sept 2021
25. Amazon advertising. https://advertising.amazon.com/. Accessed 22 Sept 2021
26. How Amazon quietly powers the internet. https://www.forbes.com/sites/danrunkevicius/2020/09/03/how-amazon-quietly-powers-the-internet/. Accessed 22 Sept 2021
27. The twenty year history of AI at Amazon. https://www.forbes.com/sites/cognitiveworld/2019/07/19/the-twenty-year-history-of-ai-at-amazon/. Accessed 22 Sept 2021
28. Explore AWS AI services. https://aws.amazon.com/machine-learning/ai-services/. Accessed 22 Sept 2021
29. Smith, B., Linden, G.: Two decades of recommender systems at Amazon.com. IEEE Internet Comput. **21**(3), 12–18 (2017)
30. Google ads help - about smart display campaign. https://support.google.com/google-ads/answer/7020281. Accessed 15 Sept 2021
31. Mahroof, K.: A human-centric perspective exploring the readiness towards smart warehousing: the case of a large retail distribution warehouse. Int. J. Inf. Manage. **45**, 176–190 (2019)
32. Faber, N., de Koster, M.B.M., Smidts, A.: Organizing warehouse management. Int. J. Oper. Prod. Manag. **33**(9), 1230–1256 (2013)
33. Boysen, N., De Koster, R., Weidinger, F.: Warehousing in the e-commerce era: a survey. Eur. J. Oper. Res. **277**(2), 396–411 (2019)
34. Dwivedi, Y.K., et al.: Artificial Intelligence (AI): multidisciplinary perspectives on emerging challenges, opportunities, and agenda for research, practice and policy. Int. J. Inf. Manage. **57**, 101994 (2019)
35. Azadeh, K., De Koster, R., Roy, D.: Robotized and automated warehouse systems: review and recent developments. Transp. Sci. **53**(4), 917–945 (2019)

36. Fragapane, G., de Koster, R., Sgarbossa, F., Strandhagen, J.O.: Planning and control of autonomous mobile robots for intralogistics: literature review and research agenda. Eur. J. Oper. Res. **294**(2), 405–426 (2021)
37. Honeywell and Fetch Robotics deliver autonomous mobile robots to DCs. https://www.robotics247.com/article/honeywell_partners_with_fetch_robotics_to_deliver_autonomous_mobile_robots. Accessed 16 Sept 2021
38. Hu, K.Y., Chang, T.S.: An innovative automated storage and retrieval system for B2C e-commerce logistics. Int. J. Adv. Manuf. Technol. **48**(1–4), 297–305 (2010)
39. Zhang, D., Pee, L.G., Cui, L.: Artificial intelligence in e-commerce fulfillment: a case study of resource orchestration at Alibaba's Smart Warehouse. Int. J. Inf. Manage. **57**, 102304 (2021)
40. Chodak, G.: Genetic algorithms in forecasting of internet shops demand. In: Świątek, J., Borzemski, L., Grzech, A., Wilimowska, Z. (eds.) Information Systems Architecture and Technology: System Analysis in Decision Aided Problems, pp. 59–68. Publishing House of the Wrocław University of Science and Technology, Wrocław (2009)
41. Azarafza, M., Ghazifard, A., Akgün, H., Asghari-Kaljahi, E.: Development of a 2D and 3D computational algorithm for discontinuity structural geometry identification by artificial intelligence based on image processing techniques. Bull. Eng. Geol. Env. **78**(5), 3371–3383 (2018). https://doi.org/10.1007/s10064-018-1298-2
42. Cao, F.: Geometric Curve Evolution and Image Processing. Springer, Heidelberg (2003). https://doi.org/10.1007/b10404
43. Shakya, S.: Analysis of artificial intelligence based image classification techniques. J. Innov. Image Process. (JIIP) **2**(01), 44–54 (2020)
44. Acharya, R.U., Yu, W., Zhu, K., Nayak, J., Lim, T.C., Chan, J.Y.: Identification of cataract and post-cataract surgery optical images using artificial intelligence techniques. J. Med. Syst. **34**(4), 619–628 (2010)
45. Tizhoosh, H.R., Zhu, S., Lo, H., Chaudhari, V., Mehdi, T.: MinMax radon barcodes for medical image retrieval. In: Bebis, G., et al. (eds.) ISVC 2016. LNCS, vol. 10072, pp. 617–627. Springer, Cham (2016). https://doi.org/10.1007/978-3-319-50835-1_55
46. da Silva, I.N., Hernane Spatti, D., Andrade Flauzino, R., Liboni, L.H.B., dos Reis Alves, S.F.: Artificial neural network architectures and training processes. In: Artificial Neural Networks, pp. 21–28. Springer, Cham (2017). https://doi.org/10.1007/978-3-319-43162-8_2
47. Youssef, S.M., Salem, R.M.: Automated barcode recognition for smart identification and inspection automation. Expert Syst. Appl. **33**(4), 968–977 (2007)
48. Yu, B., Jain, A.K.: A robust and fast skew detection algorithm for generic documents. Pattern Recogn. **29**(10), 1599–1629 (1996)
49. Liao, H.Y., Liu, S.J., Chen, L.H., Tyan, H.R.: A bar-code recognition system using backpropagation neural networks. Eng. Appl. Artif. Intell. **8**(1), 81–90 (1995)
50. Wang, L., Hou, Y., Li, L.: Barcode recognition based on improved AdaBoost algorithm. J. Liaoning Tech. Univ. (Nat. Sci.) **2** (2013)
51. Zamberletti, A., Gallo, I., Albertini, S.: Robust angle invariant 1D barcode detection. In: 2013 2nd IAPR Asian Conference on Pattern Recognition (ACPR), Okinawa, Japan, pp. 160–164. IEEE (2013)
52. Meet Scout, Amazon. https://www.aboutamazon.com/news/transportation/meet-scout. Accessed 10 Sept 2021
53. How Amazon scientists are helping the Scout delivery device find a path to success. https://www.amazon.science/latest-news/how-amazon-scientists-are-helping-the-scout-delivery-device-find-a-path-to-success. Accessed 10 Sept 2021

54. Amazon prime air. https://www.amazon.com/Amazon-Prime-Air/b?ie=UTF8& node=8037720011. Accessed 10 Sept 2021

55. How do AI-based drones work? https://heartbeat.fritz.ai/how-ai-based-drones-work-a94f20e62695. Accessed 10 Sept 2021

56. Introducing Yandex.Rover, our autonomous delivery robot. https://medium.com/yandex-self-driving-car/introducing-yandex-rover-our-autonomous-delivery-robot-5c6f03796c3f. Accessed 20 Sept 2021

57. Partnership develops vertical takeoff and landing delivery drones. https://www.springwise.com/innovation/mobility-transport/delivery-drone-wingcopter-ups. Accessed 20 Sept 2021

58. Turban, E., Outland, J., King, D., Lee, J.K., Liang, T.-P., Turban, D.C.: Order fulfillment along the supply chain in e-commerce. In: Electronic Commerce 2018. STBE, pp. 501–534. Springer, Cham (2018). https://doi.org/10.1007/978-3-319-58715-8_13

59. Why combine artificial intelligence and 3D printing? https://www.3dnatives.com/en/artificial-intelligence-and-3d-printing-060120204/. Accessed 20 Sept 2021

60. Artificial intelligence market size, share & trends analysis report by solution, by technology (deep learning, machine learning, natural language processing, machine vision), by end use, by region, and segment forecasts, 2021–2028. https://www.grandviewresearch.com/industry-analysis/artificial-intelligence-ai-market. Accessed 22 Sept 2021

61. Guha, A., et al.: How artificial intelligence will affect the future of retailing. J. Retail. **97**(1), 28–41 (2021)

Early Warning Indicators for Financial Crisis During Covid-19

Aakash Jignesh Modi[1], G. Jyothish Lal[1(✉)], E. A. Gopalakrishnan[1],
V. Sowmya[1], K. P. Soman[1], and R. Vinayakumar[2]

[1] Center for Computational Engineering and Networking (CEN), Amrita School
of Engineering, Amrita Vishwa Vidyapeetham, Coimbatore, India
g_jyothishlal@cb.amrita.edu
[2] Center for Artificial Intelligence, Prince Mohammad Bin Fahd University,
Khobar, Saudi Arabia

Abstract. The impact of covid-19 on the financial market is considered a 'black swan event', i.e., the occurrence of a highly unpredictable event with far-reaching consequences. Prediction of such events in prior is essential due to the financial risk associated. In this paper, we study critical slowing down as an early warning signal to forewarn such unpredictable and sudden transitions concerning the Indian stock market for the covid-19 period. This is the first study to predict covid-19 financial crisis based on critical slowing down theory. We analyze the evolution of first-order autocorrelation and standard deviation using the sliding window approach to predict any impending transition. We found that both the early warning measures could forewarn an impending transition for almost all the stock indices considered for the analysis.

Keywords: Financial market · Early Warning Signal (EWS) · Critical transition · Critical slowing down · Complex systems

1 Introduction

Financial markets are subject to sudden changes due to external events, which can be local like a disaster [23,36] (earthquake, volcanic eruption, acts of terrorism, etc.) or changes in the geopolitical stage [9] that are confined to a region or can be global like worldwide recession [2,30] or world war. These unforeseen events can result in the regime shift of the stock market or a change of stock market behaviour to be bearish or bullish. The covid-19 pandemic financial crisis is the first of its kind unique event in terms of its global scope and sheer scale of economic disruption in the history of the market crisis. This makes the study of the financial market in context to the covid-19 pandemic important.

A stock market collapse is a rapid and often unforeseen drop in stock prices. Figure 1 shows the change in the closing price index for different Nifty stock indices during the covid-19 financial crisis in India. Nifty 50 index observed a 52 week low on 23 March, 2020 [11], as it dipped by 35% since the onset of the

© Springer Nature Switzerland AG 2022
D. Garg et al. (Eds.): IACC 2021, CCIS 1528, pp. 229–243, 2022.
https://doi.org/10.1007/978-3-030-95502-1_18

pandemic in India (30 January, 2020 [15]). As seen in Fig. 1, the worst affected sectoral indices are banking, realty, media, automobile, financial services, metal, oil and gas, information technology, and consumer durables. The least affected indices were healthcare, pharmaceutical and FMCG[1].

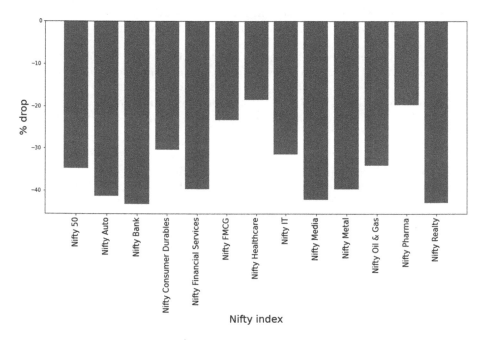

Fig. 1. Percentage change in the closing price for different Nifty indices between 30 January, 2020 (first confirmed case of covid-19 in India) and 23 March, 2020 (lowest point to which Nifty plummeted).

Prediction of the stock market collapse in prior will help curtail risk associated with such events in the future. Several methods for prediction and analysis of stock market behaviour using historical stock data based on linear models [1, 10, 29] (AR[2], MA[3], ARIMA[4] and its variations) and non-linear models [16, 18, 22, 33] (TAR[5], ARCH[6] and its variations, deep learning algorithms) for different timeline respect to a particular region have been employed in recent times. Jiang *et al.* [19] employed a log-periodic power model (LPPL) to analyze and anticipate two Chinese stock market financial bubbles and subsequent market crashes between May 2005 and July 2009. Selvin S. *et al.* [33] used the

---

[1] Fast Moving Consumer Goods.
[2] Auto-Regression model.
[3] Moving Average model.
[4] Auto-Regressive Integrated Moving Average model.
[5] Threshold Auto-Regressive model.
[6] Auto-Regressive Conditionally Heteroscedastic model.

moving window approach for predicting future stock price values on a short time basis using RNN[7], LSTM[8] and CNN[9] for NSE[10] listed companies. Of the three models used for analysis, CNN gave the best results.

One of the appealing frameworks widely used in ecology or physics is to consider that systems are complex, which is the case in financial markets due to a lot of dynamics involved. Due to the stock market's unpredictable and dynamic behaviour, an analogy can be drawn between the financial market and critical slowing down theory. In their pioneering study, Scheffer et al. [31] proposed a plethora of indicators based on critical slowing down theory to forewarn the onset of asthmatic attacks and epileptic seizures, imminent shifts in ecosystems, and the collapse of financial markets. Following that, these early warning measures are widely used to predict critical transitions in ecological models [4,6], palaeoclimate records [24,26], medicinal [34], biological systems [5,28], chemical [20], and structural behaviour [25]. A financial market is a complex dynamic system that, when subject to small external perturbations, local or global events can result in an abrupt change in its landscape, depicting a critical transition from a normal state to a crisis state. Change of state occurs when the considered system, the financial market, reaches a critical point known as the tipping point [6,7]. The convergence of the system towards the tipping point results in its inability to absorb any external shocks [21], and hence, its ability to recover from such perturbation slows down, similar to the fold catastrophe model by Scheffer et al. [31], which have similar dynamics as financial markets. This slowing down reduces the potential of a system to recover, exhibiting a recovery rate of zero and a rise in recovery time [35]. In addition, the dynamic system shows a decreasing resilience [5], resulting in loss of efficiency and can trigger critical transition due to accumulation of small perturbations [4,31]. Such a phenomenon is called critical slowing down [31,35,37].

Under the slowing down phenomenon, the pattern of fluctuations undergoes modifications characterized by auto-correlation, standard deviation, skewness and kurtosis indicators. Such indicators act as a warning measure for a system approaching a tipping point [3,4,7,8,13]. They can be considered critical slowing down indicators or, more precisely, early warning signals that can detect in prior significant future transition in the dynamical system [32] or forthcoming downward shifts in the financial market or financial crisis.

This paper analyses different critical slowing down indicators (auto-correlation and standard deviation) in context with the financial crisis due to the covid-19 pandemic for the Nifty 50 index and other Nifty sectoral indices. The remaining part of the paper is organized as follows. Section 2 describes the proposed methodology for finding the critical transition in the financial time series. Section 3 provides a detailed description and illustration of EWS for time series from different sectors. Finally, Sect. 4 concludes the paper with future directions.

---

[7] Recurrent Neural Network.
[8] Long Short Term Memory.
[9] Convolutional Neural Network.
[10] National Stock Exchange.

2   Methodology

The study is based on the metric-based methods suggested by Dakos *et al.* [6] to compute Early Warning Signal (EWS) indicators for impending transition in stock market data. Figure 2 describes the proposed methodology used to identify critical transitions in the stock market. The approach requires a univariate time series with a clear critical transition from normal to a depressed state or vice versa. Therefore, closing index data of Nifty 50 and other Nifty sectoral indices (Nifty Auto, Nifty Bank, Nifty Financial Services, Nifty Healthcare, Nifty Pharma, Nifty FMCG, Nifty Consumer Durables, Nifty IT, Nifty Media, Nifty Metal, Nifty Oil & Gas and Nifty Realty) are collected for the covid-19 financial crisis period from the official website of NSE *(https://www1.nseindia.com/)*.

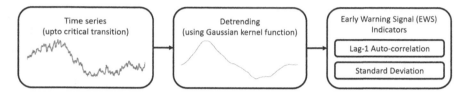

Fig. 2. Proposed methodology to identify critical transition (financial crisis) in stock index time series data.

To compute leading indicators, we first selected the part of the time series of each index that preceded the probable market transition. All stock index time series are considered from 01 October, 2019 to 23 March, 2020, the lowest point after the emergence of covid-19 in India [11]. Critical points for each sectoral time series are the points after which the fall of the stock index was observed before the lowest point (23 March, 2020). The summary of critical points considered for each time series is shown in Table 1. We ensured that for all the time series under consideration, there were no missing values or only trading days are considered for analysis. The time series under consideration are regular, i.e., closing index data are equally spaced in time, $\Delta t = 1$ trading day. Regular time series is an essential factor for computing auto-correlation indicators because it estimates memory in time series. The sample data size (T) considered for analysis is shown in Table 1 with a rolling window of length $n = 0.5T$. The time series is then detrended using the Gaussian kernel function, and leading indicators are computed to identify critical transition.

2.1   Detrending

Detrending of time series involves removing effects of the trend from a dataset to show only the differences in the value from the trend known as residuals, to identify underlying cyclical and other patterns associated with the time series. For financial market data, detrending helps to achieve stationarity in the mean

Table 1. Summary of critical dates and sample size for each index upto which time series is considered for analysis.

Index	Critical point	Sample size (T)
Nifty 50	20 February, 2020	98
Nifty Auto	20 February, 2020	98
Nifty Bank	20 February, 2020	98
Nifty Financial Services	20 February, 2020	98
Nifty Healthcare	5 March, 2020	108
Nifty Pharma	5 March, 2020	108
Nifty FMCG	19 February, 2020	97
Nifty Consumer Durables	19 February, 2020	97
Nifty Metal	20 February, 2020	98
Nifty Oil & Gas	19 February, 2020	97
Nifty IT	19 February, 2020	97
Nifty Media	19 February, 2020	97
Nifty Realty	7 February, 2020	89

of financial time series to identify any cyclical price fluctuation in the stock index, which can help to time position entry and exit. Detrending of time series is done using moving average method. In our study, to remove trends in each stock indices, we detrend all the time series by smoothing across time using the Gaussian kernel function given as

$$K(y) = \frac{1}{\sigma\sqrt{2\pi}} e^{-(y)^2/2\sigma^2} \tag{1}$$

and the moving average as

$$MA_j = \frac{\sum_{i=j-T}^{j-1} K(i) y_j - i}{\sum_{i=j-T}^{j-1} K(i)} \tag{2}$$

where y is the original time series with time-step, $\Delta t = 1$ and σ is the bandwidth. Only the time series before the critical point is considered for the smoothing step. The residual time series is given by

$$z_j = y_j - MA_j \tag{3}$$

The choice of bandwidth σ is an important parameter, as it involves a bias-variance trade-off. The bandwidth is chosen to capture slower trends from the time series while retaining the details of the fluctuations around the local equilibrium value [12]. This paper considers a bandwidth σ of 5 trading days for all sectoral index time series.

2.2   Early Warning Signal (EWS) Indicators

Early warning statistical metric-based measures like return rate, auto-correlation, standard deviation, skewness, and kurtosis are well established and used in various applications to prevent impending transition. Auto-correlation and standard deviation is able to predict the stock market crash due to covid-19 effectively and will be discussed in the results and discussion section. We have also explored return rate, skewness and kurtosis measures for our analysis and the results of these measures are mentioned in the appendix. "Early Warning Signal Toolbox" (http://www.early-warning-signals.org/) is used for our analysis. All the parameters are calculated based on a rolling window of length $0.5T$. Mann-Kendall test [27] is used to calculate the temporal trend value of all measures. The trend value is the concurrent increase or decrease in the values of a parameter, measured in Kendal-τ.

3   Results and Discussion

We compute Early Warning Signal (EWS) indicators for identification of transition of market closing index (CI) time series for Nifty 50 and different sectors due to covid-19 pandemic using metric-based methods suggested by Dakos *et al.* [6]. The following measures are considered in this study to measure critical slowing down: lag-1 autocorrelation (AC) and standard deviation (SD). We analyze Nifty 50 and all the sectoral time series for pre-covid financial crisis sample size T and with sliding window length $n = 0.5T$.

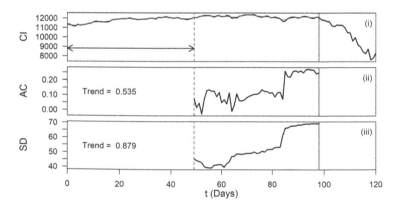

Fig. 3. Early warning indicators for covid-19 financial crisis based on Nifty 50 index with pre-covid crisis sample size $T = 98$ and window length $n = 0.5T$. **(i)** Daily closing index time series. **(ii)** lag-1 auto-correlation (AC) indicator. **(iii)** standard deviation indicator. The vertical solid blue line indicates the critical point. The double headed arrow in (i) represents the length of sliding window. The red graph in (i) denotes the smoothed time series obtained by filtering. Trend is the Kendal-τ value. (Color figure online)

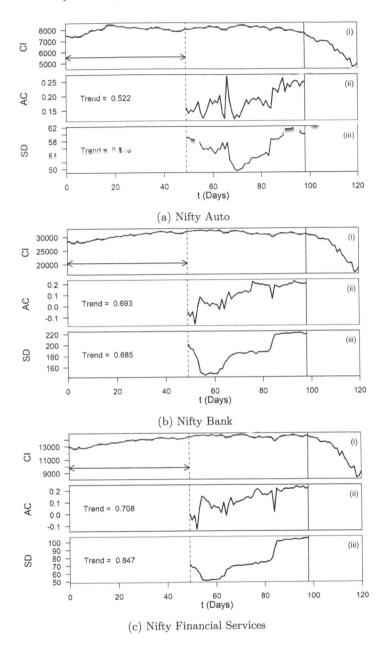

(a) Nifty Auto

(b) Nifty Bank

(c) Nifty Financial Services

Fig. 4. Early warning indicators for covid-19 financial crisis based on (**a**) Nifty Auto, (**b**) Nifty Bank & (**c**) Nifty Financial Services index with pre-covid crisis sample size T = 98 and window length $n = 0.5T$. (**i**) Daily closing index time series. (**ii**) lag-1 autocorrelation (AC) indicator. (**iii**) standard deviation indicator. The vertical solid blue line indicates the critical point. The double headed arrow in (i) represents the length of sliding window. The red graph in (i) denotes the smoothed time series obtained by filtering. Trend is the Kendal-τ value. (Color figure online)

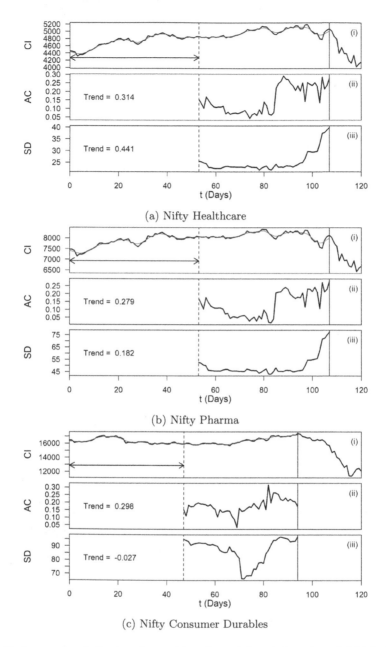

(a) Nifty Healthcare

(b) Nifty Pharma

(c) Nifty Consumer Durables

Fig. 5. Early warning indicators for covid-19 financial crisis based on **(a)** Nifty Health-care, **(b)** Nifty Pharma & **(c)** Nifty Consumer Durables index with pre-covid crisis sample size $T = 108$ (Nifty Healthcare and Nifty Pharma), $T = 97$ (Nifty Consumer Durables) and window length $n = 0.5T$. **(i)** Daily closing index time series. **(ii)** lag-1 auto-correlation (AC) indicator. **(iii)** standard deviation indicator. The vertical solid blue line indicates the critical point. The double headed arrow in (i) represents the length of sliding window. The red graph in (i) denotes the smoothed time series obtained by filtering. Trend is the Kendal-τ value. (Color figure online)

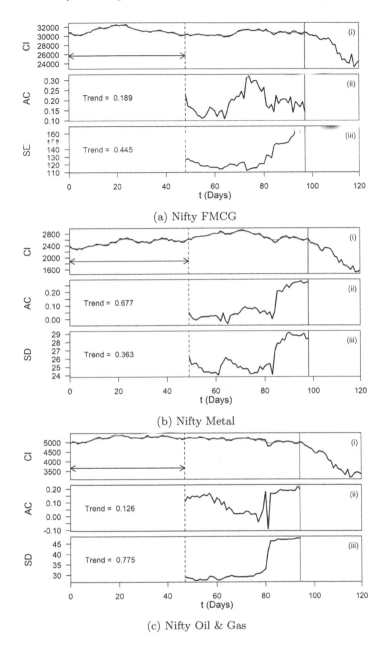

(a) Nifty FMCG

(b) Nifty Metal

(c) Nifty Oil & Gas

Fig. 6. Early warning indicators for covid-19 financial crisis based on **(a)** Nifty FMCG, **(b)** Nifty Metal & **(c)** Nifty Oil & Gas index with pre-covid crisis sample size $T = 97$ (Nifty FMCG and Nifty Oil & Gas), $T = 98$ (Nifty Metal) and window length $n = 0.5T$. **(i)** Daily closing index time series. **(ii)** lag-1 auto-correlation (AC) indicator. **(iii)** standard deviation indicator. The vertical solid blue line indicates the critical point. The double headed arrow in (i) represents the length of sliding window. The red graph in (i) denotes the smoothed time series obtained by filtering. Trend is the Kendal-τ value. (Color figure online)

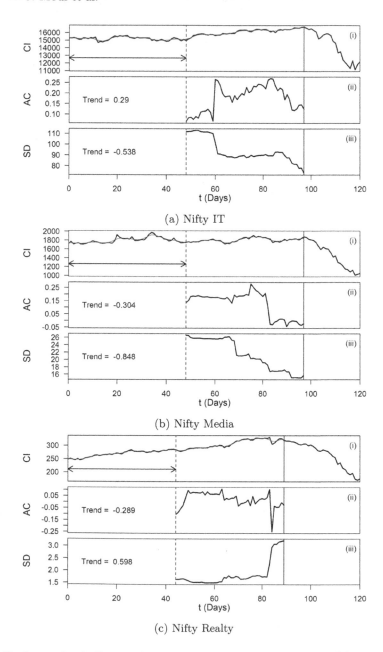

Fig. 7. Early warning indicators for covid-19 financial crisis based on **(a)** Nifty IT, **(b)** Nifty Media & **(c)** Nifty Realty index with pre-covid crisis sample size $T = 97$ (Nifty IT and Nifty Media), $T = 89$ (nifty Realty) and window length $n = 0.5T$. **(i)** Daily closing index time series. **(ii)** lag-1 auto-correlation (AC) indicator. **(iii)** standard deviation indicator. The vertical solid blue line indicates the critical point. The double headed arrow in (i) represents the length of sliding window. The red graph in (i) denotes the smoothed time series obtained by filtering. Trend is the Kendal-τ value. (Color figure online)

Auto-correlation is the simplest method to measure critical slowing down. When a system moves closer to a critical transition, auto-correlation increases much before the actual transition [8]. Similarly, it induces an increased amplitude of fluctuations that do not decay fast, resulting in the increase of variance prior to a complete transition [31]. Variance is the second moment of the distribution and is measured using standard deviation. Slowing down also causes an increase in the short term memory of the system before an impending transition [17], and hence auto-correlation at low lags would increase. We compute auto-correlation with lag-1. Trend value or Kendall-τ should be greater than 0 for the system approaching critical transition for both the early warning measures. Figure 3 to 7 shows the trend and variation of the EWS indicator for all the Nifty stock indices under consideration with rolling window length, $n = 0.5T$. (i) in each plot is the time series plot for the closing price of particular stock indices. The vertical solid blue line shows the critical point. (ii) and (iii) plot shows the change in lag-1 autocorrelation (AC) and standard deviation (SD) as the stock index approaches critical transition or crash for all sectors (Fig. 3–Fig. 7).

Lag-1 auto-correlation plot for Nifty 50 (Fig. 3), Nifty Auto (Fig. 4a), Nifty Healthcare (Fig. 5a), Nifty Pharma (Fig. 5b), Nifty Metal (Fig. 6b) and Nifty Oil & Gas (Fig. 6c) detects the transition well before the indices approach critical points. For Nifty 50, Nifty Auto, Nifty Metal and Nifty Oil & Gas lag-1 auto-correlation detected transition on the 86th day or on 3 February, 2020, while for Nifty Healthcare and Nifty Pharma transition is detected on 89th day or on 6 February, 2020 whose critical point are on 20 February, 2020 and 5 March, 2020 respectively. Nifty Bank (Fig. 4b) and Nifty Financial Services (Fig. 4c) plot for lag-1 auto-correlation does not show any sign of transition. However, it depicts an increase in auto-correlation values with time. In comparison, Nifty Consumer Durables (Fig. 5c), Nifty FMCG (Fig. 6a), Nifty IT (Fig. 7a), Nifty Media (Fig. 7b) and Nifty Realty (Fig. 7c) shows a decrease in the value of lag-1 auto-correlation after reaching a peak forewarning impending transition. All sector indices Kendal-τ or trend value shows a positive trend except Nifty Media and Nifty Realty.

The standard deviation plot for all sectors except Nifty IT (Fig. 7a) and Nifty Media (Fig. 7b) shows an increase in standard deviation value with time and distinctly detects the impending transition in prior before the indices reach critical points. Nifty IT and Nifty Media shows a continuous drop in standard deviation value with time. For Nifty 50, Nifty Auto, Nifty Bank, Nifty Financial Services, Nifty Consumer Durables, Nifty FMCG, Nifty Metal and Nifty Realty, standard deviation detected transition on the 86th day or on 3 February, 2020, while for Nifty Healthcare and Nifty Pharma transition is detected on 99th day or on 20 February, 2020 whose critical points are after 5 or 15 days. Standard deviation predicted the upcoming transition for Nifty Oil & Gas on 27 January, 2020. All sector indices Kendal-τ or trend value shows a positive trend except Nifty Consumer Durables, Nifty IT and Nifty Media.

Lag-1 auto-correlation and standard deviation early warning measures with window length $0.5T$ were able to sight the upcoming transition or market crash much prior to the system critical point, which is in accordance with the slowing down theory. Compared to lag-1 auto-correlation, standard deviation plots showed better regime shift points. The potential transition was clearly noted for all the indices with both the early warning measures except for Nifty Media.

4   Conclusion

An imminent critical transition is characterised by an increasing first order auto-correlation and standard deviation based on critical slowing down theory. Due to the complexity and dynamics involved in the stock market, we utilised these indicators to predict stock market collapse due to the covid-19 pandemic for Nifty 50 and 12 different sectoral indices listed on National Stock Exchange (NSE) India considering the market as a complex system. Our results showed that both the early warning measures could apprehend the upcoming transition or collapse for most of the indices with an analysis window length of 0.5T much before (5 to 15 days prior) than the critical point of transition. The method was able to identify transitions for all indices for covid-19 financial crisis, except the Nifty Media index. The study can further be extended to check the robustness of the proposed methodology with other early warning indicators like model-based indicators as proposed by Dakos *et al.* [6].

Appendix: Return Rate, Skewness and Kurtosis Early Warning Measure

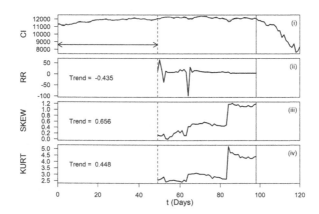

Fig. 8. (i) Closing index time series depicting stock market crash or transition for Nifty 50 index. Plot depicting the change in **(ii)** return rate (RR), **(iii)** skewness and **(iv)** kurtosis as the market approaches critical transition or crash. We observed that the plot for (ii) return rate showed little or no variation as it approached the market collapse, while the plots for (iii) skewness and (iv) kurtosis clearly identify the transition much ahead of actual critical transition or crash.

Table 2. Early warning indicators (RR: Return Rate; SKEW: Skewness; KURT: Kurtosis) trend measured in Kendall-τ, for critical transitions in different sectoral indices of Nifty Stock Exchange (NSE) for sample size T and window length n. Highlighted numbers shows incorrect trend.

Index	RR	SKEW	KURT
Nifty 50	−0.435	0.656	0.448
Nifty Auto	0.500	0.342	−0.096
Nifty Bank	−0.195	0.647	0.144
Nifty Financial Services	−0.44	0.624	0.358
Nifty Healthcare	−0.343	0.321	0.394
Nifty Pharma	−0.29	0.321	0.161
Nifty FMCG	−0.218	**−0.445**	0.122
Nifty Consumer Durables	−0.33	**−0.34**	**−0.213**
Nifty IT	−0.29	0.752	**−0.185**
Nifty Media	−0.404	**−0.68**	**−0.582**
Nifty Metal	−0.463	0.334	0.726
Nifty Oil & Gas	−0.167	0.103	0.406
Nifty Realty	**0.001**	0.768	0.668

Any system approaching a critical transition due to some (minor) perturbation slows down the rate of return of that system to equilibrium [37]. This slowing-down phenomenon is expressed as return rate, which would decrease before transition, and hence, trend value must be less. As seen in Fig. 8 (i), the variation of return rate is not able to identify the impending transition for the Nifty 50 index, which is the same for all other sectoral indices. However, the trend value or Kendal-τ value is negative for all indices except Nifty Realty which is close to 0, as shown in Table 2.

Skewness measures the asymmetry of data distribution across its mean, i.e., whether the distribution is biased to one side or the other. In most of the cases, due to asymmetry associated with the distribution of time series near to transition, a rise in skewness is observed [14,31]. Kurtosis gives information about whether a distribution is heavily tailed due to rare values in the time series. A system undergoing transition may reach more extreme values resulting in the rise of kurtosis of time series [6]. We see an apparent increase in the variation of skewness and kurtosis as shown in Fig. 8 (iii) and (iv) for the Nifty 50 index and is the same for other indices except for Nifty Media and Nifty IT. Also, we observed that the trend value of skewness and kurtosis was more significant than 0 for almost 8 out of the 12 indices, as shown in Table 2.

References

1. Abinaya, P., Kumar, V.S., Balasubramanian, P., Menon, V.K.: Measuring stock price and trading volume causality among nifty50 stocks: the Toda Yamamoto method. In: 2016 International Conference on Advances in Computing, Communications and Informatics (ICACCI), pp. 1886–1890. IEEE (2016)
2. Bellalah, M., Masood, O., Thapa, P.D.P., Levyne, O., Triki, R.: Economic forces and stock exchange prices: pre and post impacts of global financial recession of 2008 (2012)
3. Carpenter, S.R., Brock, W.A.: Rising variance: a leading indicator of ecological transition. Ecol. Lett. **9**(3), 311–318 (2006)
4. Carpenter, S.R., et al.: Early warnings of regime shifts: a whole-ecosystem experiment. Science **332**(6033), 1079–1082 (2011)
5. Dai, L., Vorselen, D., Korolev, K.S., Gore, J.: Generic indicators for loss of resilience before a tipping point leading to population collapse. Science **336**(6085), 1175–1177 (2012)
6. Dakos, V., et al.: Methods for detecting early warnings of critical transitions in time series illustrated using simulated ecological data. PLoS ONE **7**(7), e41010 (2012)
7. Dakos, V., Scheffer, M., van Nes, E.H., Brovkin, V., Petoukhov, V., Held, H.: Slowing down as an early warning signal for abrupt climate change. Proc. Natl. Acad. Sci. **105**(38), 14308–14312 (2008)
8. Dakos, V., Van Nes, E.H., d'Odorico, P., Scheffer, M.: Robustness of variance and autocorrelation as indicators of critical slowing down. Ecology **93**(2), 264–271 (2012)
9. Das, D., Kannadhasan, M., Bhattacharyya, M.: Do the emerging stock markets react to international economic policy uncertainty, geopolitical risk and financial stress alike? North Am. J. Econ. Financ. **48**, 1–19 (2019)
10. De Gooijer, J.G., Hyndman, R.J.: 25 years of time series forecasting. Int. J. Forecast. **22**(3), 443–473 (2006)
11. Dhillion, M., Tyagi, D.V., et al.: Impact of Covid-19 on Indian stock market. J. Contemp. Issues Bus. Gov. **27**(1), 2663–2671 (2021)
12. Diks, C., Hommes, C., Wang, J.: Critical slowing down as an early warning signal for financial crises? Empirical Economics **57**(4), 1201–1228 (2018). https://doi.org/10.1007/s00181-018-1527-3
13. Drake, J.M., Griffen, B.D.: Early warning signals of extinction in deteriorating environments. Nature **467**(7314), 456–459 (2010)
14. Guttal, V., Jayaprakash, C.: Changing skewness: an early warning signal of regime shifts in ecosystems. Ecol. Lett. **11**(5), 450–460 (2008)
15. Ritchie, H., et al.: Coronavirus pandemic (covid-19). Our World in Data (2020). https://ourworldindata.org/coronavirus
16. Heaton, J., Polson, N.G., Witte, J.H.: Deep learning in finance. arXiv preprint arXiv:1602.06561 (2016)
17. Held, H., Kleinen, T.: Detection of climate system bifurcations by degenerate fingerprinting. Geophys. Res. Lett. 31(23) (2004)
18. Jia, H.: Investigation into the effectiveness of long short term memory networks for stock price prediction. arXiv preprint arXiv:1603.07893 (2016)
19. Jiang, Z.Q., Zhou, W.X., Sornette, D., Woodard, R., Bastiaensen, K., Cauwels, P.: Bubble diagnosis and prediction of the 2005–2007 and 2008–2009 Chinese stock market bubbles. J. Econ. Behav. Organ. **74**(3), 149–162 (2010)

20. Kramer, J., Ross, J.: Stabilization of unstable states, relaxation, and critical slowing down in a bistable system. J. Chem. Phys. **83**(12), 6234–6241 (1985)
21. Kuehn, C.: A mathematical framework for critical transitions: bifurcations, fast-slow systems and stochastic dynamics. Physica D **240**(12), 1020–1035 (2011)
22. Kuttichira, D.P., Gopalakrishnan, E., Menon, V.K., Soman, K.: Stock price prediction using dynamic mode decomposition. In: 2017 International Conference on Advances in Computing, Communications and Informatics (ICACCI), pp. 55–60. IEEE (2017)
23. Lee, K.J., Lu, S.L., Shih, Y.: Contagion effect of natural disaster and financial crisis events on international stock markets. J. Risk Financ. Manag. **11**(2), 16 (2018)
24. Lenton, T., Livina, V., Dakos, V., Van Nes, E., Scheffer, M.: Early warning of climate tipping points from critical slowing down: comparing methods to improve robustness. Philos. Trans. Roy. Soc. A Math. Phys. Eng. Sci. 370(1962), 1185–1204 (2012)
25. Livina, V., Barton, E., Forbes, A.: Tipping point analysis of the NPL footbridge. Journal of Civil Structural Health Monitoring **4**(2), 91–98 (2013). https://doi.org/10.1007/s13349-013-0066-z
26. Livina, V.N., Vaz Martins, T.M., Forbes, A.: Tipping point analysis of atmospheric oxygen concentration. Chaos Interdisc. J. Nonlin. Sci. **25**(3), 036403 (2015)
27. Mann, H.B.: Nonparametric tests against trend. Econ. J. Econ. Soc. **13**, 245–259 (1945)
28. Meisel, C., Klaus, A., Kuehn, C., Plenz, D.: Critical slowing down governs the transition to neuron spiking. PLoS Comput. Biol. **11**(2), e1004097 (2015)
29. Menon, V.K., Vasireddy, N.C., Jami, S.A., Pedamallu, V.T.N., Sureshkumar, V., Soman, K.: Bulk price forecasting using spark over NSE data set. In: International Conference on Data Mining and Big Data, pp. 137–146. Springer, Heidelberg (2016). doi: 10.1007/978-3-319-40973-3
30. Sain, M., Mittal, A.: Impact of recession on India. Int. J. Manag. Soc. Sci. 1(4) (2013)
31. Scheffer, M., et al.: Early-warning signals for critical transitions. Nature **461**(7260), 53–59 (2009)
32. Scheffer, M., et al.: Anticipating critical transitions. Science **338**(6105), 344–348 (2012)
33. Selvin, S., Vinayakumar, R., Gopalakrishnan, E., Menon, V.K., Soman, K.: Stock price prediction using LSTM, RNN and CNN-sliding window model. In: 2017 International Conference on Advances in Computing, Communications and Informatics (ICACCI), pp. 1643–1647. IEEE (2017)
34. Trefois, C., Antony, P.M., Goncalves, J., Skupin, A., Balling, R.: Critical transitions in chronic disease: transferring concepts from ecology to systems medicine. Curr. Opin. Biotechnol. **34**, 48–55 (2015)
35. Van Nes, E.H., Scheffer, M.: Slow recovery from perturbations as a generic indicator of a nearby catastrophic shift. Am. Nat. **169**(6), 738–747 (2007)
36. Wang, L., Kutan, A.M.: The impact of natural disasters on stock markets: Evidence from japan and the us. Comp. Econ. Stud. **55**(4), 672–686 (2013)
37. Wissel, C.: A universal law of the characteristic return time near thresholds. Oecologia **65**(1), 101–107 (1984)

Facial Recognition Based Attendance Monitoring System

Amitava Choudhury[1]([✉]), Tanmay Bhowmik[2], and Samya Muhuri[2]

[1] Department of Computer Science and Engineering,
Pandit Deendayal Energy University, Gandhinagar, Gujrat, India
a.choudhury2013@gmail.com
[2] Department of Computer Science Engineering, Bennett University, Greater Noida,
Uttar Pradesh, India
samya.muhuri@bennett.edu.in

Abstract. Proper monitoring of regular attendance is a strenuous as well as the cumbersome process in manual mode of operation. However, an automated computerized system can be designed for managing attendance utilizing several features of biometrics. The intervention of deep convolutional neural networks (CNNs) has simplified the process of face recognition. Maneuvering the promising results of CNN in terms of accuracy, a modified framework for attendance supervising based on the face recognition approach is proposed in the current manuscript. The facial recognition apparatus can acknowledge a similar human face from any digital image or video frame relying on an existing database of known faces. It operates by revealing and quantifying the features of the faces of an input image. The proposed framework can be used to verify users through ID verification services. The model is developed based on state-of-the-art approaches like CNN cascade for face detection and face embedding. The motivation of the work is to implement benchmark deep learning approaches in facial recognition tasks for real-life applications. In the recent era, facial recognition systems are used in all smart devices including mobiles, laptops, and robotics. The proposed recognition model can be used as a stand-alone system or may be incorporated in some other model for an automated monitoring process.

Keywords: Automated attendance monitoring · Convolutional neural network · Deep learning · Face recognition · Facial features

1 Introduction

The issue on attendance monitoring and surveillance system has been going on for a very long time. Proper maintenance and control of student attendance are one of the main concerns of every university. Every organization implements its own rules and regulations in this regard. Some existing traditional solutions of attendance monitoring have produced good results from a certain point of view. Certainly, most of the systems have different kinds of associated problems. Manual attendance is time-consuming as well as an uncertain method. It is very

© Springer Nature Switzerland AG 2022
D. Garg et al. (Eds.): IACC 2021, CCIS 1528, pp. 244–253, 2022.
https://doi.org/10.1007/978-3-030-95502-1_19

difficult to manage the attendance of classes with a large number of students. There are always more chances of marking fake attendance as it is quite difficult to recognize each person from a large number of students within a short duration.

One popular method, convolutional neural network (CNN) based 'FaceTime' application is a competitive approach for the augmentation of image and recognition of face [2]. Another important method is designed based on RFID [7]. The approach is laborious as individual learners need to appear for indicating their attendance. These systems are also very costlier to implement especially in a developing country like India. A smart attendance based on low energy Bluetooth devices is proposed where a student can easily give a proxy by bringing the phone of another student [1]. Also, students can mark the attendance from outside of the class too. A method is developed based on fingerprint scanner as shown in [10]. The drawback of the system is that the individuals must wait in a long queue to register their attendance. It takes interminable time for an organization with huge attendees. In some of the educational institutes where it is found a large number of students in a single classroom, it would be quite difficult to monitor the process repetitively. In the barcode enabled system [9], individuals have to exhibit their unique ID card with a barcode to put attendance. This is considered a prolonged process of attendance marking. Many other approaches like speech-based [4] and Near-Field Communication (NFC) empowered attendance system [3] are proposed. However, all the above-mentioned systems have certain limitations including cost and time. Therefore, there is a need for automated arrangements that would take care of all these disadvantages and produce efficient or reliable attendance marking methodologies. These systems have relied heavily on machine learning and artificial intelligence techniques. The latest development in the field of computer vision, especially deep learning, provide possibilities to find real-time solutions. These automated approaches can be more flexible to reduce human error and biases.

Facial Recognition is one of the most searched areas of the modern era of automation and machine learning. A model combining the attendance system with facial recognition has been proposed in this study. In this manuscript, an automated attendance system utilizing the face recognition method has been suggested. The framework can be used to take attendance of the students sitting in a classroom all at once. The smart system can terminate the issue of fake attendance and proxies by the employees and students. The proposed framework would be an effective way to conserve the attendance data of all the stakeholders of the institution. The proposed system is designed utilizing the modified face recognition technique for the automatic attendance of students in the physical classroom scenario without any manual intervention.

In our proposed method, the face detection and recognition technique is comprised of two broad parts. At first, faces are detected from the given digital image. Next, these already detected faces are matched with the database images for affirmation. We have used *HaarCascade* procedure as mentioned in [6] for detecting the faces. After detecting the faces captured by the camera, the Siamese Network is used for the recognition of the face. At the back end, the

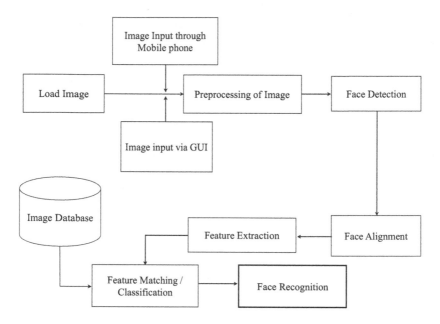

Fig. 1. Basic block diagram of face detection and recognition

proposed attendance system would mark the attendance of students according to the database information. In the front-end web portal, the attendance of the students can be viewed. The aim of the proposed work is to deploy a real-time attendance system that accurately calculates the presence of the students. In Fig. 1, the basic block diagram is represented for the face detection and recognition task.

2   Literature Study

In reference to the facial recognition task, some existing study is found. Arsenovic et al. have suggested facial recognition technique by extracting the features from one's face [2]. That is a very important as well as challenging task to perform. The mentioned paper has also observed that a single face can give various information each time while extracting its features. The features include the amount of light in the image, different patterns of facial hair, color of the face to some extent, and so on. These features can be very helpful to develop a new solution for facial recognition. Sabri et al. have proposed the RFID-based attendance system [7] and suggested some simple ways to recognize a person by detecting the facial image through a camera. In their method, the face is taken as a 2-Dimensional image, and then further image processing takes place. It includes a new notion of Eigenfaces that uses Eigenvectors. These eigenvectors make the task of identification simpler and even faster. Apoorv and Mathur have proposed the low energy Bluetooth and Android-based smart attendance system [1]. It has shown the way to identify a person even from the complex as well higher lightning-colored backgrounds. Their method has detected the region with skin color over the entire image and taken different basic facial features for verifying any person relying on the existing data set. In another work, proposed by Song et al., a mask learning strategy has been proposed. An innovative built paired differential siamese network is also used. A mask dictionary [8] is utilized to capture the relationship between occluded face areas and corrupted feature elements (FDM). We have also created the FDM by merging appropriate dictionary items while working with facial images with random partial occlusions. We have multiplied it with the original features to remove the corrupted feature elements from recognition. In the technique proposed by Zhang et al., the approach has created and implemented SiameseFace1, a new Siamese network model. It can take pairs of face photos as inputs and translates them to target space. The target space 'L2' norm distance can be represented as the semantic distance in input space [11]. In supervised learning, the neural network represents the mapping. Furthermore, SiameseFace2, a more lightweight Siamese network model, is meant to reduce network parameters without sacrificing accuracy. In the current manuscript, we have also provided a new strategy for generating training data and increasing the number of training samples in AR and labeled faces in the wild (LFW) data sets, which increases the models' recognition accuracy.

3   Methodology

3.1   Framework

In this work, the *PyTorch* has been adopted. *PyTorch* is one of the open-source libraries of Python, mostly utilized for the applications on natural language processing. The two main high-level features of *PyTorch* are:

- Working with Tensor utilizing the strong computation power of GPU.
- Deep Neural Network based module is improved in performance using tape-based autograd system.

The model that has been used in this work is Siamese Network [5]. Based on this model, thousands of layers can be trained with a convincing performance. As it has the powerful representational capability, high-end computing works including object detection and face recognition can be done in less time.

The procedure to implement the proposed system has been depicted in Fig. 2. The six-phase system has been represented here. The details have been described in the following section.

4   Design Approach

The design procedure is going to deploy the following six subsections:

- Module 1: Pi Camera has been deployed to capture image of a person.

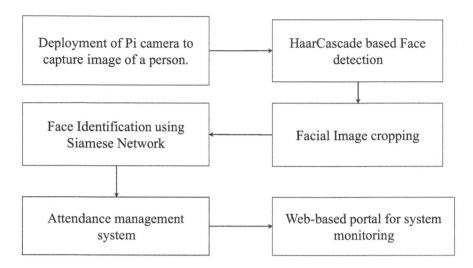

Fig. 2. The six-phase approach to implement the proposed system

- Module 2: Face detection is performed using *HaarCascade* [6].
- Module 3: In this module image cropping has been done. Once the image of the person is captured, it needs to be cropped in such format that only the face is presented inside the cropped rectangle.
- Module 4: Face identification using Siamese network.
- Module 5: Attendance management System [9].
- Module 6: Web based portal for keeping an eye on the activities per-formed by the attendance management system.

In reference to the implementation, Siamese Network for calculating similarity and dissimilarity between faces has been utilized. Unlike a traditional CNN, the Siamese Network does not categorize or label the photos; instead, it simply calculates the distance between any two images. If the images have the same label, the network should learn the parameters, such as weights and biases, in such a way that the distance between them is lower; if the images have different labels, the distance should be bigger. A basic functional flow of a Siamese Network has been depicted in Fig. 3. The module-wise description is given in the following sections:

4.1 Module 1

- A Pi Camera has been deployed to capture an image of a person.
- Images of faculty and student's faces are captured.
- It is processed to match the face from databases.
- Update attendance according to time slots.

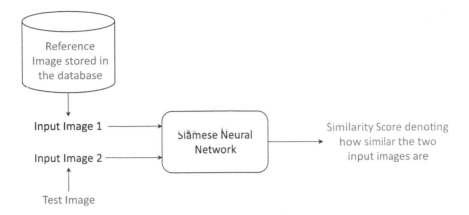

Fig. 3. The functional flow of Siamese Network

Bounding boxes around the faces and the eyes

Fig. 4. Bounding box around the faces and eyes

4.2   Module 2

- *HaarCascade* classifier is used to detect the faces from an image captured.
- Bounding box is created around the faces and eyes. An example image has been shown in Fig. 4

4.3   Module 3

- The image cropping procedure is executed in this module.
- After the generation of the bounding box around the face, it needs to copy the faces from the image and they are stored in a separate database.
- These separate images are input to the next module and work as proof of the person's presence in the room.
- This helps to get more images of the person and assist in increasing the efficiency of the model.

4.4 Module 4

- Face identification using Siamese network is the most important module for this system.
- This allows identifying a person correctly so that attendance can be marked.
- First faculty is recognized so that branch and subject can be identified from Room-No and time slot.
- Then each present student is individually identified and marked present.

4.5 Module 5

- The attendance management system that works at the back-end are utilized for updating value.
- It allows to connect with the databases and update the records such as classes held for a batch, classes attended by every individual, attendance percentage of every individual.

4.6 Module 6

- Web-based portal for keeping an eye on the activities performed by the attendance management system.
- Web portal is created for students to check attendance percentage.
- Timetable can be checked by students online.
- Faculty can update the attendance if any discrepancy.
- Faculty can follow their timetable.

5 Results and Analysis

In reference to the results, in Fig. 5 some set of output screens are observed. There are number of advantages of this work.

- With Deep face, which uses the Siamese architecture, the developers would have the advantage to classify a new user.
- This work is capable of detecting and recognizing faces from side angles also. In Fig. 5, it has been observed that in the first image the dissimilarity index is high when the front face are different to the side face. The dissimilarity index is low in case of both the image is of same person. In the last image it as been mentioned that how the attendances would be recorded.
- The One-shot learning allows to build a classifier that can correctly show results with one input. In Fig. 6, a one-shot learning of a siamese network has been depicted. Siamese is a term that refers to twins. Here we have used two copies of the same Convolutional Neural Networks, and thus, these are known as Siamese Networks. They are essentially the same in terms of parameters. The ConvNet is used to construct a fixed length feature vector h(x1) and h(x2) where two input images are x1 and x2, respectively. After the neural network models are properly trained, we can conclude that the feature vectors

of two input photos that belong to the same character must be comparable. However, the feature vectors of two input images that belong to separate characters must be distinct.

- This method also works well when the complete face is not visible.
- This network can be modelled into Binary classification if the images of employees can be stored as image encodings and match those encoding to the new image.

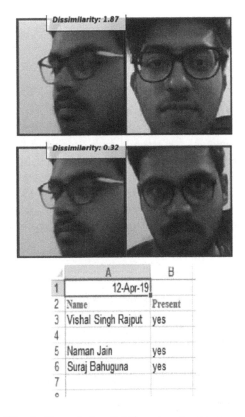

Fig. 5. Snapshots of different output screens

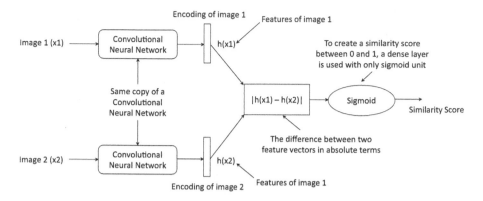

Fig. 6. One-shot learning of Siamese network

6   Conclusion and Future Work

The entire work is developed for attendance monitoring for the stakeholders of any organization. However, the challenges encountered in the existing systems have been addressed and corrected in the current framework. In the future, we shall try to improve the recognition rate of our framework in some special cases like the faces of the students are half-covered or they are partially visible. The proposed model can be developed with an Android app for ease of accessibility.

References

1. Apoorv, R., Mathur, P.: Smart attendance management using Bluetooth Low Energy and android. In: 2016 IEEE Region 10 Conference (TENCON), pp. 1048–1052. IEEE (2016)
2. Arsenovic, M., Sladojevic, S., Anderla, A., Stefanovic, D.: FaceTime-deep learning based face recognition attendance system. In: 2017 IEEE 15th International Symposium on Intelligent Systems and Informatics (SISY), pp. 000053–000058. IEEE (2017)
3. Baykara, M., Gürtürk, U., Karakaya, E.: NFC based smart mobile attendance system. In: 2017 International Conference on Computer Science and Engineering (UBMK), pp. 937–941. IEEE (2017)
4. Dey, S., et al.: Speech biometric based attendance system. In: 2014 Twentieth National Conference on Communications (NCC), pp. 1–6. IEEE (2014)
5. Guo, Q., Feng, W., Zhou, C., Huang, R., Wan, L., Wang, S.: Learning dynamic Siamese network for visual object tracking. In: Proceedings of the IEEE International Conference on Computer Vision, pp. 1763–1771 (2017)
6. Padilla, R., Costa Filho, C., Costa, M.: Evaluation of Haar cascade classifiers designed for face detection. World Acad. Sci. Eng. Technol. **64**, 362–365 (2012)
7. Sabri, M.Y., Aziz, M.A., Shah, M.M., Abd Kadir, M.: Smart attendance system by suing RFID. In: 2007 Asia-Pacific Conference on Applied Electromagnetics, pp. 1–4. IEEE (2007)

8. Song, L., Gong, D., Li, Z., Liu, C., Liu, W.: Occlusion robust face recognition based on mask learning with pairwise differential Siamese network. In: Proceedings of the IEEE/CVF International Conference on Computer Vision, pp. 773–782 (2019)
9. Sudha, K.L., Shinde, S., Thomas, T., Abdugani, A.: Barcode based student attendance system. Int. J. Comput. Appl. **119**(2), 1–5 (2015)
10. Zainal, N.I., Sidek, K.A., Gunawan, T.S., Manser, H., Kartiwi, M.: Design and development of portable classroom attendance system based on Arduino and fingerprint biometric. In: The 5th International Conference on Information and Communication Technology for the Muslim World (ICT4M), pp. 1–4. IEEE (2014)
11. Zhang, J., Jin, X., Liu, Y., Sangaiah, A.K., Wang, J.: Small sample face recognition algorithm based on novel Siamese network. J. Inf. Process. Syst. **14**(6), 1464–1479 (2018)

Transfer Learning Using Variational Quantum Circuit

Rajashekharaiah Karur Mudugal Mathad[1]($^{(\boxtimes)}$)(iD), Abhishek Saurabh[1](iD),
Aditya Mishra[1](iD), Sambhav Jain[1](iD), Purushottam Kumar[1](iD), Vardaan[1](iD),
and Satyadhyan Chickerur[2](iD)

[1] School of Computer Science and Engineering, K L E Technological University,
Hubballi 580 031, Karnataka, India
kmmr@kletech.ac.in
[2] Centre for High Performance Computing, K L E Technological University,
Hubballi 580 031, Karnataka, India
chickerursr@kletech.ac.in

Abstract. Quantum computing and particularly quantum machine learning has witnessed a surge in the direction of fruitful research being done in recent years. Variational quantum algorithms have gained popularity due to their resilience to error, which is a common occurrence in the near term intermediate scale quantum (NISQ) hardware. In such an algorithm, an optimal function is mapped by a quantum circuit which is designed using weighted parameterized gates to be trained based on a cost function that is optimized using gradient descent. A Variational Quantum Classifier (VQC) is such an algorithm and is used for supervised learning to perform data classification. But since the quantum hardware available today is not powerful enough for a VQC to come of any practical use in the current setting, we implement a transfer learning pipeline in which a pre-trained image processing model is fine tuned using a dressed VQC; for a specific, binary classification task. Our aim was to study the working of a VQC and test it's behaviour with respect to multiple hyperparameters such as circuit depth, number of qubits, etc. We trained our transfer learning-VQC model for 4 different datasets and for different hyperparameters and were able to get close to state of the art performance in most of our tests, solidifying the prospect of VQC as an efficient quantum-classical hybrid supervised learning algorithm. It should be noted that the study of VQC was chosen over that of other algorithms available for classification because recent advancements in the understanding of VQCs that show promise in favour of the algorithm.

Keywords: Quantum computing · Machine learning · Transfer learning · Binary classification

K L E Technological University.

D. Garg et al. (Eds.): IACC 2021, CCIS 1528, pp. 254–267, 2022.
https://doi.org/10.1007/978-3-030-95502-1_20

1   Introduction

Quantum computing [1,2] expands the domain of information science and provides a model of computation that's based on the laws of quantum mechanics. The promise of quantum computers is that they will be able to solve some specific important problems much faster than classical computers. The development of efficient algorithms to be deployed on quantum computers is an active area of research as of the time of writing. Merging of the field with that of machine learning has resulted in the proposal of multiple novel algorithms in the recent years [3–7]. One such algorithm is a Variational Quantum Classifier(VQC) [8] which is a hybrid quantum-classical supervised machine learning algorithm [9–11] that can be used for classifying data into binary labels. In this algorithm, the parameters of a quantum circuit are optimized in a training phase based on a cost function built for the data and labels. Machine learning and quantum computing are both technological directives that have the potential to change how computation should be performed to solve problems that were previously said to be unsolvable when dealt with classical approaches. The procedure followed here is to fine tune a pre-trained classical machine learning model with a variational quantum classifier and study the pros and cons of using such an approach by testing it in multiple scenarios.

We'll be discussing our hybrid model in Sect. 4 including the system architecture for our experiment and design principles which guide the testing choices made in Sect. 5. Sections 6 and 7 concludes our work with a discussion on results obtained and inferences that can be derived from them.

2   Background

This section covers the background knowledge required to get to the context of this paper. It contains three sub-sections, first is dedicated to quantum computing, second to VQC and third to transfer learning.

Quantum Computing and quantum circuits:

Fig. 1. Quantum circuit

A quantum circuit defines a computation to be performed on a quantum computer. Figure 1 shows a generic quantum circuit made using the GUI available on the cloud based IBM quantum platform. Qubits are the basic unit of computation in a quantum computer whose states can be defined by a 2D vector in the complex hilbert space. Operations, defined by quantum gates, can be performed to change the states of these qubits such that their measurement gives some desired output and because of the inherent randomness of quantum mechanics as we know it, these operations need to be performed multiple, say a thousand, times and an average over all the measured outputs is taken as the final answer.

The quantum circuit shown has 2 qubits initialized in the $|0\rangle$ state and quantum gates being applied on them in the order from left to right until they are measured, which disrupts the states of the qubits and gives out an answer with respect to the type of the measurement.

Simulation: The state of one qubit can be completely defined, and represented mathematically, by a 2D complex vector and a quantum operation on one qubit is defined by a 2×2 complex unitary matrix. The resultant state of the qubit, after the operation is performed, is given by multiplying the qubit state by the operation matrix. Furthermore, a measurement operation on a single qubit is given by a 2×2 complex hermitian matrix, and the outcome of the measurement is given by a similar matrix multiplication. When dealing with multiple qubits, we need to work with the tensor product of all the individual qubit states and operations.

A qubit state can be visualized as a unit vector on the surface of a bloch sphere [12] and quantum operations can be visualized as change in the direction of this state vector.

Variational quantum classifier(VQC):

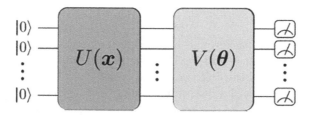

Fig. 2. Variational quantum circuit

Variational or parametrized quantum circuits are a class of hybrid quantum-classical machine learning algorithms that use trainable parameters to approximate a mapping function [13]. A variational quantum classifier is an algorithm (or model) proposed to perform binary classification of classical data in a supervised learning scenario. Figure 2 shows a generic VQC having the following conceptual divisions -

1. Converting classical data to quantum data: This process is called embedding and it plays a major role in the performance of a VQC. Multiple approaches have been proposed for this task, some major ones being basis embedding,

amplitude embedding, angle embedding and trainable embeddings. The most common approach, and the one we have used, is the angle embedding technique. In this approach, classical data is embedded into qubits by performing parameterized rotations of their state vectors on the bloch sphere using any one of the three pauli rotation gates.

2. Parameterized quantum circuit: A repeating circuit ansatz consisting of parameterized pauli rotation gates and cnot gates. The parameters are trained through gradient descent and are made to settle on values that make the circuit act as a binary classifier for the classical data that is embedded in the circuit. The number of repetitions of this ansatz is a hyperparameter for VQC and is known as depth.

3. Measurement and optimization: Upon measuring the qubits, the gradients for all the parameters are calculated by the parameter shift rule [14] based on an objective function of choice. The calculation of gradients and tuning of parameters can now be handled in the background by libraries such as pennylane and qiskit and thus the realization of a VQC has become quite simple these days.

Transfer learning: Transfer learning is a method in machine learning that involves using the knowledge gained while solving one problem, applying it to another related problem [16]. For example, knowledge gained while learning to recognize cars could apply when trying to recognize trucks. VQCs as we know them now are not able to handle high dimensional data due to hardware limitations and thus are essentially useless for any practical problems. Transfer learning provides a way to use and test VQCs in a practical setting, the approach involves using a pretrained model that was trained for a general task, such as classification of images, and fine tuning it using a VQC for a particular task say for classification of ants and bees (Fig. 3).

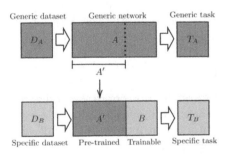

Fig. 3. Transfer learning (source [15])

3   Related Works

This work is inspired by [15]. Here the authors propose the use of transfer learning for testing and using VQCs in a practical setting. They test their approach on three different datasets and are able to prove the viability of VQCs. For the exploration of VQCs one may refer [17]. Here the authors propose the variational quantum classifier as an alternative to the classical neural network and explore its performance as a standalone binary classifier. In [5] the authors propose and experimentally implement two novel machine learning methods, including the VQC, and demonstrate the role of the high dientionality of the quantum hilbert space in achieving an enhanced solution. In [18] the authors talk about how the encoding of data governs the expressive potential of a quantum circuit and propose a trainable embedding technique.

4   The Hybrid Model

This section discusses our proposed model which is a combination of a classical CNN and a dressed quantum model. The transfer learning approach is discussed first and then the idea is built upon to create a VQC based transfer learning pipeline that can be used as a hybrid model to be trained for the binary classification of images.

4.1   Transfer Learning

For our hybrid model, the use of transfer learning was inspired by [15] and was justified to us by the fact that the currently feasible VQCs are not able to handle high-dimensional data such as images due to the lacking quantum hardware. Therefore, for our work, we used a pre-trained classical CNN model, specifically Resnet [19] 18, got the outputs from the last layer and attached a dressed VQC at the end to perform binary classification on multiple different image datasets.

Resnet 18 is a pretrained convolutional neural network that is 18 layers deep. It is trained on the Imagenet dataset and can classify images into 1000 object categories. We take the outputs from the last layer of the model and feed it to the dressed quantum circuit.

4.2   Proposed Model

The architecture for our system incorporates a design where an input image is passed through resnet-18 and the outputs from it's last layer are then passed through a dressed quantum circuit(a quantum circuit surrounded by dense classical NN-layers). Figure 4 shows the flow of operations.

Dense layers make up what are the 'dressed' part of the dressed quantum circuit, where every neuron of one layer is connected to every neuron of previous layer. Dense layers are used to strengthen feature propagation from the pretrained model to the quantum circuit and from the quantum circuit to the output layer.

The classical data point x is translated into a set of gate parameters in a quantum circuit which, when applied, create a quantum state $|\psi\rangle$ that is representative of the data point.

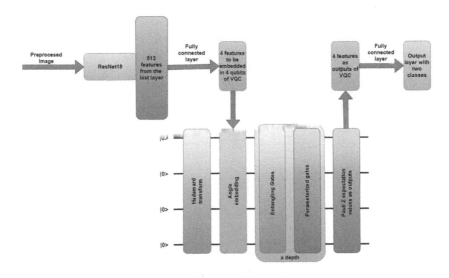

Fig. 4. Proposed model

4.3 Dressed Quantum Circuit

We use a dressed quantum circuit for fine tuning our pretrained model and propose a specific version of VQC that gave us optimal results and was consistent across all the datasets that we tested it on (Fig. 5).

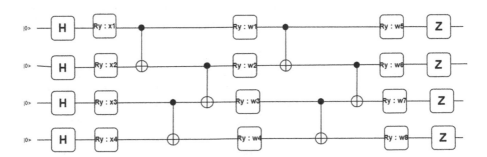

Fig. 5. Generic VQC - depth 2

First have a look at a generic VQC circuit (Fig. 1) of depth two. Four qubits are used and a hadamard transform is applied to put the qubits in superposition state. Then comes the embedding layer, the inputs to which are given by the outputs of the pretrained model after passing them through a fully connected/dense layer of 4 classical neurons (Fig. 4). Pauli Y rotation gates are used for this embedding step.

After embedding comes the repeating ansatz comprising the three cnot gates and a parameterized Pauli Y rotation layer for the four qubits. The final step is the measurement of qubits, which was done in the Z basis.

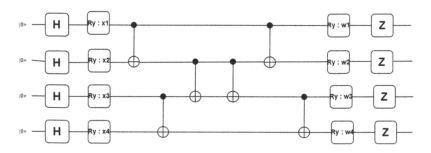

Fig. 6. Optimal VQC - depth 1

Figure 6 shows the proposed circuit having similar structure except for the ansatz, which has six cnot gates and a similar parameterized Pauli Y rotation layer for the four qubits. For making a case close to an apples to apples comparison, in the testing phase this ansatz was repeated half the number of times as the one in the generic VQC. Some important points to note here are that the cnot gate, being a two-qubit gate, is more error prone for operations running on actual quantum hardware. Secondly, the time required to calculate the gradients of the parameters in the ansatz varies linearly with the number of parameters when using the parameter shift rule. When this optimal circuit is used with half depth of the generic circuit, the result is a 50% reduction in the number of parameters and thus a sizable reduction in computation time is achieved. The circuit architecture proposed is a result of thought guided by the intuition of lateral symmetry of the entangling gates in the ansatz. In our testing, any ansatz that had laterally symmetrical entangling gates gave comparable or better results when compared to the ones which did not have such a structure.

After getting the Pauli Z expectation values of the four qubits as outputs from the VQC, we pass it through a dense layer of two neurons(Fig. 4) and apply the softmax activation function to get the output of the classification.

5   Testing

Google colab environment was used in the testing process.

The hybrid model was tested with a circuit of 4 and 5 qubits with a depth of 4, and the training time, loss and accuracy value on four different datasets were observed. The results were compared against the generic model [20]. In each scenario, a dataset is chosen, split in a 7:3 training and validation ratio and training was done multiple times with different set of hyperparameters. The results of which are discussed in following section. It should be noted that the testing process was carried on a quantum simulator and not on an actual quantum computer but since the variational algorithms are known to be less prone to error, we can expect similar results from actual quantum hardware.

6 Results

The results as compared to the generic model are discussed below.

When tested on the hymenopetra dataset containing 300 labelled images of ants and bees, our hybrid model was able to perform better and train faster. A graphical representation of the comparison of performance on the validation set can be seen in Fig. 7. Upon increasing the number of qubits from 4 to 5 while keeping a similar circuit structure, we see that our model gave consistent if not better results (Fig. 8).

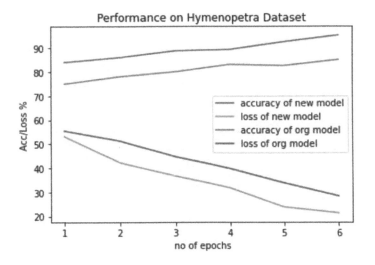

Fig. 7. Comparison on Ants-bees dataset

Figure 9 shows the performance of our model when training for image classification of cats and dogs for 4 qubits and Fig. 10 shows the performance when training was done with 5 qubits. These images were taken from the cifar10 dataset. Also for the case of classification of planes and cars, the images were taken from the same dataset. The results in the same manner are presented in Fig. 11 for the case of 4 qubits and in Fig. 12 for the case of 5 qubits. Figure 13 shows the performance of the model on the diabetic retinopathy dataset when using 4 qubits and Fig. 14 shows the outputs of classification on the same dataset as generated by our model.

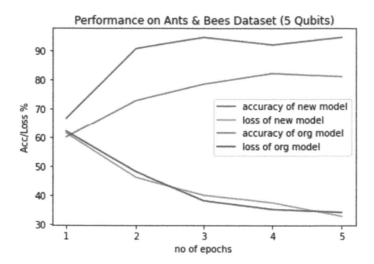

Fig. 8. Comparison on Ants-bees dataset with 5 qubits

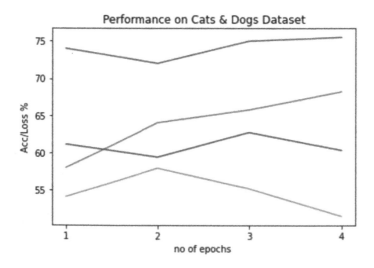

Fig. 9. Comparison on Cats-dogs dataset

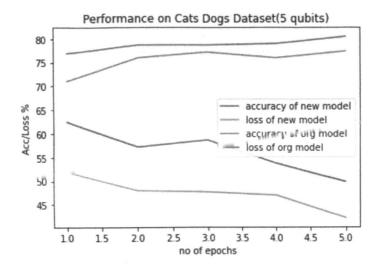

Fig. 10. Comparison on Cats-dogs dataset with 5 qubits

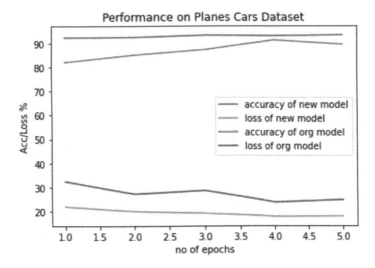

Fig. 11. Comparison on Cars-planes dataset with 4 qubits

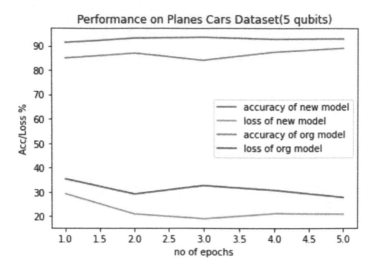

Fig. 12. Comparison on Cars-planes dataset with 5 qubits

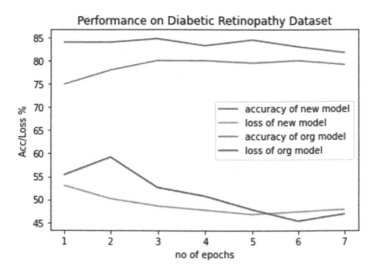

Fig. 13. Comparison on Diabetic-Retinopathy dataset

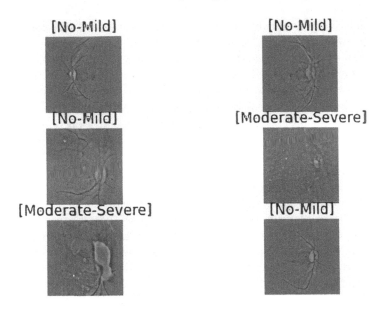

Fig. 14. Outputs of classification of diabetic retinopathy images

Table 1. .

No. of qubits	Ants-bees	Cats-dogs	Planes-cars	Diabetic retinopathy
4	95.12	76.4	94.2	87.6
5	96.06	80.05	95.7	91.4

Table 2. .

No. of qubits	Ants-bees	Cats-dogs	Planes-cars	Diabetic retinopathy
4	20.42	51.4	20.2	47.9
5	17.6	42.05	20.7	42.6

Table 1 summarizes the accuracy score for 4 and 5 qubits and Table 2 summarizes the validation loss.

7   Discussion

Our hybrid model performed consistently across all datasets, which reinforces the usability of VQCs in a transfer learning setting. It was seen that in any general case, increasing the depth of the variational form increased the complexity of the model, and helped in getting an overall better accuracy for any dataset at the cost of training/computation time. For any variational circuit, having a greater depth implies the use of more gates to be applied and more parameters to be optimized for the qubits leading to a greater error rate. And therefore care must be taken in choosing a circuit with optimum depth.

With respect to the number qubits used, it was generally observed that increasing the number of qubits increased the overall accuracy of the model at the cost of computation time. We can say that being able to access the data points in a higher dimensional hilbert space helps with being able to separate the datapoints in a process of classification at the cost of encountering barren plateaus in the training process.

With respect to the design of the variational form we are not able to show any definitive results that proved if a particular form was 'better' than the others but on analyzing the results from different circuits, we came to the conclusion that any variational ansatz with a laterally symmetric entanglement structure can be expected to perform decently.

There still remain many unexplored properties that we should enquire about in the context variational quantum classifiers such as the significance of learning rate and barren plateaus in the hilbert space, which we saw was a recurring problem with the current architecture.

8   Future Work

We have leveraged transfer learning to make optimal use of a variational quantum classifier since a currently feasible VQC will not be able to handle high dimensional data when used with angle embedding, and so different embedding methods can be used to work for different kinds of data, with or without using transfer learning approach.

Future work may be done in the direction of leveraging the variational embedding technique [18] for feature embedding in the quantum circuit. In this method separate training is done for the data embedding layer of the VQC. The idea is to map the different classes of the data to distinct and easily separable parts of the hilbert space before training a variational quantum circuit for classification [21].

References

1. Nielsen, M.A., Chuang, I.: Quantum computation and quantum information (2002)
2. Yanofsky, N.S., Mannucci, M.A.: Quantum Computing for Computer Scientists. Cambridge University Press, Cambridge (2008)
3. Rebentrost, P., Mohseni, M., Lloyd, S.: Quantum support vector machine for big data classification. Phys. Rev. Lett. 113(13), 130503 (2014)
4. Amin, M.H., Andriyash, E., Rolfe, J., Kulchytskyy, B., Melko, R.: Quantum Boltzmann machine. Phys. Rev. X 8(2), 021050 (2018)
5. Havlíček, V., et al.: Supervised learning with quantum-enhanced feature spaces. Nature 567(7747), 209–212 (2019)
6. Otterbach, J.S., et al.: Unsupervised machine learning on a hybrid quantum computer. arXiv preprint arXiv:1712.05771 (2017)

7. Kerenidis, I., Landman, J., Luongo, A., Prakash, A.: q-means: a quantum algorithm for unsupervised machine learning. arXiv preprint arXiv:1812.03584 (2018)

8. Schuld, M., Bocharov, A., Svore, K.M., Wiebe, N.: Circuit-centric quantum classifiers. Phys. Rev. A **101**(3), 032308 (2020)

9. Biamonte, J., Wittek, P., Pancotti, N., Rebentrost, P., Wiebe, N., Lloyd, S.: Quantum machine learning. Nature **549**(7671), 195–202 (2017)

10. Schuld, M., Killoran, N.: Quantum machine learning in feature Hilbert spaces. Phys. Rev. Lett. **122**(4), 040504 (2019)

11. Lloyd, S., Mohseni, M., Rebentrost, P.. Quantum algorithms for supervised and unsupervised machine learning. arXiv preprint arXiv:1307.0411 (2013)

12. The Qiskit Team: Representing qubit states, August 2021. https://qiskit.org/textbook/ch-states/representing-qubit-states.html

13. Variational circuits. https://pennylane.ai/qml/glossary/variational_circuit.html

14. Parameter-shift rules. https://pennylane.ai/qml/glossary/parameter_shift.html

15. Mari, A., Bromley, T.R., Izaac, J., Schuld, M., Killoran, N.: Transfer learning in hybrid classical-quantum neural networks. Quantum **4**, 340 (2020)

16. Transfer learning, August 2021. https://en.wikipedia.org/wiki/Transfer_learning

17. Gil Fuster, E.M.: Variational quantum classifier (2019). diposit.ub.edu

18. Schuld, M., Sweke, R., Meyer, J.J.: Effect of data encoding on the expressive power of variational quantum-machine-learning models. Phys. Rev. A **103**(3), 032430 (2021)

19. ResNet. https://pytorch.org/hub/pytorch_vision_resnet

20. Quantum transfer learning. https://pennylane.ai/qml/demos/tutorial_quantum_transfer_learning.html

21. Nghiem, N.A., Chen, S.Y.C., Wei, T.C.: Unified framework for quantum classification. Phys. Rev. Res. **3**(3), 033056 (2021)

Problem Solving Using Reinforcement Learning and Analysis of Data

Gait Learning Using Reinforcement Learning

Bharath Raj Mahadeva Rao[1]($\boxtimes$) and Sharmila Chidaravalli[2]($\boxtimes$)

[1] University of Groningen, 9714 CP Groningen, Netherlands
[2] Global Academy of Technology, Bangalore, India

Abstract. This paper provides a practical way of implementing gaits for robots using the powerful reinforcement learning techniques, offering vivid applications in areas ranging from defense, last mile delivery, firefighting, search and rescue operations and entertainment. We first survey existing approaches of generating gaits and then propose a an agent based on the Proximal policy optimisation algorithm. However, agent suffers from jittery motions due to the continuous action space.

Keywords: Gait · Reinforcement learning · Proximal policy · Deep Q learning

1 Introduction

Gait is the manner of walking of any animal, human, or a robot. As humans we have a bipedal gait which corresponds to making use of the two legs to move forward. However, in robots gait refers to the locomotion achieved by the robot through the movement of its limbs or actuators. In this paper we explore the methods to generate a gait for a quadruped in a simulated environment and later interface it with a real world quadruped. In general gait is broadly classified as periodic and non-periodic. Figure 1 shows the classification of gaits.

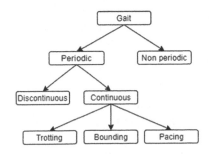

Fig. 1. Broad classification of gaits

D. Garg et al. (Eds.): IACC 2021, CCIS 1528, pp. 271–278, 2022.
https://doi.org/10.1007/978-3-030-95502-1_21

In this paper we discuss about the non-periodic gait generated using rein-forcement learning. Non periodic gait refers to free gait, which means there is no particular repetition of the movement of legs between time intervals. Hard coding gaits for locomotion of robots is very tedious as it involves careful study of each scenario and the angles at which each actuator, motor and the servo has to move. Adding to that, the torque required and the timing of each of these is also very crucial. Taking the above challenges into consideration in a dynamic ever changing environment of the robot, there is a need to design gaits which enable the robot to adapt and move from one point to another point. This gives an edge over a standardized hard coded gait.

Consider another scenario where the robot might lose one of its limbs, or a failure of its motors, or another case where one of it's limbs are stuck in a puddle, for these cases there should be a mechanism for the robot to overcome this challenge and make use of its remaining functional entities to move form one point to another. This calls for a new age of smart gait to be learnt. By making use of reinforcement learning, we are addressing the issue of stabilized movement and flexibility of locomotion in a free gait. Once gaits are automated and made completely autonomous, the entire robotic industry can be revolutionized. There are immense applications in the fields of Defense, Space Exploration, Search and Rescue operations, multi-terrain bots, mining industry and Hazardous environment explorations.

To understand the approach of implementing reinforcement learning to gen-erate gaits, this paper is split into the following sections: Sect. 2 is about related work, Sect. 3 discusses design and learning process, Sect. 4 shows the simulation results, Sect. 5 explains how the interfacing is done with a real world quadruped, and Sect. 6 summarizes the results and gives the conclusion

2   Related Work

In Mustafa et al. [1] they explore reinforcement learning on a six legged robot. Here they use a reinforcement signal which comprises of measuring the stability of a new state $P*$ after transitioning from the old state P. Only if this stability is above a given threshold, then the state-transition table is updated with this new value, and the agent takes the steps greedily with little room for exploration. They explore the stability signal in a 5-legged robot and a 6-legged robot. In their simulations they found the instability issues of a 5 legged robot, as it's stability cannot be guaranteed. One particular drawback is the transition from an even terrain to an uneven terrain, their approach does not cover this situation, however their initial approach gave rise to further research in this field.

In another paper by Alessio et al. [2], they explore generating gait on uneven terrain for a humanoid robot. In their simulations they try the Model Predictive Control scheme on a linear surface. From here they draw the trajectory of the motion of the legs and later consider the stability and zero-momentum points to traverse. This was later verified on the NOA robot. Their approach was a significant improvement considering they took the surface into account and the respective path planning of a bipedal robot.

Another research by Anton Orell Wiehe et al. [7], developed an offline actor-critic algorithm titled *Sampled Policy Gradient* for continuous state space. Their algorithm suffered from exploration as the model continued to exploit known state spaces.

Taking these researches into account, we were motivated to use a reinforcement learning approach in a dynamic environment setup. While exploring different reinforcement learning techniques we wanted the agent to have a simple policy, have low latency and low memory utilization. Proximal policy optimization introduced by Schulman et al. [3], is one of the prime algorithms in this area. The key advantages of PPO are listed as follows:

– It ensures slight deviation from previous policy
– No replay buffers are present (unlike Deep Q learning) but instead, learn directly from whatever the agent encounters
– Once experience is used to make a policy update the experience is discarded.
– Simple implementation and ease of use

Keeping these in mind we proceed to the design and learning process used by us.

3   Design and Learning Process

The experiment took place in a simulated environment made using PyBullet [5] in Python. This allowed us to reuse the features of physics concepts such as gravity and force provided by PyBullet. The quadruped is designed in Universal Robotic Description Format to describe all the elements of the quadruped and the joints and the types of joints.

In the pybullet environment, the quadruped has to walk in a 3d surface to reach a goal station. The quadruped walks across the field in this environment for a specified amount of time or until it reaches the goal. The episode terminates if the quadruped topples upside down, or if it accumulates a threshold of negative rewards. The goal is to reach a particular position in the X axis, where X axis is the forward axis for the quadruped.

Since, the goal of the quadruped is to reach a particular position in the X axis, we measure the distance between this point and the coordinates of the quadruped to reward it. The reward function takes into account the direction the quadruped is facing, the displacement of the quadruped with respect to its start position and the goal. The quadruped is negatively rewarded when it sways in the Y axis direction, when it stands still in the same position without taking any action for more time steps and if it goes in the opposite direction away from the goal.

The learning algorithm used is Proximal Policy Optimization [1]. This was made available on python which interfaces with the simulated world. The interfacing of the simulated environment and OpenAi Gym is depicted in Fig. 2

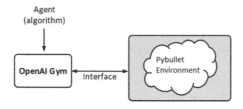

Fig. 2. Interfacing of OpenAi Gym environment, the algorithm and the simulated environment.

The observation space consists of the current angles of 8 servos which the policy has to observe and the distance from the quadruped to its goal. The action space consists of setting the correct angle for these 8 servos. There are a set of initial parameters assumed before the learning process is initiated, these are:

- Collectively there are 8 servos
- Each leg of the quadruped has 2 servos, one connects the leg to the body helping it to rotate and the other one is used to lift the limb.
- Each servo is allowed to move freely between $-45°$ to $+45°$ with $0°$ being the mean position. This continuous range of values to be predicted by the agent is tedious, so we use the values $[+45, 0, -45]$, as three discrete values for the servos. Hence, with 8 servos there are 3×8 state-action space.

Reward function in our scenario is defined as follows:

- For every step in the positive x axis direction - positive reward is given
- If the agent keeps its stability after a step towards its goal - positive reward is given
- For every step it stays in the same position - negative reward is given.
- For every step in the direction away from the goal - negative reward is given.

The design of the model was based on an open source design by Konredus [6]. Figure 3 shows a CAD rendering of the model with the servos (in blue). The blue blocks in the image are servos which control the movement of the legs, which are connected to the main body.

For our simulated environment we use an implementation by Ruben Chevez [8] on PyBullet. In this environment PPO has is ready to be deployed, however we tweak the new reward function to observe it in a dynamic environment. After the simulation was setup, the next step was to start training in this environment. During training, PPO was interfaced with this setup and Fig. 4 shows a screenshot of how the quadruped is being trained. During training we can see the agent handling and tweaking the angles of the joints of the quadruped, trying to reach the goal. The reward gained by the quadruped is also shown in the GUI which tells us how much reward the agent received for the current episode.

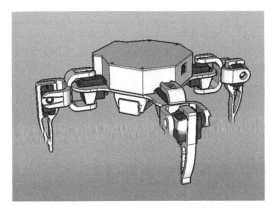

Fig. 3. 3D model of the quadruped [6]. (Color figure online)

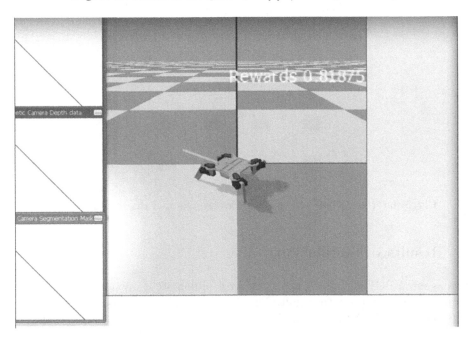

Fig. 4. Training of the quadruped in a simulated world. The X axis is marked Red in colour, the model has to move along this path to reach it's goal position.

4   Interfacing with the Real World Quadruped

The real world quadruped is built by taking advantage of the 3D printing technology. The quadruped is printed out in a PLA plastic material. Each servo is fixed and the servos are controlled by an ArduinoUNO microcontroller. This board is interfaced serially with the PPO agent. The entire working structure of the Arduino-Python interface is given in Fig. 5, which clearly indicates how the interfacing is done between devices. We use the trained agent to control the quadruped in the real world. The agent reads the servo positions as its observation over a serial communication with the quadruped and takes appropriate action to move forward by outputting the next set of servo positions for the quadruped. This output is serially sent to the quadruped and the servos move accordingly.

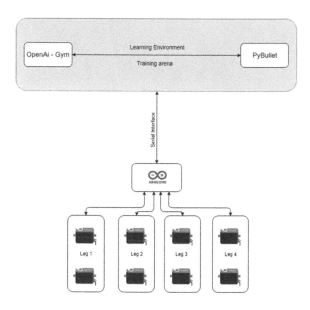

Fig. 5. Interfacing between the hardware system and the software system

5   Results of Simulation

The agent (PPO) was allowed to train for 4 billion steps on the simulated environment to come up with a gait. The results achieved are consolidated in the Figs. 6 and Fig. 7. After about 3.78 billion steps of training, the result achieved is shown in Fig. 7

The agent struggles with a lot of back and forth movement while reaching its target with jittery motion.

approxkl	0.0009594701
clipfrac	0.0014648438
ep_rewmean	nan
eplenmean	nan
explained_variance	-1.56
fps	450
nupdates	2
policy_entropy	14.189719
policy_loss	-0.015171743
serial_timesteps	256
time_elapsed	4.05e-06
total_timesteps	1024
value_loss	0.2522758

Fig. 6. Mid-way through the training we can observe that the loss seen is about 0.2522 for 1024 time steps.

approxkl	0.0002343525
clipfrac	0.0
ep_rewmean	nan
eplenmean	nan
explained_variance	-6.01
fps	1138
nupdates	7813
policy_entropy	37.50491
policy_loss	-0.0050025107
serial_timesteps	1000064
time_elapsed	3.78e+03
total_timesteps	4000256
value_loss	9.1157496e-14

Fig. 7. After training for 3.78 billion timesteps we can observe that the loss is $10e-15$

6 Discussion

The system as a whole worked accordingly in the real world, with the quadruped walking forward. There are instances where the quadruped sways left and right which can be further fine-tuned by making use of a better reward function and a better simulation model. The model swayed back and forth due to a simple reward function, which can later be fine-tuned. The gait generated was not as efficient as a human coded gait, but a major inference can be observed here which shows how adaptable reinforcement learning is for any given scenario.

When we tested the model on a real world environment, we observed a key difference between the real world environment and the simulated environment,i.e. friction. The friction in the simulated world was far too less compared to the real world quadruped. In few scenarios, when the model tries to move forward with huge steps, the friction between the legs and the floor does not let it complete its motion. This can be improved with a more comprehensive design.

7 Conclusion and Future Work

While taking the stability into consideration, there's a semantic gap between the real world and the simulated environment. In the real world, the robot either falls, or is stable, but having a continuous feedback loop with real values is not handled in our implementation. However, an intrinsic reinforcement signal to handle these values, it'd be more easier.

However, in this paper we present a proximal policy based gait generation on quadruped robots. Our method has proven to be effective in the simulated arena but there is a semantic gap between the simulated world and the real world which needs to be bridged. We feel that our work can benefit as a ground work for future research in this field and can be carried forward by taking numerous other observations like the orientation of the bot distance measurements, and also adding extra sensory information as observations can greatly influence the algorithm. A key improvement would be having pressure sensors on the feet to make sure the agent senses the edge of a table/ground and does not continue its motion.

Another approach would be utilizing a curiosity driven approach, which enables sufficient exploration by allowing the agent to create its own feedback based on the reward [4].

With these key improvements we can expect a paradigm shift in how future robots can travel on their own in every situation.

References

1. Erden, M.S., Leblebicioğlu, K.: Free gait generation with reinforcement learning for a six-legged robot. Robot. Auton. Syst. **56**, 199–212 (2008). https://doi.org/10.1016/j.robot.2007.08.001
2. Zamparelli, A., Scianca, N., Lanari, L., Oriolo, G.: Humanoid gait generation on uneven ground using intrinsically stable MPC. IFAC-PapersOnLine **51**(22), 393–398 (2018). https://doi.org/10.1016/j.ifacol.2018.11.574
3. Schulman, J., Wolski, F., Dhariwal, P., Radford, A., Klimov, O.: Proximal policy optimization algorithms. arXiv:1707.06347 [cs.LG]
4. Burda, Y., Edwards, H., Pathak, D., Storkey, A., Darrell, T., Efros, A.A.: Large-scale study of curiosity-driven learning. arXiv:1808.04355 [cs.LG]
5. Coumans, E., Bai, Y.: PyBullet, a Python module for physics simulation for games, robotics and machine learning. http://pybullet.org
6. 3D STL files of the quadruped model by Konredus. https://www.thingiverse.com/thing:2540774
7. Wiehe, A.O., Ansó, N.S., Drugan, M.M., Wiering, M.A.: Sampled policy gradient for learning to play the game Agar.io. arXiv:1809.05763
8. Existing 3D simulated environment for quadruped. https://github.com/rubencg195/WalkingSpider_OpenAI_PyBullet

Data Science in the Business Environment: Architecture, Process and Tools

Jing Lu[(✉)]

University of Winchester, Winchester SO22 5HT, UK
Jing.Lu@winchester.ac.uk

Abstract. Data science involves the collection, management, processing, analysis, visualisation and interpretation of huge amounts of data. It is a multi-disciplinary field that integrates systematic thinking, methodology, process and technology to develop intelligence with respect to real-world problems. This paper focuses on the business environment and identifies the components of data science forming a conceptual architecture before proposing a composite data-driven process model. Representative tools and techniques are applied to relevant case studies demonstrating innovation in undergraduate programme design, customer analytics and the marketing of insurance.

Keywords: Applied data science · Business analytics · Conceptual architecture · Process modelling · Knowledge discovery · Innovative case studies

1 Introduction

A vast amount of complex data is being generated in the business environment which requires detailed exploration and sophisticated processing to develop intelligence in the discovery of insights for informed decision making. This advanced understanding from knowledge can be derived from data-driven processes in order to create significant business value. Data science is a multi-disciplinary field which provides a bridge to data-driven decision making across organisations through an umbrella of techniques from a range of subject areas to generate insights from data.

Often companies find it challenging to become data-driven organisations due to the focus, time, persistence and commitment required. They need some guidance on "quick wins" to realise value and build creditability for their investments in data [2]. The contribution of this paper lies in bringing together key elements of the data science journey to promote understanding of the opportunities now available. An overarching process model for decision making is made accessible and explained through analysis of case studies applied to the business environment. The three main sections focus on data science architecture and corresponding frameworks, process models and methodology as well as tools and techniques – each part includes a brief review of the topic and a related case study.

Section 2 starts by identifying the components of data science, providing some comparison with data science frameworks and then showcasing the development of a Data Science degree apprenticeship programme. Based on the discussion of several

© Springer Nature Switzerland AG 2022
D. Garg et al. (Eds.): IACC 2021, CCIS 1528, pp. 279–293, 2022.
https://doi.org/10.1007/978-3-030-95502-1_22

data science methodologies, a composite data-driven process model is then proposed in Sect. 3. This guides business decision making through data exploration and insight generation – a representative example is given from customer analytics. Section 4 considers relevant tools and techniques in the context of data science skills and analytical technology before providing a more detailed exposition of the process model – highlighting an application from the insurance industry through predictive analytics. The paper then draws to a close with some concluding remarks.

2 Architecture and Framework

This section presents a novel architecture for data science and makes some comparison with corresponding frameworks, in particular the EDISON competence framework.

2.1 Data Science Conceptual Architecture

Data science has been considered as lying at the intersection of computer science, statistics and substantive application domains [19]. It is a blend of exploration, discovery and practice involving the collection, management, processing, analysis, visualisation and interpretation of huge amounts of data [6]. Domain knowledge cannot be separated from analysis and therefore it should form an integral part with data science components [17] – data professionals need both the analytical skills and the business understanding. Cao (2017) uses a formula to describe this discipline-based data science as [3]:

Data   Science = {Statistics ∩ Informatics ∩ Computing ∩ Communication ∩ Sociology ∩ Management ∩ Domain ∩ Thinking}.

The six key components of data science identified in this paper are linked graphically in Fig. 1. They form a conceptual architecture (or fan) containing five significant first-level intersections representing closely related areas. The foundation which provides a substantive connection to the business environment is domain-based knowledge and expertise.

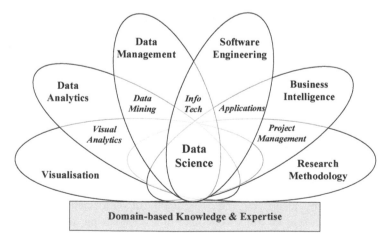

Fig. 1. A conceptual architecture for data science

2.2 EDISON Data Science Framework

In terms of Data Science frameworks, DASCA (Data Science Council of America) suggests that key components of data science are big data analytics and visualisation; programming and data engineering; big data strategy and management ecosystem; industry and applications; professions and career [5]. Donoho (2017) proposed a broader data science framework in the 50 years of Data Science article which classified the activities into six divisions at a relatively high level, preparing professionals for gaining insights from data while applying best practice [6].

The EU-funded EDISON (Education for Data Intensive Science to Open New science frontiers) project has focused on activities to establish the new profession of Data Scientist [7]. The EDISON Data Science Framework (EDSF) was developed to provide a platform for consistency in definitions supporting the data science profession – it is also integrated with practice and methodology as specified in related standards and frameworks.

The Competence Framework (CF-DS) provides a foundation for EDSF by including the common competences required for successful work of data scientists in industry and research, from data management through data analytics to domain-based business analytics. CF-DS defines five groups of competences which have been illustrated in Fig. 2 below.

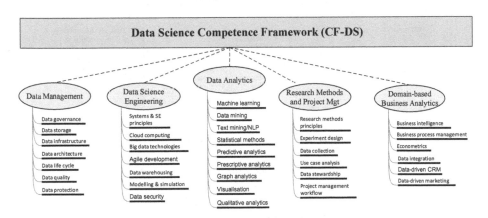

Fig. 2. EDISON data science competence framework

EDISON offers a conceptual roadmap for education, training, professional certification and organisational skills management which can inform future teaching and learning.

Successful data scientists must also be able to view business problems from a data perspective in order to improve decision making. Provost and Fawcett (2013) proposed several fundamental principles which can be used as guidance when extracting useful knowledge and insights from data [16]. Prominent among these are regarding data as a key strategic asset; treating the solution of business problems systematically by following a well-defined process; using information technology to discover relevant information from a large mass of data; with the evaluation of resulting solutions proceeding in light of the context where they will be deployed.

The next sub-section introduces the development of an undergraduate Data Science apprenticeship programme as a case study, with a focus on the application of the above concepts in the business environment.

2.3   Case Study: Data Science Degree Apprenticeship

Previously the University of Winchester Business School has developed a full-time BSc (Hons) Data Science with a distinctive structure and pedagogy, integrating themes in (e.g.) information management, predictive analytics, business intelligence and strategy [14]. The Skills Framework for the Information Age provided a basis for mapping employability skills in the context of data science [18].

Degree apprenticeships in the UK are business-led and government-supported nationally recognised qualifications developed in close collaboration with employers. In partnership with an international insurance company, the University has subsequently developed a part-time Data Science degree apprenticeship – see Fig. 3 for its programme structure.

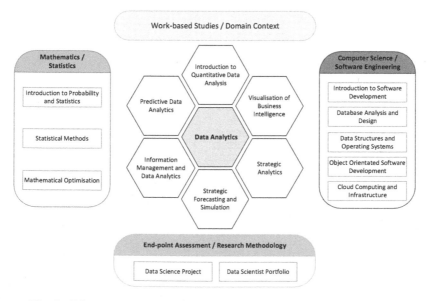

Fig. 3. BSc Data Science (Apprenticeship) – programme module structure

The specialist modules for the BSc Data Science (Apprenticeship) can be categorised under the following subject areas: Mathematics/Statistics, Data Analytics and Computer Science/Software Engineering. Work-based Studies topics and the final-year End-point Assessment are also included in the programme, representing the business environment and research methodology respectively. Moving into its second year of operation, the further development and delivery of this degree apprenticeship will be reported elsewhere.

3   Methodology and Process

This section reviews some established methodologies for data science and analytics before proposing a composite process model for data-driven decision making.

3.1   Range of Approaches

It is important to note that while each data science project is unique, they can usually benefit from following a well-established methodology which recommends the steps to follow in a clear process [4]. This will not only underpin credibility for the project path but also provide a structure for handling data and actionable insights. There are some established approaches available to help data science practitioners and businesses to follow the process principle of data-analytic thinking [10].

A foundational methodology for data science has been proposed by IBM Analytics which includes ten stages incorporating various iterative processes and corresponding technologies designed for insight generation [9]. The methodology has been redrawn here in the middle of Fig. 4 to provide a central spine facilitating comparison with other frameworks, such as PPDAC [21] and SMART [15].

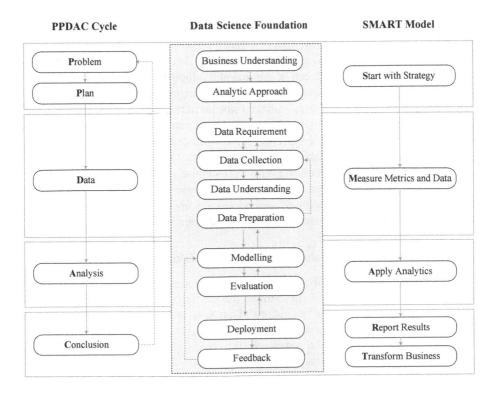

Fig. 4. Sample methodologies for data science and analytics

According to the foundational methodology [9], business problems and/or management issues will have been addressed/defined during the initial business understanding stage. Subsequently, the selection of suitable analytic approaches is required to identify the appropriate types of pattern (e.g. association rules, decision trees or clusters) to address business requirements. The next four stages represent comprehensive tasks working in and around the data, i.e. data requirements, collection, understanding and preparation – including data quality and consistency control. The final four stages involve iterations of modelling and evaluation – to deliver insights/answers for the business – before the deployment stage is reached for the first time and feedback provided.

The left-hand side of Fig. 4 illustrates the traditional PPDAC investigative cycle, which aims to solve a specific problem as part of a larger project – therefore domain knowledge is important at the early stages [21]. PPDAC begins with an appreciation of system dynamics before defining the problem in hand then moving onto the planning stage, where statistical sampling design and piloting are important. Data collection, management and cleaning proceed ahead of the analysis stage, where data exploration and various analyses are performed to inform hypothesis generation. Interpretation of results takes place at the conclusion stage, where new ideas and onward communication are key before the cycle may be repeated by adjusting the problem definition.

While PPDAC suggests starting with a problem, in reality the business environment can often be strategy-led. For example, as illustrated on the right-hand side of Fig. 4, the SMART model initiates a (big) data analytics project with business strategy [15]. This method will narrow down the requirements for data gathering into manageable areas – therefore the framework can be applied and adopted even in small to medium-sized enterprises (SMEs). Although using a different naming convention, the measure metrics stage aligns with working around data similar to the foundational methodology. Applying analytics and reporting results again aim to convey insights to stakeholders ahead of realising the potential impacts in business transformation.

Other approaches are available depending on the nature of the project (scientific, technological, business), the starting point (data-centric or decision centric analysis) and the level of analysis required (macro solutions or micro solutions). Although there is no single standard analytics solution methodology, some common features exist such as being systematic, creating believable results and being repeatable [4].

3.2   A Process Model for Data-Driven Decision Making

The methodologies reviewed above share a certain commonality – as the horizontal alignment has indicated in Fig. 4. In terms of the starting point however, is it better to consider business problems first or strategy? That said, there is more consensus going forward through data collection and pre-processing; likewise modelling, analysis and evaluation; also interpretation and communication of insights prior to deployment. This all informs the composite process model below for data-driven decision making.

Data analytics is one of the key components for data science and can be viewed as a process where a team explores and analyses data to discover organisational insights, which in turn facilitates better informed decisions. In the business environment, the extraction of knowledge from data to address management problems can be pursued by following such a systematic process with well-structured stages. A composite data-driven process model is thus proposed in Fig. 5, providing both a procedural approach and structure which all organisations can apply and adopt.

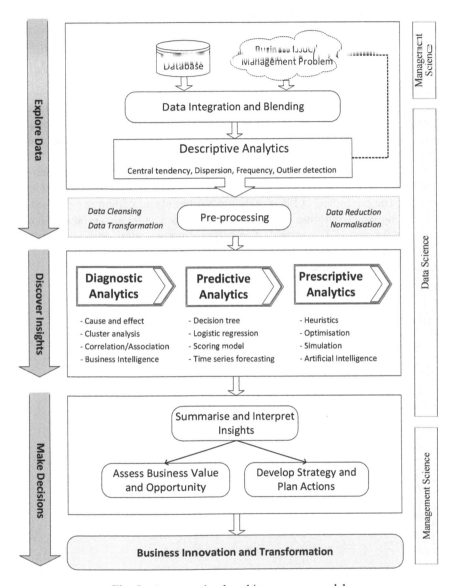

Fig. 5. A composite data-driven process model

The left-hand side of the figure indicates that this composite model comprises three distinct stages namely (i) Explore Data, (ii) Discover Insights and (iii) Make Decisions, each with its own structure. While the right-hand side of the figure points out the contributions both from data science (technical perspective – from data to insight) and management science (business context – from insight to impact).

It is worth mentioning that during the Discover Insights stage, although three levels of analytics have been indicated, it does not mean that all of these have to be applied in order to generate insights. Types of insights can be *observational* (based on description), *comparative* (providing some contrast), *causal* (factors which make another factor happen) and *predictive* (something that will likely occur in the future).

3.3   Case Study: Customer Analytics in SMEs

A representative case study from a small manufacturing organisation will be used here to illustrate an application of the process model – aiming to analyse the company's historical sales data to project increased revenue in future years by adopting the most effective sales approach [13].

Tableau visual analytics software [20] has been applied to explore this real-world SME data and discover insights through descriptive, diagnostic and predictive analytics techniques. The dashboard in Fig. 6 presents a summary of certain insights generated [13], including which customer types should be targeted and which products should be promoted in the future. The extrapolation of year-on-year sales for the next five years also shows that the USA will overtake North East Europe to become the highest revenue territory, with Asia Pacific closing in third place if trends continue.

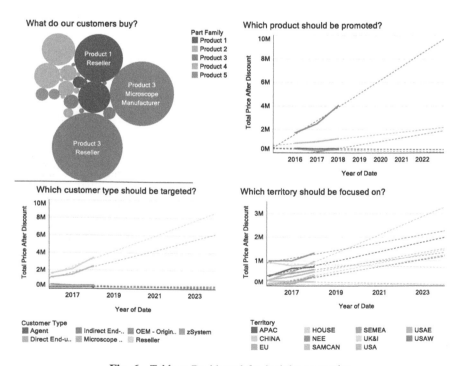

Fig. 6. Tableau Dashboard for insight generation

Insights from the analysis have enabled the SME and its management to assess the business value of innovative changes to the product portfolio, including both reduction and enhancement of products. Moreover there is the potential to target customers and markets more precisely as part of a future strategy.

4   Tools and Techniques

This section considers the technologies and skills which can be required for data science and analytics, describing a representative selection of analytical tools and techniques. A more detailed case study is explored here demonstrating insight generation in the marketing analytics domain.

4.1   EDISON Data Science Skills

Technologies related to collecting, cleansing, storing, processing, analysing and visualising big data are evolving rapidly. The capability and depth of the analytical tools and techniques are crucial to effective deployment in the business environment. While EDISON proposes a wide range of Data Science skills in relation to data analytics languages, tools, platforms and big data infrastructure, it is also clear that technology adoption can be challenging for less technical businesses and their staff. The nature and extent of the requirements are illustrated graphically in Fig. 7, which has been adapted from a forthcoming paper [12].

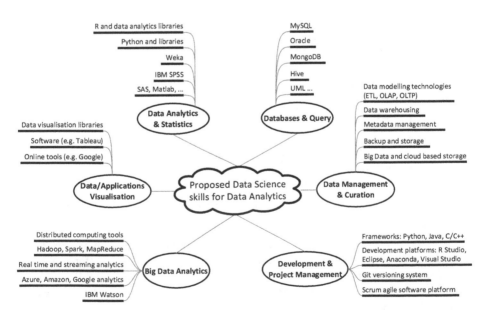

Fig. 7. EDISON Data Science skills in relation to Data Analytics

4.2   Analytical Technology

While Fig. 7 is quite extensive, some representative software tools for data analytics have been selected here based on whether suppliers offer open source versions or provide educational licences for the academic context. Following on from the data-driven process model in the previous section, Fig. 8 outlines specific tools and techniques in relation to Exploring Data and Discovering Insights. Weka is highlighted below and is well known for its industrial strength algorithms [8]. It will be used for the case study in the next sub-section.

	Explore Data	Discover Insights
Excel	Create pivot tables for missing data Graphs/charts, PivotCharts	Analysis ToolPak, PowerPivot, XLCubed
alteryx	Eliminate SQL formulae/coding Workflow for self-service data analytics	Pre-packaged procedures for predictive analysis
IBM SPSS	Validate and cleanse data, deal with unusual cases and optimal binning Chart builder, Graphboard Template Chooser	Descriptive statistics, inferential analysis, prediction
R	Correct raw data for consistency Base, grid, lattice and ggplot2	Statistics, time series, classification, clustering
iNZight	Explore data quickly for missing values Visual Inferential Tools (VIT)	Relationships, estimation, time series
WEKA	Discretise, transform, normalise, attribute selection Plot, receiver operating characteristic, tree/graph/boundary visualiser	Classification, clustering, association rules and sequential patterns mining
tableau	Use joins, pivots, splits and unions Interactive and visual analytics	Segmentation and cohort analysis, predictive analysis
FRONTLINE solvers	Data cleansing via dimensionality reduction View detailed charts of data using Chart Wizard	Simulation, optimisation and data mining
python	Standardise, cleanse, reduce, transform, normalise Matplotlib, Plotly, ggplot, Bokeh, Seaborn, pygal	Machine learning, network analysis, statistics, web applications, etc.

Fig. 8. Analytical tools and techniques

Several of the above tools are well established, including Excel from Microsoft and SPSS from IBM – Frontline Solvers produce the Analytic Solver platform used by many companies for predictive and prescriptive analytics in Excel – while the more contemporary iNZight software does as its name suggests and provides data exploration and insight generation capability. The latter was developed using R, the well-known environment for statistical computing and graphics. Alteryx primarily for data pre-processing and the flexible Python language for general-purpose programming complete the list along with Tableau, used in the previous case study.

4.3   Case Study: Marketing Analytics for Health Insurance

4.3.1   Explore Data

This case study is based on a representative insurance industry scenario where a financial services company provides various services such as loans, investment funds and insurance. The company plans to cross-sell health insurance to its existing customers, who may or may not hold insurance policies with the company. The company recommends health insurance to customers based on their profile. Customers might browse the recommended health insurance policy and consequently complete a form to make an initial application. When these customers fill out the form, their Response towards the policy is considered positive and they are classified as a *lead*. Once these leads are acquired, sales advisors approach them to convert into business – thus the company can sell proposed health insurance to these leads in a more efficient manner. Now the company is intent on building a model to predict whether a person will be interested in their proposed health plan/policy.

The health insurance dataset used here is drawn from Kaggle.com [11] – there are 50,882 instances and 14 attributes/variables. The features are a mix of customer demographics, holding policies of the customer and recommended policy information – see Table 1 for selected variables. Weka will be applied in order to demonstrate its data pre-processing and predictive model building functionalities.

Table 1. Description of selected variables.

Attribute/Variable	Description	Measurement type	Pre-processing
Customer_Age	Age of the customer	Numeric •18–75	PP5
Health_Indicator	Encoded value for health of the customer	Nominal •9 distinct labels •X1 to X9	Missing: 11,691 (23%) PP3
Holding_Policy_Type	Type of policy holding currently	Numeric •1–4	Missing: 20,251 (40%) PP1
Holding_Policy_Duration	Duration (in years) of policy that customer has subscribed to with the company	Nominal •15 distinct labels •1–14 •14 + (indicating > 14 years)	Missing: 20,251 (40%) PP2 PP4
Reco_Policy_Cat	Encoded value for recommended health insurance	Numeric •1–22	
Reco_Insurance_Type	Type of the recommended insurance	Nominal •Individual •Joint	
Reco_Policy_Premium	Premium (INR) for the recommended health insurance	Numeric •min: 2280 •max: 43350.4 •mean: ~ 14184	PP6
Response (Target)	Whether or not the customer has shown interest in the recommended policy	Numeric •0: No •1: Yes	

Data Cleansing
There are 3 variables with missing values.

- 'Holding_Policy_Type' and 'Holding_Policy_Duration': missing values indicate these are not the current customers of the company – the approach taken here is filling these null values with zero (0) **PP1 & PP2**
- 'Health_Indicator': can be assumed indicator was derived from pre-existing metric (e.g. BMI) – the missing value occurs when the user decided not to complete that part of the form – the approach taken here is filling the null values with the most common value in that category (i.e. the mode, which is X1) **PP3**

Data Transformation
A key part of data preparation is creating transforms of the dataset, through attribute selection and rescaling their values.

- Flagging long term customers if their "Holding_Policy_Duration" = 14 +
- Generating a new variable "Long_Term_Cust"
- 0: New Customer; 1: Not Long Term; 2: Long Term **PP4**

In addition, applying the Weka Discretize approach (Preprocess => Filter => Choose => unsupervised => attribute => Discretize) to create subgroups for "Customer_Age" and the "Reco_Policy_Premium".

- Dividing customer age into 5 groups – new variable "Age_Group" **PP5**
- Dividing premium into 5 groups too **PP6**

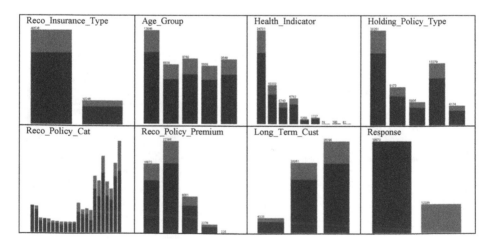

Fig. 9. Descriptive analytics for health insurance data

Figure 9 shows the visualisation of 8 variables in the context of descriptive analytics – note, due to the default colour setting for classes from Weka, the blue indicates a No response from customers and red indicates Yes.

4.3.2 Discover Insights

Before applying any predictive analytics technique, the number of input variables should be reduced to improve the effectiveness of the machine learning algorithms. For the prediction task here, certain factors have thus been eliminated from consideration. By performing the 'CorrelationAttributeEval' algorithm in Weka, several attributes were evaluated and the following selected for the predictor set: Reco_Policy_Cat, Reco_Insurance_Type, Reco_Policy_Premium, Holding_Policy_Type, Age_Group, Long_Term_Cust.

Depending on the nature of the variables (e.g. nominal vs numeric), Weka supports different categories of decision trees such as J48, Logistic Model Trees, M5P, Random Forest and Reduced Error Pruning Trees [8]. M5P is a binary regression algorithm to generate trees which are compact, where the leaves are linear regression functions that can produce continuous numerical attributes. This data mining technique follows the splitting idea of decision trees, but instead of class labels it has linear regression functions at the leaves, representing machine learning rules for prediction.

A M5P model was created for this case study by applying Weka to the pre-processed health insurance data. The complete tree is shown in Fig. 10 with 10 rectangular boxes representing the leaf nodes (i.e. regression models). The elliptical nodes each represent a test on the variable and every branch corresponds to an outcome from the test. For instance, looking at the middle path of the tree: IF Reco_Policy_Cat is encoded as 13, 16 or 18, THEN Holding_Policy_Type needs to be tested – in the case of the type being 3 or 4, THEN the predictive value for the outcome variable Response will be represented by the linear regression model LM6.

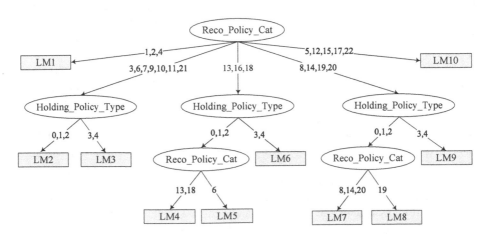

Fig. 10. M5P tree example for health insurance analysis

Continuing the example, the corresponding relationships for the LM6 model are:

LM num: 6

Response =
$$-0.0325 * \text{Age\_Group} =' 52-63',' 29-40'$$
$$+ 0.0633 * \text{Age\_Group} =' 29-40'$$
$$+ 0.0002 * \text{Holding\_Policy\_Type} = 3, 4$$
$$- 0.0893 * \text{Holding\_Policy\_Type} = 4$$
$$- 0.1437 * \text{Reco\_Policy\_Cat} = 16, 14, 20, 8, 19, 5, 17, 12, 22, 15$$
$$+ 0.2756$$

Regression is about predicting a quantity – in this case using the *Response* from LM6 as a target variable to predict a continuous value (between 0 and 1) representing the extent to which a customer is likely to show interest in an insurance policy – based on their age group, current type of policy holding and the recommended health insurance policy category. The illustration here shows the advantage of the M5P algorithm for its characterisation into simple linear relations, which can be readily used to predict the outcome values.

5 Conclusion

Companies nowadays are able to collect large amounts of customer, product and operational data about every aspect of their business – both internally and externally. Data has increasingly become an important asset to fulfill customer needs and improve decision making. Organisations are well advised to incorporate data science into their business strategy in order to optimise key processes, uncover new opportunities and create competitive differentiation.

The motivation of this research aims to help consultants and business management gain confidence in using data science and analytics to guide their recommendations and decision making. This paper provides a conceptual architecture for data science and a composite data-driven process model applicable to the business environment. Representative tools are illustrated along with supporting case studies from degree apprenticeship programme development, SME customer analytics and the marketing of insurance.

The UK insurance industry is the largest in Europe and makes it one of the most data rich markets [1]. New opportunities are available for insurance companies utilising data to gain knowledge about consumers and generate insights to remain price competitive. The majority of the Data Science degree apprentices at the University of Winchester are from the insurance industry. Further research will be carried out to investigate which analytical processes and techniques offer best practice in the market and provide the most significant business benefits.

References

1. Adams, M., Upreti, V., Chen, J.: Product-market strategy and underwriting performance in the united kingdom's property–casualty insurance market. Eur. J. Finance **25**(11), 1012–1031 (2019)
2. Bean, R.: Why is it so hard to become a data-driven company? Harvard Bus. Rev. Digital Articles **5**, 1–5 (2021)
3. Cao, L.B,: Data science challenges and directions. Commun. ACM **60**(8), 59–68 (2017)
4. Cochran, J.J.: INFORMS Analytics Body of Knowledge. John Wiley & Sons, Hoboken, NJ (2019)
5. Data Science Council of America. https://www.dasca.org
6. Donoho, D.: 50 years of data science. J. Comput. Graph. Stat. **26**(4), 745–766 (2017)
7. EDISON: Building the data science profession. https://cordis.europa.eu/project/id/675419/reporting
8. Hall, M., Frank, E., Holmes, G., Pfahringer, B., Reutemann, P., Witten, I.H.: The WEKA data mining software: an update. SIGKDD Explor. **11**(1), 10–18 (2009)
9. IBM Analytics White Paper: Foundational Methodology for Data Science. https://tdwi.org/~/media/64511A895D86457E964174EDC5C4C7B1.PDF
10. Iacobucci, D., Petrescu, M., Krishen, A., Bendixen, M.: The state of marketing analytics in research and practice. J. Market. Anal. **7**, 152–181 (2019)
11. Kaggle: Health Insurance – JOB-A-THON – Analytics Vidhya. https://www.kaggle.com/imsparsh/jobathon-analytics-vidhya
12. Lu, J.: Data science in the business environment: insight management for an Executive MBA. Int. J. Manage. Educ. **20**(1) (2022). Elsevier
13. Lu, J., Cairns, L., Smith, L.: Data science in the business environment: customer analytics case studies in SMEs. J. Model. Manag. **16**(2), 689–713 (2021)
14. Lu, J.: Data Science in the Business Environment: skills analytics for curriculum development. In: G. Nicosia et al. (eds.) Machine Learning, Optimization and Data Science. Lecture Notes in Computer Science, Vol. 11331, Springer International Publishing AG, pp.116–128. ISBN 978–3–030–13708–3 (2019)
15. Marr, B.: Big Data: Using Smart Big Data, Analytics and Metrics to Make Better Decisions and Improve Performance. John Wiley & Sons, Chichester (2015)
16. Provost, F., Fawcett, T.: Data Science for Business: What You Need to Know About Data Mining and Data-Analytic Thinking. O'Reilly Media, California (2013)
17. Sedkaoui, S.: Data Analytics and Big Data. Wiley (2018)
18. SFIA: The Skills Framework for the Information Age. https://www.sfia-online.org/en
19. Skiena, S.: The Data Science Design Manual. Texts in Computer Science, Springer (2017)
20. Tableau: Visual analytics platform. https://www.tableau.com
21. Wild, C. J., Pfannkuch, M.: Statistical thinking in empirical enquiry. Int. Stat. Rev. **67**(3), 223–265 (1999)

A Logarithmic Distance-Based Multi-Objective Genetic Programming Approach for Classification of Imbalanced Data

Arvind Kumar[1]([✉]), Shivani Goel[1], Nishant Sinha[2], and Arpit Bhardwaj[3]

[1] Computer Science Engineering Department, Bennett University,
Greater Noida, India
ak2815@bennett.edu.in,shivani.goel@bennett.edu.in
[2] Pitney Bowes Software, Noida, India
[3] Computer Science and Engineering Department, Mahindra University,
Hyderabad, India
arpit.bhardwaj@mahindrauniversity.edu.in

Abstract. Standard classification algorithms give biased results when data sets are imbalanced. Genetic Programming, a machine learning algorithm based on the evolution of species in nature, also suffers from the same issue. In this research work, we introduced a logarithmic distance-based multi-objective genetic programming (MOGP) approach for classifying imbalanced data. The proposed approach utilizes the logarithmic value of the distance between predicted and expected values. This logarithmic value for the minority and the majority classes is treated as two separate objectives while learning. In the final generation, the proposed approach generated a Pareto-front of classifiers with a balanced surface representing the majority and the minority class accuracies for binary classification. The primary advantage of the MOGP technique is that it can produce a set of good-performing classifiers in a single experimental execution. Against the MOGP approach, the canonical GP method requires multiple experimental runs and a priori objective-based fitness function. Another benefit of MOGP is that it explicitly includes the learning bias into the algorithms. For evaluation of the proposed approach, we performed extensive experimentation of five imbalanced problems. The proposed approach's results have proven its superiority over the traditional method, where the minority and majority class accuracies are taken as two separate objectives.

Keywords: Imbalanced data classification · Genetic programming · Fitness function · Multi-objective optimization · Pareto front

1 Introduction

Classification of imbalanced datasets imposes a major challenge in artificial intelligence (AI). A dataset is called imbalanced when the proportion of one class

© Springer Nature Switzerland AG 2022
D. Garg et al. (Eds.): IACC 2021, CCIS 1528, pp. 294–304, 2022.
https://doi.org/10.1007/978-3-030-95502-1_23

sample is lower compared to another class. The class with a lower sample data count is the minority class, and the class with a higher sample data count is the majority class. Standard AI algorithms suffer from a higher proportion of the majority class samples and produce biased classifiers inclined toward the majority class [8,14]. As the majority class samples count is high, overall accuracy will still be high though the generated classifiers produced very lower accuracy for the minority class samples. Genetic Programming (GP), a nature inspired technique, was also influenced by the imbalanced nature of data and produced bias classifiers. In real-world problems, like disease patient classification, fraud detection in a financial transaction, e-commerce, national security, spatial planning, and many more, the minority class accuracies are more important than the other one [4,10,15,16]. Therefore, generating a classifier with good and balanced accuracies on both classes is a vital area of research.

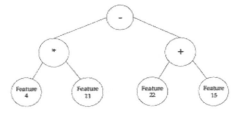

Fig. 1. Program's tree representation.

One approach to address the challenges of imbalanced data classification is to introduce the over-sampling of the minority class samples or the under-sampling of the majority class samples so that the influence of higher sample count can be minimized [17,20]. The second approach is to adjust the cost, intending to give higher weightage to the minority class samples [7,18,29]. This work emphasized the second approach based on multi-objective evolutionary optimization (MOEO) to tackle the performance trade-off during model learning. In the MO approach, a set of solutions, having a good trade-off between both class accuracies, is evolved. These trade-off solutions generate a Pareto-front in a single execution by keeping both class performance objectives distinct during the evolution. Bhowan et al. (2013), proposed multi-objective Genetic Programming (MOGP) for the classification of an imbalanced data set [1]. In their work, the author used the majority class accuracy and the minority class accuracy as to competing objectives during the training process. The authors utilized an existing Pareto-based optimization technique Non dominated sorting genetic algorithm II (NSGA-II) by Deb et al. (2002) [2,3]. For generating Pareto-front, NSGA-II, uses dominance rank, which is the count of all solutions in population, dominating a given solution [28,30]. NSGA-II is applied to solve various research problems [11,19,26,27].

Again, based on NSGA-II, Fernandes et al. (2019) proposed an ensemble of classifiers based on the multi-objective genetic sampling for imbalanced classification (EMOSAIC) technique [6]. In this work, we presented a logarithmic distance-based MOGP approach to classifying imbalanced data. The proposed approach utilizes the logarithmic value of the distance between predicted and expected values. This logarithmic value for the minority and the majority classes are treated as two separate objectives while learning. In the final generation, the proposed approach generated a Pareto-front of classifiers with a balanced surface representing the majority and the minority class accuracies for binary classification. The primary motive behind this research work is to generate a better Pareto-front, compared to the standard MOGP method. The comparison will be done in the form of a higher hyper-front area and diversified solutions spread throughout the Pareto-front.

The rest of this paper is organized as follows. Section 2 gives details of MOGP, proposed MOGP approach, GP parameter setting, followed benchmark data set. Section 3 summarizes results and discussion followed by the conclusion in Sect. 4.

2   Materials and Methods

2.1   Multi-Objective Genetic Programming (MOGP)

GP is a population-based, nature-inspired technique based on Darwin's theory of survival of the fittest. As per this theory, new solutions are generated in nature by reproduction, crossover, and mutation. Based on some evaluation criteria (call fitness function in GP terminology), the survival of solutions increases generation by generation in any environment representing the problem domain. An individual also called a program, is shown in Fig. 1

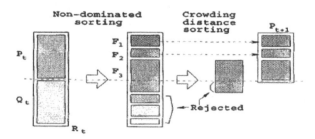

Fig. 2. NSGA-II procedure [3]

In traditional MOEO, the algorithm cultivates the set of non-dominated solutions until a Pareto Optimal front is generated. Our proposed technique is based on a well-known MOEO technique called NSGA-II. In NSGA-II, a new population is generated by crossover and mutation, and this newly generated population is merged with the parent population at each generation. After that, this intermediate population is sorted by the fitness of individuals, and the best individuals are copied to the new generation. These two objective-based sorting are done by a fast non-dominated sorting approach [3, 25]. Thus, the population size is fixed in each generation, and this intermediate population ensures elitism in the population. The final generation corresponds to the set of evolved individuals with the generated Pareto front in the last step. Figure 2, gives a brief of this procedure.

In the traditional MOGP approach, the minority class accuracy ($F_{m_{std}}$) and the majority class accuracy ($F_{M_{std}}$) are taken as two objective fitness functions (Eq. 1 and 2).

$$F_{m_{std}} = \frac{TP}{TP + FN} \tag{1}$$

$$F_{M_{std}} = \frac{TN}{TN + FP} \tag{2}$$

where TN is *true negative*, TP is *true positive*, FN is *false negative* and FP is *false positive* prediction counts.

2.2 Proposed MOGP Approach

The standard fitness functions mentioned in the previous section may suffer from under-fitted modeling. To understand this, let's assume that there are three classifiers, C1, C2, and C3, predicting any minority class sample (value = 1). If predicted values for C1, C2, and C3 are 0.60, 0.70, and 0.99, respectively, all the three predictions indicate values 1, and all are correct. But the classifier C3 is better than C2, and C2 is better than C1. Therefore, we can generate better-fitted classifiers if we consider the distance factor, i.e., how far the prediction values compare to the expected value. Also, if we sum up these distance values for all samples, some worst predicted values may nullify the correct or near-correct predicted values. Therefore, before sum-up these individual distance values, these values should be bounded. For bounding these values, we may take the logarithmic of the distance values. Based on these facts, We propose a logarithmic distance-based MOGP approach, in which we define two objective functions as Eq. 3 and 4.

$$F_{m_{prop}} = \sum_{i=1}^{N_{min}} \frac{log\left(1 + |dist_{min i}|\right)}{N_{min}} \tag{3}$$

$$F_{M_{prop}} = \sum_{i=1}^{N_{maj}} \frac{log\left(1 + |dist_{maj i}|\right)}{N_{maj}} \tag{4}$$

where,

N_{min}: Minority samples count in training data.
N_{maj}: Majority samples count in training data.

$dist_{\text{maj}}$ ₁: Distance of actual value from predicted value in ith majority class sample.

$dist_{\text{min}}$ ₁: Distance between expected value and predicted value in ith minority class sample.

Thus, the $F_{m_{prop}}$ replace the $F_{m_{std}}$ and $F_{M_{prop}}$ replace the $F_{M_{std}}$, in the standard MOGP framework. After completion of GP run, we recalculate Pareto-front based on the minority class accuracy and the majority class accuracy. Thus the main difference with the standard GP method is that the proposed approach utilized the logarithmic value of the distance between predicted and expected values. In this way, the proposed method generates better-fitted classifiers.

2.3   Trapezoidal Rule for Area Under Generated Pareto-Front

The trapezoidal rule (TR) is utilized for calculating the hyper-area under generated Pareto-front curve. The TR divides the curve into small trapezoids and performs the summation of all the areas of the small trapezoids to calculate the total area under the curve [22].

Let $y = f(x)$ be continuous function on interval [a, b]. We can divide the interval [a, b] into n equal sub-intervals, each of width h (Eq. 5 and 6).

$$a = x_0 < x_1 < x_2 < \cdots < x_n = b \tag{5}$$

$$h = \frac{(b - a)}{n} \tag{6}$$

Now, area under Pareto-front curve is defined as Eq. 7.

$$\int_a^b f(x)dx \approx \frac{h}{2} * \left[f(x_0) + 2 * \sum_{i=1}^{n-1} f(x) + f(x_n) \right] \tag{7}$$

2.4   GP Parameter Setting

For population initialization, we used the "ramped half and half" method. This method generates a wide variety of individuals of various sizes, and shapes [13]. The tree initialization depth is taken as (2, 6). The function set contains +, −, *, /, log, sin and cos functions. The crossover and mutation probability is set to 0.60 and 0.40, respectively. Population size is set to 512, and max generation is set to 50. We use tournament selection, with tournament size 2. For simplicity, sub-tree crossover, sub-tree mutation, and tournament selection with tournament size two are taken.

2.5   Benchmark Data Set

The proposed MOGP approach is assessed for five imbalanced benchmark problems. These benchmark problems are based on data available on the UCI machine learning repository [5]. Table 1 shows a summary of these data-sets. These imbalanced classification problems are briefly described as follows:

Abalone (ABL-9-18). The abalone dataset is a popular imbalanced real-world problem used in various research work [7,12,21]. In this benchmark problem, a classifier is evolved to predict the age of abalone shellfish. The abalone dataset has 8 attributes and a multi-class classification problem. We have converted this to a binary class classification problem by selecting class 9 vs. class 9 plus 18. Thus out of 731 total samples, 42 samples (6%) belong to the minority class.

Yeast (YEAST1 and YEAST2). The yeast dataset has 1484 samples. The objective is to predict the protein localization sites in yeast cells [9]. Based on the properties of amino acid sequences, there are 8 input features. There are nine classes in this dataset, which makes it a multi-class classification problem. We converted this multi-class problem to a binary class classification problem by considering only one class samples at a time (the minority class), and rest as the majority class samples. Two sets of datasets, YEAST1 and YEAST2, are generated. In YEAST1 dataset is generated by considering MIT versus all, and YEAST2 is generated by considering MEA3 versus all. YEAST1 have 16%, and YEAST2 have 11% of minority samples count.

Table 1. Benchmark datasets

Data set name	Imbalanced factor	Features count	Minority sample	Majority sample count	Total sample count
ABL-9-18	06:94	8	42	689	731
YEAST2	11:89	8	163	1321	1484
YEAST1	16:84	8	244	1240	1484
ION	36:64	34	126	225	351
WDBC	37:63	31	212	357	569

Ionosphere (ION). The ionosphere dataset has 351 samples of radar signals based on high-frequency antennas aiming for free electrons in the ionosphere [23]. In this dataset, there are 126 minority class samples ("good" signals) and 225 majority class samples ("bad" signals). Thus, there are 36% minority class samples and 34 real-number input features.

Wisconsin Diagnostic Breast Cancer (WDBC). WDBC dataset has samples of 569 patients [24]. It has 31 input features. The patient may belong to be either the Benign or Malignant breast tumor group. From 569 samples, 212 patients belong to the minority (Benign (37%))class.

3   Results and Discussion

The proposed approach is implemented in Python. We use Python 3.6.6, installed on Microsoft Windows 10, powered by an Intel Core i7 processor with 32 GB RAM. For each benchmark problem, 30 runs of standard MOGP and proposed MOGP approaches are executed. In every run, the hyper-area of generated Pareto front is calculated. For calculating the hyper area under generated Pareto-front, we use trapezoidal rule [22]. The trapezoidal rule is a technique to approximate the integral of a curve (area) on a given interval [a, b]. The mean and standard deviation of these 30 runs for each benchmark problem is calculated. Generated Pareto-front for each imbalanced problem is plotted in Fig. 3 and 4. The left part of the figure shows the generated front for the proposed MOGP approach, and the right part shows the generated front for the standard MOGP approach. If we do a visual comparison of these fronts, we can see that the generated Pareto-front by the proposed method contains a much higher diversity of generated classifiers, compared to the standard method.

Table 2. Pareto front hyper area

Data set name	Imbalanced factor	Front hyper area GP_{prop}	Front hyper area GP_{std}
ABLN-9-18	06:94	**0.840** ± 0.031	0.632 ± 0.030
Yeast-2	11:89	**0.941** ± 0.005	0.813 ± 0.071
Yeast-1	16:84	**0.818** ± 0.004	0.788 ± 0.027
ION	36:64	**0.733** ± 0.159	0.292 ± 0.041
WDBC	37:63	**0.960** ± 0.009	0.109 ± 0.023

For all the five benchmark problems, the generated front by the proposed method outperforms the front produced by the standard MOGP technique. Figure 3 and 4, clearly show the visual of this conclusion. The mean value of generated Pareto-front is summarized in Table 2. In the case of the standard MOGP method, for ABL-9-18, YEAST2, YEAST1, ION, and WDBC datasets, the generated front hyper-area are 0.632, 0.813, 0.788, 0.292, and 0.1094, respectively. Against this, in the case of the proposed logarithmic-distance-based MOGP method, the generated front for ABL-9-18, YEAST2, YEAST1, ION, and WDBC datasets hyper-area are 0.840, 0.941, 0.818, 0.733, and 0.960, respectively. Thus the proposed logarithmic distance-based MOGP method beats the standard MOGP method in all considered imbalanced problems.

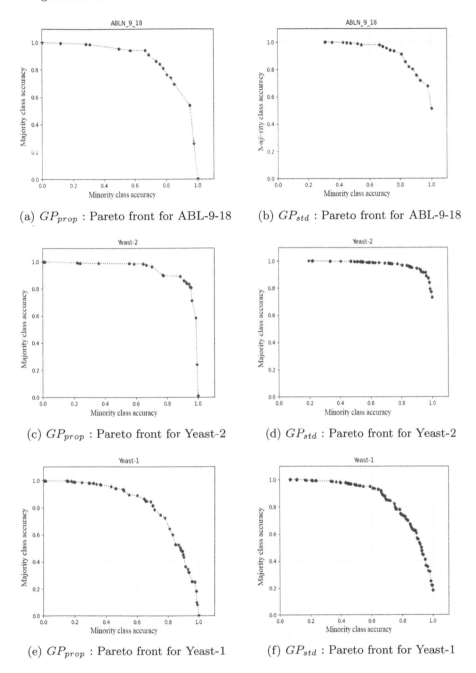

(a) GP_{prop} : Pareto front for ABL-9-18

(b) GP_{std} : Pareto front for ABL-9-18

(c) GP_{prop} : Pareto front for Yeast-2

(d) GP_{std} : Pareto front for Yeast-2

(e) GP_{prop} : Pareto front for Yeast-1

(f) GP_{std} : Pareto front for Yeast-1

Fig. 3. Generated pareto front by multi-objective genetic programming

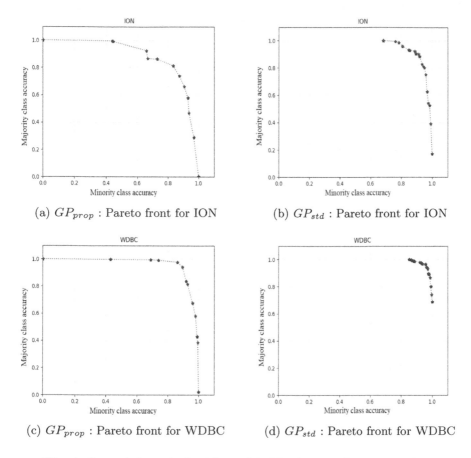

(a) GP_{prop} : Pareto front for ION   (b) GP_{std} : Pareto front for ION

(c) GP_{prop} : Pareto front for WDBC   (d) GP_{std} : Pareto front for WDBC

Fig. 4. Generated pareto front by multi-objective genetic programming

4   Conclusions

Many of the real-world classification problems are imbalanced, and this imbalanced nature of data highly influences the performance of standard AI techniques. GP also suffers from a similar issue. In this research work, we introduced a logarithmic distance-based multi-objective genetic programming approach to classifying imbalanced data. The proposed MOGP method generate a better Pareto-front, compared to the standard MOGP method. We evaluated its performance in the form of a higher hyper-front area and diversified solutions spread throughout the Pareto-front. Based on our extensive experimentation results, we can conclude that the proposed logarithmic distance-based MOGP approach outperforms the standard MOGP method.

References

1. Bhowan, U., Johnston, M., Zhang, M., Yao, X.: Evolving diverse ensembles using genetic programming for classification with unbalanced data. IEEE Trans. Evol. Comput. **17**(3), 368–386 (2013)
2. Deb, K.: Multi-objective optimisation using evolutionary algorithms: an introduction. In: Multi-objective Evolutionary Optimisation for Product Design and Manufacturing, pp. 3–34. Springer, Cham (2011) https://doi.org/10.1007/978-0-85729-652-0_1
3. Deb, K., Pratap, A., Agarwal, S., Meyarivan, T.: A fast and elitist multiobjective genetic algorithm: NSGA-II. IEEE Trans. Evol. Comput. **6**(2), 182–197 (2002)
4. Dhote, S., Vichoray, C., Pais, R., Baskar, S., Shakeel, P.M.: Hybrid geometric sampling and AdaBoost based deep learning approach for data imbalance in e-commerce. Electron. Commer. Res. **20**(2), 259–274 (2020)
5. Dua, D., Graff, C.: UCI machine learning repository (2017). http://archive.ics.uci.edu/ml
6. Fernandes, E., de Leon Ferreira, A.C.P., Carvalho, D., Yao, X.: Ensemble of classifiers based on multiobjective genetic sampling for imbalanced data. IEEE Trans. Knowl. Data Eng. **32**, 1104–1115 (2019)
7. Galván-López, E., Vázquez-Mendoza, L., Trujillo, L.: Stochastic semantic-based multi-objective genetic programming optimisation for classification of imbalanced data. In: Pichardo-Lagunas, O., Miranda-Jiménez, S. (eds.) MICAI 2016. LNCS (LNAI), vol. 10062, pp. 261–272. Springer, Cham (2017). https://doi.org/10.1007/978-3-319-62428-0_22
8. Guan, D., Yuan, W.: A survey of mislabeled training data detection techniques for pattern classification. IETE Tech. Rev. **30**(6), 524–530 (2013)
9. Horton, P., Nakai, K.: A probabilistic classification system for predicting the cellular localization sites of proteins. In: ISMB, vol. 4, pp. 109–115 (1996)
10. Huang, S., Lei, K.: IGAN-IDS: an imbalanced generative adversarial network towards intrusion detection system in ad-hoc networks. Ad Hoc Netw. **105**, 102177 (2020)
11. Jemai, J., Zekri, M., Mellouli, K.: An NSGA-II algorithm for the green vehicle routing problem. In: Hao, J.-K., Middendorf, M. (eds.) EvoCOP 2012. LNCS, vol. 7245, pp. 37–48. Springer, Heidelberg (2012). https://doi.org/10.1007/978-3-642-29124-1_4
12. Kang, Q., Shi, L., Zhou, M., Wang, X., Wu, Q., Wei, Z.: A distance-based weighted undersampling scheme for support vector machines and its application to imbalanced classification. IEEE Trans. Neural Netw. Learn. Syst. **29**(9), 4152–4165 (2017)
13. Koza, J.: Genetic Programming: On the Programming of Computers by Means of Natural Selection (1992)
14. Kumar, A., Sinha, N., Bhardwaj, A.: A novel fitness function in genetic programming for medical data classification. J. Biomed. Inform. **112**, 103623 (2020)
15. Kumar, A., Sinha, N., Bhardwaj, A.: Predicting the presence of newt-amphibian using genetic programming. In: Advances in Data and Information Sciences, vol. 318, pp. 1–10. Springer, Cham (2021). https://doi.org/10.1007/978-981-16-5689-7_19
16. Kumar, A., Sinha, N., Bhardwaj, A., Goel, S.: Clinical risk assessment of chronic kidney disease patients using genetic programming. Comput. Meth. Biomech. Biomed. Eng. 1–9 (2021). https://doi.org/10.1080/10255842.2021.1985476

17. Lee, D., Kim, K.: An efficient method to determine sample size in oversampling based on classification complexity for imbalanced data. Expert Syst. Appl. **184**, 115442 (2021)
18. Li, J., Fong, S., Wong, R.K., Chu, V.W.: Adaptive multi-objective swarm fusion for imbalanced data classification. Inf. Fusion **39**, 1–24 (2018)
19. Li, Y., Wang, S., Duan, X., Liu, S., Liu, J., Hu, S.: Multi-objective energy management for Atkinson cycle engine and series hybrid electric vehicle based on evolutionary NSGA-II algorithm using digital twins. Energy Convers. Manage. **230**, 113788 (2021)
20. Liu, B., Tsoumakas, G.: Dealing with class imbalance in classifier chains via random undersampling. Knowl.-Based Syst. **192**, 105292 (2020)
21. Nash, W.J., Sellers, T.L., Talbot, S.R., Cawthorn, A.J., Ford, W.B.: The population biology of abalone (Haliotis species) in Tasmania. I. Blacklip abalone (H. rubra) from the north coast and islands of bass strait. Sea Fisheries Division, Technical Report 48, p. 411 (1994)
22. Rahman, Q.I., Schmeisser, G.: Characterization of the speed of convergence of the trapezoidal rule. Numer. Math. **57**(1), 123–138 (1990)
23. Sigillito, V.G., Wing, S.P., Hutton, L.V., Baker, K.B.: Classification of radar returns from the ionosphere using neural networks. J. Hopkins APL Tech. Dig. **10**(3), 262–266 (1989)
24. Street, W.N., Wolberg, W.H., Mangasarian, O.L.: Nuclear feature extraction for breast tumor diagnosis. In: Biomedical Image Processing and Biomedical Visualization, vol. 1905, pp. 861–870. International Society for Optics and Photonics (1993)
25. Wang, P., Emmerich, M., Li, R., Tang, K., Bäck, T., Yao, X.: Convex hull-based multiobjective genetic programming for maximizing receiver operating characteristic performance. IEEE Trans. Evol. Comput. **19**(2), 188–200 (2014)
26. Wang, S., Zhao, D., Yuan, J., Li, H., Gao, Y.: Application of NSGA-II algorithm for fault diagnosis in power system. Electr. Power Syst. Res. **175**, 105893 (2019)
27. Xu, X., Fu, S., Li, W., Dai, F., Gao, H., Chang, V.: Multi-objective data placement for workflow management in cloud infrastructure using NSGA-II. IEEE Trans. Emerg. Top. Comput. Intell. **4**(5), 605–615 (2020)
28. Yusoff, Y., Ngadiman, M.S., Zain, A.M.: Overview of NSGA-II for optimizing machining process parameters. Procedia Eng. **15**, 3978–3983 (2011)
29. Zhang, C., Tan, K.C., Li, H., Hong, G.S.: A cost-sensitive deep belief network for imbalanced classification. IEEE Trans. Neural Netw. Learn. Syst. **30**(1), 109–122 (2018)
30. Zhao, B., Xue, Y., Xu, B., Ma, T., Liu, J.: Multi-objective classification based on NSGA-II. Int. J. Comput. Sci. Math. **9**(6), 539–546 (2018)

Multiview Classification with Missing-Views Through Adversarial Representation and Inductive Transfer Learning

Mukhtar Opeyemi Yusuf[1]($\boxtimes$) (iD), Divya Srivastava[1] (iD),
Shashank Sheshar Singh[1] (iD), and Mahtab Alam[2] (iD)

[1] Bennett University, Greater Noida, Uttar Pradesh, India
{e20soe814,divya.srivastava,shashank.singh}@bennett.edu.in
[2] Mewar University, Chittorgarh, Nigeria

Abstract. The importance of Multiview learning in classification task cannot be further stressed. Over the years, there is an increasing interest among researchers to enhance Multiview classification models. However, very little attention has been paid to handling the missing-view(s) problem in existing systems. Missing-view can be caused by various reasons. It can be a technical fault during data measurement which can occur in real-world applications. Handling such occurrences is paramount to determine the success of the classification model on real-world data. In this paper, a Multiview deep classification model is proposed. The model implements an adversarial network that learns a latent space of semantic knowledge of the Multiview data. Further, the model used an inductive transfer style to train a neural classifier network from the learned latent space. Therefore, understanding the semantics is required to recreate any corresponding alternate view from a given view. The proposed model is trained and evaluated on MNIST and Noisy MNIST datasets. Its performance was compared with existing systems in terms of accuracy and normalized mutual information (NMI). The proposed model achieved better performance. The model is evaluated across different missing rates which further demonstrated that it is capable of handling missing-view(s) effectively.

Keywords: Multiview learning · Classification · Missing view · Adversarial learning · Inductive transfer learning

1 Introduction

Multiview learning is an interesting kind of machine and deep learning approach that consider the multiple views of a datapoint to enhance the model's generalization. These views can be representations of each datapoint in several forms; like, in face recognition, a combination of LBP (to extract salient features of textures as regards skin color) and HoG (to extract facial shape) can be

© Springer Nature Switzerland AG 2022
D. Garg et al. (Eds.): IACC 2021, CCIS 1528, pp. 305–317, 2022.
https://doi.org/10.1007/978-3-030-95502-1_24

used to achieve encouraging success [14,18,33]. However, a direct combination of these two feature representations can easily lead to over-fitting when variance in the training data is large (especially if the number of available training data is small). Therefore, it is much safer and justifiable to train a system that learns the underlying statistics from both representations (LBP and HoG). Encourage mutual correlations to infer the giving datapoint. This underlying statistical learning of mutual connections between different representations is what coined Multiview learning. Multiview data are describe in this paper as either *organic* or *inorganic*. Organic Multiview data refers to the data curated directly from the source. That is data that is captured organically from the source. For example, Fig. 1(A) depicts multiple views of a Mini Van captured from different angles. Another example can be seen in [2], which observed several news articles and translated into 5 different languages. Each language represents a different view. In contrast, inorganic Multiview data as seen in Fig. 1(B), are the data that were either; generated/synthesized or represented using different features descriptors, like in [30,31]. Multiview data are increasing today and the need to utilize these data in the most efficient way is important [24]. Various studies across multi-disciplines have incorporated different Multiview learning approaches to achieve better generalization in their respective task. These tasks could be either in Clustering [21,29,38,46], in classification [22,41,48] and many more. However, the interest of this paper is focused on Multiview learning for a classification task.

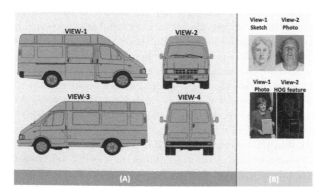

Fig. 1. A pictorial description of organic and inorganic Multiview data. (A) Depicts an organic simulation capturing different views of a minivan. (B) Depict a description of inorganic Multiview data of sketch generated from the photo, and HOG feature descriptor generated from photo image.

Multiview learning classification aims at enhancing the generalization performance in the classification task. The principle of maximum entropy [8] is used in most conventional single-view machine/deep learning classification systems. Theoretically, these single-view systems train a model that learns several encodings from a pool of prior data for each class. Then maximize the Entropy. The encodings with the maximum entropy are chosen as the representation for the specific class. The process of learning such encodings is often referred to as the feature extraction process. Which simply involves extracting statistical information about the giving datapoint. After extracting these features (or encodings), a supervised classifier is trained to map the learned encodings to a given class label. This classical approach has tremendously shown great success in different domains of machine learning and deep learning applications. One of such successes is the Alexnet [11] which won the ILSVR image recognition competition and became a pivotal achievement for deep learning models in 2012. Yushi Chen et al. [7] successfully classify hyperspectral data. Heba Mohsen et al. [19] were able you achieve a decent classification of four classes of brain tumors. Omar Ahmed et al. [1] uses a similar approach to classify gene expressions. Despite the continued success of all these models, one of the challenges in the classification task is data bias. Especially in a multi-modal setting. This is because most existing systems train their models on a specific view using the principle of maximum entropy. Therefore, eliminating other hidden information that may have been considered as less informative, noise, or even redundant. However, some of these discarded information may be an indication to infer a different outcome. These gaps are what Multiview learning tries to fit. Multiview learning have seen success in various inter-disciplinary areas of research and application. Like in medical diagnosis [9,42], in finance [4,28], in social behavior [6,10], and many more areas.

Multiview learning has been able to achieve interesting growth of success in classification tasks. However, few challenges are faced by many researchers in the domain. One of which is the missing-view(s) or incomplete-view(s) problem [15]. Missing-view is a problem attributed to Multiview data where certain view(s) of a datapoint does not contain enough information to describe that datapoint [37]. Sometimes such view(s) may be completely missing in the Multiview data. This situation can occur due to some technical problems faced either during the curation/measurement of organic Multiview data. Or during the generation of synthetic Multiview data.

1.1 Motivation and Contributions

The proposed system is motivated by the gaps identified in the extensive literature survey. Summary of these gaps are;

i Conventional single-view classification systems pose a risk of data biases. Especially if the classification is based on multi-modal data. The single-view classification approach forces the model to select the best performing (maximum entropy) single-view datapoint. However, the effect of such an approach can sometimes lead to incorrect classification. As hidden indicators may exist in the data that may have contributing factors towards the final inference. However, these data are discarded in single-view learning. Therefore, it is paramount to allow such inclusiveness in the model. This ability can be provided through Multiview learning.

ii Many existing Multiview classification systems have not considered the problem of missing-views. Which can cause over-fitting of data. Even when overfitting prevention mechanisms like regularization, dropout, and others are
applied to the model. This paper opines that handling missing-views should
be incorporated in Multiview classification systems. Such that, the model can
perform well on test data and generalize even better on real-world data.

The following are the summarized contributions of the proposed model;

1. A novel deep Multiview learning architecture is proposed to incorporate multiple views of data and properly classify them.
2. Adversarial learning combined with inductive transfer learning is used to
handle the missing-view(s) problem in Multiview classification.

The rest of the paper is organized as follows. Section 2 highlights some existing related work. Section 3 discusses the methodology of the proposed system.
Section 4 explains the experimental setup. Section 5 presents and discusses the
results obtained. Lastly, Sect. 6 gives the conclusion of the paper.

2   Related Work

Existing systems have proposed several approaches to solve the missing-view
problem in Multiview data. Some of these approaches like dimensionality reduction [25,36,43,44], multi-kernel learning [5,32], matrix completion [17,23,26] and
subspace learning [13,35,39,40,47]. The proposed work considered the subspace
learning approach to both solve the missing view problem and provide Multiview classification. Subspace learning is an isomorphic approach where a model
is trained to learn the engineering of its latent embeddings. This technique is syn-
onymous with dimensionality reduction as used in data compression. However,
unlike dimensionality reduction which removes less-salient features or views. Subspace learning of Multiview data enhances the property of inclusiveness of these
diverse views. After an extensive literature survey of this topic. Some closely
related existing systems are highlighted in this section.

L. Zhang et al. [45] proposed an Isomorphic Linear Correlation Analysis
(ILCA). That learns latent space of correlating features across the different
views. The missing-views are then modeled by a combination of a low-rank
matrix (for inter-class difference) and a sparse matrix (for intra-class difference). Furthermore, they proposed an Identical Distribution Pursuit Completion (IDPC) algorithm to recover the missing views in the data. The IDPC is
based on the identical distribution constraint of the missing view to other available views in the feature-isomorphic subspace. However, this approach is based
on the assumption that missing-views obey normal distribution as in principal
component analysis (PCA). Meanwhile, the proposed system is capable of recon-
structing the latent space of a missing-view without constraining them to normal
distribution.

Cai Xu et al. [34] proposed an adversarial incomplete Multiview clustering (AIMC). They explored the adversarial learning of generative adversarial networks (GAN) to train each view's latent representation. Firstly, they generate each view's encoding Z_i^v. Then they used an average pooling to combine all the Z_i^v into Z. The decoder uses element-wise reconstruction loss to reconstruct each view from Z. They further added a Kullback-Liebler aligned clustering loss to minimize the divergence between the clustering distribution estimated by Z^v and target distribution estimated by Z. Although the proposed system uses an adversarial learning technique, the objectives of the proposed system are focused on enhancing Multiview classification. Hence, the architecture and objective functions differ.

Yijie Lin et al. [16] proposed the COMPLETER model to solve the missing-view problem in Multiview clustering. The model uses two autoencoders (assuming two views). Each learning the corresponding latent view representation as Z^{v1} and Z^{v2}. Then uses additional two autoencoders (G^{v1} and G^{v2}) to learn the mappings from Z^{v1} to Z^{v2}. And lastly, uses contrastive learning to maximize the correlations between Z^{v1} and Z^{v2}. The proposed system is somewhat similar to the COMPLETER since it also learns how to reconstruct cross-view latent space and complete missing-views if any. However, the proposed system combines adversarial learning and transfer learning to complement the missing-view. The overall objective function in the proposed system is towards classification tasks, which is quite different from that of COMPLETER.

3 Proposed Methodology

For simplicity and clarity, the proposed system has been divided into two subsections. Figure 2 depicts the architecture of the proposed system.

3.1 Adversarial Cross-View Latent Learning

This phase of the proposed system is responsible for learning the latent representation Z_i^v of each view. The is achieved through adversarial learning of cross-view latent representation. A generative adversarial network (GAN) with cycle consistency is implemented. The GAN is used to construct and reconstruct cross-view semantic encodings. For the sake of simplicity, only two views are demonstrated in this paper.

The proposed model uses two generators G_b and G_a to construct encodings Z_{v_a} and Z_{v_b} that is further used to reconstruct cross-view inputs X_{v_a} and X_{v_b} respectively. Then, two adversarial discriminators D_{v_a} and D_{v_b} are trained to compete with the generators and help the model to differentiate complete and incomplete views. This adversarial training helps the proposed model to learn the semantic embeddings required to reconstruct the corresponding view. Equation (1) and (2), gives the loss function for the implemented GAN.

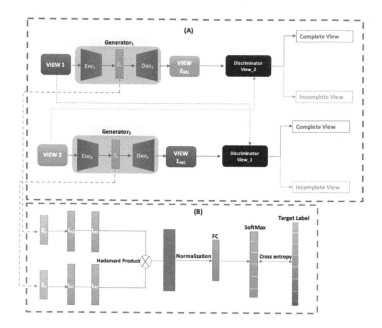

Fig. 2. Architecture of the proposed model. (A) Depicts the adversarial learning of cross-view latent semantics Z_1 & Z_2. (B) Depicts inductive transfer of Z_1 & Z_2 to train a neural classifier network.

$$L_{GAN}(G_a, D_{v_b}, X_{v_a}, X_{v_b}) = E_{v_a=>p(v_a)}[logD_{v_a}(X_{v_a})]$$
$$+ E_{v_b=>p(v_b)}[log(1 - D_{v_a}(G_a(X_{v_b})))] \quad (1)$$

Where G_a is the generator of view A (i.e. X_{v_a}) from view B (X_{v_b}). D_{v_b} is the discriminator of view B (D_{v_b}). X_{v_a} and X_{v_b} are the ground-truth input view A and B respectively. This loss is derived from the cross-entropy loss which encourages the discriminators to properly identify a complete or incomplete view. Therefore, simultaneously forcing the generators to improve their efforts and generate complete view(s). In this model, a complete view is regarded as any encoding that is as close to the ground-truth input. Hence, the discriminator network is simply encodes its input view and make such comparison. Equation 1 demonstrate the generator G_a loss. The same is repeated for generator G_b.

$$L_{cyc}(G_a, G_b, X_{v_a}) = E_{x_{va}=>p(x_{va})}[||G_a(G_b(X_{v_a})) - X_{v_a}||_1]$$
$$+ E_{x_{vb}=>p(x_{vb})}[||G_b(G_a(X_{v_b})) - X_{v_b}||_1] \quad (2)$$

In Eq. (2), $G_a(G_b(X_{v_a}))$ is the reconstructed view-A from generated view-B. $G_b(G_a(X_{v_b}))$ is the reconstructed view-B from generated view-A. An L1 norm was used to minimize the loss between the reconstructed view and the ground-truth input of view. This loss maintains the cycle consistency of the GAN. Both losses are trained through back-propagation and optimized through a gradient descent algorithm.

The overall loss function for the GAN is given in Eq. (3)

$$L(G_a, G_b, D_{va}, D_{vb}) = L_{GAN}(G_a, D_{vb}, X_{va}, X_{vb})$$
$$+ L_{GAN}(G_b, D_{va}, X_{vb}, X_{va})$$
$$+ \lambda * L_{cyc}(G_a, G_b, X_{va}) \qquad (3)$$

λ is an hyper-parameter that was set as 5.0 for this experiment.

3.2   Classification Through an Inductive Transfer of Encodings

This phase uses the inductive transfer learning approach [27]. The learned view representation Z_{v_a} and Z_{v_b} are transferred as inputs to train a neural classifier $F(.)$. As seen in Fig. 2(B), the neural classifier consist of two multilayer perceptron L_{i1} and L_{i2}. Both layers serve as a vacuum container to further learn correlating information among the given latent views. To achieve this, a cosine similarity loss is applied to intrinsically learn correlating features.

$$cosine\_similarity = \frac{enc_1.enc_2}{max(||enc_1||_2.||enc_2||_2, \epsilon)} \qquad (4)$$

In Eq. (4) $||.||_2$ refers to the L2 norm, and ϵ is a control parameter to avoid division by zero. After the similarity property is embedded in each latent vector. A Hadamard product $H(.)$ of the two layers was used to fuse both views into a unified latent view. Next, max-pooling and normalization are applied to the resultant latent. Finally, the latent is connected to a fully connected (FC) layer and a SoftMax activation function is applied to it. Cross-entropy [20] is combined to predict the class label. The classifier network is trained in a supervised learning approach through a back-propagation and optimized using the gradient descent algorithms.

The overall loss function for the Neural Classifier Network (NCN) is given by:

$$NCN = \alpha * cosine\_similarity(A, B) + \beta * cross\_entropy. \qquad (5)$$

where α and β are hyper-parameters that were set to 5.0 and 10.0 respectively. $cos\_sim(A, B)$ is the cosine similarity of embedding A and B.

4   Experimental Setup

Several experiments of the proposed system were conducted in a Python 3.9.5 environment on Ubuntu-18.04 OS with an NVIDIA DGX-1 V100 GPU.

4.1 Datasets

The publicly available MNIST digits dataset [12] was used to evaluate the performance of the proposed model. The dataset contains a total of 70,000 handwritten images and was divided into 60,000 and 10,000 for training and testing respectively.

Inorganic View Generation. In this paper, the inorganic Multiview data is implemented. The original view of the MNIST dataset is used as view-1 and a view-2 is generated. Similarly as used in [30], a Noisy MNIST dataset is generated to represent view 2. To introduce missing-views in the Multiview data. Some number of views were randomly removed from the dataset. And the missing rate is estimated by η which is defined by Eq. (6).

$$\eta = \frac{(n - m)}{n}. \tag{6}$$

where n is the total of data in the dataset, and m is the number of complete views.

4.2 Evaluation Metrics

The proposed system is evaluated using two metrics which are described below:

1. Accuracy: the objective of the proposed system is to enhance the efficiency of classification tasks using mutual discriminative information from Multiview data. Higher accuracy in the proposed model tells that the said objective is being achieved. The accuracy is calculated as follow:

$$Accuracy = ((T_n - F_n)/N) * 100 \tag{7}$$

Where T_n is the total number of correctly classified inputs, F_n is the total number of misclassified inputs, and N is the total number of inputs in the dataset.

2. Normalized Mutual Information (NMI): The proposed model ensures the mutual dependency of the Multiview embedding. Hence, the NMI is responsible for measuring these mutual dependencies. Higher dependencies signify higher dependencies. And therefore, higher correlations.

$$NMI(A, B) = \frac{2MI(A, B)}{H(A) + H(B)} \tag{8}$$

Where MI(A, B) refers to the mutual information between Multiview embedding A and B. $H(A)$ and $H(B)$ are the maximum entropy of embedding A and B respectively.

5 Results Analysis and Discussion

The performance of the proposed model is measured across several existing state-of-the-art models. The performance and comparison are discussed in this section.

5.1   Performance on Existing Multiview State-of-the-Art Systems

When the proposed system is compared to the existing state-of-the-art systems. The comparison shows that the proposed system achieves better accuracy on the same datasets. Table 1 shows the accuracy performances of the proposed system on the MNIST and Noisy MNIST datasets. Compared existing systems include COMPLETER [16], DCCAE [30], and DCCA [3].

Furthermore, the NMI of the trained embeddings in the proposed system is measured. Table 1 also reports the NMI of the proposed system. When compared to existing systems, like COMPLETER [16]. The proposed system performs competitively better in some of the existing systems. This is because the compared existing systems are focused on Multiview clustering. Therefore, they are expected to achieve higher NMI in their model since their objective functions are designed to increase higher NMI among Multiview clusters.

Table 1. Evaluation performance of the proposed model on MNIST and Noisy MNIST dataset. In the table below, (A) signifies complete views is used (i.e. $\eta = 0$). (B) signifies incomplete views is used (i.e. $eta = 0.5$).

Methods	Accuracy (A)	NMI (A)	Accuracy (B)	NMI (B)
COMPLETER [16]	89%	88.86%	80.01%	75.23%
DCCA [3]	61.82%	60.55%	61.82%	60.55%
DCCAE [30]	61.79%	59.49%	61.79%	59.49%
Proposed model	**91.2%**	**86.4%**	**81.1%**	**73.38%**

To give a complete evaluation of the major objectives of the proposed system. Evaluation has to be carried on the Multiview data with several missing rates.

5.2   Performance Evaluation on Handling the Missing-Views in Multiview Data

The missing rates (η) in Eq. 6, artificially introduce the problem of missing-view in Multiview data. A higher missing rate is expected to decline the classification accuracy of any model. However, bridging this declination gap is one of the objectives of the proposed model.

Figure 3 shows the evaluation performance on different missing rates. The evaluation is carried out using $0 =< \eta <= 0.9$. Meanwhile, the figure shows that for all the missing rates considered, the proposed system has achieved relatively good accuracy and NMI. However, the interesting development to note is the close differential gap in the accuracy performance for all different missing rates. As expected the NMI declined at higher missing rates. However, the proposed model at $\eta = 0.9$ performs better than DCCA and DCCAE when at ($\eta = 0.5$). This is because the proposed system is trained to reconstruct cross-view data from a given view. Therefore, it can properly handle missing-view representation.

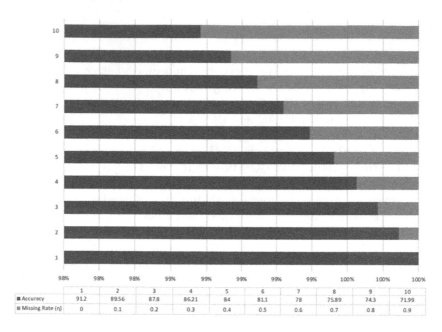

	1	2	3	4	5	6	7	8	9	10
■ Accuracy	91.2	89.56	87.8	86.21	84	81.1	78	75.89	74.3	71.99
■ Missing Rate (η)	0	0.1	0.2	0.3	0.4	0.5	0.6	0.7	0.8	0.9

Fig. 3. Missing-view evaluation performance on Accuracy and NMI for the proposed model at several η.

Hence, the NMI is not very much affected as compared to other existing systems that tries to statistically complete missing-view instead.

6   Conclusion and Future Perspectives

Multiview learning in classification tasks aims at improving the generalization of any classifier with multiple sources of data. Multiview learning achieves this by encouraging the contributions of hidden complementary information in different data forms. Although, several successes have been recorded in this area. However, this area is also faced with several challenges. One of these many challenges is the missing-view problem. A Multiview classification with a missing-view model is proposed in this paper. The proposed model adopts the combination of adversarial learning and inductive transfer learning to handle the problem of missing-view(s). The adversarial network learns the cross-view representation to reproduce the missing-view. The learned representation is transferred to train a neural classifier network. Evaluation of the proposed model is carried out on two standard metric systems. The evaluation results are compared to the existing state-of-the-art systems. Which shows that the proposed model achieves better performance.

Future works will be focused on improving the similarity of the view embedding. Also, further extending this work to inter-disciplinary areas to assert the generalization of the model.

References

1. Ahmed, O., Brifcani, A.: Gene expression classification based on deep learning. In: 2019 4th Scientific International Conference Najaf (SICN), pp. 145–149. IEEE (2019)
2. Amini, M.R., Usunier, N., Goutte, C.: Learning from multiple partially observed views-an application to multilingual text categorization. In: Advances in Neural Information Processing Systems, vol. 22, pp. 28–36 (2009)
3. Andrew, G., Arora, R., Bilmes, J., Livescu, K.: Deep canonical correlation analysis. In: International Conference on Machine Learning, pp. 1247–1255. PMLR (2013)
4. Ben-Ami, Z., Feldman, R., Rosenfeld, B.: Using multi-view learning to improve detection of investor sentiments on Twitter. Computación y Sistemas **18**(3), 477–490 (2014)
5. Bhadra, S., Kaski, S., Rousu, J.: Multi-view kernel completion. Mach. Learn. **106**(5), 713–739 (2016). https://doi.org/10.1007/s10994-016-5618-0
6. Chen, C.W., Aghajan, H.: Multiview social behavior analysis in work environments. In: 2011 Fifth ACM/IEEE International Conference on Distributed Smart Cameras, pp. 1–6. IEEE (2011)
7. Chen, Y., Lin, Z., Zhao, X., Wang, G., Gu, Y.: Deep learning-based classification of hyperspectral data. IEEE J. Sel. Top. Appl. Earth Observ. Remote Sens. **7**(6), 2094–2107 (2014)
8. Guiasu, S., Shenitzer, A.: The principle of maximum entropy. Math. Intell. **7**(1), 42–48 (1985). https://doi.org/10.1007/BF03023004
9. Hazarika, A., Dutta, L., Barthakur, M., Bhuyan, M.: A multiview discriminant feature fusion-based nonlinear process assessment and diagnosis: application to medical diagnosis. IEEE Trans. Instrum. Meas. **68**(7), 2498–2506 (2018)
10. Jiang, Z., et al.: Muti-view mouse social behaviour recognition with deep graphic model. IEEE Trans. Image Process. (2021)
11. Krizhevsky, A., Sutskever, I., Hinton, G.E.: ImageNet classification with deep convolutional neural networks. In: Advances in Neural Information Processing Systems, vol. 25, pp. 1097–1105 (2012)
12. LeCun, Y., Bottou, L., Bengio, Y., Haffner, P.: Gradient-based learning applied to document recognition. Proc. IEEE **86**(11), 2278–2324 (1998)
13. Li, J., Yong, H., Wu, F., Li, M.: Online multi-view subspace learning with mixed noise. In: Proceedings of the 28th ACM International Conference on Multimedia, pp. 3838–3846 (2020)
14. Li, T., Hou, W., Lyu, F., Lei, Y., Xiao, C.: Face detection based on depth information using HOG-LBP. In: 2016 Sixth International Conference on Instrumentation & Measurement, Computer, Communication and Control (IMCCC), pp. 779–784. IEEE (2016)
15. Li, Y., Yang, M., Zhang, Z.: A survey of multi-view representation learning. IEEE Trans. Knowl. Data Eng. **31**(10), 1863–1883 (2018)
16. Lin, Y., Gou, Y., Liu, Z., Li, B., Lv, J., Peng, X.: COMPLETER: incomplete multi-view clustering via contrastive prediction. In: Proceedings of the IEEE/CVF Conference on Computer Vision and Pattern Recognition, pp. 11174–11183 (2021)
17. Luo, Y., Liu, T., Tao, D., Xu, C.: Multiview matrix completion for multilabel image classification. IEEE Trans. Image Process. **24**(8), 2355–2368 (2015)
18. Mady, H., Hilles, S.M.: Face recognition and detection using random forest and combination of LBP and HOG features. In: 2018 International Conference on Smart Computing and Electronic Enterprise (ICSCEE), pp. 1–7. IEEE (2018)

19. Mohsen, H., El-Dahshan, E.S.A., El-Horbaty, E.S.M., Salem, A.B.M.: Classification using deep learning neural networks for brain tumors. Future Comput. Inform. J. **3**(1), 68–71 (2018)
20. Murphy, K.P.: Machine Learning: A Probabilistic Perspective. MIT Press, Cambridge (2012)
21. Nie, F., Li, J., Li, X., et al.: Self-weighted multiview clustering with multiple graphs. In: IJCAI, pp. 2564–2570 (2017)
22. Qi, C.R., Su, H., Nießner, M., Dai, A., Yan, M., Guibas, L.J.: Volumetric and multi-view CNNs for object classification on 3D data. In: Proceedings of the IEEE Conference on Computer Vision and Pattern Recognition, pp. 5648–5656 (2016)
23. Qin, M., Du, Z., Zhang, F., Liu, R.: A matrix completion-based multiview learning method for imputing missing values in buoy monitoring data. Inf. Sci. **487**, 18–30 (2019)
24. Shen, X., Shen, F., Liu, L., Yuan, Y.H., Liu, W., Sun, Q.S.: Multiview discrete hashing for scalable multimedia search. ACM Trans. Intell. Syst. Technol. (TIST) **9**(5), 1–21 (2018)
25. Shen, X., Sun, Q.: A novel semi-supervised canonical correlation analysis and extensions for multi-view dimensionality reduction. J. Vis. Commun. Image Represent. **25**(8), 1894–1904 (2014)
26. Tan, Q., Yu, G., Domeniconi, C., Wang, J., Zhang, Z.: Multi-view weak-label learning based on matrix completion. In: Proceedings of the 2018 SIAM International Conference on Data Mining, pp. 450–458. SIAM (2018)
27. Torrey, L., Shavlik, J.: Transfer learning. In: Handbook of Research on Machine Learning Applications and Trends: Algorithms, Methods, and Techniques, pp. 242–264. IGI global (2010)
28. Wang, C., Yu, F., Zhang, Z., Zhang, J.: Multiview graph learning for small-and medium-sized enterprises' credit risk assessment in supply chain finance. Complexity **2021** (2021)
29. Wang, Q., Chen, M., Nie, F., Li, X.: Detecting coherent groups in crowd scenes by multiview clustering. IEEE Trans. Pattern Anal. Mach. Intell. **42**(1), 46–58 (2018)
30. Wang, W., Arora, R., Livescu, K., Bilmes, J.: On deep multi-view representation learning. In: International Conference on Machine Learning, pp. 1083–1092. PMLR (2015)
31. Wang, Y., Lin, X., Wu, L., Zhang, W., Zhang, Q., Huang, X.: Robust subspace clustering for multi-view data by exploiting correlation consensus. IEEE Trans. Image Process. **24**(11), 3939–3949 (2015)
32. Williams, D., Carin, L.: Analytical kernel matrix completion with incomplete multi-view data. In: Proceedings of the International Conference on Machine Learning (ICML) Workshop on Learning with Multiple Views, pp. 80–86. Citeseer (2005)
33. Xie, Z., Jiang, P., Zhang, S.: Fusion of LBP and HOG using multiple kernel learning for infrared face recognition. In: 2017 IEEE/ACIS 16th International Conference on Computer and Information Science (ICIS), pp. 81–84. IEEE (2017)
34. Xu, C., Guan, Z., Zhao, W., Wu, H., Niu, Y., Ling, B.: Adversarial incomplete multi-view clustering. In: IJCAI, pp. 3933–3939 (2019)
35. Xu, C., Tao, D., Xu, C.: Multi-view learning with incomplete views. IEEE Trans. Image Process. **24**(12), 5812–5825 (2015)
36. Xu, X., Yang, Y., Deng, C., Nie, F.: Adaptive graph weighting for multi-view dimensionality reduction. Signal Process. **165**, 186–196 (2019)
37. Yang, Y., Wang, H.: Multi-view clustering: a survey. Big Data Min. Anal. **1**(2), 83–107 (2018)

38. Yang, Z., Liang, N., Yan, W., Li, Z., Xie, S.: Uniform distribution non-negative matrix factorization for multiview clustering. IEEE Trans. Cybern. **51**(6), 3249–3262 (2020)
39. Yin, Q., Wu, S., Wang, L.: Incomplete multi-view clustering via subspace learning. In: Proceedings of the 24th ACM International on Conference on Information and Knowledge Management, pp. 383–392 (2015)
40. Yin, Q., Wu, S., Wang, L.: Unified subspace learning for incomplete and unlabeled multi-view data. Pattern Recogn. **67**, 313–327 (2017)
41. Yu, J., Rui, Y., Tang, Y.Y., Tao, D.: High-order distance-based multiview stochastic learning in image classification. IEEE Trans. Cybern. **44**(12), 2431–2442 (2014)
42. Zhang, C., Adeli, E., Zhou, T., Chen, X., Shen, D.: Multi-layer multi-view classification for Alzheimer's disease diagnosis. In: Proceedings of the AAAI Conference on Artificial Intelligence, vol. 32 (2018)
43. Zhang, C., Cui, Y., Han, Z., Zhou, J.T., Fu, H., Hu, Q.: Deep partial multi-view learning. IEEE Trans. Pattern Anal. Mach. Intell. (2020)
44. Zhang, C., Fu, H., Hu, Q., Zhu, P., Cao, X.: Flexible multi-view dimensionality co-reduction. IEEE Trans. Image Process. **26**(2), 648–659 (2016)
45. Zhang, L., Zhao, Y., Zhu, Z., Shen, D., Ji, S.: Multi-view missing data completion. IEEE Trans. Knowl. Data Eng. **30**(7), 1296–1309 (2018)
46. Zhang, Z., Liu, L., Shen, F., Shen, H.T., Shao, L.: Binary multi-view clustering. IEEE Trans. Pattern Anal. Mach. Intell. **41**(7), 1774–1782 (2018)
47. Zhao, D., Gao, Q., Lu, Y., Sun, D.: Two-step multi-view and multi-label learning with missing label via subspace learning. Appl. Soft Comput. **102**, 107120 (2021)
48. Zhu, X., Li, X., Zhang, S.: Block-row sparse multiview multilabel learning for image classification. IEEE Trans. Cybern. **46**(2), 450–461 (2015)

Deep Reinforcement Learning Based Throughput Maximization Scheme for D2D Users Underlaying NOMA-Enabled Cellular Network

Vineet Vishnoi[1]([✉]), Praveen Kumar Malik[2], Ishan Budhiraja[3], and Ashima Yadav[3]

[1] School of Electronics and Electrical Engineering, Lovely Professional University, Phagwara, Punjab, India
`vishnoivineet@gmail.com`
[2] Lovely Professional University, Phagwara, Punjab, India
`praveen.23314@lpu.co.in`
[3] Bennett University, Greater Noida, Uttar Pradesh, India
{`ishan.budhiraja,ashima.yadav`}`@bennett.edu.in`

Abstract. Device-to-Device (D2D) communication is a potential technology that efficiently reuses spectrum resources with CMUs in a fifth-generation (5G) underlay and even beyond the network. It improves network capacity and spectral efficiency at the cost of co-channel interference. Moreover, massive connectivity has not been fully exploited for efficient spectral efficiency usage in the existing solutions. To resolve the aforementioned issues, we combine non-orthogonal multiple access (NOMA) approaches with cellular mobile users (CMUs) in order to improve their throughput while preserving the signal-to-interference noise ratio (SINR) offered by CMUs and D2D mobile pairs (DMPs). The problem of power allocation is formulated as mixed-integer non-linear programming, which is then transformed to machine learning using the markov decision process (MDP). Then, a deep reinforcement learning (DRL) approach is proposed for solving the continuous optimisation problem in a centralised fashion. Furthermore, to achieve better performance and a faster convergence rate, the higher proximal policy optimization (PPO) scheme is employed. Numerical results reveal that the proposed algorithm outperformed state-of-the-art schemes in terms of throughput.

Keywords: D2D · DRL · MDP · NOMA · PPO · Throughput

1 Introduction

The explosive growth in the use of smart phones, smart devices, and internet-based services is causing massive data traffic on wireless networks. D2D communication is a key candidate that increases network spectrum efficiency by

© Springer Nature Switzerland AG 2022
D. Garg et al. (Eds.): IACC 2021, CCIS 1528, pp. 318–331, 2022.
https://doi.org/10.1007/978-3-030-95502-1_25

sharing radio resources between DMPs and CMUs in the underlay scenario [1]. D2D communication uses the concept of low power transfer, which enhances energy efficiency. Also, in D2D enabled networks, network throughput increases due to sharing of frequency spectrum. Despite the many advantages of D2D communication, its performance has deteriorated in ultra-dense networks due to in-cooperation between nearby BSs and intra-user interference.

To improve the network performance, the authors proposed a promising technique called NOMA for 5G and beyond. The NOMA scheme serves more than one user at the same time and same frequency via power domain multiplexing [2]. Different CMUs get different power from BS based on their channel gain conditions. CMUs having high channel gain get low power signals, and users having low channel gain get high power signals. However, NOMA causes intra-user interference among CMUs. Successive interference cancellation (SIC) is used to decode and compensate for intra-user interference at the receiver end [3]. Therefore, integrating the NOMA scheme with the D2D network improves SE, throughput, sum rate, and capacity of the entire network at the cost of additional interference. Some challenges in implementing the NOMA scheme are degradation in bit error rate, complexity at the receiver side, CMUs location, and physical security.

Reinforcement Learning (RL) is a subfield of machine learning in which an agent can make decisions on a regular basis, track the outcomes, and then change its strategy automatically to obtain the best policy [4]. It has been proven that the learning process in RL converges, but it takes a very long time to arrive at the best policy. The reason for this is that RL must explore and learn about the whole system. So RL becomes unsuitable and inappropriate for large-scale networks. As a result, RL implementations in practise are extremely limited in ultra-dense networks.

DRL schemes are used to overcome RL's limitations by combining RL and deep learning. DRL schemes take advantage of deep neural networks to improve the learning process. The RL algorithm learns faster and performs better using DRL schemes. Therefore, DRL schemes are used in a variety of RL applications, including speech recognition, natural language processing, computer vision, and robotics [5]. DRL schemes are widely used in the field of wireless communication and networking to handle different challenges and issues.

1.1 Related Work

The authors proposed incorporating the DRL scheme DQN into an overlay D2D communication network in order to reduce mutual interference among DMPs and improve the SE [6]. In [7], the authors solved the energy-efficiency resource allocation issue for underlay D2D networks to maximise the user experience by using deep queue learning (DQL), Double DQL and Duelling DQL DRL techniques. The authors solved the problem of power allocation for underlay D2D communication networks in a changing environment and proposed a DRL-based approach, DQN, to improve the capacity of the system and user experience quality for the entire network [8]. Ji et al. [9] studied the issue of resource allocation in underlay D2D networks, for which the DRL based scheme DQN was used to improve energy efficiency with respect to network throughput. The authors used a DRL-based technique named deep deterministic policy gradient (DDPG) to study an energy efficiency (EE) maximisation problem in terms of mode selection and resource allocation for an uplink D2D scenario and achieved greater EE and a faster convergence rate than state-of-the-art schemes [10]. Chen et al. [11] addressed the issue of channel allocation in the overlay D2D communication network and then developed the DRL scheme, DQN, to maximise the sum rate. The authors mitigate the co-channel interference in overlay D2D communication networks via a distributed DRL-based algorithm [12]. To optimise the aggregate of the fairness utility function with respect to scheduling of RB and power control, the authors combined the traditional computational scheme with the DDPG [13]. Tang et al. [14] suggested DQL and DQN algorithms for D2D-assisted cache-enabled IoT to reduce the energy cost of efficient traffic.

1.2   Motivation and Contributions

In contrast to the previous work, we only employ the NOMA technique in this work to schedule a set of CMUs on the RBs, while DMUs reuse these resource blocks (RBs) in an orthogonal manner for the cellular tier, subject to interference protection. The motivation for using traditional DMPs rather than NOMA-based DMPs is to minimise the computation on the resource-constrained D2D devices, hence making it more feasible. Furthermore, if interference is adequately handled, then more DMPs can join the network, because in the NOMA scheme, two or more DMPs can be scheduled to sustain minimal SIC receiver complexity. This inspires us to work on a solution for underlay DMPs that coordinates with NOMA-based CMUs. Furthermore, the delay in the centralised learning and the processing time in their optimisation algorithms is huge for real-time use cases. To get the better of these aforementioned shortcomings, in this paper, we propose efficient DRL algorithms by optimising the power allocation of the BS and the DTs for maximising the network throughput.

The main contributions of this paper are as follows:

- The throughput problem is formulated for the downlink scenario with the power restrictions. To optimise the throughput network performance, we propose a centralised DRL technique for solving the power allocation at the BS and DTs.
- To improve the network performance, we introduced the PPO algorithm with a new better sampling technique.
- The numerical results demonstrated that the proposed methods efficiently solve the optimisation problem with the dynamic environmental setting and outperform the other benchmarks.

1.3   Organization

The remainder of the paper is arranged in the following manner. The system model and problem formulation are described in Sect. 2. Section 3 demonstrates the suggested scheme. The suggested scheme's performance was evaluated in Sect. 4. Section 5 contains the conclusion.

2   System Model and Problem Formulation

Consider a model comprising a BS, a set of $\mathcal{I}$ CMUs as $\mathcal{I} = \{1, 2, ...i...I\}$, a set of $\mathcal{J}$ D2D mobile pairs (DMPs) as $\mathcal{J} = \{1, 2, ...j...J\}$, and a set of $\mathcal{N}$ RB as $\mathcal{N} = \{1, 2, ...n...N\}$ shown in Fig 1. The BS provides service to a group of CMUs through the NOMA scheme in a downlink scenario. On the other hand, D2D transmitters and receivers communicate with each other through the orthogonal multiple access (OMA) scheme. In this model, CMUs and DMPs share the same RB.

In this model, the BS used NOMA to schedule with the CMUs through a RB, and the D2D transmitter communicates with the D2D receiver using the OMA scheme in each DMP. The CMUs and DMPs form a cluster. Furthermore, the total number of users can vary from 2 to $|I| + |J|$ in each cluster. In NOMA based systems, if the number of users increases in the same RB, then SIC implementation complexity at the receiver increases. So, to keep the receiver complexity to a minimum, this model considers only two CMUs in each cluster. There is no limit on DMPs on a RB. Let $\mathcal{N}$ represent the clusters set with each RB assigned to one of them. Let $\mathcal{N}$ is the set of clusters, i.e., each RB is allocated to each cluster. Also, assume that the BS is aware of the channel state information (CSI) of all CMUs and DMPs. Furthermore, this model considers quasi-static Rayleigh fading, in which each channel's gain is constant and follows a Gaussian complex distribution.

2.1   Channel Model

Assume that CMU and DMP on the rth cluster are represented by I_n and J_n, respectively. Let P_T represent the power transmitted by the BS and P_i represent the power assigned to CMU. The received message at CMUs i from BS in the nth cluster is given as:

$$y_{b-i}^n = \sqrt{P_i^n} g_i^n x_i^n + \sum_{i' \neq i, i' \in I_n} \sqrt{P_{i'}^n} g_{i'}^n x_{i'}^n$$
$$+ \sum_{j \in J_n} \sqrt{P_j^n} g_{j-i}^n x_j^n + \zeta_i^n, \tag{1}$$

where x_i represent the transmitted symbol for CMUs, g_{j-i}^n represent the channel gain between CMUs i and DP j. P_j^n is the power of DP j and ζ_i^n is the additive white noise.

Let a_i^n is the channel coefficient for CMU i and b_i^n is the channel coefficient for D2D user j and is defined as:

$$a_i^n = \begin{cases} 1 & \text{if CMU } i \text{ is scheduled on the } n^{th} \text{ RB,} \\ 0 & \text{otherwise.} \end{cases} \tag{2}$$

$$b_j^n = \begin{cases} 1 & \text{if DMP } j \text{ is scheduled on the } n^{th} \text{ RB,} \\ 0 & \text{otherwise.} \end{cases} \tag{3}$$

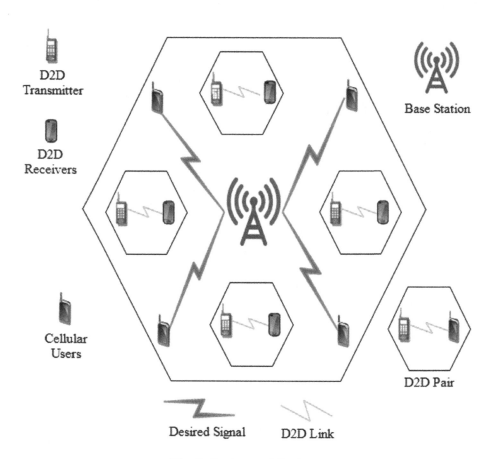

Fig. 1. System architecture.

2.2   Throughput Calculation

The desirable throughput for i^{th} CMU in the nth cluster using (1) is given as:

$$D_i^n = B \log_2 \left[1 + \frac{P_i^n |g_i^n|^2}{\mathcal{IF}_{i'-i}^n + \mathcal{IF}_{j-i}^n + \xi_j^n} \right], \tag{4}$$

where B represents the amount of bandwidth allotted to every one RB and $\mathcal{IF}_{i'-i}^n$ is the intra-user interference produced by other CMUs on CMU i and can be given as:

$$IF_{i'-i}^n = \sum_{i' \neq i, i' \in I_n} \alpha_i^n P_i^n |g_i^n|^2. \tag{5}$$

and IF_{j-i}^n is the interference produced by DMP j on CMU i is specified as follows:

$$IF_{j-i}^n = \sum_{j \in J} \beta_j^n P_j^n |g_{j-i}^n|^2. \tag{6}$$

Similarly, the desired throughput for DMP j on the nth cluster is specified as:

$$D_j^n = B \log_2 \left[1 + \frac{P_j^n |g_j^n|^2}{IF_{j'-j}^n + IF_{BS-j}^n + \xi_j^n} \right], \tag{7}$$

where $IF_{j'-i}^n$ is the co-tier interference caused by other DMPs on DMP j which is given as:

$$IF_{j'-i}^n = \sum_{j' \neq j, j' \in J_n} \beta_{j'}^n P_{j'}^n |g_{j'}^n|^2. \tag{8}$$

and IF_{BS-j}^n represents the cross-tier interference produced by BS on all DMPs and is defined as:

$$I_{BS-j}^n = \sum_{j \in J} \beta_j^n P_j^n |g_{BS-j}^n|^2, \tag{9}$$

where g_{BS-j}^n represent the channel gain between BS and j^{th} DMP.

Now, the total throughput of the overall network obtained from (4) and (7) is given as:

$$D_T^n = \sum_{n=1}^N \left[\sum_{i=1}^I D_i^n + \sum_{j=1}^J D_j^n \right]. \tag{10}$$

2.3   Problem Formulation

The aim of this paper is to increase the total network's throughput by reducing interference. The following is the problem's mathematical formulation:

$$\max_{P_i^n, P_j^n} D_T^n, \tag{11}$$

$$s.t. \ V_1 : P_i^n \leq P_i^{n,\max},$$
$$V_2 : P_j^n \leq P_j^{n,\max},$$
$$V_3 : P_i^n, P_j^n \geq 0,$$
$$V_4 : 2 \leq \sum_{j=1}^J b_j^n \leq |I| + |J|,$$
$$V_5 : \sum_{j=1}^J b_{j,i}^n P_j |g_{j,i}|^2 \leq I_i^{\text{threshold}},$$

where the constraints V_1 and V_2 ensure that the power transmitted by the BS and the DT must be less than the maximum transmission power. Constraint V_3 shows that the transmitted power must be a non-negative integer. The constraints V_4 shows that the total number of users can vary from 2 to $|I| + |J|$ in each cluster. The highest interference threshold assigned by CMUs to a resource block is represented by Constraints V_5.

3 Proposed Solution

3.1 Centralised Optimisation

In this model, consider that information is processed at a centralised location in a centralised manner (e.g., at the base station). In each sharing resource block, the next action for each system element will be transferred. As a result, we consider the central processing point as an agent (BS) for optimising throughput at CMUEs and DMPs. The optimisation problem can be defined by MDP as:

$$MDP = (\mathbb{S}, \mathbb{A}, \mathbb{P}, \mathbb{R}, \Gamma). \tag{12}$$

With respect to the above model, the game with a centralised optimisation approach is described as:

State Space: In order to achieve maximum throughput, the agent interacts with the environment. Therefore, the agent is solely aware of local information such as different channel gains and interferences. The state space is defined as:

$$\mathbb{S} = \left[g_i^n, g_{BS-j}^n, g_{j-i}^n, \mathcal{IF}_{j-i}^n, \mathcal{IF}_{BS-j}^n, \mathcal{IF}_{i'-i}^n \right]. \tag{13}$$

Action Space: In NOMA based systems, our aim is to optimise the throughput at BS. So, action space is represented as:

$$\mathbb{A} = \left[(P_1^n, P_2^n, \ldots, P_i^n); (P_1^n, P_2^n, \ldots, P_j^n) \right]. \tag{14}$$

At the state s^t, agent perform the action a^t. After performing action a^t, agent moves at the next state s^{t+1}.

Reward Function: To maximise the throughput, the reward function is expressed as:

$$\mathbb{R} = \sum_{i=1}^{I} \sum_{j=1}^{J} D_T^n. \tag{15}$$

After defining the throughput model, a DRL approach is proposed to identify the optimal policy. The DDPG is a hybrid model with a value function-based actor component and a policy search-based critic component. To enhance the convergence speed and reduce unnecessary calculations, we apply experienced replay buffer and target network approaches to the DDPG algorithm. A finite memory of capacity C is utilised to store the executed transition $\left(s^t, a^t, r^t, s^{t+1} \right)$

in the experience replay buffer. We select a small batch E at random from the finite size memory C after collecting enough samples. This small batch trains the neural network. For updating the new sample and deleting the old ones, memory C is assigned to a finite size. The target value is estimated by using target networks for both the critic and the actor network.

Let $\mathbb{Q}(s, a; \phi_x)$ represents the critic network along with variable ϕ_x and $\mathbb{Q}'(s, a; \phi_{x'})$ represents the target critic network along with variable $\phi_{r'}$. Similarly, $\nu(s, a; \phi_\nu)$ represents the actor network along with the variable ϕ_ν and $\nu'(s, a, \phi_{\nu'})$ represents the target actor network along with variable $\phi_{\nu'}$. Stochastic gradient descent (SGD) is used to train the actor and critic network over a small batch of E samples. Now the critic is updated by minimising

$$M = \frac{1}{E} \sum_i^E \left(y^i - \mathbb{Q}(s^i, a^i, \phi_x)\right)^2.$$ (16)

with the target

$$y^i = r^i(s^i, a^i) + \Gamma \mathbb{Q}(s^{i+1}, a^{i+1}; \phi_{x'})|_a^{i+1} = \nu'(s^{i+1}; \phi_{\nu'}).$$ (17)

The actor network parameter is updated as follows:

$$\vec{\nabla}_{\phi_\nu} K \approx \frac{1}{E} \sum_i^E \vec{\nabla}_{a^i} \mathbb{Q}(s^i, a^i; \phi_x)|_{a^i = \nu(s^i)} \vec{\nabla}_{\phi_\nu} \nu(s^i; \phi_\nu).$$ (18)

Soft target updates are used to update the target actor network parameters ϕ_x and the target critic network parameters ϕ'_ν as follows:

$$\phi_{x'} \hookleftarrow \chi \phi_x + (1 - \chi)\phi_{x'}$$ (19)

$$\phi_{\nu'} \hookleftarrow \chi \phi_\nu + (1 - \chi)\phi_{\nu'},$$ (20)

where χ is defined as a hyperparameter and has a range between 0 and 1.

The deterministic policy is trained in an off-line manner in the DDPG approach. So, a noise process is added and defined as $\mathcal{Z}[0, 1]$. Therefore, the target actor network is defined as follows:

$$\nu'(s^t; \phi_{\nu'}^t) = \nu(s^t; \phi_\nu^t) + \mathcal{Z}\chi(0, 1).$$ (21)

In the suggested algorithm, we give the of the DDPG algorithm-based method for power allocation and the NOMA-based BS in the downlink scenario. In the proposed algorithm, Θ represent the number of maximum episodes and $\mathcal{T}$ denotes time step.

3.2   Proximal Policy Optimization

In order to achieve better performance, we consider a policy approach denoted as proximal policy optimization (PPO) in this model. Current and obtained

Algorithm 1. Throughput Maximzation for D2D Users Using Centralised Optimization Technique.

Input

- Environment: (a) DMPs (b) CUEs (c) NOMA-integrated BS.
- $D_i^n \geq D_i^{n,\min}$: Minimum requirement of CUE
- $D_j^n \geq D_j^{n,\min}$: Minimum Requirements of DPs

Initialization:

- $\mathbb{Q}(s, a, \phi_x)$ = Critic network along with variable ϕ_x.
- $\nu(s; \phi_\nu)$ = Actor network along with variable ϕ_ν.
- $\mathbb{Q}'(s, a, \phi_x')$ = Target critic network along with variable $\phi_{x'}$
- $\nu'(s; \phi_{\nu'})$ = Target actor networkalong with variable $\phi_{\nu'}$.
- C = Experience Replay

Output: α, β

1: **for** episode $= 1, \ldots, \Theta$ **do**
2:     Begin a process of action exploration
3:     Obtain the starting state of observation s^0
4:     **for** iteration $= 1, \ldots, \mathcal{T}$ **do**
5:         Execute the action a^t achieved at state s^t
6:         Modify the reward r^t in accordance with (27)
7:         Notice the next state s^{t+1}
8:         save the transition (s^t, a^t, r^t, s^{t+1}) in the
9:         replay buffer
10:        Sample randomly a mini-batch of E transitions
11:        (s^i, a^i, r^i, s^{i+1}) from C
12:        Update critic parameter by stochastic gradient
13:        descent using loss function in (27)
14:        Update the actor policy parameter in (30)
15:        Update the target critic network parameters
16:        $(\phi_{x'}, \phi_{\nu'})$ according to (31) and (32)
17:        Update the state $s^t = s^{t+1}$
18:    **end for**
19: **end for**

policies are compared in the PPO algorithm and then the objective function is maximised as:

$$\mathscr{F}(s, a; \phi) = \mathcal{E}\left[\frac{\pi(s, a; \phi)}{\pi(s, a; \phi_{old}}W^\pi(s, a)\right]$$

$$= \mathcal{E}P_\phi^t W^\pi(s, a), \tag{22}$$

where P_ϕ^t represents the probability ratio and $W^\pi(s, a) = \mathbb{Q}^\phi(s, a) - \mathscr{V}^\pi s$ is a function that approximates the advance function in. To maximise the goal, SGD is applied for training networks with a mini-batch E. As a result, the policy is updated via

$$\phi^{t+1} = \arg\max \mathcal{E}\left[\mathscr{F}(s, a; \phi^t)\right] \tag{23}$$

To avoid excessive changes, we employ the clipping method function clipp $(p_\pi^t, 1 - \lambda, 1 + \lambda)$ in this work to limit the objective value as follows:

$$\mathscr{F}^{clipp}(s, a; \phi)$$

$$= \mathcal{E}\left[\min(p_\phi^t, W^\pi(s, a), clipp(p_\phi^t, 1 - \lambda, 1 + \lambda)W^\pi(s, a)\right], \tag{24}$$

where λ is a constant of low value. When the advantage $W^\pi(s, a)$ is greater than zero then upper bound is defined as $1 + \lambda$. In this condition, the objective is defined as:

$$\mathscr{F}^{clipp}(s, a; \phi) = \min\left[\frac{\pi(s, a; \phi)}{\pi(s, a; \phi_{old})}, (1 + \lambda)\right] W^\pi(s, a). \tag{25}$$

When the advantage $W^\pi(s, a)$ is less than zero then lower bound is defined as $1 - \lambda$. In this condition, the objective is defined as:

$$\mathscr{F}^{clipp}(s, a; \phi) = \min\left[\frac{\pi(s, a; \phi)}{\pi(s, a; \phi_{old})}, (1 - \lambda)\right] W^\pi(s, a). \tag{26}$$

In (25), if advantage $W^\pi(s, a)$ is greater than zero, then the value of the objective increases. But the minimum term puts a limit on the increased value. When $\pi(s, a; \phi) > (1 + \lambda)\pi(s, a; \phi_{old})$, then factor $(1 + \lambda)W^\pi(s, a)$ limits the objective value within the range.

Similarly, in (26), if advantage $W^\pi(s, a)$ is less than zero, then the value of the objective decreases. But the maximum term puts a limit on the decreased value. When $\pi(s, a; \phi) < (1 - \lambda)\pi(s, a; \phi_{old})$, then factor $(1 - \lambda)W^\pi(s, a)$ limits the objective value. Thus, the minimum and maximum terms put conditions on the objective in such a way that the new policy does not deviate from the old policy. An advantage function is denoted as [15]:

$$W^\pi(s, a) = r^t + \Gamma \mathscr{V}^\pi(s^{t+1}) - \mathscr{V}^\pi(s^t). \tag{27}$$

4   Performance Evaluation

The performance of the suggested strategy is examined and described in this section. It is divided into two sections: (i) Numerical Settings (ii) Results and Discussion.

4.1   Numerical Settings

Simulation Parameters for DMPs and CMUs. The BS is considered to be deployed at a fixed location in the simulation, and I CMUs and J DMPs are deployed according to a homogeneous Poisson point process (PPP). The main parameters used in simulations are taken from [3,13] and are presented in Table 1.

Table 1. Underlay D2D network simulation parameters.

Parameters	Values
Cellular radius of a cell	300 m
The distance between D2D links	20 30 m
Count of CMUs	20
Count of RBs, (N)	20
Count of DMPs	$10, 20, 30, \ldots, 180$
Each RB's bandwidth	180 kHz
Frequency of carrier	2 GHz
Density of noise power spectrum	-174 dBm/Hz
D2D pathloss exponent	4
Shadowing standard deviation	8 dB
CMU highest power, (P_i^n)	25 dBm
DMP highest power, (P_j^n)	10–25 dBm
CMU links pathloss model	$128.1 + 37.6 \log d$
DMP links pathloss model	$148 + 40 \log d$

DRL Simulation Parameters. A totally connected neural system is used in the DQN learning model. There are three layers in this network system: an input layer, a hidden layer, and an output layer. There are 250 neurons in the input layer, 250 neurons in the hidden layer, and 150 neurons in the output layer, respectively. The ReLu is employed as an activation function in the suggested model, while the adaptive moment is used as an optimizer. In the PPO algorithm, we use the learning rate = 0.00001. Table 2 contains the other parameters associated with the DQN model. Tensorflow 2.23 on the Python 5 platform is used to simulate the model.

4.2 Results and Discussion

The performance of the entire network's throughput is evaluated in relation to several factors, such as the number of DMPs, the number of CMUs, and the interference threshold.

The convergence behaviour of the proposed algorithm in relation to the number of iterations is shown in Fig. 2(a). Our suggested algorithm obtains maximum throughput in fewer than 30 iterations. The cause for this behaviour is that the proposed algorithm maximises the power of both the CMU and the DT, minimising co-channel interference. As a result, each agent educated themselves multiple times and utilised previously trained networks to acquire the best policy in less time.

The change in the throughput of the entire network in relation to the number of DMPs is shown in Fig. 2(b). The statistics suggest that as the number of DMPs increases, the network's throughput decreases due to increased co-channel

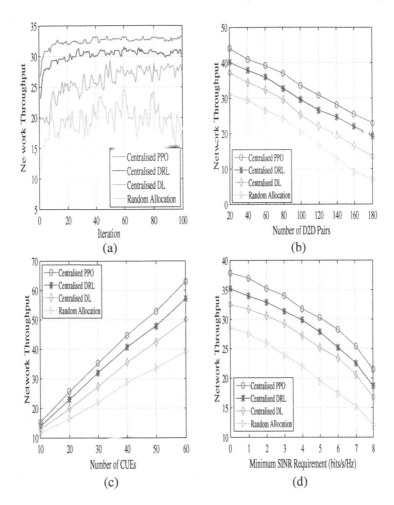

Fig. 2. Comparative Analysis (a) Network Throughput v/s number of Iterations (b) Network Throughput v/s number of D2D pairs (c) Network Throughput v/s number of CUEs (d) Network Throughput v/s Minimum SINR requirement

interference among DMPs. Figure 2(b) also shows the comparison of the PPO algorithm with other algorithms. The results suggest that the existence of multi-DQN and prioritised experience replay in PPO reduces the size of the action spaces and eliminates redundant samples, resulting in increased throughput. Also, when the number of DMPs in a cell reaches 100, the suggested scheme achieves 10.25%, 18.97%, and 32.34% higher throughput than the compared algorithms.

The network throughput is shown in Fig. 2(c) in relation to the number of CMUs. The results suggest that as the number of CMUs increases, the network's throughput decreases due to an increase in the number of RBs, with constant

Table 2. DRL simulation parameters.

Parameters	Values
Learning rate of actor network	0.01
Learning rate of critic network	0.01
Discount factor	0.9
Exploration in the starting	1
Final exploration	0.01
Number of exploratory steps	1000
Capacity of the replay buffer	1000
Size of mini-batch	32
In every epoch, number of steps	20
Reward function weights	1, 1
Discretization level of power l	10
Updated interval of weights	10
Activation function	ReLu
Optimizer	Adam

DMUs. Thus, DMPs have the option of obtaining the best RBs in order to meet their data rates with less interference.

Figure 2(d) depicts the throughput variation in relation to the lowest SINR requirements for DMPs. The result indicates that while the SINR need of DMPs is low, the network's throughput is likewise high. However, when the SINR need of DMPs is high, the network's throughput begins to fall at a quicker rate. This occurred as the number of D2D transmission pairs increased in response to increased SINR requirements, resulting in increased co-channel interference between the DMPS. Furthermore, the results reveal that the suggested algorithm gives improved results than the compared existing algorithms because, in existing approaches, transmission power is solely managed by the DDPG.

5   Conclusion

In this paper, our main goal is to optimise the total network throughput while keeping the SINR of the CMUs and DMPs as high as possible. To achieve the target, a power allocation scheme is designed. First of all, the centralised optimisation scheme is applied across the NOMA-based BS and DTs to reduce cross channel and co-channel interference. Next, to achieve better performance, train the model quickly, and faster convergence rate, the PPO is used to optimise the power of the BS and DTs. The evaluated results reveal that the proposed approach accomplishes better throughput than the state-of-the-art schemes.

References

1. Shafi, M., et al.: 5G: a tutorial overview of standards, trials, challenges, deployment, and practice. IEEE J. Sel. Areas Commun. **35**(6), 1201–1221 (2017)
2. Budhiraja, I., et al.: A systematic review on NOMA variants for 5G and beyond. IEEE Access **9**, 85573–85644 (2021)
3. Budhiraja, I., et al.: ISHU: interference reduction scheme for D2D mobile groups using uplink NOMA. IEEE Trans. Mob. Comput. (2021)
4. Goodfellow, I., et al.: Deep Learning. MIT Press, Cambridge (2016)
5. Luong, N.C., et al.: Applications of deep reinforcement learning in communications and networking: a survey. IEEE Commun. Surv. Tutor. **21**(4), 3133–3174 (2019)
6. Budhiraja, I., Kumar, N., Tyagi, S., Tanwar, S., Han, Z.: An energy efficient scheme for WPCN-NOMA based device-to-device communication. IEEE Trans. Veh. Technol. **70**(11), 11935–11948 (2021)
7. Nguyen, K.K., et al.: Non-cooperative energy efficient power allocation game in D2D communication: a multi-agent deep reinforcement learning approach. IEEE Access **7**, 100480–100490 (2019)
8. Bi, Z., et al.: Deep reinforcement learning based power allocation for D2D network. In: 2020 IEEE 91st Vehicular Technology Conference (VTC2020-Spring), pp. 1–5, March 2020
9. Ji, Z., et al.: Power optimization in device-to-device communications: a deep reinforcement learning approach with dynamic reward. IEEE Wirel. Commun. Lett. **10**(3), 508–511 (2021)
10. Zhang, T., et al.: Energy-efficient mode selection and resource allocation for D2D-enabled heterogeneous networks: a deep reinforcement learning approach. IEEE Trans. Wirel. Commun. **20**(2), 1175–1187 (2021)
11. Chen, M., et al.: Continuous incentive mechanism for D2D content sharing: a deep reinforcement learning approach. In: 2020 IEEE International Conference on Communications Workshops (ICC Workshops), pp. 1–6, June 2020
12. Tan, J., et al.: Deep reinforcement learning for joint channel selection and power control in D2D networks. IEEE Trans. Wirel. Commun. **20**(2), 1363–1378 (2021)
13. Budhiraja, I., et al.: Deep-reinforcement-learning-based proportional fair scheduling control scheme for underlay D2D communication. IEEE Internet Things J. **8**(5), 3143–3156 (2021)
14. Tang, J., et al.: Energy minimization in D2D-assisted cache-enabled Internet of Things: a deep reinforcement learning approach. IEEE Trans. Ind. Inf. **16**(8), 5412–5423 (2020)
15. Mnih, V., et al.: Asynchronous methods for deep reinforcement learning. In: International Conference on Machine Learning, pp. 1928–1937, June 2016

An Intrusion Detection System for Blackhole Attack Detection and Isolation in RPL Based IoT Using ANN

C. Prajisha$^{(\boxtimes)}$ ⓘ and A. R. Vasudevan ⓘ

Department of Computer Science and Engineering, National Institute of Technology Calicut, Calicut, India
vasudevanar@nitc.ac.in

Abstract. Routing Protocol for Low Power and Lossy Networks (RPL) is a simple and lightweight routing protocol for Internet of Things (IoT). RPL-based IoT networks are prone to various security attacks because of their constrained nature. Black hole attack is one of the most destructive threats in RPL. This paper proposes INSULATE (**I**oT **N**etwork Sec**U**rity in RPL using **A**NN based In**T**rusion Detection and **E**viction), an Intrusion Detection System (IDS) against black hole attack using Artificial Neural Network (ANN). The proposed IDS combines data from multiple watchdog nodes using Dempster-Shafer's theory of evidence to estimate the likelihood of an attacker node. Experiments in real-world dataset shows that our proposed model exhibits a maximum detection rate of 99.23%, and achieves better network performance that is 1%–2% higher compared to existing techniques.

Keywords: IoT · Black hole attack · RPL · Security

1 Introduction

The IoT plays a remarkable role in our environment, society, and economy. IoT is a Low power and Lossy Network (LLN) of smart objects/things that comprises various physical objects, sensors, cloud services, IoT protocols, consumers, and developers [1]. IoT devices are deployed in various areas, including healthcare, entertainment, industrial appliances, agriculture, and transportation [2]. The vast economic prospects available in the IoT area resulted in a massive boost in smart device's usage and self-configuring services available in IoT networks.

However, IoT objects' wide distribution and openness bring many security and privacy challenges, including data manipulation and unauthorized access [3]. IoT attacks are becoming more complex, posing more hurdles in detecting intrusions effectively. Therefore, special tools, strategies, and techniques are needed for safeguarding IoT networks. Furthermore, in object-driven IoT networks, traditional user-driven security architectures are ineffective [4]. Therefore insecure IoT environments require security defenses such as IDS. Machine

© Springer Nature Switzerland AG 2022
D. Garg et al. (Eds.): IACC 2021, CCIS 1528, pp. 332–347, 2022.
https://doi.org/10.1007/978-3-030-95502-1_26

Table 1. Acronyms used in this paper

Acronym	Full wording
RPL	Routing Protocol for Low power and lossy network
Internet of Things	IoT
Artificial Neural Network	ANN
Low power and Lossy Network	LLN
Intrusion Detection System	IDS
Border Router	BR
Black List Table	BLT
Destination Oriented Directed Acyclic Graph	DODAG
Objective Function	OF
DODAG Information Object	DIO
DODAG Information Solicitation	DIS
Destination Advertisement Object	DAO
Destination Advertisement Object Acknowledgement	DAO-ACK
Local Decision Table	LDT
Local Analysis Result Generator	LARG
Mean Square Error	MSE

learning has been applied to strengthen intrusion detection over the previous few decades [5]. However, little effort has been put into developing machine learning-based intrusion detection for RPL attacks [6]. This paper proposes an ANN-based IDS for RPL protocol in IoT. IoT devices are resource-limited and power-constrained. Because of these limitations, IoT security measures must be efficient and light, with as little computing and communication overhead as possible on end devices. The proposed approach puts less strain on the network element because it needs only the network packet traces for attack detection, collected externally by watchdog nodes. The proposed method has two phases: local detection and global detection, and eviction. Watchdogs collect data from sensor nodes and make decisions locally in the local detection process. All watchdogs use an ANN classifier, and the ANN is trained to generate a real value between 0 and 1, representing whether the data is normal or malicious. Global detection is performed via a sink node/border router (BR) based on the data provided by the watchdogs. The BR calculates a belief function using Dempster-Shafer theory of evidence [7] to find the trustworthiness of every node by using the data from watchdogs. It is the amount of belief that directly supports either the given node is malicious or trustworthy. The BR also creates a Black_List Table (BLT) that contains IDs of all attacker nodes that should be removed from the network. All nodes in the network will receive a warning message notifying them not to join the nodes in BLT again in the future, thus isolating it from the rest of the network. The major contributions of the proposed INSULATE approach are as follows:

- Propose an intrusion detection system to detect black hole attack in RPL using ANN.
- Implements a trust aggregation method based on Dempster-Shafer theory of evidence for attack detection in IoT network.
- Introduce a blacklist table concept to evict the attacker nodes from the network.

Table 1 lists the acronyms used in this paper. The rest of the paper is organized as follows. Section 2 explains the black hole attack in the RPL scenario. Section 3 deals with the related works, Sect. 4 gives a comprehensive description of the suggested technique, and Sect. 5 explains the simulation environment, the performance metrics used and the results obtained in the proposed IDS. Section 6 concludes the paper.

2   Black Hole Attack in RPL Scenario

RPL is a standardized routing protocol for LLN [8]. RPL runs at the network layer and performs routing using the distance-vector algorithm. The network topology is specified as a Destination Oriented Directed Acyclic Graph (DODAG) in RPL [9]. The DODAG represents a routing tree with a single destination, known as sink node or BR. Each participating node in DODAG should select its parent carefully based on some routing metrics to create an optimum path to DODAG root. Every node uses an Objective Function (OF) [10] to convert routing metrics into a node rank. The rank indicates the distance between a node and the BR. The attack simulated in this paper is a black hole attack with RPL as the routing protocol. In RPL, every sensor node forwards the packet to its parent node, which transfers it to its corresponding parent, and the packet finally reaches the sink node via the multi-hop path.

RPL uses ICMPv6 control messages for building DODAG [11]. The four control packets used in this protocol are DODAG Information Object (DIO), Destination Advertisement Object (DAO), DODAG Information Solicitation (DIS), and DAO Acknowledgement (DAO-ACK). A new node requests to enter the network by multi-casting DIO to neighbor nodes and access network topology information. DIO messages are multi-cast downstream from root to leaf nodes to set up and update network topology information. DAO informs the sender that it has been chosen as a preferred parent for data transfer and serves as a confirmation to DIO. DAO-ACK message is uni-cast downward from the source to the destination, indicating that the DAO message has been acknowledged.

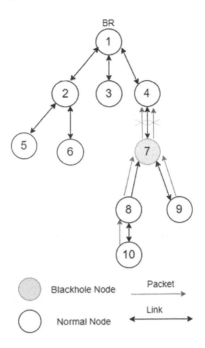

Fig. 1. Blackhole attack scenario in RPL

The RPL protocol is susceptible to various routing attacks [12] in the IoT environment, including a black hole attack [13]. When an sensor node wants to deliver a message to the BR, it first tries to forward it to the preferred parent. The black hole attack affects the routing process in RPL by forging a bogus DIO with a lower rank, thereby misleading the sensor node into believing that the malicious node has the shortest route to the BR. Sensor node chooses the attacker node as their parent node and begins sending data packets; the black hole node then quietly discards all received packets. Figure 1 shows a sample scenario of a black hole attack in the RPL network. In Fig. 1, node 7 acts as the black hole node and drops the packets from sensor nodes 8 and 9.

3   Related Work

To the best of our knowledge, the black hole attack detection and mitigation approaches for RPL base IoT network is limited. This section, discuss about the existing related works in this area.

The case study in [13] highlights the Contiki OS and RPL routing protocol flaws, leading to an easy infusion of various malicious activities, including black hole attacks. However, the authors did not propose any countermeasures for the black hole attack. A black hole attack mitigation using a trust-based technique was proposed in [14], in which every sensor nodes observe the communication behavior of its neighboring nodes. These observations are used to determine neighbor trust values, which are then used to choose the best parent. However, the attacker nodes are not mitigated globally. Every node has to repeat the same selection procedure in every parent selection. Ahmed et al. [15] proposed a mitigation technique against black hole attacks in which suspicious nodes are determined using a local decision process and verified as attackers using a global verification process. A verification message sends to the DODAG root, and the reply to this verification message from the root node is used to confirm the identity of a black hole node. In this approach, communication overhead is high due to the use of additional verification messages along with RPL control messages. In [16], a hybrid learning technique was used for intrusion detection. In this approach, special nodes called data sniffers uses a supervised learning technique to generate correctly classified instances (CCIs). These CCIs are collected at a super node. The super node detects attacker nodes using the linear regression technique. The proposed approach required a long time for detecting malicious activity. Ribera et al. [17] proposed a heartbeat-based detection method for black hole attacks. In this approach, a dedicated node will send ICMPv6 echo queries to the rest of the network's nodes. If the ICMPv6 echo request source does not obtain a reply, it indicates the probability of a black hole attack. Due to the requirement of additional packets, the protocol adds some overhead to communication.

An anomaly-based approach called SIEWE to detect black hole attacks in RPL was proposed in [18]. In SIEWE, the difference in RSSI value is used to create a suspicious node list. Hence this approach is unsuitable for RPL with other objective functions such as ETX, hop count, and remaining energy. Furthermore, declaring a node as an attacker, the root must receive at least four comparable votes from four separate nodes. As a result, the false-negative ratio is high with this method. In [19], a strategy for detecting a black hole attack at the IOT network layer was proposed. However, the proposed method is only applicable in AODV based IoT network. The suggested logistic regression-based trust model in [20] is an easy technique to find and isolate the RPL's black hole nodes. But it lacks a detailed comparison with existing approaches.

4   INSULATE - The Proposed Intrusion Detection System

This section explains the system model of INSULATE, local detection process, and the global detection and eviction process in detail.

4.1   System Model

This section shows the architecture of INSULATE. The proposed approach assumes an IoT network with numerous constrained network devices. The proposed method uses three watchdogs, and they monitor an area of 1000 m^2. As represented in Fig. 2, the proposed INSULATE has two modules: The watchdog module (Local Detection) and the BR module (Global Detection and Eviction).

In the local detection process, every watchdog uses a collector to collect information on sensor nodes' communication behavior by monitoring the data packets sent and received by sensor nodes. These are first-hand data created through promiscuous mode, which decreases the amount of false data gathered by direct reporting from nodes themselves. Every watchdog generates a data set instance per reporting time (Rt) for every node except BR. The watchdog combines the data set instances to a test data set, and it is given to a pre-trained ANN classifier to detect malicious and benign data. The output of the ANN classifier is a table, Local Decision Table (LDT), which contains the node IDs and corresponding classification report (CR). The LDT is fed to a Local Analysis Result Generator (LARG) for local analysis result calculation. The LARG maps the result of ANN classifier to a local analysis result (LAR) denoted by L_x^i for every node i observed by the watchdog x. To detect the attacker nodes, the watchdogs sends the intermediate results to the BR.

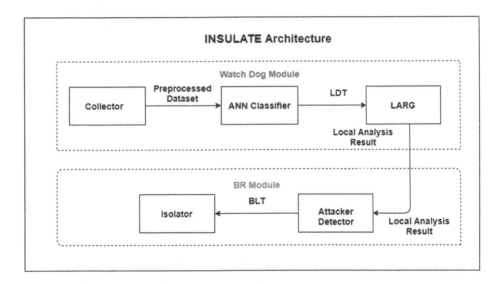

Fig. 2. Architecture of INSULATE

To detect the attacker nodes, the watchdogs sends the intermediate results to the BR. The BR module performs two progressive steps: attacker detection and eviction. Once the BR collects the LARs from each watch dogs at stage two, an attacker detection process using a belief function is performed by the attacker detection module. The attacker detection module stores the IDs of the malicious nodes in the BLT. Then the BLT is forwarded to the Isolator module. The Isolator will then send an alert message to all nodes in the network, notifying them that they should not join the nodes in BLT in the future, thereby evicting them from the network.

4.2 Local Detection

The watchdog module is responsible for local detection. The proposed approach assumed a promiscuous wireless network where watchdog nodes can monitor the communication behavior of sensor nodes in its coverage area, and all the watchdogs are trustworthy. Components of watchdog modules are as follows:

Collector. The collector module within the watchdog node monitors the incoming and outgoing packets of sensor nodes. Packet traces are collected from the network layer, and a raw data set is created during every Rt interval. From this raw dataset, features are extracted for further processing. The packets collected for analysis are DAO, DIO, DIS, and DAO-ACK and data packets. The features are extracted based on the communication information captured by the watchdogs. A total of 14 potential characteristics are produced as a result of this approach, which is given in Table 1 and the collector algorithm is presented in Algorithm 1. First, calculate the Transmitted and Received Packets Counts (TPC and RPC) for each sensor node in Rt. Also, calculate Data Packets Created and Transmitted as a source node (DPC and DPT) for each node in Rt. Total Transmission Time (TTT) is calculated by adding the duration of each packet sent, and Total Reception Time (TRT) is calculated by adding the duration of each received packet in Rt. Transmission Rate (TR), Reception Rate (RR), and Dropped Packet Count are calculated as follows:

$$TR = \frac{TPC}{1000} \tag{1}$$

$$RR = \frac{RPC}{1000} \tag{2}$$

$$DPC = RPC - TPC \tag{3}$$

The other features are the count of ICMPv6 packets, DAO, and DIO. The count of transmitted ICMPv6 packets of each sensor node in Rt time interval is calculated. Then the dataset is produced using collected data and preprocessed before feeding into the pre-trained ANN classifier. The computational complexity of Algorithm 1 is $O(kn)$, where k is the number of raws in the raw dataset and n is the total number of sensor nodes. The number of nodes (n) remain constant where as the number of raws (k) varies. Hence the complexity of Algorithm 1 is $O(k)$.

ANN Classifier. The proposed IDS uses an ANN classifier [21] to detect malicious data from normal data. The training dataset was generated with features listed in Table 2 using the open-source Contiki/Cooja simulator. Each dataset instance was labeled as benign or malicious for training. Feature selection was performed on the dataset to remove the irrelevant features before running the classification algorithm. The ANN classifier uses the sequential model to build the deep neural network. It uses Mean squared error (MSE) as the loss function and the Sigmoid function as the activation function for the output layer.

Table 2. Extracted features list.

Number	Name of attribute	Description
1	InstanceNumber	Instance sequence number
2	Node Id	IP Address of Monitored Node
3	TR	Transmission Rate
4	RR	Reception Rate
5	TTT	Total Transmission Time
6	TRT	Total Reception Time
7	DP	Dropped Packet Count
8	DPC	Data Packets Created
9	DPT	Data Packets Transmitted
10	DAO	DAO Packets Count
11	DIO	DIO Packets Count
12	TPC	Transmitted Packets Count
13	RPC	Received Packets Count

Algorithm 1. Collector algorithm

Input:
Raw dataset : Communication data collected by the collector module
Output:
Preprocessed Dataset : Dataset after feature extraction and selection
Algorithm:
1: *Feature Extraction*
2: Set window size= 1000ms
3: Calculate feature values within 1000ms
4: *Feature selection*
5: Drop insignificant features

Algorithm 2. ANN classifier algorithm

Input:
Preprocessed dataset
Output:
Local Decision Table, LDT:
Algorithm:
1: *Classification*
2: Load the datasets as dfclass
3: Xclass,Yclass ← dfclass
4: Xclass ← Scaled Xclass
5: Produce Classification Result
6: Create LDT using classification result

Algorithm 3. LAR generation algorithm

Input:
Local decision table, LDT
Output:
L_x^i : LAR for all node i observed by watchdog X
Algorithm:
  1: **for** *each node i with CR $\alpha_i \in LDT$* **do**
  2:    **if** $\alpha_i \geq 0.5$ **then**
  3:       $L_x^i(T) = \alpha_i$
  4:       $L_x^i(M) = 0$
  5:       $L_x^i(U) = 1 - \alpha_i$
  6:    **else if** $\alpha_i < 0.5$ **then**
  7:       $L_x^i(T) = 0$
  8:       $L_x^i(M) = 1 - \alpha_i$
  9:       $L_x^i(U) = \alpha_i$
10:    **end if**
11: **end for**

The ANN classifier contains five layers. The input layer includes 11 neurons. The input layer neuron count must be equal to the number of features in the dataset. The fifth layer is the output layer that contains only a single neuron. The remaining three middle layers are hidden layers. The second and fourth layer contains 50 neurons, and the third layer contains 100 neurons. If the Sigmoid neuron's output is greater than or equal to 0.5, it is trustworthy; it is malicious if the output is less than 0.5. During the prediction time, the watchdog stores the communication data collected during Rt as a raw dataset, and after feature extraction, the preprocessed dataset is given to the ANN classifier. The output of the ANN classifier is stored in LDT and forwarded to the LARG. The detailed algorithm of ANN classifier is presented in Algorithm 2. The computational complexity of Algorithm 2 is O(n), where n is the number of nodes.

LAR Generator. The last step in the local detection process is to convert the ANN classifier's outcome into a LAR. We propose an attacker detection technique that uses the Dempster-Shafer theory of evidence. Dempster-Shafer is a mathematical theory that calculates a degree of trust in a hypothesis based on data from various sources. In Dempster-Shafer, if a node N verifies the trustworthiness of another node i with probability p, it does not imply that i is fraudulent with probability $1 - p$. As a result, N would have a p degree of belief in the trustworthiness of i and 0 degrees of belief in i's maliciousness. Let $\Omega = \{T, M, U\}$ is a hypothesis set where T indicates the trustworthiness of node i; M indicates that i is malicious; and U indicates the uncertainty in i's trustworthiness or maliciousness. The local analysis result of a node i assigned by watch dog X, denoted by LAR_x^i represents a mapping function of the set Ω to a real-value between 0 and 1. In our proposal, the LAR for an sensor node is equal to the output value of the ANN classifier for the dataset instance of that sensor node.

In other words, suppose that the output of ANN classifier of watchdog X for a dataset instance of node i is α. If $\alpha >= .5$, then L_x^i would be: $L_x^i(T) = \alpha$, $L_x^i(M) = 0$, and $L_x^i(U) = 1 - \alpha$. Conversely, if ANN classifies the data instance from i as malicious, i.e. $\alpha < .5$, then L_x^i would be: $L_x^i(T) = 0$, $L_x^i(M) = 1 - \alpha$, and $L_x^i(U) = \alpha$. All watchdogs generate the L_x^i for every node i and sent this to the BR for attacker detection and eviction. The algorithm of LAR generation is presented in Algorithm 3. The computational complexity of Algorithm 3 is $O(n)$, where n is the number of nodes.

4.3   Global Detection and Eviction

Intruder detection and eviction are essential in any security framework to maintain the sustainability of the network. Once the BR collects $LARs$ from all three watchdogs, it will initiate the global detection and eviction phase to detect and isolate intruders from the network. The components of the BR module is as follows

Attacker Detector. Dempster's rule is used for combining discrete pieces of evidence from different parties [22]. Unlike the Bayesian technique, which needs complete understanding of both prior and conditional probability, the Dempster-Shafer technique can represent ambiguity or a lack of a clear knowledge. Therefor, it is well suited for aggregating the classification results from various watchdogs. In the proposed approach, the attacker detector module aggregate the $LARs$ from the watchdogs, and uses the Dempster's rule for combination to calculate a belief function. The belief function maps H to a real-valued number between 0 and 1 and indicates total belief in a particular hypothesis H. The belief of BR in trustworthiness, maliciousness and uncertainty of sensor node i using the $LARs$ from three watchdogs, X1, X2, and X3 is calculated as follows:

$$blf_{BR}^i(T) = L_{x1}^i(T) \oplus L_{x2}^i(T) \oplus L_{x3}^i(T) \tag{4}$$

Where:

$$L_{x1}^i(T) \oplus L_{x2}^i(T) = \frac{1}{k}[\, L_{x1}^i(T)\, L_{x2}^i(T) \; + L_{x1}^i(T)\, L_{x2}^i(U) \; + L_{x1}^i(U)\, L_{x2}^i(T)\,] \tag{5}$$

$$blf_{BR}^i(M) = L_{x1}^i(M) \oplus L_{x2}^i(M) \oplus L_{x3}^i(M) \tag{6}$$

Where:

$$L_{x1}^i(M) \oplus L_{x2}^i(M) = \frac{1}{k}[\, L_{x1}^i(M)\, L_{x2}^i(M) \; + L_{x1}^i(M)\, L_{x2}^i(U) \; + L_{x1}^i(U)\, L_{x2}^i(M)\,] \tag{7}$$

$$blf_{BR}^i(U) = L_{x1}^i(U) \oplus L_{x2}^i(U) \oplus L_{x3}^i(U) \tag{8}$$

Where:

$$L_{x1}^i(U) \oplus L_{x2}^i(U) = \frac{1}{k}[\ L_{x1}^i(U)\ L_{x2}^i(U)\ ] \tag{9}$$

The constant k can be calculated as follows:

$$k = \sum_{h \cap h'} L_{x1}^i(h)\ L_{x2}^i(h'), h = \{T, M, U\} \tag{10}$$

Consider a scenario where the BR wants to combine $LARs$ from watchdogs W1, W2, and W3 about a node i. Suppose that watchdogs W1, W2,and W3 ratings indicate that i is trustworthy with probability 0.9 and malicious with probabilities 0.6 and .7, respectively. Thus, the $LARs$ of the three watchdogs about node i is given as follows:

- W1: $L_{w1}^i(T) = 0.9$, $L_{w1}^i(M) = 0$, and $L_{w1}^i(U) = 0.1$
- W2: $L_{w2}^i(T) = 0$, $L_{w2}^i(M) = 0.6$, and $L_{w2}^i(U) = 0.4$
- W3: $L_{w3}^i(T) = 0$, $L_{w3}^i(M) = 0.7$, and $L_{w3}^i(U) = 0.3$

The total degree of belief in i's trustworthiness is 0.54 while the belief in i's maliciousness is 0.43. Although W2 and W3 report that i is malicious, the combined belief in i's trustworthiness is high. Watchdogs W2 and W3 make up the majority in this scenario, but their evidence is much reduced in the combined belief function. Thus, a majority vote may result in a wrong decision.

The attacker detector module will calculate the belief in the trustworthiness and maliciousness of every node under observation. Finally, the BR will create a BLT with node IDs whose belief in maliciousness is greater than trustworthiness.

Isolator. The proposed INSULATE IDS contains an Isolator module to add extra security and isolate the malicious nodes from the network. The Isolator alerts all neighbor nodes of BR to avoid communication with nodes in BLT using a DIO message. These DIOs will be forwarded to nodes in all levels until it reaches the leaf nodes.

5 Performance Evaluation

This section explains the simulation environment, the performance metrics used and the simulation results obtained in the proposed approach.

5.1 Simulation Setup and Performance Metrics

The simulations were run on the Contiki OS 3.0 under different conditions and its simulator Cooja [23]. The sensors in the simulated network use RPL as the routing protocol. Three nodes were designated as watchdogs in a network of 10–50 nodes that collect data from the sensor nodes promiscuously. In this simulation, only one node was designated as the sink. The communication range of each node is 50 m and the total deployment area is 1000 m². 10% of total nodes

Table 3. Simulation parameters

Parameter	Value
Simulator	Cooja
Number of nodes	10–50
Transmission range	50 m
Deployment area	$1000\,\mathrm{m}^2$
Simulation time	5 min
Reporting time, Rt	1000 ms
Physical layer	IEEE 802.15.4
MAC layer	Contiki MAC
Network layer	RPL
Transport layer	UDP
Objective function	ETX

were assigned as malicious nodes to simulate attack scenarios. The simulation parameters are given in Table 3.

The simulation of the black hole attack was conducted in the Cooja simulator. Network communication data with normal nodes and malicious nodes were collected separately for the performance analysis of proposed INSULATE method. In the simulated network, Cooja saved radio messages as PCAP files. After that, Python data preprocessing package was used to convert the PCAP file to CSV. The produced CSV files were then submitted to a feature extraction method. The features with less importance were dropped and a preprocessed dataset was created that was fed into a feed-forward ANN classifier with five layers. The ANN classifier was implemented using Python libraries such as KERAS, Scikit and Numpy. The performance of the proposed approach was evaluated in terms of packet delivery ratio (PDR), end-to-end delay (EED), true positive rate (TPR), and false-positive rate (FPR).

PDR: It is the ratio of the total count of data packets received by the BR to the total count of data packets generated during simulation.

$$PDR = \frac{\sum RPC(BR)}{\sum_{i=1}^{N} DPC(i)} \qquad (11)$$

EED: The EED is the time required to deliver a packet from source to destination.

$$EED = \frac{\sum(Packet\ send\ time - Packet\ received\ time)}{Total\ number\ of\ packets\ received} \qquad (12)$$

TPR: It is the ratio of the number of wrong classifications to all the classifications for the testing of normal nodes.

$$TPR = \frac{TP}{TP + FN} \tag{13}$$

where TP stands for true positive (a malicious node is found to be malicious by a detection approach) and FN stands for false negative (detection technique determines a malicious node to be normal).

FPR: This is the ratio of the number of incorrect attacker detections to the total number of detections made during testing of normal nodes.

$$FPR = \frac{FP}{TN + FP} \tag{14}$$

where FP stands for false positive (a normal node is classified as malicious by the detection technique) and TN stands for true negative (the detection technique classifies a normal node to be normal).

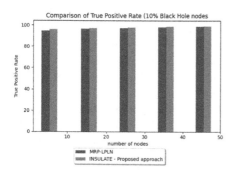

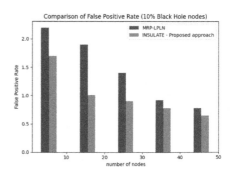

Fig. 3. Comparison of true positive rate   **Fig. 4.** Comparison of false positive rate

5.2   Simulation Results and Performance Comparison

Figure 3 shows the TPR as nodes vary from 10 to 50, with malicious nodes accounting for 10% of the total nodes. According to the graph, the TPR increases with increase in node count. The increase in TPR shows that the trained ANN in INSULATE can accurately identify normal and attack data with less negative rates when compared with MRP-LPLN. Figure 4 shows that FPR decreases when the node count varies from 10 to 50. The accuracy of intrusion detection increases by using the ANN model, which has more ability to generalize than the traditional ML model.

Figures 5 and 6 show the PDR and EED with varying nodes, where attacker nodes account for 10% of the total nodes. The proposed technique is compared with SIEWE [18] and MRP-LPLN [15]. As displayed in Fig. 2, the PDR for all approaches is significantly reduced with increase in node count. The decrease in PDR is understandable because packets can drop for a variety of reasons in congested networks. On the other hand, the proposed technique appears to be effective in decreasing the attack effect with a maximum PDR of 97.8 compared to SIEWE and MRP-LPLN. Figure 3 shows that the EED of RPL with attacker node, INSULATE, and MRP-LPLN increases as the number of nodes increases. The EED of RPL with attacker nodes is higher than the other two approaches because the attacker nodes delay packets reaching BR. Since MRP-LPLN requires additional time for verification of suspicious nodes, the suggested INSULATE method has a lower delay than MRP-LPLN. The INSULATE has an EED of 0.89s that is 0.21 s–0.7 s less than the existing methods.

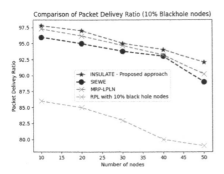

Fig. 5. Comparison of packet delivery ratio

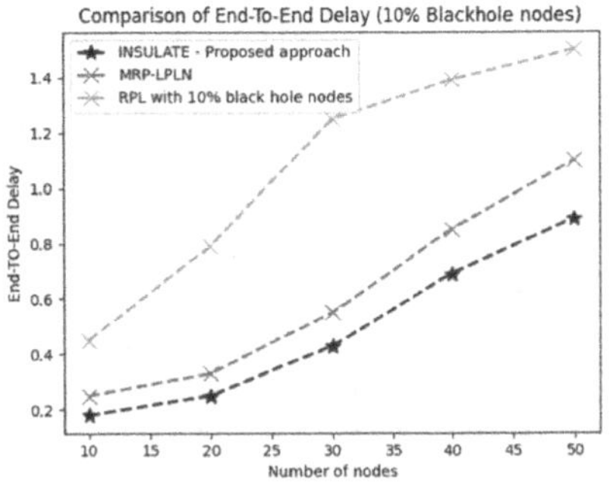

Fig. 6. Comparison of end-to-end delay

6   Conclusion

Efficient intrusion detection and eviction mechanism were presented to mitigate blackhole attacks in RPL based IoT networks. The proposed ANN-based IDS determines a blackhole attack by performing a local detection using watchdogs and mitigating attacker nodes using global detection. The BR performs the global detection by aggregating the classification results using Dempster- Shafer theory of evidence. The simulation results showed that the proposed approach significantly increased the TPR and PDR and reduced the FPR and EED. This work can be enhanced by modifying the IDS to detect more routing attacks in RPL based IoT. We're looking on adding more features to build a single model that can detect many forms of attacks. We intend to create scenarios with varying rates of malicious and non-malicious nodes, as well as a bigger number of nodes.

References

1. Ray, P.P.: A survey on Internet of Things architectures. J. King Saud Univ.-Comput. Inf. Sci. **30**(3), 291–319 (2018)
2. Atzori, L., Iera, A., Morabito, G.: The Internet of Things: a survey. Comput. Netw. **54**(15), 2787–2805 (2010)
3. Alaba, F.A., et al.: Internet of Things security: a survey. J. Netw. Comput. Appl. **88**, 10–28 (2017)
4. Nandhini, P.S., Mehtre, B.M.: Intrusion detection system based RPL attack detection techniques and countermeasures in IoT: a comparison. In: 2019 International Conference on Communication and Electronics Systems (ICCES). IEEE (2019)
5. Khraisat, A., Gondal, I., Vamplew, P., Kamruzzaman, J.: Survey of intrusion detection systems: techniques, datasets and challenges. Cybersecurity **2**(1), 1–22 (2019). https://doi.org/10.1186/s42400-019-0038-7
6. Verma, A., Ranga, V.: Machine learning based intrusion detection systems for IoT applications. Wirel. Pers. Commun. **111**(4), 2287–2310 (2019). https://doi.org/10.1007/s11277-019-06986-8
7. Wahab, O.A., et al.: Towards trustworthy multi-cloud services communities: a trust-based hedonic coalitional game. IEEE Trans. Serv. Comput. **11**(1), 184–201 (2016)
8. Kharrufa, H., Al-Kashoash, H.A., Kemp, A.H.: RPL-based routing protocols in IoT applications: a review. IEEE Sens. J. **19**(15), 5952–5967 (2019)
9. Sobral, J.V., et al.: Routing protocols for low power and lossy networks in Internet of Things applications. Sensors **19**(9), 2144 (2019)
10. Djedjig, N., et al.: New trust metric for the RPL routing protocol. In: 2017 8th International Conference on Information and Communication Systems (ICICS). IEEE (2017)
11. Sharma, D., Mishra, I., Jain, S.: A detailed classification of routing attacks against RPL in Internet of Things. Int. J. Adv. Res. Ideas Innov. Technol. **3**(1), 692–703 (2017)
12. Pongle, P., Chavan, G.: A survey: attacks on RPL and 6LoWPAN in IoT. In: 2015 International Conference on Pervasive Computing (ICPC). IEEE (2015)
13. Chugh, K., Aboubaker, L., Loo, J.: Case study of a black hole attack on LoWPAN-RPL. In: Proceedings of the Sixth International Conference on Emerging Security Information, Systems and Technologies (SECURWARE), Rome, Italy (2012)
14. Airehrour, D., Gutierrez, J., Ray, S.K.: Securing RPL routing protocol from blackhole attacks using a trust-based mechanism. In: 2016 26th International Telecommunication Networks and Applications Conference (ITNAC). IEEE (2016)
15. Ahmed, F., Ko, Y.B.: Mitigation of black hole attacks in routing protocol for low power and lossy networks. Secur. Commun. Netw. **9**(18), 5143–5154 (2016)
16. Amouri, A., Alaparthy, V.T., Morgera, S.D.: Cross layer-based intrusion detection based on network behavior for IoT. In: 2018 IEEE 19th Wireless and Microwave Technology Conference (WAMICON). IEEE (2018)
17. Ribera, E.G., et al.: Heartbeat-based detection of blackhole and greyhole attacks in RPL networks. In: 12th International Symposium on Communication Systems, Networks and Digital Signal Processing (CSNDSP), p. 2020. IEEE (2020)
18. Patel, H.B., Jinwala, D.C: Blackhole detection in 6LoWPAN based Internet of Things: an anomaly based approach. In: TENCON 2019–2019 IEEE Region 10 Conference (TENCON). IEEE (2019)

19. Kale, S.: Detection of blackhole attack in IoT. Inf. Technol. Ind. **9**(3), 700–709 (2021)
20. Prathapchandran, K., Janani, T.: A trust-based security model to detect misbehaving nodes in Internet of Things (IoT) environment using logistic regression. In: Journal of Physics: Conference Series, vol. 1850, no. 1. IOP Publishing (2021)
21. Yavuz, F.Y., Ünal, D., Gül, E.: Deep learning for detection of routing attacks in the Internet of Things. Int. J. Comput. Intell. Syst. **12**(1), 39–58 (2018)
22. Chen, T.M., Venkataramanan, V.: Dempster-Shafer theory for intrusion detection in ad hoc networks. IEEE Internet Comput. **9**(6), 35–41 (2005)
23. Osterlind, F., et al.: Cross-level sensor network simulation with COOJA. In: Proceedings of 2006 31st IEEE Conference on Local Computer Networks. IEEE (2006)

Evaluating the Efficacy of Different Neural Network Deep Reinforcement Algorithms in Complex Search-and-Retrieve Virtual Simulations

Ishita Vohra[1], Shashank Uttrani[2] (ID), Akash K. Rao[2(✉)] (ID),
and Varun Dutt[2] (ID)

[1] International Institute of Information Technology Hyderabad, Hyderabad,
Telangana, India
[2] Applied Cognitive Science Laboratory, Indian Institute of Technology Mandi,
Shimla, Himachal Pradesh, India
akashk_rao@projects.iitmandi.ac.in,
varun@iitmandi.ac.in

Abstract. In recent years, Deep Reinforcement Learning (DRL) has been extensively used to solve problems in various domains like traffic control, healthcare, and simulation-based training. Proximal Policy Optimization (PPO) and Soft-Actor Critic (SAC) methods are DRL's latest state of art on-policy and off-policy algorithms. Though previous studies have shown that SAC generally performs better than PPO, hyperparameter tuning can significantly impact the performance of these algorithms. Also, a systematic evaluation of the efficacy of these algorithms after hyperparameter tuning in dynamic and complex environments is missing and much needed in literature. This research aims to evaluate the effect of the number of layers and nodes in SAC and PPO algorithms in a search-and-retrieve task developed in the Unity 3D game engine. In the task, a bot had to navigate through the physical mesh and collect 'target' objects while avoiding 'distractor' objects. We compared the SAC and PPO models on four different test conditions that differed in the ratios of targets and distractors. Results revealed that PPO performed better than SAC for all test conditions when the number of layers and units present in the architecture was the lowest. When the number of targets was more than the distractors (9:1), PPO outperformed SAC, especially when the number of units and layers were large. Furthermore, increasing the layers and units per layer was responsible for increasing PPO and SAC performance. Results also implied that similar hyperparameter settings might be used while comparing models developed using DRL algorithms. We discuss the implications of these results and explore the possible applications of using modern, state-of-the-art DRL algorithms to learn the semantics and idiosyncrasies associated with complex and dynamic environments.

Keywords: Proximal Policy Optimization · Soft-Actor Critic · Deep reinforcement learning · Virtual environments · Unity3D

D. Garg et al. (Eds.): IACC 2021, CCIS 1528, pp. 348–361, 2022.
https://doi.org/10.1007/978-3-030-95502-1_27

1 Introduction

The use of reinforcement learning algorithms amalgamated with deep learning methods to execute/navigate complex simulation environments has risen in the past few years [1]. Researchers are continually designing and developing novel algorithms and upgradations to the state-of-the-art algorithms, showing markedly improved performance in complex environments such as Atari, Go, Shogi etc. [2, 3]. The use of deep reinforcement learning algorithms in simulation environments has gained much traction in the past 5–6 years, with problems ranging from solving large state spaces to learning policies to solving simple stochastic transitions [3]. Many platforms like OpenAI Gym, Arcade Learning, and Unity ML-Agents have been launched to test these algorithms' robustness and efficacy in different simulation settings [4]. For instance, VizDoom is a classical rendition of the popular first-person shooter game Doom. VizDoom enables the design and development of agents that can execute the objectives in the game using a screen buffer [5]. Similarly, using Unity ML-Agents, researchers in [6] utilized the propensity of state-of-the-art reinforcement learning algorithms like Proximal Policy Optimization (PPO) and Soft Actor-Critic (SAC) to make an agent learn the classic ping-pong game. In addition, researchers in [7] used BicNet, an actor-critic-based reinforcement learning agent in the Unity ML-agents platform using a bidirectional neural network to learn to collaborate and solve advanced problems in the popular StarCraft game.

A considerable amount of research is currently being carried out in the design of state-of-the-art reinforcement learning algorithms incorporating different deep learning methods. However, testing the effectiveness of manipulating different hyperparameters in neural networks is missing and much needed in the literature. In addition, varying the number of layers and the number of nodes could be very crucial. This research aims to evaluate the effect of the number of layers and number of units present in the layers in SAC and PPO algorithms. We intend to assess the efficacy of these algorithms in a search-and-retrieve task called the 'food collector environment' in the Unity ML-agents platform [19].

In what follows, first, we provide a brief background of the research involving different reinforcement learning algorithms and the incorporation of reinforcement learning algorithms and deep le$arning methods for learning to execute dynamic virtual environments. Next, we evaluate the efficacy of two state-of-the-art reinforcement learning algorithms, PPO and SAC, and the effect of the number of layers and the number of nodes in these algorithms in a food collector environment. The food collector is a pre-existing environment built on Unity, where the task is to collect targets while avoiding distractors. The food collector environment was further improvised to have different types of targets and distractors. We then discuss the results obtained in the investigation and underscore the various implications of these results on learning different complex virtual environments.

2 Background

Researchers in [8] explored the possibility and the efficacy of employing state-of-the-art deep learning algorithms like convolutional neural networks (CNNs) to extract visual representations from the data to learn optimal value functions in an arcade learning environment. The researchers claimed that the learning was performed end-to-end with no simulation knowledge incorporated in the architecture. They discovered that deep learning-based visual feature extraction architectures performed significantly compared to other reinforcement learning architectures [8].

Similarly, researchers in [9] proposed a novel deep Q-learning architecture using functional approximation via deep neural networks to estimate the value function for all action state integrations and the generalizable property of their algorithms. They developed the same by training them on a relatively small number of scenarios and analyzing them on a massive number of simulations. They discovered that the agents were able to generalize successfully to previously unseen scenarios [9].

Reinforcement learning algorithms and deep learning methods have been widely used to learn to play different game environments, ranging from simple 2D games to complex games like Atari and Doom [10]. For instance, researchers in [10] investigated the efficacy of the MuZero algorithm, which incorporated both tree-search planning and a trained model of an environment to learn to play complex games such as Chess and Atari. Even though the researchers obtained excellent efficacy scores in training the algorithms to play both the games, stochastic transitions and how they need to be dealt with was not investigated [10].

Other studies, such as [11], have evaluated the efficacy of different reinforcement learning algorithms in custom-made simulations. In a customized ping-pong game, reinforcement learning techniques like Deep-Q Networks (DQNs), PPOs, and asynchronous Advantage Actor-Critic (A3C) were compared [11]. Results showed that the PPO method achieved significantly higher cumulative rewards compared to the A3C method and the DQN method. Researchers in [12] also investigated the potency of reinforcement learning algorithms like the Soft-Actor Critic (SAC) method and imitation learning to program an agent to play Snoopy Pop using Unity ML-Agents [12]. Results showed that both SAC and imitation learning yielded similar cumulative rewards.

Researchers in [13] had also compared the effectiveness of both PPO and SAC in minimal simulations like Lily's Garden [13]. Even though the researchers found out that SAC performed relatively better than PPO, a comprehensive investigation of PPO and SAC with varied neural network parameters (like the number of layers/number of nodes) is still missing in the literature. In our study, we removed this gap by comparing the performance of PPO and SAC based on the network architecture. Further, we have evaluated the performance of these algorithms on four different testing scenarios.

2.1   Proximal-Policy Optimization (PPO)

Many different approaches have been proposed for reinforcement learning which involves neural network function approximators [14, 15]. However, these approaches have their limitations. Deep Q-Learning fails on problems involving continuous actions spaces [14]. Policy gradient methods have poor data efficiency and robustness [15]. Trust Region Policy Optimization (TRPO) is hard to use with architectures with multiple outputs and performs poorly on tasks requiring deep CNNs and RNNs [16]. PPO overcomes all these limitations.

Proximal Policy Optimization (PPO) is a reinforcement learning algorithm that works on the policy gradient [17]. It can be used for continuous as well as discrete action spaces. The algorithm trains a stochastic policy in an on-policy manner while utilizing the actor-critic method. In the actor-critic paradigm, the actor's observations are mapped to actions, and the critic expects the rewards for a given observation [17]. For each epoch, a set of trajectories are collected by sampling from the latest policy. Later, the policy is updated, and the value function is fitted based on computed advantage estimates and the rewards [17]. Finally, the gradient ascent optimizer updates the policy and gradient descent algorithm to fit the value function [17].

It attains data efficiency and reliable performance of TRPO while using only first-order optimization [17]. It is easier to implement, is applicable in more general settings (both discrete and continuous action spaces) and has better overall performance. Figure 1 shows the architecture diagram for PPO.

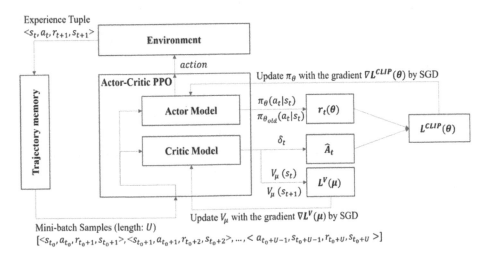

Fig. 1. Model architecture for PPO

2.2   Soft-Actor Critic (SAC)

The PPO algorithm above suffers from sample insufficiency because it uses an approach like on-policy for training [18]. In comparison, off-policy algorithms such as Deep Deterministic Policy Gradient (DDPG) use experience replay buffers to learn efficiently from past samples [18]. However, this involves a substantial amount of hyperparameter tuning to make them converge. The Soft Actor-Critic (SAC) algorithm uses a stochastic policy for optimization in an off-policy way by using a middle ground between PPO and DDPG algorithms [18].

Though SAC is considered to have better performance over PPO [18], hyperparameters like network architecture, batch size, and step size can vary policy gradient methods. Figure 2 shows the model architecture for SAC.

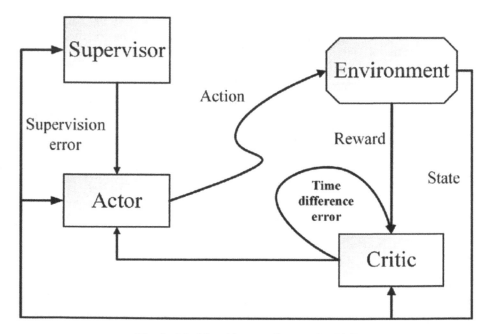

Fig. 2. Model architecture diagram for SAC

3   Methods

3.1   Experimental Design

A virtual food collector simulation [19], as shown in Fig. 3, was developed to investigate the influence of neural network parameters such as the number of hidden layers and number of nodes on the model agent's performance using state of the art reinforcement learning algorithms as PPO and SAC. The simulation consisted of the pre-existing environment on Unity, and a game development framework called the food collector environment [19]. Unity's ML-Agent toolkit [20] implemented the PPO and the SAC algorithms on the food collector environment. Various targets (items to collect) and distractors (items to avoid) were present in this environment. The targets were assigned pink, white, and green colors, whereas the distractors were red, purple, and yellow. The model agents developed for the food collector environment had three continuous actions to explore and collect items in the environment. For every target that the agent collect, +1 points were rewarded and for every distractor collected by the agent, −1 points were rewarded. We used different model configurations (by varying the number of hidden layers and number of nodes of the neural network) and different environment configurations (by varying the number of targets and distractors) to analyze the performance of model agents using different reinforcement learning algorithms, i.e., PPO and SAC.

Fig. 3. An image of the food collector environment in Unity3D

The model agents were trained and tested in different environmental conditions and varying model configurations to evaluate the performance. In the training as well as test conditions, we used four different model configurations. First model with one hidden layer and 32 nodes in the neural network, second model with one hidden layer and 512 nodes in the neural network, third model with three hidden layers and 32 nodes, and fourth model with three hidden layers and 512 nodes in the neural network. However, the number of targets and distractors varied in the train and test environments. The maximum steps that an agent can take in the training environment were fixed to 1,000,000 steps. However, no such constraint was implemented in the testing environment. The model agents were free to take as many steps as possible until all the targets were collected. The training environment consisted of 25 target and 25 distractor items, and the items (targets and distractors) were respawned at another position within the environment, once collected by the agent.

In contrast, in the test environment, we varied the proportions of targets and distractors. The items collected in the test environment did not respawn once collected by the model agent. While training the model agents, the behaviour parameters of all the model agents were kept the same. The behaviour parameters are a set of agent's properties that help the agent decide for every game instance. These properties include input and output values of decision processes, type of agent behaviour (default, heuristic, or inference), and neural network model to be used. The properties associated with each algorithm were set to their default parameter values.

4 Performance Metric

The models were trained for 1 million steps using PPO and SAC algorithms. We plotted the graphs of target versus episodes and calculated the slopes of collected targets versus episodes (i.e., target slope). Similarly, we plotted the graphs of distractors versus episodes and calculated the slopes of collected distractors versus episodes (i.e., distractor slope) in the test conditions. The performance measure for each model was evaluated as

$$Performance = normsinv\ (target\ slope) - normsinv\ (distractor\ slope) \qquad (1)$$

where *normsinv()* function returns the inverse of the standard normal cumulative distribution. The positive value of the performance parameter indicates that the agent collected more targets compared to distractors. When comparing the *performance* of different models, a higher value of *performance* parameter would suggest a better model. We calculate the *performance* value for all models in the training and test conditions.

For the calculation of the *targetslope*, we initially calculated the number of targets left, the number of distractors collected, and the number of distractors left corresponding to each episode. We tested it as long as the targets left in the environment were greater than zero. We then plotted the number of targets collected (y) versus the number of episodes it took to collect those targets (x). We took the last (x, y) coordinate in the graph (i.e. point representing the number of episodes it took to collect all the targets) and the graph's origin to calculate the slope between these two points. This was called the *targetslope*.

We also plotted the graph of the number of distractors collected (y') versus the number of episodes it took to collect those distractors (x'). We took the last (x',y') coordinate in the graph (i.e. point which represents the number of episodes where all targets are collected and some y' distractors are left) and the graph's origin to calculate the slope between these two points. This is called the *distractorslope*. A calculation of these slopes is shown in Fig. 4.

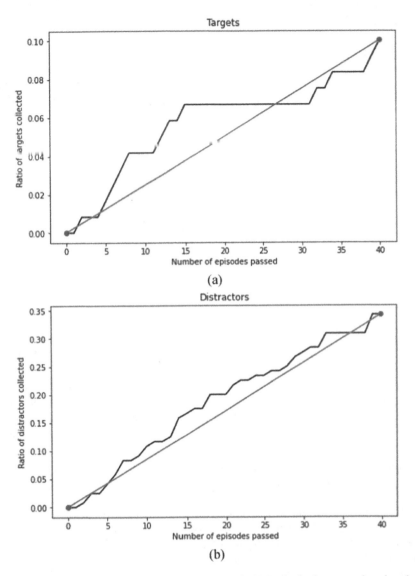

Fig. 4. The calculation of slope for (a) targets and (b) In both these graphs, the slope is represented as the red line. These graphs represent the scenario where the number of targets are 12 and number of distractors are 48. The model has been trained on PPO. Here, target slope = 0.0024 (a) and distractor slope = 0.081 (b). Thus, performance measure = normsinv (0.0024) - normsinv(0.081) = −0.42 (Color figure online)

5   Results

5.1   Training Results

The performance of models in the training condition was evaluated by plotting the graph between the collected cumulative reward and the number of steps taken by the model. Figure 5(a) shows the training performance of all four models in the food collector environment using the PPO algorithm. Similarly, Fig. 5(b) shows the training performance of all four models in the food collector environment using the SAC algorithm. The fourth model, i.e., model with three hidden layers and 512 nodes in the neural network, shows the best performance when the PPO algorithm is used. However, Fig. 5(c) shows the best performance by the fourth model for the initial part of the training when the SAC algorithm is used. The cumulative reward for all the model configurations steeply declined by the end. The SAC algorithm helped models with three hidden layers to reach high cumulative dividends in a smaller number of steps; however, the cumulative reward fell with the increase in the number of steps, and models performed poorly compared to models using the PPO algorithm.

5.2   Test Results

We evaluated model performance for both algorithms in test conditions using Eq. 1. To investigate the influence of neural network parameters, i.e., number of hidden layers and number of nodes, on the model's performance, we trained and tested the models on different sets of neural network parameters. Also, we evaluated the model performance by changing the number of targets and distractors in the test environment. Table 1 below summarizes models' performance with different configurations and environment variables, i.e., number of targets and distractors, using PPO and SAC algorithms.

5.3   Influence of Number of Hidden Layers of the Neural Network on Model Performance

From Table 1, we can observe that increasing the number of hidden layers while keeping the number of nodes constant increases the performance parameter value for both PPO and SAC algorithms. Additionally, on comparing the performance of models between two algorithms, SAC performs better than PPO in most of the model configurations except with one hidden layer and 32 nodes.

5.4   Influence of Number of Nodes of the Neural Network on Model Performance

It can be observed from Table 1 that increasing the size of nodes within a neural network helps improve the model's performance. This increase in the performance is visible for all the model configurations when PPO is used. However, when using SAC, there was an increase in the model's performance with an increase in nodes for models having one hidden layer only.

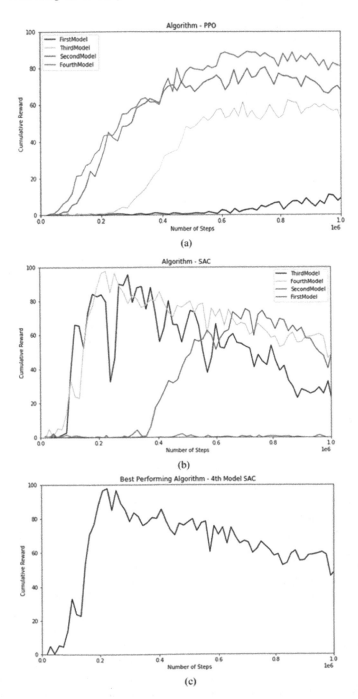

Fig. 5. Evaluating Model agent performance in an environment with 75 signals and 75 distractors using reinforcement learning algorithms, (a) PPO and (b) SAC. (c) The best-performing algorithm, the 4th model with SAC (with 3 layers and 512 nodes, as shown in Table 1).

Table 1. Performance of models with different configurations and environments variables us-ing PPO and SAC.

S. No.	Model configuration [layers, nodes]	Environment configuration [targets, distractors]	Performance (PPO)	Performance (SAC)
1.	[1, 32]	[12, 108]	-0.42	-11.99
2.	[3, 32]	[12, 108]	-0.26	0.20
3.	[1, 512]	[12, 108]	-0.48	-0.21
4	[3, 512]	[12, 108]	-0.44	-0.09
5.	[1, 32]	[18, 42]	-0.20	-11.99
6.	[3, 32]	[18, 42]	0.21	0.63
7.	[1, 512]	[18, 42]	0.43	0.11
8.	[3, 512]	[18, 42]	0.64	0.64
9.	[1, 32]	[108, 12]	0.73	-11.99
10.	[3, 32]	[108, 12]	0.89	1.37
11.	[1, 512]	[108, 12]	1.23	1.26
12.	[3, 512]	[108, 12]	1.49	1.33
13.	[1, 32]	[42, 18]	0.30	-11.99
14.	[3, 32]	[42, 18]	0.68	1.26
15.	[1, 512]	[42, 18]	0.53	0.74
16.	[3, 512]	[42, 18]	0.59	1.48

6 Discussion

Prior research in deep reinforcement learning has extensively used neural networks to develop state of the art reinforcement learning algorithms such as DQN that approximates the Q value function using deep neural networks. Recent policy optimization development using policy gradient focuses on developing reinforcement learning algorithms approximating policy using deep neural networks. Some of these algorithms are DDPG, PPO, and SAC. Research has reported SAC to perform better PPO [18]. However, little was known about these algorithms' performance in a simulated game environment with varied neural network parameters. The primary objective of this study was to investigate the influence of neural network parameters such as the number of hidden layers and number of nodes on model agents' performance using PPO and SAC algorithms. We trained and tested 16 different model agents using PPO and SAC algorithms in other environment conditions (by varying the number of targets and distractors), analyzed and compared their performance.

Our training results indicate that PPO performs better than SAC in collecting cumulative rewards in the long run, although an on-policy algorithm performs better. However, SAC tries to collect maximum cumulative rewards immediately as soon as the game starts. Also, the model with the highest number of hidden layers and nodes (hidden layers = 3 and nodes = 512) performs the best with the PPO algorithm in training conditions. This shows that PPO utilizes the complexity of the neural network models to train the model better. However, in the case of SAC, the performance peaked in the initial phase but declined drastically later. Therefore, PPO performs better than SAC with more hidden layers and nodes when significant step count.

In the test conditions, we observed better performance by models with more hidden layers while keeping the nodes constant for PPO and SAC. However, increasing the number of nodes while keeping the hidden layers constant proved beneficial for PPO in all the model configurations. However, the same cannot be said for SAC. Therefore, increasing the number of hidden layers help PPO and SAC to improve their performance. Whereas increasing the number of nodes helps PPO boost the performance, the performance of SAC remains the same.

7 Future Scope

Numerous ideas can be taken forward from this research to investigate, improve and analyze the performance of different deep reinforcement learning algorithms. First, researchers can develop an environment with various complexities enemies and competitors to evaluate the performance of model agents using PPO and SAC under competitive scenarios. Next, cognitive models such as the instance-based learning (IBL) model [21] can be developed to mimic human-like exploration and exploitation techniques in the food collector environment. Additionally, multiplayer simulations can be designed to investigate how model agents using PPO or SAC can help improve human performance in such target-distractor tasks. Further, we would extend our approach and do a comprehensive comparison on other reinforcement algorithms like Deep Q-Network (DQN) [22] and SARSA [23]. We plan to advance our research with these ideas in mind.

8 Conclusion

In this study, we observed the effect of network architecture on reinforcement learning algorithms and found that PPO can perform better than SAC in some conditions. This finding is contrary to the existing literature's observation, which suggests that SAC performs better than PPO. This finding demonstrates that researchers should report the hyperparameters while comparing these algorithms as it can give fair insights into the baseline results. We also give new insight into measuring the model's performance in various testing scenarios. We believe this can serve as a benchmark for testing in deep reinforcement learning agents.

Acknowledgements. A grant supported this research from Center for Artificial Intelligence and Robotics, Defence Research and Development Organization titled "Replicating human cognitive behavior on robots' models using ACT-R cognitive architecture for search-and-retrieve missions in virtual environments" (Project number: IITM/DRDO/VD/324) to Prof. Varun Dutt.

References

1. Bellemare, M., Naddaf, Y., Veness, J., Bowling, M.: The arcade learning environment: an evaluation platform for general agents. IJCAI Int. Joint Conf. Artif. Intell. **2015**, 4148–4152 (2015)
2. Zahavy, T., Haroush, M., Merlis, N., Mankowitz, D., Manor, S.: Learn what not to learn: action elimination with deep reinforcement learning. In: Advances in Neural Information Processing Systems, pp. 3562–3573 (2018). http://arxiv.org/abs/1809.02121. Accessed 11 Oct 2021
3. Zhang, A., Satija, H., Pinaeu, J.: Decoupling Dynamics and Reward for Transfer Learning (2018). http://arxiv.org/abs/1804.10689. Accessed 11 Oct 2021
4. Kristensen, J., Burelli, P.: Strategies for using proximal policy optimization in mobile puzzle games. In: International Conference on the Foundations of Digital Games (FDG 2020) (2020)
5. Kempka, M., Wydmuch, M., Runc, G., Tonzek, J., Jaskowski, W.: ViZDoom: a doom-based AI research platform for visual reinforcement learning. In: 2016 IEEE Conference on Computational Intelligence and Games (CIG), pp. 1–8 (2016)
6. Gao, Y., Tebbe, J., Zell, A.: Optimal Stroke Learning with Policy Gradient Approach for Robotic Table Tennis (2016). arXiv:2109.03100
7. Peng, P., et al.: Multiagent Bidirectionally-Coordinated Nets: Emergence of Human-level Coordination in Learning to Play StarCraft Combat Games (2017). arXiv preprint arXiv: 1703.10069
8. Dwibedi, D., Vemula, A.: Playing Games with Deep Reinforcement Learning (2020)
9. Kurzer, K., Schorner, P., Albers, A., Thomsen, H., Daaboul, K., Zollner, M.: Generalizing decision making for automated driving with an invariant environment representation using deep reinforcement learning. In: IEEE Intelligent Vehicles Symposium (2021)
10. Schrittwieser, J., et al.: Mastering Atari, Go, Chess and Shogi by Planning with a Learned Model (2019). arXiv:arXiv:1911.08265
11. Kamaldinov, I., Makarov, I.: Deep reinforcement learning in match-3 game. In: 2019 IEEE Conference on Games (CoG), pp. 1–4 (2019)
12. Teng, E.: https://blogs.unity3d.com/2019/11/11/training-your-agents-7-times-faster-with-ml-agents/
13. Haarnoja, T., Zhou, A., Abbeel, P., Levine, S.: Soft actor-critic: off-policy maximum entropy deep reinforcement learning with a stochastic actor. In:35th International Conference on Machine Learning, ICML 2018, pp. 2976–2989 (2018)
14. Rao, A.K., Chahal, J.S., Chandra, S., Dutt, V.: Virtual-reality training under varying degrees of task difficulty in a complex search-and-shoot scenario. In: Tiwary, U.S., Chaudhury, S. (eds.) Intelligent Human Computer Interaction: 11th International Conference, IHCI 2019, Allahabad, India, December 12–14, 2019, Proceedings, pp. 248–258. Springer International Publishing, Cham (2020). https://doi.org/10.1007/978-3-030-44689-5_22
15. Rao, A.K., Satyarthi, C., Dhankar, U., Chandra, S., Dutt, V.: Indirect visual displays: influence of field-of-views and target-distractor base-rates on decision-making in a search-and-shoot task. In: 2018 IEEE International Conference on Systems, Man and Cybernetics, pp. 4326–4332 (2018)
16. Schulman, J., Wolski, F., Dhariwal, P., Radford, A., Klimov, O.: Proximal policy optimization algorithms (2017). arXiv preprint arXiv:1707.06347
17. Wang, Y., He, H., Tan, X.: Truly proximal policy optimization. In: Uncertainty in Artificial Intelligence, pp. 113–122 (2020)

18. Haarnoja, T., et al.: Soft actor-critic algorithms and applications (2018). arXiv preprint arXiv:1812.05905
19. Pierre, V.: (2021). https://github.com/Unity-Technologies/ml-agents/blob/main/docs/Learning-Environment-Examples.md
20. Juliani, A., et al.: Unity: a general platform for intelligent agents (2018). arXiv preprint arXiv:1809.02627
21. Lejarraga, T., Dutt, V., Gonzalez, C.: Instance-based learning: a general model of repeated binary choice. J. Behav. Decis. Making. 25, 143–153 (2012)
22. Mnih, V., et al.: Playing Atari with deep reinforcement learning (2013). arXiv preprint arXiv:1312.5602
23. Zhao, D., Wang, H., Shao, K., Zhu, Y.: Deep reinforcement learning with experience replay based on SARSA. In: 2016 IEEE Symposium Series on Computational Intelligence (SSCI), pp. 1–6 (2016). https://doi.org/10.1109/SSCI.2016.7849837

Post-hoc Explainable Reinforcement Learning Using Probabilistic Graphical Models

Saurabh Deshpande[1], Rahee Walambe[1(✉)], Ketan Kotecha[1], and Marina Marjanović Jakovljević[2]

[1] Symbiosis Centre for Applied Artificial Intelligence, Symbiosis Institute of Technology, Symbiosis International University, Pune 412 115, India
{saurabh.deshpande.phd2019,rahee.walambe,director}@sitpune.edu.in
[2] Faculty of Technical Sciences, Singidunum University, Belgrade, Serbia
mmarjanovic@singidunum.ac.rs

Abstract. Reinforcement learning (RL) has recently enjoyed significant success in games, robotics, bioinformatics, etc. Soon, it will not be uncommon to see AI models employing RL agents integrated with various hardware and software solutions. Due to its generality and robustness, RL is applied in several disciplines such as game theory, control theory, multi-agent systems, swarm intelligence, robotics, and NLP. Despite these advances and successes, reinforcement learning faces many challenges for real-world adoption. Some of the major difficulties being, operator's trust and ability of an agent to explain the actions taken in a human-understandable manner. Traditionally the AI systems are blackbox models. With the advent of various legal regulations worldwide, notably the European General Data Protection Regulation (GDPR) [29], it has started becoming mandatory that the AI models be transparent, interpretable, and secure. If an RL agent can effectively and accurately explain the actions carried out by the RL system to the observers/operators, it will be a tangible step towards developing the ART (accountable, reliable and trustworthy) RL agent. This can effectively facilitate the adoption of RL systems in real-world domains. Various explainable AI (XAI) methods have been reported in the literature. However, there is a considerable lacuna in the availability of Explainable RL (XRL) methods. This paper introduces a novel RL algorithm agnostic approach of generating human-understandable explanations using the probabilistic graphical model. This method is based on Probabilistic Graphical Models (PGM) [36]. It is algorithm agnostic in that it is not dependent on any specific RL method and can be integrated with any RL algorithm. We also introduce a PGM model, which is learned along with an agent's training via classic methods and used for generating explanations at run time. Specific case studies are considered, and results are presented which demonstrate our approach. Our experiments show that the PGM-based approach is highly intuitive and a definitive step towards generating the human understandable explanations. It is a promising approach for discrete as well as continuous real-world systems employing RL.

© Springer Nature Switzerland AG 2022
D. Garg et al. (Eds.): IACC 2021, CCIS 1528, pp. 362–376, 2022.
https://doi.org/10.1007/978-3-030-95502-1_28

Keywords: Explainability · Artificial intelligence (AI) ·
Interpretability · Explainable AI (XAI) · Reinforcement learning
(RL) · Probabilistic graphical models (PGM)

1   Introduction

In recent years, Artificial intelligence (AI) and machine learning (ML), have
enjoyed exceptional success in several application areas from autonomous driving to healthcare, etc. Specifically, deep learning (DL) approaches [21], trained on
a huge amount of data, have outperformed even humans in many tasks. Another
branch of AI, namely Reinforcement Learning, has gained unprecedented success
and exceeded human performance in a focused domain, particularly in robotics
systems. The central problem of all these AI models is that they are considered as black-box models, more so in the case of deep learning and RL models.
Although it is possible to understand the supporting mathematical premise,
these models lack an explicit declarative knowledge representation. It is essentially a challenging task to generate the underlying explanatory structures. This
requires systems and models that enable the algorithms to explain the decisions
that humans understand. It is also important to note that deploying the explainable models is no longer a feature but a necessity with rising legal and privacy
laws worldwide. The new European General Data Protection Regulation [29],
which came into effect in May 2018, has made it difficult to use such black-box
approaches in business. This does not imply that automatic learning methods are
banned or that every output must be explained. However, it does stipulate that
the models should be such that their outcomes must be re-traceable on demand
[13,39]. In low-risk environments, it is sufficient to know the 'what' of the problem, but in others such as healthcare (e.g., disease diagnosis) and autonomous
vehicles, knowing the 'why' is essential to understand more about the problem,
the training data and the reasons for a possible failure of the model. The explainability of results obtained through automatic decision support systems is of vital
importance in such cases.

2   Related Work

Substantial research has been carried out and reported in the field of explainable artificial intelligence (XAI), for machine learning and deep learning, from
various approaches such as philosophy, psychology, computer science and neu-
roscience [7–9,13,27,30,39] for various ML/RL techniques. Overview of existing
XAI research, concepts and taxonomies have been presented in [3]. The notion
of 'explanations' from a social sciences perspective and how humans perceive
explanations have been discussed in [25]. Various methods for explaining black-
box models have been surveyed in [1]. However, the development of explainable
models for RL is not reported widely. This section discusses the related work
reported in literature towards the explainability and interpretability of RL systems.

The work, related to explainable or interpretable RL can be broadly divided into following categories - visual methods [10, 11, 14, 23, 26, 28, 41], methods based on decision trees [5, 6, 15, 24, 31, 35, 37] and methods based on reward decomposition [16, 19].

Visual methods predominantly use saliency maps for generating visually interpretable images of the RL agent's policy. These saliency maps can then be interpreted to understand the agent's actions. Saliency maps using gaussian blur are used in [10] on parts of the images. Saliency maps are generated using a difference between value functions and the policy of the perturbed state. Saliency maps based on a difference between Q values of the current and perturbed state are generated in [14]. Saliency maps based on a difference between Q values of the current and perturbed state are computed in [11]. The proposed method also considers whether the change in Q values after the perturbation is only due to action 'a' or other actions by computing the difference between relative expected rewards before and after perturbation. The soft top-down attention mechanism is used in [28] to focus on relevant information related to the task of the agent and generate saliency maps resulting in improved interpretation. Important regions are automatically learned in [41] from the pixel-based image that are important from the decision-making perspective.

Decision tree-based methods use a decision tree as a function approximator. Then the inherent explainability of the decision tree helps to generate the policy explanations. The main difficulty of using decision trees as a function approximator is that they are not differentiable because of their rule-based/binary nature and thus cannot be directly used in stochastic gradient descent. Differentiable decision trees (DDT) introduced by [35] are used by [15] as function approximator. Policy data is recorded while training the RL agent with well-known RL algorithms such as SARSA [32] and REINFORCE [40] by [5]. Then this data is used to train the ensemble of trees to predict the states from actions. Decision tree-based methods are independent reinforcement learning methods and are not designed to be used to augment the existing reinforcement learning methods for explainability.

Reward decomposition methods split reward scalar into multiple reward types and try to interpret the action in terms of these different reward types. A new method to train RL agents in terms of decomposed reward is introduced and mathematically proved by [16]. The bellman update for Q learning is split into multiple equations for each reward type. Now for explainability, they define the reward difference method. Given a state and an action, difference in the vector for value functions related to multiple reward types is calculated. From that, we can infer if an agent is favoring a particular action because the value function associated with that reward type is maximum.

Formalizing the RL problem (or sometimes called optimal control problem) as probabilistic inference using the framework of probabilistic graphical models has been well studied in the literature. Detailed discussion and the derivations for the same can be found in [22]. A similar discussion about probabilistic graphical models and variational inference in deep RL can be found in [33].

Our approach varies from the methods mentioned above [22,33]. In traditional methods, the RL problem is treated and formalized as the probabilistic inference and solved for optimal policy. The traditional RL algorithms are modified to offer explainability. The novelty of our approach lies in that; our approach is completely algorithm-agnostic. The classic RL algorithm is integrated with the probabilistic graphical model for generating probabilistic explanations. Such an algorithm agnostic method is essential for generalization, comparison and better implementation of the RL into the production.

In summary, the contribution of this research is threefold; firstly, we introduce and formalize the novel approach for XRL using probabilistic graphical models (PGM); secondly, we demonstrate and validate the use of this PGM based approach for generating the human-understandable explanations for RL agent's actions and lastly, we introduce an approach to effectively generate data in the learning phase of RL agent for training the probabilistic graphical model.

The paper is organized as follows. The Sect. 3 discusses the methods employed in this paper. The Sect. 5 presents the experimental setup. The Sect. 6 presents the results and subsequent analysis. The Sect. 7 presents the limitations and future work. The Sect. 8 concludes the article.

3   Methods

3.1   Reinforcement Learning (RL)

RL (detailed introduction can be found in [34], surveyed in [17]) is sequential decision making under uncertainly. An RL agent interacts with its environment and learns to map the actions to the state for maximizing the long-term average rewards. There is no instructor or training data set, and the agent learns only by interacting with the environment. With every interaction (action taken) with the environment, the agent receives the new state of the environment and a numeric scalar reward signal. The agent must learn the optimal policy 'π' to maximize the total discounted reward received in the long run. The following diagram summarizes this behavior (Fig. 1),

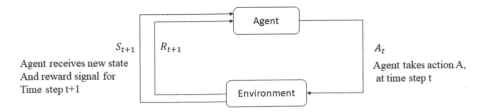

Fig. 1. Reinforcement Learning Agent's interaction with the Environment.

A Markov Decision Process (MDP) is generally used to formulate the RL problem. An MDP is a tuple (S, A, ρ, γ, R), where 'S' is set of possible states,

'A' is set of possible actions, 'ρ' is the transition probability matrix and 'R' is reward signal. $\rho(s, a, s')$ specifies the probability of transitioning to state s' from s if action a is taken. R(s,a) is a reward for taking action 'a' in state 's'. 'γ' is a discount factor indicating weightage of recent rewards vs. past rewards. The goal in the RL problem is to learn optimal policy 'π^*', which is a mapping between S $\rightarrow$ A, maximizing future expected reward.

The value $V_\pi(S)$ (Value function) of a policy π, for state S can be calculated as [34],

$$V_\pi(s) = E_\pi \left[\sum_{k=0}^{\infty} \gamma^k R_{t+k+1} \middle| s_t = s \right] \tag{1}$$

A value function for a policy represents the discounted expected rewards that can be achieved by an agent for each state if an agent follows policy π.

An optimal policy $V^*(S)$, attains the highest values of the value function for all states ($V_{\pi^*}(s) > V_\pi \ \forall \pi, s$). An optimal policy for an MDP can be calculated by applying the Bellman optimality equation (2) iteratively.

$$V_{\pi^*}(s) = \max_{a \in A} \left[R(s, a) + \gamma \sum_{s' \in S} \rho(s'|s, a) V^*(s') \right] \tag{2}$$

Theoretical analysis of convergence of such value function based learning has been done in [36].

3.2 Explainable Reinforcement Learning (XRL)

Explainability in the case of RL agent is more complex compared to a supervised or unsupervised machine learning problem. For supervised or unsupervised machine learning problem, explaination need to be generated for a the point in time result of a regression or classification model. But in the case of an RL agent, explainability methods have to explain the action taken by that agent and suggest a more strategic explanation considering an overall policy. The approach based on PGM proposed in this work generates probabilistic explanations at the policy level.

We need better explanations for RL agents for the following reasons:

1. To increase the trust in RL agents, which in turn will increase its adoption in real-world use cases.
2. To increase the adoption of RL to newer domains beyond robotics.
3. For compliance regulations such as GDPR [38].
4. For debugging the behavior of an RL agent in case of disaster or failure (This can be critical in scenarios like an accident of a self-driving car).

3.3 Probabilistic Graphical Model (PGM)

A probabilistic graphical model is a framework for graphically modeling random variables and exploiting the structure in the complex network of random variables to calculate conditional probability distributions. Then using these conditional probability distributions, posterior probabilities can be calculated based on the conditional evidence. The detailed discussion of the probabilistic graphical model framework can be found in [20].

The primary idea is to gather policy metadata during the training phase of an RL agent and fit a PGM model with that data. Once we have fitted the PGM model, we can make inferences and predict the agent behavior at runtime. We have tried our approach on two OpenAI Gym [4] environments, FrozenLake-V0 (stochastic, discrete state discrete action space) and Taxi-V2 (deterministic, discrete state discrete action space).

For generating meaningful explanations, we introduce the following PGM (Fig. 2),

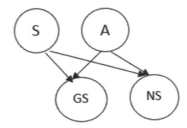

Fig. 2. Probabilistic Graphical Model for generating meaningful explanations

Where,

S: State random variable

A: Action random variable

GS: Goal state, which is 'final state' for which we want to reason about. For example, in episodic tasks, it can be final episode state (for example, success or failure) or any intermediate state to help to understand the action 'a' taken in state 's'. For example, for Taxi-V2 environment 'Successful Passenger Drop' is final episode state, but 'Hitting a wall' can be intermediate goal state which when captured in the given PGM, helps to explain why a certain action was not taken in a given state (high probability of 'Hitting a wall')

NS: Next state. This can help in certain deterministic environments to predict the 'Most probable path' taken by an agent.

The real-world applications have infinite state-action combinations and multiple policies. Our approach is RL algorithm-agnostic and generic, it is extendable to more complex, continuous systems. However, for demonstration, we have considered simpler cases to effectively validate our approach. We have considered two environments namely, FrozenLake-V0 and Taxi-V2 (OpenAI Gym).

4   Explainability and Reinforcement Learning

Dealing with the notion of explainability in reinforcement learning is tricky. As discussed in Subsect. 3.2 the goal for the XRL system is to explain why a particular action is taken in a specific state. We consider the following types of explanations relevant to reinforcement learning,

1. Explain why an action is taken in a state
2. Explain why an action is not taken in a state
3. Predict future actions based on explanations from prior decisions

Reinforcement learning has been applied in a variety of settings ranging from classic control tasks to strategic tasks. Not all kinds of explanations will make sense in every environment. For example, in continuous state environments (for example, Cartpol-v0 from OpenAI gym), generating explanation at each micro-level state is not very helpful in understanding an agent's overall behavior.

5   Experimental Setup

The SARSA [32] (detailed description can be found in [34]) is used to train agents for OpenAI Gym environments FrozenLake-V0 and Taxi-V2.

SARSA is on policy TD control algorithm. An action value function is learnt rather than state value function. It is on policy because we estimate $q_\pi(s, a)$ for current policy π and for all states 's' and actions 'a'. The following update rule is applied [34],

$$Q(S_t, A_t) \leftarrow Q(S_t, A_t) + \alpha \left[R_{t+1} + \gamma Q(S_{t+1}, A_{t+1}) - Q(S_t, A_t) \right] \qquad (3)$$

SARSA algorithm is modified to collect the trajectories data at the time of the training (the basic algorithm is taken as described in [34]). Once the training is finished, the PGM model is fitted with the data collected and conditional probabilities are calculated using Bayesian Estimator [20]. The Bayesian estimator is similar to maximum likelihood estimator' only difference being, it uses a prior distribution for the calculation of the joint probability distributions. We have used Bayesian Dirichlet equivalent uniform (BDeu) [12] as a prior type.

After training the agent and the graphical model, inferences are made at runtime by the variable elimination technique. At any point in time, a running agent is in a state s ∈ S, selects the action a ∈ A according to learned optimal policy Q(S, A). Now by inference from the PGM, we can calculate the probability distribution of GS,

$$P(GS|S = s, A = a)$$

Then the most probable explanation is *"Action 'a' is taken by an agent in state 's' because it sees the maximum probability of happening"*,

$$g \in GS \leftarrow \text{argmax}(P(GS|s, a))$$

The inference for *'Why not'* type of queries can be made as follows,

$$P(GS|S = s, A = a')$$

Where a' is an action other than the optimal policy action in that state and *'Why not'* explanation is *"Action 'a' is not taken by an agent in state 's' because it sees the maximum probability of happening"*,

$$g \in GS \leftarrow \text{argmax}(P(GS|S = s, A = a')).$$

6   Results and Discussions

OpenAI gym [4] is a library for developing and comparing RL algorithms. An agent's environment is a major variable factor in RL research. The OpenAI gym library standardizes the RL environments using which RL algorithms can be benchmarked and results can be compared. It provides a standard interface for defining an agent's interaction with the environment and the reward function. Custom environments can also be developed using this library.

The OpenAI Gym python library [4] is used for gym environments and pgmpy python library [2] for probabilistic graphical model learning and inference. As of now, pgmpy does not support learning and inference for hybrid Bayesian networks (the mixture of continuous and discrete random variables). In such cases, Bayesian Net Toolbox [29] is another good alternative to explore.

6.1   Environment I : Taxi-V2

In this grid-based task, the agent needs to pick up a passenger at one location and drop off in another. The agent gets +20 reward for successful drop-off, −1 for each time step and −10 for illegal pick and drop off. Possible actions - 0: Go South, 1: Go North, 2: Go East, 3: Go West, 4: Pick up passenger, 5: Drop passenger (Fig. 5).

Generating Explanations For Taxi-V2 environment from OpenAI Gym, the following goal states are defined,
    'Wrong Pickup',
    'Successful Pickup',
    'Wrong Drop',
    'Successful Drop',
    'Hitting Wall'
Sample results,

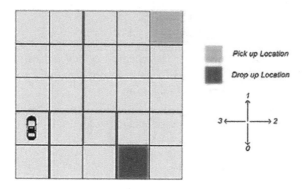

Fig. 3. Initial position and legends (0,1,2,3 are actions)

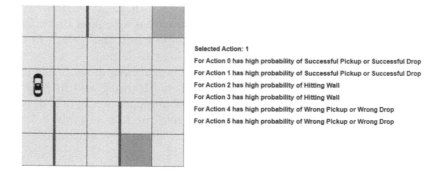

Fig. 4. State after action 1 is taken and the explanations for the action taken

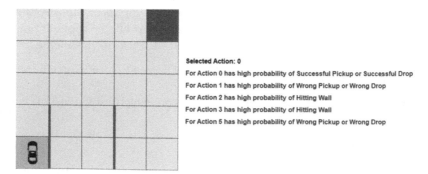

Fig. 5. Another sample (different episode) after selected action is taken and corresponding explanations

(All figures show the state after the selected action has been taken.)

As it can be seen in Fig. 3, the agent starts in the given state. It takes action 1, receives a new state (moves north). At this point, using the trained PGM model, as described in Sect. 5, we generate probability distributions for 'GS' for all possible actions in a given state So, for a given state, we can infer for each possible action what goal state is most probable. In other words, what agent perceives as the most probable goal state for each action in a given state.

Predicting Most Probable Path Taken by the Agent. It is also possible to predict the most probable path that will be taken by an agent in a given state. Such path can be generated by recursively applying the inference procedure.

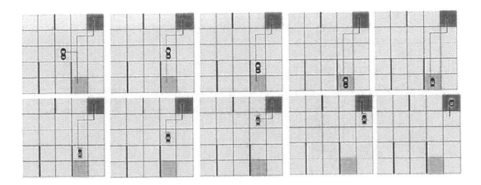

Fig. 6. Most probable path predicted and actual

As seen in Fig. 6, an agent is in state 's', and using the trained PGM model the most probable path is generated from that state. Then the agent takes action 'a' in state 's' and moves to the next state. Again, the same procedure is repeated and the actual path and predicted paths are tracked.

6.2   Environment II: FrozenLake-V0

In this grid-based task, there is a fixed start state and destination state. An agent needs to navigate successfully (without falling in a hole) from the start state to the destination state. The environment is stochastic. Meaning thereby, if an agent takes an action to move to the right square, there is around 33% probability that the agent will land up in the square other than the expected square.

Possible actions - 0: Go West, 1: Go South, 2: Go East, 3: Go North. The agent gets reward '1' if it reaches destination state, otherwise for each time step reward is '0'. The episode ends either if the agent reaches goal state or falls in the hole (marked red) (Figs. 7, 8 and 9).

Generating Explanations. The following goal states are defined for this environment,
'Successfully reached destination state'
'Fails to reach the destination state'

1
2
3
4
5
6
7
8
9
10
11
12
13
14
Start
Destination
3
0
2
1

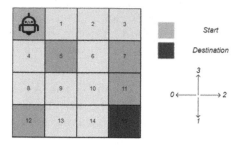

Fig. 7. Initial position and legends (0, 1, 2, 3 are actions)

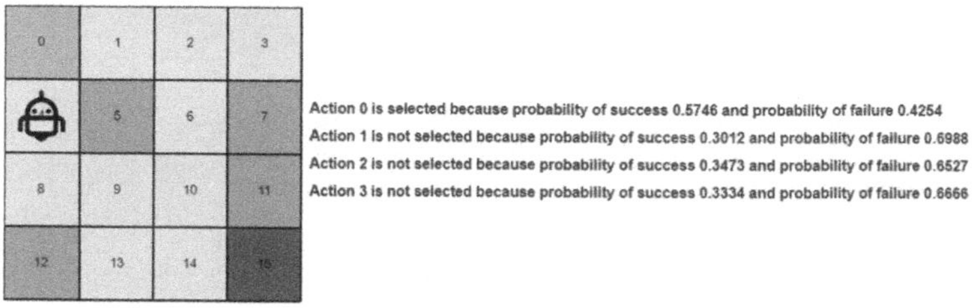

Action 0 is selected because probability of success 0.5746 and probability of failure 0.4254
Action 1 is not selected because probability of success 0.3012 and probability of failure 0.6988
Action 2 is not selected because probability of success 0.3473 and probability of failure 0.6527
Action 3 is not selected because probability of success 0.3334 and probability of failure 0.6666

Fig. 8. Sample results

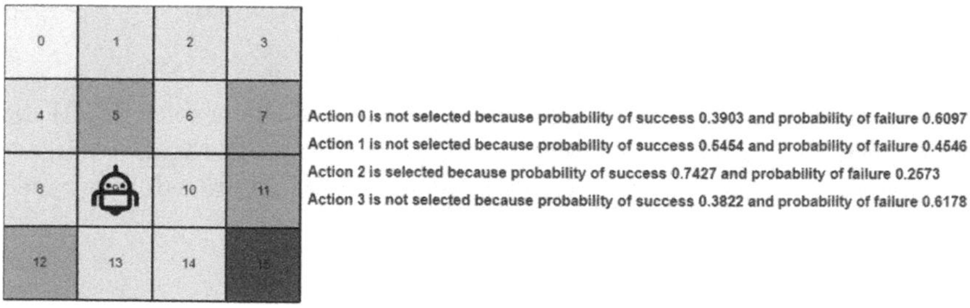

Action 0 is not selected because probability of success 0.3903 and probability of failure 0.6097
Action 1 is not selected because probability of success 0.5454 and probability of failure 0.4546
Action 2 is selected because probability of success 0.7427 and probability of failure 0.2573
Action 3 is not selected because probability of success 0.3822 and probability of failure 0.6178

Fig. 9. Sample results

Sample results,

(All figures show the state after the selected action has been taken).

Explanations are generated as described in the Taxi-V2 environment. 'Failure' or 'Fails to reach goal state' in this case means falling in one of the holes.

6.3 Discussion

Let's see how the results can be interpreted. All the results shown are generated using a trained PGM model at run time. Please refer to the Environment I: Taxi-V2 results. The probability distribution over the goal state is generated using the PGM for the given state and action. Then the explanations are generated as follows. The Fig. 3 is the initial position. The Fig. 4 is the position when the agent has taken action 1 (go up) in state Fig. 3 as per the optimal policy. For this action, both *'why'* and *'why not'* explanations are generated. In the state Fig. 3, the action '1' has the highest probability of success in the longer run. In other words, the agent chooses the action '1' in the state Fig. 3 as there is the highest probability of success in the longer run. The action '3' is not chosen as there is a high probability of 'hitting the wall'.

Currently, there are no clear metrics and established methods for benchmarking XAI for the reinforcement learning. So no such attempt has been made in this work towards it.

7   Limitations and Future Work

Generating human-understandable explanations for an RL agent's policy is a challenging problem. Several approaches to this problem are reported; however, they are either restricted to a specific type of input (such as pixel-based inputs for visual domains) or not algorithm agnostic. They fall short while generalization of the explainable method. In this work, we have presented and demonstrated a novel method for XRL, which is RL algorithm agnostic. The PGM is a promising framework for generating policy-level probabilistic explanations. This framework is flexible and can be extended for several use cases in various domains. It has the potential to generate explanations for *'why'* and *'why not'* questions about the agent's actions.

We also believe that this framework can be extended for a multi-agent systems. The PGM model can be extended to include goal states for the communications between agents to generate probabilistic explanations for multi-agent settings. The current work mainly focuses on discrete state environments.

Another issue with which reinforcement learning systems usually struggle is the scenario of the rare event. Such a situation can be handled effectively, as shown in the [18] by using data augmentation using generative adversarial networks (GAN). As our framework augments existing RL methods, such an approach will work, and the augmentation data generated by GANs can be used in PGM training. It will certainly help in generating explanations for rare events.

8   Conclusion

The development and deployment of explainable AI models is the need of the hour. With the highly state-of-the-art technology such as driverless cars, robot assistive surgery, etc., which is currently under development, it is essential to investigate the accountable, reliable and trustworthy RL model development. Understandably some of these aspects are futuristic and full proof technology is not yet in common use and production. However, this work is a concrete and promising step in the direction to develop the explainable methods for RL models and will prove impactful in the future to come- when the robot assistive surgery and completely autonomous cars will be a reality.

The primary contribution of this work lies in formalizing and demonstrating the PGM based explainable RL model and its use for specific discrete state environments namely, FrozenLake-V0 and Taxi-V2. Additionally, an approach to effectively generate data in the learning phase of an RL agent for training the probabilistic graphical model is also discussed in detail. Considering the utility of our approach it will prove extremely useful in creating robust XRL models. We have demonstrated and validated the model on the simple single-agent discrete systems. However, it will be further extended to the continuous state and continuous action problems for multi-agent systems.

Conflict of Interest. No conflict of interest is declared by the authors.

References

1. Adadi, A., Berrada, M.: Peeking inside the black-box: a survey on explainable artificial intelligence (XAI). IEEE Access **6**, 52138–52160 (2018)
2. Ankan, A., Panda, A.: pgmpy: probabilistic graphical models using python. In: Proceedings of the 14th Python in Science Conference (SCIPY 2015). Citeseer (2015)
3. Arrieta, A.B., et al.: Explainable artificial intelligence (XAI): concepts, taxonomies, opportunities and challenges toward responsible AI. Inf. Fusion **58**, 82–115 (2020)
4. Brockman, G., et al.: OpenAI gym (2016)
5. Brown, A., Petrik, M.: Interpretable reinforcement learning with ensemble methods. ArXiv abs/1809.06995 (2018)
6. Coppens, Y., et al.: Distilling deep reinforcement learning policies in soft decision trees. In: IJCAI 2019 (2019)
7. Crawford, K.: Artificial intelligence's white guy problem. The New York Times, 25 June 2016
8. Doshi-Velez, F., Kim, B.: Towards a rigorous science of interpretable machine learning. arXiv preprint arXiv:1702.08608 (2017)
9. Ferris, P.: An introduction to explainable AI, and why we need it (2018). https://www.freecodecamp.org/news/an-introduction-to-explainable-ai-and-why-we-need-it-a326417dd000/
10. Greydanus, S., Koul, A., Dodge, J., Fern, A.: Visualizing and understanding Atari agents. ArXiv abs/1711.00138 (2017)
11. Gupta, P., et al.: Explain your move: understanding agent actions using focused feature saliency. arXiv preprint arXiv:1912.12191 (2019)
12. Heckerman, D., Geiger, D., Chickering, D.M.: Learning Bayesian networks: the combination of knowledge and statistical data. Mach. Learn. **20**(3), 197–243 (1995)
13. Holzinger, A., Biemann, C., Pattichis, C.S., Kell, D.B.: What do we need to build explainable AI systems for the medical domain? arXiv preprint arXiv:1712.09923 (2017)
14. Iyer, R., Li, Y., Li, H., Lewis, M., Sundar, R., Sycara, K.: Transparency and explanation in deep reinforcement learning neural networks. In: Proceedings of the 2018 AAAI/ACM Conference on AI, Ethics, and Society, pp. 144–150 (2018)
15. Jimenez Rodriguez, I.D., Killian, T., Son, S.H., Gombolay, M.: Interpretable reinforcement learning via differentiable decision trees. arXiv preprint arXiv:1903.09338 (2019)

16. Juozapaitis, Z., Koul, A., Fern, A., Erwig, M., Doshi-Velez, F.: Explainable reinforcement learning via reward decomposition. In: Proceedings of the IJCAI 2019 Workshop on Explainable Artificial Intelligence, pp. 47–53 (2019)
17. Kaelbling, L.P., Littman, M.L., Moore, A.W.: Reinforcement learning: a survey. J. Artif. Intell. Res. **4**, 237–285 (1996)
18. Kasgari, A.T.Z., Saad, W., Mozaffari, M., Poor, H.V.: Experienced deep reinforcement learning with generative adversarial networks (GANs) for model-free ultra reliable low latency communication. arXiv preprint arXiv:1911.03264 (2019)
19. Khan, O.Z., Poupart, P., Black, J.P.: Minimal sufficient explanations for factored Markov decision processes. In: Nineteenth International Conference on Automated Planning and Scheduling (2009)
20. Koller, D., Friedman, N.: Probabilistic Graphical Models: Principles and Techniques. MIT press, Cambridge (2009)
21. LeCun, Y., Bengio, Y., Hinton, G.: Deep learning. Nature **521**(7553), 436–444 (2015)
22. Levine, S.: Reinforcement learning and control as probabilistic inference: tutorial and Review. arXiv preprint arXiv:1805.00909 (2018)
23. Li, Y., Sycara, K., Iyer, R.: Object-sensitive deep reinforcement learning. arXiv preprint arXiv:1809.06064 (2018)
24. Liu, G., Schulte, O., Zhu, W., Li, Q.: Toward interpretable deep reinforcement learning with linear model U-trees. In: Berlingerio, M., Bonchi, F., Gärtner, T., Hurley, N., Ifrim, G. (eds.) ECML PKDD 2018. LNCS (LNAI), vol. 11052, pp. 414–429. Springer, Cham (2019). https://doi.org/10.1007/978-3-030-10928-8_25
25. Miller, T.: Explanation in artificial intelligence: insights from the social sciences. Artif. Intell. **267**, 1–38 (2019)
26. Mishra, I., Dao, G., Lee, M.: Visual sparse Bayesian reinforcement learning: a framework for interpreting what an agent has learned. In: 2018 IEEE Symposium Series on Computational Intelligence (SSCI), pp. 1427–1434 (2018)
27. Mohanty, S., Vyas, S.: Inside the black box: understanding AI decision making. In: How to Compete in the Age of Artificial Intelligence, pp. 91–124. Apress, Berkeley (2018). https://doi.org/10.1007/978-1-4842-3808-0_4
28. Mott, A., Zoran, D., Chrzanowski, M., Wierstra, D., Rezende, D.J.: Towards interpretable reinforcement learning using attention augmented agents. In: Advances in Neural Information Processing Systems, pp. 12329–12338 (2019)
29. Murphy, K.: The Bayes net toolbox for Matlab. Comput. Sci. Stat. **33**(2), 1024–1034 (2001)
30. O'neil, C.: Weapons of Math Destruction: How Big Data Increases Inequality and Threatens Democracy. Broadway Books, New York (2016)
31. Roth, A.M., Topin, N., Jamshidi, P., Veloso, M.: Conservative Q-improvement: reinforcement learning for an interpretable decision-tree policy. arXiv preprint arXiv:1907.01180 (2019)
32. Rummery, G.A., Niranjan, M.: On-Line Q-Learning Using Connectionist Systems, vol. 37. University of Cambridge, Department of Engineering Cambridge, UK (1994)
33. Sun, X., Bischl, B.: Tutorial and survey on probabilistic graphical model and variational inference in deep reinforcement learning. arXiv preprint arXiv:1908.09381 (2019)
34. Sutton, R.S., Barto, A.G.: Reinforcement Learning: An Introduction. The MIT Press, Cambridge (2011)
35. Suárez, A., Lutsko, J.F.: Globally optimal fuzzy decision trees for classification and regression. IEEE Trans. Pattern Anal. Mach. Intell. **21**(12), 1297–1311 (1999)

36. Tutsoy, O., Brown, M.: An analysis of value function learning with piecewise linear control. J. Exp. Theor. Artif. Intell. **28**(3), 529–545 (2016)
37. Vasic, M., Petrovic, A., Wang, K., Nikolic, M., Singh, R., Khurshid, S.: MoËt: interpretable and verifiable reinforcement learning via mixture of expert trees. arXiv preprint arXiv:1906.06717 (2019)
38. Voigt, P., von dem Bussche, A.: The EU General Data Protection Regulation (GDPR). Springer, Cham (2017). https://doi.org/10.1007/978-3-319-57959-7
39. Weng, S.F., Reps, J., Kai, J., Garibaldi, J.M., Qureshi, N.: Can machine-learning improve cardiovascular risk prediction using routine clinical data? PloS One **12**(4) (2017)
40. Williams, R.J.: Simple statistical gradient-following algorithms for connectionist reinforcement learning. Mach. Learn. **8**(3–4), 229–256 (1992)
41. Yang, Z., Bai, S., Zhang, L., Torr, P.H.: Learn to interpret Atari agents. arXiv preprint arXiv:1812.11276 (2018)

Ghostbusters: How the Absence of Class Pairs in Multi-Class Multi-Label Datasets Impacts Classifier Accuracy

Sidharth Kathpal[1]([✉]) [iD], Siddha Ganju[2] [iD], and Anirudh Koul[3] [iD]

[1] Carnegie Mellon University, Pittsburgh, PA, USA
skathpal@andrew.cmu.edu
[2] NVIDIA Corporation, Santa Clara, USA
[3] Pinterest, San Francisco, USA

Abstract. Compositional bias is common in Multi-Class Multi-Label datasets where certain classes frequently co-occur together. Classification performance due to non-iid behavior of Multi-Class Multi-Label datasets is largely unexplored. We evaluate the potential impact of this compositional bias on Multi-Class Multi-Label classifiers, and, propose a novel framework of representing bias through "Degree of Separation", and demonstrate its effectiveness on two datasets. Consider an image with a cat and a person - our work effectively strives to answer questions along the lines of "Is the classification accuracy of cat impacted by the presence of the person in the image?" and more importantly, **"Is the classification accuracy of cat impacted by the absence of the person in the test image?"**. Interestingly our experiments show that class pairs that are present in a test image, but do not appear together elsewhere in the training dataset do impact the recognition accuracy and thus we refer to them as ghost class pairs. We make a surprising discovery: lower the degree of separation between classes (based on class pairs appearing within the same images), higher the classification accuracy. Based on this observation, we develop a greedy data augmentation strategy that recommends which missing pairs need to be added to the training dataset in order to improve F1 score with minimal data addition. This ultimately is able to improve classification accuracy by 25–30% in several scenarios.

Keywords: Multi-Class Multi-Label · Compositional bias · Non IID

1 Introduction

Compositional bias which is a common non independent and identically distributed (non-iid) property refers to which classes frequently co-occur in a particular image. Machine learning classifiers like Naive Bayes, Convolutional Neural Networks assume independent and identically distribution (iid), yet most real-world datasets exhibit non-iid properties, like class imbalance. Instead of all potential class pairs occurring equally (pure iid), most pairs don't occur, some pairs occur, and few pairs occur frequently (i.e. long tailed distribution of pairs). While in an ideal scenario we assume that the training and test distributions are identical, but in the real world (in-the-wild) test-time

© Springer Nature Switzerland AG 2022
D. Garg et al. (Eds.): IACC 2021, CCIS 1528, pp. 377–398, 2022.
https://doi.org/10.1007/978-3-030-95502-1_29

Fig. 1. We show that a model is able to intuit both the presence and absence of other co-occuring classes and its impact on accuracy - i.e. even though the model has only seen *person-cat*, and *person-dog* during training time, it may still encounter *cat-dog* together at test time and as such can we improve the F1 score of such absent ghost class pairs? We define the class pair *cat-dog* as the absent ghost class pair.

examples can't always be anticipated (Fig. 1). A common example is the MSCOCO dataset [25], within the validation split, there are 224 unique pairs that do not appear in the training set such as $bicycle + giraffe$, $car + toaster$, $motorcycle + toilet$, $airplane + wineglass$, $bus + knife$ and $cow + donut$. At the same time, there also are 948 unique pairs that are possible but do not appear in either the training or validation set like $bicycle + hairdrier$, $motorcycle + zebra$, $airplane + banana$, $bus + scissors$.

The potential impact of non-iid behavior of Multi-Class Multi-Label datasets on Multi-Class Multi-Label classifiers has not been explored in detail. Applying MCML classifiers to non-iid distributions may not be utilizing the classifier's full potential. We investigate the effect of co-occurrence of classes, both their presence and absence (ghost class pair) in a MCML dataset on the classification task. We apply multiple kinds of combination biasing techniques (while keeping individual class frequencies balanced) on a MCML version of the MNIST dataset, which we call MCML-MNIST, and study the impact of the introduced biases on Convolutional Neural Networks (CNN) classification performance. Our experiments on various biasing techniques show that there is a significant impact on the F1 score which in turn is dependent on the co-occurrence of classes, and degree of separation or connectedness between classes. We use the terms degree of separation and connectedness interchangeably throughout this paper. We build a retrospective algorithm that recommends minimal additional training examples (synthetically generated or manually collected) needed to increase the connectedess of classes in the dataset, and significantly improve the classification performance.

Our key contributions are two-fold: **(1)** Empirically show an impact of presence and absence of co-occurring classes through "Degree of separation" by introducing different kinds of biases **(2)** Develop a greedy augmentation strategy that recommends which missing pairs need to be added to the training dataset in order to improve F1 score with minimal data addition. Our augmentation strategy is automated, generalizable, and scalable on annotated datasets like MSCOCO and thus impacts production real-world classifiers where test-time examples can't anticipated. Our analysis can also be utilized as a reference to compare and contrast a practitioners dataset with our benchmarked scenarios and figure out how much the accuracy can be improved further. All code, models, and additional details will be made available post-publication.

2   Related Work

Data distributions of Multi-Class Single-Label settings and its varying impacts on classification accuracy has been well explored along directions of class imbalance [35], properties and contextual relationship of objects [34], and representing bias in various ways [21, 36] however a similar breadth and depth of research is not available for understanding bias for Multi-Class Multi-Label datasets. Additionally, for both Multi-Class Single-Label and Multi-Class Multi-Label datasets, there is limited research on how to solve or eradicate bias. Prior work related to fixing the impact of class imbalance looks at varying class frequencies, through techniques like undersampling of majority classes, oversampling of minority classes or a combination of both like SMOTE [2, 5, 6, 15, 16]. Limitations and improvements on SMOTE have been widely researched [2, 4, 5, 7, 10, 13–17, 20, 20, 26, 28, 29, 32, 33, 37]. Another oversampling technique, Localized Random Affine Shadowsampling [3] looks at the data manifold of the minority class. Our work is orthogonal to traditional class imbalance demonstrated through single class frequencies since we focus on the class pairs that co-occur together in images, while keeping the individual class frequencies equal.

Object properties and contextual relationship of objects in MCSL have been explored by research including [35], which explores the impact of context and semantics of objects within an image, where they construct a probabilistic framework establishing a relationship between object properties, like object location on canvas and context, while [34] provides comparative studies on relative data bias, cross-dataset generalization, effects of closed-world assumption, and sample value. Our research is generalizable and can represent similar contextual relationship such as relationship between different objects in MCML, and object and properties relationship in MCSL datasets. Ultimately we provide a greedy data augmentation strategy that improves F1 score with minimal data addition, and in developing such a framework our work can be considered similar to a discriminative framework providing improved generalization and reducing the effect of bias in a classification and detection tasks [21], and visual relations between pairs of objects represented as subject-predicate-object relations [27], although, we model the class pairs both which are present and absent through correlation matrices.

The Reveal Visual Biases tool [36] produces metrics to distinguish amongst dataset biases such as object based bias, gender bias, geography or location bias with statistical inputs like, object frequency and co-occurrence, scale, diversity of objects, placement on the canvas, context etc. whereas in our work we provide steps to mitigate bias in MCML and MCSL datasets. Machine learning classifiers assume that training and test data distributions are iid but this assumption in itself is fragile in the real world where minimizing error over the validation dataset does not guarantee performance in the wild [22]. With rising privacy concerns, applications of Federated learning [19, 38] for edge devices with the non iid setting are also prominent. In the medical domain, non iid learning in machine learning workflows has been considered previously [1, 8, 11]. Our experiments bear resemblance to [18] where multiple types of non iid behavior is introduced in the dataset through varying the degree of distribution of the background of objects (i.e. their context) in test and training datasets. We introduce non iid behavior through various compositional biasing techniques and study its impact on classification performance of a MCML classifier. Prior work like [9] removes class instances to boost classification performance. We also consider how our work effects data collection similar to [34]. The seminal ImageNet research [30] details how distinctive background classes can help identify objects in the foreground. Such background-foreground pairs often co-occur in the real world like the whale class with ocean in the background. Our work considers classes at separate locations within the image rather than the background and foreground pairs, such that visual patterns per category appear independently at different locations.

3 Experimental Setup

Our aim is to create a reproducible way to study the impact of the presence and absence of certain class pairs in the query image on classification performance. One way is to start with a base iid dataset and generate multiple datasets by modifying the base dataset by applying different compositional bias strategies - i.e. by adding or removing co-occurring classes from images. Since most real-world datasets possess non-iid characteristics, and moreover, our experiments require the ability to add or remove classes from images, we adopt the path of generating a synthetic dataset that gives us control on which classes to keep or remove.

Standard datasets like MNIST [24] with their handwritten digits contain intra-class variation, which inhibits CNNs to perform template matching, making the results more realistic and conclusive. The performance on the MNIST dataset is well known and this allows us to compare our performance with other work on the standardized dataset. To distinguish the impact of data from the model in the overall classification task, we try to create datasets that can be trained with the same standard model, MobileNetV2 [31]. This also enables future practitioners to build on this work to easily run the publicly accessible code and models on the limited amount of compute available. Thus, we synthesize two different datasets to compare our hypothesis - the MCML-MNIST dataset, and, MCML-ABCD dataset (Multi-Class Multi-Label Alphabets dataset).

MCML-MNIST: The MCML-MNIST base dataset is a multi-class multi-label greyscale image dataset of 96×96 resolution with each image containing a combination of any 3 digits selected from a total of 10 numerical digits from MNIST, i.e. images contains $\{012, 013, 014 \ldots 789\}$ combinations. Each character represents the corresponding class in the image. There are 120 unique combinations ($^{10}C_3$), with the individual classes randomly placed in a non-overlapping fashion on the image as shown in Appendix Fig. 6. Thus, the dataset has three features - (1) variance in location, (2) co-occurrence i.e., which classes occur together, and (3) intra-class variation which allows us to incorporate the entire 60,000 MNIST training images.

MCML-ABCD: The MCML-ABCD base dataset is a multiclass multilabel greyscale image dataset of 64×64 resolution with each image containing a combination of any 3 characters selected from a total of 26 capitalized English alphabets, i.e. images contains $\{ABC, ABD, ABE \ldots XYZ\}$ combinations. Each character represents the corresponding class in the image. There are 2600 unique combinations ($^{26}C_3$), with the individual characters randomly placed anywhere in a non-overlapping fashion on the image as shown in Appendix Fig. 6.

Thus, the dataset has two features - variance in location and co-occurrence i.e., which characters occur together. These allow us to introduce bias in the dataset in the following two ways:

(1) Ratio Bias: With the MCML-MNIST base dataset indexed as $\{0 : 012, 1 : 013, 2 : 014 \ldots . 119 : 789\}$ or $\{0 : ABC, 1 : ABD, 2 : ABE \ldots . 2599 : XYZ\}$ in case of the MCML-ABCD base dataset, this strategy picks every n^{th} combination with $n \in [2, 64]$ for the training datasets, leading to a uniform distribution of each individual character, and hence negligible individual class imbalance. With $n = 2$ pairs like $\{012, 014, \ldots . 789\}$ as shown in Appendix Fig. 7 will be picked, i.e. half of all the pairs are picked. As the dataset size is increased beyond $120/n$ items in case of the MNIST dataset, multiple images containing the same unique combination may be seen

(2) Parity Bias: Datasets like MSCOCO have specific combinations present or absent, like bicycle and giraffe do not appear together in the training dataset. To replicate this, we explicitly allow combinations based on the parity of the index. With the digits indexed as checked $\{0 : 0, 1 : 1, 2 : 2 \ldots . 9 : 9\}$ in the MCML-MNIST dataset and the alphabets indexed as $\{0 : A, 1 : B, 2 : C \ldots . 25 : Z\}$ in the MCML-ABCD dataset, this strategy generates a training dataset where either odd indexed classes or even indexed classes appear in each image but not both. In other words, odd indexed classes $\{1 : 1, 3 : 3 \ldots . 9 : 9\}/\{1 : B, 3 : D \ldots . 25 : Z\}$ occur exclusively with other odd indexed classes giving combinations like $\{135, 137 \ldots 579\}/\{BDF, BDH \ldots VXZ\}$ or, while even indexed digits $\{0 : 0, 2 : 2 \ldots 8 : 8\}/\{0 : A, 2 : C \ldots 24 : Y\}$ occur only with other even indexed digits resulting in combinations like $\{024, 026, 246, 248 \ldots 468\}/\{ACE, ACG, BDF, BDH \ldots VXZ\}$ as shown in Appendix Fig. 8. Because there are 5 even indices and 5 odd indices that co-occur with each other each character occurs the same amount of time i.e. in a uniform distribution. Similar to the strategy of generating ratio bias, in parity bias, even though the number of unique combinations (i.e. 20) is fixed, the dataset larger than 20 images can contain several images of the same combination with digits appearing at different locations. Whereas, in case of the ABCD dataset since we have 13 even indices and 13 odd indices that co-occur, we have 572 possible unique combinations.

Various training datasets are summarized in Appendix Table 5, with the class frequencies distributed equally. The test set for all our experiments is generated similar to the base dataset with all possible 120 ($^{10}C_3$) class combinations, one combination per image with each character placed randomly non-overlapping, except that the digits for the test dataset are extracted from the MNIST test images. By randomly varying the location of the extracted digit, and taking advantage of the intra-class variation amongst the handwritten MNIST test images, we generate 5000 images for our test dataset. Since each image contains 3 classes we incorporate all the 10,000 digits present in the MNIST test dataset. Hence, the test set also contains ghost class pairs which have been removed by ratio and parity bias from the training sets. The test set spans the entire space, which also means that differently biased models have seen different fractions of test set combinations, albeit not the exact digit or class instance in the test image. To ensure that the choice of test set is not a confounding factor, we report results averaged over five test/train splits. For the MCML-ABCD usecase we similarly create a unique test set, consisting of all the 2600 ($^{26}C_3$) combinations, one combination per image with each character placed randomly non-overlapping. Hence, the test set also contains ghost class pairs which have been removed by ratio and parity bias. To ensure variety in the dataset we consistently increase the number of images by first randomly choosing digit/character combinations, the digit/character image from MNIST or ABCD datasets and then location of the MNIST digit or ABCD characters to generate the MCML-MNIST/MCML-ABCD image, until we reach the desired number of images. We used the same MobileNetv2 model for all our experiments.

4   Experiments

We first take a look at the impact of unique combinations present or absent in the training dataset. We hypothesize that absence of certain combinations in the training dataset reduces the model's ability to recognize other classes in the query image. Effectively, we ask "If $bicycle + giraffe$ is not present in any image in the training dataset, does this impact the models ability to recognize either this pair or $bicycle + otherclass$ or $giraffe + anotherclass$ at test time?". To test this hypothesis, we employ different strategies (via ratio bias and parity bias) to introduce bias in the training dataset. Note that neither of these strategies introduce class imbalance.

4.1   Experiment 1: Impact of Ratio Bias

When $n = 2$, the total number of images can be between 60/1300 to a maximum of 20000 for MCML-MNIST/MCML-ABCD datasets. The test dataset remains the same across all experiments and contains all 120/2600 unique combinations for both the datasets respectively. Our results with our predefined model architecture and training strategy are summarised in Fig. 2. We compare F1 scores for all training datasets with the baseline of ratio bias $n = 1$ as the maximum potential F1 score. We observe that with an increase in ratio bias (n increasing from 2 to 32), the F1 score, precision and recall values of the classifier decrease for the same amount of training samples. This means that for the same amount of images, while each digits's chances of occurrence remains about the same during increasing ratio bias, the model's ability to recognize digits in the test set decreases. Interestingly if we keep the ratio bias constant (i.e. fixed n), and keep adding more images by varying the location of the digits, the F1 score and precision increases. All three eventually plateaus (Fig. 2). Hence we prove that beyond a certain threshold, the addition of more images doesn't help the model. Since we keep the model architecture, training strategy, and test dataset consistent, the changes observed in the F1 scores are solely attributed to the change in the training dataset. The class combinations vary in the generated training datasets and thus have the absence of certain ghost class pairs that are present in the test dataset.

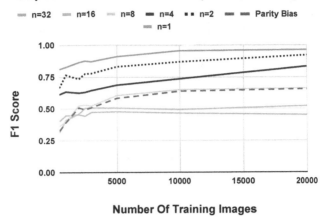

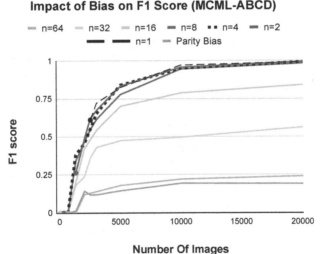

Fig. 2. Impact of different compositional biasing strategies on a classifiers F1 score. With a similar number of unique combinations and size of the training dataset, the two models trained on parity bias and ratio bias n = 4 should perform similarly but we note the disparate performance. This observation allows us to focus on the kinds of combinations rather than the number of unique combinations in the training dataset. Note that recall with its false negatives appears to be a better measure of the presence or absence of ghost class pairs rather than the false positives (precision). Best viewed in color. (Color figure online)

4.2 Experiment 2: Impact of Parity Bias

Through the ratio bias experiment, we observed that missing combinations in the training dataset significantly impacts the F1 score of the model. We now consider how a different biasing technique like the parity bias impacts the F1 score. Having a total of 20/572 combinations, we observe the model trained on the parity bias dataset for both MCML-MNIST/MCML-ABCD respectively gets worse test classification performance as compared to training on the dataset with ratio bias though both have a similar number of unique combinations, (Fig. 2) (ratio bias $n = 8, 16, 32$). For example, we observe a disproportionate drop in the F1 score at 5000 training dataset size, parity bias training dataset with 20/572 unique combinations has an F1 score of 0.581/0.197 while the ratio bias training dataset with $n = 4$; 30/650 unique combinations has an F1 score of 0.72/0.809 for both MCML-MNIST/MCML-ABCD respectively.

Why does the model trained on the ratio bias dataset perform significantly better than the model trained on the parity bias dataset when tested on the same test dataset? The number of combinations (20 versus 30)/(572 versus 650) for MCML-MNIST/MCML-ABCD respectively is within similar bounds, the training dataset size is consistent at 5000 images and both datasets are perfectly balanced. This hints that it is not the number of unique combinations but rather the kind of combinations, or the absence of combinations (ghost class pairs) which affects the final F1 score. Additionally, we hypothesize that recall is a better measure of the presence or absence of ghost class pairs, as recall takes into account the false negative class combinations rather than the false positives (precision).

4.3 Experiment 3: Impact of Degree of Separation

We observe that the ratio bias dataset has images whose combinations exhibit unique "relatedness" or "connectivity" that the parity bias dataset does not. In the parity bias dataset, either the even indexed characters occur together or the odd indexed characters occur together, in a mutually exclusive or disjoint manner. In other words, any even indexed character like 0/A is never connected to any odd indexed character like 1/B. This property is the stark difference between the parity bias dataset and the ratio bias dataset. The ratio bias dataset has images with combinations like $\{012, 126 \dots 579\}/\{ABC, ABG \dots XYZ\}$, where even though character 3/C and character 6/G never occur together, they are still connected to each other through a transitive relationship i.e. character 3/C is connected to character 6/G both via characters 0/A and 1/B. Greater connectivity signifies a shorter degree of separation. Armed with this observation, we speculate that the transitive nature of connectedness between the classes or characters in the unique combinations somehow impacts the classifier's F1 score. We want to quantify "how" transitively connected two characters or classes are, and what is the impact of connectivity amongst characters? We breakdown the quantification into two discrete steps:

(1) Identify which classes or characters are connected directly or explicitly. The explicit relations are defined as classes or characters co-occurring in the same image. If we consider the co-occurrence of the characters as being a symmetric relation, eg if an image contains ABC as characters, then the exhaustive set of singleton relationships include $\{(A, B), (B, C), (A, C), (B, A), (C, B), (C, A)\}$. Given that this is an unordered set, we can reduce the singleton relationships and establish symmetry amongst the characters or classes. Thus, for an image containing $\{ABC\}$, it has $\{(A, B), (B, C), (A, C)\}$ as individual symmetric relations. Assuming the co-occurrence of characters to be symmetric, we are able to summarize the number of relations, or which classes co-occur together in the images of the dataset in a correlation matrix.

(2) Identify which characters are connected indirectly or via a transitive relation. The implicit or transitive relation as defined previously is considering a dataset of images $\{ABC, FCD\}$, A is transitively connected to D and F via C The correlation matrix tells us which classes appear together i.e. connected explicitly or within the same image, but it does not provide information about the characters that may be transitively connected. Additionally, the transitive connections may also be of a variable length, class A connected to B through only C, or first through C and then through D. As an example, a dataset with images with labels $\{ABW, BCD, DEF\}$ - class A is explicitly co-occurring with B, B explicitly co-occurs with D thus A is transitively connected to D, through B. The length of this transitive relation is 2. For character E, which also explicitly co-occurs with D, A is transitively connected to E, first through B, and then through D resulting in a transitive relation of length 3. In the case of explicit relations, for example, A to B or B to A relation, the transitive relation is symmetric and thus the length of this transitive relation is one. Using this logic, we develop an algorithm 1 that counts the connected components (transitive and symmetric relations.) i.e. calculates the multiple transitive jumps required to reach from one connected class to the other. Similar concept applies to MCML-MNIST dataset as well.

Our algorithm builds on the binary correlation matrix and quantifies the "degree of separation" or length of transitive relations and generates a "connectedness matrix". We step through our algorithm (Tables 1, 2, 3 and 4 to generate the connectedness matrix utilizing an example dataset with six character classes $\{A, B, C, D, E, F\}$ generating 20 unique combinations (of three characters each) using ratio bias $n = 4$, i.e. 5 unique combinations to create the training dataset. The stepwise "connectedness matrix" are shown in Tables 2, 3 and 4. Using the same character classes we generate another dataset with parity bias. And its correlation matrix and "connectedness matrix" are shown in Tables 1 and 4 respectively.

From the MCML-ABCD connectedness matrices (Tables 7, 8 and 9) on both the ratio bias and the parity bias, we observe that among 572 unique combinations of parity bias, while the maximum transitive distance for connected components is one, the maximum degree of separation can be infinite. This is because none of the even indexed characters are connected to any of the odd indexed characters. In other words, out of 25 possible connections, each character has just 12 connections (with other characters in the even or odd indexed family). At the same time, in the case of ratio bias with n = 4 (650 unique combinations), each character is connected directly and indirectly to the other 25 characters, with a maximum transitive connected distance of 3. With such densely connected classes, or a closer degree of separation, the performance of the ratio bias dataset is significantly better than that of the parity bias (0.809 vs 0.197) at 5000 training data size (Fig. 2). We observe that the degree of separation is related inversely to the F1 score - when the classes have lower degrees of separation (e.g. one degree of

Table 1. Taking MCML-ABCD as the example dataset, we first generate the **binary correlation matrix** using standard functions.

	A	B	C	D	E	F
A	0	1	1	1	0	1
B	1	0	1	0	0	1
C	1	1	0	1	0	1
D	1	0	1	0	1	1
E	0	0	0	1	0	0
F	1	1	1	1	1	0

Table 2. Based on the generated correlation matrix, we initialize an empty matrix of identical size and apply our algorithm to generate the connectedness matrix. In the first step for ratio bias $n = 4$, we consider character A and fill in the degree of separation between A and different characters. For each column, we first check if a direct connection exists i.e., is the value in the binary correlation matrix true or false. For column B, C and D, it is true, so A is directly connected to B, C and D. For column E, we look for previous transitive connections, in this case E is connected to D, and D is also connected to A, so E is transitively connected to A via D with a degree of separation of two.

	A	B	C	D	E	F
A	0	1	1	1	2	1
B	1	0	0	0	0	0
C	1	0	0	0	0	0
D	1	0	0	0	0	0
E	2	0	0	0	0	0
F	1	0	0	0	0	0

separation between classes A and B in the connectedness matrix in the Supplementary), they are densely connected like in the case of ratio bias and the corresponding F1 score is higher (value of 0.809). For parity bias, where the numerical value of the degree of separation is higher, the connections are sparse and the F1 score is significantly lower. To support this observation we make a scatter plot Fig. 4 between an image's average degree of separation and the corresponding average F1 score for that degree of separation. Each point signifies the average degree of separation in different ratio bias datasets, with n = 16, 32, 64. We don't plot points from the parity bias dataset as that has a degree of separation of 1 or infinity. All the trend lines for n = 16, 32, 64 exhibit a gradual gradient change, i.e. for all the F1 score decreases with the increase in the average degree of separation. We also observe that ratio bias n=64 with the lowest average F1 score performs poorly when compared to the other ratio bias datasets. This poor performance of n = 64 is in line with our earlier observation that the degree of separation is related inversely to the F1 score. We note a similar trend in the MCML-MNIST dataset, where we additionally average the degree of separation for each combination in Fig. 5.

Table 3. In the next step, we consider the next character, B and apply the algorithm iteratively to all characters and fill in their corresponding degrees of separation.

	A	B	C	D	E	F
A	0	1	1	1	2	1
B	1	0	1	2	3	1
C	1	1	0	0	0	0
D	1	2	0	0	0	0
E	2	3	0	0	0	0
F	1	1	0	0	0	0

Table 4. The final **generated connectedness matrix** using our algorithm. We apply the insights from the connectedness matrix to generate new combinations as follows: classes B and E are separated by a larger degree of separation (distance of three), thus we add images containing classes B and E to the training dataset which helps to improve the F1 score by 35–40% as shown in Fig. 3

	A	B	C	D	E	F
A	0	1	1	1	2	1
B	1	0	1	2	3	1
C	1	1	0	1	1	1
D	1	2	1	0	1	1
E	2	3	1	1	0	2
F	1	1	1	1	2	0

4.4 Experiment 4: Adding Connected Examples to the MCML Classifier

We now consider how our observations could be applied to improve real world large scale datasets where non-iid distributions are common. In particular, we build on the observation that the degree of separation of each unique combination is related to the F1 score (Sect. 4.3 - Impact of Degree of Separation). To improve F1 score of a dataset, we hypothesize that specific image examples need to be added, which decrease the degree of separation (both direct and transitive). This entails enhancing the data distribution by augmenting new images with densely connected classes. One simple baseline option is randomly generating class combinations, with the hope that eventually it will lead to class combinations with higher connectedness i.e. lower degree of separation. While simple, this approach could be further optimized (Table 6).

Our approach involves generating new data samples involving class combinations with the lowest connectedness. For a given dataset, we first create a covariance matrix (based on direct appearance of class combinations in the same image) and then derive a "degree of separation" among class combinations in the entire dataset. Based on the degree of separation, we pick one or more class combination pairs to help augment the training dataset. Finally, to prove the effectiveness of this algorithm, we apply this augmentation technique on various poor performing datasets with varying training dataset size: ratio bias with $n = 16$, $n = 32$ and the parity bias dataset. Additionally, we also compare with our baseline method of randomly generating class combinations. In all cases, the original training dataset is increased from 5000 to 20000 for both datasets, and then classifiers are trained at regular intervals. The resultant F1 scores on the default test dataset (identical to base dataset) are shown in Fig. 3. We see that with the addition of the new combinations, the F1 score jumps drastically. There is also a significant difference between our greedy data augmentation technique that picks combinations based on connectedness vs random data augmentations. Moreover, even a few thousand addition of images shows a sizable jump in accuracy.

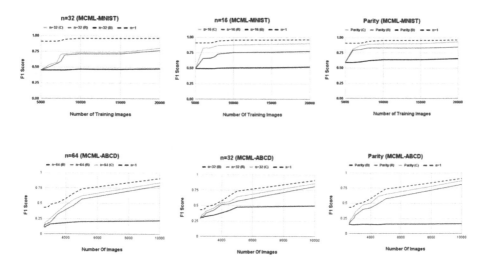

Fig. 3. Effectively adding new images post the augmentations based on degree of separation selection (C) improves the classifier accuracy more so than the random selection (R). Base dataset (B) and $n = 1$ provided for comparison. F1 score on the Y axis, and number of images on X axis. Best viewed in color. Top row is for MCML-MNIST, and bottom row is MCML-ABCD. Details in Sect. 4.4 - Adding connected examples to the MCML classifier. (Color figure online)

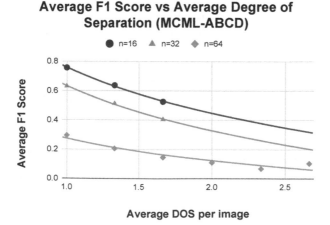

Fig. 4. Impact of increase in the average Degree of Separation (DOS) of images in n = 16, 32 and 64 which contain similar images, on the Average F1 score per image per DOS, for MCML-ABCD dataset

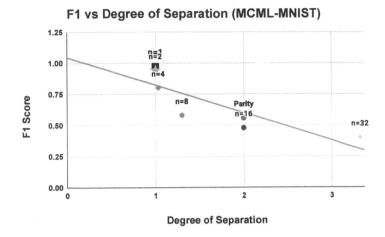

Fig. 5. Impact of increase in the degree of separation of various biased datasets on the F1 score. ⋆ indicates F1 score of $n = 2$ at .94, ■ indicates F1 score for $n = 1$ at .97. For MCML-MNIST dataset.

5 Discussion

We now consider how to utilize our observations on both the MCML-MNIST and MCML-ABCD datasets - of varying complexities, and apply them to real world large scale datasets where non-iid distributions are common. In particular, we build on the following observations: **(1) Observation from experiments on the impact of ratio and parity bias** - While comparing an iid dataset vs a non iid dataset with comparable number of class instances for each class across the datasets, we see that there is performance disparity. Since the number of class instances are equal, the disparity has to be because of the only variable amongst the datasets i.e. the class combinations that never occurred in the training dataset, like the mutually exclusive odd or even digits or alphabets in the parity bias training dataset. **(2) Impact of transitive connectedness and adding connected examples to the MCML classifier** - The F1 score of a classifier on an image is related to the degree of separation of the unique class combinations in the image. Then, if we augment the dataset with new images containing classes with a lower degree of separation, we note an increase in the F1 score.

Thus, we learnt that there is a significant impact of degree of separation (both direct and transitive) between classes on the F1 score of a classifier. Given a dataset, we can generate its degree of separation and then utilize this measure to benchmark its current performance and compare it against a fixed dataset with added combinations and see the increase in connectedness and eventually F1 scores.

Classifiers assume the class distribution to be iid but when certain classes are absent the classifier starts drawing a dependence on the absence of those classes or in the case of a CNN representative features of classes. Taking the example of parity bias vs iid, the dataset has comparable instances of character classes for a similar sized dataset but gives poor performance when an odd indexed and even digits occur together in the test image. The interdependence between classes overshadows the visual features that a CNN learns. Concretely the presence of a relatively few examples increases the connectedness thereby reducing the interdependence between classes thus making the classifier more robust. The model learns that the even indexed classes are dependent on the absence of odd indexed classes rather than just being dependent on the visual features of the even indexed classes. A practitioners work traditionally focuses on class imbalance that manifests in the form of varying class frequencies. Our research sheds light towards the fact that even if class frequencies are similar, there is still imbalance based on the combinations of classes which occur together.

For our algorithm to work on real world datasets, a key question to answer is how to generate or synthesize images with the missing class combinations? Augmenting datasets with synthetic images is a common way to increase training samples. One can extract class instances using bounding boxes or segmentation masks from annotated datasets like MSCOCO or OpenImages [23], and then create new images with random backgrounds and the foreground as the segmented object [12]. Additionally cropping objects from MSCOCO or OpenImages and synthesizing complete images with multiple classes with Blender would result in more realistic images with complete control. Other ways of synthesizing data include utilizing predefined 3D models of object, placing multiple objects in a scene (background) and taking images from various viewpoints. The focus is not to teach the model on what the object looks like, and is instead on the class combinations that the model sees during training time. Effectively we enable the model to intuit that even though it's only seen class *cat* and class *person* together, and class *dog* and class *person* together, it may still encounter class *cat* and class *dog* together. It should be noted that images cannot be synthesized for all datasets but this algorithm can be used by data collectors to prioritize which class combinations are essential for the model to perform better.

Applying simple random augmentations and collecting data in a random order will eventually arrive at a high F1 score, but our greedy algorithm can achieve the same F1 score quicker by addressing the most impactful class combinations. It is worth mentioning that our algorithm which generates the connectedness is $O(n^3)$, so a random approach might be much quicker to implement if generating more images at scale is not a bottleneck. Alternately on large datasets like MSCOCO with 80 classes or OpenImagesV6 with 600 classes, the update step for the connectedness can occur after generating a larger batch size like 100, rather than after every class combination to amortize the cost involved.

6 Future Work

In our work, we explored the impact of presence and absence of class combinations on a classifiers F1 score on an image dataset. We also considered how to improve the classifier performance by adding images containing high leverage class combinations. For numerical tabular datasets with class imbalance, techniques like SMOTE are already applied to generate synthetic examples through extrapolation. Depending on the type of tabular dataset, it may be possible to similarly generate synthetic data. Applications of this method beyond image datasets to tabular, text, audio datasets where sparse class combinations occur may be feasible but we keep this for future work. For future improvements we consider scaling the dataset creation by reinforcement learning methods - once the objects are extracted from the MSCOCO dataset, the reinforcement learning algorithm can combine multiple objects and create a single image such that the objects are placed non-overlapping. The objects are cropped or segmented from the ground truth. For real scene image datasets to increase the robustness of the system we are also experimenting with transferring the context of the chosen objects via extending the area occupied by the segmentation mask. We also consider transferring this knowledge of classification tasks to detection and segmentation tasks.

7 Conclusion

In this paper we observe a strong dependence between the presence and more importantly the absence of class combinations (i.e. ghost pairs). The classification performance of images is related to the degree of separation of class combinations occurring in the particular test image through two synthesized datasets - the MCML-MNIST and MCML-ABCD. Through our work we highlight a new facet of data imbalance such that even if class frequencies are similar, imbalance may exist based on the combinations of classes which occur together in images. By synthesizing missing combinations through a greedy algorithm and adding those images to the training dataset we are able to show improved F1 score by an average of 25–30%.

8 Appendix

Fig. 6. Random images from base dataset with 120 combinations in case of the MCML-MNIST dataset and 2600 combinations in the MCML-ABCD dataset. The test dataset for all our experiments is identical to the base dataset.

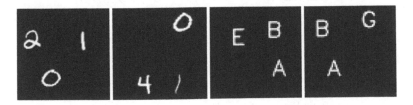

Fig. 7. Images from training dataset with Ratio Bias n=2. We pick every other combination resulting in a uniform distribution with negligible individual class imbalance.

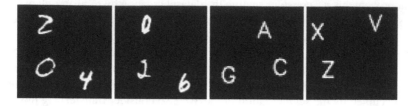

Fig. 8. Images from training dataset with Parity Bias where odd and even indexed digits occur in a mutually exclusive or disjoint manner. First two images with even digits/characters and last two images with odd digits/characters.

Table 5. Number of unique combinations in the base dataset and various training datasets generated as a result of introducing Ratio and Parity bias on the base dataset. *"Unq Comb"* indicates the total number of unique combinations in each dataset and *"# 0, 9 per 5k"* reflects the total number of 0 and 9 in a dataset with 5000 images showing negligible imbalance and near equal frequencies. Other classes exhibit a similar distribution.

Training dataset	# Unq Comb	# 0, 9 per 5k
Base dataset	120	0: 756, 9: 746
Ratio Bias: n = 2	60	0: 756, 9: 748
Ratio Bias: n = 4	30	0: 756, 9: 756
Ratio Bias: n = 8	15	0: 835, 9: 790
Ratio Bias: n = 16	8	0: 939, 9: 1250
Ratio Bias: n = 32	4	0: 1250, 9: 1250
Parity Bias	20	0: 750, 9: 750

Table 6. Number of unique combinations in the base dataset and various training datasets generated as a result of introducing Ratio and Parity bias on the base dataset. *"Unq Comb"* indicates the total number of unique combinations in each dataset and *"# A, Z per 5k"* reflects the total number of characters A and Z in a dataset with 5000 images showing negligible imbalance and near equal frequencies. Other character classes exhibit a similar distribution.

Training dataset	# Unq Comb	# A, Z per 5k
Base Dataset	2600	A: 578, Z: 577
Ratio Bias: n = 2	1300	A: 577, Z: 577
Ratio Bias: n = 4	650	A: 577, Z: 554
Ratio Bias: n = 8	325	A: 585, Z: 524
Ratio Bias: n = 16	163	A: 583, Z: 521
Ratio Bias: n = 32	82	A: 610, Z: 610
Ratio Bias: n = 64	41	A: 610, Z: 490
Parity Bias	572	A: 580, Z: 580

Algorithm 1: Connectedness Matrix Algorithm

Input: $corrMat$, $numOfClasses$
Output: $connMat$

```
1   connMat ← np.zeros([numOfClasses, numOfClasses]);
2   for i ← 0 to numOfClasses do
3       for j ← 0 to numOfClasses do
4           if corrMat[i][j] == 1 and connMat[i][j] == 0 then
5               connMat[j][i] ← 1;
6               connMat[i][j] ← 1;
7           end
8           else if connMat[i][j] == 0 then
9               for k ← 0 to numOfClasses do
10                  if corrMat[k][j] == 1 and k ≠ i and j ≠ k then
11                      if corrMat[i][k] == 1 then
12                          if corrMat[i][k] + 1 < connMat[i][j] or connMat[i][j] == 0
                            then
13                              connMat[j][i] ← corrMat[i][k] + 1;
14                              connMat[i][j] ← corrMat[i][k] + 1;
15                          end
16                      end
17                      else if connMat[i][k] ≠ 0 then
18                          tempVal = connMat[i][k] + 1;
19                          if tempVal < connMat[i][j] or connMat[i][j] == 0 then
20                              connMat[j][i] ← tempVal;
21                              connMat[i][j] ← tempVal;
22                          end
23                      end
24                  end
25              end
26          end
27      end
28  end
```

Table 7. Binary correlation matrix, n = 32 generated using standard functions.

	A	B	C	D	E	F	G	H	I	J	K	L	M	N	O	P	Q	R	S	T	U	V	W	X	Y	Z
A	0	1	1	1	0	1	1	0	1	0	1	1	1	1	0	0	1	0	1	0	1	1	1	1	1	1
B	1	0	1	0	1	1	0	1	0	1	0	1	1	0	1	0	0	1	1	1	0	1	1	1	1	0
C	1	1	0	1	1	0	1	1	1	1	0	1	0	0	1	1	0	1	0	0	1	1	1	1	1	1
D	1	0	1	0	1	1	0	1	1	1	0	1	0	1	1	1	0	1	1	0	1	1	1	0	1	1
E	0	1	1	1	0	0	1	0	1	0	1	0	1	1	0	1	0	1	1	0	0	0	0	0	0	1
F	1	1	0	1	0	0	1	0	1	0	1	0	1	0	1	1	0	1	0	1	1	1	0	0	1	0
G	1	0	1	0	1	1	0	1	1	1	0	1	0	0	1	1	0	1	1	1	1	0	1	1	0	1
H	0	1	1	1	0	0	1	0	1	0	1	1	1	0	1	1	1	0	1	1	1	0	1	1	0	1
I	1	0	1	1	1	1	1	1	0	1	1	1	1	0	1	0	0	1	1	0	0	1	1	0	0	0
J	0	1	1	1	0	0	1	0	1	0	1	1	1	0	1	0	1	0	1	1	0	1	0	1	0	1
K	1	0	0	0	1	1	0	1	1	1	0	1	0	1	1	1	1	1	0	0	1	1	0	1	1	1
L	1	1	1	1	1	0	0	1	1	1	1	1	0	0	0	1	0	0	1	1	1	1	1	0	1	0
M	1	1	0	0	1	1	0	1	1	1	0	0	0	1	0	0	1	0	1	0	1	1	1	0	0	0

(continued)

Table 7. (*continued*)

	A	B	C	D	E	F	G	H	I	J	K	L	M	N	O	P	Q	R	S	T	U	V	W	X	Y	Z
N	1	0	0	1	1	0	0	0	0	0	1	0	1	0	0	0	1	0	1	0	1	0	0	0	1	0
O	0	1	1	1	0	1	1	1	1	1	1	1	0	0	0	0	1	1	1	1	1	1	0	1	1	1
P	0	0	1	1	1	1	1	1	1	1	0	0	1	0	0	0	0	0	0	1	0	1	0	0	0	1
Q	1	0	0	0	0	0	0	1	0	1	1	0	1	1	1	0	0	0	1	1	1	1	0	0	0	0
R	0	1	1	1	1	1	1	1	0	1	0	1	1	0	0	1	1	0	0	1	1	0	1	1	1	1
S	1	1	0	1	1	0	1	1	1	1	0	1	1	1	1	0	1	1	0	1	0	0	1	1	1	1
T	0	1	0	0	0	1	1	1	0	1	0	1	0	0	1	1	1	1	1	0	0	1	0	0	0	1
U	1	0	1	1	0	1	1	1	0	0	1	1	1	1	1	0	1	0	0	0	0	0	0	0	1	0
V	1	1	1	1	0	1	0	0	1	1	1	1	1	0	1	0	1	1	0	1	0	0	1	0	0	1
W	1	1	1	1	0	0	1	1	1	0	0	1	1	0	0	0	0	1	1	0	0	1	0	0	1	1
X	1	1	1	0	0	0	1	1	0	1	1	0	0	0	1	0	0	1	1	0	0	0	0	0	1	0
Y	1	1	1	1	0	1	0	0	0	0	1	1	0	1	1	0	0	0	1	0	1	0	1	1	0	1
Z	1	0	1	1	1	0	1	1	0	1	1	0	0	0	1	1	0	1	1	1	0	1	1	0	1	0

Table 8. Connectedness matrix - n = 32, generated using the Algorithm defined in Sect. 1

	A	B	C	D	E	F	G	H	I	J	K	L	M	N	O	P	Q	R	S	T	U	V	W	X	Y	Z
A	0	1	1	1	2	1	1	2	1	2	1	1	1	1	2	2	1	2	1	2	1	1	1	1	1	1
B	1	0	1	2	1	1	2	1	2	1	2	1	1	2	1	2	2	1	1	1	2	1	1	1	1	2
C	1	1	0	1	1	2	1	1	1	1	2	1	2	2	1	1	2	1	2	2	1	1	1	1	1	1
D	1	2	1	0	1	1	2	1	1	1	2	1	2	1	1	1	2	1	1	2	1	1	1	2	1	1
E	2	1	1	1	0	2	1	2	1	2	1	2	1	1	2	1	2	1	1	2	2	2	2	2	2	1
F	1	1	2	1	2	0	1	2	1	2	1	2	1	2	1	1	2	1	2	1	1	1	2	2	1	2
G	1	2	1	2	1	1	0	1	1	1	2	1	2	2	1	1	2	1	1	1	1	2	1	1	2	1
H	2	1	1	1	2	2	1	0	1	2	1	1	1	2	1	1	1	2	1	1	1	2	1	1	2	1
I	1	2	1	1	1	1	1	1	0	1	1	1	1	2	1	2	2	1	1	2	2	1	1	2	2	2
J	2	1	1	1	2	2	1	2	1	0	1	1	1	2	1	2	1	2	1	1	2	1	2	1	2	1
K	1	2	2	2	1	1	2	1	1	1	0	1	2	1	1	1	1	1	2	2	1	1	2	1	1	1
L	1	1	1	1	2	2	1	1	1	1	1	0	2	2	1	2	2	1	1	1	1	1	2	1	1	2
M	1	1	2	2	1	1	2	1	1	1	2	2	0	1	2	2	1	2	1	2	1	1	1	2	2	2
N	1	2	2	1	1	2	2	2	2	2	1	2	1	0	2	2	1	2	1	2	1	2	2	2	1	2
O	2	1	1	1	2	1	1	1	1	1	1	1	1	2	0	2	1	1	1	1	1	1	2	1	1	1
P	2	2	1	1	1	1	1	1	1	2	2	1	2	2	2	0	2	1	2	1	2	2	2	2	2	1
Q	1	2	2	2	2	2	2	1	2	1	1	1	2	1	1	1	0	2	1	1	1	1	2	2	2	2
R	2	1	1	1	1	1	1	2	1	2	1	1	2	2	1	1	2	0	1	1	2	1	1	1	2	1
S	1	1	2	1	1	2	1	1	1	1	2	1	1	1	1	2	1	1	0	1	2	2	1	1	1	1
T	2	1	2	2	2	1	1	1	2	1	2	1	2	2	1	1	1	1	1	0	2	1	2	2	2	1
U	1	2	1	1	2	1	1	1	1	2	2	1	1	1	1	1	2	1	2	2	0	2	2	2	1	2
V	1	1	1	1	2	1	2	2	1	1	1	1	1	2	1	2	1	1	2	1	2	0	1	2	2	1
W	1	1	1	1	2	2	1	1	1	2	2	1	1	2	2	2	2	1	1	2	2	1	0	2	1	1
X	1	1	1	2	2	2	1	1	2	1	1	2	2	2	1	2	2	1	1	2	2	2	2	0	1	2
Y	1	1	1	1	2	1	2	2	2	2	1	1	2	1	1	2	2	2	1	2	1	2	1	1	0	1
Z	1	2	1	1	1	2	1	1	2	1	1	2	2	2	1	1	2	1	1	1	2	1	1	2	1	0

Table 9. Correlation matrix and Connectedness matrix for, Parity Bias are the same because the Even characters are only connected to Even and Odd characters are only connected to Odd characters.

	A	B	C	D	E	F	G	H	I	J	K	L	M	N	O	P	Q	R	S	T	U	V	W	X	Y	Z
A	0	0	1	0	1	0	1	0	1	0	1	0	1	0	1	0	1	0	1	0	1	0	1	0	1	0
B	0	0	0	1	0	1	0	1	0	1	0	1	0	1	0	1	0	1	0	1	0	1	0	1	0	1
C	1	0	0	0	1	0	1	0	1	0	1	0	1	0	1	0	1	0	1	0	1	0	1	0	1	0
D	0	1	0	0	0	1	0	1	0	1	0	1	0	1	0	1	0	1	0	1	0	1	0	1	0	1
E	1	0	1	0	0	0	1	0	1	0	1	0	1	0	1	0	1	0	1	0	1	0	1	0	1	0
F	0	1	0	1	0	0	0	1	0	1	0	1	0	1	0	1	0	1	0	1	0	1	0	1	0	1
G	1	0	1	0	1	0	0	0	1	0	1	0	1	0	1	0	1	0	1	0	1	0	1	0	1	0
H	0	1	0	1	0	1	0	0	0	1	0	1	0	1	0	1	0	1	0	1	0	1	0	1	0	1
I	1	0	1	0	1	0	1	0	0	0	1	0	1	0	1	0	1	0	1	0	1	0	1	0	1	0
J	0	1	0	1	0	1	0	1	0	0	0	1	0	1	0	1	0	1	0	1	0	1	0	1	0	1
K	1	0	1	0	1	0	1	0	1	0	0	0	1	0	1	0	1	0	1	0	1	0	1	0	1	0
L	0	1	0	1	0	1	0	1	0	1	0	0	0	1	0	1	0	1	0	1	0	1	0	1	0	1
M	1	0	1	0	1	0	1	0	1	0	1	0	0	0	1	0	1	0	1	0	1	0	1	0	1	0
N	0	1	0	1	0	1	0	1	0	1	0	1	0	0	0	1	0	1	0	1	0	1	0	1	0	1
O	1	0	1	0	1	0	1	0	1	0	1	0	1	0	0	0	1	0	1	0	1	0	1	0	1	0
P	0	1	0	1	0	1	0	1	0	1	0	1	0	1	0	0	0	1	0	1	0	1	0	1	0	1
Q	1	0	1	0	1	0	1	0	1	0	1	0	1	0	1	0	0	0	1	0	1	0	1	0	1	0
R	0	1	0	1	0	1	0	1	0	1	0	1	0	1	0	1	0	0	0	1	0	1	0	1	0	1
S	1	0	1	0	1	0	1	0	1	0	1	0	1	0	1	0	1	0	0	0	1	0	1	0	1	0
T	0	1	0	1	0	1	0	1	0	1	0	1	0	1	0	1	0	1	0	0	0	1	0	1	0	1
U	1	0	1	0	1	0	1	0	1	0	1	0	1	0	1	0	1	0	1	0	0	0	1	0	1	0
V	0	1	0	1	0	1	0	1	0	1	0	1	0	1	0	1	0	1	0	1	0	0	0	1	0	1
W	1	0	1	0	1	0	1	0	1	0	1	0	1	0	1	0	1	0	1	0	1	0	0	0	1	0
X	0	1	0	1	0	1	0	1	0	1	0	1	0	1	0	1	0	1	0	1	0	1	0	0	0	1
Y	1	0	1	0	1	0	1	0	1	0	1	0	1	0	1	0	1	0	1	0	1	0	1	0	0	0
Z	0	1	0	1	0	1	0	1	0	1	0	1	0	1	0	1	0	1	0	1	0	1	0	1	0	0

References

1. Bang, H., Robins, J.M.: Doubly robust estimation in missing data and causal inference models. Biometrics **61**(4), 962–973 (2005). https://doi.org/10.1111/j.1541-0420.2005.00377.x, https://onlinelibrary.wiley.com/doi/abs/10.1111/j.1541-0420.2005.00377.x
2. Barua, S., Islam, M.M., Yao, X., Murase, K.: MWMOTE-majority weighted minority oversampling technique for imbalanced data set learning. IEEE Trans. Knowl. Data Eng. **26**(2), 405–425 (2014). https://doi.org/10.1109/TKDE.2012.232, ISSN: 1041-4347
3. Bej, S., Davtyan, N., Wolfien, M., Nassar, M., Wolkenhauer, O.: LoRAS: an oversampling approach for imbalanced datasets. Mach. Learn. **110**, 279–301 (2020)

4. Blagus, R., Lusa, L.: Smote for high-dimensional class-imbalanced data. BMC Bioinform. **14**(1), 106 (2013). https://doi.org/10.1186/1471-2105-14-106, ISSN: 1471-2105

5. Bunkhumpornpat, C., Sinapiromsaran, K., Lursinsap, C.: Safe-Level-SMOTE: safe-level-synthetic minority over-sampling technique for handling the class imbalanced problem. In: Theeramunkong, T., Kijsirikul, B., Cercone, N., Ho, T.-B. (eds.) PAKDD 2009. LNCS (LNAI), vol. 5476, pp. 475–482. Springer, Heidelberg (2009). https://doi.org/10.1007/978-3-642-01307-2_43

6. Chawla, N.V., Bowyer, K.W., Hall, L.O., Kegelmeyer, W.P.: SMOTE: synthetic minority over-sampling technique. J. Artif. Int. Res. **16**(1), 321–357 (2002)

7. Chawla, N.V., Lazarevic, A., Hall, L.O., Bowyer, K.: SMOTEBoost: improving prediction of the minority class in boosting. In: European Conference on Principles of Data Mining and Knowledge Discovery, pp. 107–119 (2003). https://doi.org/10.1007/978-3-540-39804-2_12, ISBN: 978-3-540-39804-2

8. Darrell, T., Kloft, M., Pontil, M., Rätsch, G., Rodner, E.: Machine learning with interdependent and non-identically distributed data (Dagstuhl Seminar 15152). Dagstuhl Rep. **5**(4), 18–55 (2015). http://drops.dagstuhl.de/opus/volltexte/2015/5349, https://doi.org/10.4230/DagRep.5.4.18

9. Dekel, O., Shamir, O.: Multiclass-multilabel classification with more classes than examples. In: Teh, Y.W., Titterington, M. (eds.) Multiclass-Multilabel Classification with More Classes than Examples. Proceedings of Machine Learning Research, vol. 9, pp. 137–144. JMLR Workshop and Conference Proceedings, Chia Laguna Resort, Sardinia, Italy, 13–15 May 2010). http://proceedings.mlr.press/v9/dekel10a.html

10. Douzas, G., Bacao, F.: Geometric smote a geometrically enhanced drop-in replacement for smote. Inf. Sci. **501**, 118–135 (2019). https://doi.org/10.1016/j.ins.2019.06.007, http://www.sciencedirect.com/science/article/pii/S0020025519305353

11. Dundar, M., Krishnapuram, B., Bi, J., Rao, R.B.: Learning classifiers when the training data is not IID. In: Proceedings of the 20th International Joint Conference on Artificial Intelligence, pp. 756–761, IJCAI 2007. Morgan Kaufmann Publishers Inc., San Francisco, CA, USA (2007)

12. Dwibedi, D., Misra, I., Hebert, M.: Cut, paste and learn: surprisingly easy synthesis for instance detection (2017)

13. Elhassan, T., Aljurf, M., Al-Mohanna, F., Shoukri, M.: Classification of imbalance data using Tomek Link (T-Link) combined with random under-sampling (RUS) as a data reduction method. Global J. Technol. Optim. **1**, 2–11 (2016). https://doi.org/10.21767/2472-1956.100011, ISSN: 2472-1956

14. Gao, M., Hong, X., Chen, S., Harris, C.J.: On combination of SMOTE and particle swarm optimization based radial basis function classifier for imbalanced problems. In: The 2011 International Joint Conference on Neural Networks, pp. 1146–1153. IEEE, July 2011. https://doi.org/10.1109/IJCNN.2011.6033353, ISBN: 978-1-4244-9635-8

15. Haibo, H., Yang, B., Garcia, E., Shutao, L.: ADASYN: adaptive synthetic sampling approach for imbalanced learning. In: 2008 IEEE International Joint Conference on Neural Networks, June 2008. https://doi.org/10.1109/IJCNN.2008.4633969, ISBN: 2161-4393

16. Han, H., Wang, W.Y., Mao, B.H.: Borderline-smote: a new over-sampling method in imbalanced data sets learning. In: Huang, D.S., Zhang, X.P., Huang, G.B. (eds.) Advances in Intelligent Computing. ICIC, vol. 3644, pp. 878–887. Springer, Heidelberg (2005), https://doi.org/10.1007/11538035_91, ISBN: 978-3-540-31902-3

17. Hanifah, F.S., Wijayanto, H., Kurnia, A.: SMOTE bagging algorithm for imbalanced dataset in logistic regression analysis (Case: Credit of Bank X). Appl. Math. Sci. **9**(138), 6857–6865 (2015). https://doi.org/10.12988/ams.2015.58562, ISSN: 0066-5452

18. He, Y., Shen, Z., Cui, P.: NICO: a dataset towards Non-I.I.D. image classification. CoRR abs/1906.02899 (2019). http://arxiv.org/abs/1906.02899

19. Hsieh, K., Phanishayee, A., Mutlu, O., Gibbons, P.B.: The Non-IID data quagmire of decentralized machine learning (2020)
20. Hu, S., Liang, Y., Ma, L., He, Y.: MSMOTE: improving classification performance when training data is imbalanced. In: Second International Workshop on Computer Science and Engineering, vol. 2, pp. 13–17, January 2009. https://doi.org/10.1109/WCSE.2009.756, ISBN: 978-0-7695-3881-5
21. Khosla, A., Zhou, T., Malisiewicz, T., Efros, A.A., Torralba, A.: Undoing the damage of dataset bias. In: Fitzgibbon, A., Lazebnik, S., Perona, P., Sato, Y., Schmid, C. (eds.) ECCV 2012. LNCS, vol. 7572, pp. 158–171. Springer, Heidelberg (2012). https://doi.org/10.1007/978-3-642-33718-5_12
22. Kuang, K., Xiong, R., Cui, P., Athey, S., Li, B.: Stable prediction across unknown environments. CoRR abs/1806.06270 (2018). http://arxiv.org/abs/1806.06270
23. Kuznetsova, A., et al.: The open images dataset V4: unified image classification, object detection, and visual relationship detection at scale. IJCV **128**, 1956–1981 (2020)
24. LeCun, Y., Cortes, C.: MNIST handwritten digit database (2010). http://yann.lecun.com/exdb/mnist/
25. Lin, T.Y., et al.: Microsoft COCO: common objects in context (2015)
26. Mathew, J., Luo, M., Khiang Pang, C., Leng Chan, H.: Kernel-based smote for SVM classification of imbalanced datasets. In: IECON 2015–41st Annual Conference of the IEEE Industrial Electronics Society, pp. 001127–001132. IEEE, November 2015. https://doi.org/10.1109/IECON.2015.7392251, ISBN: 978-1-4799-1762-4
27. Peyre, J., Laptev, I., Schmid, C., Sivic, J.: Weakly-supervised learning of visual relations. In: ICCV, abs/1707.09472 (2017). http://arxiv.org/abs/1707.09472
28. Puntumapon, K., Waiyamai, K.: A pruning-based approach for searching precise and generalized region for synthetic minority over-sampling. In: Tan, P.-N., Chawla, S., Ho, C.K., Bailey, J. (eds.) PAKDD 2012. LNCS (LNAI), vol. 7302, pp. 371–382. Springer, Heidelberg (2012). https://doi.org/10.1007/978-3-642-30220-6_31
29. Ramentol, E., Verbiest, N., Bello, R., Caballero, Y., Cornelis, C., Herrera, F.: SMOTE-FRST: a new resampling method using fuzzy rough set theory. In: World Scientific Proceedings Series on Computer Engineering and Information Science, vol. 7, pp. 800–805 (2012). https://doi.org/10.1142/9789814417747_0128, ISBN: 9789814417730
30. Russakovsky, O., et al.: ImageNet large scale visual recognition challenge. Int. J. Comput. Vision **115**(3), 211–252 (2015). https://doi.org/10.1007/s11263-015-0816-y
31. Sandler, M., Howard, A.G., Zhu, M., Zhmoginov, A., Chen, L.: Inverted residuals and linear bottlenecks: mobile networks for classification, detection and segmentation. In: CVPR, abs/1801.04381 (2018). http://arxiv.org/abs/1801.04381
32. Santoso, B., Wijayanto, H., Notodiputro, K.A., Sartono, B.: Synthetic over sampling methods for handling class imbalanced problems: a review. IOP Conf. Ser. Earth Environ. Sci. **58**, 012–031 (2017). https://doi.org/10.1088/1755-1315/58/1/012031, ISSN: 1755-1315
33. Suh, Y., Yu, J., Mo, J., Song, L., Kim, C.: A comparison of oversampling methods on imbalanced topic classification of Korean news articles. J. Cogn. Sci. **18**, 391–437 (2017)
34. Torralba, A., Efros, A.A.: Unbiased look at dataset bias. In: CVPR 2011, pp. 1521–1528 (2011). https://doi.org/10.1109/CVPR.2011.5995347
35. Torralba, A., Murphy, K.P., Freeman, W.T.: Using the forest to see the trees: exploiting context for visual object detection and localization. Commun. ACM **53**(3), 107–114 (2010). https://doi.org/10.1145/1666420.1666446
36. Wang, A., Narayanan, A., Russakovsky, O.: REVISE: a tool for measuring and mitigating bias in visual datasets. In: Vedaldi, A., Bischof, H., Brox, T., Frahm, J.-M. (eds.) ECCV 2020. LNCS, vol. 12348, pp. 733–751. Springer, Cham (2020). https://doi.org/10.1007/978-3-030-58580-8_43

37. Wang, K.J., Makond, B., Chen, K.H., Wang, K.M.: A hybrid classifier combining SMOTE with PSO to estimate 5-year survivability of breast cancer patients. Appl. Soft Comput. **20**, 15–24 (2014). https://doi.org/10.1016/J.ASOC.2013.09.014, ISSN: 1568-4946
38. Zhao, Y., Li, M., Lai, L., Suda, N., Civin, D., Chandra, V.: Federated learning with Non-IID data. CoRR abs/1806.00582 (2018). http://arxiv.org/abs/1806.00582

ReLearner: A Reinforcement Learning-Based Self Driving Car Model Using Gym Environment

Hiren Kumar Thakkar[1]([✉]) [iD], Ankit Desai[2], Priyanka Singh[3],
and Kamma Samhitha[3]

[1] Department of Computer Engineering, Marwadi University,
Rajkot 360003, Gujarat, India
[2] Bangalore 560068, India
[3] Department of Computer Science and Engineering, SRM University,
Amaravati 522240, Andhra Pradesh, India
{priyanka.s,kamma_samhitha}@srmap.edu.in

Abstract. In the recent past, Artificial intelligence and its sister technology such as Machine Learning, Deep Learning, and Reinforcement learning have grown rapidly in several applications. The self-driving car is one of the applications, which is the need of the hour. In this paper, we describe the trends in autonomous vehicle technology for the self-driving car. There are many different approaches to mathematically formulate a design for the self-driving car such as deep Q-learning, Q-learning, and machine learning. However, in this paper, we propose a very basic and less compute-intensive simplistic self-driving car model called "ReLearner" using the Gym environment. To simulate the self-driving car model, we preferred to create a simple small environment OpenAi gym which is a deterministic environment. The OpenAi gym provides the virtual simulation environment and parameter tuning to train and test the model. We have focused on two methods to test our model. The basic approach is to compare the performance of the car when tested using Q-Learning and another using a random action agent, i.e., No reinforcement learning. We have derived a theoretical model and analyzed how to use Q-learning to train cars to drive. We have carried out a simulation and on evaluating the performance and found that Q-learning is a more optimal approach to solve the issue of a self-driving car.

Keywords: Self-driving car · Deep Q-learning · Q-Learning · Reinforcement learning · Machine learning · Deterministic environment · Virtual simulation

1 Introduction

In the recent past, artificial intelligence technology and its subsidiary technologies such as Machine Learning (ML), Deep Learning (DL), and Reinforcement

A. Desai—Data Scientist, Independent Researcher.

D. Garg et al. (Eds.): IACC 2021, CCIS 1528, pp. 399–409, 2022.
https://doi.org/10.1007/978-3-030-95502-1_30

Learning (RL) are rapidly developing. Several applications such as image recognition [4], voice recognition [1], text summarization [7,13], image recognition, healthcare data analysis using machine learning [6,8] are commonly used these days. It is also noticeable that reinforcement learning is growing rapidly and are used in diversified research areas including the self-driving car [17] and cloud computing [10]. In addition to the ML and RL approaches, the conventional approaches are also prominently used to solve real-life problems such as Mobile Robot Navigation using the Breadth-First Search [15]. Health care is an important avenue and several AI-enabled models are proposed to predict future health conditions using ML [11,12,14]. In the recent past, there are several attempts to automate the work procedures such as industrial automation. In this regard, researchers are trying to build a prototype of a self-driving car. One of the examples is Tesla, which is one of the leading companies and it has employed embedded automation technology in a car. The central idea of this paper is reinforcement learning, which is being used for automated self-driving cars. We are using the Q-learning algorithm in reinforcement learning for designing a self-driving model called "ReLearner", which attempts to decide the path from the source to the destination.

In the proposed "ReLearner", we have used the Q-learning algorithm which is quite popular these days. In the past few decades, there is a significant change in automated technology from the 1920s, when the first radio-controlled vehicle was designed. In the same period, various automatic electric cars are built by using embedded circuits on the roads. By the time of the 1960s, we had electronic guide systems and in the 1980s there was a drastic change in the field of automation and the field of Technology. In modern intelligent cars, several semi-automatic features are available such as automated lane keeping, automatic braking, automatic brakes, and adaptive cruise control. Considering the busy lifestyle of an individual, it is predicted that several companies will transform into intelligent car manufacturing industries to launch automated vehicles. Therefore, it is evident that the future is the era of automated vehicles and transportation. Autonomous vehicles are usually categorized into five levels. In level 0, the automated system generates the warning for anticipated problems and may momentarily takes the control of the vehicle. However, the level 0 system has no absolute and sustained control over the system. In the level 1 system, the human and system share the controls and work cooperatively. For instance, the human may control the steering and at the same time system may control the vehicle cruising speed. Level 2 is an up-gradation of level 1 system, where the system takes full control of the vehicle such as braking, cruising speed, accelerating, etc., and the driver will monitor the overall driving and may immediately take the control whenever it deems fit to do it. Level 3 is towards automated driving, where drivers can keep their eyes off the vehicle and continue doing the other things. However, the driver still needs to intervene upon the prior warning generated by the system to take over. In level 4, it is assumed that the system is so adaptable that a driver may go to sleep and completely leave the driver's seat. In level 5, the system will be controlled and no human intervention will be required. It is assumed that the vehicle will move around on any surface and irrespective of the weather condition.

This paper focuses on the issue of a self-driving car based on simple reinforcement learning, we took the pre-created environment from OpenAi gym for the training and testing of our model. The environment is having everything, all the parameters required for training the self-driving car. The car we will be using to train and test the model is also provided with the environment. The car is a hypothetical entity. The training and testing will be performed using python in google co-laboratory. The simulation of the model will also be demonstrated in the co-laboratory itself. The car was trained using different methods in the environment for many episodes. At last, the car was able to learn a good policy to drive itself with minimum error.

2   Related Works

A self-driving car is the most popular application of Machine Learning. They are used in video games, racing cars, traffic control, etc. An MIT-based project called Deep traffic uses Deep Reinforcement Learning, a robot called AWS Deep Racer uses Reinforcement Learning, and self-driving cars are also used in Traffic Control. Most of the previous self-driving car applications use Reinforcement learning or Deep Reinforcement learning but other Machine Learning algorithms like Linear Regression and CNN are also used. However, linear regression was not the best-suited method as it assumes that data is independent whereas in a self-driving car model data may not be available. Andrew Ng has said that Deep Learning requires a lot of computations and Deep Q-learning requires even more computations. However, Deep Q-learning is used these days in most applications because it can compute a large number of q values efficiently. Simply using Reinforcement Learning is also not efficient because, it will take several time steps, make many wrong moves, and still not be able to learn. In [9] a deep reinforcement learning framework is proposed for autonomous driving. In [16], an automated lane change maneuver is proposed using reinforcement learning. In [5], a self-driving and driver relaxing vehicle design is proposed. In [3], the application of reinforcement learning in a self-driving car is demonstrated. In [2], end-to-end reinforcement learning for self-driving car is proposed. Our main purpose is to demonstrate the working of a self-driving car in a Gym Environment using Reinforcement Learning. Our approach to solving the environment is very basic and simple. Gym Environment is used for developing and comparing Reinforcement Learning algorithms like Q-learning, SARSA, and Deep Q-learning. In Gym Environment, we have used Taxi-v3 where the environment is already developed for our agent (taxi). The most popular and simple among the three is Q-learning which we have used. Q-learning Algorithm is based on updating the q-table records by updating the state, action pair. First, we have compared how the agent performs without Q-learning and with Q-learning. In this condition, our agent does not perform well as it takes too many time steps, many penalties have also been incurred, this means that the agent is not intelligent. Then the agent performs by using the Q-learning method which is much more efficient and gives us better results.

3   ReLearner Model

Our prototype of a self-driving car is very simple as discussed in this paper. The first step to solve the problem is to create an environment for our car. Fortunately, OpenAi Gym is having an already created environment named "Taxi-v3". "Taxi-v3" is the environment in which we worked.

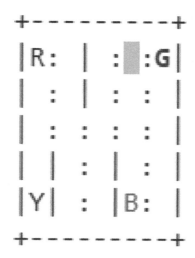

Fig. 1. "Taxi-v3" environment by OpenAi gym (Color figure online)

"Taxi-v3" consists of all the required parameters we need to train our algorithm, so we used this environment as it is. The environment is having four designated locations indicated by "R", "G", "Y", and B". There are 500 states and 6 deterministic actions. There is a reward of +20 for dropping the passenger at the destination, a reward of −10 for executing illegal pickup and drop-off and there is a reward of −1 for each action. Figure 1 shows the "Taxi-v3" environment. While Rendering the environment we observed color codes that defined the environment. 'Blue' color indicates the passenger, the 'magenta' color indicates the destination, the 'yellow' color indicates the empty taxi and the 'green' color indicates the taxi is full. To solve this environment we have focused on two methods which we have implemented using python in google co-laboratory.

3.1   No Reinforcement Learning

By the name, we understand that we are solving the environment without using reinforcement learning. As discussed above our environment is deterministic, which means our agent will perform an action with a probability of 1.0 at any state. Therefore, it was very easy to solve the environment without using reinforcement learning. The agent interacts with the environment by taking some actions, on which the environment returns rewards and the agent moves to the next state. By reading this sentence, you might think that it is the same as reinforcement learning, then why the method is called no reinforcement learning? Because in this method the agent is not learning from its experience. The agent will perform random actions from its state. Based on the random action, the agent will either get a reward or will be penalized.

$$\overline{a} = \{0, 1, 2, 3, 4, 5\}$$
$$a \leftarrow random(\overline{a})$$
(1)

Here, $\overline{a}$ is a collection of all the actions. a is any random action selected from all the actions.

We tested the method for 100 episodes. Each episode starts with the agent spawning at a random state. In this current state, the agent will perform some random action and move into the next state, based on the action the agent performed, the environment will return some reward. An episode will end when the agent successfully drops the passenger at the destination. This whole process will run for 100 episodes. Throughout the 100 episodes, no learning is happening and thus it is called the no reinforcement learning method.

3.2   Q-learning

Q-learning is another approach for solving the environment. The steps to solve the environment are the same as the steps that were in the no reinforcement learning method. The agent will perform some action on a state, on performing the action, the agent will move on to the next state and will get some reward from the environment. Through multiple interactions with the environment, the agent will gain experience and will seek the optimal strategy to solve the environment. You will again have a question that, what is the difference between no reinforcement learning and the Q-learning method? In this method every action the agent performs on a state, a value is calculated for that action and that value is stored in a table corresponding to the state in which currently the agent is and the active agent performs on that state. This table is called Q-Table. It records the quality of actions performed on states.

Before getting into Q-learning we have to create a Q-Table, Q(s,a). The size of the Q-Table will be $s \times a$. The Q-learning process consists of $< s, a, r, \ldots, \overline{s}, \overline{a} >$: $s = \{0, 1, 2, 3, \ldots, 498, 499\}$. Here, s is the collection of all the states. In our environment, we are having 500 states. $a = \{0, 1, 2, 3, 4, 5\}$, a is the collection of all the actions. In our environment, we are having six actions. $r = r(s, a)$ r is reward function, it will return the reward of taking action a under state s. α is the learning rate. $\alpha \in [0, 1]$. γ is the discount rate. $\gamma \in [0, 1]$ $\overline{a}$ is all the actions that can be performed under state s. $\overline{s}$ is the next state. Defining the Q-learning equation as follows in Eq. 2.

$$Q(s, a) \leftarrow Q(s, a) + \alpha \times [r + \gamma \times \max_{\overline{a}} Q(\overline{s}, \overline{a}) - Q(s, a)]$$
(2)

During the training period, in each episode, the values in the Q-table will continuously be updated using this equation. In the initial episodes, the agent will explore the environment by taking random actions, but after few episodes, the agent will start exploiting the environment. Now the agent will take the action based on the values in the Q-table. The agent will perform the action a which is having the maximum Q-value among all the other actions under that state s.

$$a \leftarrow argmax(Q(s,a)) \tag{3}$$

Now there must be a question that how to decide when to end the exploration and start the exploitation? The answer to this is, After some random exploration of actions, the q-values tend to converge which our agent will take as an action-value function and it can exploit to pick the most optimal action from a given state. There is a trade-off between exploration and exploitation. We want to prevent our agents from always taking the same route. So we introduce another parameter called epsilon. Instead of selecting the best-learned q-value, an agent will sometimes perform random action, i.e., it will explore the environment.

Initially, the epsilon value is set to 1, where $\epsilon \in [0,1]$. Our exploration-exploitation trade off value will be randomly selected from the range (0,1) at each time step. At any time step, if the value of the exploration-exploitation trade-off is greater than the epsilon, then the agent will start exploiting the environment. Else, the agent will explore the environment. After each episode, the epsilon value will decrease a little, as we are adding one more parameter called decay rate. Decay rate will make sure that the agent does not always explore the environment.

$$\epsilon \leftarrow min(\epsilon) + [max(\epsilon) - min(\epsilon)] \times e^{-decay\_rate \times episode} \tag{4}$$

Minimum and Maximum values of epsilon are variable, i.e., we can set the values of these parameters by testing the result with different values and comparing the results in the end. The values which gave optimal output can be set as min./max. epsilon value. In our case, the maximum value that epsilon can have is 1.0, and the min-max value can be any number between (0,1). After training is completed, the q-values will be updated in the q-table. Figures 2 and 3 shows the q-table before training and the q-table after training, respectively.

Now using this q-table, we can test our agent's performance. While testing the performance of the agent, the action 'a' that the agent will take under state s will be decided using this q-table. That action with the maximum q-value under state s will be the action that the agent will perform.

4   Experimental Results

Here, we will compare the results produced when using a no reinforcement learning methodology to our Q-learning agent. With Q-learning agent commit errors initially while exploring the environment but once it has explored enough, it

Q-Table		Actions					
		South (0)	North (1)	East (2)	West (3)	Pickup (4)	Drop off (5)
States	0	0	0	0	0	0	0
	...	...	...	...	...	...	...
	327	0	0	0	0	0	0
	...	...	...	...	...	...	...
	499	0	0	0	0	0	0

Fig. 2. Q-table initial values.

Q-Table		Actions					
		South (0)	North (1)	East (2)	West (3)	Pickup (4)	Drop off (5)
States	0	0	0	0	0	0	0
	...	...	...	...	...	...	...
	327	-2.30	-1.97	-2.30	-2.21	-10.36	-8.55
	...	...	...	...	...	...	...
	499	9.97	4.02	12.96	29	3.32	3.38

Fig. 3. Q-table updated values.

starts exploiting the environment and makes smart moves to reach the destination with high rewards and fewer penalties. Let's see how much better our Q-learning agent is when compared to the agent making just random moves. We evaluate our agents according to three metrics. First, an average number of penalties per episode: The smaller the number the better the performance of our agent. Ideally, we would like this metric to be zero or very close to zero. Second, the average number of time steps per trip: We want a small number of time steps per episode as well since we want to make our agent take minimum steps to reach our destination. Third, average rewards per move: The larger the reward means the agent is doing the right thing. That's why deciding rewards is a crucial part. In our case, as both timesteps and penalties are negatively rewarded, a higher average reward would mean that the agent reaches the destination as fast as possible with the least penalties.

Table 1. The evaluation results for $\alpha = 0.3$ and $\gamma = 0.2$

Measure	Random agent	Q-learning
Avg reward per move	−3.91	0.64
Avg # penalties per episode	62.51	0.0
AVg # timesteps per trip	192.37	12.80

Table 2. The evaluation results for $\alpha = 0.6$ and $\gamma = 0.2$

Measure	Random agent	Q-learning
Avg reward per move	−3.97	0.56
Avg # penalties per episode	65.99	0.0
AVg # timesteps per trip	192.22	13.40

These metrics were computed over 100 episodes. Here, you can observe that the average rewards per move of a random agent are negative i.e., an agent chooses the wrong direction many times while making a move as it doesn't learn anything from the environment where as Q-learning agent learns from the environment after each action and get higher rewards. The higher average reward would mean that the agent is reaching the destination as fast as possible. And you can also see that the average number of penalties per episode is 0 for Q-learning agent i.e., it can reach its destination without making any wrong steps whereas random agent makes many wrong steps and gets higher penalties. To complete

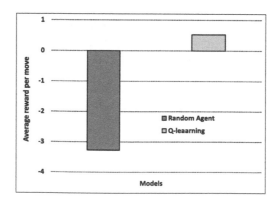

Fig. 4. Experimental results for average reward per move.

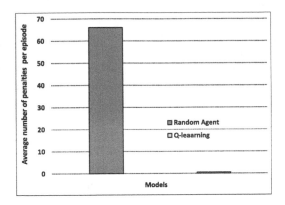

Fig. 5. Experimental results for average penalties per episode.

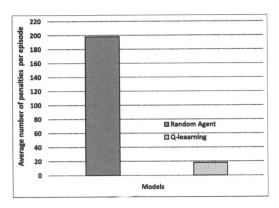

Fig. 6. Experimental results for average number of timesteps per episode.

one episode, a random agent took nearly 200 timesteps and also took more time whereas the Q-learning agent reached its destination on average 13 steps i.e., in a minimum number of steps. The following graphs show the performance of the model. Figure 4 shows the average reward per move for both models. Figure 5 shows an average number of penalties per episode for both models. Figure 6 shows an average number of timesteps per episode for both models.

5   Conclusion

In this paper, we have used the Q-learning method to solve the environment. The approach was very simple and easy to understand. As discussed above we are comparing the model without reinforcement learning and the model with reinforcement learning. Based on the Experimental results shown in Tables 1 and 2, Q-learning is better than no reinforcement learning because average timesteps per episode of Q-learning is less than no reinforcement learning and average rewards per move are also high for Q-learning agent and it has 0 penalties. Also by visualizing the results on a bar graph shown in Figs. 4, 5 and 6, we can say that the performance of the Q-learning agent was much better than the performance of the random agent. So we can conclude that the performance of the Q-learning model is better than the no reinforcement learning model. Now in the Q-learning model, we evaluated the performance with two different values of alpha and gamma. And by looking at the results show in Tables 1 and 2, we can conclude that low learning rate and low discount rate gave much optimal or better output. Limitations: The approach of solving the model was very simple as we used the deterministic approach and in the real world, there is stochasticity in the environment and this deterministic approach is not feasible for the real world.

References

1. Anh, M.N., Bien, D.X.: Voice recognition and inverse kinematics control for a redundant manipulator based on a multilayer artificial intelligence network. J. Robot. **2021**, 5805232 (2021)
2. Chopra, R., Roy, S.S.: End-to-end reinforcement learning for self-driving car. In: Pati, B., Panigrahi, C.R., Buyya, R., Li, K.-C. (eds.) Advanced Computing and Intelligent Engineering. AISC, vol. 1082, pp. 53–61. Springer, Singapore (2020). https://doi.org/10.1007/978-981-15-1081-6_5
3. Kendall, A., et al.: Learning to drive in a day. In: 2019 International Conference on Robotics and Automation (ICRA), pp. 8248–8254. IEEE (2019)
4. Keysers, D., Deselaers, T., Gollan, C., Ney, H.: Deformation models for image recognition. IEEE Trans. Pattern Anal. Mach. Intell. **29**(8), 1422–1435 (2007)
5. Memon, Q., Ahmed, M., Ali, S., Memon, A.R., Shah, W.: Self-driving and driver relaxing vehicle. In: 2016 2nd International Conference on Robotics and Artificial Intelligence (ICRAI), pp. 170–174. IEEE (2016)
6. Mishra, S., Thakkar, H., Mallick, P.K., Tiwari, P., Alamri, A.: A sustainable IOHT based computationally intelligent healthcare monitoring system for lung cancer risk detection. Sustain. Cities Soc. **72**, 103079 (2021)
7. Prudhvi, K., Bharath Chowdary, A., Subba Rami Reddy, P., Lakshmi Prasanna, P.: Text summarization using natural language processing. In: Satapathy, S.C., Bhateja, V., Janakiramaiah, B., Chen, Y.-W. (eds.) Intelligent System Design. AISC, vol. 1171, pp. 535–547. Springer, Singapore (2021). https://doi.org/10.1007/978-981-15-5400-1_54
8. Rai, D., Thakkar, H.K., Rajput, S.S., Santamaria, J., Bhatt, C., Roca, F.: A comprehensive review on seismocardiogram: current advancements on acquisition, annotation, and applications. Mathematics **9**(18), 2243 (2021)
9. Sallab, A.E., Abdou, M., Perot, E., Yogamani, S.: Deep reinforcement learning framework for autonomous driving. Electron. Imaging **2017**(19), 70–76 (2017)
10. Thakkar, H.K., Dehury, C.K., Sahoo, P.K.: MUVINE: multi-stage virtual network embedding in cloud data centers using reinforcement learning-based predictions. IEEE J. Sel. Areas Commun. **38**(6), 1058–1074 (2020)
11. Thakkar, H.K., Liao, W.w., Wu, C.y., Hsieh, Y.W., Lee, T.H.: Predicting clinically significant motor function improvement after contemporary task-oriented interventions using machine learning approaches. J. NeuroEngineering Rehabil. **17**(1), 1–10 (2020)

12. Thakkar, H.K., Sahoo, P.K.: Towards automatic and fast annotation of seismocar-diogram signals using machine learning. IEEE Sens. J. **20**(5), 2578–2589 (2019)
13. Thakkar, H.K., Sahoo, P.K., Mohanty, P.: DOFM: domain feature miner for robust extractive summarization. Inf. Process. Manage. **58**(3), 102474 (2021)
14. Thakkar, H.K., Shukla, H., Patil, S.: A comparative analysis of machine learning classifiers for robust heart disease prediction. In: 2020 IEEE 17th India Council International Conference (INDICON), pp. 1–6. IEEE (2020)
15. Tripathy, H.K., Mishra, S., Thakkar, H.K., Rai, D.: Care: a collision-aware mobile robot navigation in grid environment using improved breadth first search. Comput. Electr. Eng. **94**, 107327 (2021)
16. Wang, P., Chan, C.Y., de La Fortelle, A.: A reinforcement learning based app-roach for automated lane change maneuvers. In: 2018 IEEE Intelligent Vehicles Symposium (IV), pp. 1379–1384. IEEE (2018)
17. Zhang, Q., Du, T., Tian, C.: Self-driving scale car trained by deep reinforcement learning. arXiv preprint arXiv:1909.03467 (2019)

Automating Paid Parking System Using IoT Technology

Ankit Desai[1(✉)], Anurag Deotale[2], Atharva Bapat[2],
and Chaitanya Khinvasara[3]

[1] IIM, Ahmedabad, Gujrat 380015, India
[2] VIT, Pune, Maharashtra 411037, India
[3] University of Southern California, Los Angeles, CA 90007, USA

Abstract. The system aims to propose an efficient pay and park method developed based on use of domains like deep learning, server and app management. The system so developed detects entry of vehicle in parking facility. The database is created and modified with each incoming car and registrations in the system. The user can register his all the vehicles in the system database through an android based PayPark app. The app incorporates Google Pay services to provide the user with a safe and secure payment facility. At the entry and exit of a parking facility, the vehicle is detected along with the time for which it was parked. The corresponding entries are made in the database and saved. Through the PayPark app the charges are deducted from a pre- registered app user. The charges deduction is depending on the time for which the vehicle uses parking facility.

Keywords: Deep learning · Android app development · Server management · IoT

1 Introduction

Stepping forward in the complete new Technology driven generation of interconnected things, the world has moved past the limits that allows you to create an intelligent area and lead a smart life-style. We are hastily adapting to the constantly evolving generation at a quicker pace than ever, consequently marking the generation of smart city that has been dreamt since. As the technology is growing rapidly and along with the increase in the number of vehicles there is burden on the parking facility. Every time a vehicle enters a parking lot it has wait to take the parking ticket and because the waiting time increases, the queue will increase, and this causes waste of time. So, if we have parking space statistics, we will plan for increase parking space need based totally on our requirement. Along with waiting time we have another problem i.e., we need to traverse through multiple parking slots so that we can find free parking slot, and this becomes a tedious problem too. To overcome these problems, there is a need for an

D. Garg et al. (Eds.): IACC 2021, CCIS 1528, pp. 410–418, 2022.
https://doi.org/10.1007/978-3-030-95502-1_31

automated parking system that helps in efficient parking and keeping human intervention minimum. This problem can be addressed through the use of IOT (Internet of Things).

Internet of Things can be stated as Real Objects along with the use of sensors and controllers that have the ability to transfer data over a network without requiring human-to-human interaction. The most critical factors for the emergence of smart cities are systematic parking structures. due to the advancements inside the sensor technology and the low-price capabilities of the Embedded systems, we say that systems can be created using internet of things.

Here our proposed idea will be applied using a smartphone, so the consumer of application can get their parking data and reserve the vacant spaces over internet. Due to the fact that smartphones and internet has come to be the basic necessity of the modern lifestyle.

2 Literature Review

Singh, H – "An IOT -based E-Parking System for Smart Cities" This system talks about automated parking system which eliminates the space problems and human intervention. Booking for parking slots is done through Bluetooth device, as each Bluetooth device has unique registration number.

Mr. Basavaraju S R – "Automatic Smart Parking System using Internet of Things" - This system helps the user to find the nearest parking spot and gives availability of parking slots in that respective parking area and it also avoids the unnecessary traversing the entire parking slots in a parking area [13].

M Kumar Gandhi – "A Prototype for IoT based Car Parking Management System for Smart Cities" - In this paper, user can book slots. Space depending upon the availability. Use of IOT is for processing and collection of data. This system is flexible and handles issues of theft.

Abhirup Khana, Rishi Anand – "IoT based Smart Parking System" - This system is used to check the availability of parking slots in the area.

3 Architectural Diagram

See Fig. 1.

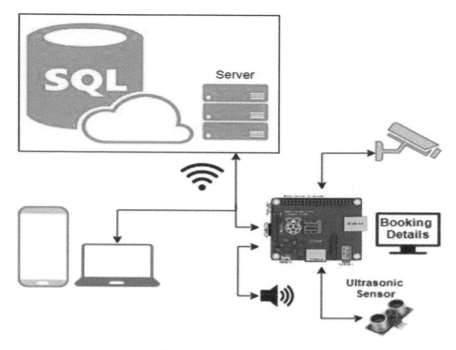

Fig. 1. Architectural diagram

4 Proposed Model

The mentioned system can be categorized in two parts as - Real time number plate detection and character extraction. Server, database and app management.

The system works using two cameras, one at entry point and another at exit point. Vehicle is detected at entry of parking facility through a number plate. The number from number plate is sent to the parking system server which adds it in the database with date and time. The database is formed and appended with each new user account registration. The owner of the vehicle number so detected is identified in database. The modification is made under the user ID profile and updated through a mobile server in the PayPark app. The PayPark app is the part of system introduced to provide an efficient, safe and secure account management for user. On detection of same number at the exit point, the same process is repeated, and the bill is generated according to the time for which it was parked. For adding balance, Google Pay services have been integrated in the PayPark app. A predefined amount is deducted according to client's requirements depending on car parking time.

Number plate detection and extraction using computer vision is very difficult when the vehicle color and color of number plate is same [11]. So, for vehicle number plate detection and extraction convolutional neural network (CNN) [3, 4] and Region Proposal Network (RPN) [2] are implemented using TensorFlow API. Database management is implemented on MySQL. App management with server and database has back end programming in PHP [6]. Server management is the key area which is implemented using an online server. The two main parts i.e. the part of deep learning and user interaction are connected through the server and database.

4.1 Classification of Vehicles

Two classes are created Bike and Car. Around 400 images are used for training both classes. Model is created using 'KERAS' API. Model created contained 3 convolution layers and 2 hidden layers. First hidden layer is activation function called RELU (Rectified linear Unit). Second Hidden layer uses SoftMax.

Model uses Adam Optimizer is used for error back propagation between expected output and found output. Loss function is categorical cross entropy. Model is trained for 100 steps. The classifier gives around 96% accuracy.

4.2 Real Time Number Plate Detection

The real time number plate detection is a key factor for the flawless system working. for neural network construction Faster R-CNN architecture is used. The image dataset consisting of 330 images of number plates was used for training a neural network [1, 2].

Dataset Preparation
To prepare dataset 330 images were used as input. We followed the following steps to prepare the dataset. Step 1 – The images were labelled according to the location of number plate in that image using image annotation tool. Step 2 – The labelled images then converted into an.xml file. Step 3 – A '.csv' file is created for all the images combined which has 4 columns, name, height and width and co-ordinates where the number plate is located in that image. Step 4 – This file is converted to 'tf.record' and then fed to TensorFlow API as an input.

Region Proposal Network
RPN moves a 3 * 3 sliding window over feature map and maps it to lower dimension. For each sliding-window location, it generates multiple possible regions where number plate might be located. For each region proposed, there is a fixed "objectness" score assigned and the 4 co-ordinates of that bounding box are obtained. Figure 2 shows objectness loss which shows reduction in error between expected value on objectness value obtained. In other words, it looks at each location in last feature map and consider different boxes centered around it. For each of those boxes, it is determined whether it contains the number plate or not and what co-ordinates are for that box [2].

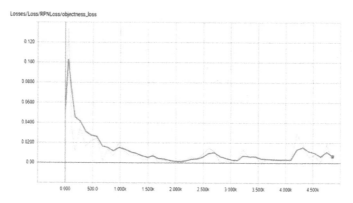

Fig. 2. Objectness loss

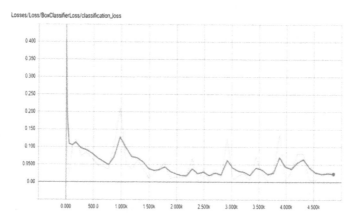

Fig. 3. Classifier loss

Convolutional Neural Network

RPN proposes the regions of the boxes which is worked up on by the CNN [4]. It takes these regions as input and works as a classifier to determine whether there is number plate in the region or not. It gives a confidence value as output which shows the possibility of a number plate being present in a particular region of interest [3]. Figure 3 shows the classifier output for the dataset that shows loss in the error of classifier after nearly 5000 steps. Considering the objectness loss output and classifier loss, total loss function for the used neural network to detect a number plate in a live video can be calculated [5]. Total loss function shows entire system loss including classification and RPN. Figure 4 shows total loss of the system in number plate detection.

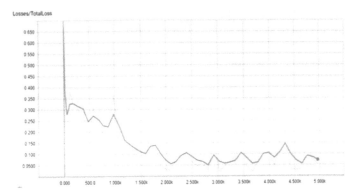

Fig. 4. Total loss

4.3   Character Segmentation and Recognition

Tesseract is open-source OCR engine that was developed in one of labs of HP from 1984 to 1994. It was one of best in 1995 UNLV Annual Accuracy Test of OCR. In 2005, HP publicly released Tesseract. Tesseract has multilingual support, and provides easy to use libraries for these supported languages [9]. In addition, it also provides methods for training of custom character sets as per the requirements (Fig. 5).

Fig. 5. Character segmentation

The Tesseract engine was created with aim of recognizing printed text, but constant efforts are being made to use it for recognizing character from other sources [10]. For text gathered from other sources such as sensors, images etc., we first use image processing to remove noise and convert image into either black or white depending on the image.

Initially, the image of number plate is scaled to 1200 by 300 pixels to make it uniform for all future image processing. Then the image is converted to grayscale and bilateral filter is applied to smoothen the image. During image processing, the character segmentation is performed based on the area of each contour detected [8]. This allows to filter out unwanted contours detected for objects such as screws, etc. Then using canny edge filter and contour detection all the shapes and characters are detected. All the shapes are sorted based on area and only those are selected whose area is between lies between 90,000 and 900. After this only character remain whose bounding box is found to separate them.

All the characters segmented previously are scaled to 100 by 100 pixels and a white border of width 20 pixels is added on all sides. This image of each character is feed to tesseract OCR engine. List of whitelists characters is also provided to it. This results in more accurate results.

4.4 IOT Using RPi

In parking, raspberry pi (RPi) acts as controller for gathering information from the arrived vehicle as well as the parking itself. RPi has a connected camera to record an image of the arrived vehicle [12]. All this processing such as vehicle classification and number plate detection is done remotely, on a server to reduce processing on RPi. After all the processing is done, the details are confirmed with user before his/her entry. In the parking premises, to ensure whether the vehicle is parked properly or not, we use metal wedges and ultrasonic sensors. The lateral boundary is restricted using metal wedges which are kept parallel to each other, while to make sure that the vehicle is not crossing its frontal and pivotal boundaries of parking, ultrasonic sensors are used. If the ultrasound detects a vehicle, then the sensor sets echo to 1, to indicate vehicle detection. If a vehicle is detected, then the buzzer is on notifying vehicle is not parked correctly.

4.5 PayPark Application

PayPark application is introduced as a part of this system to provide user with an interface to access the system facilities. PayPark application is developed on android studio. To avail the services of auto pay and park facility, user should register in the system using this application. While registration, user can give information about more than one vehicle under his ID. App has incorporated Google Pay Services for safe, secure and reliable payment. It can be used to add balance in the app wallet as per user convenience and all the stored data about a vehicle's entries can be viewed anytime. At the exit point, if the enough balance is not present in the user's account, it can be refilled easily [7].

5 Observations and Results

The number plate detection system has a detection accuracy of around 98–99%. If the number plate is in front of the camera it is detected and highlighted with a box around it. In live video, the timespan between two consecutive character string generation is approximately 0.8 s i.e. every 0.8 s, a new string is generated in the character recognition system.

The character recognition system's accuracy is affected by technical constraints like processing power requirement for training a large dataset and camera quality resolution. Figure 6 shows the output of the strings recorded when the frame having number "MH12DS2666" was tried to be detected.

Fig. 6. Number plate detection

6 Conclusion

The main motive of this model is to develop a smart parking system with the help of Internet of Things which reduces human intervention and provides an efficient way to park vehicles. The system extracts number plates from a live video with a good accuracy. Some technical constraints like processing power for training a neural network and camera resolution quality have altered the character recognition accuracy from live video template which can be worked upon. Using a smartphone application for reserving a parking space has resulted in ease of use of the user and enablement of online payment adds on the amazing end user experience. Here, we have enchased cost effectiveness, ease of use and low maintenance features of Raspberry-pi [13]. The PayPark application have successfully incorporated Google Pay Services to provide safe and secure funds transfer and easy to use. The system can be used by airports, multiplexes, big residential societies and even at offices.

7 Future Scope

In future, certain changes can be incorporated as per the requirements of the organizations implementing the system. Various tools and algorithms can be used to analyze the data and implement dynamic pricing. The model can be converted to a transfer-learning model so that it can learn continuously from the data being gathered during its working. The proposed model can be further extended to public places and open parking. Also, the mobile application can be built to support all platforms and not just android. The parking reservation support can be further extended as a website to increase the platform reach.

References

1. Ozbay, S., Ercelebi, E.: Automatic vehicle identification by plate recognition. World. Acad. Sci. Eng. Technol. Int. J. Comput. Inf. Eng. **1**, 1–9 (2007)
2. Ren, S., He, K., Girshick, R., Sun, J.: Faster R- CNN: towards real-time object detection with region proposal networks. IEEE Trans. Pattern Anal. Mach. Intell. **39**(6), 1137–1149 (2017)
3. Lecun, Y., Bottou, L., Bengio, Y., Haffner, P.: Gradient-based learning applied to document recognition. Proc. IEEE **86**(11), 2278–2324 (1998). https://doi.org/10.1109/5.726791
4. Zeiler, M.D., Fergus, R.: Visualizing and understanding convolutional networks. In: Fleet, D., Pajdla, T., Schiele, B., Tuytelaars, T. (eds.) Computer Vision – ECCV 2014: 13th European Conference, Zurich, Switzerland, September 6-12, 2014, Proceedings, Part I, pp. 818–833. Springer International Publishing, Cham (2014). https://doi.org/10.1007/978-3-319-10590-1_53
5. Yusnita, R., Norbaya, F., Bashruddin, N.: Intelligent parking space detection system based on image processing. Int. J. Innov. Manage. Technol. **3**, 232–235 (2012)
6. Maggo, S., Aswani, R.: AutoPark: a sensor based automated, secure and secure efficient parking guidance system. India IOSR J. Comput. Eng. (IOSRJCE) **8**(3), 47–56 (2013)
7. Android app development documentation. https://developer.android.com/reference/packag
8. Wang, J., Zhou, W., Xue, J., Liu, X.: The research and realization of vehicle license plate character segmentation and recognition technology. In: 2010 International Conference on Wavelet Analysis and Pattern Recognition, Qingdao, 11–14 July 2010
9. Smith, R.: An overview of the Tesseract OCR engine in ninth international conference on document analysis and recognition (ICDAR 2007)
10. Li, Q., An, W., Zhou, A., Ma, L.: Recognition of offline handwritten Chinese characters using the Tesseract open source OCR engine. In: 2016 8th International Conference on Intelligent Human-Machine Systems and Cybernetics (2016)
11. Yang, J., Hu, B., Yu, J., An, J., Xiong, G.: A License Plate Recognition System Based on Machine Vision. In: IEEE 978–1–4799–0530–0/13
12. Smart Parking Assist System using Internet of Things (IoT), Int. J. Control Theory App. **9**, 40 (2016)
13. Basavaraju, S.R.: Automatic smart parking system using Internet of Things (IoT). Int. J. Sci. Res. Publ. **5**(12), 1–10 (2015)

Farmers' Survey App - An Interactive Open-Source Application for Agricultural Survey

Aditya Ghodgaonkar[1]([✉]), Bhavya Surana[1], Parteek Kumar[1], Karun Verma[1], Balakrishna Kommanaboina[1], and Yosi Shacham-Diamand[2]

[1] TIET-TAU Center of Excellence for Food Security, Thapar Institute of Engineering and Technology, Patiala, Punjab, India
Aghodgaonkar_me20@thapar.edu
[2] TIET-TAU Center of Excellence for Food Security, Tel Aviv University, Ramat Aviv, Israel

Abstract. Agricultural sector has become an indispensable part of the Indian economy. In the past few years, traditional methods of agriculture have fraternized with technological solutions. This marked the beginning of precision agriculture. In perpetuation of these efforts, this study introduces a survey application that gives a new definition to surveys and other manual methods of data collection. Data collected through Drones and IoT sensors are often the most reliable and preferred choice while working with agriculture data, but these methods often ignore the knowledge and experience of a farmer. Field surveys ensure that the minute details and knowledge of farmers are captured properly. This study introduces a mobile-based application - "Survey App" to conduct field surveys in remote locations and further outlines a model through which the collected data could be analyzed. The presented research paper lays down the underlying architecture of the application and the implementation details. This application intends to provide a free open-source framework to conduct agriculture surveys. Additionally, to back the theoretical framework of this paper, a real-time case study has been presented to showcase the advantages of field surveys and mobile applications in such scenarios. The data analysis model presented in this study is further implemented in the Digital Village Project at TIET-TAU Center of Excellence for Food Security.

Keywords: Agricultural survey · Mobile application · Precision agriculture · Cloud data analysis

1 Introduction

Precision Agriculture is the decade's most valuable innovation. Its amalgamation with traditional agricultural practices has paved novel ways of crop management through Information and Communication Technologies. In traditional farming

D. Garg et al. (Eds.): IACC 2021, CCIS 1528, pp. 419–430, 2022.
https://doi.org/10.1007/978-3-030-95502-1_32

techniques, many variables are involved such as lack of expertise, equipment usage, funds, labor skills, etc. These variables are often ignored when data is collected through Drones, IoT sensors, and Satellites [1,2]. It is then the need for field surveys comes into the picture. From time to time if field surveys are conducted, then the collected data could prove to be a powerful tool to study important parameters involved in agriculture. If the knowledge and experience of farmers could be channelized through technological means then this can prevent the degradation of soil, increase agricultural productivity, detect plant diseases, and do great wonders [3]. Thus, there is an inevitable need to re-adopt surveying with a modern touch of technology. Thus, the agricultural data must be collected through surveys to derive important findings [4]. Survey data can assist farmers in identifying techniques that led to increased production and profits. Moreover, the data captured through surveys could be used as a training repository for machine learning algorithms, thus in turn it helps in Precision agriculture [5]. In the agricultural sector, most of the surveys are collected manually by a field engineer, which means a person will go to farms and fill the information using pen and paper; then this data is entered manually to excel sheets for further analysis. Manual data collection and data entry has their consequences, a lot of errors and fallacies get added unintentionally to the data [6]. To address this problem, we built a mobile-based survey application as a part of the Digital Village Project [7]. This Android application can collect field data in a phased manner i.e. weekly, monthly, and seasonal progress of crops could be captured through the developed application. The developed application captures information of fields right from the land preparation to the harvesting, and the collected data get collected on a secure cloud from where it could be downloaded in form of CSV files and further analysis becomes easy. The whole process of data analysis through the developed application- Survey App becomes swift and error less. Currently, a multitude of applications are available in the app market such as SurveyCTO [8], Zoho forms [9], etc. But most of these app services charge users heavily or demand subscriptions. Keeping the Indian scenario in mind, the developed application is open-source and offers all its services free of cost. The application features an Interactive GUI and is extensible. To use the application for conducting surveys in chosen fields of Patiala (Punjab, India) some field engineers were hired. These field engineers surveyed around 60 fields of Patiala using the developed Survey App. The application uses in-app verification techniques to validate the authenticity of data collected by a surveyor. Hence, the data presented in this study and its analysis could be used as a reference to work in Indian fields. Additionally, these forms record various field information - crop details, fertilizer details, pesticide details, machinery details, etc. In Sect. 2 of this study, some of the distinct key features of the developed Survey App have been presented. Further, Sect. 3 pinpoints the architectural dynamics of the application and summarizes the different kinds of surveys that can be taken through the app. Ultimately, in Sect. 4 a real-time case study is discussed to give the reader a wholesome idea of the application and the succeeding data analysis.

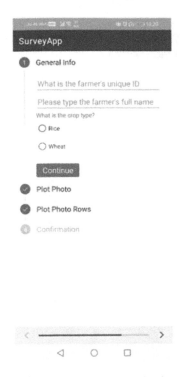

Fig. 1. Vertical stepping layout of forms in the Survey App

2   Key Features of the Android Application

Survey App offers a unique set of features to serve Indian researchers working in the field of Precision Agriculture. Some of the key features offered by the developed application are as follows:

– **Open Source** - The competitors such as SurveyCTO, Zoho forms [8,9] could not be extended or customized at the programming level because these are closed source apps. But the Survey App is free-to-use software, and the users of the app are not charged in any way. The entire source code of the application is available on GitHub for contributions and extensions.
– **Interactive** - The application has been designed based on Google's Material design guidelines, hence the Survey App is more interactive and even the farmers can fill their field's data through the app in a hassle-free manner.
– **Secure** - The application uses Firebase Real-time database and Storage for its data transactions. Hence, the security of the app is enforced by server-side rules. Also, the data is securely pushed to the cloud.
– **Vertical Stepper Layout** - Instead of burdening the user with the whole form, the application uses a modified version of Vertical Stepper API [10] to display instances of forms. For instance, Fig. 1 shows one of the forms designed

Fig. 2. Real time validation of images in the Survey App

using the modified vertical stepper API. This makes the whole process of filling forms easy and more interactive.

- **Real-time data validation** - One of the main features of this application is to validate images and data with the field coordinates in real-time. For instance, when a farmer uploads a cropped image of his field the application captures the current GPS coordinates and uses an algorithm based on Geo-location API [11] to validate the authenticity of the image and data. If the images or data is not captured at the respective field of the farmer an exception is thrown. The usage of mobile applications for collecting GPS coordinates reduces the redundancy of using external GPS devices, which are frequently used in surveys [12]. The whole process of authenticating a captured image is shown in Fig. 2.
- **Wide Range of Surveys** - At present, the app features 6 different surveys. The app can easily be customized at the programming level to add more surveys.
- **In-app Image Capture Module** - The app also flaunts an image capture module that is used for capturing images of crops, fields, machinery, and

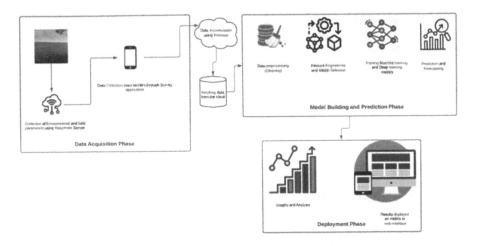

Fig. 3. Survey App in the overall architecture of Digital Village Project

other relevant objects. This module then stores the images on the cloud. The captured images are first compressed before they are sent to the Firebase storage. This reduces the data usage of the application, considering the remote locations of farmer fields.

3   Application Interface and Architecture of Survey App

3.1   Application Interface

In this section, each component of the Application Interface is explained in detail along with steps to navigate through the application from a users' point of view. The Survey App presented in this study will be used as one of the methods of data collection in the Data acquisition phase of the Digital Village Project [7] as highlighted in Fig. 3.

The Digital village project aims at incorporating the latest trends and techniques of modern-day agriculture in a phased manner. This application will play a key role in the Data Acquisition phase of the Digital Village Project. The mobile app will be a one-stop destination for researchers and farmers. Surveyors or Field Engineers will feed field data using the app. Based on the cropping season, a specific form will be filled. Thus, the forms featured in the application relate to each other, this can be explained in the systematic study on Digital Village Project.

The developed application will take the following surveys:

– **Farmer's Profile Survey** - This survey is a one-time registration form. Whenever some farmer gets associated with the project his important details such as - Farmer Name, District, Village, Household information, Plot Information, etc. are collected through this survey.

- **Plot Tracker Survey** - In succession to Farmer's survey, a plot tracker survey is taken. This form collects details such as the Plot Status, Plot Pictures, Method of irrigation used in the field, crop details, cropping season, and other relevant cropping information. It also captures information on water sources and specifications of machinery used on the field etc. Relevant Pictures of the field and machinery are also taken through this survey.
- **Weekly Surveys** - There are two weekly surveys on the application namely - Weekly Survey 1 and Weekly Survey 2. These surveys run every week and are conducted on the same day.
- **Weekly Survey 1** - This survey captures before and after plantation details. Information about Irrigation, Fertilizers, Weedicides, Herbicides, General Work, Machinery used, Harvesting, and marketing information is captured through this survey.
- **Weekly Survey 2** - This is also a weekly survey undertaken to capture general cropping information and crop measurements. Data such as the average height of the plant, the number of leaves, etc. are collected in weekly survey 2. These surveys are very useful in monitoring the growth of crops. Hence, these surveys mainly focus on the after-plantation parameters.
- **Crop Disease Surveys** - Damages to crops can occur anytime. Through this survey details of crop damage such as - number of damaged crops and their respective images are captured. This data could further be used to train machine learning models.
- **Image Capture Module** - This module is used when some images or data is required that cannot fit any of the above forms. So all the additional information, images are captured through this form. This module also validates the location of the captured images.
- **Crop Measurement Module** - Traditionally, the height of the plant is measured using a yardstick. Since Precision Agriculture involves collecting data precisely, The height of each plant needs to be observed throughout the crop lifetime. The height of the wheat plant is measured using FREE- MANS IKON 7.5 m × 25 mm Blade Measurement Tape. This tool helps to measure even the parts of a plant such as a spike, leaf, stalk including the overall plant. There are other tools or techniques which give plant height more accurately but a strenuous process [13]. The details are filled in the application as shown in Fig. 4.

These surveys are conducted in a pre-planned manner. The Schedule of these surveys based on the Indian cropping season is depicted in Fig. 5. The survey App showcasing these surveys can be seen in Fig. 6.

3.2   The Architecture of the Survey App

The architecture of the developed Survey App is depicted in Fig. 7. The interfaces offered through the application have been discussed in part A of this section. If the user of the app selects the option to fill a survey form, then he is presented with survey forms in the vertical stepper interface. On submitting the form,

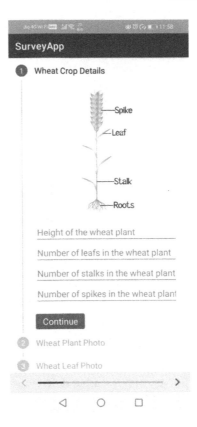

Fig. 4. Crop measurement survey in Survey App

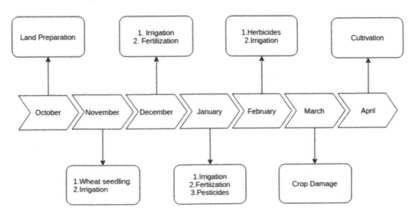

Fig. 5. Schedule for conducting different surveys enlisted in Sect. 3 for the Wheat crop.

the values get stored in Firebase RealTime Database. All the images captured through the application's Image Capture module are stored on Firebase Storage. These images are compressed and validated using a Geolocation Module before

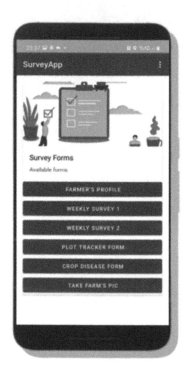

Fig. 6. Survey App featuring different surveys.

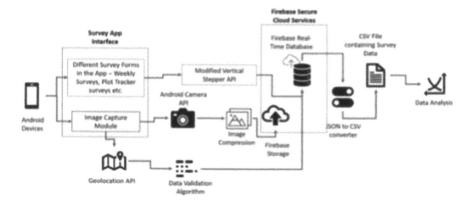

Fig. 7. Architecture of the Survey App.

they are pushed to the cloud. In the cloud, JSON files are collected and subjected to a customized JSON to CSV converter. This converter converts JSON data into CSV files which can be downloaded from the Admin Dashboard.

These files are then given to the Data Scientists who further analyze them and infer useful results.

4   Case Study: Analysis of Survey Data

As mentioned this Mobile App has been developed as part of the ongoing Digital Village Project [7] for conducting surveys in chosen fields of Patiala (Punjab, India). We have analyzed the data collected through this app from various farmers to get the on-field information. In the section, we are presenting the insights of data collection for the wheat crop during the 'Rabi' season i.e. between October to April 2021 from the fields of a village near Patiala. The timeline of various activities carried by farmers for the wheat crop is shown in Fig. 5. The whole data is analyzed based on per acre of the field. Some of the insights from this data analysis have been given below.

- **Land Preparation** - It has been observed that land is prepared in two phases by the farmers for the wheat crop. In the first phase, the crop residuals of the previous crop have been destroyed [14] by using a paddy destroyer and after this plowing has been performed by using tractors and land labeling has been performed by using laser technique.
- **Use of Fertilizers, Pesticides, Herbicides** - Since the data has been captured every week by conducting weekly surveys and from this we can analyze the average consumption of fertilizers, pesticides, and herbicides on a per-acre basis in different fields. This data is very vital to understand the over or under consumption of fertilizers, pesticides, and herbicides in the fields. This will further help to investigate the reduction in usage of these chemicals in the fields after implementing Precision agriculture in the fields [15, 16].
- **Irrigation** - We are also able to analyze the exact use of the water for the whole irrigation cycle of the wheat crop by using these surveys. Since we have stored the information about the irrigation sources used by the farmers in the Plot Tracker Survey and we are also collecting the amount of time taken for irrigation by the farmers on the daily basis through weekly surveys, this way we can know the exact amount of water used by the farmer for a whole crop cycle. This information is very vital to understand the usage of water resources for irrigation. The idea is also to measure the impact of implementing PA in the fields in turn reducing food insecurity [17], by measuring the consumption of water before the implementation of PA and after implementing PA in the fields to know the overall saving of natural resources due to PA.
- **Crop Damage** - We are also storing the information of crop damage if any due to bad weather [18], due to disease, or due to weed, animals [19], etc. during the whole cycle. This data is helpful to understand the damage incurred to farmers and will also be useful for insurance companies and government agencies to decide about the compensation to the farmers. This data is also vital to the impact of implementing artificial intelligence-based early detection systems for weed and disease detection in the fields.
- **Growth of Crops** - The growth of crops is also measured on the weekly basis by capturing the size spikes, leaves, and stalks as shown in Fig. 4 every week. This data is helpful to decide about the overall health and growth of

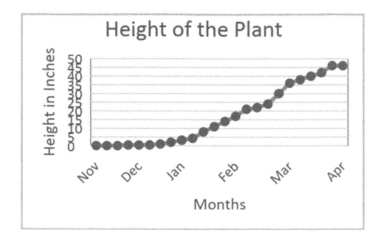

Fig. 8. Illustration of plant growth (in inches) through-out the crop season.

crops in the fields. This information can be used to alert the farmers about the need for possible intervention [20]. The data collected for crop growth indicates its growth with time as shown in Fig. 8. This information is also helpful to decide about the time of harvesting.

- **Overall Revenue to Farmers** - Through these surveys, we are also capturing the information of all the input costs incurred to farmers at various stages of the crop cycle and we are also storing the revenue information by the sale of the yield. Thus, we are also able to know the exact profit or loss to the farmers after the crop cycle. This data is very vital to understand how PA is helping the farmer to raise his income. Since we are storing the yield information, it also helped to build futuristic machine learning-based yield prediction systems.

We can conclude that this data analysis shows that these survey forms are very vital to get on-ground information about the crops and to analyze the impact of implementing PA in the fields.

5 Conclusion

It has been concluded that modern agriculture is driven by continuous improvements in digital tools. In today's scenario, sensor-based data collection methods have cascaded the potential of surveys and old methods of data collection. In this study, a surveying application has been presented. The open-source app can be used in Indian scenarios to capture before and after plantation details of crop fields. It offers out-of-the-box features to the farmers living in remote regions of the country. This study presents the application framework and talks in-depth about the developed application's features and surveys so that other researchers could implement it in their project and ripe out benefits. A case study has also been presented in the study to showcase a real-time implementation of the application and the data analysis that flows with it. This case study helps in understanding the operations that need to be performed on data collected through surveys; it starts with data preparation and delves deeper with an analysis of important parameters. On a side note, the survey data collected from this application is used in the TIET-TAU Digital Village project's data acquisition phase [7].

Acknowledgement. This work was supported by Thapar-TAU Center for Excellence in Food Security (T2CEFS), under research project "A Data-Driven Approach to Precision Agriculture in Small Farms Project".

References

1. Tsouros, D.C., Triantafyllou, A., Bibi, S., Sarigannidis, P.G.: Data acquisition and analysis methods in UAV-based applications for precision agriculture. In: 2019 15th International Conference on Distributed Computing in Sensor Systems (DCOSS), pp. 377–384 (2019)
2. Sishodia, R.P., Ray, R.L., Singh, S.K.: Applications of remote sensing in precision agriculture: a review. Remote Sens. **12**(19) (2020). https://www.mdpi.com/2072-4292/12/19/3136
3. Bolfe, L., et al.: Precision and digital agriculture: adoption of technologies and perception of Brazilian farmers. Agriculture **10**(12) (2020). https://www.mdpi.com/2077-0472/10/12/653
4. Friedman, S.: A farmer's perspective: 4 reasons why collecting data is important (2015). http://blogs.edf.org/growingreturns/2015/02/11/a-farmers-perspective-4-reasons-why-collecting-data-is-important/. Accessed 27 May 2021
5. Patel, H., Patel, D.: Survey of android apps for agriculture sector. Int. J. Inf. Sci. Tech. **6**, 61–67 (2016)
6. National Research Council (U.S.): Understanding American Agriculture: Challenges for the Agricultural Resource Management Survey. The National Academies Press, Washington, DC (2008). https://www.nap.edu/catalog/11990/understanding-american-agriculture-challenges-for-the-agricultural-resource-management-survey
7. Fishman, R., et al.: Digital villages: a data-driven approach to precision agriculture in small farms. In: Proceedings of the 9th International Conference on Sensor Networks - WSN4PA, INSTICC. SciTePress, pp. 161–166 (2020)
8. Christopher Robert, L.L.: Survey CTO - because we care about your data, too. https://www.surveycto.com/. Accessed 27 May 2021
9. Sridhar Vembu, S.K.T.T., Thomas, T.G.: Zoho forms - simplify data collection with online forms. https://www.zoho.com/forms/. Accessed 27 May 2021
10. Google-LLC. API reference for angular material stepper. https://material.angular.io/components/stepper/api. Accessed 7 June 2021
11. Google-developers. Geolocation API. https://developers.google.com/maps/documentation/geocoding/overview. Accessed 7 June 2021
12. DD-Larix-LLC. Selecting the right GPS receiver for your job. http://resource-analysis.com/geospatial/gps-collection-devices/. Accessed 7 June 2021

13. Yuan, W., Li, J., Bhatta, M., Shi, Y., Baenziger, P.S., Ge, Y.: Wheat height estimation using LiDAR in comparison to ultrasonic sensor and UAS. Sensors **18**(11), 3731 (2018). https://www.mdpi.com/1424-8220/18/11/3731
14. Shibusawa, S., Hache, C.: Data collection and analysis methods for data from field experiments (2020)
15. Bryce, E.: Here's how precision agriculture could help farmers reduce fertilizer use (2019). https://www.anthropocenemagazine.org/2019/04/heres-how-precision-agriculture-could-help-farmers-reduce-fertilizer-use/. Accessed 7 June 2021
16. Balafoutis, A., et al.: Precision agriculture technologies positively contributing to GHG emissions mitigation, farm productivity and economics. Sustainability **9**(8), 1339 (2017). https://www.mdpi.com/2071-1050/9/8/1339
17. Mungarwal, A.K., Mehta, S.: Why farmers today need to take up precision farming (2019). https://www.downtoearth.org.in/blog/agriculture/why-farmers-today-need-to-take-up-precision-farming-64659. Accessed 7 June 2021
18. Mauldin, M.: Excessive rain creates many problems for growers (2013). https://nwdistrict.ifas.ufl.edu/phag/2013/07/12/excessive-rain-creates-many-problems-for-growers/. Accessed 7 June 2021
19. Rao, K., Maikhuri, R., Nautiyal, S., Saxena, K.: Crop damage and livestock depredation by wildlife: a case study from Nanda Devi biosphere reserve, India. J. Environ. Manage. **66**(3), 317–327 (2002). https://www.sciencedirect.com/science/article/pii/S0301479702905876
20. Folnovic, T.: Benefits of using precision farming: producing more with less. https://blog.agrivi.com/post/benefits-of-using-precision-farming-producing-more-with-less. Accessed 7 June 2021

Advance Uses of RNN and Regression Techniques

Improving Recognition of Handwritten Kannada Characters Using Mixup Regularization

Chandravva Hebbi, Anirudh Maiya$^{(\boxtimes)}$, and H. R. Mamatha

Department of Computer Science and Engineering, PES University, Bengaluru
560085, Karnataka, India
{chandravvahebbi,mamathahr}@pes.edu

Abstract. Recognition of handwritten characters is essential for the digitization of old and degraded documents. The recognition of handwritten characters differs from its printed counterpart in terms of consistency in character size, spacing, thickness. This work aims to tackle the problem of recognizing handwritten characters for the Kannada language, an official language of the Karnataka state. We develop a novel dataset called Kannada84 considering a variety of factors such as age, profession, and native language of the authors, hence representing individuals from all walks of life. State-of-the-art Convolutional Neural Networks such as VGG Network, Squeeze-and-Excitation Network, and Residual Neural Network are employed to solve the task of handwritten character recognition. To enhance the performance of these networks, we performed mixup regularization leading to a reduction in generalization error. Quantitative results such as top-1 and top-3 test accuracy on Kannada84 are demonstrated in our study in which Residual Neural Network combined with mixup had the best top-1 test accuracy of 96.92% and Squeeze-and-Excitation Network combined with mixup had the best top-3 test accuracy of 99.57%.

Keywords: Convolutional neural networks · Empirical risk minimization · Mixup regularization · Residual neural network · Squeeze-and-excitation network · VGG network

1 Introduction

Optical Character Recognition (OCR) is the process of conversion of handwritten or printed text to machine editable form or machine-understandable text. This conversion helps in automating the laborious task of data entry to the machine which involves manually entering data from various sources like automatic form processing, postal automation, cheque processing in banks etc. OCR is particularly in significant demand for the recognition of handwritten characters. These handwritten characters have varying characteristics from time to time depending on an individual. Handwritten characters also differ from their printed counterpart in terms of:

© Springer Nature Switzerland AG 2022
D. Garg et al. (Eds.): IACC 2021, CCIS 1528, pp. 433–447, 2022.
https://doi.org/10.1007/978-3-030-95502-1_33

1. **Thickness, slope:** Handwritten characters from the same author may have varying levels of thickness, height, width, slope.
2. **Size consistency:** Size consistency between words, letters can vary.
3. **Slant:** Often authors tend to slant the letters towards left, right, or no slant.
4. **Spacing:** Spacing between letters, words vary from one author to another.
5. **Pen Pressure:** Closely related to thickness, pen pressure refers to the fact whether the author applies a varying amount of pressure when performing a downward/upward stroke.

Hence considering the above characteristics of handwritten text, the OCR model must be capable to handle a diverse range of characters.

In this work, the problem of recognizing handwritten letters for the Kannada language is tackled. Kannada is a popular language in the southern region of India, mainly spoken in the state of Karnataka. The Indian Government has also granted classical language status to Kannada. The character set (Varnamale) of Kannada comprises 49 alphabets of which 13 are vowels (Swara), 2 are partly vowel/consonant (Yogavahaka), 25 are structured consonants (Vargeeya Vyanjana) and 9 are unstructured consonants (Avargeeya Vyanjana). The diverse range of similar and complex letters in the character set of Kannada increases the complexity of the OCR model that must be used. Hence all the above-mentioned characteristics of handwritten text are applicable predominantly in Kannada.

The rest of the paper is organized as follows. Section 2 explains the existing work done in the recognition of handwritten Kannada letters. Section 3 briefs about the process of creation of the novel dataset used in the present study. The proposed methodology and architecture of state-of-the-art convolutional neural networks are comprehensively discussed in Sects. 4 and 5 respectively. Section 6 briefs about the hyperparameter and training configuration used in the present study. The results of our proposed methodology are discussed in Sect. 7. Conclusion and future work are presented in Sect. 8.

2 Literature Survey

The work in the field of handwritten character recognition is continuous and ongoing. A considerable amount of work is present in recognizing handwritten characters for languages such as English, Arabic, Chinese along with languages native to India such as Hindi, Bengali, Devanagari, Tamil, Kannada, and Telugu. Some of the work is presented below.

In [21] authors have carried out the task of recognition of Chinese, Bangla, and Devanagari characters using traditional machine learning techniques such as decision trees, random forests, and support vector machines (SVM). The recognition of handwritten Arabic characters using various traditional and deep learning models is presented in [19]. Binary Whale Optimization Algorithm with Neighbourhood Rough Set (BWOA-NRS) is used for feature selection. Most efficient features are extracted using BWOA-NRS. The selected features are fed to various traditional machine learning models like k-nearest neighbors (KNN), multilayer perceptron (MLP), linear discriminant analysis (LDA), and support vector machine (SVM). Average accuracy of 88.5% is reported with these models. They also compare their results with deep learning models like VGG Network (VGGNet), Residual Neural Network (ResNet), Inception Network, and MobileNet. The accuracy of the proposed method is good. Recognition of handwritten Kannada characters using Convolutional Neural Nets (ConvNets) is discussed in [17]. Various pre-processing techniques such as gray-scale conversion, noise removal, contrast normalization, binarization have been applied to enhance the features. The Bounding box method is used for the segmentation of text lines into words and words are further segmented to an individual character. The authors use char74K dataset in their study. char74K dataset consists of hand-drawn characters using a tablet/PC rather than handwritten characters which are written using tools like pen or pencil by the people on a paper. An accuracy of 86% was reported for the char74K dataset.

Recognition of handwritten Kannada characters using Capsule Networks is discussed in [11]. The dataset consists of 23,500 characters written by a heterogeneous group of people. The performance of the model is good compared to the ConvNet model. Pre-processing techniques such as resizing and gray-scale conversion are applied to the input data which are of size 28 × 28. The accuracy of the model was 93.2% and 78.73% for the two datasets which were considered for experimentation. In [5] authors have employed a ConvNet for the recognition of handwritten Kannada characters. The dataset for the work was collected from online documents using the Tesseract tool. Various combinations of the characters were obtained and an accuracy of 86% was reported.

In [12] authors solve the problem of recognition of handwritten Kannada characters using the char74K dataset. ConvNet when compared to the other techniques such as Multinomial Naive Bayes Classifier and Random Forest Classifier outperformed with considerable accuracy. In [1] authors have considered Local Binary Pattern for feature extraction and use a support vector machine as the classifier. Recognition of deformed handwritten and printed characters is presented in [16]. The dataset consists of 10,400 deformed handwritten and printed characters. The authors used a ConvNet and reported an accuracy of 87%. In [2] authors employ Hu's invariant moments along with horizontal and vertical moments which are extracted from the images and are fed to Probabilistic Neural Network (PNN). The experiment was carried out with Kannada characters and a good recognition rate of 94.69% was reported.

Literature survey reveals that the work in the field of handwritten character recognition for various languages around the world is in continual progress. The goal of achieving a high recognition rate with diverse/varying handwritten characters is a work in progress. Some of the studies mentioned above have considered a small dataset, while others have used hand-drawn characters instead of handwritten characters. Such datasets fail to represent real-world scenarios and tend to overfit. Contrarily in our work, we create a dataset that is collected from a heterogeneous group of people belonging to different age groups, professions, etc. This work aims to enhance the accuracy of the recognition rate with a real-world dataset that is large enough for Deep Convolutional Neural Networks to take advantage of. Additionally, we employ State-of-the-art ConvNets and boost the performance of these ConvNets with mixup regularization. Hence the scope of recognizing handwritten Kannada characters is immense considering its applications in the field of education as a learning tool.

3   Dataset

3.1   Kannada84

In our present study, the development of Kannada84 dataset is accomplished by considering a variety of factors. These factors were chosen to diversify the distribution of the dataset:

1. **Age:** Age group of the authors spanned from 9–60 years.
2. **Profession:** Student, teacher, homemaker, clerk
3. **Native Language:** Both native and non-native speakers of Kannada.

Hence the instances in our Kannada84 dataset represents people from all walks of life. A total of 495 authors were identified to create the dataset. The authors were asked to write a total of 84 letters with a reference copy of 84 letters (13 vowels, 36 consonants, 14 modifiers, 19 vattakshara's) to aid them. Some of the letters written by the authors were discarded from the dataset since they were not written correctly. A sample collection of all 49 letters (only consonants and vowels) is shown in Fig. 1. The remaining characters are modifiers and vattakshara's. For our work consonants and vowels are considered.

Fig. 1. Sample collection of handwritten Kannada letters in Kannada84

A total of 24,265 letters which are of size 50×50 are chosen to form the dataset for the task of classification of handwritten Kannada letters. The performance of our classification model can only be assessed when we split the dataset into train and test sets since using the same train set for inference leads to a biased estimate. Therefore, a separate test set is created as a proxy to estimate the performance of the classification model. Hence, we split the dataset with a 70–30 split-ratio to form a train and test set. A bar chart that represents the number of training and testing samples for vowels and consonants in Kannada84 is shown in Fig. 2 and Fig. 3.

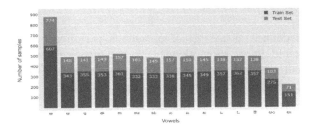

Fig. 2. Distribution of vowels in train and test set in Kannada84

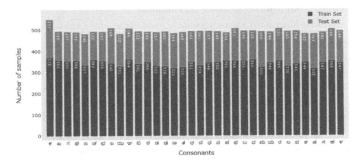

Fig. 3. Distribution of consonants in train and test set in Kannada84

3.2 Char74K

Char74K developed by [3] is an annotated database of characters from English and Kannada language. The images in the Char74K dataset consists of characters from natural street scenes captured in the city of Bengaluru. In addition to the natural street scene images, hand-drawn characters are also added to Char74K to increase the size of the dataset. In the present study, we consider the hand-drawn characters from Kannada character set of Char74K. Hence the hand-drawn Kannada character set consists of 1225 samples of size 1200 × 900 comprising of 49 letters with 25 samples each. We resize the images of Char74K to size 50 × 50 for saving computational cost. Analogous to Kannada84, we split the Char74K dataset with a 70–30 split ratio to form a train and test set.

4   Proposed Methodology

In the present work, the workflow to classify images from Kannada84 and Char74K consists of 3 stages: Pre-Processing, Augmentation, and finally training/inference of the model. The workflow is demonstrated in Fig. 4.

4.1 Pre-processing

Pre-Processing is defined as the set of operations performed on any raw data to eliminate undesirable information along with enhancement of the features. Pre-Processing is usually the first step carried out before conducting any task in machine learning. In this paper, for the pre-processing step, we normalize the images based on the training set's mean and standard deviation. This value of mean and standard deviation from the training set is used to normalize the test set. To sum up the procedure the dataset is split into train and test sets, in which the mean and standard deviation of the training set is used to normalize the test set. The normalization is done in this way rather than using the mean and standard deviation of the entire dataset to avoid data leakage which leads to biased evaluation.

4.2 Augmentation

Augmentation is the process of increasing the size of the dataset by using the principle of Vicinal Risk Minimization (VRM). To define it formally it is the process of choosing samples that are similar but different from the samples in the existing dataset. VRM operates under the assumption that the samples chosen from the vicinity of the training dataset have the same class/label as the training dataset. Hence domain knowledge is important while choosing samples from the vicinity as choosing wrong augmentation techniques might lead to change in class/label. E.g., Flipping the number 6 vertically results in number 9. Some popular data augmentation techniques are horizontal flipping, vertical flipping, the addition of Gaussian noise, rotation, etc. We use the following augmentation techniques for both Kannada84 and Char74K:

1. **Random Rotation:** The image is rotated by an angle ranging from −10° to 10°. On rotation of the image, the pixels located outside the rotated image are filled with the value 0.
2. **Random Crop:** The image is padded along left, right and top/bottom of the image with a value of 0. After padding, the image is cropped at a random location to get the desired size. E.g., For an image of size 50 × 50, we pad the image along the four sides so that the padded image size is 54 × 54. After padding, image is cropped at a random location so that its size reverts to 50 × 50.

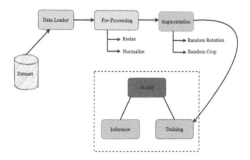

Fig. 4. Workflow to classify handwritten images

5 Architecture

Convolutional Neural Networks presented in [7] (ConvNets) are a variant of Neural Networks where convolution operator is used. ConvNets are shift-invariant and also share weights (filters) between neurons. This weight-sharing property reduces the number of parameters used and in turn, serves as implicit regularization thereby reducing the problem of over-fitting when compared to fully connected networks. ConvNets also eliminate the tedious task of feature engineering and hence require minimal pre processing of the data. ConvNets have convolutional layers in the initial part of the network and have fully connected layers at the later stages of the network. They also comprise dropout, normalization, and pooling layers. ConvNets have been used for a wide variety of tasks ranging from recognizing zip code numbers [15] to segmenting brain tumors [18]. Due to their increasing popularity, they have also been used to win ImageNet Large Scale Visual Recognition Challenge [4] over recent years. In the present study, we use different flavors of ConvNets which have been used to win various competitions like [4]. In this paper, some of the most commonly used Deep Convolutional Neural Networks (Deep ConvNets) which have a proven track record in terms of both efficiency and accuracy for other image classification tasks mainly [4] and [13] are considered.

5.1 VGG Network

The VGG Network (VGG Net) introduced by [20] is the successor of AlexNet [14]. VGG Net addresses the problem of AlexNet using a larger receptive field (11×11) and replaces it with three layers of 3×3 convolutional layer. This in turn helps the decision function to be more discriminative. The VGG Net also eliminates the use of Local Response Normalization and argues that such normalization techniques do not help in improving the performance rather increases memory consumption. A modified version of VGG Net is considered for the present work. The original 16 layered VGG Net had 13 convolutional layers followed by 3 fully connected layers with dropout regularization. It also had max-pooling layers to reduce the spatial dimension. We employ a similar architecture, but we differ in the number of convolutional and fully connected layers used. We use 13 convolutional layers and 1 fully connected layer with maxpooling after successive convolutional layers to reduce spatial dimension. Batch Normalization layer introduced by [10] is used after each convolutional layer followed by ReLU non-linearity. The fully connected layer in the later part of the network is followed by a softmax classifier since the present work is involved in solving a multi-class classification problem.

5.2 Residual Neural Network

Residual Neural Networks (ResNet) introduced by [8] addresses the problem of degradation of deep neural networks when stacked with a large number of convolutional layers. Degradation problem refers to the decrease in train and test accuracy with the increase in the depth of the network. ResNets solve this problem of degradation by introducing a residual learning framework. The residual learning framework consists of skip connections across convolutional layers that are not adjacent to each other and are governed by a learnable skip weight matrix $W^{i+2,i}$ (layer i) in case of Highway Networks [22], and identity matrix $W^{i+2,i}$ which is parameter free for ResNets. We follow the exact architecture mentioned in the original version of ResNet [8] and choose the 18-layered version. The network consists of 17 convolutional layers with batch normalization and ReLU non-linearity ending with 1 fully connected layer followed by a softmax classifier. The only difference is that we have 49 neurons in the fully connected layer. Mathematically it can be represented as follows,

Consider a ResNet with n layers. Consider a single shortcut where a skip connection exists between layer i and $i+2$. Let $W^{i,i+1}$ be the weight matrix between layers i and $i+1$ and $W^{i,i+2}$ between layers i and $i+2$. Hence,

$$
\begin{aligned}
z^{i+1} &= W^{i+1,i} \cdot a^i \\
a^{i+1} &= g(z^{i+1}) \\
z^{i+2} &= W^{i+2,i+1} \cdot a^{i+1} \\
a^{i+2} &= g(z^{i+2} + W^{i+2,i} \cdot a^i)
\end{aligned}
\tag{1}
$$

where:

$g(\cdot)$ is the activation function.

a^{i+1} is the output after the activation function is applied on layer $i+1$.

$W^{i+2,i}$ is the skip weight matrix between non-consecutive convolutional layers i and $i+2$.

Highway Networks learn the skip weight matrix $W^{i+2,i}$, while its counterpart ResNet, converts $W^{i+2,i}$ into an identity matrix which is parameter-free.

5.3   Squeeze-and-Excitation Networks

Squeeze-and-Excitation Networks introduced by [9] proposes a novel architectural unit that uses channel-wise information to increase the performance of the network. They introduce a Squeeze-and-Excitation block (SE block) which is capable of modeling inter-channel dependencies. An SE block consists of two operations namely squeeze and excitation. Squeeze operation captures the global information across channels and is parameter-free. This global information is obtained by a global average pooling operation. Mathematically the squeeze operation can be formulated as,

$$
z^{1 \times 1 \times C} = \mathcal{F}_{\text{squeeze}}\left(U^{H \times W \times C}\right) = \frac{1}{H \times W} \sum_{i=1}^{H} \sum_{j=1}^{W} U^C(i,j)
\tag{2}
$$

where:

$H \times W \times C$ is the dimension of the feature map and $U^{H \times W \times C}$ is a feature map that serves as an input to the squeeze operation.

Excitation operation works on the output of the squeeze operation. It captures the non-linear interaction between channels and gives importance to all the channels rather than a single channel. Mathematically $\mathcal{F}_{\text{excitation}}(z^{1\times1\times C})$ can be calculated as,[1,2]

$$
\begin{aligned}
y_1^{1\times\frac{C}{r}} &= W_1^{\frac{C}{r}\times C} \cdot z^{1\times1\times C} \\
a_1^{1\times\frac{C}{r}} &= g\left(y_1^{1\times\frac{C}{r}}\right) \\
y_2^{1\times C} &= W_2^{C\times\frac{C}{r}} \cdot a_1^{1\times\frac{C}{r}} \\
a_2^{1\times C} &= \sigma\left(y_2^{1\times C}\right)
\end{aligned}
\tag{3}
$$

where:

W_1 and W_2 are fully connected layers.

$g(\cdot)$ is ReLU non-linearity.

$\sigma(\cdot)$ is sigmoid non-linearity.

r (Reduction ratio) is a hyper parameter that decides the computational cost of the SE block.

Hence after excitation operation, the original feature map $U^{H\times W\times C}$ is rescaled with $a_2^{1\times1\times C}$. Therefore, the final output is,

$$
X^{H\times W\times C} = U^{H\times W\times C} \odot a_2^{1\times1\times C}
\tag{4}
$$

where:

$\odot$ is an element-wise multiplication operation.

The simplicity of the SE block is its trademark feature. It can be easily integrated into any state of the art (SOTA) architecture with minimal overhead. The authors of the squeeze-and- excitation network integrate SE blocks before/after residual block. We choose the SE-Pre block variant where a residual block is placed before the SE block. Hence, we use the 18 layered version of ResNet mentioned in the previous section with additional SE blocks.

5.4   Improving Performance with Mixup

Mixup introduced by [23] is an augmentation/regularization technique that reduces the generalization error of the network. It introduces linear behavior between two training instances and their corresponding labels by creating virtual training samples on the fly with little overhead. This linear behavior reduces undesirable oscillation when the prediction has to be done outside the training set, thereby reducing the generalization error. The entire procedure to train a network using mixup augmentation is shown in Algorithm 1.

A representative diagram of mixup between two characters is shown in Fig. 5. In Fig. 5 the letters ಚ and ಭ are considered to demonstrate the effectiveness of mixup. ಚ is multiplied by mixup coefficient λ which is sampled from a Beta distribution. ಭ is scaled

---

[1] $z^{1\times1\times C}$ is reshaped to $z^{1\times C}$.

[2] $a_2^{1\times C}$ is reshaped to $a_2^{1\times1\times C}$.

Algorithm 1: Mixup

Require: Dataset $\mathcal{D}$ consisting of $1,2,...,n$ I.I.D samples

Require: $f(\cdot\,;\theta)$ is a ConvNet with parameters θ

Require: $\mathcal{L}(\cdot)$ is the objective function that must be minimized

Require: η is the step size

Require: α, β are the parameters for Beta distribution

Result: Parameters θ^* after the model has converged

while θ not converged do

    Sample minibatch of m samples $\mathcal{A} = \{(X_1, y_1), ..., (X_m, y_m)\}$ from $\mathcal{D}$;

    Create a shuffled minibatch of m samples $\mathcal{B}$ from $\mathcal{A}$ such that

$$\mathcal{A}_i \neq \mathcal{B}_i \;\forall i \in \{1,2,....,m\};$$

$\mathcal{A}^X, \mathcal{A}^y = \{X_1,...,X_m\}, \{y_1,...,y_m\}$ such that $X_i \in \mathcal{A}$ and $y_i \in \mathcal{A}$;

$\mathcal{B}^X, \mathcal{B}^y = \{X_1,...,X_m\}, \{y_1,...,y_m\}$ such that $X_i \in \mathcal{B}$ and $y_i \in \mathcal{B}$;

$\lambda \sim Beta(\alpha, \beta)$;

$X' = \lambda \cdot \mathcal{A}^X + (1-\lambda) \cdot \mathcal{B}^X$;

$y' = \lambda \cdot \mathcal{A}^y + (1-\lambda) \cdot \mathcal{B}^y$;

$\hat{y} = f(X'; \theta)$;   ▷ Forward Propagation

$G = \nabla_\theta \mathcal{L}(\hat{y}, y')$;   ▷ Compute derivative of the objective function

    w.r.t parameters θ

$\theta = \theta - \eta \cdot G$;   ▷ Perform a step with gradient descent

---

by a factor of $1 - \lambda$. Similarly, the labels of α and β which are onehot encoded are multiplied by λ and $1 - \lambda$ respectively. Although the end product of mixup may not be visually pleasing for the human eye, ConvNets can make a lot of sense from the mixed image. Hence mixup is a convex combination of two images that are mixed on the fly during the training phase. Although the complexity of gradient descent is problem dependent, the shuffling step of mixup in Algorithm 1 uses Fisher-Yates shuffling algorithm [6] which has a time complexity of $\mathcal{O}(n)$ where n is the number of elements to be shuffled.

6 Training

In the proposed work, the training regime is identical for both Kannada84 and Char74K datasets. ConvNets are trained with two different variations, the variation being mixup regularization and Empirical Risk Minimization (ERM) (without mixup regularization). All the ConvNets regardless of their variation are configured with the same hyperparameters. We use categorical cross-entropy loss for both mixup and ERM. Stochastic gradient descent with momentum (SGD-M) is used as an optimizer to minimize the categorical cross-entropy loss for a total of 200 epochs with a batch size of 128. The learning rate is set to 0.01 for the first 100 epochs and is decayed by a factor of 10 at the end of 100, 150 epochs. Momentum is set to 0.9 with a weight decay of 10^{-4}. The parameters for the Beta distribution (α and β) mentioned in Sect. 5.4 are both set to a value of 1.

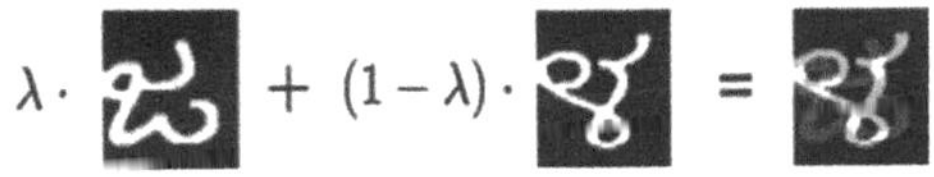

$$\lambda \cdot \boxed{} + (1 - \lambda) \cdot \boxed{} = \boxed{}$$

Fig. 5 Visual representation of mixup augmentation on Kannada84 dataset

7 Results

In the present study, the efficacy of three different ConvNets with two variations (mixup and ERM) are compared for Kannada84 and Char74K datasets. We report top-1 and top-3 test accuracy for all the models. Top-1 test accuracy for Kannada84 ranged from 96.03% to 96.49% for ERM and 96.56% to 96.92% for mixup. ResNet-18 on Kannada84 with mixup outperformed all other models with an accuracy of 96.92%. Top-3 test accuracy for Kannada84 ranged from 99.28% to 99.49% for ERM and 99.43% to 99.57% for mixup. Similarly, Char74K had a top-1 test accuracy ranging from 86.96% to 93.75% for ERM and 92.11% to 94.84% for mixup. Top-3 test accuracy for Char74K ranged from 95.65% to 98.13% for ERM and 97.28% to 98.37% for mixup. Table 1 shows the test accuracy of various ConvNets with ERM and mixup for Kannada84 and Char74K. Table 2 tabulates the per-class test accuracy and F1-score for ResNet-18 with mixup for Kannada84 to better assess the sanctity of our model. Train and test accuracy evolution for ConvNets trained with ERM and mixup is shown in Fig. 6 and Fig. 7.

8 Conclusion and Future Work

In the present work, a new dataset called Kannada84 is developed by considering a diverse set of individuals from all walks of life. The dataset is created to simulate a real-world scenario, where individuals belong to different age groups and have distinctive professions. Additionally, Kannada84 dataset is large enough for deep learning models to take advantage of. We employ state-of-the-art Deep Convolutional Neural Networks for the recognition of handwritten Kannada characters for both Kannada84 and Char74K. Further, the performance of these networks is enhanced by adding mixup augmentation/regularization on the fly. Mixup in turn introduces linear behaviour between training samples and reduces variance. We report top-1 and top-3 test accuracy for all the networks along with per-class test accuracy and F1-Score. The future scope of this work is to recognize modifiers, words with modifiers and vattakshara's.

Table 1. Test accuracy of various architectures trained with mixup and ERM for Kannada84 and Char74K. All values are shown in percent

Model	Method	Kannada84		Char74K	
		Top-1 Test Accuracy	Top-3 Test Accuracy	Top-1 Test Accuracy	Top-3 Test Accuracy
VGG-14	ERM	96.03	99.28	86.96	95.65
	mixup	96.56	99.43	92.11	97.55
ResNet-18	ERM	96.49	99.47	93.75	98.10
	mixup	**96.92**	99.56	**94.84**	97.28
SE-ResNet-18	ERM	96.16	99.49	92.66	98.13
	mixup	96.90	**99.57**	94.30	**98.37**

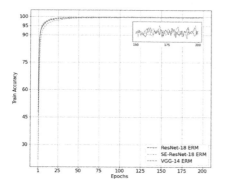
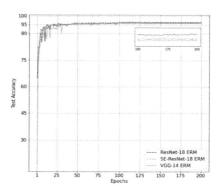

Fig. 6. Train (left) and Test (right) accuracy evolution for ConvNets trained with ERM for Kannada 84

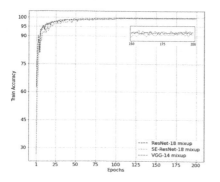
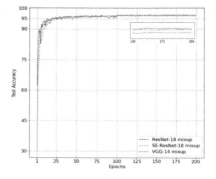

Fig. 7. Train (left) and test (right) accuracy evolution for ConvNets trained with mixup for Kannada 84

Table 2. Per-class test accuracy and F1-score for ResNet-18 with mixup for Kannada84

Letter	Classification Rate	F1-Score	Accuracy
ಆ	142/148	0.9793	95.95
ಇ	141/141	0.9964	99.29
ಈ	149/149	1.0	100.0
ಉ	155/157	0.9936	98.73
ಊ	163/163	1.0	100.0
ಋ	148/149	0.9966	99.33
ಎ	154/157	0.9904	98.09
ಏ	148/150	0.9933	98.67
ಐ	143/145	0.9930	98.62
ಒ	133/138	0.9815	96.37
ಓ	126/132	0.9767	95.45
ಔ	138/138	1.0	100.0
ಅಂ	103/103	1.0	100.0
ಅಃ	71/71	1.0	100.0
ಕ	174/177	0.9915	98.31
ಖ	134/135	0.9963	99.26
ಗ	136/137	0.9963	99.28
ಘ	126/133	0.9730	94.74
ಙ	134/146	0.9571	91.78
ಚ	131/132	0.9962	99.24
ಛ	134/137	0.9889	97.81
ಜ	162/165	0.9908	98.18
ಝ	151/152	0.9967	99.34
ಞ	144/144	1.0	100.0
ಟ	147/152	0.9833	96.71
ಠ	140/142	0.9929	98.59
ಡ	152/157	0.9838	96.82
ಢ	158/163	0.9844	96.93
ಣ	164/164	1.0	100.0
ತ	162/165	0.9908	98.18
ಥ	111/143	0.8740	77.62
ದ	154/161	0.9778	95.65
ಧ	126/147	0.9230	85.71
ನ	141/143	0.9929	98.60

ಪ	127/131	0.9844	96.95
ಫ	144/151	0.9763	95.36
ಬ	130/139	0.9665	93.52
ಭ	129/135	0.9773	95.56
ಮ	163/166	0.9909	98.20
ಯ	142/144	0.9930	98.61
ರ	148/151	0.9900	98.01
ಲ	162/163	0.9969	99.39
ವ	149/154	0.9834	96.75
ಶ	124/133	0.9650	93.23
ಷ	149/163	0.9551	91.41
ಸ	136/142	0.9784	95.77
ಹ	149/149	1.0	100.0
ಳ	148/149	0.9966	99.33

References

1. Basarkod, B.U., Patil, S.: Recognition of printed and handwritten Kannada characters using SVM classifier. J. VLSI Des. Signal. Process. **2**, 1–10 (2018)
2. Belagali, N., Angadi, S.: OCR for handwritten Kannada language script. Int. J. Recent. Trends. Eng. Res. **2**, 1–10 (2016)
3. de Campos, T., Babu, B., Varma, M.: Character recognition in natural images. In: VISAPP 2009 - Proceedings of the 4th International Conference on Computer Vision Theory and Applications 2, pp. 273–280 (2009)
4. Deng, J., et al.: ImageNet: A large-scale hierarchical image database. In: 2009 IEEE Conference on Computer Vision and Pattern Recognition, pp. 248–255 (2009)
5. Fernandes, R., Rodrigues, A.P.: Kannada handwritten script recognition using machine learning techniques. In: 2019 IEEE International Conference on Distributed Computing, VLSI, Electrical Circuits and Robotics (DISCOVER), pp. 1–6 (2019)
6. Fisher, R., Yates, F.: Statistical Tables For Biological, Agricultural and Medical Research. Statistical Tables. 3rd edn. Oliver and Boyd, Edinburgh (1949)
7. Fukushima, K., Miyake, S.: Neocognitron: a self-organizing neural network model for a mechanism of visual pattern recognition. In: Amari, S.I., Arbib, M.A. (eds.) Competition and Cooperation in Neural Nets, Lecture Notes in Biomathematics, **45**, 267–285. Springer, Berlin, Heidelberg (1982). https://doi.org/10.1007/978-3-642-46466-9_18
8. He, K., Zhang, X., Ren, S., Sun, J.: Deep residual learning for image recognition. In: 2016 IEEE Conference on Computer Vision and Pattern Recognition (CVPR), pp. 770–778 (2016). https://doi.org/10.1109/CVPR.2016.90
9. Hu, J., Shen, L., Sun, G.: Squeeze-and-Excitation Networks. In: 2018 IEEE/CVF Conference on Computer Vision and Pattern Recognition, pp. 7132–7141 (2018)

10. Ioffe, S., Szegedy, C.: Batch normalization: accelerating deep network training by reducing internal covariate shift. In: Bach, F., Blei, D. (eds.) Proceedings of the 32nd International Conference on Machine Learning. Proceedings of Machine Learning Research, vol. 37, pp. 448–456. PMLR, Lille, France, 07–09 Jul 2015
11. Jagadeeshan, M.B., Sharma, G.: Recognition of off-line kannada handwritten characters by deep learning using capsule network. Int. J. Eng. Adv. Technol. **8**, 2249–8958 (2019). https://doi.org/10.35940/ijeat.F8726.088619
12. Joe, K.G., Savit, M., Chandrasekaran, K.: Offline character recognition on segmented handwritten Kannada characters. In: 2019 Global Conference for Advancement in Technology (GCAT), pp. 1–5 (2019)
13. Krizhevsky, A.: Learning multiple layers of features from tiny images. Technical report (2009)
14. Krizhevsky, A., Sutskever, I., Hinton, G.E.: ImageNet classification with deep convolutional neural networks. In: Pereira, F., Burges, C.J.C., Bottou, L., Weinberger, K.Q. (eds.) Advances in Neural Information Processing Systems, vol. 25, pp. 1097–1105. Curran Associates, Inc. (2012)
15. LeCun, Y., et al.: Back propagation applied to handwritten zip code recognition. Neural Comput. **1**(4), 541–551 (1989)
16. Rani, N.S., Chandan, N., Jain, S., Kiran, H.: Deformed character recognition using Convolutional Neural Networks. Int. J. Eng. Technol. **7**, 1599 (2018)
17. Rao, A., et al.: Exploring deep learning techniques for Kannada handwritten character recognition. IJAST **29**, 11078–11093 (2020)
18. Saba, T., Sameh Mohamed, A., El-Affendi, M., Amin, J., Sharif, M.: Brain tumor detection using fusion of hand crafted and deep learning features. Cogn. Syst. Res. **59**, 221–230 (2020)
19. Sahlol, A., Elaziz, M.A., Al-qaness, M.A., Kim, S.: Handwritten Arabic optical character recognition approach based on hybrid whale optimization algorithm with neighborhood rough set. IEEE Access **8**, 23011–23021 (2020)
20. Simonyan, K., Zisserman, A.: Very deep convolutional networks for large-scale image recognition. In: Bengio, Y., LeCun, Y. (eds.) 3rd International Conference on Learning Representations, ICLR 2015, San Diego, CA, USA, May 7–9, 2015, Conference Track Proceedings (2015)
21. Singh, A., Bist, A.: A wide scale survey on handwritten character recognition using machine learning. Int. J. Comput. Sci. Eng. **7**, 124–134 (2019). https://doi.org/10.26438/ijcse/v7i6.124134
22. Srivastava, R.K., Greff, K., Schmidhuber, J.: Highway Networks. CoRR abs/1505.00387 (2015)
23. Zhang, H., Cissé, M., Dauphin, Y.N., Lopez-Paz, D.: mixup: beyond empirical risk minimization. In: 6th International Conference on Learning Representations, ICLR 2018, Vancouver, BC, Canada, April 30-May 3, 2018, Conference Track Proceedings (2018). OpenReview.net

Research on the Detection and Recognition Algorithm of Click Chinese Character Verification Code

Duo Wang, Chongwen Wang$^{(\boxtimes)}$, and Xiaotian Long

Beijing Institute of Technology, Beijing, China
wcwzzw@bit.edu.cn

Abstract. Network security has always been a hot topic of people's attention. In recent years, click Chinese character verification codes have been used by major Chinese websites to prevent malicious attacks and malicious batch operations. How effective this verification code is and whether it will be cracked at a low cost is a worthy of discussion and research question. In response to this problem, this paper proposes a two-step cracking method of detection and classification. Using the more commonly used detection and classification networks, combined with some targeted changes, achieved an 83.33% cracking success rate on the test set at a relatively low cost, and made a partial answer to this question.

Keywords: Network security · Verification code

1 Introduction

Network security has always been a hot topic. As a relatively simple Turing test, verification code can distinguish whether the visitor is a normal user or a machine according to the answers submitted by the user. It has been used to prevent the program from cracking the password according to the dictionary sequence [1]. Nowadays, with the gradual maturity of the Internet, verification codes have been widely used by major websites to prevent information leakage, malicious attacks, malicious batch operations and so on.

Cracking and protection are often conflicting and mutually reinforcing. The emergence and development of Verification Code technology has also accelerated the emergence and update of Verification Code technology. Text-based Verification Code is initially a simple combination of Roman numerals and English letters without image enhancement. With the birth of OCR [2] technology, such verification codes can also be easily recognized by the machine for further development. To distinguish between normal users and machines, text-based authentication codes incorporate image enhancement operations such as character rotation, character gluing, and adding shadows.

In recent years, a Chinese character click verification code has appeared on Chinese websites. The verification code is divided into two parts. The upper part is transformed by the style transfer of the background picture and the rotation and stretching of the

Chinese characters and the second half is easy to read as a title. The recognition needs to click on the position of the upper part according to the order of the lower part of the Chinese characters. As a more mainstream information security verification method, what steps should be taken to crack the possible Chinese character click verification code? What's the cost of cracking it? Is there a way to improve its security? Only by answering these questions, can people have a clearer understanding of verification code, which will promote the further development of verification code technology and improve the security of personal accounts.

The article can be divided into the following parts: the first is the overall solution idea, and then is the experimental content of the detection experiment, finally is the idea and implementation details of the identification part.

2 Solution Idea

Through the introduction of the first chapter, it can be seen that the steps to give the answer to the verification code are mainly divided into two steps: first, it need to correspond to the same character above and below, and then it need to point out the top text position in turn. Intuitively, OCR technology seems to meet our needs, but after a simple attempt, it can found that it doesn't work well with character in the top half of the image, which is also the advanced point of this type of verification code. The author have also considered the idea of object detection, that is, use the detector to predict the position and category of the text. The main disadvantage of this method is how many categories there are in the training set, and the prediction is limited to these categories. The problem with this shortcoming is that the model is poor generalization.

So the idea of this experiment is to summarize the whole task into two sub-tasks, detection and classification, to solve the problems mentioned above.

For the detection task, it can directly follow the solution idea of the object detection task. Object detection is a classic problem in the field of computer vision. Popular detection algorithms are mainly divided into two types: one-stage and two-stage. The representative of the two-stage type is Faster RCNN. The main idea is to first use the RPN network to extract regions that may have targets, and then further classify and fine-tune these regions. It has high accuracy [3]. The representative of one-stage is the YOLO series. This type of algorithm directly predicts categories and position [4–6]. Its advantage is that it is faster and the detection accuracy is also within an acceptable range. For the task of detecting the position of the text in the verification code image, the number of objects in a single image is small, and the size is relatively fixed. The requirement for detection accuracy is not high, so this paper intends to use one-stage idea to solve the detection task.

For the recognition task, the solution ideas are mainly divided into two types: similarity judgment and accurate classification.

The idea of accurate classification is to accurately classify each detected Chinese character, and then correspond up and down according to the classification results. The main defect of this idea is similar to the direct detection idea mentioned above, its generalization is poor. The idea of similarity judgment is to directly compare the question image and the answer image one by one, and match according to the similarity. Since the order of the question images can be directly determined by the coordinates, the order of the corresponding answer images can also be determined. The advantage of this method is that it does not need a full-covered training set, nor does it need to accurately identify the types of Chinese characters, and is robust; it has a certain generalization performance for verification forms such as verification codes such as similar graphics. This paper adopts the similarity judgment method to solve the task corresponding to the character.

3   Detection Experiment

3.1   K-means Clustering Generates Anchor Size

The size of the Chinese character target in the verification code is relatively fixed, so the K-means clustering method is used to generate the anchor size to improve the convergence speed and make the result more accurate. Because the shape of Chinese characters is often relatively fixed, and the aspect ratio does not change much, the Euclidean distance is used instead of IoU as the method for distance calculation.

Finally obtained three large medium and small anchors of different sizes in three dimensions, as follows (Table 1):

Table 1. Anchor size.

	Scale1	Scale2	Scale3
Small	(25, 25)	(29, 28)	(34, 32)
Medium	(63, 59)	(67, 59)	(74, 68)
Large	(75, 67)	(79, 73)	(86, 67)

3.2   Class Imbalance

In Yolo, in which grid the center point of the target object is, all bounding boxes and target objects predicted by the grid are used for IoU calculation, and the bounding box with the largest IoU is selected as a positive example. The positive example participates in the error calculation of the position and size of the bounding box, the object confidence error calculation and the classification error calculation, and the negative example only participates in the object confidence error calculation. The limitation of this processing is that it cannot cope with the situation shown in Fig. 1.

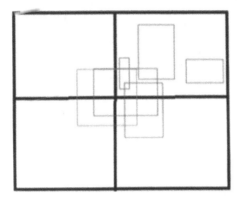

Fig. 1. Limitation scene

In the above figure, the red is the truth object, the three blue boxes are the bounding boxes predicted by the grid where the center point of the truth object is located, and the yellow and green are one of the bounding boxes predicted by other surrounding grids. Obviously, in this situation, the effects of the yellow and green boxes are better than the blue boxes. However, according to Yolo's traditional selection strategy, the blue box with inferior effect was finally selected.

Because of this, many reproduced Yolo codes do not use Yolo's traditional selection strategy, and even the author of Yolov3 had improved the strategy in the code implemented: setting an IoU threshold. The bounding box of all grid predictions with objects are calculated for IoU, the one with the largest IoU value and exceeding the threshold is a positive example, and the rest are negative examples. This strategy can be adapted to the scenarios illustrated above, but it still has the problem of imbalance between positive and negative examples.

In YOLOv3, inputting a 416 × 416 picture will generate 10647 bounding boxes. For the verification code detection task, there are most only 8 positive examples in a picture, which means that the proportion of positive examples and negative examples is seriously unbalanced during back propagation, which is not conducive to the convergence of the model. Taking the common cross entropy loss function as an example, its expression is as follows:

$$Loss = -[ylog(p) + (1-y)log(1-p)] = \begin{cases} -\log(p), y = 1 \\ -log(1-p), y = 0 \end{cases} \quad (1)$$

Where y is the real value and p is the predicted value.

It can be seen that in the above formula, the impact of positive and negative examples on loss is of the same magnitude. In the case where the ratio of positive and negative cases mentioned above is seriously unbalanced, the loss caused by negative cases is large, which largely covers the loss of positive cases, resulting in the slowdown of model convergence speed.

For the positive and negative case imbalance problem, RetinaNet proposes a solution, Focal Loss [7], which is expressed as follows:

$$Loss = \begin{cases} -\alpha(1-p)^{\gamma}logp, y = 1 \\ -(1-\alpha)p^{\gamma}log(1-p), y = 0 \end{cases} \tag{2}$$

Compared with the general cross-entropy function, Focal Loss balances their impact on Loss by weighting positive and negative cases, giving higher weights to fewer positive cases and lower weights to more negative cases.

However, in actual use, it was found that Focal Loss did not perform well in solving the problem of Yolo's imbalance of positive and negative cases, which was also mentioned in the reference about Yolov3. In the reference, the author believes that the reason for the poor performance of Focal Loss is that Yolo itself has a certain degree of robustness to the problem of imbalance of positive and negative examples. Yolo separates object detection and classification for regression. Many negative examples are not participating in the back prop. But in fact, the effect of Yolo is really limited by the imbalance of positive and negative examples. Therefore, the author more inclined to think that the poor performance of Focal Loss is more likely due to the absence of suitable hyperparameters, or more likely because the ratio of positive and negative cases of Yolo is too imbalanced, and the adjustment effect of Focal Loss is diluted.

In order to solve this problem, the experiment used the following positive and negative example selection strategy:

1. The IoU with all target objects is less than the threshold is a negative example.
2. If the IoU with at least one target object is greater than or equal to the threshold, but the IoU value is not the maximum value, it will be ignored.
3. The highest IoU value with a target object (even if it does not exceed the threshold) is a positive example.
4. Positive cases participate in the calculation of bounding box position and size loss, object confidence loss calculation, and classification loss calculation; negative cases only participate in the object confidence loss calculation; ignoring cases do not participate in the calculation.

This strategy refers to the concept of "ignoring cases" in the RetinaNet, it alleviates the imbalance of positive and negative cases. The difference is that RetinaNet summarizes neglected cases through double thresholds, while this strategy is summarized through single threshold. The double threshold is difficult to guarantee the number of ignored cases, and there may be only a few ignored cases at the end; the single threshold ensures that most of the bounding boxes that are dispensable for loss are filtered out, reducing the interference of loss calculation.

4   Recognition Experiment

4.1   Main Idea

The purpose of this section is to classify the characters that are same character up and down in the detected state in the previous step into the same category. Its essence is judging the similarity of up and down character pictures, and classifying the highest similarity into the same category. For this purpose, the following ideas can be used: the task can be treated as a classification task during training, and the similarity of the features is finally compared. The two characters pictures with the highest similarity of the features are regarded as characters of the same category.

4.2   Feature Extraction Network

Image classification is a classic task in computer vision field. There are many classic classification networks. The data set in this article is a single character cut out, and the features are easy to extract. Therefore, the author choose to complete this part of the task based on the ResNet18 network.

The advantage of the ResNet network is that the design of its residual module is conducive to weakening the phenomenon of over-fitting and gradient explosion [8], so it has become a classic recognition network and is widely used in the feature extraction part of various tasks. The ResNet18 network consists of 17 convolutional layers and a fully connected layer. The fully connected layer is responsible for classifying the features extracted in the previous part.

This experiment uses classification as the target during training, and back-propagates the loss that is accurately classified, trains a targeted feature extraction network, and removes the final classification layer when using it, and only retains the previous feature extraction part (Fig. 2).

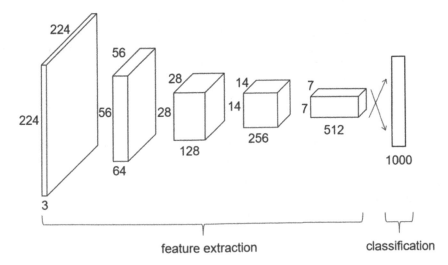

Fig. 2. Training network architecture

Fig. 3. Data example

At the same time, in order to improve the classification accuracy and reduce the cost of data mark, the experiment adopts a variety of data enhancement methods, and compares their effects.

The data example is shown in the Fig. 3. Observing the data set, it can be seen that the transformation of characters mainly includes rotation, stretching, and blurring of the background. Therefore, the experiment also added data enhancement operations such as rotation and shear in the recognition part to increase the number of data sets; in order to avoid the influence of the background, the experiment also added grayscale operations and the difference of Gaussian algorithm to improve the model's performance of convergence speed and accuracy.

Rotation: Use the midpoint of a single character as the center of rotation to rotate each character. In this experiment, the rotation angle is limited to between $-45°$ and $45°$, and the angle is randomly selected for each enhancement operation. The rotation formula centered on the coordinate origin is shown below.

$$\begin{bmatrix} x \\ y \end{bmatrix} = \begin{bmatrix} cos\theta & sin\theta \\ -sin\theta & cos\theta \end{bmatrix} \begin{bmatrix} x_0 \\ y_0 \end{bmatrix} \tag{3}$$

Where x and y are the coordinates after rotation, x_0 and y_0 are the coordinates of the points in the original image, and θ is the rotation angle.

Shear: Shear can divide into the x-axis direction and the y-axis direction, in the present experiment were randomly selected binary manner shearing direction. The x-axis direction shear formula shown below.

$$\begin{bmatrix} x \\ y \end{bmatrix} = \begin{bmatrix} 1 & tan\varphi \\ 0 & 1 \end{bmatrix} \begin{bmatrix} x_0 \\ y_0 \end{bmatrix} \qquad (4)$$

Where x and y are the coordinates after shear, x_0 and y_0 are the coordinates of the points in the original image, and φ is the shear angle.

Two operations are adopted to eliminate background noise: grayscale and difference of Gaussian. Among them, gray scale is an enhancement method based on point operation, which converts a three-channel image into a single channel to reduce the influence of noise. However, the noise introduced in this kind of verification code includes not only color noise, but also a lot of color distortion. It is difficult to achieve the desired effect only by gray-scale transformation. In order to make it easier for humans to distinguish, the outlines of Chinese characters are relatively clear in the figure. If the outlines of Chinese characters can be extracted, a relatively good effect may be achieved. For this purpose, this experiment introduced the enhancement method of difference of Gaussian.

4.3 Difference of Gaussian

Scale invariant feature conversion realizes similarity comparison by detecting and describing some local features of the image [9]. The so-called local features refer to points with rotation invariance and scale invariance.

Scale refers to the degree of blurring of the picture. Looking at an object with close range and looking at an object with a distance, the degree of blurring is not the same; the process from near to far is a process where the image becomes more and more blurred, and it is also a process where the scale of the image becomes larger and larger.

Gaussian pyramids are often used to construct scale spaces. First, the image is converted into a scale space representation, that is, multiplied by Gaussian functions of different sizes, and then down-sampled according to the scale. The size of the Gaussian function to be multiplied and the frequency of downsampling are usually selected as a power of 2. That is to say, in the process of each iteration, the image will be multiplied by a Gaussian function of a fixed size, and the length and width of the image will be multiplied 0.5. If stack the pictures of the downsampling process one by one, it will appear as a pyramid, so this process is called a Gaussian pyramid. As shown in the figure below, σ in the figure represents the scale space coordinates, S represents the number of layers, and samples are taken down in the same direction as the arrow (Fig. 4).

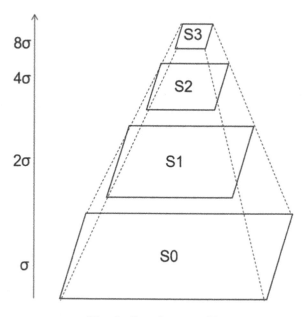

Fig. 4. Gaussian pyramid

Once the scale space is constructed, the SIFT algorithm finds the feature points of the picture. First, the difference between two pictures of different scales is called the difference of Gaussians. Obviously, the Gauss difference should also be a pyramid with one fewer layers than the Gauss pyramid. Then, for each point in the Gauss difference, compare it with a total of 26 points at eight surrounding points, nine points at two adjacent scales, and a total of 26 points. If the point is larger or smaller than 26 points, it is characteristic.

SIFT algorithm is based on scale space theory and identifies feature points by constructing scale pyramids. Generally speaking, Gaussian filters are the most common operators for building scale space. By sampling pictures with different Gaussian filters, pictures of different sizes and scales can be obtained, which form a Gaussian pyramid. Difference the adjacent scales of the Gaussian pyramids. It can get a new pyramid, called the difference pyramid, and the process of getting this pyramid is called the difference of Gaussian (Fig. 5).

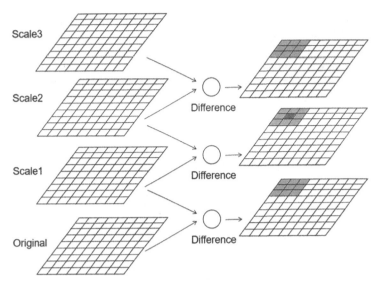

Fig. 5. Difference of Gaussian

Essentially, the difference of Gaussian is an approximation of the Laplace operator. Because a Gaussian filter suppresses only high frequency information, and a difference between two images preserves the spatial information contained in the bands maintained by the two images, the difference of Gaussian is essentially a band pass filter that removes all frequency information except those preserved in the original image.

As an enhancement algorithm, the difference of Gaussian can be used to increase the visibility of edges and other details. Most edge sharpening operators use methods to enhance high-frequency signals, but because random noise is also high-frequency signals, many sharpening operators also enhance the noise. The high-frequency signal removed by the difference of Gaussian algorithm usually contains random noise, so this method is the most suitable for processing those images with high-frequency noise. One of the main disadvantages of this algorithm is that the amount of information is reduced in the process of adjusting the image contrast.

Difference of Gaussian is also used for spot detection in scale invariant feature transformation. In fact, the difference of Gaussian as the difference between two multivariate normal distributions usually totals zero, and it is meaningless to convolve it with a constant signal. When K is approximately 1.6, it is a good approximation of the Laplace transform of Gaussian, and when K is approximately 5, it is a good approximation of the visual field of the ganglion cells on the retina.

In this verification code, it is easy to extract and learn the background as a feature directly into the feature extractor because there is too much background interference in the validation code. To solve this problem, a simple Gauss difference is used in the experiment, that is, two different of Gaussian filters are used to filter the grayscale image, and then the two filters are used to make a difference. The purpose of this is to use the difference of Gaussian for image enhancement and to highlight the edges of the text. In other words, the experimental recognizer does not recognize the whole text, but instead recognizes the outline of the text, so as to avoid situations where background and problem colors are similar and cause the text not to stand out. Figures 6 and 7 show the effect of the same graph before and after the Gauss difference processing, respectively. You can see that with Gauss difference, the color and background inside the text are almost the same, but the outline of the text has a very strong contrast with the color and background inside the text. This makes it easier for the network to extract features according to the structure of the text, rather than the text itself.

Fig. 6. Before introducing the difference of Gaussian

Fig. 7. After introducing the difference of Gaussian

This experiment uses the above methods to enhance the image, and uses the feature extractor trained by the classification task to extract the feature. For each detected character, the corresponding 512-dimensional vector is extracted as the feature for the next step of similarity calculation.

This experiment compares different enhancement methods. It can be seen that simple grayscale processing does not bring significant improvement and it's result is similar to the original image, data enhancement and difference of Gaussian are helpful to improve the accuracy when the experimental dataset is small data magnitude. And difference of Gaussian accelerates the convergence rate of the model (Fig. 8).

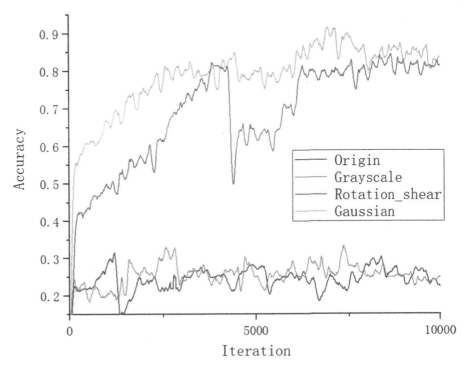

Fig. 8. Comparison of training effect of enhancement method

4.4 Similarity Calculation

Similarity calculation is generally divided into two methods, distance measurement method and similarity function method.

The more commonly used distance calculation method in the distance measurement method is Euclidean distance, which is a special form when the Minkowsky distance coefficient is 2. Compared with the Manhattan distance with a coefficient of 1, it's characteristic is that although the calculation amount has been increased, it is to a certain extent amplifies the effect of larger element loss in distance measurement, so it is widely used in various fields. The calculation formula is as follows:

$$d(x,y) = \left(\sum\nolimits_{i=1}^{N} |x_i - y_i|^2\right)^{\frac{1}{2}} \tag{5}$$

Where x and y respectively represent two vectors.

Common similarity functions include Cosine Similarity method, Correlation Coefficient method, generalized Dice coefficient method and generalized Jaccard coefficient method. The latter three similarity functions are evolved on the basis of the Cosine Similarity method. In the application, the two methods of Cosine Similarity and Correlation Coefficient are used more frequently [10].

The formula of Cosine Similarity method is as follows:

$$sim(x,y) = \frac{\sum_{i=1}^{n} x_i \cdot y_i}{\left(\sum_{i=1}^{n} x_i^2 \cdot \sum_{i=1}^{n} y_i^2\right)^{\frac{1}{2}}} \tag{6}$$

The formula of Correlation Coefficient method is as follows:

$$sim(x,y) = \frac{\sum_{i=1}^{n} (x_i - \bar{x}) \cdot (y_i - \bar{y})}{\left(\sum_{i=1}^{n} (x_i - \bar{x})^2 \cdot \sum_{i=1}^{n} (y_i - \bar{y})^2\right)^{\frac{1}{2}}} \tag{7}$$

It can be seen from the two formulas that the Correlation Coefficient method is essentially a centralized Cosine Similarity method.

We annotated a total of 245 images and divided 10% of them, namely 24 images, into validation sets.

This experiment carried out a comparative experiment on the above three methods, using the two steps of detection and identification comprehensively, that is, simulating the experiment in the real verification code scenario, and keeping the above process using the same model, manually counting 24 verification sets, the detection and classification results are both correct, they are recorded as correct, and divided by the total number of verification sets, the result is as follows (Table 2):

Table 2. Comparing accuracy of similarity calculation.

Calculation method	Accuracy
Euclidean distance	79.17%
Cosine similarity	83.33%
Correlation coefficient	83.33%

It is worth noting that the 24 validation sets contain 2 examples of not finding all the Chinese characters, so the comparison of accuracy above will be relatively conservative. However, from the comparison above, can see that the accuracy of the three methods is very small, so it can infer that for this experiment, the accuracy depends more on the effect of feature extraction than on the method of similarity calculation (Fig. 9).

Fig. 9. Final results

The figure above shows the final effect of verification code recognition.

5 . Conclusion

This article divides the cracking of the clicked Chinese character verification code into two steps: detection and recognition. For detection, this article designs a character detector based on YOLO v3, which divides the up and down words into two categories, And for the positive and negative examples unbalance of the verification code, set a separate positive and negative example selection strategies is designed for unbalanced scenes; secondly, for this kind of similarity ranking scene, this paper designs a feature extractor for a single character with classification as the training target, and combines the feature similarity calculation method, the corresponding characters are classified into the same kind. Using the above method to crack the verification code of the clicked Chinese character, the final accuracy rate can reach more than 80%.

For the solution of this problem, this paper designs a set of feasible solutions, which is easy to reuse and expand, and there is no high requirement for the scale of the data set. On this basis, the correct rate of the solution can reach 83.33%. In addition, in the implementation details of the detection part, this paper designs a set of positive and negative example selection strategies designed for the imbalance of positive and negative examples. By introducing the design of ignoring examples, the coverage effect of negative example loss on positive example loss is reduced. This speed up the convergence of the model. The recognition part is designed to implement a feature extractor with classification as the training target, combined with multiple image enhancement methods, to perform feature extraction on the detected single character. Finally, combined with the method of feature similarity calculation, a more accurate classification of the verification code is achieved.

References

1. Von Ahn, L., Blum, M., Langford, J.: Telling humans and computers apart automatically. Commun. ACM **47**(2), 56–60 (2004)
2. Mori, S., Nishida, H., Yamada, H., et al.: Optical character recognition. Comput. Sci. Commun. Dictionary **8**(4), 191–195 (1999)
3. Shaoqing, R., Kaiming, H., Ross, G., et al.: Faster R-CNN: towards real-time object detection with region proposal networks. In: Conference and Workshop on Neural Information Processing Systems, Montreal, pp. 91–99 (2015)
4. Joseph, R., Santosh, D., Ross, G., et al.: You only look once: unified, real-time object detection. In: IEEE Conference on Computer Vision and Pattern Recognition, Las Vegas (2016)
5. Joseph, R., Ali, F.: YOLO9000: better, faster, stronger. In: IEEE Conference on Computer Vision and Pattern Recognition, Hawaii (2017)
6. Joseph, R., Ali, F.: YOLOv3: an incremental improvement. In: IEEE Conference on Computer Vision and Pattern Recognition, Salt Lake City (2018)
7. Tsung-Yi, L., Priya, G., Ross, G., et al.: Focal loss for dense object detection. In: IEEE International Conference on Computer Vision, Venice (2017)
8. Kaiming, H., Xiangyu, Z., Shaoqing, R., et al.: Deep residual learning for image recognition. In: Proceedings of the IEEE Conference on Computer Vision and Pattern Recognition, Las Vegas (2016)
9. Von Ahn, L., Blum, M., Langford, J.: Distinctive image features from scale-invariant keypoints. Int. J. Comput. Vis. **60**(2), 91–110 (2004)
10. Yu, Z., Yudong, L., Zhao, J.: Vector similarity measurement method. Acoust. Technol. **28**(04), 532–536 (2009)

Multihead Self-attention and LSTM for Spacecraft Telemetry Anomaly Detection

Sharvari Gundawar[1]($\boxtimes$), Nitish Kumar[1], Prajjwal Yash[1], Amit Kumar Singh[2], M. Deepan[2], R. Subramani[3], B. R. Uma[1], G. Krishnapriya[1], B. Shivaprakash[1], and D. Venkataramana[1]

[1] U R Rao Satellite Centre, Bengaluru, India
sharvari@ursc.gov.in
[2] ISRO Telemetry, Tracking and Command Network, Bengaluru, India
[3] Master Control Facility, Hassan, India

Abstract. In spacecraft operations, a significant amount of resources is invested on constant monitoring of the health parameters of various subsystems. Any deviation from the normal in the telemetry data remains a cause of serious concern and requires immediate attention and appropriate action. In this paper, Multihead Self Attention (MHSA) and Long Short-Term Memory (LSTM) blocks have been applied for detection of spacecraft anomalies using Nominal Behaviour Modelling approach of telemetry for different subsystems. The performance of the algorithms has been compared. The required threshold to classify a particular point as anomaly has been attained by employing Non-Parametric Dynamic Thresholding (NPDT) method.

Keywords: Multihead self-attention · LSTM · Spacecraft health monitor · NPDT · Nominal Behaviour Modelling

1 Introduction

Presently the health check of the telemetry data is performed based on Out-Of Limit (OOL) method for LEO and GEO satellites. Anomaly detection methods for spacecraft telemetry primarily consist of tiered alarms indicating when values exceeds pre-defined limits and inspection of visual representations are performed. These approaches have well-documented limitations such as the requirement of extensive expert knowledge and human resources to update nominal ranges as well as to perform analysis of telemetry. Statistical and limit-based approaches are susceptible to missing anomalies that occur within defined limits [2].

© Springer Nature Switzerland AG 2022
D. Garg et al. (Eds.): IACC 2021, CCIS 1528, pp. 463–479, 2022.
https://doi.org/10.1007/978-3-030-95502-1_35

The approach adopted for anomaly detection in this paper is the use of neural networks instead of statistical approaches (such as Autoregression [13], Exponential smoothening [6], ARIMA [17]) or classical machine learning algorithms (such as Clustering [1], DBSCAN [4], LOF [3], Isolation forest [11]). In a spacecraft, various subsystems are codependent and are interacting with each other continuously. Statistical approaches model the system and therefore, can be a tricky preposition in spacecraft applications. In recent years, neural network algorithms have been preferred over classical machine learning algorithms [2] as they show better promise of identifying contextual anomalies.

In this paper, a nominal behavior modelling method has been employed to train the models. These techniques learn the nominal features from within the data-set and facilitates detection of outliers which do not conform to the modelled behavior. The continuous supply of telemetry data from a spacecraft makes nominal behavior modelling methods an attractive preposition for anomaly detection in this field as the anomaly in spacecraft telemetry are infrequent. Moreover, this technique facilitates detection of unforeseen and singular anomalies.

Hundman et al. [9] proposed a method that uses Long-Short Term Memory (LSTM) algorithm and combines it with non-parametric dynamic thresholding (NPDT) method in order to correctly distinguish between anomalous and non-anomalous behaviour. Another method to detect the presence of anomalies is the use of transformers' self-attention mechanism [15] to model the nominal behaviour of the system. Both the Multi-head self attention (MHSA) and the LSTM models have advantage over Recurrent Neural networks (RNN) - they avoid the issue of gradient exploding and vanishing. Here, NPDT method has been used with MHSA model as well as LSTM model.

The paper is structured as follows: the first section is a brief introduction to LSTM model, the second section briefly discusses the methodology of MHSA model, the third section is the description of the NPDT method for obtaining appropriate threshold, the fourth section contains the results obtained for selected spacecraft telemetry and finally, the fifth section discusses the results and scope for further work.

2   LSTM Model for Anomaly Detection

LSTM (Long Short-Term Memory) networks belong to the RNN forms [8] (Recurrent Neural Networks) of deep learning networks. When compared to dense Deep Neural Networks (DNN) and early RNNs, LSTMs have been shown to improve the ability to maintain memory of long-term dependencies due to the introduction of a weighted self-loop conditioned on context that allows them to forget past information in addition to accumulating it.

LSTM approaches have been shown to model complex nonlinear feature interactions that are often present in multivariate time-series data streams, a feature that is appealing for spacecraft health monitoring. They can also handle multivariate time-series data without the need for dimensionality reduction or domain knowledge of the specific application, allowing for generalization across different types of spacecraft and application domains. For details on the working of the model, readers are directed to [8]. The details of the LSTM model parameters configuration have been mentioned in Table 1 and the architecture has been illustrated in Fig. 1.

Table 1. LSTM model parameters configuration

Sr. No.	Parameters	Values
1	Hidden layers	2
2	No. of units per layer	80
3	Sequence length	250
4	Dropout	0.3
5	Max no. of epochs	35
6	Batch size	10
7	Optimiser	Adam

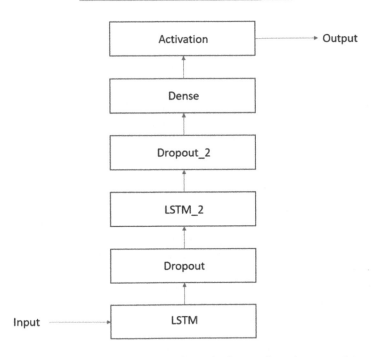

Fig. 1. Architecture of LSTM. The flow through the two lstm layers and two dropout layers followed by a dense layer and an activation layer is shown.

3   MHSA Model for Anomaly Detection

Vaswani et al. [15] had shown that transformers outperform any RNN or CNN model on translation benchmarks. The use of MHSA algorithm is credited with the edge the transformers have displayed. Transformer architecture eliminates the recurrence as well as enables parallelization [15]. This overall reduces the computational requirements - a particularly remarkable property which is appealing for applications demanding faster results with lower computational needs. This is desirable in spacecraft anomaly detection as faster processing could lead to timely detection of important events. Details of positional encoding and the architecture of the model employed here is mentioned below.

3.1   Positional Encoding

The sinusoidal functions used for positional encoding in a time-series of Natural Language Processing (NLP) is not promising as the inputs are not tokens anymore. The method used is the Time2Vec model [10]. This method works by representing a $k + 1$ input time-series as a Fourier series -

$$
t2v(\tau)[i] = \begin{cases} \omega_i \tau + \phi_i & \text{if } i = 0, \\ F(\omega_i \tau + \phi_i) & \text{if } 1 \leq i \leq k, \end{cases} \tag{1}
$$

where t2v(τ) is the i-th element of the time series and F is a periodic activation function. Unlike the sinusoidal function for NLP, the Time2Vec method is a learnable back propagation method with ω and ϕ as the learnable parameters. Readers are referred to [10] for further details on the method.

3.2   Architecture

Unlike the transformers model, the architecture used here does not have a decoder but only a stacked series of attention blocks with the Query, Key and Value matrices updated with training of the model. The attention block, like in [15], consists of a self-attention, layer normalization and Feed-forward network (FFN).

The number of heads in the MHSA model architecture was selected as two for the purpose of simplicity. A higher batch size is selected than that in the LSTM architecture as it was observed that MHSA has lower time complexity (see Sect. 6.2). The details of the MHSA model parameters configuration have been mentioned in Table 2 and the architecture has been illustrated in Fig. 2.

Table 2. MHSA parameters configuration

Sr. No.	Parameters	Values
1	No. of Heads in Attention Block	2
2	Head size	128
3	Sequence length	250
4	Max no. of epochs	35
5	Batch size	64
6	Optimiser	Adam

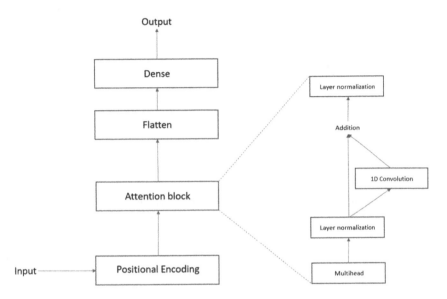

Fig. 2. Architecture of MHSA. The flow through the attention layer of the model followed by a flattening and a dense layer is shown here.

4 Non-parametric Dynamic Thresholding (NPDT) Method

For monitoring large and continuous telemetry data, an unsupervised learning method with general capability of flagging anomalous behavior is desired. Non-Parametric Dynamic Thresholding technique [9] has been employed here, as it does not require any statistical assumptions and minimal domain knowledge is required. It has been shown by the author in [9] that the method has a far lesser computational demand than distance based methods. Moreover, newer anomaly types can also be detected.

The output of the Nominal Behaviour Modelling model - LSTM and MHSA models - consists of a single channel and the predicted values can be represented as $\hat{y}$, whereas the ground truth array is represented by y.

The prediction error at time t is calculated as:

$$e^{(t)} = |\hat{y}^{(t)} - y^{(t)}| \tag{2}$$

To analyse and evaluate the current error, an error array e of size $h + 1$ is considered which consists of current error and h "historical" errors of the previous predictions. The set of errors e are then smoothed to dampen spikes in errors that frequently occur with LSTM-based predictions - abrupt changes in values are often not perfectly predicted and result in sharp spikes in error values even when this behavior is normal.

$$\mathbf{e_s} = [e_s^{(t-h)}, e_s^{(t-h+1)}, \ldots, e_s^{(t-1)}, e_s^{(t)}] \tag{3}$$

The next step is to analyse and evaluate if these values of the smoothed error array are nominal (or) anomalous using a threshold (dynamic). The values corresponding to smoothed errors above the threshold are classified as anomalies. A set of thresholds is constructed:

$$\epsilon = \mu(\mathbf{e_s}) + z\sigma(\mathbf{e_s}) \tag{4}$$

where, z is an ordered set of positive values representing the number of standard deviations above the mean $\mu(e_s)$. An ϵ out of the above set is selected by [9]

$$\epsilon = argmax_\epsilon \left(\frac{\Delta\mu(\mathbf{e_s})/\mu(\mathbf{e_s}) + \Delta\sigma(\mathbf{e_s})/\sigma(\mathbf{e_s})}{|\mathbf{e_a}| + |E_{seq}|^2} \right) \tag{5}$$

such that:

$$\Delta\mu(\mathbf{e_s}) = \mu(\mathbf{e_s}) - \mu(\{e_s \in \mathbf{e_s} | e_s < \epsilon\}) \tag{6}$$

$$\Delta\sigma(\mathbf{e_s}) = \sigma(\mathbf{e_s}) - \sigma(\{e_s \in \mathbf{e_s} | e_s < \epsilon\}) \tag{7}$$

$$\mathbf{e_a} = \{e_s \in \mathbf{e_s} | e_s > \epsilon\} \tag{8}$$

$$E_{seq} = \text{continuous sequences of } e_a \in \mathbf{e_a} \tag{9}$$

The modulus in the denominator of Eq. 5 represents the count of the parameter.

For a data set with lot of anomalous (as compared to typical setup) examples, a scoring method for showing the severity of the anomaly can be used which can be calculated as follows after the ϵ is selected:

$$s^{(i)} = \frac{max(e_{seq}^{(i)}) - argmax(\epsilon)}{\mu(\mathbf{e_s}) + \sigma(\mathbf{e_s})} \tag{10}$$

Anomaly score is a method to quantitatively give a measure of severity to the different anomalies that a model predicts. These scores should be compared for different anomalies in the data-set across the same algorithm. In order to compare anomaly score from different algorithms, a normalized anomaly score is calculated in this paper. The anomaly scores are normalized with respect to the highest anomaly score obtained by the model in the data-set.

5   Results and Analysis

The aim of the work here is to build a generalized algorithm which would not require an extensive domain expertise post training. A variety of telemetry data-sets have been analyzed by experts and anomalies have been detected. These data-sets have been then modelled here by LSTM and MHSA models but with no labels for nominal or anomalous behavior. Without specifying the spacecrafts, the following are the data-sets and the corresponding results

5.1   Detection of Solar Array Drive Assembly (SADA) Anomaly

North and South arrays of solar panels rotate about the pitch-axis for optimizing sun-pointing to maximize power generation for the spacecraft. Spacecraft has a potentiometer to provide position of the solar array with respect to the body axis. Solar Array Drive Assembly (SADA) [5] reads 120° at 6 PM spacecraft time and increase with time in the on-orbit mode for the sun tracking with forward direction selected for open-loop.

If the reading crosses beyond the set limit, alarms are generated for appropriate actions. Since Resolver angle value changes from 0–360° in a day, setting a limit check for this type of parameter is not feasible. Non-linear variation are observed at angles near roll over (360 to 0) and therefore, frozen data condition are also expected during this period. On occurrence of such stuck, solar panel sun sensor (SPSS) output deviates from zero angle and indicate the actual period of SADA stuck as shown in plot below (Fig. 3(d)). The figure below relates SADA with SPSS telemetry.

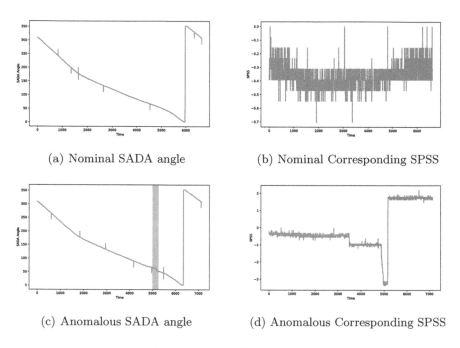

(a) Nominal SADA angle

(b) Nominal Corresponding SPSS

(c) Anomalous SADA angle

(d) Anomalous Corresponding SPSS

Fig. 3. SADA angle and SPSS values for a single day.

A single-channel LSTM training has been performed in this case. The training data is the nominal telemetry data of SPSS of a single day. The test has been performed on an anomalous Solar Panel Sun Sensor (SPSS) data. The normalized anomaly scores for the identified anomalies for both models is given in the Table 3 below.

Table 3. Normalized anomaly score for SADA anomaly for MHSA and LSTM

	MHSA	LSTM
Normalized anomaly scores	1,1,0.97	1,1

An interesting observation was the presence of a third anomaly in the NPTD-MHSA model compared to the NPDT-LSTM model. The anomaly was before the 'dip' in the telemetry signal was seen. In spacecraft anomaly detection, such a 'signature' of a possible anomaly could be invaluable. Further work is planned in this direction (Fig. 4).

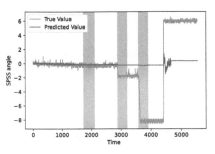

(a) Prediction and true value by MHSA

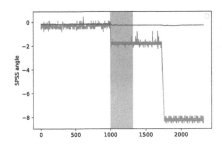

(b) Closer look at 1st dip anomaly zone by MHSA

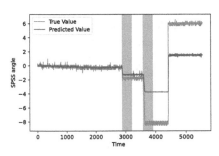

(c) Prediction and true value by LSTM

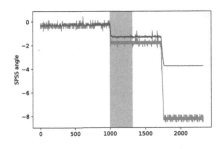

(d) Closer look at 1st dip anomaly zone by LSTM

Fig. 4. SADA anomaly prediction by looking at SPSS telemetry by the models. Red stripes are the anomalies detected with NPDT

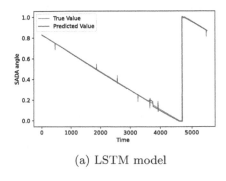

(a) LSTM model

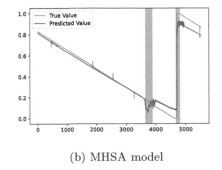

(b) MHSA model

Fig. 5. Dual channel SADA anomaly prediction by LSTM and MHSA models. SPSS telemetry and SADA telemetry are the two channels used to make progress towards multi-channel training.

A dual channel training and prediction by both the models has also been performed in an attempt to move towards multi-channel anomaly detection using the models. The models were trained using two channels - SPSS telemetry and SADA angle telemetry - and the predictions for the SADA angle were obtained. The data used for inference testing contained a single anomaly as show in Fig. 3(c). The LSTM model detected no anomaly whereas the MHSA model detected two anomalies, including a false positive. The scores of the true positive anomaly, 1.2, suggests significantly low severity. The false positive anomaly has a even lower score and can be pruned (Fig. 5).

The detection of SADA anomaly could be further improved by inclusion of telecommand data.

5.2   Detection of Momentum Wheel Anomaly

LSTM and MHSA training was performed on single-channel for telemetry of momemtum wheel [12]. The training data is the telemetry data of the same satellite's momentum wheel current for a period of 2 weeks. The test has been performed on the next five days' telemetry. Both the models detect the presence of anomaly (true positive) as shown in the figure given below (Fig. 6).

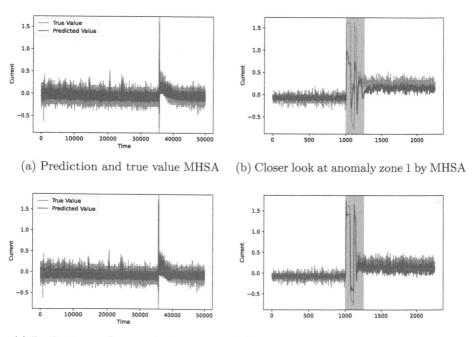

(a) Prediction and true value MHSA   (b) Closer look at anomaly zone 1 by MHSA

(c) Prediction and true value by LSTM   (d) Closer look at anomaly zone 1 by LSTM

Fig. 6. MW current anomaly prediction by the models. Red stripes are the anomalies detected with NPDT (Color figure online)

This result is corroborated by the LSTM and MHSA models when trained for earth sensor telemetry data. The algorithms were able to identify the anomaly in the earth sensor data as well, as shown in Fig. 7.

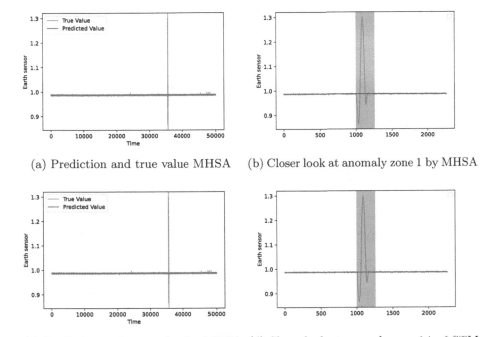

(a) Prediction and true value MHSA   (b) Closer look at anomaly zone 1 by MHSA

(c) Prediction and true value by LSTM   (d) Closer look at anomaly zone 1 by LSTM

Fig. 7. Earth sensor anomaly prediction by the models. Red stripes are the anomalies detected with NPDT (Color figure online)

5.3 Detection of Reaction Wheel Anomaly

DFC (Dyanmic Friction Compensation) torque is a parameter which will show the increase/decrease in friction component on the reaction wheel [14]. If such changes are well within a set limit, it may not come to the notice of operation team and may rise alarm only after it deviated largely away.

The prospect of detecting this failure earlier was the motivation behind trying to detect such changes in DFC. Single-channel LSTM training was performed in this case. The telemetry data of DFC torque for a period of about 50 days is chosen for training of the model. The test has been performed on the data for the next two weeks (Fig. 8).

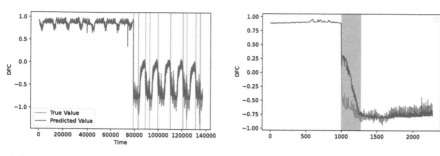

(a) Prediction and true value by MHSA (b) Closer look at anomaly zone by MHSA

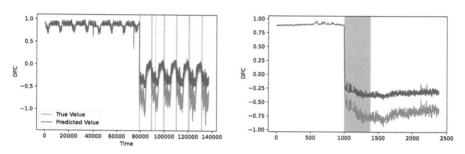

(c) Prediction and true value by LSTM (d) Closer look at anomaly zone by LSTM

Fig. 8. RW anomaly prediction by the models. Red stripes are the anomalies detected with NPDT (The telemetry values are normalised) (Color figure online)

The DFC value steeply decreased and then maintained the trend which became the new normal. Both NPDT-LSTM and NPDT-MHSA were able to identify the first anomaly (drop in the data) correctly as shown in the plots above. The models also identified anomalies after the drop - indicating that the anomaly persists.

6   Comparison of the Models

In this section, the LSTM and the MHSA models are compared empirically. The section compares the number of parameters indicating the space complexity and run-time (indicating the time complexity) of the models.

6.1   Number of Parameters

The number of parameters in the LSTM model's architecture and the MHSA model's architecture are given in Tables 5 and 6, respectively (Table 4).

Table 4. LSTM parameters number

Sr. No.	Layer type	No. of parameters
1	LSTM	26240
2	LSTM1	51520
3	Dense	81
4	Activation	0
5	Total no. of parameters	77,841

Table 5. MHSA parameters number

Sr. No.	Layer type	No. of parameters
1	Time2VecLayer	4
2	AttentionBlock	3986
3	Dense	751
4	Flatten	0
5	Total no. of parameters	4741

The number of parameters in the MHSA model is significantly lower, implying a more optimized algorithm. This does not come as a surprise as multi-headed self-attention models have shorter path length for forward and backward signals in the network.

Both the models have been created used Keras 2.0.0 and since the memory usage is proportional to the number of parameters and the batch size [7], the MHSA model uses significantly lesser memory.

6.2 Empirical Time Complexity of the Models

In addition to differentiating the number of parameters of the models, an experiment was performed to observe the time taken by the models for training as well as for inference.

The configuration of computational facility used for both training and inference was a NVIDIA Tesla K80 GPU and 25 GB RAM with disk space of 157 GB.

Shown in Fig. 9(a) and Fig. 9(b) are the empirical time complexities [16] for one epoch of the MHSA and LSTM models for different combinations of sequence length and number of sequences for a batch size of 32. For both the models, higher was the number of sequences, more was the training time, as is expected. Figure 10(a) shows that, for LSTM, increase in sequence length leads to linear increase in the time complexity, with higher slope for higher number of sequences. Whereas, for MHSA, the time complexity is significantly lower.

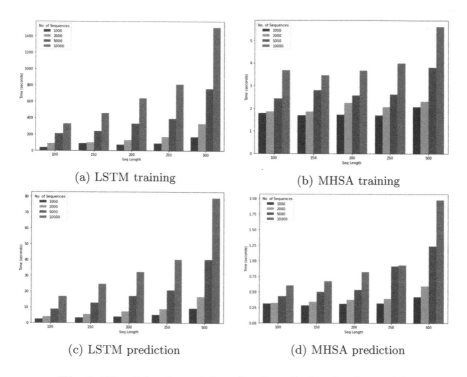

(a) LSTM training

(b) MHSA training

(c) LSTM prediction

(d) MHSA prediction

Fig. 9. Time taken for training of and predictions by the models

The empirical time complexity for prediction using LSTM and MHSA is lower than training, as expected. They follow similar trends to training time complexity as shown in Fig. 10(b). For the MHSA model the time cost was lower than LSTM for any combination, reiterating the faster computation of the MHSA model. Significantly, the rise in time complexity with increase in sequence length for MHSA was not as pronounced as LSTM model.

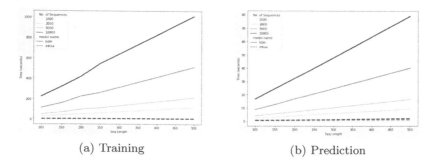

(a) Training

(b) Prediction

Fig. 10. Comparison of empirical time complexity for training of and predictions by the models

6.3   Comparing Normalized Anomaly Scores

A comparison of the normalized anomaly scores of the two models (MHSA and LSTM) with XGBoost [18] for the multiple anomalies observed in the Momentum wheel telemetry has been performed and is shown in the table here.

Table 6. Normalized anomaly score for RW anomaly for MHSA and LSTM

Normalized anomaly scores	MHSA	LSTM	XGBoost
First dip	1	1	1
Other anomalies average	0.21	0.95	0.95

The anomaly scores (Eq. 10) of MHSA model conforms to the definition of 'the new normal' as it detects the first dip as the most severe among all. However, the anomaly scores in LSTM model and the XGBoost model are same for all the detected anomalies.

7   Discussions and Conclusions

In this paper, three subsystems of different spacecrafts have been successfully modelled and the NPDT method finds appropriate threshold for correctly detecting any anomalous behaviour. It has been shown that with adequate training, the algorithms were able to detect the anomalies in telemetry data without the requirement of traditional method's domain knowledge and expertise.

The performance of the two models (LSTM and MHSA) has been compared. MHSA model shows better results than LSTM in terms of number of parameters involved in the architecture and time complexity. Both of these factors are significant in spacecraft application.

The LSTM model and MHSA model with NPDT method can be developed as the cornerstone of Spacecraft Health Monitoring System. Such a system would save considerable human resource for an organization. Further development of the spacecraft health monitoring system can be achieved by supplementing the algorithm with relevant information such as telecommand data for the corresponding telemetry. Multi-channel training for the models is an extension to the existing approach that is aimed to be explored in order to advance the system.

Acknowledgements. This work was supported by U.R. Rao Satellite Centre (URSC), Indian Space Research Organization (ISRO).

References

1. Astakhova, N.N., Demidova, L.A., Nikulchev, E.V.: Forecasting method for grouped time series with the use of k-means algorithm. Appl. Math. Sci. **9**, 4813–4830 (2015). https://doi.org/10.12988/ams.2015.55391

2. Braei, M., Wagner, S.: Anomaly detection in univariate time-series: a survey on the state-of-the-art. CoRR abs/2004.00433 (2020). https://arxiv.org/abs/2004.00433

3. Breunig, M.M., Kriegel, H.P., Ng, R.T., Sander, J.: LOF: identifying density-based local outliers. SIGMOD Rec. **29**(2), 93–104 (2000). https://doi.org/10.1145/335191.335388

4. Celik, M., Dadaser-Celik, F., Dokuz, A.: Anomaly detection in temperature data using DBSCAN algorithm, June 2011. https://doi.org/10.1109/INISTA.2011.5946052

5. Chen, J.P., Cheng, W., Wang, Y.F.: Modeling and simulation of solar array drive assembly disturbance driving a flexible load. In: Aerospace and Mechanical Engineering. Applied Mechanics and Materials, vol. 565, pp. 67–73. Trans Tech Publications Ltd., July 2014. https://doi.org/10.4028/www.scientific.net/AMM.565.67

6. Ding, N., Gao, H., Bu, H., Ma, H., Si, H.: Multivariate-time-series-driven real-time anomaly detection based on Bayesian network. Sensors **18**(10), 3367 (2018). https://doi.org/10.3390/s18103367

7. Gao, Y., et al.: Estimating GPU memory consumption of deep learning models. In: Proceedings of the 28th ACM Joint Meeting on European Software Engineering Conference and Symposium on the Foundations of Software Engineering, ESEC/FSE 2020, pp. 1342–1352. Association for Computing Machinery, New York (2020). https://doi.org/10.1145/3368089.3417050

8. Hochreiter, S., Schmidhuber, J.: Long short-term memory. Neural Comput. **9**(8), 1735–1780 (1997)

9. Hundman, K., Constantinou, V., Laporte, C., Colwell, I., Soderstrom, T.: Detecting spacecraft anomalies using LSTMS and nonparametric dynamic thresholding. In: Proceedings of the 24th ACM SIGKDD International Conference on Knowledge Discovery & Data Mining, July 2018. https://doi.org/10.1145/3219819.3219845

10. Kazemi, S.M., et al.: Time2Vec: learning a vector representation of time. CoRR abs/1907.05321 (2019). http://arxiv.org/abs/1907.05321

11. Liu, F.T., Ting, K.M., Zhou, Z.H.: Isolation forest. In: 2008 Eighth IEEE International Conference on Data Mining, pp. 413–422. IEEE (2008)

12. Narayan, S., Nair, P., Ghosal, A.: Dynamic interaction of rotating momentum wheels with spacecraft elements. J. Sound Vib. **315**, 970–984 (2008). https://doi.org/10.1016/j.jsv.2008.02.020

13. Rushe, E., Namee, B.M.: Anomaly detection in raw audio using deep autoregressive networks. In: ICASSP 2019–2019 IEEE International Conference on Acoustics, Speech and Signal Processing (ICASSP), pp. 3597–3601 (2019). https://doi.org/10.1109/ICASSP.2019.8683414

14. Urakubo, T., Tsuchiya, K., Tsujita, K.: Attitude control of a spacecraft with two reaction wheels. J. Vib. Control **10**(9), 1291–1311 (2004). https://doi.org/10.1177/1077546304042042

15. Vaswani, A., et al.: Attention is all you need. In: Advances in Neural Information Processing Systems, pp. 5998–6008 (2017)

16. Woeginger, G.J.: Space and time complexity of exact algorithms: some open problems. In: Downey, R., Fellows, M., Dehne, F. (eds.) IWPEC 2004. LNCS, vol. 3162, pp. 281–290. Springer, Heidelberg (2004). https://doi.org/10.1007/978-3-540-28639-4_25

17. Zhang, G.P.: Time series forecasting using a hybrid ARIMA and neural network model. Neurocomputing **50**, 159–175 (2003). http://dblp.uni-trier.de/db/journals/ijon/ijon50.html#Zhang03

18. Zhang, Y., Cai, Y., Roca, X., Kwoh, C.K., Fullwood, M.J.: Chromatin loop anchors predict transcript and exon usage. Briefings Bioinform. **22**, bbab254 (2021). https://doi.org/10.1093/bib/bbab254

Validity and Reliability Assessment of a Smartphone Application for Measuring Chronic Low Back Pain

Jake Fenech[1], Vijay Prakash[2(✉)], Lalit Garg[3], Conti Carlo[1], and Anshul Sharma[4]

[1] Department of Physiotherapy, University of Malta, Msida, Malta
[2] Department of Computer Science and Engineering, Thapar Institute of Engineering and Technology, Patiala, Punjab, India
vijay.prakash@thapar.edu
[3] Faculty of Information and Communication Technology, University of Malta, Malta, Msida, Malta
lalit.garg@thapar.edu
[4] Open Assessment Technologies, 40, Parc d'Activities, Capellen, 8308 Mamer, Luxembourg

Abstract. Chronic low back pain (CLBP) is treated as one of the most severe issues confronting Western public health systems. Physiotherapists rely on the patient's self-reporting to collect the essential information, subsequently transcribed into a paper format. While paper-based techniques are helpful, they have drawbacks, requiring patients to recall their pain episodes retrospectively. As a result, the information reported may be incorrect. Such issues can be avoided with mobile phone applications. However, studies on similar technologies revealed a lack of user, clinician, or healthcare-system involvement in their development and little study on their efficacy. An issue that has been highlighted in numerous studies is the lack of healthcare professionals' involvement in designing and creating the application for pain recording. Furthermore, none of the already existing applications has been tested for their validity, reliability, usability, etc. This paper aims to see if a newly developed application is valid and reliable. For this study, an app called "Pain in the App" was created. The results show that Smartphone apps in healthcare have many potentials and provide a good proof-of-concept.

Keywords: Chronic low back pain · Numerical rating scale · Smartphone · Application · Validity · Reliability

1 Introduction

Chronic pain is more complex as it carries a bio-psychosocial aspect to it [1]. The gold standard in assessing pain is by self-reporting its characteristics when it is felt [2]. Limitations in diagnostic tools, imperfect options, and flawed structures for treatment delivery make treatment of pain more difficult [3]. Studies have shown that when assessing with a paper-based Numerical Rating Scale (NRS), there are many

© Springer Nature Switzerland AG 2022
D. Garg et al. (Eds.): IACC 2021, CCIS 1528, pp. 480–491, 2022.
https://doi.org/10.1007/978-3-030-95502-1_36

retrospective data whereby the patient must recall on memory to give a value of the intensity of their pain for the previous days [4–6]. In the last two decades, technological advancements have allowed this exponential increase in mobile phones, increasing their potential for healthcare implementation [7].

Physiotherapists rely on the patient's self-reporting to gather the necessary information about the discomfort, subsequently transcribed into paper format. Although paper-based techniques are helpful, they have drawbacks, requiring patients to recall their pain episodes retrospectively. As a result, the information recorded may be erroneous. Such issues can be avoided with the use of mobile phone applications. However, investigations on similar technologies revealed a lack of a user, clinician, or health-care-related involvement in their development, as well as a bit of study on their efficacy.

The study aims to design a patient-centred Smartphone application serving as a pain assessment tool with the primary function of recording and tracking pain. The data collected will then confirm or negate the validity and reliability of the application when compared to the NRS, which is the gold standard in pain assessment. This scientific evaluation will help approve or disprove the feasibility of such an application for both the patient and the health care professional to collect data.

The rest of the paper is organised as Sect. 2 discusses the related work. Section 3 describes the problem formulation. Section 4 describes the methodology used in detail to find the solution. Results and Discussion is presented in Sect. 5, followed by Conclusion and Future Scope in Sect. 6.

2   Related Work

Pain is one of the main reasons people opt to seek medical attention; as stated, pain is "an unpleasant sensory and emotional experience." Hence, pain is an experience, including emotion, cognition, memory, interpersonal and social contexts, and interpretation.

2.1   Chronic Pain: More Than Just a Physical Problem

Chronic pain is most commonly defined by its persistence beyond an expected time frame from healing, i.e., lasting more than three months and related to prolonged functional impairment and loss of function [8–10]. According to IASP and the European Federation of IASP (EFIC), "chronic and recurrent pain is a specific healthcare problem, a disease in its own right [11]."

2.2   Chronic Low Back Pain (CLBP): Definition and Epidemiology

CLBP is defined as pain without a clear pathophysiological cause [12, 13], localised at the lumbar region, possibly radiating down the legs. However, the chronicity of this condition is not based solely on the physical impairment but also on the recurrence of the pain [12]. CLBP poses a significant economic and socio-economic impact highlighted and exposed by the researches [14–23].

2.3   Mode of Assessment

To obtain any form of information regarding one's intensity, quality, location, and temporal nature of pain, health care professionals depend on self-reporting from the patient [10]. Information from the patient is then transcribed into a paper format whereby numerous information fields, such as intensity and location, are obtained [25]. Validated and standardised tools such as the Visual Analogue Scale (VAS), Numerical Rating Scale (NRS), and the 2-dimensional (2-D) representation of the human body are used to identify the intensity and the location, respectively [10]. Valid retrospective questionnaires are also used to recall the intensity and location of the pain in the previous days [4]. The information obtained can then guide the physiotherapist towards the proper treatment for that patient.

3   Problem Formulation

Developing a Smartphone-based application accessible in one's pocket could be a vital tool to facilitate self-reporting of their painful episodes. With current pain assessment applications, healthcare professionals' input is minimal. Hence, the tools required to carry out a proper assessment are either not present or not as effective as they need to be. Therefore, the aim behind the development of this application would be to include the health care professionals to find out what is essential in a pain assessment tool to make assessments far more effective. Analysing and transcribing data from paper to digital form into the national logging system for other health care professionals to view takes time and is sometimes not performed. Using a mobile phone-based application to assess pain facilitates this process since the information is already in digital form.

4   Methodology

On mobile devices, mobile language learning delivers solutions that enable asynchronous and casual language learning [26]. However, a shortage lies in the number of pain applications available on the market and the studies behind their validity. Therefore, with this in mind, the idea of creating a Smartphone-based application that can record pain in real-time was harboured. The application will then undergo a scientific evaluation to confer its validity and reliability. This study aimed to investigate the validity and reliability of a newly developed Smartphone application on chronic low back pain (CLBP) patients. This was investigated through analysing data for a correlation between the Smartphone application and the numerical rating scale (NRS) results.

4.1   Unit Study Design

A "within-participant" experimental design was used for the data collection. This benefits the study by reducing the potential variance error, which is the variability that occurs by chance or uncontrolled variables [27]. The mobile phone application and the modified questionnaire were used as the data collection tools for this study. The Smartphone application incorporates both the colour scheme with which the body could be shaded and the NRS.

4.2   Tools

The numerical rating scale (NRS) is a valid and straightforward objective measure that is used to measure the intensity of pain. Due to its validity, the NRS was chosen as the gold standard for data comparison and interpretation. To compare and interpret the data, the NRS is integrated into the application whereby the participant had to select a value that best described their pain. The vertical numerical rating scale [28] is used for the application. The correlation was observed by comparing the colour chosen with which to draw on the body, which indicates the intensity of pain to the score selected on the NRS.

4.3   Testing Procedure

Their physiotherapist refers participants fulfilling the inclusion criteria for this study to the principal researcher. The study was briefly described, and an information letter and a consent form were handed to the participant by the physiotherapist during the out-patient visit. A demonstration of the application was given on the researcher's Smartphone and then explained in further detail. If interested, the participant signed the consent form, and subsequently, the researcher transferred the application onto the participant's phone.

Fig. 1. The Splash screen appears until the loading of the application

The researcher then explained the process of how to input data into the application. A set of instructions was also handed, to which the participant wrote their specific username and their chosen password, which would allow them to access the application securely. After registration, the participant could input the data when the pain was being felt. The participant was encouraged to input data ideally three times a day and at least once a day. According to the individual's sleeping habits or working hours, an acoustic alarm was included to remind patients to use the application. On clicking the Application icon, a splash screen (Fig. 1) appeared until the application was loading, and then the log-in screen appeared (Fig. 2). Here, the participant inputted their specific username and password and logged in to their profile. The application was given on the researcher's Smartphone and then explained in further detail to the patients.

Fig. 2. Login screen

A set of instructions was also handed, to which the participant wrote their specific username and their chosen password, which would allow them to access the application securely. After registration, the participant could input the data when the pain was being felt. The participant was encouraged to input data ideally three times a day and at least once a day. According to the individual's sleeping habits or working hours, an acoustic alarm was included to remind patients to use the application.

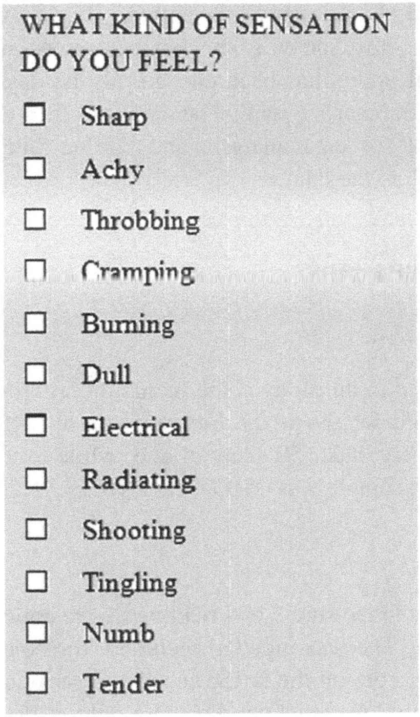

WHAT KIND OF SENSATION
DO YOU FEEL?

☐ Sharp

☐ Achy

☐ Throbbing

☐ Cramping

☐ Burning

☐ Dull

☐ Electrical

☐ Radiating

☐ Shooting

☐ Tingling

☐ Numb

☐ Tender

Fig. 3. The selected word describes the pain.

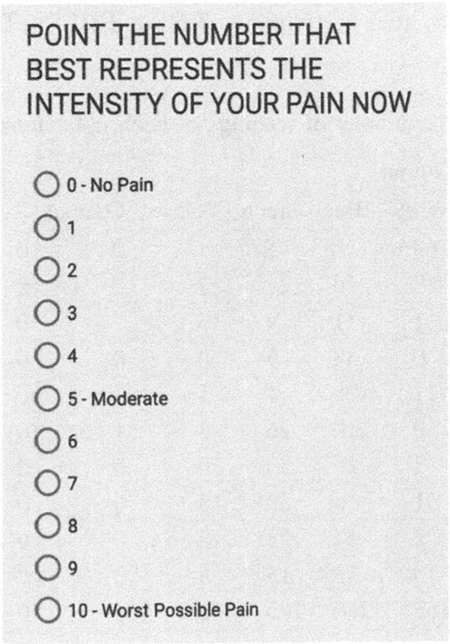

POINT THE NUMBER THAT
BEST REPRESENTS THE
INTENSITY OF YOUR PAIN NOW

○ 0 - No Pain
○ 1
○ 2
○ 3
○ 4
○ 5 - Moderate
○ 6
○ 7
○ 8
○ 9
○ 10 - Worst Possible Pain

Fig. 4. The selected number describes the intensity of pain.

The participant could choose many descriptions (Fig. 3) which best described the sensation of the pain. The next screen is an 11-point numerical scale for pain intensity (Fig. 4). Once the e-mail option has been chosen, all the data inputted will automatically transfer into the researcher's e-mail. The data was then extrapolated and inputted into an SPSS document for data analysis and further interpretation. A period of 1 month was established as the data.

5   Results and Discussions

5.1   Participants

Participants were recruited in the study if the inclusion criteria were met. A total of 10 participants were recruited for the study. Seven of these participants were male, and three were female. Six were under 50 years of age, while four were above 50 years of age. The mean age of the sample was 45.17 years (SD = 15.27, range 22 to 71 years).

5.2   Readings

Out of the 10 participants in the study, 694 readings were collected, giving a maximum margin of error of 3.73%. The data inputted included: the colouration with which they shaded the body and the score on the NRS; and the description/s chosen. On average, each participant entered two readings per day. The colour most frequently chosen was blue (Mild) (260 readings), whereas the less frequently chosen was red (Unbearable) (0 readings), followed by orange (Very Severe) (4 readings). The colour orange (Very Severe) was recorded by three participants (LBP2, LBP3 & LBP6), whereas white (No Pain) was not recorded by two participants (LBP4, LBP6) (Table 1).

Table 1. The number of readings of each color for each patient

ID/ reading	Colour						
	White	Blue	Green	Yellow	Orange	Red	Total
LBP1	69	6	5	4	0	0	**84**
LBP2	19	36	27	7	2	0	**91**
LBP3	1	11	19	13	1	0	**45**
LBP4	0	58	5	0	0	0	**63**
LBP5	11	28	1	1	0	0	**41**
LBP6	0	10	26	3	1	0	**40**
LBP7	2	25	50	6	0	0	**83**
LBP8	31	6	30	18	0	0	**85**
LBP9	22	27	25	2	0	0	**76**
LBP10	10	53	15	8	0	0	**86**
Total	**165**	**260**	**203**	**62**	**4**	**0**	**694**

The highest score obtained from the NRS was eight by one participant (LBP6), whereas all the participants inputted the lowest score of 0 except for 2 (LBP4, LBP6) (Table 2).

Table 2. Numerical rating scale readings

ID/reading	NRS										
	0	1	2	3	4	5	6	7	8	9	10
LBP1	69	0	6	4	1	4	0	0	0	0	0
LBP2	19	3	33	4	21	3	6	2	0	0	0
LBP3	1	2	9	10	10	9	3	1	0	0	0
LBP4	0	9	50	4	0	0	0	0	0	0	0
LBP5	11	14	13	1	1	1	0	0	0	0	0
LBP6	0	0	9	7	20	3	3	0	1	1	1
LBP7	2	16	9	33	17	6	0	0	0	0	0
LBP8	31	0	6	6	24	4	14	0	0	0	0
LBP9	22	10	19	19	5	0	1	0	0	0	0
LBP10	10	52	5	11	1	7	0	0	0	0	0
Total	**165**	**106**	**156**	**99**	**100**	**37**	**27**	**3**	**1**	**0**	**0**

5.3 Analysis of Data

The quantitative data collected has been analysed using SPSS Statistics v.20 to determine the normality of the data acquired and, subsequently, the statistical tests required to determine the validity and reliability and of the application.

Normality

To check the normality of the data, the Kolmogorov- Smirnov test was used. A level of significance of less than 0.05 shows that the data is not normally distributed. A p-value of <0.001 was obtained (Table 3) in this study, indicating non-normality and skewness in the data.

Table 3. Test of normality

	Kolmogorov-Smirnov			Shapiro-Wilk		
	Statistic	df	p-value	Statistic	df	p-value
NRS	0.149	694	0.000	0.917	694	0.000

Correlation

The Spearman Correlation Coefficient is used to observe a positive correlation between the colouration scheme and the NRS scores. A p-value of 0.960 was obtained, indicating a strong positive correlation between the two scores (Table 4).

Table 4. Testing correlation

	Spearman's rho	Colour	Correlation coefficient	p-value (1-tailed)	Sample size
NRS			0.960	0.000	694

Validity

The validity of the application is assessed by comparing the colouration with which the participants drew on the body- diagram with the score obtained from the NRS. The Kruskal Wallis test is used to assess the construct validity of the application. The application is said to be valid if the mean NRS scores varied positively with the colour chosen and were accepted if the p-value is less than the 0.05 level of significance. A p-value of <0.001 is obtained in the study (Table 5).

Table 5. Testing the validity using the Kruskal Wallis Test

Colour	N	Mean NRS	Standard deviation	Standard error	95% Confidence level for mean	
					Lower bound	Upper bound
White	165	0.00	0.000	0.000	0.000	0.000
Blue	260	1.62	0.533	0.033	0.155	0.168
Green	203	3.49	0.616	0.043	0.340	0.357
Yellow	62	5.39	0.583	0.074	0.524	0.554
Orange	4	7.25	0.500	0.250	0.645	0.805

Reliability

The reliability is obtained by comparing the mean absolute difference scores between the participants and observing their consistency in inputting data. A discrepancy is expected as an 11- numerical point scale is compared to a 6-point colouration scheme. The Kruskal Wallis test yielded a p-value of <0.001, indicating that some participants inputted data more consistently and accurately than others (Table 6).

Table 6. Testing the reliability using the Kruskal Wallis Test

ID/reading	Sample size	Mean	Standard deviation	Standard error	95% Confidence level for mean	
					Lower bound	Upper bound
LBP1	94	0.10	0.295	0.032	0.03	0.16
LBP2	81	0.13	0.340	0.036	0.06	0.20
LBP3	45	0.58	0.583	0.087	0.40	0.75
LBP4	63	0.24	0.465	0.059	0.12	0.36
LBP5	41	0.39	0.494	0.077	0.23	0.55
LBP6	40	0.25	0.439	0.069	0.11	0.39
LBP7	83	0.66	0.476	0.052	0.56	0.77
LBP8	85	0.12	0.324	0.035	0.05	0.19
LBP9	76	0.46	0.576	0.066	0.33	0.59
LBP10	86	0.93	0.428	0.046	0.84	1.02

5.4   Discussions

With the increase in technological advancements in Smartphones, a Smartphone-based application was created to record pain in real-time. This application incorporated a three-dimensional (3-D) body diagram with a colouration scheme to identify the location of the pain, several evidence-based descriptions, an 11-point NRS, and an open-ended description. Following data collection, a questionnaire was handed to assess the reliability and validity of the application. The data gathered was then analysed for the application's construct reliability and validity.

For this study, CLBP patients were selected due to the frequent presence of pain and the number of individuals suffering from such a condition in western countries, making it one of the most typical causes of chronic pain [18].

5.5   Limitations

Though positive results have been obtained in the study, the researcher recognises several limitations. One of the most significant limitations is that though a considerable number of readings were gathered from the study (694), it has been evaluated on a relatively small population. This study has looked at a very narrow section of CLBP patients, as the inclusion criteria set eliminated several participants from taking part in the study. This possibly could have given non-representative results, especially when it came to the questionnaire.

The application was developed in English and worked on Android 4.0 and onwards, excluding several participants. It was assumed that the participants who owned a Smartphone could understand English as well. However, participants may not have adequately understood the terms and instructions, so some participants may have either stuck to one term or inserted the data incorrectly.

6 Conclusions and Future Scope

The results confirm that the application is valid and reliable for CLBP patients. Therefore as a recommendation, the application should be tested on several other musculoskeletal conditions and see whether results regarding reliability change. Ideally, the reliability is tested via the "test-retest reliability" testing, significantly showing the reliability. For the application to be used in different conditions, further development would be required to operate on other operating systems and for older versions of these operating systems. This would increase the likelihood of finding participants with a particular musculoskeletal condition, both acute and chronic, which may yield different results to the ones obtained.

Further development of the application would be required to increase accuracy in locating the pain. Thus, including regional views rather than just a generalised 3-D body diagram may aid even further, especially in areas like the shoulder and the knee, to precisely localise the pain to 1 particular point. With this feature, the possibility of capturing several images rather than just having one image may also help to give a better representation of the pain. The colouration scheme adopted can also be placed under scrutiny as a pretty generic colour scheme was adopted. Possibly further research would show chronic conditions to be represented by a different colouration scheme.

References

1. Portenoy, R.: Development and testing of a neuropathic pain screening questionnaire: ID pain. Curr. Med. Res. Opin. **22**(8), 1555–1565 (2006)
2. Cohen, M.J., Jangro, W.C., Neff, D.: Pathophysiology of pain. In: Challenging Neuropathic Pain Syndromes: Evaluation and Evidence-Based Treatment, pp. 1–5 (2018)
3. Collins, J.: Oxford handbook of pain management. Anaesthesia (2012)
4. Gaertner, J., Elsner, F., Pollmann-Dahmen, K., Radbruch, L., Sabatowski, R.: Electronic pain diary: a randomized crossover study. J. Pain Sympt. Manage. **28**(3), 259–267 (2004)
5. Stinson, J.N., et al.: e-Ouch: usability testing of an electronic chronic pain diary for adolescents with arthritis. Clin. J. Pain **22**(3), 295–305 (2006)
6. Stone, A.A., Shiffman, S., Schwartz, J.E., Broderick, J.E., Hufford, M.R.: Patient non-compliance with paper diaries. Br. Med. J. **324**(7347), 1193–1194 (2002)
7. Luxton, D.D., McCann, R.A., Bush, N.E., Mishkind, M.C., Reger, G.M.: mHealth for mental health: Integrating smartphone technology in behavioral healthcare. Prof. Psychol. Res. Pract. **42**(6), 505–512 (2011)
8. Cassel, C.K., Leipzig, R.M., Cohen, H.J., Larson, E.B., Meier, D.E., Capello, C.F.: Geriatric Medicine: An Evidence-Based Approach. Springer, New York (2003). https://doi.org/10.1007/b97639
9. Argoff, C.E., McCleane, G.: Pain Management Secrets (2009)
10. Lalloo, C., Kumbhare, D., Stinson, J.N., Henry, J.L.: Pain-QuILT: clinical feasibility of a web-based visual pain assessment tool in adults with chronic pain. J. Med. Internet Res. **16**(5), e127 (2014). https://doi.org/10.2196/jmir.3292
11. IASP. Unrelieved Pain is a Major Global Healthcare Problem (2004)
12. Maher, C., Underwood, M., Buchbinder, R.: Non-specific low back pain. Lancet **389**(10070), 736–747 (2017)

13. Gordon, R., Bloxham, S.: A systematic review of the effects of exercise and physical activity on non-specific chronic low back pain. Healthcare **4**(2), 22 (2016)
14. Breivik, H., Collett, B., Ventafridda, V., Cohen, R., Gallacher, D.: Survey of chronic pain in Europe: prevalence, impact on daily life, and treatment. Eur. J. Pain **10**(4), 287–287 (2006)
15. Woolf, A.D.: Driving musculoskeletal health for Europe: EUMUSC.NET, Reumatismo, 63 (1) (2011)
16. Saravanan, A., Tell, D., Mathews, H., Bajaj, P., Janusek, L.W.: (121) Pain, sleep disturbances, fatigue, mood changes, and underlying inflammation: a study of patients with chronic low back pain (CLBP). J. Pain **20**(4), S6–S7 (2019)
17. Shmagel, A., Foley, R., Ibrahim, H.: Epidemiology of chronic low back pain in US adults: data from the 2009–2010 national health and nutrition examination survey. Arthritis Care Res. **68**(11), 1688–1694 (2016)
18. Knezevic, N.N., Mandalia, S., Raasch, J., Knezevic, I., Candido, K.D.: Treatment of chronic low back pain - New approaches on the horizon. J. Pain Res. **10**, 1111–1123 (2017)
19. Gerhart, J.I., et al.: Variability in negative emotions among individuals with chronic low back pain: relationships with pain and function. Pain **159**(2), 342–350 (2018)
20. Foster, N.E., et al.: Prevention and treatment of low back pain: evidence, challenges, and promising directions. Lancet **391**(10137), 2368–2383 (2018)
21. Buchbinder, R., et al.: Low back pain: a call for action. Lancet **391**(10137), 2384–2388 (2018)
22. Urquhart, D.M., et al.: Efficacy of low-dose amitriptyline for chronic low back pain: a randomised clinical trial. JAMA Intern. Med. **178**(11), 1474–1481 (2018)
23. Paolucci, T., Attanasi, C., Cecchini, W., Marazzi, A., Capobianco, S.V., Santilli, V.: Chronic low back pain and postural rehabilitation exercise: a literature review. J. Pain Res. **12**, 95–107 (2019)
24. Poling, T.: A systematic review of the effects of yoga therapy for chronic low back pain (2019)
25. Spyridonis, F., Ghinea, G., Frank, A.O.: Attitudes of patients toward adoption of 3d technology in pain assessment: qualitative perspective. J. Med. Internet Res. **15**(4), e55 (2013). https://doi.org/10.2196/jmir.2427
26. Vassallo, K., Garg, L., Layfield, C.: Mobile language learning: providing tools that allow the asynchronous, casual and sometimes gamified learning of languages on mobile devices (2016)
27. Jackson, S.L.: Research methods: a modular approach (2014)
28. Chukwu, E., Garg, L., Eze, G.: Mobile health insurance system and associated costs: a cross-sectional survey of primary health centers in Abuja, Nigeria. JMIR mHealth uHealth **4**(2), e37 (2016). https://doi.org/10.2196/mhealth.4342

Predicting Disasters from Tweets Using GloVe Embeddings and BERT Layer Classification

Aabha Ranade[1(✉)], Saurav Telge[1(✉)], and Yash Mate[2(✉)]

[1] B.E. Computer Engineering, Vivekanand Education Society's Institute
of Technology, Mumbai, India
{2018.aabha.ranade,2018.saurav.telge}@ves.ac.in
[2] MS Computer Science, University of Southern California, California, USA
ymate@usc.edu

Abstract. Twitter, a social media platform, has quickly become one of the most reliable sources of news and other information. With an ever-increasing number of users and tweets, it's feasible to use Twitter data to learn about a variety of interesting things that are happening around us. During a disaster, people can get real-time information from Twitter to give and receive help. This paper deals with the extraction of Twitter data in order to identify the tweets that give information about disasters. This is essentially a binary classification problem. GloVe Global Vectors for Word Representation embeddings have been implemented to convert the tweets into vectors which are then trained using the BERT (Bidirectional Encoder Representations from Transformers) model to classify the tweets into two categories: tweets related to disasters and tweets unrelated to disasters. This can be helpful to know how many tweets are related to disasters and are truly informative. Existing research focus on using LSTM, classification models (Random forest, Decision trees, Naive Bayes) which do not give accurate results. The results obtained in the proposed solution got an accuracy of around 87% in both training and validation parts. Thus, the BERT model is better as compared to other models.

Keywords: Disaster prediction · GloVe embeddings · BERT classification · Tweets classification · NLP

1 Introduction

As of 2021, Twitter is one of the most used social media platforms with approximately 200 million daily active users and over 500 million tweets sent per day [1]. This provides an enormous opportunity for data mining and analysis of tweets.

During a crisis, this medium is seen as an excellent place for harvesting information to determine what is happening on the ground. The increased usage of social media, especially during crises provides new information sources from which the relevant authorities can get better insights into the situation under consideration, which is commonly regarded as a vital component of making successful and effective emergency response decisions. Exploiting and analyzing disaster-related tweets is critical since the knowledge gleaned can be utilized to improve disaster response. The subject

© Springer Nature Switzerland AG 2022
D. Garg et al. (Eds.): IACC 2021, CCIS 1528, pp. 492–503, 2022.
https://doi.org/10.1007/978-3-030-95502-1_37

and content of tweets vary greatly, and the influx of tweets, especially in the aftermath of a catastrophe, can be overwhelming. It consists of socio-behavioral patterns such as intensified information seeking and increased information dissemination. Using the Twitter Search APIs [2], NodeXL [3] and other such tools, data from Twitter can be retrieved with the help of Twitter hashtags. The tweets can then be categorized as relevant (related to disasters) or irrelevant. There are three main approaches to this issue: Filtering tweets based on factors such as location and the presence of keywords or hashtags, crowdsourcing, and machine-learning approaches.

This paper presents a novel approach for predicting disasters through Tweets. We have performed data analysis on a dataset from a Kaggle competition called Real or Not? NLP with Disaster Tweets [4], which consists of training and testing sets having the text of the tweets, keywords present in the tweets, and the location the tweet was sent from. The task is to predict whether a given tweet is about a real disaster or not. To address this text classification problem we have used word embedding transformation followed by a BERT model. Word embedding is the representation of text data into numerical vector format which can be given as an input to machine learning models. In this project, we have made use of Stanford's GloVe (Global Vectors for Word Representation) embeddings. Next, we have employed a pre-trained BERT model to perform the classification. The performance of the model is tested by calculating the precision, recall, F1 score, and accuracy.

2 Literature Survey

2.1 Text Classification Using Machine Learning Techniques

Authors M. Ikonomakis, S. Kotsiantis, and V. Tampakas illustrate the text classification process using machine learning techniques in their paper. The major goal of this work is to propose text classification strategies that will perform efficiently even when additional information besides the pure text, such as the hierarchical structure of the texts or date of publication, etc. is not available [5].

2.2 Sentimental Analysis of Twitter Data Using Classifier Algorithms

Authors Sharvil Shah, K Kumar, and Ra. K. Saravanaguru offer a method to detect a user's current attitude toward a specific issue in this work. They have provided not only a binary classification of positive and negative data, but also a hashtag classification for topic modeling, an emoticon analysis for assessing post polarity, and multiple language support using tools like Google Language Detector and Langid.

They've also used Google Chart Tools to create a graphical depiction of the sentiment analysis. The polarity shifter using Naïve Bayes classification algorithm and topic modeling are two critical steps in their method, which leads to a high 81% accuracy [6].

2.3 Event Classification and Retrieving User's Geographical Location Based on Live Tweets on Twitter and Prioritizing Them to Alert the Concern Authority

Authors Sarthak Vage, Sarvesh Wanode, Kunal Sorte, and Dipak Gaikar have presented a system where the user can enter keywords related to a situation and the application runs live to show the priority and classified tweets dynamically. The proposed method employs the Naive Bayes algorithm, a stochastic model that belongs to a class of simple probabilistic classifiers based on Bayes theorem application.

Various models were tested to classify as per priority, with XGBoost, a decision tree-based Machine Learning method that uses a gradient boosting framework, providing the best results. The geo-location of the tweet is an essential characteristic as it's necessary to know the user's location in specific scenarios [7].

2.4 Automatic Classification of Disaster-Related Tweets

In this work, authors Beverly Estephany Parilla-Ferrer, Proceso L. Fernandez Jr., and Jaime T. Ballena IV have constructed a machine learning model that categorizes disaster-related tweets as informative or uninformative, as well as assesses the performance of two of the most used machine classification methods, Naive Bayes and Support Vector Machine. Their findings show that SVM surpassed Naive Bayes in terms of accuracy, recall, AUC, and F-measure using 10-fold cross-validation, but Naive Bayes outperformed SVM in precision [8].

2.5 Comparing BERT Against Traditional Machine Learning Text Classification

In this work, four distinct text classification experiments have been carried out by the authors Santiago Gonzalez-Carvajal and Eduardo C. Garrido-Merch´an. In order to compare the results, they have employed two distinct classifiers in all of the experiments: the BERT classifier and a conventional classifier that trains machine learning algorithms in features retrieved by the Term Frequency - Inverse Document Frequency (TF-IDF) technique. Their findings show that BERT not only outperforms the traditional NLP approach but is also comparatively easier to implement [9].

2.6 Usage and Analysis of Twitter During 2015 Chennai Flood Towards Disaster Management

This work by authors Meera R. Nair, G. R. Ramya, and P. Bagavathi Sivakumar focuses on tweets regarding the 2015 Chennai Flood. Extensive data exploration and analysis of these tweets show that the tweets fall under five distinct categories. Three machine learning techniques were employed to classify the tweets: Random Forests, Decision Trees, and Naive Bayes. Precision, recall, and F-measure was used to evaluate performance. It was found that Random Forests was more suited for twitter analysis and classification. This paper also focuses on identifying the most influential users of the Chennai flood using data mining techniques [10].

2.7 A Comparative Analysis of Machine Learning Techniques for Disaster-Related Tweet Classification

In this work, authors Abhinav Kumar, Jyoti Prakash Singh, and Sunil Saumya have implemented five deep neural network-based models and seven machine learning classifiers on tweets related to earthquakes, hurricanes, floods, and wildfires. The tweets are classified into six different categories. Their findings show that deep neural networks give better classification results than traditional classifiers even when there is data imbalance. GloVe embeddings gave the best results for wildfire-related tweets while Crisis embeddings proved to be better in case of earthquakes [11].

2.8 Multimodal Analysis of Disaster Tweets

In this work, authors Akash Kumar Gautam, Luv Misra, Ajit Kumar, Kush Misra, Shashwat Aggarwal, Rajiv Ratn Shah have analyzed multimodal data related to various natural calamities from the CrisisMDD dataset consisting of both textual and image data extracted from Twitter. They have proposed a novel decision diffusion technique in this paper to classify the data as informative or non-informative [12].

3 Methodology

The basic outline of the project is as follows (Fig. 1):

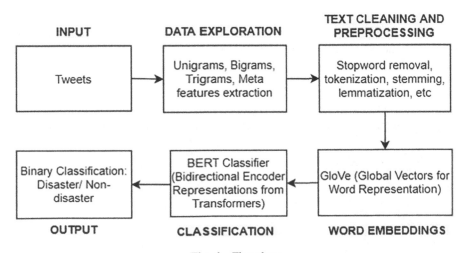

Fig. 1. Flowchart

3.1 Data Exploration

The dataset we used contains 7613 rows of text along with the location, keywords and the target, that is, whether it is a disaster or not. For testing purposes, we have a separate CSV containing 3263 rows. A small dataset gives rise to the problem of overfitting especially in a dataset involving textual features. Thus this amount is sufficient to create a robust and reliable model. Data gathered from tweets contains a lot of ambiguity and hence needs to be processed before passing it to the model. For this firstly we segregate the data into unigrams, bigrams, and trigrams, as usually unigrams are sufficient for training but using bigrams and trigrams allows for complex meanings to be processed by the model efficiently (Fig. 2).

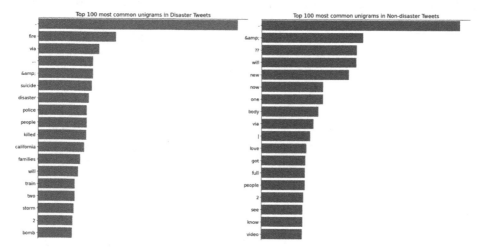

Fig. 2. Unigrams list

The most frequent unigrams in disaster tweets already provide information about disasters. Some of the terms are quite difficult to use in other situations. Verbs are the most prevalent unigrams in non-disaster tweets. Because the phrases are originating from individual users, the majority of them have an informal active structure (Fig. 3).

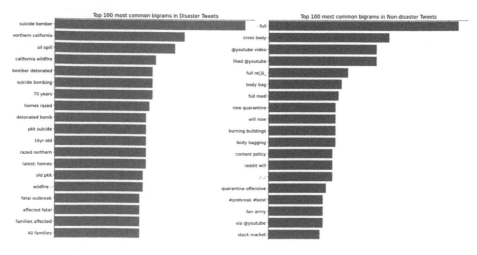

Fig. 3. Bigrams list

The most common bigrams provide additional information about the disasters as compared to unigrams. However, punctuations have to be removed from these words (Fig. 4).

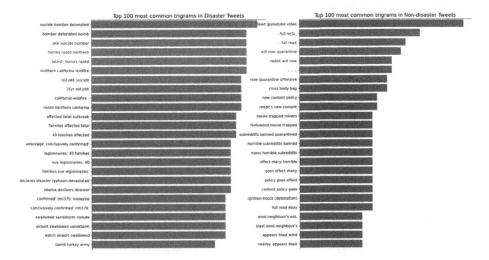

Fig. 4. Trigrams list

Trigrams are extremely similar to the most prevalent bigrams in disaster tweets. They provide a lot of information related to disasters, however, they may not supply any extra information beyond bigrams.

3.2 Meta Features Extraction

Meta-feature distributions in classes and datasets can assist identify disaster tweets. Because the majority of the tweets come from news organizations, it may be deduced that disaster tweets are written more professionally with lengthier words than non-disaster tweets. Because they come from individual people, non-disaster tweets have more mistakes than disaster tweets. The meta-features used for the analysis are:

- word_count number of words in the text
- unique_word_count number of unique words in the text
- stop_word_count number of stop words in the text
- url_count number of URLs in text
- mean_word_length average character count in words
- char_count number of characters in the text
- punctuation_count number of punctuations in text
- hashtag_count number of hashtags (#) in text
- mention_count number of mentions (@) in text

All of the meta-features in the training and test sets have extremely similar distributions, indicating that the training and test sets are from the same sample. All of the meta-features provide information on the target, although some of them, such as URL count, hashtag count, and mention count, are useless. For disaster and non-disaster tweets, however, word count, unique word count, stop word count, mean word length, char count, and punctuation count have significantly different distributions. These characteristics are beneficial in models.

3.3   Text Cleaning and Preprocessing

The preprocessing of tweets is a crucial step for any text mining task. Tweets often include personal opinions and views in addition to factual information. Tweets that have not been preprocessed are very unstructured and may contain a lot of redundant data. Text cleaning helps us to get rid of noisy and inconsistent data which may hamper the efficiency of our machine learning model. Multiple steps are taken in the preprocessing of tweets as mentioned below:

- Lowercasing the entire text
- Removal of punctuation marks
- Removal of URLs
- Removal of hashtags and usernames
- Removal of numbers and special characters
- Correction of typos, informal abbreviations are written in their long forms.
- Tokenization
- Stemming and Lemmatization
- Removal of stop words

Tokenization is the process of converting a sequential piece of text into smaller units called tokens. These tokens are then used to build a vocabulary. In traditional NLP approaches, the vocabulary is used as a feature to train the model.

Both Stemming and lemmatization are methods to convert words into their root forms. This eliminates the need to store all forms of words and prevents the overfitting of the model.

Stopwords are common words such as 'the', 'on', 'an', etc. which do not provide any important meaning to the text. It is important to remove such stopwords from the data as they do not contribute to the classification task and take up the valuable processing time.

3.4   Cardinality and Target Distribution

Locations and keywords are a part of the tweets. Locations are generally given by the user. Hence, there are far too many unique values for the locations. Therefore, locations should not be used as a feature. Keywords, on the other hand, are context-specific. So a keyword can be used as a feature. It is also feasible to utilise target encoding on keywords if the training and test sets are from the same sample (Figs. 5 and 6).

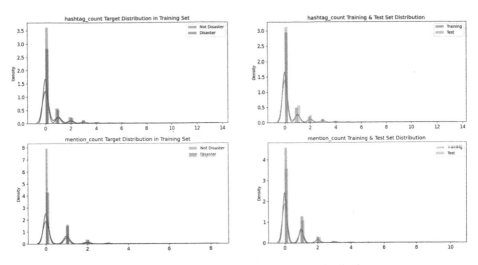

Fig. 5. Hashtag and mention count target distribution

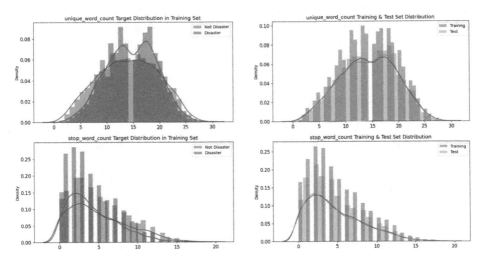

Fig. 6. Unique word count and stop-word count target distribution

3.5 Target Features

The class distributions for 0 (Not Disaster) and 1 (Disaster) are 57% and 43%, respectively. Because the classes are almost similar in size, cross-validation does not need stratification by the target (Fig. 7).

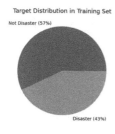
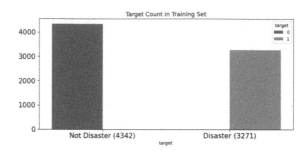

Fig. 7. Target distribution graph

3.6 Architecture of the Disaster Detector Function

The preprocessed input text is fed into the DisasterDetector(), a wrapper function, that includes the above-mentioned cross-validation and metrics. The FullTokenizer class [15] performs the tokenization of input text. The max sequence length (set to 128) property can be used to adjust the length of text sequences. During the learning phase, parameters like Learning Rate (0.0001), Epochs (10), and Batch size (32) produced the best results. After the last layer of BERT, no dense or pooling layers are introduced. Because other optimizers have issues converging, SGD is employed as an optimizer (Fig. 8).

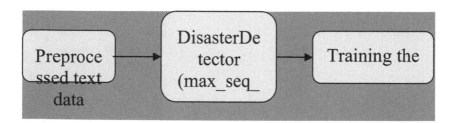

Fig. 8. Architecture

3.7 Word Embedding Using GloVe

Word embedding is an essential part of any natural language processing problem. Machine learning models cannot directly work on textual data. Hence, it is necessary to convert the text into a numerical format. Word embeddings are numerical representations of text. There are several methods for this such as Bag of Words.

TF-IDF, Word2Vec, etc. In this work, we have employed Stanford's GloVe (global vectors for word representation) Pre-Trained Word Embedding [13]. The gloVe helps to capture the semantic and syntactic meaning of words by deriving the relationship between the words using simple statistics. GloVe encodes the information of the probability ratio in the form of word vectors. Using a pre-trained model has two major advantages: Firstly, as it is trained on very large datasets having a rich vocabulary, it performs well even if the data has a lot of rare, uncommon words. Moreover, they are much faster than learning embeddings from scratch. Another benefit of GloVe is that, unlike Word2vec, it includes global statistics (word co-occurrence) to generate word vectors instead of just depending on local statistics (local context information of words) as it uses matrix factorization techniques on the word-context matrix.

3.8 Classification Using BERT Model

This research requires the BERT family of transformers from the TensorFlow Models repository on GitHub [14]. Each token of input text is processed by the BERT family of models (utilizing a Transformer encoder architecture), in the full context of all tokens before and after, therefore the name: Bidirectional Encoder Representations from Transformers. It uses L = 12 hidden layers, that is, Transformer blocks, a hidden size of H = 768, and A = 12 attention heads. The entire BERT is pre-trained for English on Wikipedia and BooksCorpus. All the text is converted to lower-case before tokenization into word pieces, and all the accent markers are cleaned. This Neural network-based approach is implemented as traditional techniques like Naive Bayes, Term Frequency Inverse Document Frequency (TF-IDF), Count Vectorizer only take into account the frequency of the words and not their semantics, that is, their meaning, hence the performance hinders when the amount of data and the complexity of the sentences increases. Therefore, implementing a Neural Network centric method (BERT) is more preferential.

4   Results

After data preprocessing and feature extraction, the dataset was trained on the BERT layer. We froze the outcomes of training and testing at 10 epochs as the curve started plateauing after 6 epochs, hence it was redundant to train the model for more epochs. The classification reports presented in the figure clearly show the values of different parameters used for evaluation after training the model for 2 folds segregated using Stratified K-Fold. The results obtained are Training Precision: 0.873517, Training Recall: 0.854729, Training F1: 0.860643, Validation Precision: 0.824855, Validation Recall: 0.809625, Validation F1: 0.814241 for 0th Fold and Training Precision: 0.884135, Training Recall: 0.867071, Training F1: 0.872638, Validation Precision: 0.85964, Validation Recall: 0.842464, Validation F1: 0.847904 for 1st Fold. From these results, we can infer that the BERT model is successful in understanding the texts and can be employed in detecting disasters from tweets (Fig. 9).

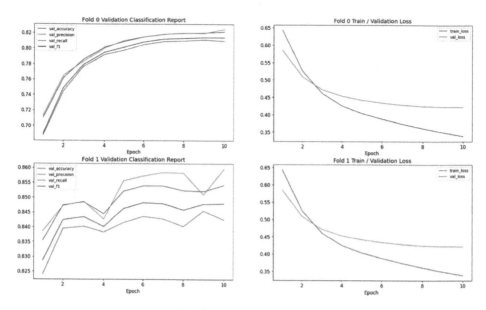

Fig. 9. Classification report

5 Conclusion

Twitter has proved to be a rich source of information for data mining and analysis. This can be especially useful during calamities and disasters as many individuals, NGOs, and government agencies rely on Twitter for information transfer. In this work, we have dealt with the binary classification of disaster-related tweets. We have employed trained glove embeddings and BERT classification models for this purpose. Utilizing GloVe we generated word vector representations using aggregated global word-word co-occurrence statistics. The actual classification task is done using Google's BERT model. BERT scans the full sequence of words at once, unlike typical NLP models that read the text from left to right or right to left. BERT utilizes a Transformer, which is essentially a mechanism for establishing relationships between the words in a dataset. The predictions made are robust and can accurately differentiate between a disaster-related tweet (target) and an unrelated tweet. In the future, we can make it a multi-class classification problem, wherein we can also predict what kind of disaster is mentioned in the tweet. e.g. Earthquake, Forest Fire, Tsunami, Flood. A web application that informs the concerned government authorities in case of disasters through email and SMS notifications to send relief is a plus.

References

1. https://www.omnicoreagency.com/twitter-statistics/
2. https://developer.twitter.com/en/docs/twitter-api/v1/tweets/search/api-reference/get-search-tweets
3. https://www.smrfoundation.org/nodexl/
4. https://www.kaggle.com/c/nlp-getting-started/data
5. Ikonomakis, E., Kotsiantis, S., Tampakas, V.: Text classification using machine learning techniques. WSEAS Trans. Comput. **4**, 966–974 (2005)
6. Shah, S., Kumar, K., Sarvananguru, R.K.: Sentimental analysis of Twitter data using classifier algorithms. Int. J. Electr. Comput. Eng. **6**(1), 357 (2016). https://doi.org/10.11591/ijece.v6i1.pp357-366
7. Vage, S., Wanode, S., Sorte, K., Gaikar, D.: Event Classification and Retrieving User's Geographical Location based on Live Tweets on Twitter and Prioritizing them to Alert the Concern Authority (2020)
8. Parilla-Ferrer, B.E., Fernandez, P.L., Ballena, J.T.: Automatic classification of disaster-related tweets. In: Proceedings of the International conference on Innovative Engineering Technologies (ICIET), December 2014, vol. 62 (2014)
9. González-Carvajal, S., Garrido-Merchán, E.C.: Comparing BERT against traditional machine learning text classification (2020). https://arxiv.org/abs/2005.13012
10. Nair, M.R., Ramya, G.R., Sivakumar, P.B.: Usage and analysis of Twitter during 2015 Chennai flood towards disaster management. Procedia Comput. Sci. **115**, 350–358 (2017)
11. Kumar, A., Singh, J.P., Saumya, S.: A comparative analysis of machine learning techniques for disaster-related tweet classification. In: 2019 IEEE R10 Humanitarian Technology Conference (R10-HTC) (47129), pp. 222–227 (2019). https://doi.org/10.1109/R10-HTC47129.2019.9042443
12. Gautam, A.K., Misra, L., Kumar, A., Misra, K., Aggarwal, S., Shah, R.R.: Multimodal analysis of disaster tweets. IEEE Fifth Int. Conf. Multim. Big Data **2019**, 94–103 (2019). https://doi.org/10.1109/BigMM.2019.00-38
13. Pennington, J., Socher, R., Manning, C.: Glove: global vectors for word representation. EMNLP. **14**, 1532–1543 (2014). https://doi.org/10.3115/v1/D14-1162
14. https://github.com/tensorflow/models/tree/master/official/nlp/bert
15. https://github.com/tensorflow/models/blob/master/official/nlp/bert/tokenization.py

Contextual Quality Assessment of the Newspaper Articles Based on Keyword Extraction

Samya Muhuri[1]([⊠]) and Susanta Chakraborty[2]

[1] School of Computer Science Engineering and Technology, Bennett University, Greater Noida, Uttar Pradesh, India
samya.muhuri@bennett.edu.in
[2] Department of Computer Science and Technology, Indian Institute of Engineering Science and Technology, Shibpur, Howrah, West Bengal, India
sc@cs.iiests.ac.in

Abstract. It is often seen that the same news or stories are portrayed in different newspapers from a separate perspective. It always confuses the readers to determine which newspaper publishes better quality news with the rich content in a specialized domain. Thus, contextual quality analysis of any document or newspaper report is always a research concern. In this work, we have proposed a novel graph theoretic method to decide the quality of the newspaper articles written on any specific subject. Different node centrality measuring metrics of the complex graph like degree centrality, betweenness centrality, and clustering coefficient are considered for judging the association among the keywords in any concerned text piece. The amount of necessary and contextual words are presented in an article related to the specific subject represents the quality of the document. The method can be operated to rank the published news articles based solely on contextual quality. Our approach performs without any semantics and prerequisite knowledge. As a case study, we analyze some match reports of FIFA men's football world cup, 2018 published in three popular newspapers circulated in India. The analytical results reveal the newspaper that published the best quality news reports about the tournament. Our model depicts the unbiased answer than the human perspective and can be used as an alternative procedure in interdisciplinary research areas.

Keywords: Contextual words · Document quality analysis · Football world cup · Graph centrality · News articles

1 Introduction

Newspapers or daily play an important role to circulate the ongoing events to the common mass. News is usually classified in various groups including political, social, business, cultural, entertainment, advertisements, sports and many more. Often on a single event, different newspapers share their opinion from

D. Garg et al. (Eds.): IACC 2021, CCIS 1528, pp. 504–518, 2022.
https://doi.org/10.1007/978-3-030-95502-1_38

independent angles and create confusion among the readers. Use of unnecessary words and context, make the story attractive for the readers but sooner or later, distorted the originality and importance of the news. People always have their personal choices or biased towards any particular newspaper based on language, availability, price or regular habit. In the commercialized world, the constant increment of the news gossip demands an unorthodox method to assess the contextual quality of the newspaper articles and rank them based on any unbiased method. In this paper, we propose a graph theoretic method to judge the quality of the articles by realizing the number of contextual words exists in any published article.

Any news article or report is usually a representation of a group of related sentences where each sentence is a cluster of associated words. The association of the words as a whole reflects the main essence of the news story. Sometimes, the news is replete with lots of extraneous words or subject and create ambiguity within the readers. In the computational field, the content of any report can be represented as a graph of some words those are connected among themselves. The corresponding graph can be analyzed with computational metrics to find valuable words or keywords related to the concerned subject. The keywords and their ties with the neighbouring words in the generated graphs depict suitability and quality of the concerned text document. The keywords can be extracted from any word graph using various node centrality measuring parameters, namely degree centrality, betweenness centrality and clustering coefficient.

As the generated graph is unaware of any semantic knowledge, it is robust and independent of the corpus. In this paper, we compare some sports reports published by different newspapers to review similar matches. We categorize them based on the proposed quality parameter. As a case study, we choose online reports of three newspapers and twelve random matches of FIFA (The Fédération Internationale de Football Association) men's football world cup, 2018 held in Russia. Result differentiate the newspaper which publishes superior quality match review reports. Results are also generated from the available benchmark data set to establish the prospect of the proposed method. Our method is unbiased, language independent and can be used as an alternative framework for document quality analysis.

2   Related Works and Our Contributions

For the last few decades, topic modeling [1] and sentiment analysis [2] are getting tremendous attention within text mining and natural language processing (NLP) research community. Both of these methods are heavily dependent on the appropriate keywords extraction. Most of the NLP methods are mostly relies on Latent Dirichlet Allocation (LDA) method and 'bag of word' model [3]. For vectorization of the text data, 'text2vec' framework [4] has been explored. But in most of the existing works, only topics or polarity of the documents are analyzed. In this manuscript, we would focus only on finding the contextual quality of any article based on the keywords used for elaborating the theme.

Automatic keyword extraction [5] can be broadly divided into three approaches which are statistical, machine learning and graph based method. Term frequency (TF) [6] and inverse document frequency (IDF) [7] identification from any report are the most popular approaches in statistical method. Machine learning approaches [8] take advantage of the initial corpus and make the decision based on it. TextRank [9], DegExt [10], and KeyGaph [11] methods are explored for graph based keyword extraction. Most of the statistical and machine learning methods depend on the corresponding corpus and work well only for a specific subject or only on the trained corpus. The machine learning methods suffer from different problems, mainly like overfitting, underfitting and also need some predefined knowledge of the experts. On the other hand, existing graph based methods are more generic but work well for topic modeling, word scoring, or finding word positional importance.

Quality of the transparent text is assessed with the convolutional neural network in [12]. But those works are mostly taken advantage of the supplied dictionary and limited over a certain topic. The works also suffer from "order effects", i.e. different results are generated if the order of training data is varied [13]. In this paper, we propose a method to examine the significance of the correlated words that are presented in the report and establish the contextual quality of the article based on the corresponding topic.

3 Preliminaries

3.1 Quality of Document

Classifying the news reports according to the contextual quality is quite subjective and can be debatable at times. Quality of any published document mostly depends on the targeted readers. There is no defined measuring parameter exists for the quality of the documents. In the text, context is the setting of words respect to an event. Contextual quality mostly depends on the grammar, quality of the words chosen, readability and its usefulness based on the subject. The words quality and relevance is not similar respect to any document. Relevance depends on the time and scenario, in which a particular word or set of words is used. Here, we focus only on the quality but not on the relevance of any report.

3.2 Graph Centrlity Metrics

We use some graph centrality metrics, namely degree and betweenness centrality, to measure the correlation within the words that are used in the document.

Degree Centrality [14]. Degree centrality of a node is defined as the number of links incident upon the corresponding node. The value defines the total number of immediate neighbours of any node. It can be denoted as

$$C_D(i) = deg(i) \tag{1}$$

where $deg(i)$ is the degree of node i.

Betweenness Centrality. In graph, there exists a shortest path between the vertices such that the path minimizes the number of edges by which it passes through. The betweenness centrality for each vertex is the number of these shortest paths that pass through the corresponding vertex [15]. The betweenness centrality of a node i is given by the expression

$$C_b(i) = \sum_{x \neq i \neq y \in v} \frac{\sigma(x, y, i)}{\sigma(x, y)} \tag{2}$$

where $\sigma(x, y)$ is the total number of shortest paths from node x to node y and $\sigma(x, y, i)$ is the number of those paths that pass through i. Betweenness centrality value is always high for any influential node in the network.

3.3   Clustering Coefficient

Clustering co-efficient [16] can express the internal relationship among the neighbours. Clustering Coefficient $CC(i)$ of a node i can be measured by

$$CC(i) = \frac{no.\ of\ edges\ between\ neighbour\ of\ node\ i}{max\ no.\ of\ edges\ may\ exists\ between\ neighbours} \tag{3}$$

A maximum number of C_2^n edges may exist among n neighbours of node i. $CC(i)$ value 1 represents that every neighbour connected to i is also connected within themselves, and 0 otherwise. Every node shows $CC(i)$ value 1 in a complete graph and it represents that the nodes are not dependent on each other.

3.4   Mantel Test

To quantify statistical significance of the two data sets [17], Mantel test [18] is utilized. It calculates the association between two matrices A and B by calculating Pearson correlation coefficient $[r(AB)]$. The value of $[r(AB)]$ lies between -1 to $+1$, where being close to -1 specifies strong negative correlation, $+1$ specifies strong positive correlation, and 0 specifies no correlation.
Mantel test is based on the following cross product term:
$Z = \sum_{i=1}^{n} \sum_{j=1}^{n} x_{ij} y_{ij}$ where x and y are the variables measured at locations i and j respectively, and n is the number of elements in the distance matrices. The Z-standardized of Mantel statistic $[r(AB)]$ is computed by calculating the Pearson correlation coefficient [19] between the two matrices A and B.

4   Our Approach for Quality Detection of Any Article

Our Approach for quality detection of any article is based on two major steps which are i) representing the whole text with its equivalent graph consists of words and their relation and ii) analyzing the obtained graph to extract the hidden keywords that reflect the main essence of the text body.

4.1   Representation of the Text Report with Graph

Any document or report is collection of some statements or lines l and can be represented as $d = \{l_1, l_2, \ldots, l_n\}$. l is collection of words w, $l = \{w_1, w_2, \ldots, w_n\}$. The tokens are generated from the document after tokenization i.e. $T_d = \{t_1, t_2, \ldots, t_n : t_i \in d\}$. The stopwords are removed from the tokens and stemming is done for the rest of the words as described in [20]. This will give filtered words W_f. For a document d, total number of filtered words, $W_f = \{W_1, W_2 \ldots W_n\}$ where W_i denotes filtered words per line. Now, a window of size s is taken where $(2 \leq s << q)$ and $q = max|W_i|$; $(W_i \in W_f)$. This window states the number of filtered words that would be connected directly to each other in the graph. This model restricts the connection if a full-stop period (.) comes in between two words. Edge list E is prepared using the tokens where $E = \{(t_i, t_{i+1}), (t_i, t_{i+2}), \ldots, (t_i, t_{i+s}), \forall t \in T_d\}$. After generating the edge list, a non-weighted and undirected equivalent graph, $G = (V, E)$ is initiated where V $(V \in T_d)$ and E represent nodes and edges respectively. In this graph, words are represented as nodes and their relationships in the source text are depicted as edges.

4.2   Analysing the Generated Graph

The influential keywords are to be discovered from the already generated graph to examine the quality of the document. At first, the topic is extricated by discovering the intermediate keywords. Then these intermediate keywords is mined again for quality analysis. Higher degree nodes denote the words which are much more important than the rest of the words. The nodes are associated with a high number of associate nodes or words and show superiority over the remaining nodes. A higher value of betweenness centrality signifies a large number of associated nodes are highly dependent on the specific node and maximize the influence of the corresponding word. The lower value of the clustering coefficient indicates the nodes have more influence over the rest of the words as the associate nodes are not connected within themselves. We assume that the superior words are the representative of the concerned topic. Thus, the the nodes having degree greater than the average degree, the coefficient of cluster less than average clustering coefficient and betweenness centrality greater than average betweenness centrality of the graph have been extracted. The extracted nodes are the intermediate keywords, and they represent the concerned topic.

A subgraph $\hat{G}$ of the graph G is generated from the tokens T_d. The subgraph $\hat{G} = (\hat{V}, \hat{E})$ show the relation within the intermediate keywords and their acquaintance. Here $\hat{V} = \{v_1, v_2, \ldots v_j | v_i \in$ intermediate keywords$\}$ and $\hat{E} = \{e_1, e_2, \ldots e_m | e_i = \{u_i, v_i\}\}$ where $e_i \in E$ & $(u_i, v_i) \in \hat{V}$. Further processing is needed to extract the most influential nodes of the subgraph. Now we look for the association among the words. In the resultant subgraph, the connections between one intermediate keyword and its acquaintance are less compared to the connection between two intermediate keywords. The bonding within the keywords examine the essence of the document.

Now again extraction of the nodes from $\hat{G}$ is done in the same manner. This process refines the intermediate keywords and determines the final set of influential keywords from the whole document. This process will go on in repetitive manner until the final keywords(from the last subgraph) is matched with the gold standard keywords. From our assumption about the quality of any document, we can conclude that the population of the influential keywords $V_f(V_f \subset \hat{V})$ in any published document mostly regulate the quality of the corresponding report.

Table 1. An Example data set

Description	Example 1	Example 2
Raw Text (d)	Python is an interpreted high-level programming language for general purpose programming. Python has a design philosophy that emphasizes code readability, notably using significant whitespace	Python features a dynamic type system and automatic memory management. It supports multiple programming paradigms, including object-oriented, imperative, functional and procedural, and has a large and comprehensive standard library
Collection of words (l)	{'python','is', 'an', 'interpreted', 'high level', 'programming', 'language', 'for','general', 'purpose', 'programming', '.', 'Python', 'has', 'a', 'design','philosophy', 'that', 'emphasizes', 'code', 'readability', ',', 'notably', 'using', 'significant', 'whitespace', '.'}	{'python', 'features', 'a', 'dynamic', 'type', 'system', 'and', 'automatic', 'memory','management', '.', 'It', 'supports', 'multiple', 'programming', 'paradigms', ',' 'including', 'object', 'oriented', ',', 'imperative', ',', 'functional','and', 'procedural', ',', 'and', 'has', 'a', 'large', 'and', 'comprehensive','standard', 'library', '.'}
Filtered words (W_f)	['python','interpret', 'high level', 'program', 'language', 'general' 'purpose', 'program'], ['python', 'design', 'philosophi', 'emphas', 'code', 'read', 'notab', 'use', 'signific', 'whitespace']	['python','feature', 'dynamic','type', 'system', 'auto', 'memory', 'manage'], ['support', 'multiple','program', 'paradigm', 'include', 'object', 'oriented','imper','function', 'procedure','large', 'compre', 'standard', 'library']]

Table 2. Intermediate and final keywords from the example documents

	Example 1	Example 2
intermediate Keywords	Python, notab, emphas, code, read, signific, program	System, large, type, paradigm, include, object, imper, function, procedure, memory, standard
final (influential) Keywords	Python, notab, emphas, read	Large, paradigm, object, imper, function, procedure

4.3   Features

Now we extract some features from each document to determine the contextual quality. We extract filtered, intermediate and final keyword percentage from each article. In the document, let the total number of filtered words are (W_f), tokens are (T_d), intermediate keywords are V and the total number of influential keywords are (V_f). Then,

$$Filtered\ keywords(\%) = \frac{W_f}{T_d} * 100 \qquad (4)$$

$$intermediate\ keywords(\%) = \frac{V}{W_f} * 100 \qquad (5)$$

$$Final\ keywords\ (\%) = \frac{V_f}{T_d} * 100 \qquad (6)$$

The filtered keyword percentage denotes the percentage of information embedded in the document. These words may or may not related to the actual topic but present some relative information. Percentage of intermediate keywords designate the number of words that are presented to describe the topic. These words are true evidence of the contextual information. Final keyword percentage is the genuine reflection about the correlation of the contextual words and exhibits their presence in the article. Based on the majority, the document with populated filtered, intermediate and final keywords would be distinguished as the quality document from the class of articles on a similar topic. The quality of the document manifests its qualitative richness than the other similar reports.

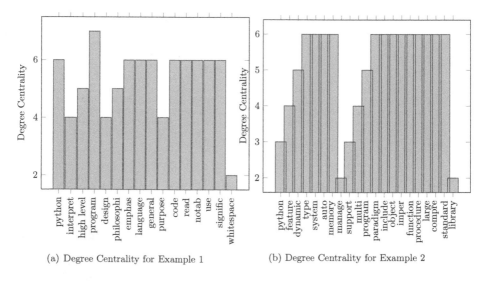

(a) Degree Centrality for Example 1   (b) Degree Centrality for Example 2

Fig. 1. Degree centrality for initial graph extracted from examples

4.4   Illustration with an Example

We illustrate our proposed method with a small example. In Table 1, two texts are given to describe the 'Python' programming language. Now, based on our method, we examine which example is rich in contextual quality and truly represents the hidden information. Figure 1a and 1b illustrate degree centrality of the filtered nodes from the example 1 and 2, respectively. The average node degree for the first example is 5.34, whereas for the second graph the value is 5.04. Now the nodes with degree centrality more than the average value are considered for each case. Clustering coefficient and betweenness centrality of the

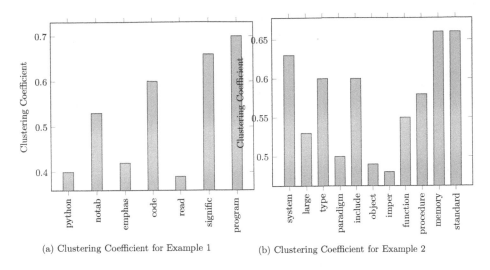

(a) Clustering Coefficient for Example 1

(b) Clustering Coefficient for Example 2

Fig. 2. Clustering coefficient for high degree nodes extracted from examples

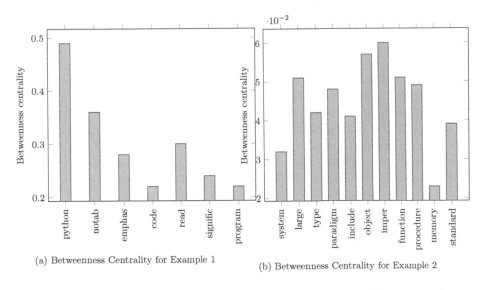

(a) Betweenness Centrality for Example 1

(b) Betweenness Centrality for Example 2

Fig. 3. Betweenness centrality for high degree nodes extracted from examples

corresponding nodes are calculated as portrayed in the Figs. 2a, 2b and 3a, 3b respectively. The union of the nodes having a degree greater than the average degree of the graph, the coefficient of cluster less than average clustering coefficient and betweenness centrality greater than average betweenness centrality is considered. The extracted nodes are the intermediate keywords, and they represent the concerned topic. Now the intermediate keywords are further analysed as shown in the Fig. 4a and 4b. The intermediate and final keywords are shown

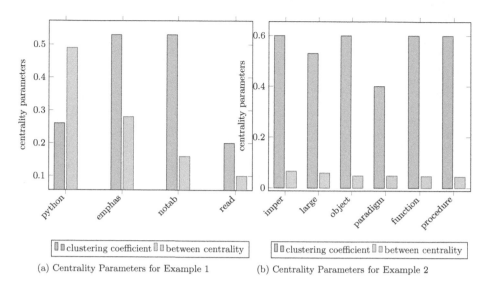

(a) Centrality Parameters for Example 1   (b) Centrality Parameters for Example 2

Fig. 4. Comparison of different centrality values of final keywords in the examples

from both the examples in Table 2. The percentage of filtered, intermediate and final keywords from both the examples are shown in Table 3. The result reflects that the second document is of better quality as it consists of a greater percentage of contextual information. It is a significant observation that the word 'Python' is missing in both the set of the intermediate and influential keyword of example 2. But more significant words are present in the extracted word set that truly define any programing paradigm. As a result, the words distinguished themselves as more superior than example 1. The experiment concludes that our method only depends on the relationship of the words but not their semantic.

Table 3. Keyword percentage from the example documents

	Parameters	Filtered keywords %	Intermediate keywords %	Final keywords %
Example 1	$W_f = 18$ $T_d = 24$ $V = 7$ $V_f = 4$	75.00	38.89	16.67
Example 2	$W_f = 22$ $T_d = 30$ $V = 11$ $V_f = 6$	73.33	50.00	20.00

Table 4. Performance evaluation

Data set	Method	Precision	Recall	F1-Score
Krapivin2009	**PositionRank**	36.95	40.90	38.82
	sCAKE	42.48	48.78	46.57
	Our Method	42.02	48.46	45.41
NLM500	**PositionRank**	19.69	26.60	22.63
	sCAKE	24.88	34.00	29.58
	Our Method	24.62	33.21	29.08

5 Result and Analysis

5.1 Comparison with Other Existing Methods

We have extracted keywords in three different layers, which are filtered, intermediate and final keywords. Filtered keywords are moreover comparable with the filtered word data set of the existing methods. In our approach, intermediate and final keywords denote the topic and the quality of the concerned document, respectively. It has been established that the conventional parameters like accuracy, precision, recall, F1-score are always not suitable to decide the correctness of any quality measuring method. The parameters take decision based on the 'gold standard' which is debatable over time, specially to judge 'quality'. We have tested our method on two publicly available data sets which are Krapivin2009 [21] and NLM500 [22]. The gold standard keywords are also available for these data sets. Krapivin2009 and NLM500 contain 2304 and 500 documents in the corpus, respectively. As no other alternatives are available, we compare the performance of our method with two state-of-the-art algorithms which are PositionRank [23] and sCAKE [5]. For evaluation, we consider the number of intermediate keywords extracted from our method. The comparative results are shown in Table 4. Our method outperforms PositionRank algorithm and works equally well like the sCAKE approach. We want to mention here that, like the existing methods [5,9,10,23], our method does not concern about the number of keywords extracted in each step. As mentioned earlier, keyword extraction is a very subjective procedure and depends upon the user assumption. More number of keywords do not necessarily judge the superiority of the algorithm. We are only worried about the extraction of the keywords that are strongly tied with all the associated words and robustly depict the theme as well as the quality of the report.

Table 5. Result on movie review data set

Type of reviews	Number of reviews	Filtered keyword %	Intermediate keyword %	Final keyword %
Mixed	73860	50.80	43.34	41.09
Negative	4990	50.56	43.94	41.90
Positive	10207	50.91	43.07	40.71

5.2 Result on Real-Life Application

We have taken 73860 movie reviews from the online available benchmark data set [24] to check the quality of the reviews given by the viewers. Three types of reviews are there, which are positive, negative and mixed. Here, positive, negative and mixed review express the emotional feeling of the reviewer on a particular movie. The percentage of filtered, intermediate and final keywords from all the documents for mixed, negative and positive reviews are shown in Table 5. It has been found that about 41.09% of reviews were of good quality in the mixed category. 4990 negative reviews have been taken to check the quality of the reviews given by the viewers. The result shows that about 41.90% of reviews are of good quality and crowded with contextual words. 10207 positive reviews also have been taken to examine. The method shows that about 40.71% of reviews are of good quality. We may conclude from the above results that reviewers usually use an enormous number of non-contextual words in movie reviews to share their experiences. In reality, more number of positive reviews compared to negative reviews are actually given by the people who didn't watch the movie or unable to get the essence of the movie and express their views with non-contextual words and our results depict the same.

Table 6. Mantel test or association of betweenness centrality for the newspapers

Mantel test for association	Newspapers A and B	Newspapers B and C	Newspapers A and C
Betweenness	0.854	0.946	0.895

Table 7. Keyword percentage (%) of Newspapers A, B and C

Newspapers	Final keywords %
Newspaper A	14.33
Newspaper B	12.86
Newspaper C	14.92

5.3   Result on Newspaper Data

The model has been tested over the reports of FIFA Football World Cup Men's 2018 matches which have been published in three popular newspapers anonymous as A, B, and C, respectively. We collect the reports of twelve specific matches from these three newspapers. So, a total of thirty-six match reports is gathered and analysed. We examine the top ten words in the match reports of A, B, and C as depicted in Fig. 5a, 5b and 5c respectively. The Y-axis of these figures represents the number of each word used in each daily. The correlation analysis of the words used in these three newspapers using Mantel test is shown in Table 6. Correlation analysis is done on the betweenness centrality values as it represents the dependence of each associate on a corresponding word. The results show that The Hindu and The Telegraph share high correlation and depict reasonable similarities within their choice of words. Average of final keywords percentage (%) of A, B, and C are shown in Table 7. In our method filtered keywords and intermediate keywords are dependent on the main graph and filtered keywords respectively. The final keywords depend on intermediate keywords and give us the set of influential keywords. By analysing the data very precisely, it has been found that the articles of The Telegraph were of good quality based on the use of contextual words. Deccan Chronicle and The Hindu can be ranked in number two and three, respectively. The ranking has no relation

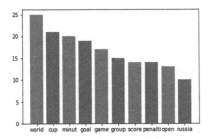

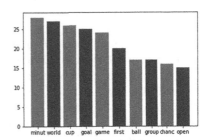

(a) Top 10 influential words in Newspaper A

(b) Top 10 influential words in Newspaper B

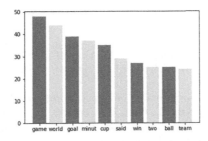

(c) Top 10 Influential Words in Newspaper C

Fig. 5. Top 10 influential words from different newspapers

with the general sports reports quality of these newspapers. Our method does not represent the overall quality of these specific newspapers at all. Here, the quality of some specific reports is solely judged based on the population of the keywords and their association with the remaining words used in the article. Our proposed method would assist the readers in nominating a specific daily which publishes superior quality articles on any desired topic, for example, reports on world cup football, from the bracket of top quality newspapers.

5.4   Limitations

Our study has some limitations. Though the study is not restricted only to a particular topic, it would compare the quality of the articles over a distinct subject. The extracted keywords from each topic can be aggregated to reveal the overall quality of any newspaper. Our study period was for a single year and few match reports. A comprehensive study is needed to conclude the overall grade of the dailies. For the time being, we have concluded our study on the English language. Availability of the NLP tools for other languages would definitely enhance our research in the future. For the time being, we have manually extracted specific newspaper reports. Availability of the benchmark data set of different newspapers would strengthen the accuracy of the method.

6   Conclusions

In this work, we have proposed a graph mining method to judge the contextual quality of any number of published articles. As a case study, we compare the sports reports of three popular newspapers and classify them according to the word used in the documents. The proposed model shows satisfying results and can be employed as a parameter to judge the document quality. In future, as an extension of this work, a surveillance system can be generated to censor the newspapers from publishing violent, unethical or unconstitutional stories. The model can be employed as an expert system to advise the journalists and the editors to raise the quality of the reports.

References

1. Fang, Y., Huang, H., Jian, P., Xin, X., Feng, C.: Self-adaptive topic model: a solution to the problem of "rich topics get richer". China Commun. **11**(12), 35–43 (2014)
2. Subrahmanian, V.S.: Mining online opinions. Computer **42**(7), 88–90 (2009)
3. Cummins, N., Amiriparian, S., Ottl, S., Gerczuk, M., Schmitt, M., Schuller, B.: Multimodal bag-of-words for cross domains sentiment analysis. In: 2018 IEEE International Conference on Acoustics, Speech and Signal Processing (ICASSP), pp. 4954–4958. IEEE (2018)

4. Makuch, E.: Hagrid Was Too Small in the Movies, Director Says (2016). http://text2vec.org/
5. Duari, S., Bhatnagar, V.: SCAKE: semantic connectivity aware keyword extraction. Inf. Sci. **477**, 100–117 (2019)
6. Luhn, H.P.: A statistical approach to mechanized encoding and searching of literary information. IBM J. Res. Dev. **1**(4), 309–317 (1957)
7. Jones, K.S.: A statistical interpretation of term specificity and its application in retrieval. J. Documentation **28**(1), 11–21 (1972)
8. Hulth, A.: Improved automatic keyword extraction given more linguistic knowledge. In: Proceedings of the 2003 Conference on Empirical Methods in Natural Language Processing. Association for Computational Linguistics, pp. 216–223 (2003)
9. Mihalcea, R., Tarau, P.: Textrank: bringing order into text. In: Proceedings of the 2004 Conference on Empirical Methods in Natural Language Processing (2004)
10. Litvak, M., Last, M., Aizenman, H., Gobits, I., Kandel, A.: Degext-a language-independent graph-based keyphrase extractor. In: Mugellini, E., Szczepaniak, P.S., Pettenati, M.C., Sokhn, M. (eds.) Advances in Intelligent Web Mastering-3, pp. 121–130. Springer, Heidelberg (2011). https://doi.org/10.1007/978-3-642-18029-3_13
11. Ohsawa, Y., Benson, N.E., Yachida, M.: Keygraph: automatic indexing by co-occurrence graph based on building construction metaphor. In: Proceedings IEEE International Forum on Research and Technology Advances in Digital Libraries-ADL 1998-, pp. 12–18. IEEE (1998)
12. Östling, R., Grigonyte, G.: Transparent text quality assessment with convolutional neural networks. In: Proceedings of the 12th Workshop on Innovative Use of NLP for Building Educational Applications, pp. 282–286 (2017)
13. Agrawal, A., Fu, W., Menzies, T.: What is wrong with topic modeling? and how to fix it using search-based software engineering. Inf. Softw. Technol. **98**, 74–88 (2018)
14. Tang, X., Wang, J., Zhong, J., Pan, Y.: Predicting essential proteins based on weighted degree centrality. IEEE/ACM Trans. Comput. Biol. Bioinform. (TCBB) **11**(2), 407–418 (2014)
15. Freeman, L.C.: A set of measures of centrality based on betweenness. Sociometry **40**, 35–41 (1977)
16. Watts, D.J., Strogatz, S.H.: Collective dynamics of 'small-world'networks. Nature **393**(6684), 440 (1998)
17. Legendre, P., Fortin, M.J.: Comparison of the mantel test and alternative approaches for detecting complex multivariate relationships in the spatial analysis of genetic data. Mol. Ecol. Resou. **10**(5), 831–844 (2010)
18. Mantel, N.: The detection of disease clustering and a generalized regression approach. Cancer Res. **27**(2(1)), 209–220 (1967)
19. Benesty, J., Chen, J., Huang, Y.: On the importance of the pearson correlation coefficient in noise reduction. IEEE Trans. Audio Speech Lang. Process. **16**(4), 757–765 (2008)
20. Bhamidipati, N.L., Pal, S.K.: Stemming via distribution-based word segregation for classification and retrieval. IEEE Trans. Syst. Man Cybern. Part B (Cybern.) **37**(2), 350–360 (2007)
21. Krapivin, M., Autaeu, A., Marchese, M.: Large dataset for keyphrases extraction. University of Trento, Tech. Rep. (2009)
22. Aronson, A.R., et al.: The NLM indexing initiative. In: Proceedings of the AMIA Symposium. American Medical Informatics Association, p. 17 (2000)

23. Florescu, C., Caragea, C.: A position-biased pagerank algorithm for keyphrase extraction. In: Thirty-First AAAI Conference on Artificial Intelligence (2017)
24. Maas, A.L., Daly, R.E., Pham, P.T., Huang, D., Ng, A.Y., Potts, C.: Learning word vectors for sentiment analysis. In: Proceedings of the 49th Annual Meeting of the Association for Computational Linguistics: Human lLanguage Technologies, vol. 1, pp. 142–150. Association for Computational Linguistics (2011)

GEDset: Automatic Dataset Builder for Machine Translation System with Specific Reference to Gujarati-English

Margi Patel[1(✉)] and Brijendra Kumar Joshi[2]

[1] Indore Institute of Science and Technology, Indore, India
[2] Military College of Telecommunication Engineering, Mhow, India

Abstract. Datasets have been instrumental in advancing machine learning research. They are the foundation for the models we develop and implement, as well as our primary means of measuring and assessing them. Furthermore, the techniques utilized to collect, construct, and share these datasets have an impact on the sorts of problems tackled by the field as well as the methodology employed in algorithm development. This study provides method for creating a large number of new bilingual dictionaries automatically. In recent years, number of people who use the internet has exploded drastically. Because English is the most often used language on the internet, most documents are written in this language. If a user's mother tongue is Gujarati, he or she will naturally want to access info in Gujarati if at all feasible. Our algorithm generates word translations from the source language Gujarati to the target language English. This bilingual dataset dictionary is suitable for Machine Translation (MT).

Keywords: Dataset · Machine learning · Machine translation

1 Introduction

Language is a very effective way of communication. It clearly reflects the thoughts and expressions of the human intellect. The globe has numerous languages, representing the diversity of the world's languages. A single person will never be able to know and understand all of the world's languages. As a result, utilizing the translation process, messages were delivered from one language to another. As a consequence of improvements in information, communication and technology, MT has experienced a revolution. The automatic translation of text from one language to another is known as machine translation [1]. Machine Translation System (MTS) is an application of artificial intelligence in Natural Language Processing (NLP).

MT is a difficult process. The MT work is fraught with difficulties, such as referential ambiguities and complicated structures in the source and target languages, idioms, collocations, synonym metaphors, polysemy, homonymy, and lexical and structural mismatches between the source and destination languages [2]. This is the main reason why we don't have a good MT system right now. Through this article we are focusing on automated method to create a bilingual dictionary dataset which in turn can be useful in MT with a specific concentration on Gujarati-English language pair.

D. Garg et al. (Eds.): IACC 2021, CCIS 1528, pp. 519–528, 2022.
https://doi.org/10.1007/978-3-030-95502-1_39

The importance of datasets in machine learning research is impossible to underestimate. Datasets have long been seen as a stumbling block to algorithmic development and scientific progress [3, 4], and some of the most noteworthy findings in the field have been inspired by a relatively small number of benchmark datasets. Benchmark datasets have also had a substantial impact on the machine learning public's goals, ideals, and research priorities [5]. When tested on benchmark datasets such as the GLUE benchmark for English textual comprehension, machine learning systems have been reported to perform at a 'stupendous' level [6]. Datasets are also required for Meta-Learning. Meta-learning, often known as learning to learn, is the utilization of previously accumulated information about a learning activity to give an automated selection, recommendation, or assistance for a future task.

As the area of machine learning transitioned to data-driven techniques, the competent and meticulous human annotation employed in previous dataset gathering practices was criticized as 'expensive and time-consuming to get' and a trend toward unrestricted gathering of ever huge volumes of data obtained via the internet, as well as an increasing dependence on crowdworkers who aren't experts, was regarded as a bonus to Machine Learning [3, 7].

Bilingual dictionaries are useful in applications such as natural language processing, machine translation, information retrieval, documents in multiple languages, automatic disambiguation of the meaning of words, evaluation of similarities between texts, and improvement of translation accuracy [8]. Ordinary readers may also benefit from bilingual dictionaries if they need help in translating material from one language to their mother tongue or another language with which they are already acquainted. These dictionaries might be valuable for intelligence purposes, especially when dealing with small languages from vulnerable regions of the world. Developing new multilingual dictionaries is a completely intellectual endeavor and scholarly effort that is essential to humanists and other intellectuals.

2 Motivation and Significance

In recent years, the advent of Artificial Intelligence (AI), and particularly Machine Learning (ML) approaches, has aided a substantial number of translation apps in their data processing procedure [9]. When it comes to machine learning, the availability of a suitably big and statistically representative dataset becomes critical [10–13]. A large amount of data is required to train the neural network selected for a certain application and this issue highlights all of the issues associated with Big Data and its handling. 60% effort of Data scientists is devoted for cleaning and organizing data. Data collection takes up 19% of their time, implying that around 80% of data scientist's effort is spent preparing and managing data for analysis. Data preparation is the least fun aspect of data scientists' jobs, according to 76% of them. Cleaning and organizing data is the least fun aspect of data scientists' jobs, according to 57%, while acquiring data sets is the least enjoyable component of their jobs, according to 19%. Collecting, generating, arranging, and cleansing data is a time-consuming task that irritates researchers because it is viewed as the least pleasurable aspect of data processing [14], as shown in Fig. 1. Still, it is an essential step before they may focus on the most intriguing aspect of their own work.

The purpose of this work is to show an automated dataset builder's architecture, as well as a thorough description of the various components that comprise it. As a result, an innovative tool will be made accessible to researchers for them in order to create datasets for applications of Artificial Intelligence (AI) in context to Machine Translation. The program automates the tedious and repetitive tasks, allowing the researcher to devote his or her time to more productive endeavors. According to advanced analysis, the existence of such systems is quite restricted, particularly for Gujarati Language.

What Data Scientists spend the most time doing ?

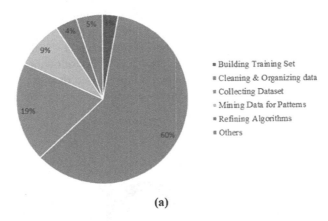

(a)

What is the least enjoyable part of Data Science ?

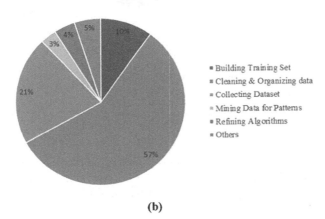

(b)

Fig. 1. (a): Data science tasks that take the most time, (b): Data science activities that are the least fun [14].

3 Software Description

Section 3.1 gives a brief description of the tool. Section 3.2 provides insights into the current implementation of each functional block.

3.1 Software Architecture

As previously stated, the suggested architecture provides a tool meant to create acceptable datasets for Machine Translation Systems in an easy and automated manner. Figure 2 depicts the process of generating a Data Set in the Target Language. A suite of Python scripts enables the user to perform a meta search using any accessible search engine. We built the dataset generator in Python since it is simple to use and is becoming increasingly popular in scientific computing. Section 3.2 depicts the process for Dataset generation, which includes numerous functional blocks, each of which handles a certain job. The various functional blocks will be discussed in the following subsections. It's well worth noting that, both the raw data and the processed data are kept in separate folders during the process that the user may access as and when needed.

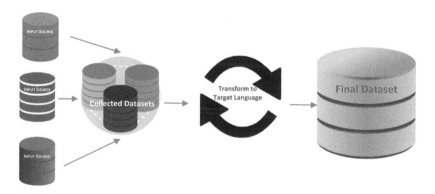

Fig. 2. Software architecture.

3.2 Software Functionalities

Uploader
The File Uploader component enables an end user to upload the files in Source Language. An end user can select files that are in dot csv, doc, docx, xls format. This module is in charge of verifying file type and handling files that have been uploaded.

Filter
The uploaded document may contain diagrams, flowcharts, pictures, and other elements that are not needed to be included in the dataset. As a result, only translation segments should be recognized. For each uploaded file, this module will first remove diagrams, flowcharts, pictures, and other elements. Later on punctuation marks and stop words will be removed.

Splitter

In this module, the paragraphs and complex sentences are simplified. It will be based on coordinating conjunctions (અને (ane), પણ (paN), અથવા (athavA), એટલે (eTale), etc.), subordinating conjunctions (તોપણ (topaN), પછી (paChI), કારણ (kAraN), કે (ke), etc.), and connectives such as relative pronouns (જે (je), તે (te), etc.). Hence sentences will split in to words

Cleaner

In some cases, it may happen that words are already there in the raw list. In such cases those words are filtered out and newly encountered words are automatically inserted in a separate dot csv file. At this phase user will get a raw list of words in source language.

Search Request

The suggested architecture, as stated, describes a tool meant to create acceptable datasets for MT applications in a straightforward and automated manner. Hence a set of Python script is used that allows the user to automatically search meaning in target language of the word that is there in raw list.

Previewer

User will preview the data set and the finalize the same. Output of this module will be finalized dataset from source language to target language (Fig. 7).

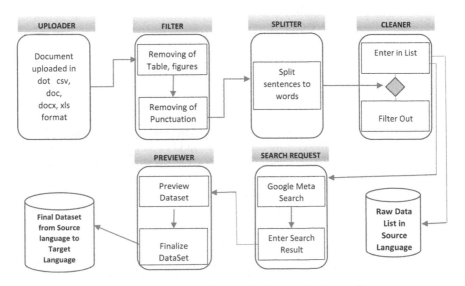

Fig. 3. Functional diagram for dataset creation tool

4   Proposed Algorithm

This section discusses a method for generating a new dataset DST(S,T), each of which translates a word in the Source language S to a word in the Target language T. Outcome of this will be dataset DST(S,T).

```
READ uploaded file
REPAT
    remove table, figure
    remove punctuation marks, stop words
UNTIL end_of_file
FOR each row on the board
    split sentences to words
    convert word to lowercase
END FOR
FOR each row on the board
    IF word exist in dataset_list THEN
        filter word
    ELSE
        add word in dataset
        SEARCH word on google
        OBTAIN search result
        COMPUTE dataset
    END IF
END FOR
PRINT dataset
```

5   Experiment and Result

After converting sentences to words, for the experimental purpose more than 90000 random words have been found from different Gujrati language e-books, e-newspapers etc. 10 separate excel documents (each file contains 10000 words) named as "Gujarati_Dictionary_1.xlsx,   Gujarati_Dictionary_2.xlsx,....,   Gujarati_Dictionary_10.xlsx" keeping one word in each row was created.

Now for the translation purpose google colaboratory is used as it's an online cloud service provided by google (standalone system having Jupiter Notebook can also be used).

Firstly, all the APIs are being installed using *pip install* command. Then importing required packages for processing of excel file (i.e. reading input and writing result) and accessing google translator API.

Figure 4 is of screenshot of sample input excel file *"Gujarati_Dictionary_1.xlsx."*

Fig. 4. Input excel file

```
df=pd.read_excel('/content/Gujarati_ Dictionary_1.xlsx',sheet_name='Sheet1')
df
```

	ઘરવાળી
0	નવ
1	શણગાર
2	નિર્મળ
3	કાળજી
4	ભેદિત
...	...
9230	વિદારી
9231	પૂષા
9232	સિંધુપુત્ર
9233	ભગવતી
9234	કાલકંઠ

9235 rows × 1 columns

Fig. 5. Reading the excel file

The Fig. 5 displays the content of "*sheet 1*" of excel file named "*Gujarati_Dictionary_1.xlsx*" using panda (*pd*) library.

Thereafter, the instance of "*Translator*" from "*googletrans*" api is calling translate function for each unique element read from the excel file and displays the result of translation. Finally, the result is being updated in the respected excel file i.e. English translation is written corresponding to each Gujarati word per row as shown in Fig. 6. Figure 7 contains screenshot of final dataset in excel format.

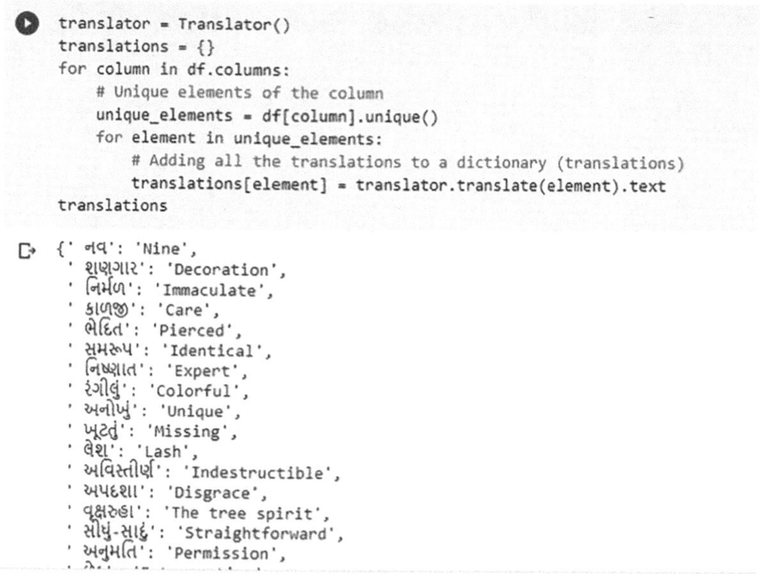

```
translator = Translator()
translations = {}
for column in df.columns:
    # Unique elements of the column
    unique_elements = df[column].unique()
    for element in unique_elements:
        # Adding all the translations to a dictionary (translations)
        translations[element] = translator.translate(element).text
translations
```

```
{' નવ': 'Nine',
 ' શણગાર': 'Decoration',
 ' નિર્મળ': 'Immaculate',
 ' કાળજી': 'Care',
 ' ભેદિત': 'Pierced',
 ' સમરૂપ': 'Identical',
 ' નિષ્ણાત': 'Expert',
 ' રંગીલું': 'Colorful',
 ' અનોખું': 'Unique',
 ' ખૂટતું': 'Missing',
 ' લેશ': 'Lash',
 ' અવિસ્તીર્ણ': 'Indestructible',
 ' અપદશા': 'Disgrace',
 ' વૃક્ષરૂહા': 'The tree spirit',
 ' સીધું-સાદું': 'Straightforward',
 ' અનુમતિ': 'Permission',
```

Fig. 6. Translation function and its result

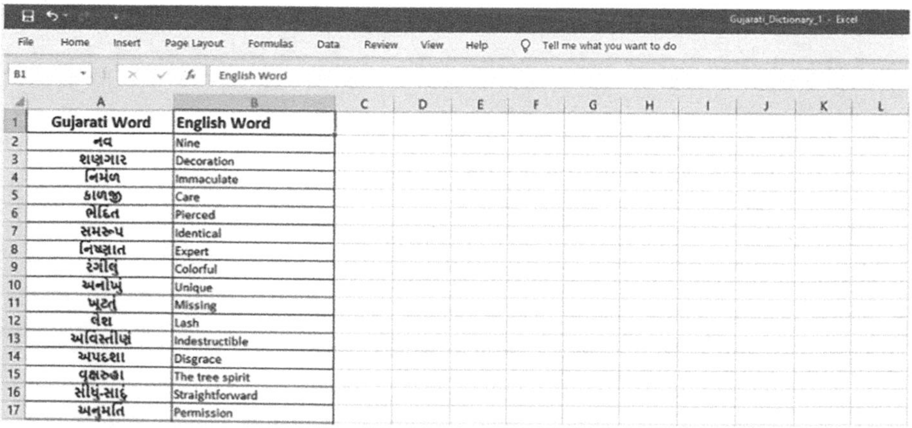

	A	B	C	D	E	F	G	H	I	J	K	L
1	**Gujarati Word**	**English Word**										
2	નવ	Nine										
3	શણગાર	Decoration										
4	નિર્મળ	Immaculate										
5	કાળજી	Care										
6	ભેદિત	Pierced										
7	સમરૂપ	Identical										
8	નિષ્ણાત	Expert										
9	રંગીલું	Colorful										
10	અનોખું	Unique										
11	ખૂટતું	Missing										
12	લેશ	Lash										
13	અવિસ્તીર્ણ	Indestructible										
14	અપદશા	Disgrace										
15	વૃક્ષરૂહા	The tree spirit										
16	સીધું-સાદું	Straightforward										
17	અનુમતિ	Permission										

Fig. 7. Final bilingual dictionary dataset

6   Conclusion

The design of an innovative tool that allows researchers to automatically produce acceptable datasets for AI applications in the context of Natural Language Processing is discussed in this study. Almost 15 lakh people of Gujarati descent live in the United States, with more than 3.5 lakh speaking Gujarati as their primary tongue. Guajaratis have made their imprint in many aspects of life in the United States, from the power corridors of Washington DC to organizations such as NASA and philanthropic and innovative circles [15]. Considering all of these facts and numbers, a more particular machine translation system that can correctly translate from English to Gujarati and vice versa is necessary. The goal of making bilingual dictionary dataset is to use them for machine translation. Our method is generic, and in order to show the efficacy and utility of our algorithm, we have chosen English as the target language and Gujarati as the source language for testing. Although this can be used with other type of language pairs viz.; Hindi-English, Punjabi-English etc.

References

1. Patel, M., Kumar Joshi, B.: Issues in machine translation of Indian languages for information retrieval. Int. J. Comput. Sci. Inf. Secur. **19**(8), 59–62 (2021)
2. Gupta, S.: A Survey of Data Driven Machine Translation. Department of Computer Science and Engineering, Indian Institute of Technology, Bombay (2012). https://www.cfilt.iitb.ac.in/resources/surveys/MT-Literature%20Survey-2012-Somya.pdf
3. Halevy, A., Norvig, P., Pereira, F.: The unreasonable effectiveness of data. IEEE Intell. Syst. **24**(2), 8–12 (2009)
4. Sun, C., Shrivastava, A., Singh, S., Gupta, A.: Revisiting unreasonable effectiveness of data in deep learning era. In: Proceedings of the IEEE International Conference on Computer Vision, pp. 843–852 (2017)
5. Dotan, R., Milli, S.: Value-laden disciplinary shifts in machine learning. In: Proceedings of the 2020 Conference on Fairness, Accountability, and Transparency, FAT'20, New York, 2020, p. 294. Association for Computing Machinery (2020). ISBN 9781450369367. https://doi.org/10.1145/3351095.3373157
6. He, H., Zha, S., Wang, H.: Unlearn dataset bias in natural language inference by fitting the residual. In: Proceedings of the 2nd Workshop on Deep Learning Approaches for Low-Resource NLP (DeepLo 2019), Hong Kong, China, November 2019, pp. 132–142. Association for Computational Linguistics (2019). https://doi.org/10.18653/v1/D19-6115. https://www.aclweb.org/anthology/D19-6115
7. Deng, J., Dong, W., Socher, R., Li, L.-J., Li, K., Fei-Fei, L.: ImageNet: a large-scale hierarchical image database. In: CVPR (2009)
8. Knight, K., Luk, S.K.: Building a large-scale knowledge base for machine translation. Proc. AAAI **94**, 773–778 (1994)
9. Del Rosso, M.P., Sebastianelli, A., Ullo, S.L.: Artificial Intelligence Applied to Satellite-based Remote Sensing Data for Earth Observation. The Institution of Engineering and Technology (IET) (2021)
10. Camps-Valls, G.: Machine learning in remote sensing data processing. In: 2009 IEEE International Workshop on Machine Learning for Signal Processing, pp. 1–6 (2009)
11. Roh, Y., Heo, G., Whang, S.E.: A survey on data collection for machine learning: a big data - AI integration perspective. IEEE Trans. Knowl. Data Eng. 1 (2019)
12. Brownlee, J.: How much training data is required for machine learning? (2019). https://machinelearningmastery.com/much-training-data-required-machine-learning/. Accessed 3 Oct 2021
13. Machine Learning Mastery. Jason Brownlee, Impact of Dataset Size on Deep Learning Model Skill and Performance Estimates (2019). https://machinelearningmastery.com/impact-of-dataset-size-on-deep-learning-model-skill-and-performance-estimates/. Accessed 3 Oct 2021

14. Gil Press. Cleaning big data: most time-consuming, least enjoyable data science task, survey says (2016). https://www.forbes.com/sites/gilpress/2016/03/23/data-preparation-most-time-consuming-least_enjoyable-data-science-task-survey-says/#11e80e496f63. Accessed 3 Oct 2021

15. https://timesofindia.indiatimes.com/nri/us-canada-news/Gujaratis-6-of-Indians-but-20-of-US-Indians/articleshow/45746350.cms. Accessed 23 Oct 2021

16. Saini, J.R., Modh, J.C.: GIdTra: a dictionary-based MTS for translating Gujarati bigram idioms to English. In: Proceedings of Fourth International Conference on Parallel, Distributed and Grid Computing (PDGC), Waknaghat, 2016, pp. 192–196 (2016). https://doi.org/10.1109/PDGC.2016.7913143

17. Antony, P.: Machine translation approaches and survey for Indian languages. Int. J. Comput. Linguist. Chin. Lang. Process. **18**(1), 47–78 (2013). https://aclanthology.org/O13-2003

18. Deng, L., Liu, Y. (eds.): Deep Learning in Natural Language Processing. Springer, Singapore (2018). https://doi.org/10.1007/978-981-10-5209-5

Power Function Algorithm for Linear Regression Weights with Weibull Data Analysis

Robert Ross$^{(\boxtimes)}$ (iD)

IWO, Zweerslaan 46 6711GC Ede, The Netherlands
r.ross@iwo.nl

Abstract. Weighted Linear Regression (WLR) can be used to estimate Weibull parameters. With WLR, failure data with less variance weigh heavier. These weights depend on the total number of test objects, which is called the sample size n, and on the index of the ranked failure data i. The calculation of weights can be very challenging, particularly for larger sample sizes n and for non-integer data ranking i, which usually occurs with random censoring. There is a demand for a light-weight computing method that is also able to deal with non-integer ranking indices. The present paper discusses an algorithm that is both suitable for light-weight computing as well as for non-integer ranking indices. The development of the algorithm is based on asymptotic 3-parameter power functions that have been successfully employed to describe the estimated Weibull shape parameter bias and standard deviation that both monotonically approach zero with increasing sample size n. The weight distributions for given sample size are not monotonic functions, but there are various asymptotic aspects that provide leads for a combination of asymptotic 3-parameter power functions. The developed algorithm incorporates 5 power functions. The performance is checked for sample sizes between 1 and 2000 for the maximum deviation. Furthermore the weight distribution is checked for very high similarity with the theoretical distribution.

Keywords: Asymptotic behavior · Power function · Similarity Index · Weighted linear regression

1 Introduction

The 2-parameter Weibull distribution is widely used for failure data where the lowest value represents the performance of a test object. E.g., the failure time of an electronic device in a destructive test is the time that a first failure is observed. The weakest path to breakdown determines the strength of the device.

Maximum Likelihood (ML) and Linear Regression (LR) can be applied to estimate the Weibull scale parameter α and shape parameter β from a set of observed failure times t_i ($1 \leq i \leq n$), where n is the sample size, i.e., the total number of tested objects. IWO aims at developing data analytics that can be implemented in office software and devices with limited computing capabilities, such as mobile phones and smart components. An advantage of LR over ML in this respect is that LR parameter estimators

D. Garg et al. (Eds.): IACC 2021, CCIS 1528, pp. 529–541, 2022.
https://doi.org/10.1007/978-3-030-95502-1_40

are analytical. An advanced LR method is weighted LR (WLR). It is preferred because of a faster declining bias and scatter in β, matches the ML standard deviation while keeping the analytical advantage of LR (6.3.2.7 in [1]). In general, the calculation of variances for WLR weights can be difficult [2]. Analytical methods do exist in case of Weibull, but are demanding for large sample sizes n and for censored data where data ranking indices i can become non-integer (see Sect. 3). The unavailability of weights for non-integer indices is recognized by IEC [3], recommending to use the weight for the nearest integer ranking instead. A precise weights algorithm would be very useful.

Here, the goal was set to develop an algorithm for the weights that on the one hand can be implemented on light-weight computing devices and in common office software and on the other hand can handle non-integer ranking indices. The development of this algorithm is based on a combination of power functions. The development of the Power model for the WLR weights for Weibull analysis is subject of the paper.

The structure of the discussion is as follows. The concept of asymptotic power functions is discussed in Sect. 2. The subject of WLR with censored data, variances and especially weights is introduced in Sect. 3. This leads to the demanding analytic expressions for WLR weights. Section 4 describes the development of a model for infinite sample sizes which serves as a basis for the algorithm for weights with finite sample sizes. Finally, the performance of the algorithm is tested for maximum deviation and agreement with the theoretical weight distribution employing a (dis)similarity index.

2 Asymptotic Power Functions

Parameter estimators are required to be consistent which means that with increasing sample size n the absolute bias (if not already zero) and scatter must asymptotically approach zero as described by Fisher [4]. This concept translates into the principle that collecting additional data is rewarded by achieving greater estimate accuracy.

A 3-parameter power function of the sample size n can be used as a model that complies with the consistency concept. E.g., it could describe the decline of the bias and the standard deviation of ML, LR and WLR estimators of the Weibull shape parameter [5]. The aimed weight model employs various asymptotic 3-parameter power functions D_n:

$$D_n = E_n - E_\infty = Q \cdot (n - R)^P \tag{1}$$

E_n is the expected value of an estimated parameter from a data set with sample size n. The asymptotic behavior of E_n is usually the study subject. E_∞ is the expected value of an estimated parameter with infinite sample size, i.e., the asymptotic value of E_n. D_n is the difference of E_n and E_∞ that asymptotically approaches zero with increasing n, the variable under consideration. P, Q and R are the 3 parameters of the power function of n that models the asymptotic behavior. In logarithmic form a linear relationship shows:

$$\log(D_n) = \log(Q) + P \cdot \log(n - R) \tag{2}$$

If $\log(D_n)$ is plotted against $\log(n\text{-}R)$, or linear regression applied, then R should be optimized to achieve a straight line. P follows from the slope, and Q from the inverse log of the intercept. Sometimes the power function will be an exact description of the asymptotic behavior, but in other cases it can be a reasonable approximation merely or just does not apply. The latter case can show as an S-shaped curve that cannot be straightened by varying R. Still, it may be worth the exercise.

Sometimes the asymptotic power function must be adjusted. E.g., if the asymptotic behavior is with a declining n, the $n-R$ term may be replaced by $R-n$. If one function asymptotically approaches another function, then E_∞ may be taken not as a constant, but be replaced by that other function. In a more complicated case (like the presently studied WLR weights) various power functions may have to be combined.

The parameters P, Q and R of the power function can be interpreted as follows. The rate of the asymptotic approach is characterized by the power P in the limit $n \to \infty$. Because D_n approaches zero and provided $n\text{-}R > 1$, it is necessary that $P<0$.

The parameter Q defines the deviation of E_n from E_∞ for small n, or to be more precise $Q = D_{n-R=1}$. It can be interpreted as an amplitude. If $D_n \neq 0$, then $Q \in \mathbb{R}$ having the same sign as D_n. If $D_n = 0$ by definition, then $Q = 0$.

Whereas the concept of consistency focuses on the limit $n \to \infty$ [4], the asymptotic 3-parameter power function introduces a parameter R that can be ignored in that limit. However, for small n, this parameter defines a singularity at $n = R$ with the negative P. The description of the bias for test sets with (very) small sample size n formed the background of the introduction of R [5].

To illustrate this, the variance σ^2 of an infinitely sized population and the expected estimated variance $\langle s_n^2 \rangle$ of an n sized sample drawn from that population are compared. The ratio $\langle s_n^2 \rangle / \sigma^2$ is well-known to be $(n - 1)/n$ and asymptotically approaches $E_\infty = 1$ with increasing n. This ratio exactly follows a 3-parameter power function, namely:

$$\frac{s_n^2}{\sigma^2} - 1 = \frac{n - 1}{n} - 1 = -1 \cdot (n - 0)^{-1} \tag{3}$$

In terms of the 3-parameter function: $P = -1$, $Q = -1$ and $R = 0$.

3   Weibull Parameter Estimation by WLR

If a series of n devices are destructively tested, a series of failure times are observed. Let the failure times t_i $(i = 1,..,n)$ be ranked such that for all i: $t_{i-1} < t_i$. If not all failure times become known in the test, some failure times may remain hidden. Such data are called *censored* or *suspended*. This may occur if a specific test object fails by another mechanism than which is studied.

E.g., devices may be tested destructively to assess the failure behavior of an on board diode. A failed device is short-circuited and has to be withdrawn from the test. If such devices also contain a transistor, some devices may fail due to transistor failure rather than diode failure. For those devices, the diode failure time then remains hidden. It is clear though that the diode failure time must be larger than the observed transistor failure time on that device. Moreover, the ranking of the unknown diode failure time among the next actually observed diode failure times remains unknown. As a consequence, part of the higher rankings of observed diode failure times becomes uncertain too. A method to deal with censored data in the ranking is the Adjusted Ranking Method [3]. Usually, this leads to non-integer expected rankings i of observed failure times.

3.1   Weighted Linear Regression

Two prominent families of Weibull parameter estimation are ML and (W)LR. The focus of the present paper is on WLR, and particularly on the weights calculation challenge, rather than the well-established regression method itself. With WLR parameter estimation a linear relationship is assumed between a plotting position Z and log-failure times $\ln(t)$ from which α and β are estimated. This plotting position Z is defined as:

$$Z(p) = \ln(-\ln(1 - p)) \equiv \beta \cdot \ln(t) - \beta \cdot \ln(\alpha) \tag{4}$$

Here p is a probability, i.e. a value of the Weibull cumulative distribution $F(t; \alpha, \beta)$. In a Weibull plot, Z and $\ln(t)$ are plotted along the vertical respectively horizontal axis to form a straight graph granted the data are Weibull distributed indeed. Each observation $\ln(t_i)$ is assigned to the ith expected plotting position, $\langle Z_{i,n} \rangle$ which are detailed in Sect. 3.2 below. The two WLR estimators a_{WLR} and b_{WLR} of respectively α and β are found as:

$$a_{WLR} = \exp\left(\overline{\ln(t)}_w - \frac{\overline{Z}_w}{b_{WLR}} \right) \tag{5}$$

$$b_{WLR} = \frac{\overline{\left(Z - \overline{Z}_w\right)^2}_w}{\left(\left(Z - \overline{Z}_w\right) \cdot \left(\ln t - \overline{\ln t}_w\right)\right)_w} \tag{6}$$

The suffix w indicates a weighted average. Such a weighted average $\overline{u}_w$ of a series observations u_i is calculated as:

$$\overline{u}_w = \frac{\sum_{i=1}^{n} \left(w_{i,n} \cdot u_i\right)}{\sum_{i=1}^{n} w_{i,n}} \tag{7}$$

The $w_{i,n}$ are the weights assigned to the data $\ln(t_i)$ in the weighted averaging. The weights do also depend on the sample size n, which is the reason for indicating both i and n in the suffix. The $w_{i,n}$ are the inverse of the variances $v_{i,n}$ of the respective plotting positions $Z_{i,n}$:

$$w_{i,n} = \frac{1}{v_{i,n}} = \frac{1}{\langle Z_{i,n}^2 \rangle - \langle Z_{i,n} \rangle^2} \tag{8}$$

The smaller $v_{i,n}$, the heavier weighs observation t_i in the estimation of a_{WLR} and b_{WLR}. The variances and weights calculations are very challenging and subject of this paper.

3.2   Variances of the Plotting Position Z

The variances $v_{i,n}$ of the Weibull plotting positions follow from the first and second moments of Z. An analytic expression for the first moment $\langle Z_{i,n} \rangle$ is:

$$\langle Z_{i,n} \rangle = \left[-\gamma + i \binom{n}{i} \sum_{j=0}^{i-1} \binom{i-1}{j} \frac{(-1)^{i-j} \cdot \ln(n-j)}{n-j} \right] \tag{9}$$

Here, γ is the Euler constant ($\gamma \approx 0.57722$). Rounding errors in the summation of alternately positive and negative terms can have a high impact. For the second moment:

$$\langle Z_{i,n}^2 \rangle = i \binom{n}{i} \sum_{m=0}^{2} \binom{2}{m} (-1)^{2-m} \frac{\partial^m}{\partial s^m} \Gamma(s+1) \Big|_{s=0} \sum_{j=0}^{i-1} \binom{i-1}{j} (-1)^{i-1-j} \frac{(\ln(n-j))^{2-m}}{n-j} \tag{10}$$

These expressions allow to calculate the variances for integer n, but become demanding with increasing n. Both are unsuitable for non-integer ranking indices i that occur with censored data. For light-weight computing these expressions do not suffice either.

Another approach is to determine the moments of Z in the probability domain by numerical integration, cf. (6). The expected j^{th} moment of $Z_{i,n}$ follows from:

$$\langle Z_{i,n}^j \rangle = \frac{\Gamma(n+1)}{\Gamma(i)\Gamma(n+1-i)} \int_0^1 [\ln(-\ln(1-p))]^j \cdot p^{i-1} \cdot (1-p)^{n-i} dp \tag{11}$$

This expression is suitable for non-integer adjusted ranking as there is no summation involved. Singularities occur at $p = 0$ and 1. Numerical integration requires care therefore [6]. The expression as such is also demanding for light-weight computing, but it was used with Mathematica software and Gauss-Legendre quadrature to generate reference tables of $v_{i,n}$ values for $n = 1(1)60$, $75(1)80$, $80(10)120$, $125(25)250(250)$ 2000 as described in [6]. The notation '$A(B)C$' means a sequence from A to C with increment B. All $v_{i,n}$ and $w_{i,n}$ were determined with 10^{-9}–10^{-14} resolution and used for the model.

Figure 1 shows the $v_{i,n}$ for all integer i and sample size $n = 1, 2, 5, 10, 20, 50, 100, 200, 500, 1000, 2000$. Also the $v_{i,n}$ is shown for $i = 1(1)10000$ and sample size $n \to \infty$.

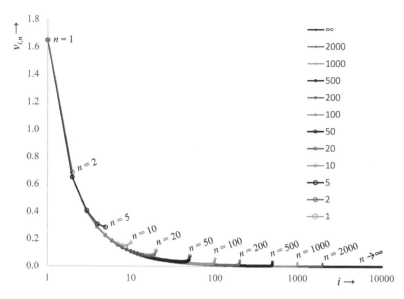

Fig. 1. The variances $v_{i,n}$ for all i with various finite n and $i \le 10000$ for infinite n.

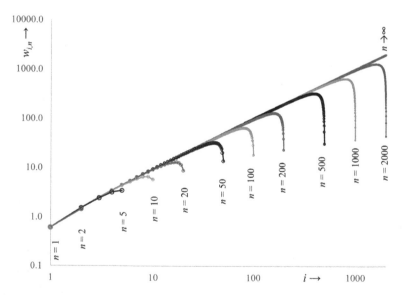

Fig. 2. The weights $w_{i,n}$ for all i with various finite n and $i \le 1500$ for infinite n.

For all finite n and $i > 1$, the $v_{i,n}$ curve curls up from the curve for infinite n. This tail is small compared to $v_{1,n}$, but with the fast decay of $v_{i,n}$ with increasing i, the curl grows larger relatively. This has a significant impact on the weights $w_{i,n}$ as shown in Fig. 2. For finite n, the weights reach a maximum for some $i \ge n/2$ and then rapidly decrease.

In the following, an algorithm is developed for $v_{i,n}$ and $w_{i,n}$ based on 3-parameter power functions. The process steps to reach the algorithm are discussed in detail. Figure 1 suggests that the $v_{i,n}$ curves might be approached as an adaption of the curve for infinite n. For that reason, firstly the $v_{i,n}$ for infinite n is studied. Secondly, the adjustment for finite $v_{i,n}$ is studied.

4   Power Model for LR Weights

4.1   Infinite Sample Size

The Eqs. (9)–(11) are not easy to interpret for infinite n. However, for $i = 1$ a simple expression follows directly from (8) and (9) that is independent of n:

$$v_{1,n} = \frac{\pi^2}{6} \tag{12}$$

The variances $v_{i,n\to\infty}$ asymptotically approach 0 with increasing i. The same holds for the difference $v_{i,n\to\infty} - v_{i+1,n\to\infty}$. Both can be approximated with an asymptotic power function as in (1). The former gives a fairly good approximation, the latter appears to yield a power function that was later proven to be an exact solution and is elaborated here further. As the difference approaches 0 with $i \to \infty$, the asymptote $E_\infty = 0$.

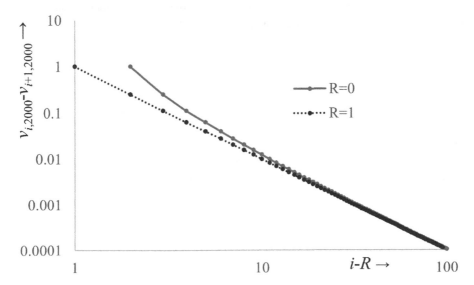

Fig. 3. The asymptotic behavior of $v_{i,n\to\infty} - v_{i+1,n\to\infty}$ for infinite n.

Figure 3 shows $v_{i,n\to\infty} - v_{i+1,n\to\infty}$ for $n = 2000$, i.e., the largest sample size. The log-log plot of D_i against i-R is straight for $R = 1$. The slope yields: $P = -2$ and the intercept $Q = 1$. With increasing n this asymptotic decay of D_i appears more and more accurate.

With power function parameters $\{P,Q,R\} = \{-2,1,1\}$, a relationship is found:

$$n \to \infty : v_{i,n} - v_{i+1,n} = \frac{1}{(i-1)^2} \tag{13}$$

Combining (12) and (13) yields an algorithm for $v_{i,n}$ with infinite n:

$$n \to \infty : \quad v_{i,n} = \frac{\pi^2}{6} - \sum_{j=2}^{i} \frac{1}{(j-1)^2} \tag{14}$$

The sum in (14) with $i \to \infty$ is known to be equal to $\pi^2/6$ (cf. Equation 23.2.24 in [7]).

It is also interesting to do a similar exercise for the weights $w_{i,n\to\infty}$. From (12) follows for $i = 1$ and all n:

$$w_{1,n} = \frac{6}{\pi^2} \tag{15}$$

When listing the values $w_{i,n\to\infty} = 1/v_{i,n\to\infty}$, these appear to asymptotically approach to $i-0.5$. However, from (15) for $i \downarrow 1$ a deviation of $6/\pi^2 - 0.5 \approx 0.108$ is found. The asymptotic approach of $w_{i,n\to\infty}$ to $i-0.5$ can again be investigated in terms of an asymptotic power function. Figure 4 shows the difference $D_i = w_{i,n\to\infty} - (i-0.5)$ against $i-R$. The asymptotic power function parameters are $\{P,Q, R\} = \{-1.04, 0.098, 0.088\}$. This yields an algorithm for $w_{i,n\to\infty}$:

$$n \to \infty : \quad w_{i,n} \approx i - 0.5 + 0.098 \cdot (i - 0.088)^{-1.04} \tag{16}$$

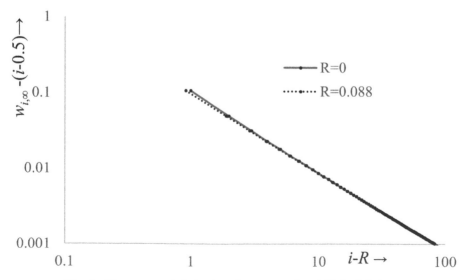

Fig. 4. The asymptotic behavior of $w_{i,n\to\infty} - (i - 0.5)$ for infinite n.

Also the variances for infinite n can be calculated through $v_{i,n\to\infty} = 1/w_{i,n\to\infty}$. This expression is suitable for non-integer i as can occur with censored failure data.

It appeared fruitful to first find an algorithm for $v_{i,n}$ and then convert to $w_{i,n}$. In the following, still, the asymptotic approach of $w_{i,n\to\infty}$ to $i-0.5$ is used as the foundation, because unlike (14) it is suitable for non-integer i. As $w_{i,n\to\infty}$ approaches $i-0.5$, likewise $v_{i,n\to\infty}$ approaches $(i-0.5)^{-1}$ with increasing i. This asymptote is a first power function with $\{P_1, Q_1, R_1\} = \{-1, 1, 0.5\}$. In a similar fashion as Fig. 4 the asymptotic behavior $D_i = v_{i,n\to\infty} - (i-0.5)^{-1}$ can be explored. The parameters of a second function are then found as $\{P_2, Q_2, R_2\} = \{-3, -0.1, 0.3445\}$. The algorithm for $v_{i,n\to\infty} = v_{i,\infty}$ is:

$$v_{i,\infty} = Q_1 \cdot (i - R_1)^{P_1} + Q_2 \cdot (i - R_2)^{P_2} \approx (i - 0.5)^{-1} - 0.1 \cdot (i - 0.3445)^{-3} \quad (17)$$

4.2   Finite Sample Size

The algorithm in (17) is suitable for the infinite n case and a good approximation for (severely) censored cases where $i \ll n$. For finite n and the limit $i \to n$, the variances increase (cf. Fig. 1) and the weights decrease sharply (cf. Fig. 2). Figure 5 shows the deviation $D_i = v_{i,n} - v_{i,\infty}$ as a function of i for various n.

For every curve, $D_i \downarrow 0$ for $i \downarrow 1$. This is due to (12). For $n \le 9$ the curves reach higher maxima $v_{n,n}$ and for $n > 9$ the maxima $v_{n,n}$ are decaying. Noticing that the summation in (14) equals $\pi^2/6$ for $i \to \infty$ (cf. Equation 23.2.24 in [7]), the $v_{n,n}$ asymptotically approach 0. These observations led to the conclusion that this behavior may be described with the product of 3 power functions as a start. In the following the parameters of these three 3-parameter power functions will be indexed 3–5.

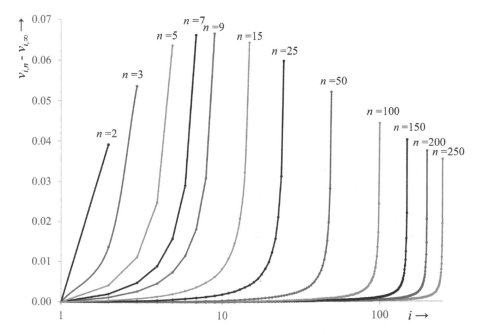

Fig. 5. The asymptotic behavior of $v_{i,n} - v_{i,\infty}$ for various sample sizes n.

The requirement to have $D_1 = 0$ can be met with a power function of i-1 (i.e., $R_3 = 1$) and a positive power P_3 (note: not asymptotic for $i \rightarrow \infty$). As for the amplitude Q_3, a product of 3 power functions will lead to a joint amplitude $Q = Q_3 \cdot Q_4 \cdot Q_5$ which is investigated as one single parameter Q. As all $D_i > 0$ for all $i > 1$ (cf. Fig. 5), the joint $Q > 0$.

The requirement of decaying $v_{n,n}$ can be met with a power function of n-R_4 and a negative power P_4. For $n \downarrow R_4$ this power function approaches its singularity on the one hand, while the power function of i-1 approaches 0. If D_i for all n and i can be described with the explored set of power functions, then $R_4 < 1$ and the singularity is not reached for any $n \geq 1$ and $i \geq 1$. It is noteworthy, that the power functions of i-1 and n-R_4 may very well describe the behavior of $v_{i,n}$ and particularly $v_{n,n}$ in the range $1 \leq i \leq 9$.

Finally, the individual curves for given n, can be described with a power function of n-i-R_5 that has a negative power P_5. Also here the singularity should not be reached for any $n - i \geq 0$ and therefore $R_5 < 0$. With $v_{i,\infty}$ as in (17), the variance model becomes:

$$v_{i,n} = v_{i,\infty} + Q \cdot (i-1)^{P_3} \cdot (n-R_4)^{P_4} \cdot (n-i-R_5)^{P_5} \tag{18}$$

The WLR weight model follows as the inverse, i.e., $w_{i,n} = 1/v_{i,n}$.

The parameters P_3, P_4, P_5, Q, R_4 and R_5 were optimized with the reference data set mentioned above [6]. A mini-max criterion was applied, i.e. the largest $\pm$ relative deviation of any *weight* $w_{i,n}$ between the model and reference was minimized. A rounded off result was: $\{P_3, P_4, P_5, Q, R_4 \text{ and } R_5\} = \{1.4, -1.656, -0.75, 0.125, -0.343, -0.8\}$. The algorithm for the variances $v_{i,n}$ thus becomes:

$$v_{i,n} \approx (i-0.5)^{-1} - 0.1 \cdot (i-0.3445)^{-3} + \left[0.125 \cdot (i-1)^{1.4} \cdot (n+0.343)^{-1.656} \cdot (n-i+0.8)^{-0.75}\right] \tag{19}$$

From (19) follows the algorithm for the WLR weights $w_{i,n}$:

$$w_{i,n} = 1/v_{i,n} \approx 1/\{(i-0.5)^{-1} - 0.1 \cdot (i-0.3445)^{-3} + \left[0.125 \cdot (i-1)^{1.4} \cdot (n+0.343)^{-1.656} \cdot (n-i+0.8)^{-0.75}\right]\} \tag{20}$$

This algorithm enables to calculate weights for WLR not only for integer ranking indices i, but also for non-integer ranking indices. As mentioned before, failure data from tests with random censoring is often treated with adjusted ranking that usually yields non-integer indices. The present algorithm is built with 3-parameter power functions. The algorithm is suitable for light-weight computing and can conveniently be embedded in common office software like spreadsheets. The performance is tested below.

5   Evaluation of the Algorithm

The variance model of (17)–(19) and weight algorithm of (20) were evaluated in two ways. The first was part of the optimization, namely, the error of each model weight $w_{i,n,mod}$ calculated with (20) compared to the theoretical or reference weight $w_{i,n,ref}$. Figure 6 shows the maximum $\pm$ relative error in $w_{i,n}$ for each sample size n that was involved in the optimization process which was the sequence detailed in Sect. 3.2 above. For all tested $n \leq 2000$ the absolute value of maximum error was $< 2.8\%$ which occurred for $i = 2000$, $n = 2000$. For all $n \leq 500$ the absolute value of max error was $\leq 1\%$. Relative to the max $w_{i,n} = w_{n,max}$ for each n, the relative error was $\leq 0.34\%$ (occurring for $n = 2$). The model parameters may be fine-tuned further. However, for the purpose of WLR, the approximation is very satisfactory with the $\leq 0.34\%$ max error.

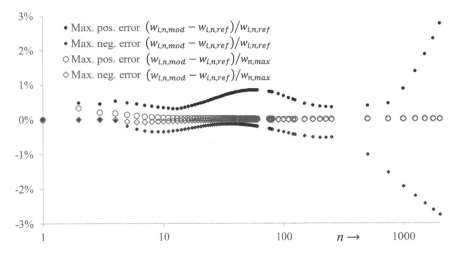

Fig. 6. The maximum relative deviations in the model $w_{i,n,mod}$ from the reference $w_{i,n,ref}$.

The second evaluation tested the shape of the weight distribution. If all model weights would deviate from theory by the same factor, then the *relative* model and theoretical weights would remain the same. The WLR results by model and theory would also be exactly the same. A Similarity Index S_{fg} [1] was employed to test the overall shape. This is a measure for how similar two distributions F and G are, judged by their respective distribution densities f and g. If the distribution densities are identical, then $S_{fg} = 1$. If f and g have nothing in common, then $S_{fg} = 0$. The general definition is:

$$S_{fg} = \frac{f \cdot g}{f \cdot f + g \cdot g - f \cdot g} \tag{21}$$

The terms $f \cdot g, f \cdot f$ and $g \cdot g$ are inner products that can be defined in various ways. In the present case, the weights can be defined as discrete distribution densities:

$$f_{i,n} = \frac{w_{i,n,mod}}{\sum_{i=1}^{n} w_{i,n,mod}}$$
$$g_{i,n} = \frac{w_{i,n,ref}}{\sum_{i=1}^{n} w_{i,n,ref}} \quad (22)$$

The S_{fg} of the model and reference can then be determined for each sample size n:

$$S_{fg} = \frac{\sum_{i=1}^{n} \left(f_{i,n} \cdot g_{i,n}\right)}{\sum_{i=1}^{n} \left(f_{i,n} \cdot f_{i,n}\right) + \sum_{i=1}^{n} \left(g_{i,n} \cdot g_{i,n}\right) - \sum_{i=1}^{n} \left(f_{i,n} \cdot g_{i,n}\right)} \quad (23)$$

Additionally, a Dissimilarity Index D_{fg} can be defined as $D_{fg} = 1 - S_{fg}$. D_{fg} can be regarded as $L2$ (sum of squared deviations) normalized by the union of F and G:

$$D_{fg} = 1 - S_{fg} = \frac{f \cdot f + g \cdot g - 2f \cdot g}{f \cdot f + g \cdot g - f \cdot g} = \frac{(f - g) \cdot (f - g)}{f \cdot f + g \cdot g - f \cdot g} \quad (24)$$

For all $n \leq 2000$, S_{fg} appeared $> 0.9999885 \approx 1$. D_{fg} was found largest for $n = 6$, namely, $1.02 \cdot 10^{-5} \approx 0$. Figure 7 shows S_{fg} of the model and theory as a function of sample size n.

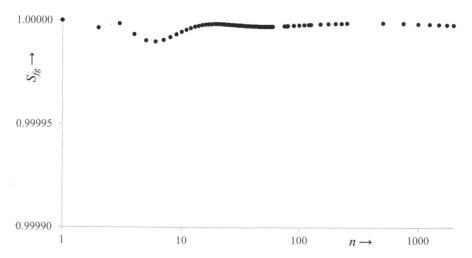

Fig. 7. The similarity of $w_{i,n,mod}$ and $w_{i,n,ref}$, i.e. between the WLR weight algorithm and theory.

6   Discussion and Conclusion

The present paper discussed the making of an algorithm to calculate the weights for WLR with two challenging boundary conditions. The first condition is that the algorithm must be able to handle failure data that have non-integer rankings i ($1 \leq i \leq n$).

The second condition comes from an on-going project that aims to develop widely accessible data analytics in support of asset management that translates into a requirement of 'light-weight computing'.

The approach of the subject is to combine asymptotic 3-parameter power functions. In earlier research, such functions were applied to cases like the bias and standard deviation of Weibull and other distribution parameters that are efficient and therefore show often a smooth asymptotic behavior. Some aspects of the present challenge, i.e., the WLR weights case, can be associated with asymptotic behavior, but it is more complex. The trajectory to reach the present results required much trial and error. The paper shows the line along which the algorithm was successfully developed.

The parameter values as in (20) are the result of an optimization process. It may be possible to find roots that make the algorithm even more accurate. The performance with the present parameter values is tested for maximum deviation of the model from theory for a wide range of sample sizes, namely, n = 1(1)60, 75(1)80, 80(10)120, 125 (25)250(250)2000 as reported in [6]. The deviation of all weights is within 1% for tested sample sizes $n \leq 500$ and within 2.8% for $n \leq 2000$. For all n, relative to the max $w_{i,n,max}$, the error < 0.34%. Secondly, the distributions of model and reference weights are tested for their similarity. The similarity index S_{fg} was practically 1, i.e. the model is almost identical to theory. The dissimilarity $D_{fg} \leq 1.02 \cdot 10^{-5}$ for all n.

This work on theory and ultimate model is supported by the Netherlands Ministry of Economic Affairs and Climate through the RvO agency, Grant ref. nr. TEUE418008, TKI Project FINDGO and by the EU H2020 R&I program and RvO under ECSEL grant agreement No 826417 (Project Power2Power).

References

1. Ross, R.: Reliability Analysis for Asset Management of Electric Power Grids. Wiley-IEEE Press, Hoboken, NJ (2019)
2. Penn State. https://online.stat.psu.edu/stat501/lesson/13/13.1.Accessed 25 Oct 2021
3. IEC TC112. IEC 62539(E):2007 Guide for the Statistical Analysis of Electrical Insulation Breakdown Data. International Electrotechnical Committee, Geneva (2007)
4. Fisher, R.A.: Theory of statistical estimation, In: Proceedings of the Cambridge Philosophical Society vol. 22(5), pp. 700–725 (1925)
5. Ross, R.: Bias and standard deviation due to weibull parameter estimation for small data sets. IEEE Trans. Dielectr. Electr. Insul. 3(1), 28–42 (1996)
6. Ross, R., Ypma, P.A.C., Koopmans, G.: Weighted linear regression based data analysis for decision making after early failures. In: Proceedings of IEEE PES ISGT-Asia 2021, paper 148, Brisbane (2021)
7. Abramowitz, M., Stegun, I.A.: Handbook of Mathematical Functions, 9th edn. Dover Publications Inc., New York (1970)

Special Intervention of AI

Shrub Detection in High-Resolution Imagery: A Comparative Study of Two Deep Learning Approaches

Katherine James and Karen Bradshaw[✉]

Rhodes University, Grahamstown, South Africa
k.bradshaw@ru.ac.za

Abstract. A common task in high-resolution remotely-sensed aerial imagery is the detection of particular target plant species for various ecological and agricultural applications. Although traditionally object-based image analysis approaches have been the most popular method for this task, deep learning approaches such as image patch-based convolutional neural networks (CNNs) have been seen to outperform these older approaches. To a lesser extent, fully convolutional networks (FCNs) that allow for semantic segmentation of images, have also begun to be used in the broader literature.

This study investigates patch-based CNNs and FCN-based segmentation for shrub detection, targeting a particular invasive shrub genus. The results show that while a patch-based CNN demonstrates strong performance on ideal image patches, the FCN outperforms this approach on real-world proposed image patches with a 52% higher object-level precision and comparable recall. This indicates that FCN-based segmentation approaches are a promising alternative to patch-based approaches, with the added advantage of not requiring any hand-tuning of a patch proposal algorithm.

Keywords: Plant species detection · Convolutional neural networks · Classification · Segmentation

1 Introduction

The ability to detect particular plants of interest in high-resolution remotely-sensed aerial imagery is essential in many ecological and agricultural applications, including distribution mapping and monitoring and in-field decision support systems.

In high-resolution aerial imagery, such as that obtained by drones, the most popular approach to detection is object-based image analysis (OBIA) [2], where pixels with some similarity are grouped to form objects, from which features can be extracted and subsequently used for classification using a machine learning classifier, such as a random forest or support vector machine (SVM). Although hand-crafted features have traditionally been extracted from the objects for training the classifiers, deep learning approaches such as convolutional neural

© Springer Nature Switzerland AG 2022
D. Garg et al. (Eds.): IACC 2021, CCIS 1528, pp. 545–561, 2022.
https://doi.org/10.1007/978-3-030-95502-1_41

networks (CNNs) that are trained with a large number of samples to rather learn features, have been shown to outperform these older methods [14].

CNNs have been used very successfully in agriculture, for example, by Milioto et al. [17] who employed a CNN for the task of detecting weeds and sugar beet plants in a field to support onboard decisions, achieving accuracy, precision and recall values over 95%. The success of deep learning in agriculture is also seen in the review by Kamilaris and Prenafetu_Boldu [11], who observed that deep learning methods nearly always outperform other image processing techniques. CNNs are learnable models, and as such, can be utilised on images other than those on which they are trained [7].

A modification of the standard CNN classification network, where dense layers are replaced with convolutional ones, allows for semantic segmentation – a pixel-wise classification of the entire image [15]. These networks are called fully convolutional networks (FCNs) and produce a pixel-wise classification instead of a single classification per image (or image patch). Mboga et al. [16] found this strategy provided better accuracy than a state-of-the-art OBIA approach when applied to the task of urban mapping, as well as having better generalisation ability as it learnt features directly from the image. FCNs have also recently been used for woody vegetation mapping [4] and pomegranate tree crown detection [26].

In this paper, we compare two deep learning approaches for the task of identifying an invasive shrub in visual spectrum (RGB) drone sourced imagery.

2   Approach

The two deep learning methods used in this investigation are (1) a CNN-based classifier combined with an image patch proposal algorithm for detection, and (2) FCN-based semantic segmentation. To evaluate these approaches, a dataset was collected and annotated, different CNN architectures were evaluated for classification on ideal image patches, with the top-performing classifier selected and applied to proposed image patches. An FCN-based segmentation architecture with different training configurations was evaluated and, finally, the top-performing classification model applied to proposed image patches was compared with the top-performing segmentation model in terms of both classification and detection.

2.1   Dataset and Target Plant

As a case study approach, a single genus of shrub, *Hakea*, was chosen to evaluate both approaches. One species of this genus, *Hakea sericea*, is the most prevalent of all woody invaders in South Africa's fynbos biome [12]. It is characterised by woody shrubs with needle-like leaves, growing three to five meters in height and forming dense stands that crowd out indigenous vegetation [12] (see Fig. 1).

The dataset used in this study was collected using a DJI Mavic Pro, with the camera facing vertically downwards, over two days, approximately a month

(a) Side profile of a *Hakea* shrub (b) Unchecked invasion results in dense stands

Fig. 1. Photographs of the target shrub genus, *Hakea*.

apart to allow for variation in environmental conditions, particularly appearance of the vegetation, illumination and cloud cover. As a result, the brightness varies across the two sets of images. The first set (train set) contains 84 images, of which 52 include at least one target shrub in the image, while the second set (unseen test set), contains 82 images of which 48 include at least one target shrub. All images contain regions that are not part of the target shrub class.

2.2 CNN-Based Detection Approach

In the task of detection, potential targets must be identified within the image (localised within an image patch, which closely bounds the shrub) and also classified into target and non-target classes. Several different CNN classification architectures were evaluated on ideal, hand-marked image patches and the best performing one was then applied to proposed image patches to evaluate detection success.

Selection of Classification Architecture. The general architecture of a CNN consists of two components: one for feature extraction and one for classification. The feature extraction portion of the network consists of convolutional and pooling layers, while the classification component consists of fully-connected layers. In this study, the Xception [3], Inception [23] and MobileNet [9] architectures were selected from the set of pre-trained models implemented in the deep-learning library Keras[1]. These models have a good balance between accuracy and model size (in MB), which is an important consideration when considering models that need to be suitable for integration with memory impoverished devices, such as a drone.

The dataset used for training, evaluation and selection of the best classification model consisted of hand-marked image patches, extracted from the full images in the train and test sets, respectively, such that these contained only

---

[1] keras.io.

a selection of closely bounded images of shrubs, both of the target and non-target varieties. This allowed for a baseline of best-possible performance to be computed and to determine whether these models were capable of distinguishing between target and non-target shrubs. The classification problem was thus formulated as: positive class → target shrub, negative class → other non-target shrub.

Each of the models was trained using the following training scheme:

- **Fine-tuning** – This is a process which exploits the behaviour whereby early layers of a CNN learn general features, which are largely dataset independent [25]. This means that the weights of a network trained to convergence on one dataset may be used for initialisation, before training further using a new dataset. In this study, the feature extraction component of each of the architectures was initialised with ImageNet[2] pre-trained weights, with a randomly initialised classification head added to distinguish between our target and non-target classes.
- **Early stopping** – This is a technique used to prevent over-fitting, which would impact the generalisation performance. A portion of the train set, called a validation set, is held out and not used to update the weights within the network. While training, the loss is also computed for the validation set and is monitored across the epochs. If the validation loss begins to increase while the training loss is still decreasing, this is an indication that the model has begun to learn noise within the training set, so training is stopped even if was originally configured to train for further epochs.
- **Data augmentation** – Data augmentation strategies were used to artificially increase the size of the training set, allowing the models to learn invariance to noise within the dataset. The augmentation strategies used were flipping, rescaling, rotating, shifting and zooming.

To evaluate the models, each was first trained using a 10-fold validation approach using the train set. This means that the train set was divided into ten portions, each of which was held-out as the validation set on one complete training iteration. This allows for the calculation of the mean performance of the model, with standard deviation, to ensure that the results are not dependent on the chance composition of the validation set. Thereafter, each of the models was trained using the complete train set. The Xception, Inception and MobileNet models were trained for 150, 50 and 100 epochs respectively, guided by observing the general training period during the 10-fold validation. These models were then evaluated on the unseen test set to gauge generalisation ability.

Proposal of Image Patches. When considering the entire image, it is necessary to identify and extract patches of the image that contain shrubs, so that the classifier can be applied to these. Vegetation indices are a well-established method for segmenting remotely-sensed imagery into foreground (vegetation)

---

[2] http://www.image-net.org/.

and background (soil) [8]. There are a number of vegetation indices suitable for use with only visual wavelength light, such as excess green (ExG) [24], normalised green-red difference (NGRDI) [6], the red, blue and green chromatic coordinates (R/B/GCC) [5], Woebbecke index (WI) [24], and visible atmospheric resistant index (VARI) [6], amongst others. A single frame was used to perform an initial assessment of the effectiveness of these vegetation indices for determining the position of bushes within the image. Indices were calculated for each pixel within the image to create a single channel index-transformed image. The most promising index for proposing shrubs was GCC, and as such, GCC transformed images were computed using Eq. 1 for the dataset.

$$GCC = \frac{G}{R + G + B} \qquad (1)$$

The GCC-transformed images were then thresholded to produce a binary image classified into foreground (shrubs) and background (other land cover). The pixel range 90 : 160 was found to yield the best segmentation into these categories.

It is necessary to convert these thresholded segmentations into plausible image patches, containing objects of interest. To do this, the contours of the thresholded image were found and filtered by area, retaining only those with an area ≥ 1000, as this threshold was found experimentally to remove areas too small to be of interest. The binary images were improved upon using the morphological 'open' operation, the contours of the binarised image found and their bounding box coordinates calculated. These bounding boxes were adjusted to have an aspect ratio of 1:1, with the smaller of the dimensions being adjusted to match the larger of the dimensions, with equal expansion on either side. If the resulting bounding box exceeded the dimensions of the image by up to half the width or height of the bounding box, then the coordinates of the bounding box were shifted such that the side exceeding the dimensions of the image rested on the edge of the image. Any bounding box exceeding the dimensions of the image by more than half the width or height of the bounding box was discarded. Image patches, suitable for classification, were then extracted from these bounding boxes.

2.3   Segmentation Approach

Semantic segmentation is obtained through pixel-level classification of images into the target and background classes, where the positive class is pixels belonging to the target shrub and the negative class is pixels belonging to any other land-cover. The U-Net architecture [21] was selected for use in this study.

A crucial component of a training scheme for a neural network is the loss function, which gives a measure of error after each iteration and is minimised across the entire training process. Several different training configurations were evaluated to determine the most optimal model in this study. Particularly, a number of loss functions were used to train the U-Net model, each of which accounts in some way for class imbalance, a problem that occurs where a local minimum in the loss function may be found by predicting all samples to be of the majority class. Class imbalance is strongly present within the dataset at pixel level, with only 8% of pixels belonging to the target class, and the remaining 92% to the non-target background class. The loss functions used were weighted binary cross-entropy (WBCE) [10], the weighted focal loss (WF) [13], the Dice loss [19] and intersection over union (IOU) loss [20]. Data augmentation was once again used, with the addition of brightness augmentation.

2.4 Evaluation

Performance of the two approaches was empirically assessed by the following metrics calculated from the confusion matrix values of true positives (TP), false positives (FP), true negatives (TN) and false negatives (FN), namely, precision, recall, accuracy, and F1-score.

In the classification task, each TP (and other confusion matrix value) corresponds to a single image patch, whereas in the segmentation task each corresponds to a single pixel within the image. Metrics calculated for classification are thus at an image-patch level, whereas metrics for segmentation are calculated per image and averaged across all images. This means that the metrics for the two approaches cannot be directly compared, but rather only used to gain a measure of performance for each task individually.

The distribution of pixels within the segmentation output is also important, as positive pixels should group into objects corresponding to target shrubs. For this reason, examining the segmentation outputs qualitatively is also important for evaluating the different trained U-Net models.

To compute comparable metrics, the top-performing model from both the patch-based CNNs and the segmentation approach were selected and the results re-analysed. First, we examine the performance on ideal hand-marked patches by extracting the same regions from the segmentation outputs, manually classifying these based on the class represented by the pixels in the binary image and using these values to compute confusion matrix values and thus metrics for 'classification', which can then be directly compared to those computed for the CNN when applied to ideal image patches.

Secondly, we evaluated the two approaches in terms of their detection ability. Again, the segmentation results were re-analysed to obtain object-level metrics which were comparable to the results of the CNN when applied to the proposed image patches. Segmentation outputs were compared to the original annotation masks produced for evaluating the trained model and notable intersections between the segmentation outputs and the masks constituted a TP detection. Overlapping bushes were counted as a single bush, unless there was a clear dividing point, and very small positive predictions were excluded. A count of true negative predictions is not possible with this method, as all regions of the image that were not part of the target plant fall into this category, which subsequently precluded the calculation of accuracy.

Table 1. Mean metrics represented as a fraction with standard deviations, calculated from 10-fold cross-validation for each model.

Model	Accuracy	Precision	Recall	F1 score
Xception	0.90 ± 0.07	0.87 ± 0.09	0.97 ± 0.05	0.91 ± 0.06
Inception	0.85 ± 0.06	1.00 ± 0.00	0.71 ± 0.11	0.83 ± 0.08
MobileNet	0.87 ± 0.07	0.99 ± 0.02	0.75 ± 0.14	0.85 ± 0.10

Table 2. Performance of each model for classification of the unseen test set

Model	Accuracy	Precision	Recall	F1 Score
Xception	0.83	0.75	0.98	0.85
Inception	0.91	0.95	0.85	0.90
MobileNet	0.98	1.00	0.95	0.97

Table 3. Performance of the MobileNet classifier on image patches proposed using the GCC vegetation index on the unseen test set, dataset 2.

Model	Accuracy	Precision	Recall	F1 Score
Ideal patches + MobileNet	0.98	1.00	0.95	0.97
Proposed patches + MobileNet	0.52	0.34	0.90	0.50

3 Experimental Evaluation

In this section, results for the three experiments are reported. In Sect. 3.1, these are the results for the different CNN classifiers when applied to ideal hand-marked image patches. Thereafter in Sect. 3.2, the best performing model is applied to non-ideal image patches, proposed using vegetation indices. In Sect. 3.3, we report the results for the contending approach, semantic segmentation using the U-Net deep learning architecture, trained with different loss functions. Finally, the patch-based CNN and segmentation approaches are compared in Sect. 3.4.

3.1 Classification of Ideal Image Patches

In this section, the performance of different CNN architectures on image patches extracted from ideal windows containing only shrubs of both classes (target and non-target) is evaluated, first through k-fold validation on the training set and then on the unseen test set. This gives a baseline of the best possible model performance that can be obtained through the use of a CNN-based classification approach.

K-fold Validation Using only Training Set. Table 1 shows that good accuracy was achieved by all models, with the Xception model the best performer in this metric, although closely followed by MobileNet and Inception. This ranking holds true for the F1-score as well, which indicates a good balance between precision and recall. When contrasting the Xception model with the Inception and MobileNet models, a trade-off between the precision and recall is noted. Looking at these two metrics, while the Xception model was able to correctly classify 97% of the target shrubs, it also incorrectly classified 13% of the non-targets as targets. In contrast, the Inception and MobileNet models respectively classified only 71% and 75% of the target shrubs correctly, but only erroneously predicted at most 1% of non-target shrubs as targets. Each of these models offers relatively strong performance, and the choice of preferable behaviour depends on the application of the model, i.e. depending on whether false positives or false negatives can be better tolerated. The best balance between precision and recall was obtained by the Xception model, as indicated by its F1-score.

| Original | Thresholded | Original | Thresholded |

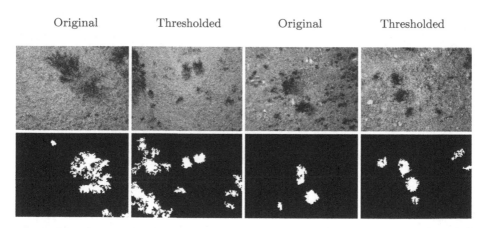

Fig. 2. A sample of segmentation results after thresholding the GCC vegetation index image.

Results for Unseen Test Set. In contrast to the 10-fold results, we find that the Xception model does not generalise as well as expected to the unseen data (see Table 2), while the MobileNet and Inception architectures do so well, with a higher accuracy and F1 score achieved by both, due to an improvement in recall score. This indicates the Xception model is likely to have overfit on some feature of the train set, impairing its ability to generalise. The MobileNet model demonstrates the best generalisation ability, with an F1-score of 0.97.

This result from the MobileNet model indicates that excellent performance is obtainable when using image patches extracted from ideal windows, and that the model is able to generalise well to unseen data. This model was thus selected for comparison in the following sections.

Table 4. Average metrics across validation set for 10-fold validation, trained with different loss functions in each case.

Average metrics		Precision	Recall	F1	Accuracy
WBCE		0.46±0.09	0.92±0.06	0.77±0.06	0.93±0.03
WF	$\gamma = 2$	0.42±0.10	0.82±0.08	0.69±0.11	0.91±0.03
	$\gamma = 1$	0.44±0.15	0.85±0.06	0.73±0.09	0.92±0.04
	$\gamma = 0.5$	0.44±0.11	0.89±0.08	0.75±0.07	0.92±0.03
Dice		0.58±0.12	0.84±0.06	0.82±0.05	0.95±0.02
IOU		0.53±0.13	0.84±0.07	0.80±0.06	0.94±0.02

3.2   Detection – Classification of Proposed Windows

The classifier in Sect. 3.1 distinguishes between the target and non-target shrubs, but not between the target shrub and other land cover. This means that the proposed image patches, used for classification, should also only contain shrubs.

Extraction of Image Patches for Classification. The GCC-transformed images were thresholded to produce segmentation into shrub and background categories, as shown by the sample in Fig. 2. Image patches were extracted from this, on which the classifier trained in Sect. 3.1 was then applied.

The segmentations produced using the GCC vegetation index were largely successful, with the shrubs detected well, although some regions of textured background vegetation were proposed as well (row one of Fig. 2).

Metrics for the results of classification of the proposed image matches may be seen in Table 3, where they are contrasted against the performance of the model on the hand-marked ideal image patches.

This table shows that when the model is applied to the proposed patches, a severe drop in precision occurs, which indicates a high number of FP detections. This poor behaviour of the classifier when applied to the same test dataset as before, but on imperfect image patches, indicates that the metrics obtained when applied to ideal image patches are indeed an upper limit of performance which is severely impacted by imperfectly proposed patches. The construction of bounding boxes from the segmentation also sometimes results in missed target shrubs, which are not bounded nor presented to the classifier as an image patch. This reduces the possible overall recall. In this case study, four target shrubs were not proposed, which means that in reality, the recall score is lower as these shrubs were excluded from the calculation. Both the poor performance on imperfect image patches and the exclusion of some target shrubs indicates that the proposal of image patches is a constraining step in the performance of this approach.

3.3   Deep Learning-Based Semantic Segmentation

The U-Net architecture was trained using different loss functions and hyper-parameter configurations, producing the results in Tables 4 and 5. Unlike the

| Input | WBCE | WF 2 | WF 1 | WF 0.5 | Dice | IOU |

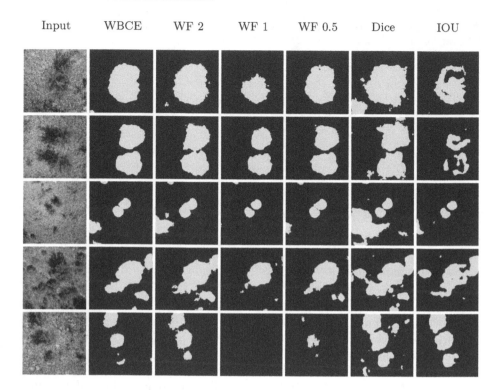

Fig. 3. A selection of images for each class, showing the resulting segmentations for each configuration.

results in Sect. 3.1, the model must both determine where in the image the target objects are located as well as providing a pixel-wise classification, instead of being provided with ideally extracted image patches.

K-fold Validation Using only Training Set. From the results for 10-fold validation in Table 4, it is seen that each of the trained models achieve high accuracy, however, this is not a particularly insightful metric for pixel-level metrics, as the vast majority of pixels form part of the background class. Of greater interest is the F1-score, which is over 0.70 for all bar one loss function. This is a relatively strong score, given that this is calculated across all the pixels in the image.

Precision and recall metrics give greater insight into the distribution of predicted positive samples. From Table 4 a high recall is observed, which indicates that nearly all true positive samples, i.e. pixels of the target shrub class, are predicted correctly, while relatively low precision values indicate that there is a fairly high number of pixels predicted as FPs.

Results for Unseen Test Set. On the whole, Table 5 shows that the models generalise well to the unseen data with fairly consistent results compared with

Table 5. Average metrics obtained on the unseen test set for each configuration, trained on dataset 1.

Average metrics		Precision	Recall	F1	Accuracy
WBCE		0.44	0.94	0.80	0.93
WF	$\gamma = 2$	0.40	0.95	0.76	0.92
	$\gamma = 1$	0.67	0.76	0.79	0.97
	$\gamma = 0.5$	0.49	0.91	0.83	0.95
Dice		0.32	0.91	0.63	0.83
IOU		0.48	0.64	0.70	0.91

Table 6. Confusion matrix values from manual examination of extracted image patches from U-Net segmentation outputs.

	Actual positives	Actual negatives
Predicted positives	58	2
Predicted negatives	41	100

those obtained in the k-fold validation. The consistency in results shows good generalisation ability across the models, with the exception of the Dice loss configuration, which experiences a substantial drop in F1-score and accuracy. Of these models, the WF loss configurations $\gamma = 0.5$ and $\gamma = 1$ achieve notably high accuracy, with 5% or fewer pixels predicted incorrectly on average across the dataset. The WBCE loss also achieves a strong F1-score.

To obtain greater insight into how these positive samples were distributed, a selection of images are shown in Fig. 3. From these images it is possible to observe that the pixels predicted to belong to the target class are generally grouped well into objects, and that all bar the IOU loss configuration detect the target shrubs well. A high number of false positive detections are predicted, where shrubs of the non-target class are predicted to belong to the target class. This is least prevalent for the WF $\gamma = 1$ configuration, most notably in row 5 where the model is the only one to correctly identify that there are no target shrubs present. These observations correspond to the values in Table 5. The trade-off between precision and recall is also visualised well through these images, with those models with higher recall achieving a fuller detection of targets (such as seen in row 1), but predicting more FPs. This is true of all models except the WF $\gamma = 1$ configuration, which achieves higher precision by almost 20%, at the cost of lower recall. Although not as many pixels within each shrub are predicted to belong to the target class, this model still detects each of the target shrubs, so has a very high visual object-level recall and predicts few false positives, which are also small. This configuration is arguably the best, as although the target plant is not fully detected in the first row, the majority of the pixels within the target shrubs are correctly predicted to be the target class and the least FP predictions are made.

Table 7. Object-level metrics for classification on the ideal hand-marked regions.

Segmentation	Classifier	Precision	Recall	F1 score	Accuracy
Ideal patches	MobileNet	1.00	0.95	0.97	0.98
U-Net (extracted)		0.97	0.59	0.73	0.82

Table 8. Confusion matrix values from manual examination U-Net segmentation outputs to count objects.

	Actual positives	Actual negatives
Predicted positives	102	16
Predicted negatives	14	–

Table 9. Object-level metrics obtained for the detection task.

Segmentation	Classifier	Precision	Recall	F1 score	Accuracy
GCC	MobileNet	0.34	0.90	0.50	0.52
U-Net (object level metrics)		0.86	0.88	0.87	–

3.4   Comparative Results

In this section, we compare the results for the two approaches, using the best model from each section, this being the MobileNet classification model and the U-Net model in the WF $\gamma = 1$ configuration. As these two models are not directly comparable as they stand, with the former providing classification at image patch level and the latter at pixel-level, we re-analyse the predictions of the two approaches to yield comparable object-level metrics. First, we compare the models' performances across all those shrubs hand-marked within ideal windows to give an indication of classification accuracy. Secondly, we compare the two models in terms of detection (localisation) performance, using the proposed patches to apply the MobileNet classifier as in Sect. 3.2 and comparing the segmentations produced by the U-Net model to hand annotated masks to obtain comparable shrub object-level metrics.

Classification of Ideal Image Patches. To facilitate direct comparison between the classification approach on ideal windows and the U-Net approach, we extract the regions corresponding to the ideal windows in Sect. 3.1 from the U-Net segmented output. As the classification in the segmentation output is pixel-wise, an overall classification for the overall extracted patch was assigned as positive if the patch contained an observable object. This allowed for the calculation of confusion matrix values (see Table 6), and from these, comparable metrics for the U-Net predictions to those obtained by the MobileNet classifier when applied to these same regions. These results are presented in Table 7.

From Table 7, it is seen that MobileNet obtains better results than U-Net, largely due to a substantially higher recall by 36%. This means that a number of positives were incorrectly predicted to be negatives by the U-Net in the region of the image patch, or were predicted poorly with the positive segmentation not centred or not largely overlapping the target plant. The precision values are however very close, which means that both approaches make few errors when classifying an image patch as the target class.

Detection of Targets Within the Entire Image. In this section, we consider the detection task, i.e. localising the target shrubs within the image. The detection results from the application of the MobileNet classifier to the proposed image patches are object-level metrics. For direct comparison with these, the segmentation outputs of the U-Net model were visually inspected, compared with the original annotation masks and a manual count of the individual objects as TP, FN and FP was performed (see Table 8 for the resulting confusion matrix). This allows for the calculation of object-level metrics from the segmentation outputs. Overlapping bushes were counted as a single bush, unless there was a clear dividing point, and very small positive predictions were excluded. A count of true negative predictions is not possible with this method, as all regions of the image that were not part of the target plant fall into this category and are thus background, not objects. This subsequently precluded the calculation of an object-level accuracy.

Table 9 shows that while a comparable recall is achieved by the two approaches, the U-Net approach achieves far better precision and hence F1-scores. This means that for the real-world task of shrub detection, the deep learning-based segmentation approach far outperforms the classification of proposed image patches approach.

4   Discussion

From the results in Sect. 3.1, we see that the MobileNet model was able to distinguish well between the target and non-target shrub classes on ideal image patches, achieving precision and recall score of 100% and 95%, respectively, on the test set. The classifier did less well when applied to image patches proposed using GCC-transformed images in Sect. 3.2, with a precision of only 34% and recall of 90%.

To obtain a comparison to the results obtained in Sect. 3.2, we consider other studies in the literature. A patch-based CNN approach (the ResNet architecture) combined with image patches proposed through thresholding grey-scale transformed images was used in [7] to detect invasive *Ziziphus lotus* shrubs in Google Earth imagery. This approach was found to yield precision, recall and F1-scores in the range 92.68 to 100%, 93.24 to 95.00% and 93.38 to 96.50%, respectively. While the recall obtained in our study is comparable at 90%, the precision is substantially lower at only 34%. The precision problem is seen elsewhere in the literature, such as in a study for detecting invasive *Iris Pseudacorus*, where a precision of 4.8% and a recall of 93% were achieved using a pixel-based random forest classification approach [1].

Vegetation index proposed image patches were used in another study [17], along with a custom CNN architecture. The NDVI vegetation index was computed with the presence of the near-infrared band in addition to the RGB band, along with a blob segmentation algorithm. This study achieved target precision of 99.42% and recall of 89.00% on the test set. This is an extremely high precision value, closer to that achieved in our study by the classifier applied to the ideal hand-marked image patches where perfect precision was achieved on the test set. This indicates that the algorithm used for segmenting the image and subsequent proposal of the image patches is of utmost importance and that such algorithms need to produce image patches that are near-ideal.

Application of the segmentation approach in Sect. 3.3 yielded 67% precision, 76% recall and 0.79% F1-score on the test set. This F1-score is comparable with that achieved by Sa et al. [22] using the SegNet FCN architecture in a three-class background-weed-crop task on near-infrared data, where F1-scores of 80% were achieved.

Using a similar dataset to that in [17], although sourced from an agricultural vehicle as opposed to a drone, an FCN approach using a custom segmentation network was used for pixel-wise classification into soil, crop and weed classes [18]. While the focus in this paper was not on pure RGB imagery, the experiment was run for comparison with the authors' augmented input representation approach and is documented here for comparison with our study's results. While both soil precision and recall were close to 100%, these metrics varied considerably for the crop and weed classes between the different test sites. Precision varied from 3.78 to 66.49% for the crop class and achieved a max of 28.97% for the weed class, while crop recall ranged from 28.95 to 82.45% and weed recall from 35.35 to 42.95%. Weighted cross-entropy loss was used to train the model. If we consider the crop and weed precision, the precision value achieved in our study is towards the higher end of the range for the crop class range, and substantially higher than that given for the weed class and similarly for recall.

Object-level metrics for segmentation outputs were also computed in [18]. The object-level precision and recall scores were higher than the pixel-wise scores. Weed precision ranged from 42.32 to 83.63%, while crop precision from 19.71 to 81.14%. Recall for weeds ranged from 42.52 to 91.99% and for crops from 23.66 to 80.42%. The object-level metrics achieved in our study were 86% for precision and 88% for recall, which are competitive with the top of the range for both metrics.

In a study on detecting pomegranate trees [26], the U-Net architecture was compared with the Mask R-CNN architecture, with the latter found to outperform the former. U-Net achieved a mean average precision of 36.2% and mean average recall of 61.2%. These metrics are calculated at object-level, through the intersection-over-union of the masks and segmentations. In contrast, the R-CNN approach achieved a mean precision of 57.5% and recall of 98.5%. This indicates that experimenting with other segmentation architectures may further improve the performance of the FCN approach, as this recall bettered our 88% object-level recall.

In our dataset, the background vegetation was mixed and of a greenish hue. This may be the reason for the poor success of the patch-based CNN approach. In situations where the candidate targets are more distinct from background vegetation and their proposal is easier, it is possible, given the results in Table 7, that the patch-based approach would provide better performance than the FCN-based segmentation approach. Such cases are likely to occur when considering the task of detecting weeds in crop fields, where a large amount of bare soil is present, such as is the case with the dataset used in [17]. However, given that the background in ecological datasets is unlikely to be perfectly bare soil, results from Table 0 illustrate that an FCN-based segmentation approach is a promising alternative, offering stronger localisation. In addition, the end-to-end training of the FCN architecture precludes the necessity for hand-tuning the algorithm for patch-proposal, such as selecting vegetation indices and setting thresholds.

5 Conclusion

A common task in ecological applications is the detection of shrubs in high-resolution remotely sensed imagery. In this paper, we conducted a comparison between two deep learning-based approaches for the task of identifying shrubs of the *Hakea* genus in drone-sourced RGB imagery. We conducted a comparison between image patched-based CNN detection, using the GCC vegetation index transformed images for patch proposal, and FCN-based semantic segmentation. Our findings show that although patch-based CNNs can produce close to perfect performance when supplied with ideal image patches, when image patches are not ideal this can severely impact their performance, particularly in terms of precision. While an FCN approach does not achieve the same level of recall at an image patch level as the ideal patch-based CNN, it substantially outperforms the patch-based approach with proposed patches, with a 52% larger object-level precision and comparable recall. This, along with the replacement of hand-performed selections associated with patch-proposal with a learnable approach, suggests that FCN-based segmentation may be a promising contender to the patch-based classification approach.

Acknowledgements. The authors acknowledge funding for this research from Rhodes University and the Telkom Centre of Excellence.

References

1. Baron, J., Hill, D., Elmiligi, H.: Combining image processing and machine learning to identify invasive plants in high-resolution images. International Journal of Remote Sensing **39**(15–16), 5099–5118 (2018). https://doi.org/10.1080/01431161. 2017.1420940
2. Blaschke, T.: Object based image analysis for remote sensing. ISPRS Journal of Photogrammetry and Remote Sensing **65**(1), 2–16 (2010). https://doi.org/10. 1016/j.isprsjprs.2009.06.004

3. Chollet, F.: Xception: deep learning with depthwise separable convolutions. In: 2017 IEEE Conference on Computer Vision and Pattern Recognition, pp. 1800–1807, July 2017. https://doi.org/10.1109/CVPR.2017.195

4. Flood, N., Watson, F., Collett, L.: Using a U-Net convolutional neural network to map woody vegetation extent from high resolution satellite imagery across Queensland, Australia. Inte. J. Appl. Earth Obs. Geoinf. **82**,(2019). https://doi.org/10.1016/j.jag.2019.101897

5. Gillespie, A.R., Kahle, A.B., Walker, R.E.: Color enhancement of highly correlated images. II. Channel ratio and "chromaticity" transformation techniques. Remote Sens. Environ. **22**(3), 343–365 (1987). https://doi.org/10.1016/0034-4257(87)90088-5

6. Gitelson, A.A., Kaufman, Y.J., Stark, R., Rundquist, D.: Novel algorithms for remote estimation of vegetation fraction. Remote Sensing of Environment **80**(1), 76–87 (2002). https://doi.org/10.1016/S0034-4257(01)00289-9

7. Guirado, E., Tabik, S., Alcaraz-Segura, D., Cabello, J., Herrera, F.: Deep-learning versus OBIA for scattered shrub detection with Google Earth imagery: Ziziphus Lotus as case study. Remote Sens. **9**(12), 1–22 (2017). https://doi.org/10.3390/rs9121220

8. Hamuda, E., Glavin, M., Jones, E.: A survey of image processing techniques for plant extraction and segmentation in the field. Computers and Electronics in Agriculture **125**, 184–199 (2016). https://doi.org/10.1016/j.compag.2016.04.024

9. Howard, A.G., .: MobileNets: efficient convolutional neural networks for mobile vision applications. arXiv preprint arXiv:1704.04861 (2017)

10. James, K., Bradshaw, K.: Detecting plant species in the field with deep learning and drone technology. Methods Ecol. Evol. **11**(11), 1509–1519 (2020). https://doi.org/10.1111/2041-210X.13473. Wiley publishing

11. Kamilaris, A., Prenafeta-Boldu, F.X.: Deep learning in agriculture: A survey. Computers and Electronics in Agriculture **147**, 70–90 (2018). https://doi.org/10.1016/j.compag.2018.02.016

12. Kluge, R., Neser, S.: Biological control of Hakea sericea (Proteaceae) in South Africa. Agriculture, Ecosystems & Environment **37**(1–3), 91–113 (1991). https://doi.org/10.1016/0167-8809(91)90141-J

13. Lin, T., Goyal, P., Girshick, R., He, K., Dollar, P.: Focal loss for dense object detection. In: 2017 IEEE International Conference on Computer Vision, pp. 2999–3007. IEEE, October 2017. https://doi.org/10.1109/ICCV.2017.324

14. Liu, T., Abd-Elrahman, A., Jon, M., Wilhelm, V.: Comparing fully convolutional networks, random forest, support vector machine, and patch-based deep convolutional neural networks for object-based wetland mapping using images from small unmanned aircraft system. GIScience & Remote Sensing **55**(2), 243–264 (2018). https://doi.org/10.1080/15481603.2018.1426091

15. Long, J., Shelhamer, E., Darrell, T.: Fully convolutional networks for semantic segmentation. In: Proceedings of the IEEE Conference on Computer Vision and Pattern Recognition, pp. 3431–3440. IEEE (2015). https://doi.org/10.1109/CVPR.2015.7298965

16. Mboga, N., Georganos, S., Grippa, T., Lennert, M., Vanhuysse, S., Wolff, E.: Fully convolutional networks for the classification of aerial VHR imagery. In: Proceedings of the 7th Geographic Object-Based Image Analysis Conference, pp. 1–12. Montpellier, France (2018). https://doi.org/10.1109/LGRS.2017.2763738

17. Milioto, A., Lottes, P., Stachniss, C.: Real-time blob-wise sugar beets vs weeds classification for monitoring fields using convolutional neural networks. ISPRS Ann.

Photogrammetry Remote Sens. Spat. Inf. Sci. **4**(2/W3), 41–48 (2017). https://doi.org/10.5194/isprs-annals-IV-2-W3-41-2017

18. Milioto, A., Lottes, P., Stachniss, C.: Real-time semantic segmentation of crop and weed for precision agriculture robots leveraging background knowledge in CNNS. In: IEEE International Conference on Robotics and Automation (ICRA), pp. 2229–2235 (05 2018). https://doi.org/10.1109/ICRA.2018.8460962

19. Milletari, F., Navab, N., Ahmadi, S.A.: V-Net: fully convolutional neural networks for volumetric medical image segmentation. In: 2016 Fourth International Conference on 3D Vision, pp. 565–571. IEEE, October 2016. https://doi.org/10.1109/3DV.2016.79

20. Rahman, M.A., Wang, Y.: Optimizing intersection-over-union in deep neural networks for image segmentation. In: International Symposium on Visual Computing. pp. 234–244. Springer (2016). https://doi.org/10.1007/978-3-319-50835-1_22

21. Ronneberger, O., Fischer, P., Brox, T.: U-Net: Convolutional networks for biomedical image segmentation. In: International Conference on Medical Image Computing and Computer-assisted Intervention. pp. 234–241. Springer (2015). https://doi.org/10.1007/978-3-319-24574-4_28

22. Sa, I., et al.: Weednet: dense semantic weed classification using multispectral images and MAV for smart farming. IEEE Rob. Autom. Lett. **20**, 588–595 (2017). https://doi.org/10.1109/LRA.2017.2774979

23. Szegedy, C., Vanhoucke, V., Ioffe, S., Shlens, J., Wojna, Z.: Rethinking the inception architecture for computer vision. In: Proceedings of the IEEE Conference on Computer Vision and Pattern Recognition, pp. 2818–2826 (2016). https://doi.org/10.1109/CVPR.2016.308

24. Woebbecke, D.M., Meyer, G.E., Von Bargen, K., Mortensen, D.: Color indices for weed identification under various soil, residue, and lighting conditions. Trans. Am. Soc. Agric. Eng. **38**(1), 259–269 (1995). https://doi.org/10.13031/2013.27838

25. Yosinski, J., Clune, J., Bengio, Y., Lipson, H.: How transferable are features in deep neural networks? In: Proceedings of the 27th International Conference on Neural Information Processing Systems, NIPS 2014, vol. 2, pp. 3320–3328. MIT Press, Cambridge (2014)

26. Zhao, T., Yang, Y., Niu, H., Wang, D., Chen, Y.: Comparing U-net convolutional network with mask R-CNN in the performances of pomegranate tree canopy segmentation. In: Larar, A.M., Suzuki, M., Wang, J. (eds.) Multispectral, Hyperspectral, and Ultraspectral Remote Sensing Technology, Techniques and Applications VII, vol. 10780, pp. 210–218. International Society for Optics and Photonics, SPIE (2018). https://doi.org/10.1117/12.2325570

Optimized Deep Neural Network for Tomato Leaf Diseases Identification

R. Sangeetha[1(✉)] ⓘ, M. Mary Shanthi Rani[1(✉)] ⓘ,
and Rabin Joseph[2(✉)]

[1] Department of Computer Science and Applications, The Gandhigram Rural
Institute (Deemed to be University), Gandhigram, Dindigul, Tamil Nadu, India
m.maryshanthirani@ruraluniv.ac.in
[2] University of South Dakota, South Dakota, USA

Abstract. Smart Farming with the transformative potential of Artificial Intelligence has emerged as a promising breakthrough in enhancing the agricultural productivity. The rapid in supercomputing facilities has redefined Deep Learning and its applications are seemingly limitless. It involves the use of deeper neural networks for greater learning capabilities eventually resulting in higher performance and precision. Its ability to discern patterns at higher calibre made it penetrate into almost all applications of computer vision including the field of Agriculture for Plant leaf disease detection, fruit counting, water management, weed and pest control. This research work deals with the prediction of Tomato leaf diseases based on image classification, using pre-trained deep convolutional networks. The accuracy of the model is evaluated using standard classification metrics namely Accuracy, Precision, Recall and F1-score. Furthermore, this paper makes a recommendation on the best optimizing function among three standard optimizers for classification of tomato leaf diseases based on performance metrics.

Keywords: Deep learning · Convolutional Neural Network · Optimizer function · TomatoPlant leaf diseases

1 Introduction

Agriculture is one of the most significant areas having a great impact on the economy of both emerging and developed states. The livelihood of the farmers depends solely on their agricultural productivity which is largely dependent on the adoption of effective farming practices like a selection of crop based on soil fertility, crop rotations, and application of organic fertilizers, weed and biological pest control etc. Unfortunately, 50% of the total crop yield is lost due to pests and diseases in crops despite preventive measures. Prior, recognizable proof of diseases in crops has been done by plant clinics, horticulture based associations or foundations. The fundamental methodology that is received by specialists for detection of infections in plants is through unaided eye perception which is a tedious cycle.

Tomato (Solanum lycopersicum) is one of the essential and edible vegetables used for the preparation of invariably all continental food items signifying its agricultural

© Springer Nature Switzerland AG 2022
D. Garg et al. (Eds.): IACC 2021, CCIS 1528, pp. 562–576, 2022.
https://doi.org/10.1007/978-3-030-95502-1_42

production which is greatly affected by leaf diseases. Seven common diseases, consisting of the target point and the mosaic, the yellow leaf curliness, the bacteria spot, the early blight, the late spot and the septorial leaf spot, are affected in the tomato leaves. In general, both living (biotic) and non-living (abiotic) agents affect tomato plants. Insects, bacteria, fungi and viruses are living agents. Non-living organisms are sudden increases in temperature, excess humidity and low pH. The highest contribution of leaf disease is by living agents. This research work implemented a new deep learning model incorporating the principle of Transfer Learning for identifying and classifying diseases in Tomatoes.

Deep Learning, an offshoot of Machine Learning has evolved as a viable solution provider in several fields such as Precision Farming [1, 4–8], Healthcare [2, 3] and much more. Deep neural networks require a great deal of data and costly computing resources to build from scratch. In the field of medicine, deep learning plays a significant role to identify and analyze the diseases [2, 3]. In addition, by avoiding complicated data mining and data-labeling initiatives, our classification task may not have enough data for training neural networks. Transfer learning is applied in a couple of ways in practice. One choice is to use our dataset as input to fine-tune the network weights; it is worth remembering that the new dataset must be resized to the pre-trained network's input scale. Another approach is to acquire from the pre-trained network the learned weights and add the weights to the target network.

Literature survey shows that several new architectures and methodologies have been proposed for plant leaf disease detection. Suneet K. Gupta et al., have proposed novel CNN based architectures for Plant leaf disease detection [6–8]. S.Srivastara et al., [9] proposed a novel vision sensing system using Principal Components Analysis for quality detection in tomato leaves. They tested four types of diseases affected by bacteria, fungi, immunity problems. The methodology involves three major steps; Preprocessing, Disease detection and Classification. In preprocessing stage, implementation of noise reduction, segmentation and scaling is done. This method achieved an accuracy of 92%. Sabrol et al., [10] designed a method by using the natural dataset for tomato plant disease classification. The tomato leaf images are categorized into six types including the healthy leaves. For classification, Adaptive neuro-fuzzy classification model based on surprised learning is proposed. This method achieved a classification accuracy of 87.2%. A. Funtes et al., [11] has analysed tomato plant diseases using three main deep learning architectures: Region based fully Convolution Network (RFCN), Single Shot multibox detector (SSD) and Faster Region based CNN. They experimented by combining each of these architecture with VGG-16 and Resnet (Residual Net) algorithms to get a high accuracy.

In order to identify the Banana leaf diseases, J.Amara et al., [12] has introduced a deep learning model. The author has proposed the Lenet architecture to detect the banana leaf diseases as a CNN model under the challenging conditions such as illumination, size, pose and real scene images. Rangarajan et al., [13] has demonstrated to classify the tomato leaf disease by using the pre-trained architectures to train the dataset consisting of 14,828 images for both the Alexnet and Googlenet. This method achieved an accuracy of 99.18%. Y. Lu et al., [14] has proposed a neural network by using deep convolution layers for automatic identification of rice diseases. Their method achieved an accuracy of 95.48% by experimenting the proposed model using a dataset of 500 natural rice images including diseased leaves with ten types of diseases and healthy leaves implementing 10 fold cross-validation strategies. D. Oppenheim et al., [15] has proposed a CNN model for potato disease classification. They simply implemented VGG16 architecture for training to predict five different classes of diseases and achieved an accuracy of 96%.

This research work uses a pre-trained convolutional Neural Network VGG16 with different combinations of Optimizing and Activation functions. The main contribution is to create a new model based on the CNN network layer and along with the different optimization function. Optimizing function is used to minimize the loss by optimal update of the weight parameters. This plays a vital role in determining the training time and accuracy of the model. Some of the commonly used optimizing functions are Gradient Descent, Mini-batch Gradient Descent, RMSProp (Root Mean Square Propogation), Momentum and Adam (Adaptive Momentum). In this work, Specifically Adam and RMSProp are used with RELU and sigmoid activation functions. Moreover, experiments are also conducted using the best model by tuning the hyper parameters such as epochs, batch size and learning.

The remaining paper is arranged in the following way. The materials and methods for the deep convolution neural networks, namely VGG16 are defined in Sect. 2. Section 3 discusses the tests and effects. The paper concludes in Sect. 4.

2   Optimized Deep Neural Network for Tomato Leaf Diseases (ODNN-TLD)

In this work. we recommend the best optimizer for predicting the tomato leaf disease by comparing the performance of two optimizing functions RMSprop and ADAM.The methodology involves the following three phases.

Step 1: Data Preparation
Step 2: Training & Testing
Step 3: Prediction and Performance evaluation

2.1   Data Preparation

The deep neural model was trained with the Plant Village open source data collection, which comprises 54,306 photos of both healthy and diseased leaves, 14 plants and 26 diseases. Table 1 lists the seven types of diseases that affect tomato crop and the causing agent.

Table 1. Seven types of diseases affecting tomato crop

Disease name	Pathogen scientific name	Type
Target spot	Corynespora cassiicola	Fungus
Septoria spot	Septoria Lycopersici	Fungal
Bacteria spot	Xanthomonas Campestris	Bacteria
Mosaic virus	(ToMV)	Viral
Early blight	Alternaria Solani	Fungal
Leaf mold	Pseudocercospora Fulingena	Viral
Late blight	Phytophthora Intestans	Oomycete

Figure 1 Shows the seven common diseases of tomato leaves which taken from the open source dataset (Plant village).

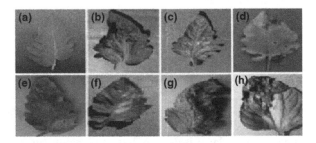

Fig. 1. a) Healthy b) Target Spot c) Mosaic Virus d) Septoria Spot e) Bacteria Spot f) Early Blight g) Late Blight h) Leaf Mold.

Figure 2 shows distribution in the plant village data collection of images under each class labels.

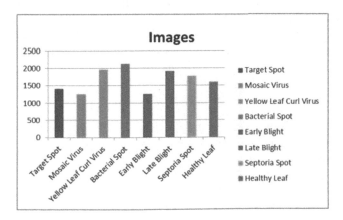

Fig. 2. Distribution of plant village dataset images under each class label

Due to computational limitations, this research work utilizes 4930 images of tomato crop type with three classes for classify the diseases, including healthy, and diseased leaves affected by Bacteria spot and Septoria.

2.2   Data Pre-processing

In the pre-processing stage, the following steps are performed:

1. As the dataset consists of mismatched leaves, the unwanted images are removed.
2. Furthermore, the images of different sizes are resized to 224 × 224 in order to make the model training process more feasible with fewer computations.
3. Next, the leaf images are manually labeled and grouped depending on their type.
4. The data set is divided into a ratio of 70:30 train data and test data that is ideal for avoiding overfitting.

As the inputs are all images represented by two- dimensional matrices, there is no necessity for handling missing values.

2.3   Training the Proposed Model with VGG16 and CNN (ODNN-TLD)

In the proposed work, we implement the pre-trained architecture VGG16. Generally, it consists of 16 CNN layers, to which five more convolution layers are added to enhance the performance by Transfer learning. Using convolution layer, the images are compared section by section and each section is referred to as a filter or feature. A pooling layer is another building block of CNN which is used to reduce the dimensions of the image. A fully connected input layer is used to flatten the inputs by converting it into a single vector. In one layer, it connects each neuron to each other layer of a neuron. The proposed methodology uses different combinations of Optimizing and Activation functions.

The activation function defines whether or not a neuron is activated by calculating a weighted sum and adding additional bias. It is used to introduce non-linearity into the model making it capable of learning unstructured data like images, audio, and video and performing complex functions during the training process. In this research work, ReLU and Softmax activation functions are used.

ReLU, abbreviated for Rectified Linear Unit is a one of the activation function are widely used to replaces the negative values by zero, mostly imported in the hidden layers of the network.

$$A(x) = \max(0, \ x) \qquad (1)$$

It generates x if x is positive and 0 if not. ReLU is less computationally expensive than other activation functions Tan H and Sigmoid because it involves simple mathematical operations.

Softmax: This is a widely used multiclass classifier. It is usually used in the classification output layer, where the possibility to set the class of each input is actually achieved.

2.4   Optimizing Functions

Optimizing functions are used in Deep Learning to update the weights optimally during the training process for minimizing the loss and boost the model's accuracy. This project work uses standard optimizing functions like RMSProp and ADAM and a performance comparison is made to recommend the best function for classification of tomato leaf diseases.

RMSProp stands for Root Mean Square Propagation which uses a different learning rate for each parameter while updating during each the iteration, thereby reducing oscillations. It utilizes the magnitude of recent gradients to normalize the gradients. It was introduced by Geoff Hinton and the main purpose is to solve the adagrad's radically diminishing learning rates. RMSProp can be expressed mathematically are shown in below formula.

$$E[g^2]t = 0.9E[g^2]\, t - 1 + 0.1g^2 t \tag{2}$$

E[g2]t denotes the exponentially average of squared gradients. The combination of the momentum and RMSProp are introducing the new optimizer that is Adam optimizer. Adam stands for Adaptive moment estimation and is an optimizing algorithm for adaptive learning speeds. It is specially designed for training the deep neural networks and is faster than other optimizers. Compare with all other optimizer, Adam is one of the best optimizer in our problem. This can be expressed based on the mathematical formula

$$vt = \gamma vt - 1 + \eta \nabla \theta J(\theta) \tag{3}$$

Here η is learning rate, J is function, γ is constant term, vt denotes the current time step, vt-1 denotes the past time step, θ defines the parameter's used in our network.

- Adam has emerged as a popular optimization algorithm replacing SGD for training neural network model in recent years.
- I t is found to very effective in handling sparse gradients.

The proposed architecture is pictorially depicted in Fig. 3.

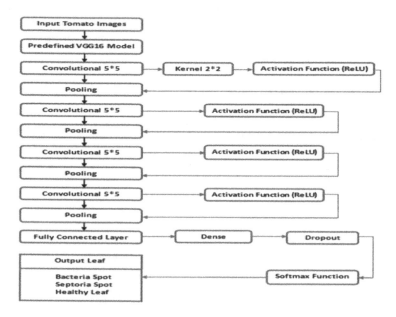

Fig. 3. Proposed architecture

The work flow of the proposed work is presented in Table 2.

Table 2. Algorithmic description

Input: Plant Village Dataset
Output: Prediction of Tomato leaf disease

Begin
Phase I: Data Preparation
1: Read the Plant Village Dataset
2: Pre-process the Data
A. Remove the irrelevant Images
B. Label the Image
3: Dataset is differentiated by training and test collection.
Phase II: Training & Testing
4: Train the pre-trained VGG16 with addition of CNN layers
5: Tune the hyper parameters for optimal performance
Phase III: Prediction and Performance evaluation
6: Test the trained model with test dataset
7: Predict the diseases
8: Measure the performance of the model in terms of precision, recall and F-1 scores.
End

3   Results and Discussion

Totally, 1098 pictures have been put for testing and 3832 for training have been used, out of the 4930 images. Optimization was achieved with the help of binary cross entropy Adam and RMSProp optimizers combined with ReLU and softmax activation functions. The model was trained for three learning rates 0.01, 0.001, and 0.0001 for a batch size of 32 and 1000 epochs.

The pretrained vgg16 model with deep CNN was trained and tested using a python programming language with Keras and Tensor flow libraries. Both the training and testing phases are done by the Colab laboratory.

Table 3. Values of hyper-parameters

Parameter	Value
Training epochs	100
Mini batch size	32
Dropout	0.1
Learning rate	0.001
Training dataset	3832
Testing dataset	1098

Performance Metrics

Accuracy is normally determined by the ratio of accurate predictions with the total number of input samples.

$$\text{Accuracy} = \frac{Number\ of\ corrrect predictions}{Total\ number\ of\ samples} \tag{4}$$

Confusion matrix defines the entire model output normally done in the testing phase. Four metrics, including accuracy, precision, recalls, and the harmonic mean of accuracy and sensitivity (f1-score), are used for quantitative evaluations and comparisons. We have called TP, TN, FP and FN as True Positive, True Negative, False positive and False Negative.

True Positives: When we predicted YES and the real performance were also yes, the data were affected by the disease.

True Negatives: If we expected NO and the actual performance was NO, the data were affected by a disease.

False Positives: When we predicted YES and the actual performance is NO, the data are affected by a disease.

False Negatives: If there are diseases in which we expected NO and the actual performance was YES, the data was affected.

Precision: It reveals the number of true positives among the total number of true positive and false positive.

$$Precision = \frac{TP}{TP + FP} \tag{5}$$

Recall: It is the ratio of the true positive to the sum of the true positive and false negative.

$$Recall = \frac{TP}{TP + FN}. \tag{6}$$

F1-Score: Two models with low precision and high recall are difficult to compare. The standard F measurements or balanced F scores (F1 scores) are the harmonic means of precision and recall.

$$F1 - Score = \frac{2 * Precision * Recall}{Precision + Recall} \tag{7}$$

Table 4 demonstrates the performance evaluation of pretrained VGG16 CNN model for classification of the tomato leaf disease using RMSPROP optimizer and RELU activation function. In Table 3, it is obvious that in terms of precision, recall and f1 score, the model suggested achieves moderate efficiency. In the test collection, 366 healthy images with a leaf and 365 unhealthy images with a septorium spot, 366 unhealthy leaf photos with the disease of the bacterial spot are included. Table 3 also shows that in the prevision of the leaves affected by the healthy, septorial spot, and bacterial spot disease, average accuracy of 0.82 is obtained from the proposed CNN classification.

Table 4. Performance analysis of proposed model using RMSPROP

Prediction	Precision	Recall	F1-score	Support
Healthy leaf	0.97	0.95	0.96	366
Bacteria spot	0.62	0.97	0.76	365
Septoria spot	0.68	0.81	0.74	366
Accuracy			0.82%	1098

The graphical representation of Table 4 is shown in Fig. 4 to compare the metrics values that are predicted in the RMSPROP optimizer.

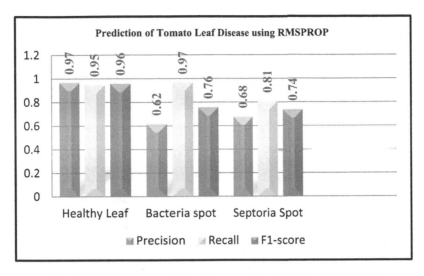

Fig. 4. Performance analysis of proposed model using RMSPROP

Table 5 presents the performance of the proposed model using ADAM optimizer and RELU activation function. Table 4 illustrates the accuracy of 0.96 for the prediction of healthy, septoria and the bacteria-spot diseases of affected leaves in the proposed CNN classification.

Table 5. The evaluation results of proposed model using ADAM optimizer

Prediction	Precision	Recall	F1-score	Support
Healthy leaf	0.98	0.95	0.96	366
Bacteria spot	0.95	0.97	0.94	365
Septoria spot	0.97	0.94	0.94	366
Accuracy	0.95			1098

The illustration of the prediction's accuracy shows in Fig. 5.

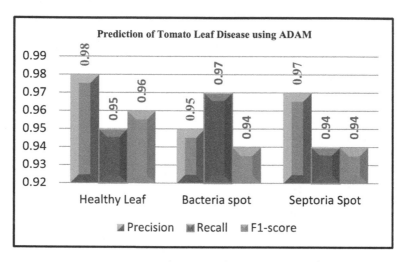

Fig. 5. Performance analysis of proposed model using ADAM

Table 6 evaluates the comparison performance of accuracy of the proposed RMSPROP and ADAM optimizers. The proposed CNN model using ADAM optimizer achieved a strong accuracy of above 95%.

Table 6. Comparison performance analysis of the proposed model

Optimizer	Accuracy
RMSPROP	0.82
ADAM	0.95

Figure 6 shows the pictorial description of the prediction's results of RMSPROP and ADAM optimizer.

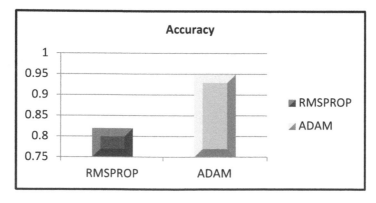

Fig. 6. Performance analysis of proposed model

Table 7 compares the precision of accuracy for healthy leaf and disease affected leaves. In that the Adam optimizer achieves the highest accuracy other than RMSProp.

Table 7. Comparison analysis of precision of proposed model

Optimizer	Precision(0)	Precision(1)	Precision(2)
RMSPROP	0.97	0.62	0.68
ADAM	0.98	0.95	0.97

Table 7 demonstrates the pictorial illustration of the results prediction by calculating the precision values.

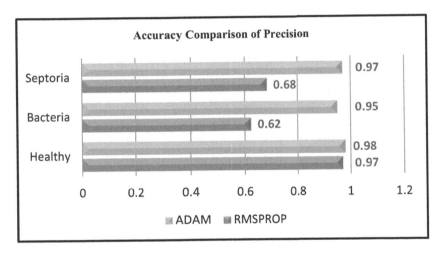

Fig. 7. Performance analysis of precision

Table 8 compares the accuracy of recall to predict the bacterial spot disease and septoria spot disease. In that we compare both the optimizer accuracy to predict the diseases.

Table 8. Comparison analysis of recall of proposed model

Optimizer	Recall(0)	Recall(1)	Recall(2)
RMSPROP	0.95	0.97	0.81
ADAM	0.95	0.97	0.94

Figure 7 displays the pictorial representation of the results prediction by calculating the recall values.

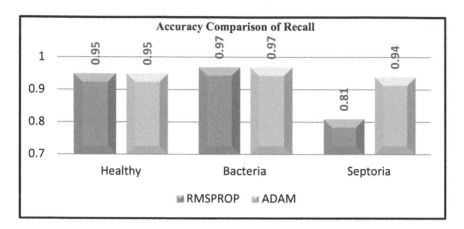

Fig. 8. Performance analysis of recall

Table 9 compares the accuracy of F1-score to predict the disease affected leaves and healthy leaves and also display the accuracy of both optimizers.

Table 9. Comparison analysis of F1score of proposed model

Optimizer/Class	F1-Score(0)	F1-Score (1)	F1-Score (2)
RMSPROP	0.96	0.76	0.74
ADAM	0.96	0.94	0.94

The visual representation of the results forecast is shown in Fig. 8.

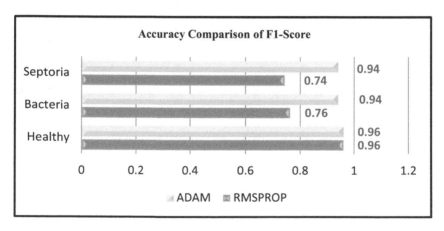

Fig. 9. Performance analysis of F1-score

The experimental results endorse the superior performance of ADAM optimizer achieving high values for all the performance metrics (Fig. 9).

Time and space complexity are the most important factors to solve and rectify problems. Time complexity is one of the important factors which are used to reduce human working hours. Space complexity is to avoid memory space and if the system lost their running process, it will take high memory to run the problem. The challenge is to reduce the space and time complexity by using the deep learning. So, the problem can be identified easily with the solution (Fig. 10). In the proposed work, running time was changed based on the optimizer and also memory stored with less number of bytes are shown in Table 10

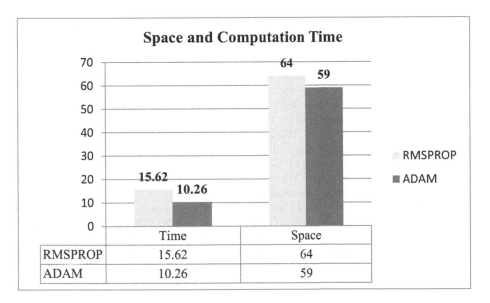

Fig. 10. Comparison representation of space and computation time

Table 10. Comparison analysis of time and space computation

Optimizer	Time	Space
RMSPROP	15.652215612000191(min)	64(mb)
ADAM	10.2607443530000064(min)	59(mb)

4 Conclusion

In this paper, we proposed a deep learning model to predict the plant leaf diseases which yielded better performance and achieved an accuracy of 95.4% on the test data set. We experimented the performance of two optimizing functions RMSPROP and ADAM in prediction of tomato leaf diseases. The hyper parameters were also fine-tuned and a model recommendation has been made based on its impact on the accuracy of prediction. In the proposed model, training time and space complexity had also been greatly reduced. This will provide endless options in terms of agricultural pricing, crop insurance, risk analysis and mitigation. The proposed model classifies only three types of classes and in future, this model can be implemented for detection of more number of diseases and extended for other crops like apple, potato, pepper ball and corn as well.

Acknowledgement. The experiments are carried out at Advanced Image Processing Lab, Department of Computer Science and Applications, The Gandhigram Rural Institute (Deemed to be University), Dindigul & funded by DST-FIST.

References

1. Sangeetha, R., Mary Shanthi Rani, M.: Tomato leaf disease prediction using convolutional neural network. Int. J. Innov. Technol. Explor. Eng **9**(1), 1348–1352 (2019)
2. Devi, M.K., Rani, M.M.S.: A comparative study of machine learning classifiers for diabetic retinopathy detection. In: Komanapalli, V.L.N., Sivakumaran, N., Hampannavar, S. (eds.) Advances in Automation, Signal Processing, Instrumentation, and Control. LNEE, vol. 700, pp. 735–742. Springer, Singapore (2021). https://doi.org/10.1007/978-981-15-8221-9_67
3. Rani, M.M.S., Shanmugavadivu, P.: 12. Deep learning based food image classification. In: Computational Intelligence, pp. 197–208. De Gruyter (2020)
4. Sangeetha, R., Mary Shanthi Rani, M.: A novel method for plant leaf disease classification using deep learning techniques. In: Gopi, E.S. (ed.) Machine Learning, Deep Learning and Computational Intelligence for Wireless Communication. LNEE, vol. 749, pp. 631–643. Springer, Singapore (2021). https://doi.org/10.1007/978-981-16-0289-4_46
5. Sangeetha, R., Rani, M.M.S.: Tomato leaf disease prediction using transfer learning. In: Garg, D., Wong, K., Sarangapani, J., Gupta, S.K. (eds.) IACC 2020. CCIS, vol. 1368, pp. 3–18. Springer, Singapore (2021). https://doi.org/10.1007/978-981-16-0404-1_1
6. Geetharamani, G., Arun, P., Mohit, A., Suneet, K.G.: Identification of plant leaf diseases using a nine-layer deep convolutional neural network. Comput. Elect. Eng. **76**, 323–338 (2019)
7. Agarwal, M., Gupta, S., Biswas, K.K.: A new conv2d model with modified relu activation function for identification of disease type and severity in cucumber plant. Sustain. Comput. Inf. Syst. **30**, 100473 (2021)
8. Agarwal, M., Gupta, S.K., Biswas, K.K.: Development of efficient CNN model for tomato crop disease identification. Sustain. Comput. Inf. Syst. **28**, 100407 (2020)
9. Srivastava, S., Boyat, S., Sadistap, S.: A novel vision sensing system for tomato quality detection. Int. J. Food Sci. **2014**, 1–11 (2014)
10. Sabrol, H., Kumar, S.: Fuzzy and neural network based tomato plant disease classification using natural outdoor images. Indian J. Sci. Technol. **9**(44), 1–8 (2016)
11. Fuentes, A., Yoon, S., Kim, S., Park, D.: A robust deep-learning-based detector for real-time tomato plant diseases and pests recognition. Sensors **17**(9), 2022 (2017)
12. Amara, J., Bassem, B., Alsayed, A.: A deep learning-based approach for banana leaf diseases classification. In: *Datenbanksysteme für Business, Technologie und Web (BTW 2017)-Workshopband* (2017)
13. Rangarajan, A.K., Purushothaman, R., Ramesh, A.: Tomato crop disease classification using pre-trained deep learning algorithm. Procedia Comput. Sci. **133**, 1040–1047 (2018). https://doi.org/10.1016/j.procs.2018.07.070
14. Lu, Y., Yi, S., Zeng, N., Liu, Y., Zhang, Y.: Identification of rice diseases using deep convolutional neural networks. Neurocomputing **267**, 378–384 (2017)
15. Oppenheim, D., Shani, G.: Potato disease classification using convolution neural networks. Adv. Anim. Biosci. **8**(2), 244–249 (2017)

Application of Distributed Back Propagation Neural Network for Dynamic Real-Time Bidding

Ankit Desai[1], Hiren Kumar Thakkar[2]([⊠]) [iD], Priyanka Singh[3], and Lakshmi Sai Bhargavi[3]

[1] Bangalore 560068, India
[2] Department of Computer Engineering, Marwadi University, Rajkot, Gujarat 360003, India
[3] Department of Computer Science and Engineering, SRM University, Amaravati 522240, Andhra Pradesh, India
{priyanka.s,lakshmisaibhargavi_g}@srmap.edu.in

Abstract. Programmatic buying popularly known as real-time bidding (RTB) is a key ascendancy in online advertising. The Ad Tech industry is experiencing sustained growth, especially due to the increased use of mobile devices. While data has become essential for targeting and ad performance, data businesses have become difficult to differentiate due to their proliferation, as well as limitations of attribution. This provides an opportunity for Big Data practitioners to leverage this data and use machine learning to improve efficiency and make more profits. Taking such an opportunity we came up with an application of a machine learning algorithm, distributed back propagation neural network (d-bpnn) to predict bid prices in a real-time bidding system. This paper depicts how d-bpnn is used to achieve less eCPM (effective Cost Per Mille) for advertisers while preserving win rate and budget utilization.

Keywords: Distributed machine learning · Back propagation neural network · Real-time bidding

1 Introduction

Demand Side Platform (DSP) tries to optimize its real-time bidding (RTB) platform to provide benefits to its customers (advertisers and/or agencies). In this paper, we have empirically evaluated the proposed strategy, namely ML bidding for dynamic RTB to reduce the eCPM (effective Cost Per Mille) of the advertiser. It is the outcome of a calculation of the ad revenue generated by a banner, divided by the number of ad impressions of that banner in units of 1000. The ad tech industry has already left its incubation phase and there have been many areas in its ecosystem where machine learning and artificial intelligence are used. For example, user targeting, CTR (click-through rate) optimization etc. [15] Due to the application of intelligence at the ad exchange side following

© Springer Nature Switzerland AG 2022
D. Garg et al. (Eds.): IACC 2021, CCIS 1528, pp. 577–587, 2022.
https://doi.org/10.1007/978-3-030-95502-1_43

scenario is observed. Given a campaign, the platform sends fix priced bid for a request, gradually ad exchange increases the winning price and/or floor price. Figure 1 shows auction price versus floor price. It can be observed that even for the lower floor prices the auction price was higher (a bottom-left region in Fig. 1). This leads to high eCPM for an advertiser. This problem persist because a non-ML RTB platform was sending bids to ML-based exchange. Introduction of ML for RTB platform at RTB platform enabled dynamic bidding strategy such that (ML-based) ad exchange is not able to learn bidding patterns and thus helped us improve eCPM for an advertiser. In this paper, a dynamic RTB strategy is proposed which uses d-bpnn to solve the eCPM problem [2]. In this regard several other applications in the domain of healthcare [6,8], summarization [9], cloud computing [7,10], self driving car [11] etc., are also possible using the AI, ML, and other conventional statistical methods.

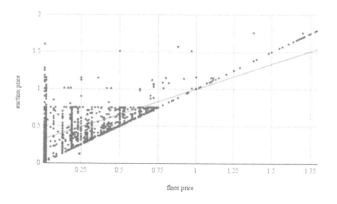

Fig. 1. Auction Price vs Floor Price - Flat Bidding

Section 2 describes the background and working of RTB and d-bpnn. Working of various bidding strategies versus ML bidding to solve problem of dynamic bidding is described in Sect. 3. In Sect. 4 using RTB data and A/B testing how we have experimentally evaluated bidding strategies is described. Section 5 concludes the paper.

2 Background

2.1 Real-Time Bidding

When a user visits a webpage with a browser, a complex process of content selection and delivery begins. Involving a video or mobile environment can make it even more complex. Breakout of that process works as follows. Keeping to a desktop environment example Fig. 2 shows how an advertiser might have placed ads posted on the website using an automated RTB system [16]. The process begins when a user visits the publisher's web page. The publisher is the website

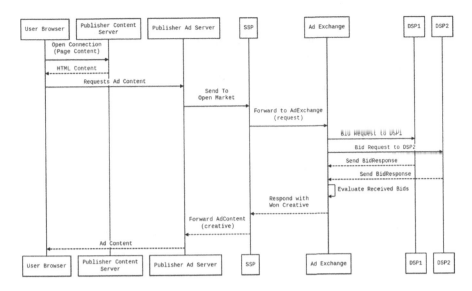

Fig. 2. RTB ecosystem sequence diagram

owner. Publishers generate content, such as news, music, information, sports, and other entertainment. These contents draw an audience and the publisher sells ad space to advertisers who want to reach that audience. Upon visiting the publisher's web page the browser opens a connection to the publisher server. The publisher server then assembles the content of the page. After returning the requested content in the form of HTML the browser begins to interpret and render it. At least one line of that HTML code represents the opportunity to display an ad. Within that one line of code, there is a URL that tells the browser where to go to retrieve ad content. The publisher has an ad server that uses built-in logic to choose what happens next by considering a series of important questions as follows. Any premium buyers? What do I know about the consumer? or Which advertiser is the best fit? If the ad space is not reserved for any specific advertiser the publisher ad server may decide to put this opportunity to open an ad market where they might get a better deal. To put this on the open market, the publisher server connects to SSPs (supply-side platforms). This is the platform that publisher uses to monetize its ad inventory. The SSP applies additional logic asking a question such as Have I seen this consumer before?, or What does my data provider say about this consumer? using that acquired knowledge, it sends the ad request to an ad exchange. Meanwhile, the ad exchange connects and communicates to a potential buying system. This system includes DSPs (demand-side platforms) and even other ad exchanges. In the same way as saying a stockbroker can buy 100 shares of some stock when a moment it falls below a certain price, buyer side system can tell the ad exchange that they will pay a dollar per 1000 ad served displayed to males of 30–35 old living in a particular area. This is called a pre-cached bid. If pre-filled, it will speed up the process of feeling real-time programmatic ads. If there are no pre-cached bids then ad exchanges send that request to all the DSPs. DSPs have to be responded to in less than 10 ms. Ad exchange selects a winning bid. The winning DSP passes instructions to ad exchange for retrieving the ad creative. The ad exchange passes those instructions to SSP. The SSP sends the request to a publisher ad server. Finally, the publisher ad server responds to the still open HTTP connection, telling the browser to go to the agency ad server for the ad. The agency ad server tracks the ad performance for advertisers. Upon receiving the ad request originating from the DSP with the winning bid the agency ad server records the request as an impression. Now the web browser can finally render the ad within the web page content. Resulting in the delivery of an ad most appropriately match to an individual user. This entire process depending on internet speed can happen in a fraction of a second. The digital landscape is complex. More systems may be involved than represented here. If an ad is served to a video player, connected tv, or a mobile device then the process may look a little different. IAB [14] defines the protocol for smooth operations of this phenomenon.

2.2 Distributed Back Propagation Neural Networks (d-bpnn)

Waikato Environment for Knowledge Analysis (Weka) is a suite of machine learning software written in Java [3]. distributedWekaSpark is a package that allows running classification, regression, or clustering algorithm of weka using Spark [5]. Handling a large volume of data was not possible until the introduction of this package in Weka. distributedWekaBase provides "map" and "reduce" functions independent of Spark and Hadoop. distributedWekaSpark provides Spark-specific wrappers and jobs for these base tasks.

An extension of distributedWekaSpark and DDTv2 [1], d-bpnn works as follow. As defined in Fig. 3, before the MapReduce phase the dataset is divided into splits. Then in the next step, i.e., Map, it creates neural networks using chunks of data that are available on each data node of Hadoop. Then in the reducing step, it collects all the models created in the map tasks. Basically, in the case of backpropagation neural networks an ensemble of the neural network is generated (the final model produced in the reduce phase is a weighted average over all prediction for an ensemble of the models learned by the mappers).

As shown in Fig. 4, distributedWekaBase determines metadata like count, sum, max, min, nominal value frequency count, etc. which is useful in training. Using metadata (summary statistics) on each chunk correlation matrix is computed. Map task produces a partial matrix of covariance. Reduce task aggregates rows to compute the final correlation matrix. Now, using weka's backpropagation neural network on each chunk mapper will train a neural network. The reduce phase will aggregate the model. As neural network comes under non-aggregatable classifier the final model in reduce phase is produced by weighted average. Using a cross-validation data bpnn is evaluated. In this process, the classifier for all folds is learned and then evaluated (details in next paragraph). Next, a trained classifier is used for prediction, no reducer is needed in this last step.

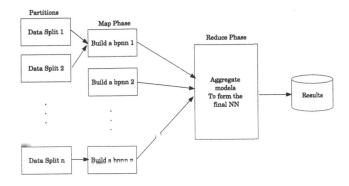

Fig. 3. MapReduce of d-bpnn

Cross-validation involves two passes over the data. Namely, model construction (Fig. 5) and model evaluation (Fig. 6). Consider simple three-fold cross-validation then the dataset gets split into three distinct partitions, and models are created by training on two out of the three folds. Therefore three models are created, each of them trained on two-thirds of the data and then tested on the fold that was held out during the training process. The model evaluation phase takes the models learned from the first phase and applies them to the holdout folds of cross-validation in each of the partitions of the dataset. It uses them to evaluate each of the holdout fold. The reducer then takes all of the partial evaluation results of the map tasks and aggregates them to the final full evaluation result, which is then written out as one model file.

3   Working of Bidding Strategies

Empirical evaluation of flat, randomized, and ML bidding as bidding strategies is performed. All three are elaborated as under.

3.1   Flat Bidding

This strategy talks about non-dynamic bidding with its advantages and disadvantages. Advantages include no processing logic required for deciding the bid to be sent over to the ad exchange for auction. In this strategy, we bid at a fixed (or flat) price for a given request from an ad exchange. Evaluating ours and bids from other DSPs, the ad exchange notifies the winning DSP with auction price (price at which bid is won). The main disadvantage for this strategy is being static bids for the same type of requests ad exchange can identify the bidding pattern and based on the same it can add some intelligence to gradually increase the auction price [4, 13].

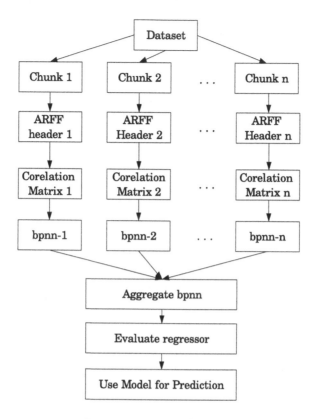

Fig. 4. Working of d-bpnn

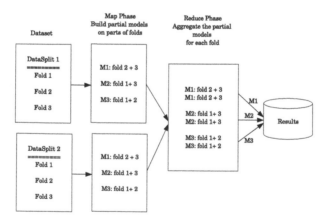

Fig. 5. Phase 1 model construction

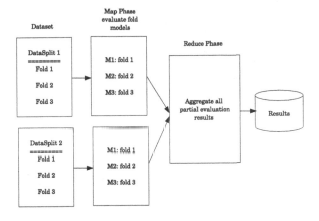

Fig. 6. Phase 2 model evaluation

3.2 Randomized Bidding

This strategy, as the title describes, is adding dynamic behavior to bidding. As described in section RTB, DSPs need to bid at least higher than the floor price which allows them to take part in an auction. Therefore the bounds of a given random bid can be in between floor price (lower bound) and maximum amount an advertiser can spend per request (higher bound). The advantage of this strategy is adding dynamic behavior while bidding. At the same time, ad exchange cannot identify the pattern easily which can overcome the disadvantage of flat price bidding. The disadvantage of randomized bidding is having no relationship with the type of request, its source (publisher), or its cost.

3.3 ML Bidding

ML bidding (machine learning-based bidding), takes historical data of winning prices prepares an ensemble of neural networks using d-bpnn to predict bid price. Similar to the strategy of DDTv2 [1] our ML bidding builds between 5–10 d-bpnn depending upon the amount of historical data. The final bid is the average prediction from all models. D-bpnn is implemented as an extension to DDTv2. The trivial difference between DDTv2 and d-bpnn is the former prepares an ensemble of trees for classification and the latter prepares an ensemble of backpropagation neural networks for prediction. DistributedWekaSpark and DistributedWekaBase are used for extending DDTv2.

Fig. 7. eCPM without bid prediction

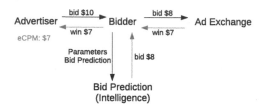

Fig. 8. eCPM with bid prediction

To explain how our strategy of ML bidding helps achieve lower eCPM for the advertiser in less than his budget Fig. 7 and 8 shows a scenario. For example, an advertiser has a budget of $10 to get 1000 impressions. Advertiser bids for $10. DSP using bid prediction places a bid at $8.0 as per prediction module whereas, without bid prediction at $10. It is possible to lose with less (predicted price), therefore it is meaningful to keep win-rate as an evaluation parameter. Next, ad exchange returns win price as per second auction bid [12]. Then we show eCPM to the advertiser. Results and discussion section will show that our instinct worked and we could win the same bids at lower prices and our advertisers got reduced eCPM (see Fig. 7, 8).

4   Empirical Evaluation and Discussion

4.1   Parameters of Evaluation

Apart from observing eCPM of the advertiser, we choose campaign WinRate (WR) and budget utilization (BU) as a parameter of evaluation. eCPM stands for effective cost per mille it is a ratio of ad revenue to the ad impressions in a unit of 1000. Win Rate is a ratio of the number of winning bids to the number of bids. Budget utilization is the daily percentage spent for a given campaign.

4.2   Description of Dataset

In the case of the dataset, due to confidentiality, we cannot provide the original features and more background information about the data. Nevertheless, sample records are as under. Here, for a given bid request what should be the optimal bidding price is considered a regression problem.

> *attrib1 (numeric), attrb2 (nominal), attrib3 (nominal), attrib4 (nominal), attrib5 (numeric), attrib6 (numeric), attrib7 (numeric), attrib8 (numeric), attrib9 (numeric), attrib10 (nominal), class (numeric), attrib12 (numeric), attrib13 (numeric)*
> *11, type1, man1, db1, ab, 3.2, 1.6, 120, 320, type1, y, 1, 12345*
> *43, type3, man2, db9, cd, 0.6, 0.3, 320, 780, type2, n, 1, 19245*
> *23, type2, man3, db2, ef, 9.0, 10.0, 780, 120, type3, n, 1, 14325*

Table 1. Budget utilization (BU), WinRate (WR) and eCPM of experiment

Bid-Type	BU (%)	WR (%)	eCPM
Flat	95.82	71.67	95.30
Randomized	93.72	59.77	92.45
ML	93.34	69.54	79.84

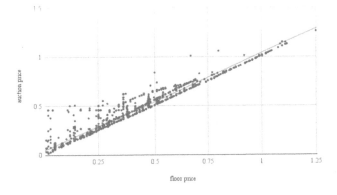

Fig. 9. Auction price vs floor price - ML bidding

4.3 Experimental Setup and Results

For training of d-bpnn Amazon Web Services (AWS) Elastic Map Reduce (EMR) cluster with 1 master (m3.large) and 2 slaves (c3.2xlarge) as server resources and one month of bid logs as data are being used.

ML bidding strategy is tested against flat bidding and randomized bidding. A/B testing setup is as follows. Three campaigns with all equal configurations (budget, targeting, creative, time, max bid, etc.) are set up for fair comparison. The first was run using a flat bid strategy. The second and third were run using random bidding and ML bidding strategies respectively. The outcome of various parameters including parameters of evaluation is shown in Table 1.

Each campaign was run five times and values in the Table 1 show an average of over 5 runs. It can be observed from the Table 1 that budget was successfully utilized in all three types of campaigns (90%) in all cases. It is natural to think that when we bid at higher rates it is more likely to win. Therefore in flat bidding, we observed comparatively high WinRate. On the other end, WinRates for randomized and ML bidding are comparable. Finally, eCPM of ML bidding has improved 16.22% and 13.64% as compared to flat and randomized bidding respectively.

It can be observed from Fig. 9 that the slope of the trendline is increased compared to Fig. 1. This means the auction prices are now distributed across instead of forming density towards lower floor prices. Given a campaign, now using ML bidding system sends dynamically priced bid for a request therefore gradually ad exchange is not able to increase the winning price and/or floor price which results in improved eCPM for an advertiser.

5 Conclusions

ML Bidding is proposed, implemented, and tested in this paper. The introduction of ML bidding at our DSP platform (the bidder) helped advertisers achieve low eCPM. It is important to note that our strategy is machine learning-based. It considers historical win prices for similar bids and decides what to bid. We observed an important behavior on the ad exchange side that, when DPSs bids higher, sometimes the win prizes also increases. ML bidding randomizes the behavior of prediction logic of bidding so it is difficult to learn by an ad exchange. WinRates and budget utilization for the campaigns are not affected. Campaigns can still utilize their 95% of the budget. Currently, ML Bidding is used in production at our bidder and it gives 15% of advantage to our advertisers.

References

1. Desai, A., Chaudhary, S.: Distributed decision tree. In: 2017 IEEE International Conference on Big Data (Big Data), vol. 2.0, pp. 929–934 (2017). https://doi.org/10.1109/BigData.2017.8258011
2. Desai, A., Chaudhary, S.: Distributed adaboost extensions for cost-sensitive classification problems. Int. J. Comput. Appl. **975**, 8887 (2018)
3. Hall, M., Frank, E., Holmes, G., Pfahringer, B., Reutemann, P., Witten, I.H.: The weka data mining software: an update. SIGKDD Explor. Newsl. **11**(1), 10–18 (2009). https://doi.org/10.1145/1656274.1656278
4. Ikonomovska, E., Jafarpour, S., Dasdan, A.: Real-time bid prediction using thompson sampling-based expert selection. In: Proceedings of the 21th ACM SIGKDD International Conference on Knowledge Discovery and Data Mining, pp. 1869–1878. KDD '15, ACM, New York, NY, USA (2015). https://doi.org/10.1145/2783258.2788586
5. Koliopoulos, A.K., Yiapanis, P., Tekiner, F., Nenadic, G., Keane, J.: A parallel distributed weka framework for big data mining using spark. In: 2015 IEEE International Congress on Big Data, pp. 9–16. IEEE (2015)
6. Mishra, S., Thakkar, H., Mallick, P.K., Tiwari, P., Alamri, A.: A sustainable ioht based computationally intelligent healthcare monitoring system for lung cancer risk detection. Sustain. Cities Soc. 103079 (2021)
7. Thakkar, H.K., Dehury, C.K., Sahoo, P.K.: Muvine: Multi-stage virtual network embedding in cloud data centers using reinforcement learning-based predictions. IEEE J. Selected Areas Commun. **38**(6), 1058–1074 (2020)
8. Thakkar, H.K., Sahoo, P.K.: Towards automatic and fast annotation of seismocardiogram signals using machine learning. IEEE Sensors J. **20**(5), 2578–2589 (2019)
9. Thakkar, H.K., Sahoo, P.K., Mohanty, P.: Dofm: domain feature miner for robust extractive summarization. Inf. Process. Manage. **58**(3), 102474 (2021)
10. Thakkar, H.K., Sahoo, P.K., Veeravalli, B.: Renda: resource and network aware data placement algorithm for periodic workloads in cloud. IEEE Trans. Parallel Distrib. Syst. **32**(12), 2906–2920 (2021)

11. Tripathy, H.K., Mishra, S., Thakkar, H.K., Rai, D.: Care: A collision-aware mobile robot navigation in grid environment using improved breadth first search. Comput. Electric. Eng. **94**, 107327 (2021)
12. Wellman, M.P., Greenwald, A., Stone, P.: Autonomous bidding agents: strategies and lessons from the trading agent competition. Mit Press (2007)
13. Wu, W.C.H., Yeh, M.Y., Chen, M.S.: Predicting winning price in real time bidding with censored data. In: Proceedings of the 21th ACM SIGKDD International Conference on Knowledge Discovery and Data Mining, pp. 1305–1314. KDD '15, ACM, New York, NY, USA (2015). https://doi.org/10.1145/2783258.2783276
14. Yang, K.C., Kang, Y.: Real-time bidding advertising: challenges and opportunities for advertising curriculum, research, and practice. In: Encyclopedia of E-Commerce Development, Implementation, and Management, pp. 1263–1278. IGI Global (2016)
15. Yuan, S., Wang, J., Zhao, X.: Real-time bidding for online advertising: measurement and analysis. In: Proceedings of the Seventh International Workshop on Data Mining for Online Advertising, pp. 1–3. ADKDD '13, ACM, New York, NY, USA (2013). https://doi.org/10.1145/2501040.2501980
16. Zhang, W., Yuan, S., Wang, J.: Real-time bidding benchmarking with ipinyou dataset. CoRR abs/1407.7073 (2014). arxiv.org/abs/1407.7073

An Efficient Minimum Spanning Tree-Based Color Image Segmentation Approach

Shahina Anwarul[✉]

School of Computer Science, University of Petroleum
and Energy Studies (UPES), Bidholi, Dehradun, 248007, India

Abstract. In the contemporary scenario, image segmentation possesses a major role in a wide spectrum of applications as a pre-processing step such as object detection, face recognition, medical imaging, aerial imaging, etc. The efficient segmentation step in the practical application of the discussed tasks can significantly enhance their accuracy. However, a fast and efficacious segmentation approach is the need of the hour. Therefore, the authors proposed an efficient graph-based approach that adapts the clustering based on the Minimum Spanning Tree for the segmentation of color images. It divides the image into various sub-regions based on the spatial and color distance in an image. The key feature of the proposed approach is that it can process the megapixel-sized image in seconds. In the present paper, Berkeley Segmentation Dataset is utilized to conduct all the experiments. The evaluation of the proposed approach is done by considering the various evaluation parameters such as precision, recall, F-measure, specificity, Negative Rate Matrix (NRM), accuracy, error rate, and segmentation speed. The proposed approach outperforms the existing state-of-the-art approach (i.e., Simple Linear Iterative Clustering (SLIC) based segmentation).

Keywords: Segmentation · Minimum Spanning Tree · Pixel · Clustering

1 Introduction

The process of dividing the image into different meaningful sub-regions based on the characteristics of pixels is termed image segmentation. It helps to encounter the objects and their boundaries (i.e., lines, curves, etc.) in an image. Each picture element (i.e., pixel) of an image is having a label, and the pixel having the same label shares some specific properties. Image segmentation is employed as a pre-processing step in numerous computer vision and image processing tasks such as remote sensing, medical imaging, aerial imaging, etc. [1–3]. A large number of segmentation approaches exist that use a graph-based approach [4, 5]. Graph-based methods follow a top-down approach that converts the images into weighted graphs and provides the segmented images by dividing the graph into sub-graphs recursively [6]. Researchers used the concept of Minimum Spanning Tree (MST) in various graph-based approaches for the segmentation process [7–10].

© Springer Nature Switzerland AG 2022
D. Garg et al. (Eds.): IACC 2021, CCIS 1528, pp. 588–598, 2022.
https://doi.org/10.1007/978-3-030-95502-1_44

A human brain segments the visual image as fast as it can, however, the same process is difficult when done by an algorithm. Therefore, an efficient segmentation algorithm is required that lessen the quantity of information to be processed for fast processing. The main motive of the proposed research is to design and develop an efficient graph-based color image segmentation approach that effectively captures all the visual objects or regions. The major contributions of the proposed research are summarized as:

- The author proposed a new approach for color image segmentation that utilized the concept of Minimum Spanning Tree (MST) which is more effective than other existing approaches.
- The authors proved the effectiveness of the presented approach both experimentally and mathematically.

The present paper is organized majorly into 6 sections. The first section confers an overview of the process of image segmentation and the major contributions of the author in the proposed research. The second section discusses the research done in the field of the addressed task. The third section provides a meticulous explanation of the proposed methodology containing a flowchart and algorithm to demonstrate the flow of the segmentation process of the proposed approach. The description of the evaluation parameters and dataset used in the proposed research is discussed in Sect. 4. The experimental results and discussion are demonstrated in Sect. 5. Last, the authors concluded the proposed work by providing the future perspective of the research.

2 Related Works

A good amount of exploration has been done in the area of the addressed task. Many segmentation algorithms have been developed based on different techniques such as region-growing [11], k-means clustering [12], watersheds [13], graph cuts [14], and sparsity-based methods [15]. With the recent surge of deep learning, image segmentation approaches result in a very high accuracy [16, 17]. But deep learning models require high computation power systems (i.e., GPU-based systems) for the processing. Therefore, graph-based approaches can be used to generate desired results in less time with less computational power systems [18]. Cigla et al. [18] used the concept of turbo-pixels for graph-based image segmentation. The TurboPixel algorithm [19] can be considered as the better algorithm in contrast to other segmentation algorithms concerning the evaluation parameters such as compactness of segments, segmentation speed, and over-segmentation errors.

Achanta et al. [20] proposed SLIC based segmentation approach using the concept of the superpixel. They have used k-means clustering to procreate superpixels in an image. The main contribution of the authors of this paper is utilizing the concept of reducing the search space to alleviate the count of distance calculations. The size and compactness of superpixels are controlled by the appropriate calculation of the edge weight. They have used the combination of spatial and color proximity to calculate the weight of an edge. This approach required human intervention to specify the number of superpixels in an algorithm.

Kruskal's algorithm is employed in the image segmentation method proposed by Felzenszwalb et al. [21]. They proposed an efficient segmentation algorithm based on the predicate defined in [21]. The defined predicate is used to measure the evidence of a boundary between two regions in image segmentation. The key feature of this method is the ability to preserve detailed information in regions of images having low variability while ignoring detailed information in regions having high variability. The algorithm is fast as compared to other existing methods and runs in O (E log E) time with E edges. The major drawback of this method is the calculation of the internal difference that is done using the extreme values of the edge weights of the components, which does not provide a precise description of the components.

3 Proposed Methodology

Figure 1 demonstrates the diagrammatic representation of the proposed graph-based segmentation approach. First, the input RGB image (X_i) of Berkeley Segmentation Dataset [22] is translated to CIELAB color space [23]. The main motive to convert the RGB image to CIELAB color space (L_i) is to cover the entire visible color spectrum. The CIELAB consists of three channels $(L^* \ rg^* \ by^*)$ where L^* presents perpetual lightness ranges from 0 to 100 (i.e., 0 represents black and 100 represents white) while rg* and by* represents four unique colors such as red, green, blue, and yellow. After converting the RGB image to CIELAB color space, the next step is to construct the proximity graph G (V, E) of the image where each pixel of the image is represented as the vertex and weighted distance between the connecting pixels are considered as edges of the proximity graph (i.e., $v_i \in V$ and $(v_i, v_j) \in E$). Each edge is having a weight represented by $\omega (v_i, v_j)$ is the measure of the variance between the adjacent pixels. Achanta et al. [20] utilized the count of superpixels in an image to define the distance measure but the authors considered a handy variable λ to define the maximum acceptable distance between the picture elements. Therefore, the weight of an edge $\omega (v_i, v_j)$ represented by ω_{ij} is calculated by considering only those pixels which are at the distance less than or equal to λ using Eq. (1). The color of the picture element in CIELAB color space is represented by $[L^* \ rg^* \ by^*]$ and the location of the pixel is (p, q), where Euclidean color distance (cd_{ij}) between the ith and j^{th} pixel is calculated using Eq. (2) and the Euclidean spatial distance (sd_{ij}) between the ith and j^{th} picture element is calculated using Eq. (3). Every pixel is represented as five-dimensional vector $[L^* \ rg^* \ by^* \ p \ q]$. The use of α in distance measure helps to contemplate the relative significance of spatial proximity and color similarity. With the larger value of c, spatial distance dominates color difference else similar color pixels combine to form a segment. The value of λ can be any integer in the range between 2 and 8 and the value of c can be in the range between 1 and 40.

$$\omega_{ij} = \begin{cases} \sqrt{(cd_{ij})^2 + \left(\frac{sd_{ij}}{\lambda}\right)^2 \alpha^2} & \text{if } sd_{ij} \leq \lambda \\ 0 & \text{otherwise} \end{cases} \tag{1}$$

$$cd_{ij} = \sqrt{(L_j - L_i)^2 + \left(rg_j - rg_i\right)^2 + \left(by_j - by_i\right)^2} \tag{2}$$

$$sd_{ij} = \sqrt{\left(p_j - p_i\right)^2 + \left(q_j - q_i\right)^2} \tag{3}$$

In the proposed approach, each picture element is connected with only those picture elements which are at a distance of maximum λ distance. Therefore, the maximum number of edges in the graph is $|V| \times \lambda^2$. So, the time complexity to construct a graph is O (V). After the construction of the graph, Prim's algorithm [24] is utilized to find out the MST (MST (V′, E′), i.e., MST contains V′ vertices and E′ edges) of the graph G (V, E). To apply clustering on MST, threshold value T is calculated by taking the sum of the average weight $\tilde{\omega}$ and standard deviation ρ of all the edges present in MST. The edges having the weight value greater than T are removed from MST that is stored in $3'$ and the remaining edges in MST generate $T_1, T_2, \ldots, T_m$ disjoint set of subtrees stored in 3. Each subtree $T_1, T_2, \ldots, T_m$ represents a cluster $C_1, C_2, \ldots, C_m$.

After getting $T_1, T_2, \ldots, T_m$ disjoint set of subtrees, a clustering algorithm based on nearest-centroid is applied to get the optimized clusters for the segmentation of an image. Here, cluster difference g_{prev}, g is utilized to discern the optimum number of clusters in an image. Cluster difference is measured by taking the ratio of the intra cluster distance $(\hat{i})$ and inter cluster $(\ddot{i})$ distance using Eq. (4). Intra cluster difference is measured as an average of the spatial distance of pixels in a cluster from the center of the cluster given in Eq. (5). Inter cluster distance is the spatial distance between the centers of two different clusters shown in Eq. (6).

$$\text{Cluster Difference } (g) = \frac{\text{Intra Cluster Difference } (\hat{i})}{\text{Inter Cluster Difference } (\ddot{i})} \tag{4}$$

$$\text{Intra Cluster Difference } (\hat{i}) = \frac{1}{N} \sum_{i=1}^{m} \sum_{h \in C_i} (h - C_i)^2 \tag{5}$$

$$\text{Inter Cluster Difference } (\ddot{i}) = \min\left(C_i - C_j\right)^2 \tag{6}$$

Where, N is the count of pixels in an image, m is the count of clusters, C_i is the ith cluster, h is the element of the ith cluster, C_i is the arbitrarily selected center of the C_i cluster, and C_j is the arbitrarily selected center of the C_j cluster. Now, find the weight of the edge having the minimum weight in $\mathfrak{Z}$' and utilized it as a new threshold value for the next iteration. Using this new threshold value, add all the edges having weight less than or equal to the new threshold to $\mathfrak{Z}$ that generates $T'_1, T'_2, \ldots, T'_m$ disjoint set of subtrees. This process continues till the cluster difference is less than or equal to the threshold value. The addition of new edges to S is done so as to reduce the number of iterations and thereby reduce the overall time to O (V) because the edge count is $|V| \times \lambda^2$. The $\mathfrak{g}$ ranges between 0 and 1. A large value of $\mathfrak{g}$ indicates that the clustering is done appropriately while a low value indicates that the clusters are in close proximity to each other and the clustering is not done as expected. After getting all the clusters, overlay these clusters over the original image to get the segmented image. {Algorithm 1} demonstrated the working of the efficient graph-based segmentation algorithm for the proposed approach.

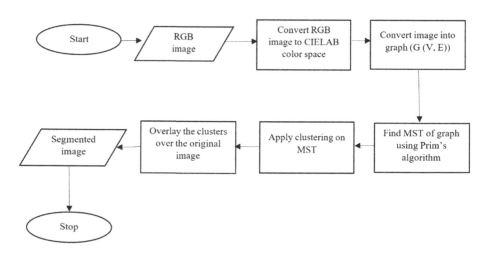

Fig. 1. The diagrammatic flow of the proposed approach.

Algorithm 1: Efficient graph-based segmentation algorithm for the proposed approach

---

Input: Dataset $D = \{X_i\}_{i=1}^n$, where, n is the count of color images in dataset
Output: Segmented images $\{Y_i\}_{i=1}^n$
function segmentation (D)
   repeat
     for all $X_i \in D$ do
       CIELAB $(L_i) \leftarrow$ RGB (X_i)
       G (V, E) $\leftarrow L_i$
       MST (V', E') $\leftarrow$ *Prims* (G (V, E))
// MST (V', E') is the MST of G (V, E)
       $T = \tilde{\omega} + \rho$
       $\mathcal{G}_{prev} = 0$
      while ($\mathcal{G}_{prev} \leq T$)
// k is the count of edges in MST of G (V, E)
       repeat
        for all $e_j \in$ E' do
         if$(\omega$ (e $\in$ E')$\geq T)$
          $\mathcal{E}' \leftarrow e$
        end for
        until k times
        if $\mathcal{E}'$ is empty **then**
         Exit
        end if
        $\mathcal{G} = \frac{(|)}{(|)}$
        if $\mathcal{G} > \mathcal{G}_{prev}$ **then**
         store the clustering using $\mathcal{G}$ threshold value
         $\mathcal{G}_{prev} = \mathcal{G}$
        end if
// Now, threshold will be updated by taking the minimum edge weight from $\mathcal{E}'$
        $T \leftarrow$ min_weight(e $\in \mathcal{E}'$)
      end while
     end for
   until n times
return $\{Y_i\}_{i=1}^n$

4 Experimental Setup

All the experiments are conducted on MATLAB R2019b using AMD Ryzen 5 4600H with Radeon Graphics, 3000 MHz processor with 8 GB RAM. The size of the images for the experimental evaluation is considered as 200×250 by taking the average height and width of all the images.

4.1   Dataset Used

The authors used the Berkeley Segmentation Dataset (BSD) Divided into two folds for training and testing. It contains 200 images for training and 100 images for testing the proposed algorithm. The dataset is available on [25].

4.2   Evaluation Parameters

The authors utilized precision, recall/sensitivity, F-measure, specificity, Negative Rate Matrix (NRM), accuracy, and error rate for the evaluation of the proposed method. The speed of the segmentation algorithm used in the discussed method is measured in seconds. Precision and recall values are used to identify the relation between the boundary pixels of the two regions. The advantage of using precision and recall parameters for the evaluation is that the comparison of the segmented outputs generated from the same or different algorithms becomes easier. Assume, O_2 is the ground truth and the achieved result from the segmentation algorithm be O_1. Precision defines the probability of the valid result while recall defines the probability of the detected ground truth. A low value for the precision parameter indicates over-segmentation whereas the low value of the recall score leads to under-segmentation. F-Measure indicates the combination of both the precision and recall score. Specificity defines the proportion of true negative samples. The Negative Rate Matrix (NRM) defines the pixelwise mismatch between the output generated after segmentation and the ground truth. Accuracy is the ratio of the total number of correctly identified pixels to the total number of pixels in an image. The error rate refers to the percentage of the inaccuracy of the predicted output values. The discussed evaluation parameters are calculated using Eqs. (7–13).

$$Precision\ (P) = \frac{Matched(O_1, O_2)}{|O_1|} \tag{7}$$

$$Recall\ (R)\ or\ Sensitivity\ (S) = \frac{Matched(O_2, O_1)}{|O_2|} \tag{8}$$

$$F - Measure = \frac{2 \times Recall \times Precision}{Recall + Precision} \tag{9}$$

$$Specificity = \frac{TN}{TN + FP} \tag{10}$$

$$Negative\ Rate\ Matrix\ (NRM) = \frac{NR_{FN} + NR_{FP}}{2} \tag{11}$$

Where, $NR_{FN} = \frac{FN}{FN + TP}$ and $NR_{FN} = \frac{FP}{FP + TN}$

$$Accuracy = \frac{TP + TN}{FP + FN + TP + TN} \tag{12}$$

Where, the total number of true negative samples is TN, FP is the count of false positives, TP is the number of true positive samples while FN is the count of false negatives.

$$Error\ Rate = 1 - Accuracy \tag{13}$$

5 Experimental Results and Discussion

Figure 2 and Fig. 3 illustrate the achieved outputs through SLIC based method and the proposed method for the segmentation of images. Experiments have been performed on various input images from BSD. For experimental purposes, the value of λ is set to 4, and the value of α is set to 10 because it offers a good balance between color similarity & spatial proximity. It is ascertained that the results achieved using the approach presented in this paper are closer to the ground truth than the results accomplished through SLIC based method. The main aim of the proposed approach is to perform an efficient segmentation of images in less time. The proposed approach outperforms SLIC based approach for the addressed task in terms of evaluation parameters and speed of segmentation as demonstrated in bar charts in Fig. 4 and Fig. 5.

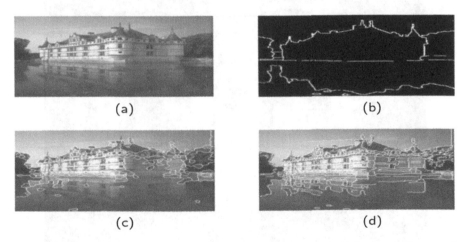

(a)

(b)

(c)

(d)

Fig. 2. Experimental results on image 1 (a) image (b) ground truth (c) segmented image using SLIC based approach (d) segmented image using proposed approach.

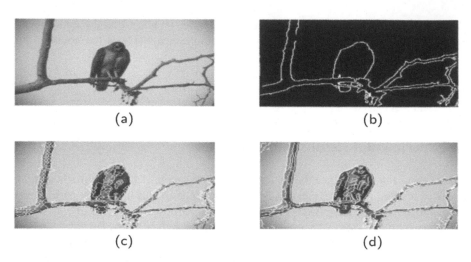

Fig. 3. Experimental results on image 2 (a) image (b) ground truth (c) segmented image using SLIC based approach (d) segmented image using proposed approach.

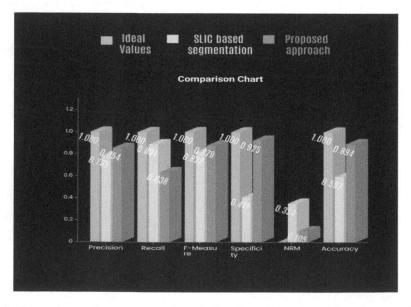

Fig. 4. Comparison of the discussed method with existing SLIC based approach for segmentation.

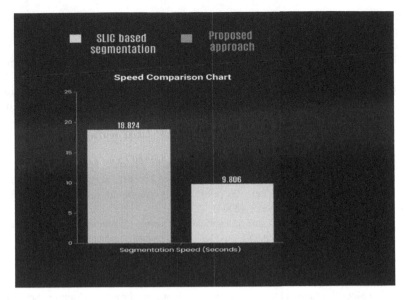

Fig. 5. Comparison of the speed of discussed method with existing SLIC based approach for segmentation.

6 Conclusion and Future Perspective

The authors proposed an efficient clustering-based approach for color image segmentation. Unlike the other segmentation algorithms, the approach discussed in the present paper does not oblige any prior number of segments, therefore it is an unsupervised approach. The proposed approach experimentally and mathematically confirms that it is more effective than previous segmentation approaches. It takes the advantage of an efficient MST to reduce the computational complexity of the segmentation approach. It can be smoothly expanded for larger dimensions. Still, there is a scope for segmentation of regions having pixels with lesser intensity difference, which is a potential area of improvement. The proposed segmentation algorithm can be used for various practical applications such as face recognition, medical imaging, object detection, etc. to achieve better results.

References

1. Su, T., Zhang, S.: Local and global evaluation for remote sensing image segmentation. ISPRS J. Photogramm. Remote. Sens. **130**, 256–276 (2017)
2. Guo, Z., Li, X., Huang, H., Guo, N., Li, Q.: Deep learning-based image segmentation on multimodal medical imaging. IEEE Trans. Radiat. Plasma Med. Sci. **3**(2), 162–169 (2019)
3. Chakraborty, M., Khot, L.R., Peters, R.T.: Assessing suitability of modified center pivot irrigation systems in corn production using low altitude aerial imaging techniques. Inf. Proc. Agricult. **7**(1), 41–49 (2020)

4. Iyer, G., Chanussot, J., Bertozzi, A.L.: A graph-based approach for feature extraction and segmentation of multimodal images. In: 2017 IEEE International Conference on Image Processing (ICIP), pp. 3320–3324, IEEE (2017)
5. Kalinin, P., Sirota, A.: A graph based approach to hierarchical image over-segmentation. Comput. Vis. Image Underst. **130**, 80–86 (2015)
6. Çiğla, C., Alatan, A.A. Efficient graph-based image segmentation via speeded-up turbo pixels. In: 2010 IEEE International Conference on Image Processing, pp. 3013–3016, IEEE (2010)
7. Zahn, C.T.: Graph-theoretical methods for detecting and describing gestalt clusters. IEEE Trans. Comput. **100**(1), 68–86 (1971)
8. Kwok, S.H., Constantinides, A.G.: A fast recursive shortest spanning tree for image segmentation and edge detection. IEEE Trans. Image Process. **6**(2), 328–332 (1997)
9. Felzenszwalb, P.F., Huttenlocher, D.P.: Efficient graph-based image segmentation. Int. J. Comput. Vision **59**(2), 167–181 (2004)
10. Xu, Y., Uberbacher, E.C.: 2D image segmentation using minimum spanning trees. Image Vis. Comput. **15**(1), 47–57 (1997)
11. Nock, R., Nielsen, F.: Statistical region merging. IEEE Trans. Pattern Anal. Mach. Intell. **26**(11), 1452–1458 (2004)
12. Dhanachandra, N., Manglem, K., Chanu, Y.J.: Image segmentation using K-means clustering algorithm and subtractive clustering algorithm. Procedia Comput. Sci. **54**, 764–771 (2015)
13. Najman, L., Schmitt, M.: Watershed of a continuous function. Sign. Proc. **38**(1), 99–112 (1994)
14. Boykov, Y., Veksler, O., Zabih, R.: Fast approximate energy minimization via graph cuts. IEEE Trans. Pattern Anal. Mach. Intell. **23**(11), 1222–1239 (2001)
15. Minaee, S., Wang, Y.: An ADMM approach to masked signal decomposition using subspace representation. IEEE Trans. Image Process. **28**(7), 3192–3204 (2019)
16. Minaee, S., Boykov, Y.Y., Porikli, F., Plaza, A.J., Kehtarnavaz, N., Terzopoulos, D.: Image segmentation using deep learning: A survey. IEEE Trans. Patt. Anal. Mach. Intell. (2021)
17. Ghosh, S., Das, N., Das, I., Maulik, U.: Understanding deep learning techniques for image segmentation. ACM Comput. Surv. (CSUR) **52**(4), 1–35 (2019)
18. Cigla, C., Alatan, A.A.: Region-based image segmentation via graph cuts. In: 2008 15th IEEE International Conference on Image Processing, pp. 2272–2275, IEEE (2008)
19. Levinshtein, A., Stere, A., Kutulakos, K.N., Fleet, D.J., Dickinson, S.J., Siddiqi, K.: Turbopixels: Fast superpixels using geometric flows. IEEE Trans. Pattern Anal. Mach. Intell. **31**(12), 2290–2297 (2009)
20. Achanta, R., Shaji, A., Smith, K., Lucchi, A., Fua, P., Susstrunk, S.: SLIC compared to state-of-the-art superpixel method. IEEE Trans. Patt. Anal. Mach. Intell. **34**(11), 2274–2281 (2012). Child Development 65(1): 13-16
21. Felzenszwalb, P., Huttenlocher, D.: Efficient graph based image segmentation. Int. J. Comput. Vision **59**(2), 167–181 (2004)
22. Martin, D., Fowlkes, C., Tal, D., Malik, J.: A database of human segmented natural images and its application to evaluating segmentation algorithms and measuring ecological statistics. In: Proceedings Eighth IEEE International Conference on Computer Vision. ICCV 2001, Vol. 2, pp. 416–423. IEEE (2001)
23. Connolly, C., Fleiss, T.: A study of efficiency and accuracy in the transformation from RGB to CIELAB color space. IEEE Trans. Image Process. **6**(7), 1046–1048 (1997)
24. GeeksforGeeks. https://www.geeksforgeeks.org/prims-minimum-spanning-tree-mst-greedy-algo-5/. Accessed 12 Sept 2021
25. Berkeley Segmentation Dataset. https://www2.eecs.berkeley.edu/Research/Projects/CS/vision/bsds/BSDS300/html/dataset/images.html

Geo-ML Enabled Above Ground Biomass and Carbon Estimation for Urban Forests

Swati Uniyal[1], Kuldeep Chaurasia[2(✉)], Saurabh Purohit[3,5], S. S. Rao[4], and Vazeer Mahammood[1]

[1] Geo-Engineering Department, Andhra University, Visakhapatnam, Andhra Pradesh, India
[2] Computer Science Engineering Department, Bennett University, Greater Noida, UP, India
kuldeep@bennett.edu.in
[3] Water Resources Department, Indian Institute of Remote Sensing, ISRO, Dehradun, Uttarakhand, India
[4] National Remote Sensing Center, NRSC, Hyderabad, India
[5] Forest Research Institute Deemed to be University, Dehradun, Uttarakhand, India

Abstract. The study of the carbon cycle and climate change in the worldwide terrestrial ecosystem relies heavily on forest aboveground biomass (AGB). Remote sensing based AGB estimate is an excellent solution for regional scale. Urban trees play an important part in carbon cycling because they sequester carbon. Above Ground Biomass (AGB) quantification is thus critical for better understanding the function of urban trees in carbon sequestration. This work was carried out for geospatial modelling of AGB and carbon with the aid of field-based data and their correlations with spectra and textural variables derived from Landsat-8 OLI data for urban forests in Jodhpur city, Rajasthan, India, using a Random Forest (RF) based machine learning (ML) approach. A total of 198 variables were retrieved from the satellite image including bands, Vegetation Indices (VIs), linearly transformed variables and Grey Level Co-occurrence textures (GLCM) were taken as independent input variables for RF regression. The RF regression model has been evaluated independently for spectral and texture variables and their integration together. Best prediction accuracy noted for the integrated model. Using RF regression a Boruta feature selection method has been applied to extract important variables from the list of variables to get a more accurate prediction. A total number of 18 variables have been identified as most important for the integrated model. Highest considerable accuracy given by the integrated model and values noted were R2 of 0.83, MAE of 11.86 t/ha and RMSE of 16.22 t/ha while for individual bands R2 value of 0.69, MAE of 16.37 t/ha and RMSE of 22.20 t/ha. For indices R2 value noted was 0.81, MAE value of 13.17 t/ha, RMSE of 17.27 t/ha. For individual textures R2 of 0.71, MAE value of 16.56 t/ha and RMSE of 21.67 t/ha have been noted. Results of the study indicate the potential efficiency of RF regression algorithm for modelling AGB and assessing the role of urban forests for carbon sequestration.

Keywords: Remote sensing · Biomass · Machine learning · Carbon estimation

© Springer Nature Switzerland AG 2022
D. Garg et al. (Eds.): IACC 2021, CCIS 1528, pp. 599–617, 2022.
https://doi.org/10.1007/978-3-030-95502-1_45

1 Introduction

Forests are vital to the world's ecosystem, environment, economy, and civilization [1]. Forests can be Natural or planted forests. Natural forests are the forests "regenerated naturally without human intervention" [2], while planted forests are defined as forest stands developed via planting and/or sowing during the afforestation or reforestation process [3]. In today's world rapid urbanisation is one of the most typical phenomena and has led to serious social, economic and environmental impacts. Tree, a major component of urban habitats, serve as a sustainable and single solution to issues like rising pollution, the impact of heat islands and many other environmental challenges. Trees in urban settings are typically seen as single trees or tiny groups, as opposed to trees in natural forests. There are many ecological benefits to a healthy, well organised, and well-managed urban forest. Well-managed forests assist to safeguard the ecosystem by preserving biodiversity, ensuring stable food and energy cycles, and reducing soil depletion and erosion [4].

Possible expansion of the forested area by the establishment of an urban forest could be effective in mitigating the build-ups of atmospheric CO2 [5] as any improvements resulting in increased forest biomass will significantly lead to sequestration of at least one portion of the 'excess carbon' emitted into the atmosphere. Accumulated growth stock in planted forests can alleviate the weight of the following commitments: CO2 reductions from forestry land use and other sources that can be deducted from emissions from other sectors [6]. Measuring and assessing the forest AGB is so critical for climate change modeling and carbon accounting. As a result, precise and rapid computation methods for AGB are required. Traditional techniques of determining AGBs (e.g. measurement of the tree height and diameter and tree harvesting) have been demonstrated to be arbitrary, time-taking, expensive and spatially restricted. Combining remote sensing technologies with ground survey based methods of calculating AGB, on the other hand, has proven to be realistic, cost-effective, and geographically explicit [7–13]. As a result, several researchers investigated empirical correlations between biomass and satellite image spectral bands and discovered substantial associations that may be used to increase the biomass inversion using geospatial techniques [14]. Primary multispectral (MX) bands, multitemporal spectral information, texture information and vegetation indices, growing syncretic characteristics from many sensors are examples of potential variables derivable from remote sensing images and progressively merged in order to develop clear or hidden associations for predicting the biomass [14]. Improved mathematical models for spatially explicit biomass quantification have been created by developing theoretical connections between biomass and remote sensing variables [15, 16] and a broad range of methods, particularly in the field of machine learning like SVR ("Support Vector Regression"), ANN ("Artificial Neural Network"), K-NN ("K-Nearest Neighbour") and RF ("Random Forest") are in use to establish empirical relationships between remote sensing-based variables and biomass. Machine-learning algorithms can generally represent complicated class signatures, take into account a wide variety of predictor data, and do not distribute data (i.e. non-parametric) assumptions.

In comparison to previous techniques, the RF algorithm gives extra knowledge in that it provides information regarding Out of Bag (OOB) error, which aids in objective generalization error computation and avoids the requirement for a separate accuracy evaluation employing the ground-truth [17, 18]. RF is an ensemble approach since it employs a large number of Decision Trees (DTs) to overcome the shortcomings of a single decision tree [19–23]. The RF method additionally evaluates the relative importance of predictor variables in the model for both the overall model and each class. Following the identification of significant factors, the RF algorithm is utilized in this work to forecast biomass and carbon. The objective of the current research work is the prediction of biomass and carbon with the help of RF regression algorithm for urban forest of Jodhpur city by integrating field observed data and various spectral and texture parameters derived from satellite data.

2 Materials and Methods

2.1 Study Area

The research work as been carried out in and around the surrounding areas of the city of Jodhpur as shown in Fig. 1. Jodhpur spread over the north-western part of Rajasthan, India between 26.2380 latitude and 73.0240 longitudes. It extends over an area of 214,5 km^2 and is located at 231 m above the datum (mean sea level). The Climate in Jodhpur is one of the deserts characterized by an average rainfall of 362 mm with large fluctuations. Noted as low as 24 mm and as high as 1,178 mm in the past. [24] In summer, high temperatures exceed 40 °C with an increase in humidity perception of heat rises in the city. April, May and October, with an average of 10 h of sunshine, were recorded as the months with the most sunshine. Annual Potential evapotranspiration noted was 6.38 mm/year. [25] In general, soils are sandy to sandy loam in texture for a few parts, while in other parts there is fine loamy sand to coarse. Sand with a high percentage of soluble salt and high pH value and low in nitrogen. Soil fertility is low because of low water retention capacity [26]. Important tree species include Acacia nilotica, Syzygium cumini, Tecomella undulata, Ziziphus mauritiana, Azadirachta indica, Millettia pinnata, Dalbergia sisoo, Broussonetia papyrifera, Phyllanthus emblica, Cassia angustifolia, Prosopis cineraria, Delonix regia, Albizia lebbek, Eucalyptus sps etc.

2.2 Satellite Data

In this analysis, Orthorectified Landsat 8 OLI (30 m spatial resolution) satellite data was used for quantified AGB and Carbon modelling. The cloud-free data is downloaded for February, May, October, and December 2019. The Strongest AGB correlation was observed with October data derived parameters, so October data was selected for AGB and Carbon modelling.

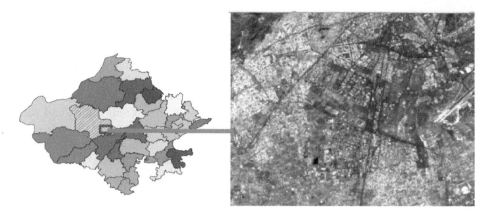

Fig. 1. Study area and classes of Urban Forest

WorldView-2 (WV-2) imagery has been used for tree crown extraction and random point generation for field observations. The Very High-Resolution WV-2 imaging has eight bands with a spatial resolution of half a meter. The first four bands are blue, green, red, and near-infrared-1, whereas the following four bands are coastal, yellow, red edge, and near-infrared-2. This study used a merged image of only standard colour bands (Fig. 2).

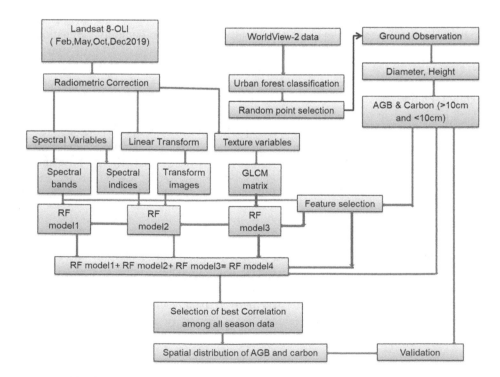

Fig. 2. Methodology for assessment of AGB and Carbon for Urban Forest

2.3 Field Sampling

Random sampling approach was adopted to obtain the field data. The study area has been divided into three major urban forest classes as shown in Table 1. Ground data from 46 sample plots of each urban forest class were collected.

2.4 Field Observed AGB and Carbon Estimation for Urban Forest

AGB for each class was estimated for >10 cm diameter tree bole using FSI developed volume equations and wood specific gravity. While the biomass of <10 cm diameter bole was estimated based on correlation between >10 cm AGB and basal areas for trees. Individual tree biomass was added together to get plot-level biomass for each class. Carbon content for individual trees as well as plot level was estimated based on AGB values.

Table 1. Urban forest classification

S. No	Stratum	Class
1	Linear	Road
		Railway
		Canal
2	Scattered	Settlement/Urban
		Agriculture
		Scrub
3	Plantation	Plantation

3 Methods

3.1 Geospatial Modelling of AGB and Carbon

It was carried out by developing a strong model between ground data along with satellite data after extracting spectral values from bands and variables derived from bands.

3.2 Variable Selection

Spectral and texture variables have been taken into consideration for the study Table 2. Spectral variables include 6 number of bands; 43 Indices; 5 linear transformed images but only tasselled cap distance (TCD) has been considered for modelling as variation in values of correlation was noted for other linear transformed images, 144 texture variables which include Grey Level Co-occurrence Matrix (GLCM) based textural features. Initially Kernels of size $3 \times 3, 3 \times 3, 5 \times 5, 7 \times 7, 9 \times 9, 7 \times 7, 9 \times 9$ were taken into consideration but variation in values of correlation has been noted for 5×5 kernel size. So kernels of size $3 \times 3, 7 \times 7, 9 \times 9$ were chosen for extraction of texture variables.

3.3   RF Based Approach

In the current study, the RF regression technique was applied for geographical analysis of AGB. When a collection of variables in many factors is chosen, RF is an ensemble strategy that integrates a large number of regression trees (as illustrated in Fig. 3). A regression tree is a hierarchical collection of conditions or constraints that extends from the tree's root to its leaf. The RF begins with a random selection of bootstrap samples from the initial training dataset, with the original training dataset being replaced. Each bootstrap sample comprises a regression tree, and a limited set of input variables selected at random from the whole set is utilized for binary partitioning for each node per tree.

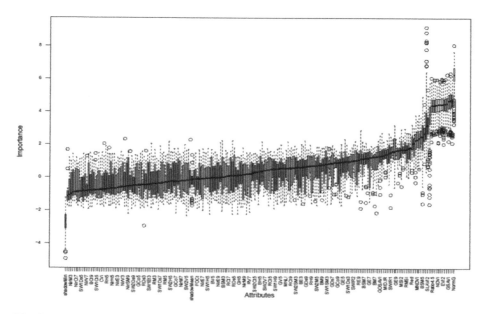

Fig. 3. The importance of the features Boruta feature selection boxplot. (Color figure online)

The regression tree partitioning criterion is based on the input variable with the lowest Gini index. The expected value is determined by averaging over all the trees [4]. RF Regression is frequently used due to its resilience and simple feature-selection techniques [2–28]. In the present study Boruta based feature selection algorithm has been applied. Boruta algorithm, which works as wrapper algorithm around random forest, uses Z-scores as a measure of band importance. It Creates shadow bands after replication of original bands. Shadow bands play the role of reference which decides the importance of variables. Figure 3 showing the Boruta boxplot where blue boxplot corresponds to Z- score of shadow variable. Z-scores for verified variables are shown by green boxplots, whereas rejected variables are represented by red boxplots. In Fig. 4, which is Importance history graph, it can be seen that green variables have higher values i.e. more importance than shadow variables, shown in blue lines.

Biomass was regarded as dependent variable, while bands, indices, linear trans-formed texture as independent variables. After selection of important variables, RF regression algorithm has been tested for 4 models using variables form bands (RF model1), indices and linear transformed images (RF model2), textures (RF model3) and integrated spectral and texture variables (RF model4). Best correlation was obtained with RF model4 so used for spatial modelling of AGB and Carbon. For modelling 70% of the samples also called as in-bag samples have been used to train the algorithm, while 30% of samples also called as OOB have been considered for cross-validation of model.

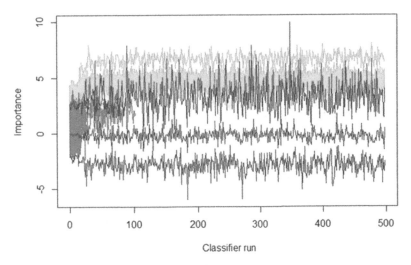

Fig. 4. Plot showing the Boruta Feature Importance history. (Color figure online)

Before executing the RF regression algorithm, 'mtry' and 'ntree' are the other parameters which need to be optimized so to minimize the generalization error. 'mtry', which tells about the number of predictor variables which have to be examined at each node, for the current research. 'ntree', which is total number of regression trees grown Fig. 6 from bootstrap sample of observation [29]. ntree and mtry parameter values were optimized at all stages of RF regression (bands, indices, textures and combinations) using the training dataset to find the finest correlation factor that could better predict AGB. After multiple iterations ntree selected was 300 and as recommended by [30, 31] 'mtry' value was taken as 1/3 of number of variables (Fig. 5).

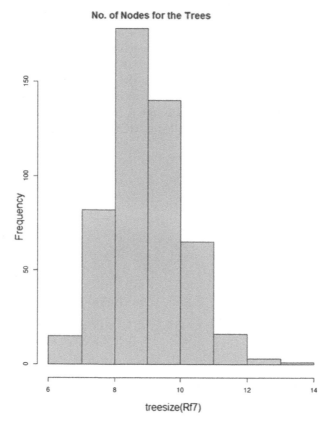

Fig. 5. Total number of regression trees grown for RF model

Table 2. List of Variables used for AGB and Carbon modelling

S. No	Independent 1 variables	Name	Details	Citation
1	Bands (6)	B2	Blue (B)	
		B3	Green(G)	
		B4	Red(R)	
		B5	NIR	
		B6	SWIR-1	
		B7	SWIR-2	
2	Vegetation Indices (43)	BNDVI- "Blue-normalised difference Vegetation Index"/ Normalized Difference NIR	NIR-B/NIR + B	[32]
		BWDRVI- "Blue-Wide Dynamic Range Vegetation Index"	(0.1*NIR-B)/(0.1*NIR + B)	[32]
		CM- Clay Minerals	R1650/R2215	
		CTVI- "Corrected Transformed Vegetation Index"	((NDVI + 0.50)/abs(NDVI + 0.50))*sqrt(abs(NDVI + 0.50))	[33]
		EVI2- Enhanced Vegetation Index	2.5 * (NIR − R)/(NIR + 6 * R − 7.5 * B) + 1	[34]
		EVI22- "Enhanced Vegetation Index"	2.5 × (NIR − R)/(NIR + 2.4 + R + 1)	[35]
		GOSAVI- "Green Optimized Soil Adjusted Vegetation Index"	(NIR-G)/(NIR + G + 0.16)	[36]

(continued)

Table 2. (*continued*)

S. No	Independent 1 variables	Name	Details	Citation
		GNDVI – "Green Normalized Vegetation Index"	(NIR − G)/(NIR + G)	[37]
		GARI- "Green Atmospherically Resistant Vegetation Index"	NIR − (G − (B − R))/ NIR − (G + (B − R))	[37]
		GRVI- "Green Ratio Vegetation Index"	(NIR/G)	[38]
		GSAVI-"Green Soil Adjusted Vegetation Index"	(NIR-G)/(NIR + G + 0.5)	[36]
		GVMI- Global Vegetation Moisture Index	((NIR + 0.1)-(SWIR + 0.02))/((NIR + 0.1)-(SWIR + 0.02))	[39]
		Intensity	(R + G + B)*(1/30.5)	[40]
		IPVI- "InfraRed Percentage Vegetation Index"	(NIR/(NIR + R)	[41]
		Iron Oxide (IO)	R/B	[42]
		logR	log(NIR/R)	
		MID IR	R1650/R2215	[43]
		MNDVI- "Modified Normalised Difference Vegetation Index"	NIR–SWIR-2/NIR + SWIR-2	[44]
		MNLI- "Modified Nonlinear Vegetation Index"	(1 + L)(NIR2 − R)/ (NIR2 + R + L)	[45]
		MSL2- Moisture Stress Index2	SWIR1/NIR	[46]
		MSL3- Moisture Stress Index-3	SWIR2/NIR	[47]
		NBR- "Normalised Burn Ratio"	(B5-B7)/(B5 + B7)	[48]
		NDII- "Normalised Difference InfraRed Index"	NIR − SWIR1/NIR + SWIR1	[49]
		NLI-	NIR − R/NIR + R	[50]
		Non Linear Index	(NIR)2 − R/(NIR)2 + R	[51]
		Normalised Green (NormG)	G/(NIR + R + G)	[52]
		Normalised NIR(NormNIR)	NIR/(NIR + R + G)	[53]
		Normalised Red (NormR)	R/(NIR + R + G)	[52]
		Red by NIR (Ratio45)	R/NIR	
		NIR by Red (Ratio54)	NIR/R	[54]
		Reciprocal of Moisture Stress Index (RMSI)	(NIR/SWIR)	[55]
		SARVI – "Soil-Adjusted and Atmospherically Resistant Vegetation Index"	(1 + L) × (NIR − R)/ (NIR + R + L)	[56]
		SI (Shape Index)	(2R-G-B)/(G-B)	[40]
		Specific Leaf Vegetation Index (SLAVI)	NIR/R + SWIR-1	[57]
		"Specific Leaf Vegetation Index" (SLAVI2)	NIR/R + SWIR-2	[57]
		Square root Infra-Red (SQIR)	Sqrt(IR)	
		Simple ratio(SR)	(1 + NDVI)/(1-NDVI)	[48]
		"Transformed Normalised Difference Vegetation Index" (TNDVI)	Sqrt((NIR-R)/(NIR + R) + 0.5)	[58]
		TVI ("Transformed Vegetation Index")	Sqrt(R − G)/ (R + G) + 0.5	[59]
		Ferrous minerals (FM)	R1650/R830	
		Ferrous Iron Oxide (FIO)	R2165/R1650	
		Ferrous oxide Composition (FOC)	R660/R560	
		Ferric Oxide Content (FOCt)	R1650/R810	

(*continued*)

Table 2. (*continued*)

S. No	Independent 1 variables	Name	Details	Citation
3	Linear Transformations (5)	Tasselled Cap angle (TCA)	arctan(TCG/TCB)	[60]
		TCB- "Tasselled Cap Brightness"	B × 0.3029 + G × 0.2786 + R × 0.4733 + NIR × 0.5599 + SWIR-1 × 0.508 + SWIR-2 × 0.1872	
		TCD- "Tasselled Cap Distance"	√(TCB)2 + (TCG)2	
		TCD- "Tasselled Cap Greenness"	B × (− 0.2941) + G × (− 0.24 3) + R × (− 0.5424) + NIR × (0.7 276) + SWIR-1 × (0.0713) + SWIR-2 × (− 0.1608)	
		TCW- "Tasselled Cap wetness"	B × (0.1511) + G × (0.1973) + R × (0.3283) + NIR × (0.3407) + SWIR × (− 0.7117) + SWIR × (− 0.4559)	
4	Texture (144)	Mean	GLCM with a 3 × 3, 7 × 7 and 9 × 9 window	[61]
		Variance		
		Homogenity		
		Contrast		
		Dissimilarity		
		Entropy		
		2nd Moment		
		Correlation		

4 Results and Discussion

4.1 Ground Observed AGB and Carbon Estimation

The estimation is based on data collected from 46 random sample plots which were laid in different Urban forest classes as described in Table 1. For Scattered areas mean basal area noted was 29.22 m^2/ha, AGB range noted from 6.91 t/ha to 104 t/ha and Carbon content range was 3.28 tC to 49.59 tC. For linear areas mean basal area was 22.17 m^2/ha, biomass range was 9.92 t/ha to 85.24 t/ha and Carbon range as 4.71 tC to 40.49 tC. In Planted areas mean basal area noted was 7.11 m^2/ha biomass ranges as 6.52 t/ha to 25.09 t/ha and Carbon content as 3.09 tC to 11.91 tC.

4.2 AGB Estimation Using RF

RF regression was conducted repeatedly with different values of mtry and ntree for each model (RF model1, Rf model2, RF model3 and RF model4) in order to achieve optimized mtry and ntree performance Table 3. The final values picked were the ones with the highest R^2 and lowest RMSE i.e. for RF model4.

Table 3. Performance analysis of the different models

Model	Description	No. of variables	mtry	ntree	R^2	RMSE (t/ha)
RF model1	Spectral Bands (SBs)	6	2	200	0.69	22.2
RF model2	Spectral Indices (SIs) + Linear transformed images (LFs)	13	3	300	0.81	17.27
RF model3	GLCM texture (Gt)	7	2	200	0.71	21.67
RF model4	SBs + SIs + LFs + Gt	18	6	300	0.83	16.22

For RF model 1, the correlation between predicted and observed demonstrated R^2 value of 0.69, MAE of 16.37 t/ha and RMSE of 22.20 t/ha Fig. 8. For RF model2 R^2 value noted was 0.81, MAE value of 13.17 t/ha, RMSE of 17.27 t/ha. With RF model3 R^2 of 0.71, MAE value of 16.56 t/ha and RMSE of 21.67 t/ha. Best values obtained with RF model4 where R^2 value of 0.83, MAE of 11.86 t/ha and RMSE of 16.22 t/ha.

Using Boruta feature selection method effective set of 18 variables were identified for RF model4 and have been taken into consideration to run RF regression algorithm, where, TVI ranked as the most important variable followed by logR, Ratio 45, GSAVI, NDVI, CTVI etc. on the basis of %IncMSE and IncNode purity Fig. 6.

Random Forest

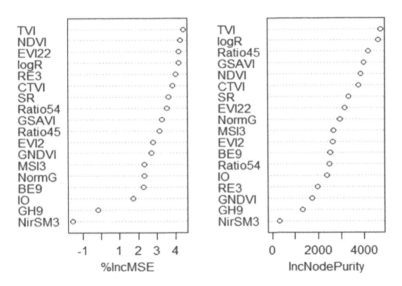

Fig. 6. Important variable selected from Boruta feature selection for prediction of AGB and Carbon

Although individual indices (15 variables identified) also formed a robust combination for modelling of AGB [51], but combination of textures and vegetation indices improved the prediction accuracy (Pham and Brabyn 2017) (Fig. 7).

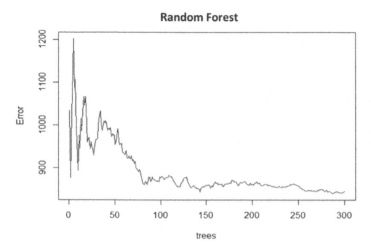

Fig. 7. Plot showing final Random Forest model error against number of trees.

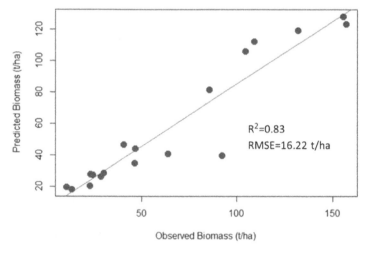

Fig. 8. Validation of field-observed AGB and RF-modelled AGB

4.3 Spatial Distribution of AGB and Carbon

The spatial distribution of AGB, Fig. 9 and Carbon, Fig. 10 was generated using 15 vegetation indices and 3 texture variables by RF regression algorithm. For urban forest in the study area the predicted value of AGB ranged from 22.22 t/ha to 121.23 t/ha and Carbon 10.55 tC to 57.58 tC. Class wise highest range noted for scattered areas as followed by linear and Plantation. Results indicated slight overestimation of values follow AGB areas while slight underestimation for high AGB areas (Table 4).

Table 4. Comparison of different methods and studies done for AGB estimation for Urban forests

S. No	Study area	Satellite data	Modelling approach	Forest type	R^2	RMSE	References
1	Xuzhou city, East China	Sentinel-2A	Boruta based Multiple linear regression	Urban forest (Low vegetation, Broadleaved Forest, Coniferous Forest, All-Type Vegetation)	0.70, 0.62, 0.64, 0.49	10.89, 57.06, 9.67, 60.19 t/hm^2	[62]
2	Nur city, Mazandaran Province, North Iran	ALOS PALSAR, Sentinel-1, Sentinel-2	SVM-genetic model	Urban forest	0.51, 0.50, 0.60	–	[63]
3	Hai Phong city, Vietnam	ALOS 2 PALSAR 2, Sentinel-2A	SVM	Mangrove plantation at Coastal area	0.596	0.187 Mg/h	[64]
4	Bhimsen Rural Muinicipality, Nepal	Worldview PAN 50 cm	Linear regression	Urban forest	0.767	–	[65]
5	Bijnor, U.P., India	IRS-P6 LISS-IV	Spectral modelling	Tree resources outside the forest	0.522	–	[66])
6	South Tangerang, Banten province, Jakarta	SPOT-7	Linear regression	Urban forest	NDVI-59.50, SAVI-54.40, ARVI-57.20	–	[67]
7	Kampong Chang Province, Cambodia	ALOS-PALSAR	Multiple Linear Regression	Cashew and rubber plantation	0.64	23.2 Mg/ha	[68]
8	Jetis and Girisekar private forest, Yogyakarta province, Indonseia	Sentinel-2	Stepwise linear regression	Private forest management unit	0.81	27 Mg/ha	[69]
9	Jilin Province, Northeast China	Sentinel-1 and Sentinel-2	Support Vector machine for regression (SVR)	Pinus koraiensis, Larix gmelinii, Betula platyphylla, Fraxinus mandschurica, Juglans mandshurica	1	0.08 Mg/ha	[58]
10	Jodhpur city, Rajasthan, India	Landsat -8 OLI	Random Forest	Urban forest	0.83	16.22 t/ha	Proposed method

Validation was performed on 30% of the sample plots. Following validation, it was discovered that the RF regression method was capable of predicting R^2 of 83.8, RMSE of 16.22 t/ha, and MAE of 11.86 t/ha.

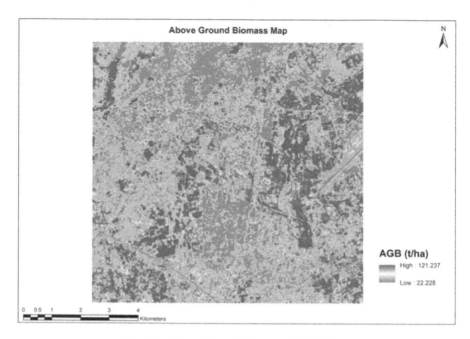

Fig. 9. Above Ground Biomass (AGB) Map

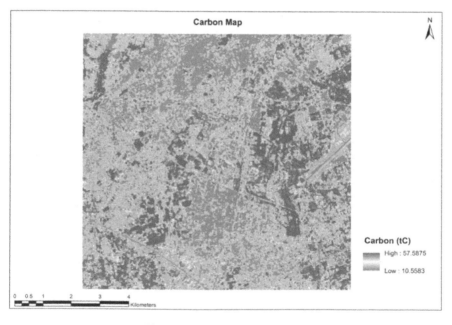

Fig. 10. Carbon distribution map

5   Conclusion

Rapid urbanisation has been one of the most prominent modern-day phenomena, with significant social, economic, and environmental consequences. Planation of trees in urban environment can be considered as important climate change mitigation option. Work on biomass estimation is increasing, using Geospatial technology combined with field research to simulate spatiotemporal biomass. This research aims to establish a RF regression-based machine learning approach based on field observations and variables retrieved from satellite data to model AGB and Carbon for Urban Forest of an arid area after identification of important variable set large number of variables. For current research using RF regression, high R^2 and RMSE indicative values show the ability of RF algorithms for quantification of AGB, thus taking the actual value in urban forest areas closer to estimates. We discovered that this approach is one of the most promising for estimating aboveground biomass with greater accuracy and a low cost budget. The results of such research may be used to educate local residents about the value of every tree and their role in mitigating global warming and climate change.

References

1. Davis, L.S., Johnson, K.N., Bettinger, P.E.T.: Forest Management: To Sustain Ecological, Economic, and Social Values (2001)
2. Carle, J., Holmgren, P.: Definitions related to planted forests. In: UNFF Intersessional Expert Meeting International Steering Group on "The Role of Planted Forests in Sustainable Forest Management. Maximising Planted Forests' Contribution to SFM", Wellington, New Zealand (2003). http://www.fao.org/forestry/5248-0d4f50dd8626f4bd6248009fc68f892fb.pdf
3. Carle, J., Vuorinen, P.: Del Lungo a, status and trends in global forest plantation development. For. Prod. J. 52(7–8), 12 (2002)
4. Kangas, A., Maltamo, M.: Forest Inventory: Methodology and Applications (Managing Forest Ecosystem). Springer, Dordrecht (2006)
5. Zhang, K., Hu, B.: Individual urban tree species classification using very high spatial resolution airborne multi-spectral imagery using longitudinal profiles. Remote Sens. 4(6), 1741–1757 (2012). https://doi.org/10.3390/rs4061741
6. Karsenty, A., Blanco, C., Dufour, T.: Forest and climate change. In: Instruments Related to the United Nations Framework Convention on Climate Change and Their Potential for Sustainable Forest Management in Africa, CIRAD, FAO (2003). ftp://ftp.fao.org/docrep/fao/011/ac836e/ac836e00.pdf
7. Sarker, L.R., Nichol, J.E.: Improved forest biomass estimates using ALOS AVNIR-2 texture indices. Remote Sens. Environ. 115(4), 968–977 (2011). https://doi.org/10.1016/j.rse.2010.11.010
8. Lottering, R., Mutanga, O.: Estimating the road edge effect on adjacent eucalyptus Grandis Forests in KwaZulu-Natal, South Africa, Using Texture Measures and an Artificial Neural Network. J. Spat. Sci. 57, 153–173 (2012). https://doi.org/10.1080/14498596.2012.733617
9. Barbosa, J.M., Melendez-Pastor, I., Navarro-Pedreño, J., Bitencourt, M.D.: Remotely sensed biomass over steep slopes: an evaluation among successional stands of the Atlantic Forest, Brazil. ISPRS J. Photogram. Remote Sens. 88, 91–100 (2014). https://doi.org/10.1016/j.isprsjprs.2013.11.019

10. Bastin, J.-F., et al.: Aboveground biomass mapping of African forest mosaics using canopy texture analysis: toward a regional approach. Ecol. Appl. **24**(8), 1984–2001 (2014). https://doi.org/10.1890/13-1574.1

11. Dube, T., Mutanga, O., Elhadi, A., Ismail, R.: Intra-and-inter species biomass prediction in a plantation forest: testing the utility of high spatial resolution Spaceborne multispectral RapidEye sensor and advanced machine learning algorithms. Sensors **14**(8), 15348–15370 (2014). https://doi.org/10.3390/s140815348

12. Dube, T., Mutanga, O.: Evaluating the utility of the medium-spatial resolution landsat 8 multispectral sensor in quantifying aboveground biomass in UMgeni Catchment, South Africa. ISPRS J. Photogram. Remote Sens. **101**, 36–46 (2015). https://doi.org/10.1016/j.isprsjprs.2014.11.001

13. Wang, G., et al.: Uncertainties of mapping aboveground forest carbon due to plot locationsusing national forest inventory plot and remotely sensed data. Scand. J. For. Res. **26**, 360–373 (2011)

14. Lu, D.: The potential and challenge of remote sensing-based biomass estimation. Int. J. Remote Sens. **27**(7), 1297–1328 (2006). https://doi.org/10.1080/01431160500486732

15. Yang, C., Huang, H., Wang, S.: Estimation of tropical forest biomass using Landsat TM imagery and permanent plot data in Xishuangbanna, China. Int. J. Remote Sens. **32**(20), 5741–5756 (2011). https://doi.org/10.1080/01431161.2010.507677

16. Tian, X., et al.: Estimating montane forest above-ground biomass in the upper reaches of the Heihe River Basin using Landsat-TM data. Int. J. Remote Sens. **35**(21), 7339–7362 (2014). https://doi.org/10.1080/01431161.2014.967888

17. Rodriguez-Galiano, V.F., Ghimire, B., Rogan, J., Chica-Olmo, M., Rigol-Sanchez, J.P.: An assessment of the effectiveness of a random forest classifier for land-cover classification. ISPRS J. Photogram. Remote Sens. **67**, 93–104 (2012). https://doi.org/10.1016/j.isprsjprs.2011.11.002

18. Lawrence, R.L., Wood, S.D., Sheley, R.L.: Mapping invasive plants using hyperspectral imagery and Breiman cutler classifications (RandomForest). Remote Sens. Environ. **100**(3), 356–362 (2006). https://doi.org/10.1016/j.rse.2005.10.014

19. Breiman, L.: Random forests. Mach. Learn. **45**, 5–32 (2001). https://doi.org/10.1023/A:1010933404324

20. Pal, M.: Random forest classifier for remote sensing classification. Int. J. Remote Sens. **26**(1), 217–222 (2005). https://doi.org/10.1080/01431160412331269698

21. Cutler, D.R., et al.: Random forests for classification in ecology. Ecology **88**(11), 2783–2792 (2007). https://doi.org/10.1890/07-0539.1

22. Belgiu, M., Drăguţ, L.: Random forest in remote sensing: a review of applications and future directions. ISPRS J. Photogram. Remote Sens. **114**, 24–31 (2016). https://doi.org/10.1016/j.isprsjprs.2016.01.011

23. He, Y., Lee, E., Warner, T.A.: A Time Series of Annual Land Use and Land Cover Maps of China from 1982 to 2013 Generated Using AVHRR GIMMS NDVI3g Data Remote Sensing of Environment a Time Series of Annual Land Use and Land Cover Maps of China from 1982 to 2013 Generated Using AVHRR GIM, vol. 199. Elsevier, Amsterdam (2017). https://doi.org/10.1016/j.rse.2017.07.010

24. https://en.climate-data.org/asia/india/rajasthan/jodhpur-2848/. Accessed 13 June 2020

25. https://www.weather-ind.com/en/india/jodhpur-climate. Accessed 13 June 2020

26. https://www.rajras.in/index.php/soils-of-rajasthan-2/. Accessed 13 June 2020

27. Greaves, H.E., et al.: High-resolution mapping of aboveground shrub biomass in arctic tundra using airborne Lidar and imagery. Remote Sens. Environ. **184**, 361–373 (2016). https://doi.org/10.1016/j.rse.2016.07.026

28. Mutanga, O., Adam, E., Cho, M.A.: High density biomass estimation for wetland vegetation using worldview-2 imagery and random forest regression algorithm. Int. J. Appl. Earth Observ. Geoinf. **18**, 399–406 (2012). https://doi.org/10.1016/j.jag.2012.03.012

29. Gwal, S., Singh, S., Gupta, S., Anand, S.: Understanding forest biomass and net primary productivity in Himalayan ecosystem using geospatial approach. Model. Earth Syst. Environ. **6**(4), 2517–2534 (2020). https://doi.org/10.1007/s40808-020-00844-4

30. Liaw, A., Wiener, M.: Classification and regression by RandomForest, vol. 2 (2002)

31. Abdel-Rahman, E.M., Ahmed, F.B., Ismail, R.: Random forest regression and spectral band selection for estimating sugarcane leaf nitrogen concentration using EO-1 hyperion hyperspectral data. Int. J. Remote Sens. **34**(?), 712–728 (2013). https://doi.org/10.1080/01431161.2012.713142

32. Hancock, D.W., Doughtery, C.T.: Relationships between blue-and red-based vegetation indices and leaf area and yield of alfalfa. Crop science **47**(6), 2547–2556 (2007). https://doi.org/10.2135/cropsci2007.01.0031

33. Perry, C.R., Lautenschlager, L.F.: Functional equivalence of spectral vegetation indices. Remote Sens. Environ. **14**(1–3), 169–182 (1984)

34. Bannari, A., Morin, D., Bonn, F., Huete, A.R.: A review of vegetation indices. Remote Sensing Reviews **13**(1–2), 95–120 (1995). https://doi.org/10.1080/02757259509532298

35. Jiang, Z., Huete, A., Didan, K., Miura, T.: Development of a two-band enhanced vegetation index without a blue band. Remote Sens. Environ. **112**(10), 3833–3845 (2008). https://doi.org/10.1016/j.rse.2008.06.006

36. Sripada, R., et al. Determining in-season nitrogen requirements for corn using aerial color-infrared photography. Ph.D. dissertation, North Carolina State University (2005)

37. Gitelson, A.A., Kaufman, Y.J., Merzlyak, M.N.: Use of a green channel in remote sensing of global vegetation from EOS- MODIS. Remote Sens. Environ. **58**, 289–298 (1996). https://doi.org/10.1016/S0034-4257(96)00072-7

38. Sripada, R., et al.: Aerial color infrared photography for determining early in-season nitrogen requirements in corn. Agron. J. **98**, 968–977 (2006)

39. Glenn, E.P., Nagler, P.L., Huete, A.R.: Vegetation index methods for estimating evapotranspiration by remote sensing. Surv. Geophys. **31**(6), 531–555 (2010). https://doi.org/10.1007/s10712-010-9102-2

40. Escadafal, R., Belghith, A., etal.: Indices spectraux pour la degradation des milieu naturels en Tunisie aride (1994)

41. Crippen, R.: Calculating the vegetation index faster. Remote Sens. Environ. **34**(1), 71–73 (1990). https://doi.org/10.1016/0034-4257(90)90085-Z

42. Segal, D.: Theoretical basis for differentiation of Ferric-Tron bearing minerals, using landsat MSS Data. In: Proceedings of Symposium for Remote Sensing of Environment, 2nd Thematic Conference on Remote Sensing for Exploratory Geology, Fort Worth, TX (1982), pp. 949–951

43. Schlerf, M., Atzberger, C., Hill, J.: Remote sensing of forest biophysical variables using HyMap imaging spectrometer data. Remote Sens. Environ. **95**(2), 177–194 (2005). https://doi.org/10.1016/j.rse.2004.12.016

44. Jurgens, C.: The modified normalized difference vegetation index (MNDVI) a new index to determine frost damages in agriculture based on Landsat TM data. Int. J. Remote Sens. **18** (17), 3583–3594 (1997). https://doi.org/10.1080/014311697216810

45. Gong, P., Ruiliang, P., Biging, G.S., Larrieu, M.R.: Estimation of forest leaf area index using vegetation indices derived from hyperion hyperspectral data. IEEE Trans. Geosci. Remote Sens. **41**(6), 1355–1362 (2003). https://doi.org/10.1109/TGRS.2003.812910

46. Raymond, H.E., Rock, B.N., Nobel, P.S.: Measurement of leaf relative water content by infrared reflectance. Remote Sens. Environ. **22**, 429–435 (1987). https://doi.org/10.1016/0034-4257(87)90094-0

47. Vogelmann, J.E., Rock, B.N.: Spectral characterization of suspected acid deposition damage in red spruce (Picea rubens) stands from Vermont. In: Airborne Imaging Spectrometer Data Anal, pp. 51–55 (1985)

48. Vermote, E., Justice, C., Claverie, M., Franch, B.: Preliminary analysis of the performance of the Landsat 8/OLI land surface reflectance product. Remote Sens. Environ. **185**, 46–56 (2016)

49. Hardisky, M.A., Smart, R.M., Klemas, V.: Seasonal spectral characteristics and above-ground biomass of the Tidal Marsh plant, Spart. Alternif. **49** (1983)

50. Tucker, C.J.: Red and photographic infrared linear combinations for monitoring vegetation. Remote Sens. Environ. **8**(2), 127–150 (1979)

51. Goel, N.S., Qin, W.: Influences of canopy architecture on relationships between various vegetation indices and LAI and FPAR: a computer simulation. Remote Sens. Rev. **10**, 309–347 (1994). https://doi.org/10.1080/02757259409532252

52. Kender, J.R.: Saturation, Hue, and Normalized Color: Calculation, Digitization Effects, and Use (1976)

53. Majasalmi, T., Rautiainen, M.: The potential of sentinel-2 data for estimating biophysical variables in a boreal forest: a simulation study. Remote Sens. Lett. **7**(5), 427–436 (2016). https://doi.org/10.1080/2150704X.2016.1149251

54. Birth, G.S., McVey, G.R.: Measuring the color of growing turf with a reflectance spectrophotometer 1. Agron. J. **60**(6), 640–643 (1968). https://doi.org/10.2134/agronj1968.00021962006000060016x

55. Huntjr, E., Rock, B.: Detection of changes in leaf water content using near- and middle-infrared reflectances. Remote Sens. Environ. **30**(1), 43–54 (1989). https://doi.org/10.1016/0034-4257(89)90046-1

56. Kaufman, Y.J., Tanre, D.: Atmospherically resistant vegetation index (ARVI) for EOS-MODIS. IEEE Trans. Geosci. Remote Sens. **30**(2), 261–270 (1992)

57. Lymburner, L., Beggs, P.J., Jacobson, C.R.: 2000_Feb_183-191. **66** (2000)

58. Chen, L., Ren, C., Zhang, B., Wang, Z., Xi, Y.: Estimation of forest above-ground biomass by geographically weighted regression and machine learning with sentinel imagery. Forests. **9**, 582 (2018). https://doi.org/10.3390/f9100582

59. Rouse, J.W., Hass, R.H., Schell, J.A., Deering, D.W.: Monitoring Vegetation Systems in the Great Plains with ERTS, vol. 1 (1973). doi:citeulike-article-id:12009708

60. Kauth, R.J.: Tasselled Cap - A Graphic Description of the Spectral-Temporal Development of Agricultural Crops as Seen by Landsat (1976)

61. Haralick, R.M.: Statistical and structural approaches to texture. Proc. IEEE **67**, 786–804 (1979). https://doi.org/10.1109/proc.1979.11328

62. Li, Z., Chen, C., Zhang, L.: Estimating urban vegetation biomass from sentinel-2A image data. Forests **11**(2), 125 (2020). https://doi.org/10.3390/f11020125

63. Tavasoli, N., Arefi, H., Samiei-Esfahany, S., Ronoud, Q.: Modelling the amount of carbon stock using remote sensing in urban forest and its relationship with land use change. Int. Archiv. Photogram. Remote Sens. Spatial Inf. Sci. **XLII-4/W18**, 1051–1058 (2019). https://doi.org/10.5194/isprs-archives-XLII-4-W18-1051-2019

64. Pham, T.D., Yoshino, K., Le, N.N., Bui, D.T.: Estimating aboveground biomass of a mangrove plantation on the Northern Coast of Vietnam using machine learning techniques with an integration of ALOS-2 PALSAR-2 and Sentinel-2A data. Int. J. Remote Sens. **39**(22), 7761–7788 (2018). https://doi.org/10.1080/01431161.2018.1471544

65. Shrestha, H.L., Rai, A., Dhakal, P.: Assessment of above ground biomass of trees outside forest (TOF) in the context of climate change. J. Ecol. Nat. Resour. (2020). https://doi.org/10.23880/jenr-16000186

66. Heyojoo, B.P., Nandy, S.: Estimation of above-ground phytomass and carbon in tree resources outside the forest (TROF): a geo-spatial approach. Banko Janakari **24**(1), 34–40 (2015). https://doi.org/10.3126/banko.v24i1.13488

67. Pitriya, A., Rokhmatuloh, R., Wibowo, A.: Biomass Estimation by Combining Field-Sampling Measurement and Vegetation Indices Derived from SPOT-7 Imagery in Urban Area: Case Study in South Tangerang, Indonesia Biomass Estimation by Combining Field-Sampling Measurement and Vegetation Indices Deri, vol. 020177 (2018)

68. Avtar, R., Suzuki, R., Sawada, H.: Natural forest biomass estimation based on plantation information using PALSAR data. PLoS ONE **9**(1), e86121 (2014). https://doi.org/10.1371/journal.pone.0086121

69. Askar, N.N., Phairuang, W., Wicaksono, P., Sayektiningsih, T.: Estimating aboveground biomass on private forest using Sentinel-2 imagery. J. Sens. **2018**, 1–11 (2018). https://doi.org/10.1155/2018/6745629

Custom Cloud: An Efficient Model for Cloud Service Selection Based on Neural Network

Abhi Bothera, Arjun Mohnot, Neha Garg, Neeraj,
and Indrajeet Gupta$^{(\boxtimes)}$

Bennett University, Greater Noida, India
indrajeet7830@gmail.com

Abstract. Cloud Computing uses a remote web-hosting network for storing, handling, and processing data, instead of a local server or a personal computer. Due to the huge demand for cloud services, the number of cloud service providers (CSPs) is expanding day by day. Each CSP has its unique offering. The availability of multiple CSPs having different offerings has confused the users in selecting an efficient service provider. It becomes much more complex if cloud users change their requirements based on demands and the comfort level of the experienced operator. This paper would resolve this downside by establishing a Custom Cloud model for the collection of cloud services by defining a trend of shifting users' needs or priorities. A combination of various Multi-Criteria Decision-Making (MCDM) methods is used to train the neural network. The trained neural network is used to select the efficient CSP based on user preferences. The improvement in the results shows the acceptability and efficiency of the proposed model in the cloud environment.

Keywords: Cloud service provider · Multi-Criteria Decision-Making · Neural network · Service selection · Quality attributes

1 Introduction

Nowadays, most organizations and users have adopted cloud-based services due to their enormous benefits [1–3]. To fulfill the ever-increasing demand many big IT organizations are in the role of the cloud service provider (CSP). Due to the increase in the number of CSPs and users many issues have taken place in the cloud. Both the academic and industrial communities have drawn significant attention to the cloud issues related to scheduling [4], energy efficiency [5–7] service selection [12, 13], etc. The explored works have a few focal points concerning their condition, applications, and limitations. Furthermore, cloud administration determination issues and cloud user necessities have additionally made numerous difficulties [8]. In this way, further investigation is required to build up a productive determination and positioning technique that will permit leaders to take powerful choices with high precision proportions by reducing the bias in the decision-making process.

Cloud Service Selection has been a hot topic for research for the past decade [8]. There have been many methods for the same and various industries have used these

D. Garg et al. (Eds.): IACC 2021, CCIS 1528, pp. 618–625, 2022.
https://doi.org/10.1007/978-3-030-95502-1_46

methods to improve their performance [9–11]. Multi-criteria decision making (MCDM) methods, analytical hierarchy process/analytical network process (AHP/ANP), outranking, simple additive weighting (SAW), Technique for Order of Preference by Similarity to Ideal Solution (TOPSIS), and VIseKriterijumska Optimizacija I Kompromisno Resenje (VIKOR), etc. are prominently used in the cloud environment [14]. The selection strategies have been mostly analyzed based on seven aspects as background, aim, representation model of data, selection techniques, parameters of selection qualitative parameter quantity methods, and methods of weighting criteria [15].

In this paper, the Custom Cloud model is proposed where users get the best of services after comparing available cloud service providers according to their usage and need. The selection of an efficient cloud service provider is based on ten attributes i.e., response time, availability, throughput, success Ability, reliability, compliance, best practices according to WS-I basic profile, latency, documentation, and Web Service Relevancy Function. The model targets the Proposed custom cloud model is user-centric and contrasts the relevant parameters.

1.1 Motivation and Contributions

Due to the COVID-19 pandemic, most people were not able to access their physical systems and will want to shift to the efficient cloud for their computational and storage needs. Cloud computing has provided a viable solution. But while mixing and matching the services, the user might be deprived of the incentives he would have received if he had stuck to CSP rather than switching to other CSPs. The big organizations utilize cloud services intensively and hence these organizations get heavy discounts if they stick to one CSP. But the small and medium enterprises (SMEs) use a limited service, so they do not receive discounts. Therefore, we are motivated to pursue this research work so that the SMEs can be benefited. The main contributions in the presented paper are as follow:

- A custom cloud model based on the neural network is proposed that targets the selection of efficient CSP for SMEs or users.
- Design an interface/portal for small businesses to aid them when they move to Cloud Computing.
- The performance of CustomCloud model based on Neural Network is compared with MCDM methods AHP and VIKOR to show the efficiency and effectiveness of the proposed model.

1.2 Paper Outline

In the next section, the proposed Custom Cloud model along with the working process is presented. Section 3 presents the case study by considering the performance value of ten CSPs from the QWS Dataset. The experimental results are presented in Sect. 4. In the last section, research work is concluded with some future directions.

2 Proposed Custom Cloud Model

In this section, the proposed Custom Cloud model and its working flow are presented. Figure 1 describes the architectural diagram of the proposed Custom Cloud model. The proposed Custom Cloud model completes its process of efficient cloud selection in the following steps.

Step 1: In the first step, the user's preferences are taken in an input excel file.

Step 2: Analytic Hierarchy Process (AHP) is applied to the input matrix to obtain weights for each user preference.

Step 3: TOPSIS (Technique of Order Preference Similarity to the Ideal Solution), WSM (Weighted Sum Model), and VIKOR (VIšekriterijumsko KOmpromisno Rangiranje) methods are then applied to rank the CSPs using weights from Step 2.

Step 4: Calculate the final performance with the help of the above results using Eq. 1.

$$Final\ Performnance = (0.2) * \left(WSM^2_{performnace}\right) + (0.3)$$
$$* \left(\left(TOPSIS^2_{performnace}\right) + (0.5) * \left(\left(1 - VIKOR^2_{performnace}\right)\right)^{\frac{1}{2}}\right) \quad (1)$$

Step 5: For the validation purpose, 80% of 2507 (2005) results are used to train the Neural Network and Neural Network is tested on the rest of the results (20% of total i.e., 502).

Step 6: Finally, mean square errors (MSE) are minimized to obtain a trained and better performing Neural Network. The loss function MSE was considered for LSTM based classification and found high loss value while using binary cross-entropy in the given dataset, while MSE outperform and provided a good result in our proposed solution The trained model is used to predict the rank based on consumers' preferences from the input file.

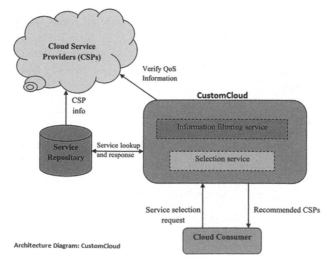

Fig. 1. Custom cloud model.

Table 1. Test input data.

CSP	Response Time (ms)	Availability(%)	Throughput (invokes/second)	Successability(%)	Reliability (%)	Compliance (%)	Best Practices (%)	Latency (ms)	Documentation (%)
A1	302.75	89	7.1	90	73	78	80	187.75	32
A2	482	85	16	95	73	100	84	1	2
A3	3321.4	89	1.4	96	73	78	80	2.6	96
A4	126.17	98	12	100	67	78	82	22.77	89
A5	107	87	1.9	95	73	89	62	58.33	93
A6	107.57	80	1.7	81	67	78	82	18.21	61
A7	255	98	1.3	99	67	100	82	40.8	4
A8	136.71	76	2.8	76	60	89	69	11.57	8
A9	102.62	91	15.3	97	67	78	82	0.93	91
A10	93.37	96	13.5	99	67	89	58	41.66	93
Impact	Negative	Positive	Positive	Positive	Positive	Positive	Positive	Negative	Positive

3   Case Study

To test the validity and performance of the Custom Cloud model against the existing Hybrid MCDM method (AHP-VIKOR), a case study is presented. Table 1 shows the sample data from QWS Dataset (2500 + Nodes) [16]. Table 2 shows the output of the Hybrid MCDM Technique (AHP-VIKOR) on the above test input data given in Table 1. In the AHP VIKOR method lowest value of performance is considered as better therefore CSP A_6 has given rank 1, CSP A_9 is given rank 2, and so on. Table 3 shows the output of the CustomCloud model on the test input data that is given in Table 1. In the CustomCloud model higher value is considered as better therefore A_6 has given rank 1, A_9 is given rank 2, and so on. Figure 2 describes the comparison plot between Custom Cloud and Hybrid MCDM (AHP VIKOR).

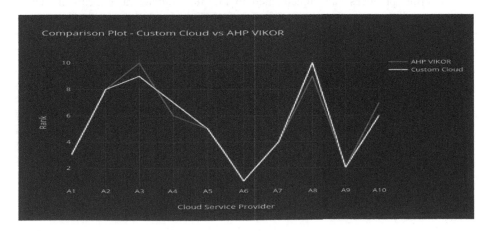

Fig. 2. Comparison plot of ranks.

Table 2. Performance of AHP VIKOR.

CSP	Performance	Rank
A1	0.3667	3
A2	0.6479	8
A3	1	10
A4	0.6198	6
A5	0.6161	5
A6	0	1
A7	0.5388	4
A8	0.8488	9
A9	0.2776	2
A10	0.624	7

Table 3. Performance of CustomCloud.

CSP	Performance	Rank
A1	0.593784	3
A2	0.347333	8
A3	0.187158	9
A4	0.385974	7
A5	0.409211	5
A6	0.881207	1
A7	0.41179	4
A8	0.182315	10
A9	0.645564	2
A10	0.403395	6

4 Experimental Results and Discussion

To implement the proposed custom cloud model, Windows 10, Ubuntu, Python 3, MATLAB, cloud platform, GitHub are used. Quality of Service for Web services (QWS) dataset [16] is used to evaluate the proposed model. The QWS Dataset is considered for accurate analysis. The provided development test data is used to create an accurate prediction of user actions. A portal is designed to submit the user preferences as shown in Fig. 2. User needs to upload his preferences in an excel sheet amongst the ten considered attributes, i.e., response time, availability, throughput, success Ability, reliability, compliance, best practices according to WS-I basic profile, latency, documentation, and web service relevancy function as shown in Fig. 4.

Numerous practices had implemented to fine-tune our neural network model to generate greater accuracy on test data. Some of the parameters and specifications of the neural model such as the number of LSTM Units, LSTM layers, changes in the learning rate, dropout and total epochs are modified. Due to unavailability of big data set, there was some overfitting when we had increased the number of epochs while training the model. Hence, some extra dropout layers within the existing layers are added. After a few iterations of testing, we had selected the final optimized hyperparameters. The activation function was considered as relu. The learning rate was set to 0.0325 with 50 epochs were used to train the resulting model. The user gets the efficient CSP as an output based on preferences. A Custom Cloud offers a more reliable and fast way of selecting the best performing CSP in the least time complexity. Figure 5 describes the performance of the most used MCDM Methods in the Custom Cloud model (Fig. 3).

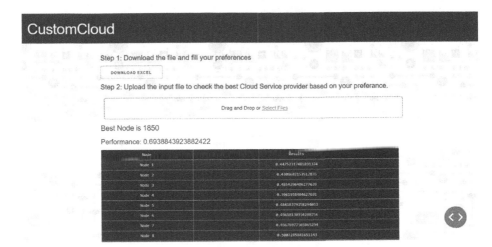

Fig. 3. User interface.

⊿	A	B	C	D	E	F	G	H	I	J	K	L
1		Response Time	Availability	Throughput	Successability	Reliability	Compliance	Best Practices	Latency	Documentation	WsRF	
2	Response Time	1	2	1	1	1	2	5	1	2	3	
3	Availability	0.5	1	3	4	5	1	2	3	4	1	
4	Throughput	1	0.33333333	1	2	2	3	4	4	5	3	
5	Successability	1	0.25	0.5	1	3	2	3	1	5	2	
6	Reliability	1	0.2	0.5	0.333333333	1	2	3	5	2	1	
7	Compliance	0.5	1	0.33333333	0.5	0.5	1	2	3	4	4	
8	Best Practices	0.2	0.5	0.25	0.333333333	0.3333333	0.5	1	1	2	3	
9	Latency	1	0.33333333	0.25	1	0.2	0.33333333	1	1	4	4	
10	Documentation	0.5	0.25	0.2	0.2	0.5	0.25	0.5	0.25	1	3	
11	WsRF	0.333333333	1	0.33333333	0.5	1	0.25	0.333333333	0.25	0.333333333	1	
12												
13												
14												

Fig. 4. Input file.

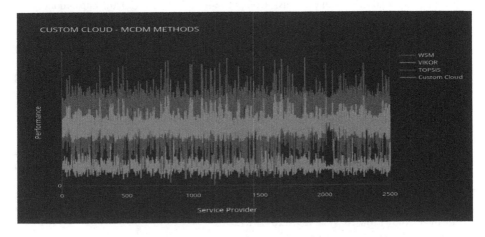

Fig. 5. Performance of Custom Cloud and MCDM methods.

5 Conclusion

In this paper, a combination of various Multi-Criteria Decision-Making (MCDM) methods is used to train the neural network. The trained neural network predicts the efficient Cloud Service Provider (CSP) based on the user preferences from more than 2500 CSPs. The model provides custom-made options to the users that best suit their needs. The improvement in the results shows the acceptability of the proposed model in the cloud environment. In the future, an easy-to-use web application supported to all platforms will be built. The Neural Network will also be enhanced to train the model over different inputs from various users.

Data and Code Availability. Data and Code used in the presented paper are available from the GitHub repository. The link for the data availability is: https://github.com/abhibothera/CustomCloud.

References

1. Zhou, J., Liu, L.-F., Sun, L.-J., Xiao, F.: A multi-criteria decision-making method for hesitant fuzzy linguistic term set based on the cloud model and evidence theory. J. Intell. Fuzzy Syst. **36**(2), 1797–1808 (2019)
2. Mishra, S., Sahoo, M.N., Bakshi, S., Rodrigues, J.J.: Dynamic resource allocation in fog-cloud hybrid systems using multicriteria AHP techniques. IEEE IoT J. **7**(9), 8993–9000 (2020)
3. Al-Faifi, A., Song, B., Hassan, M.M., Alamri, A., Gumaei, A.: A hybrid multi criteria decision method for cloud service selection from smart data. Futur. Gener. Comput. Syst. **93**, 43–57 (2019)
4. Garg, N., Goraya, M.S.: Task deadline-aware energy-efficient scheduling model for a virtualized cloud. Arab. J. Sci. Eng. **43**(2), 829–841 (2018)
5. Garg, N., Singh, D., Goraya, M.S.: Energy and resource efficient workflow scheduling in a virtualized cloud environment. Clust. Comput. **24**(2), 767–797 (2020). https://doi.org/10.1007/s10586-020-03149-4
6. Kumar, M.S., Gupta, I., Panda, S.K., Jana, P.K.: Granularity-based workflow scheduling algorithm for cloud computing. J. Supercomput. **73**(12), 5440–5464 (2017). https://doi.org/10.1007/s11227-017-2094-7
7. Garg, N., Singh, D., Goraya M.S.: Optimal virtual machine scheduling in virtualized cloud environment using VIKOR method. J. Supercomput. (2021)
8. Garg, N., Singh, D., Goraya M.S.: Power and resource-aware VM placement in cloud environment. In: 2018 IEEE 8th International Advance Computing Conference (IACC), pp. 113–118. IEEE, Greater Noida, India (2018)
9. Kumar, M.S., Indrajeet, G., Prasanta K.J.: Delay-based workflow scheduling for cost optimization in heterogeneous cloud system. In: 2017 Tenth International Conference on Contemporary Computing (IC3) (2017)
10. Nawaz, F., Asadabadi, M.R., Janjua, N.K., Hussain, O.K., Chang, E., Saberi, M.: An MCDM method for cloud service selection using a Markov chain and the best-worst method. Knowl.-Based Syst. **159**, 120–131 (2018)

11. Lee, S., Seo, K.-K.: A hybrid multi-criteria decision-making model for a cloud service selection problem using BSC, fuzzy delphi method and fuzzy AHP. Wireless Pers. Commun. **86**(1), 57–75 (2015)
12. Yadav, N., Goraya, M.S.: Two-way ranking based service mapping in cloud environment. Futur. Gener. Comput. Syst. **81**, 53–66 (2018)
13. Neeraj, G.M.S., Singh, D.: Satisfaction aware QoS-based bidirectional service mapping in cloud environment. Clust. Comput. **23**(4), 2991–3011 (2020)
14. Neeraj, G.M.S., Singh, D.: A comparative analysis of prominently used MCDM methods in cloud environment. J. Supercomput. **77**(4), 3422–3449 (2020)
15. Alabool, H., Kamil, A., Arshad, N,, Alarabiat, D.: Cloud service evaluation method-based multi-criteria decision-making: a systematic literature review. J. Syst. Softw. **139**, 161–188 (2018)
16. QWS Dataset (The Quality of Service for Web Services Dataset). https://qwsdata.github.io/

A Machine Learning-Based Approach for Efficient Cloud Service Selection

Uttam Gandhi, Abhi Bothera, Neha Garg, Neeraj,
and Indrajeet Gupta$^{(\boxtimes)}$

Bennett University, Greater Noida, India
indrajeet7830@gmail.com

Abstract. Cloud computing can be considered a revolutionizing invention of decay. The computing resources are externally supplied to the user with benefits of scalability, accessibility, pay-as-you-go, serverless, etc. With its ever-growing market, there is a multitude of cloud service providers (CSPs) with different offerings available to small and medium enterprises (SMEs) or users. Due to the availability of numerous CSPs with different offerings, it becomes complicated for the user to pick the right services. In the presented paper, a supervised learning-based model based on Random Forest Regressor is proposed. The proposed model has been trained for Multi Criteria Decision Making Methods (MCDM) methods such as Technique for Order of Preference by Similarity to Ideal Solution (TOPSIS), VlseKriterijumska Optimizacija I Kompromisno Resenje (VIKOR), and Weighted Sum Method (WSM). The score obtained from these MCDM methods has been used to rank the services. Results show the acceptability of the proposed model in the cloud environment.

Keywords: Cloud computing · Cloud Service Provider · Multi-Criteria Decision Making · Machine learning

1 Introduction

The 21st century has been revolutionized by cloud computing. Numerous web services such as YouTube, Google, Amazon, Zoom, etc. are hosted on the cloud. Researchers have presented numerous methods/models/frameworks for solving the cloud computing issues in the field of scheduling [1, 2], energy efficiency [3–6], service selection/mapping [12], etc. The unique characteristics of cloud, higher scalability, on-demand IT services, pay-as-you-go model, etc. have paved way for all the scales of industries to access IT services. To fulfill the ever-increasing demand for cloud-based services and generating more revenue, many big IT organizations are in the role of Cloud Service Provider (CSP). The CSPs offer similar services with different quality parameters. On the other hand, the users have also different requirements. The different CSPs offerings and dynamic changes in users' requirements have made the cloud service selection process more complicated.

Manually selecting a service from multiple CSPs based on the plethora of offerings and dynamic requirements is a tedious task for the user. However, there are hundreds of registered CSPs, each providing different services, but none of them address the ever-

© Springer Nature Switzerland AG 2022
D. Garg et al. (Eds.): IACC 2021, CCIS 1528, pp. 626–632, 2022.
https://doi.org/10.1007/978-3-030-95502-1_47

changing needs of the provider and provides them with the best recommendations. Numerous CSPs, such as Amazon Web Services, Google Cloud Platform, Azure Cloud, etc., provide price calculators that will assist to choose a CSP, but they do not appeal to the end user's evolving needs. Researchers have carried out an intensive study and have proposed various methods for the users to make the best decision.

Brokerage-based cloud service selection has been proposed in the literature [7]. Cloud Service Brokers (CSBs) take the user's needs into account and offer a directory of possible cloud providers to ease the user's discovery process. Some organizations such as Amazon Marketplace, Cloud Compare, Cloud Country, Clouditalia, Cloudmore, etc. are in the role of cloud broker [7]. Selecting a service having multiple quality parameters is a multi-criteria decision-making (MCDM) problem. MCDM methods such as the Weighted Sum Method (WSM), VlseKriterijumska Optimizacija I Kompromisno Resenje (VIKOR), and Technique for Order of Preference by Similarity to Ideal Solution (TOPSIS), etc. are used for assigning weights to different parameters and rank the CSPs [13, 14].

In this paper, MCDM methods, TOPSIS, VIKOR, and WSM are exploited to score the services and rank the CSPs. Based on these MCDM methods, ML model is trained on the Quality of Service for Web Services (QWS) dataset 1 [15] and had applied the trained ML regressor model on the QWS dataset 2 [15]. Comparison between the results of MCDM methods and the ML model is performed to check the accuracy of the model.

1.1 Paper Outline

The following section contains a comprehensive literature review on cloud service selection. Section 3 contains the problem statement. In Sect. 4, the proposed method along with a data flow chart is presented. Experimental results and discussion are presented in Sect. 5. The last section concludes the paper along with some future directions (Table 1).

Table 1. List of abbreviations

Abbreviation	Meaning
AHP	Analytic Hierarchy Process
ANP	Analytical Network Process
CSP	Cloud Service Provider
ELECTRE	Elimination Et Choice Translating Reality
IT	Information Technology
ML	Machine Learning
MAVT	Multi-Attribute Value Theory
MAUT	Multi-Attribute Utility Theory
MCDM	Multi Criteria Decision Making
PROMETHEE	Preference ranking organization method for enrichment evaluation
QoS	Quality of Service
QWS	Quality of Service for Web Services
TOPSIS	Technique for Order of Preference by Similarity to Ideal Solution
VIKOR	VlseKriterijumska Optimizacija I Kompromisno Resenje
WSM	Weighted Sum Method
BWM	Best Worst Method
WSCE	Web Service Crawler Engine

2 Literature Survey

In this section, a brief review of research articles related to cloud service selection using MCDM methods has been presented.

Nawaz et al. [7] proposed a cloud broker architecture for cloud service selection by defining a trend of changing customer preferences. To find the pattern, a Markov chain was employed. The Best Worst Method (BWM), a recently proposed MCDM method, is used to rate the facilities. Saroj and Dileep [8] reviewed the various MCDM (Outranking Methods, TOPSIS, (PROMETHEE), Multi-Attribute Value Theory (MAVT), Multi-Attribute Utility Theory (MAUT), Elimination Et Choice Translating Reality (ELECTRE), and AHP methods along with their strengths and limitations. Supriya et al. [9] proposed a raking method to rank the CSPs using hybrid MCDM methods, Analytic Hierarchy Process (AHP), FuzzyAHP, TOPSIS, and Fuzzy TOPSIS) based on their technical parameters. Chung and Seo [10] proposed an Analytical Network Process (ANP) based Cloud service, selection model. Lee [11] proposed a ranking method based on the AHP framework for cloud decision-making. Financial, marketing, management, and environmental requirements are included in the proposed AHP model.

3 Problem Statement

As there is unhindered growth in the cloud segment, there are many CSPs. As there is advancement in the Information Technology (IT) sector, the same can be applied to the growing number of services that each CSP can offer. Let us consider there are 'X' number of CSPs and each CSP offers 'Y' number of cloud services. So, it becomes very difficult for the user to select the appropriate services among the total '$X * Y$' options. In this paper, a model is proposed based on hybrid MCDM methods (TOPSIS, VIKOR, WSM). Numerous Quality of Service (QoS) parameters, Response time, Availability, Throughput, Success-ability, Reliability, Compliance, Best Practices, latency, and Documentation are considered while training the machine learning (ML) regression model.

Let number of CSPs are $X\{X_1, X_2, X_3, X_4, X_5, ...X_n$ and cloud services offered by each CSP are $Y\{Y_1, Y_2, Y_3, Y_4, Y_5, ...Y_n\}$. Thus the total number of options available are $X*Y = \{X_1Y_1, X_1Y_2, ..., X_1Y_n, X_2Y_1, X_2Y_2, ..., X_2Y_n, X_nY_n$. The number of criteria are $C\{C_1, C_2, C_3, C_4, C_5, C_6, C_7, C_8, C_9\}$.

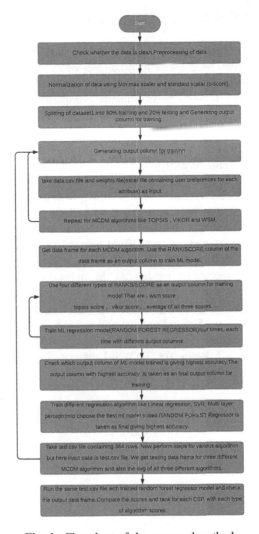

Fig. 1. Flowchart of the proposed method.

Table 2. Pre-processing methods accuracy comparison.

MCDM Methods	MIN - MAX	Z-SCALE
WSM	0.97898913	0.97886059
TOPSIS	0.98756346	0.98437200
VIKOR	0.98793540	0.98789617
AVG	0.99135257	0.99175167

Table 3. Regression model accuracy comparison.

Model	Accuracy
Linear Regression	0.841934539
Support Vector Machine	0.437492547
ML Regressor	0.972680118

4 Experimental Results and Discussion

In this research work, two datasets namely QWS1 and QWS2 [15] are used for experimentation. This dataset consists of nine QoS per web service for 365 web services. Dataset QWS version 2.0 contains a compilation of 2,507 web services and their Quality of Web Service (QWS) measurements completed in 2008 using the Web Service Broker (WSB) platform. Each row in this database represents a web service and the nine QWS measurements that go with it (separated by commas). Nine items are QWS metrics that were analyzed over six days using various Web service benchmark instruments. The QWS values are estimates of the measurements taken during the time. Dataset QWS version 2.0, referred to as dataset1 is used to train the machine learning model. The distribution of the training model while pre-processing is 80% training and 20% testing. Method is also present using flowchart as shown in Fig. 1. After the training, the testing is done on dataset QWS version 1.0, referred to as dataset 2. The Web Service Crawler Engine (WSCE) was used to retrieve the web services. The accuracy comparison of pre-processing methods is presented in Table 2. Table 3 represents that the ML regression model has the highest accuracy in comparison to linear and support vector machine regression models. Figure 2 represents the top 15 cloud services by trained model and predicted by ML Regressor for TOPSIS method. Figure 3 represents the top 15 cloud services by trained model and predicted by ML Regressor for VIKOR method. Figure 4 represents the Top 15 cloud services by trained model and predicted by ML Regressor for WSM method. The x-axis represents the top 15 rankings, and the y-axis represents the CSPs.

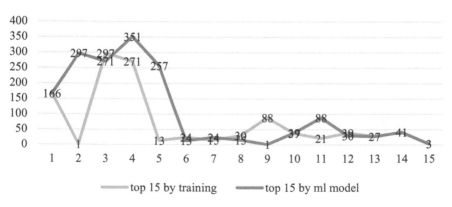

Fig. 2. Top 15 cloud services by trained model and predicted by ML Regressor for TOPSIS.

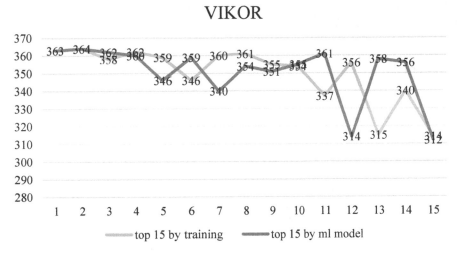

Fig. 3. Top 15 cloud service by trained model and predicted by ML Regressor for VIKOR.

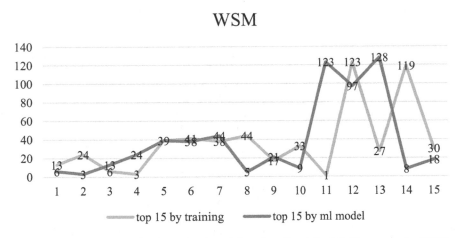

Fig. 4. Top 15 cloud service by trained model and predicted by ML Regressor for WSM.

5   Conclusion

Cloud computing is a rapidly expanding market. The number of CSPs that provide IT resources has exploded in recent years. This research work provides the users and efficient ML based method for efficient cloud service selection based on their requirements in terms of quality attributes. Proposed model is based on the MCDM methods (VIKOR, TOPSIS and WSM). The experimental results have shown the efficiency and acceptability of the proposed method in the cloud environment. In the future, results based on real world dataset of the CSP will be further explored. More parameters will be considered such as trustworthiness, financial security, legal policy, and long-term growth strategy other than no long-term performance forecast or dynamic service deployment approach.

References

1. Kumar, M.S., Gupta, I., Panda, S.K., Jana, P.K.: Granularity-based workflow scheduling algorithm for cloud computing. J. Supercomput. **73**(12), 5440–5464 (2017). https://doi.org/10.1007/s11227-017-2094-7
2. Kumar, M.S., Indrajeet G., Prasanta K.J.: Delay-based workflow scheduling for cost optimization in heterogeneous cloud system. In: 2017 Tenth International Conference on Contemporary Computing (IC3) (2017)
3. Garg, N., Goraya, M.S.: Task deadline-aware energy-efficient scheduling model for a virtualized cloud. Arab. J. Sci. Eng. **43**(2), 829–841 (2018)
4. Garg, N., Singh, D., Goraya, M.S.: Energy and resource efficient workflow scheduling in a virtualized cloud environment. Clust. Comput. **24**(2), 767–797 (2020). https://doi.org/10.1007/s10586-020-03149-4
5. Garg, N., Singh, D., Goraya M.S.: Optimal virtual machine scheduling in virtualized cloud environment using VIKOR method. J. Supercomput. (2021)
6. Garg, N., Singh, D., Goraya M.S.: Power and resource-aware VM placement in cloud environment. In: 2018 IEEE 8th International Advance Computing Conference (IACC), pp. 113–118, IEEE, Greater Noida, India (2018)
7. Nawaza, F., Asadabadia, M.R., Janjuab, N.K., Hussaina, O.K., Changa, E., Saberia, M.: An MCDM method for cloud service selection using a Markov chain and the best-worst method. Knowl.-Based Syst. **159**, 120–131 (2018)
8. Saroj, S., Dileep, V.K.: A review multi-criteria decision making methods for cloud service ranking. Int. J. Emerg. Technol. Innov. Res. **3**(7), 92–94 (2016)
9. Supriya, M., Sangeeta, K., Patra, G.K.: Trustworthy cloud service provider selection using multi criteria decision making methods. Eng. Lett. **24**(1), 1–10 (2016)
10. Chung, B.D., Seo, K.K.: A cloud service selection model based on analytic network process. Indian J. Sci. Technol. **8**(18), 1–5 (2015)
11. Lee, Y.H.: A Decision framework for cloud service selection for SMEs: AHP analysis. SOP Trans. Market. Res. **1**(1), 51–57 (2014)
12. Yadav, N., Goraya, M.S.: Two-way ranking based service mapping in cloud environment. Futur. Gener. Comput. Syst. **81**, 53–66 (2018)
13. Neeraj, G.M.S., Singh, D.: Satisfaction aware QoS-based bidirectional service mapping in cloud environment. Clust. Comput. **23**(4), 2991–3011 (2020)
14. Neeraj, G.M.S., Singh, D.: A comparative analysis of prominently used MCDM methods in cloud environment. J. Supercomput. **77**(4), 3422–3449 (2020)
15. QWS Dataset (The Quality of Service for Web Services Dataset). https://qwsdata.github.io/

Enhancing Network Robustness Using Statistical Approach Based Rewiring Strategy

Suchi Kumari[1]($\boxtimes$), Samya Muhuri[1], and Swati Chandna[2]

[1] Department of Computer Science Engineering, Bennett University,
Greater Noida, Uttar Pradesh, India
{suchi.kumari,samya.muhuri}@bennett.edu.in
[2] School of Information, Media and Design, SRH University Heidelberg,
Heidelberg, Germany
swati.chandna@srh.de

Abstract. The robustness of the time-varying graphs is one of the prominent issues in the complex network domain. The problem can be resolved by restructuring the network topology after each attack by providing a probabilistic rewiring approach. The proposed system should be structured in such a manner that some statistical network parameter such as clustering coefficient and the rich club coefficient score of the network can be enhanced. In the current manuscript, we have studied the network performance under random link attacks. We have checked the robustness status by measuring the size of the giant component and information flow in the system. The discussed statistical parameters are used to measure the performance of the proposed rewiring strategy against the random strategy. We have compared our result with a random rewiring strategy and shown the superiority of our proposed techniques on benchmark real world data sets. Our method can be utilized in any real-life complex network structure for surviving outside attacks.

Keywords: Network robustness · Probabilistic rewiring strategy · Core-periphery architecture · Centrality measures · Statistical parameters

1 Introduction

Modern real-world systems consist of the interdependent subsystem in such a way that malfunctioning of components in one subsystem may lead to the propagation of failure of the entire system due to the cascade failure. To make the system more robust, we need to make the nodes and links more resilient under random or targeted failure. Therefore, the network should be restructured in such a manner that it should be protected from any type of attacks. The network

© Springer Nature Switzerland AG 2022
D. Garg et al. (Eds.): IACC 2021, CCIS 1528, pp. 633–645, 2022.
https://doi.org/10.1007/978-3-030-95502-1_48

attack, as well as random failure, can't be avoided, but, we can protect our system from collapse by providing some restructuring mechanism using probabilistic approach. Addition of new resources always incur cost so, in this manuscript, we have considered statistical approach based rewiring mechanism for enhancing network robustness. We have measured the performance of the network by measuring statistical approach based parameters such as the average rich-club coefficient (RCC) score and clustering coefficient (*cc*) score of the network. Both the parameters, RCC and *cc* ensures larger connectivity among the nodes in the network. The more considerable value indicated larger connectivity in the network. Some other statistical parameters such as entropy (S), giant component size (GCC), correlation coefficient *corr*, are studied for the performance analysis of the network. From the analysis, we can say that the network performance is enhanced after the rewiring operations.

2   Literature Review

The real world network can be represented with the help of complex network. Many network properties help to evaluate performance of the network under various circumstances e.g., attack, failure, congestion, routing, topology design [3,6,11,23]. The real-world networks exhibit different behaviour against errors, random attack, or targeted attack. Some of the networks such as communication network [10,12], WWW [5], transportation [24], social systems[9,13], power systems [2] etc.; follow power law degree distribution. These networks are robust against high failure rate of any random components. However, these networks are fragile against targeted failure of the network components.

Some researchers worked on the robustness analysis of the network under random and targeted attack. Albert et al. [1] studied the resilience of various complex networks against some erroneous events or under some attack. Holme *et al.* [8] studied the performance of complex network model and some real-world networks under attacks on nodes and links. To cover all types of attacks, four different strategies are used: removal of higher degree nodes, higher betweenness centrality nodes, recalculated degrees, and recalculated betweenness. Researchers [4,18] studied the effect of cascading failure due to load redistribution among the live nodes at a larger scale.

In some of the literature, rewiring operations are performed to increase the robustness of the network. Many real-world systems are in-homogeneous and scale-free. Though the networks are robust under usual condition but brittle in case of any attack. To address this issue, Xiao *et al.* [25] used degree-degree correlation to increase the robustness of the nodes in the network. The network robustness is increased by using two methods; Assortative Increasing Rewiring (AIR) and Assortative Unaffecting Rewiring (AUR) techniques.Louzada *et al.* [16] converted the network into multiple layers with a similar degree and made the network a highly modular structure and named as "modular onion-like structure". By maintaining the above architecture and performing multiple rewiring, the network robustness is considerably modular. Liang et al. [15] proposed a smart edge rewiring strategy and compared with random rewiring strategy. They found that the regeneration of edges between larger degree nodes enhance the network robustness against the targeted attack and takes lesser computation time than the random rewiring strategy. The smart rewiring method also explains the reason behind the selection of nodes with positive correlation on network robustness. Paterson et al. [20] provided a hybrid approach (rewiring and addition of links) to enhance the network robustness by considering largest connected component as an evaluation parameter in the network. Geng et al. [7] proposed correlation based rewiring strategy to make the scale free network robust against the localized attack.

All the literature, as mentioned earlier, discussed multiple rewiring strategies based on degree, correlation, betweenness centrality and so on. Network robustness can be measured using some other realistic statistical parameters like k-core architecture, clustering coefficient, entropy, giant component size, rich-club coefficient and so on. All these parameters play a measure role in network connectivity and information flow in the network. By considered all the parameters, we proposed two rewiring strategies and compared with random rewiring strategy and enhanced the robustness of the network.

3   Definitions

In this section, some related statistical parameters are explained.

(i) Degree-degree correlation (DDC): It calculates the bonding between two connected vertices. Let, p_k is the probability of a any random node having degree k and $q_k = \frac{(k+1)p_{k+1}}{\langle k \rangle}$ as an excess degree distribution. The correlation coefficient r_{net} cen be formulated as $r_{net} = \langle jk \rangle - \langle j \rangle \langle k \rangle = \sum_{jk} jk(p_{e_{jk}} - q_j q_k)$ [19]. Here, $p_{e_{jk}}$ is the joint degree distribution of the link, e_{jk} and $\langle k \rangle$ is average degree of the network.

(ii) Clustering coefficient (cc): It is used to measure node's involvement in triangle formation with the neighboring nodes. In social network, we can say that cc is used to measure how many friends of your friend is connected. For an unweighted network, the clustering coefficient of a node v is calculated as $cc_v = \frac{2\Delta(v)}{k(v)k(v)-1}$, where $\Delta(v)$ is the number of triangles formed using node v and $k(v)$ is the the degree of node v.

(iii) Entropy: It defines uncertainty in any network. The entropy is represented as $S = -\sum_i k_i log(k_i)$.

(iv) Rich club coefficient: It is a ratio of two values, which are number of actual edges present in a network and the number of potential edges for nodes with degree greater than k. It is denoted as $\phi(k) = \frac{2E_k}{N_k(N_k-1)}$, where N_k is the number of nodes with degree larger than k, and E_k is the number of edges among the denoted nodes.

(v) Giant component: The component in a graph having a maximal connected sub-graph is called as giant component. We can calculate normalized giant connected component by finding the ratio of two values, which are the number of vertices in the largest connected sub-graph and total number of vertices in the network.

4   Proposed Strategies

The real-world network is prone to attack, and in the worst case, it breaks the whole network into multiple components. The network attack is inevitable, so our task is to make the system more robust against such types of attack. There may be multiple ways to enhance the network robustness and network performance. Here, we have considered rewiring of the network connection so that we can maintain connectivity and robustness of the network. The rewiring process can be done based on two strategies, random or based on some network parameter. For the rewiring operation, we may consider multiple network parameters e.g., degree, centrality measures, core-periphery architecture, clustering coefficient and so on. The degree can be used for assigning new connection (i.e., preferential attachment Π_i) in the network. The probability Π_i that a node i will be selected through preferential attachment is defined as $\Pi_i = \frac{k_i}{\sum_j k_j}$. Betweenness centrality (BC) is used to find the participation of the node in the information/data flow in the network. The clustering coefficient emphasises on finding tightly connected cluster in the network. The core-periphery (CP) architecture helps to find the nodes present in the inner cores as well as the nodes present in the periphery. These parameters are used to perform rewiring operation to enhance the network robustness under random attack.

4.1   Betweenness Centrality and Core Periphery (BCCP) Based Rewiring Strategy

The BCCP strategy is a combination of two statistical network parameters i.e., between centrality and k-core score of the nodes in the network. The network is layered into k-cores based on the connection of a node with degree k with the other nodes whose degree is $\geq k$ [21]. In the core-periphery architecture, the nodes in the inner core layers are more connected and central than the other nodes in the periphery. Hence, the probability of the selection of the nodes with higher $k-$core score is more than the nodes with lower $k-$core score after the rewiring operation. There exists multiple nodes in the inner cores so, the nodes can be ranked according to some other statistical network parameters such as betweenness centrality. If a node lies in the shortest path of the source-destination node pair with high BC, then it may be helpful for enhancement in network robustness. That's why, in the proposed strategy, the probability of the selection of a node with larger BC is more for establishing a new connection after the rewiring process. In Fig. 1(a), a link e_{ij} (connecting nodes; i and j) is selected randomly and removed from the network. Thereafter, a node v is chosen randomly from the pool of higher k-core nodes and its k-core score and BC score is evaluated. The node i will be connected with a node v if k-core score, $core(v)$

and BC score g_v of node v is greater than the core score $core(i)$ and BC score g_i of node i in the network. The steps for the rewiring operation is presented in Algorithm 1.

Algorithm 1. Betweenness Centrality and Core Periphery (BCCP) based rewiring strategy

---

1: **Input:** Initial Network $(G(\mathcal{V}, \mathcal{E}))$, BC (q), fraction of rewired links r_f.
2: **Output:** Rewired Network (G').
3: **Parameters:** $core[N], count = 0, RL = 0.$
4: $core \leftarrow core\_number(G)$. // $core\_number$ returns K-core score of the nodes in G.
5: $RL \leftarrow r_f \times E$.
6: **while** $count < RL$ **do**
7:     Remove a link e_{ij} randomly.
8:     Select a node v randomly in G.
9:     **if** $core[v] > core[i]$ AND $g_v > g_i$ **then**
10:         Add a link e_{iv}.
11:         $count \leftarrow count + 1$.
12:     **end if**
13: **end while**
    return G'

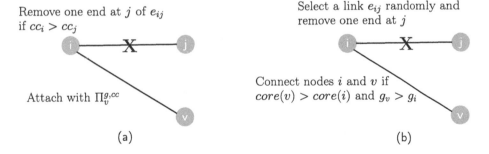

(a)   (b)

Fig. 1. Efficient rewiring strategies based on some statistical parameters; (a) Clustering Coefficient and Betweenness Centrality based strategy (CCBC) and (b) Betweennness Centrality and Core Periphery based rewiring strategy (BCCP).

4.2 Clustering Coefficient and Betweenness Centrality (CCBC) Based Rewiring Strategy

The **CCBC** rewiring strategy is a combination of clustering coefficient and betweenness centrality. In CCBC rewiring strategy, a link, e_{ij} is chosen randomly. The end nodes of the link e_{ij} is node i and node j. The node i removes connection from node j if the clustering coefficient (cc) of node i is greater than node j. The first node establishes a new connection with a new node k by preferring node with higher degree, cc and betweenness centrality (g). In Fig. 1(b), the rewiring operation using CCBC strategy is depicted. A node with high between-ness centrality (BC) will be appearing in user's route than the node with lower BC. Apart from that, a node with high clustering coefficient score is more connected to neighbors which makes the network more robust. Hence, a node with high BC, degree and clustering coefficient score is preferred for a new connection after the rewiring process. The probability, $\Pi_v^{g,cc}$ is defined for the selection of nodes v after rewiring operation. The probability $\Pi_v^{g,cc}$ that the node i to attach with node v can be expressed as,

$$\Pi_v^{g,cc} = \frac{1}{N(N-1)} k_v \times cc_v \times g_v \tag{1}$$

where, k_v is degree of node v, cc_v is clustering coefficient of node v and g_v is BC of node v. The detailed description is presented in Algorithm 2.

Algorithm 2. Clustering coefficient and betweenness (CCBC) centrality based rewiring strategy

---
1: **Input:** Initial Network $(G(\mathcal{V}, \mathcal{E}))$, cc, fraction of rewired links r_f, BC g.
2: **Output:** Rewired Network (G').
3: **Parameters:** $count = 0, RL = 0, avg\_score = 0$.
4: $RL \leftarrow r_f \times E$.
5: **while** $count < RL$ **do**
6:     $f \leftarrow 1$
7:     **while** $f == 1$ **do**
8:         Select a link e_{ij} randomly.
9:         **if** $cc_j < cc_j$ **then**
10:            Remove the link e_{ij}.
11:            $f \leftarrow 0$
12:        **end if**
13:    **end while**
14:    $flag \leftarrow 1$
15:    **while** $flag == 1$ **do**
16:        Select a node v randomly in G.
17:        $\Pi_v^{g,cc} \leftarrow k_v \times cc_v \times g_v$
18:        $avg\_score \leftarrow \frac{\sum_u k_u}{N} \times \frac{\sum_u cc_u}{N} \times \frac{\sum_u g_u}{N}$
19:        **if** $\Pi_v^{g,cc} > avg\_score$ **then**
20:            Add a link e_{iv}.
21:            $count \leftarrow count + 1$.
22:            $flag \leftarrow 0$
23:        **end if**
24:    **end while**
25: **end while**
    return G'

---

5 Results

We used three different real-world data sets and evaluated the value of five different network parameters as performance indicator of the proposed algorithms. The performance of the network is measured by evaluating five parameters; degree-degree correlation $corr$, clustering coefficient cc, entropy S, average rich-club coefficient RCC and giant component size GCC. Some links are removed from the network due to the link attack. After the network attack, $E \times r_f$ links are rewired in the network where, r_f is rewiring fractions. The removal fraction and the rewiring fraction is kept same. The r_f and removal fractions are ranging from 0.05 to 0.4 of links of the network. The data sets are Chesapeake [14], Dolphins [17] and Polbooks [22]. The information about each data set is provided in Table 1.

Table 1. Experimental setup

Network	Parameters
Chesapeake	$N = 39$, $E = 170$
Polbook	$N = 105$, $E = 441$
Dolphins	$N = 62$, $E = 159$

The network robustness of Chesapeake data set is evaluated under link attack by evaluating multiple network parameters (in Fig. 2, and Fig. 3). Initially, before the network attack, the scores of all the parameters are higher. After the network attack, some of the links removed from the network and all the parameter scores except $corr$ score got decreased. As the correlation score depends on the tendency of one node to connect with another node in the network hence, it may increase or decrease based on the type of the network and tendency of the nodes in the network.

In Fig. 2, random rewiring and CCBC strategies are compared for different network parameters. The correlation score $corr$ of the rewiring strategies are higher than the initial network for most of the r_fs. The cc score evaluated the network clustering. Higher the network clustering, higher the network robustness against attacks. The RCC score shows connectivity among the larger degree nodes. If larger degree nodes are densely connected then it signifies higher score of RCC than the smaller degree nodes. For different r_fs, the proposed CCBC approach provides higher value of cc and RCC scores than random rewiring approach. Therefore, it signifies that the proposed CCBC approach makes the network more robust than random rewiring approach. The entropy S and giant component size, GCC obtained through random rewiring approach is higher than the CCBC approach. The simulation is averaged over 20 iterations. In Fig. 3, random rewiring and BCCP strategies are compared for different network parameters. The cc and RCC scores obtained through BCCP strategy is higher than the random rewiring approach. The entropy S obtained through random and BCCP rewiring strategies are approx. same. The GCC score obtained through BCCP strategy is more than or equal to random rewiring strategy. Therefore, we can say that the proposed BCCP strategy is performing better than the random strategy for maintaining the network robustness after attack on Chesapeake data set. The simulation is averaged over 20 iterations.

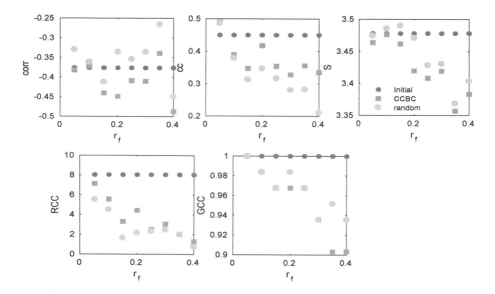

Fig. 2. Study of the network parameters before and after the CCBC rewiring operation for Chesapeake data set

In Fig. 4 and Fig. 5, the network robustness of Dolphins data set is evaluated under link attack. The fraction of removal of links and rewiring fractions (r_f) are kept the same. The r_f and removal fractions are ranging from 0.05 to 0.4 of links of the network. The performance of the network is measured by evaluating five previously discussed parameters. The clustering coefficient cc score and the RCC of the network decreases after the network attack.Both the scores depend on the total number of connection.

In Fig. 4, BCCP rewiring strategy is compared with random approach fro Dolphins data set. The cc and the RCC score obtained after the BCCP rewiring operation are always higher than the random approach. The network is fully connected even after the removal of 40% of the link. The simulation is averaged over 20 iterations.

In Fig. 5, CCBC rewiring strategy is compared with random approach fro Dolphins data set. The cc and the RCC score obtained after the CCBC rewiring operation are always higher than the random approach. The entropy score S of the network rewired using CCBC is always lower than the random approach. The simulation is averaged over 20 iterations.

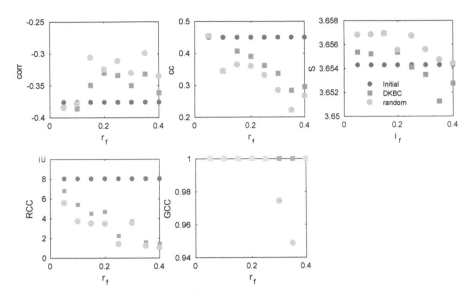

Fig. 3. Study of the network parameters before and after the BCCP rewiring operation for Chesapeake data set

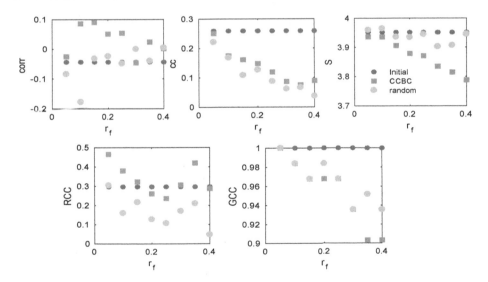

Fig. 4. Study of the network parameters before and after the CCBC rewiring operation for Dolphins data set

In Fig. 6 and Fig. 7, the network robustness of Polbook data set is evaluated under link attack. The fraction of removal of links and rewiring fractions (r_f) are kept the same. The r_f and removal fractions are ranging from 0.05 to 0.4 of

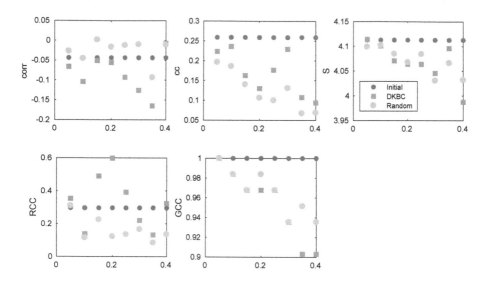

Fig. 5. Study of the network parameters before and after the BCCP rewiring operation for Dolphins data set

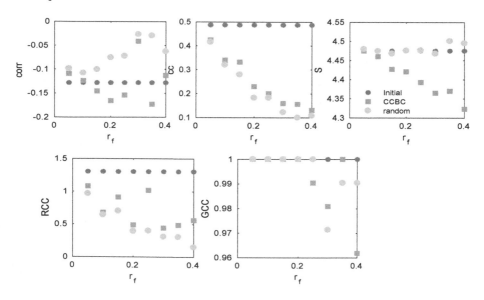

Fig. 6. Study of the network parameters before and after the CCBC rewiring operation for Polbooks data set

links of the network. The performance of the network is measured by evaluating five discussed parameters.

In Fig. 6, the network robustness of Polbook data set is evaluated using BCCP rewiring strategy after the link attack. Initially, before the network attack, the scores of cc, GCC and S are higher than the network after the attack. The cc

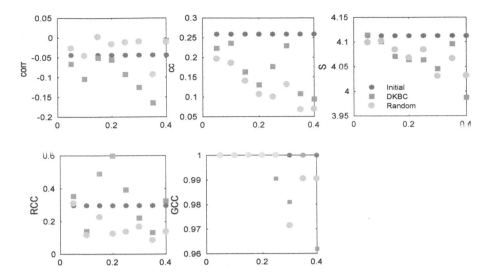

Fig. 7. Study of the network parameters before and after the BCCP rewiring operation for Polbooks data set

score and the RCC of the network after the rewiring operation are always higher than the random approach. The simulation is averaged over 20 iterations.

In Fig. 7, the network robustness of Polbook data set is evaluated using CCBC rewiring strategy after the link attack. Initially, before the network attack, the scores of cc, GCC and S are higher than the network after the attack. The cc score and the RCC of the network after the rewiring operation are always higher than the random approach. The simulation is averaged over 20 iterations.

6   Conclusions

In this paper, we have studied the network performance under random link attacks. The performance of different data sets is studied by evaluating different robustness parameters under proposed probabilistic rewiring strategies; BCCP and CCBC. We have compared the methods with a random rewiring strategy by evaluating statistical parameters. From the generated results it can be concluded that the network is more clustered and contains a larger amount of rich clubs. In some networks, the giant component size is also larger than the random rewiring strategies.

In the future, the work can be extended by considering some machine learning approaches in the rewiring operation. Other large data sets can be considered for generalizing the performance of complex networks.

References

1. Albert, R., Jeong, H., Barabási, A.L.: Error and attack tolerance of complex networks. Nature **406**(6794), 378–382 (2000)

2. Bhusal, N., Abdelmalak, M., Kamruzzaman, M., Benidris, M.: Power system resilience: Current practices, challenges, and future directions. IEEE Access **8**, 18064–18086 (2020)
3. Chen, Z., Wu, J., Rong, Z., Chi, K.T.: Optimal topologies for maximizing network transmission capacity. Physica A Stat. Mech. Appl. **495**, 191–201 (2018)
4. Crucitti, P., Latora, V., Marchiori, M.: Model for cascading failures in complex networks. Physic. Rev. E **69**(4), 045104 (2004)
5. Dorogovtsev, S.N., Mendes, J.F.: Evolution of networks: from biological nets to the Internet and WWW. OUP Oxford (2013)
6. Fronczak, P.: Theoretical approach and impact of correlations on the critical packet generation rate in traffic dynamics on complex networks. European Physic. J. B **85**(10), 1–6 (2012)
7. Geng, H., Cao, M., Guo, C., Peng, C., Du, S., Yuan, J.: Global disassortative rewiring strategy for enhancing the robustness of scale-free networks against localized attack. Physic. Rev. E **103**(2), 022313 (2021)
8. Holme, P., Kim, B.J., Yoon, C.N., Han, S.K.: Attack vulnerability of complex networks. Physic. Rev. E **65**(5), 056109 (2002)
9. Kumar, R., Kumari, S., Bala, M.: Quantum mechanical model of information sharing in social networks. Soc. Netw. Anal. Mining **11**(1), 1–12 (2021)
10. Kumari, S., Kumar, R., Kadry, S., Namasudra, S., Taniar, D.: Maintainable stochastic communication network reliability within tolerable packet error rate. Comput. Commun. **178**, 161–168 (2021)
11. Kumari, S., Saroha, A., Singh, A.: Efficient edge rewiring strategies for enhancement in network capacity. Physic. A Stat. Mech. Appl. **545**, 123552 (2020)
12. Kumari, S., Singh, A.: Time-varying network modeling and its optimal routing strategy. Adv. Compl. Syst. **21**(02), 1850006 (2018)
13. Kumari, S., Yadav, R.J., Namasudra, S., Hsu, C.H.: Intelligent deception techniques against adversarial attack on the industrial system. Int. J. Intell. Syst. **36**(5), 2412–2437 (2021)
14. Kunegis, J.: Konect: the koblenz network collection. In: Proceedings of the 22nd International Conference on World Wide Web, pp. 1343–1350 (2013)
15. Liang, B., Yan-Dong, X., Lv-Lin, H., Song-Yang, L.: Smart rewiring: Improving network robustness faster. Chin. Physics Lett. **32**(7), 078901 (2015)
16. Louzada, V.H., Daolio, F., Herrmann, H.J., Tomassini, M.: Smart rewiring for network robustness. J. Complex Netw. **1**(2), 150–159 (2013)
17. Lusseau, D., Schneider, K., Boisseau, O.J., Haase, P., Slooten, E., Dawson, S.M.: The bottlenose dolphin community of doubtful sound features a large proportion of long-lasting associations. Behav. Ecol. Sociobiol. **54**(4), 396–405 (2003)
18. Motter, A.E., Lai, Y.C.: Cascade-based attacks on complex networks. Physic. Rev. E **66**(6), 065102 (2002)
19. Newman, M.E.: Mixing patterns in networks. Physic. Rev. E **67**(2), 026126 (2003)
20. Paterson, J., Ombuki-Berman, B.: A hybrid approach to network robustness optimization using edge rewiring and edge addition. In: 2020 IEEE International Conference on Systems, Man, and Cybernetics (SMC), pp. 4051–4057. IEEE (2020)
21. Rombach, P., Porter, M.A., Fowler, J.H., Mucha, P.J.: Core-periphery structure in networks (revisited). SIAM Rev. **59**(3), 619–646 (2017)
22. Rossi, R.A., Ahmed, N.K.: The network data repository with interactive graph analytics and visualization. In: AAAI (2015). networkrepository.com
23. Singh, A., Nath Singh, Y.: Rumor dynamics in weighted scale-free networks with degree correlations. J. Complex Netw. **3**(3), 450–468 (2015)

24. Taylor, M.A., D'Este, G.M.: Transport network vulnerability: a method for diagnosis of critical locations in transport infrastructure systems. In: Critical Infrastructure, pp. 9–30. Springer (2007)
25. Xiao, S., Xiao, G., Cheng, T.H.: Robustness of complex communication networks under rewiring operations. In: 2006 10th IEEE Singapore International Conference on Communication Systems, pp. 1–5. IEEE (2006)

A Partcle Swarm Optimization Based Approach for Filter Pruning in Convolution Neural Network for Tomato Leaf Disease Classification

Mohit Agarwal[1]([✉]), Suneet Kumar Gupta[1], Deepak Garg[1], and Mohammad Monirujjaman Khan[2]

[1] Bennett University, Greater Noida 201310, India
deepak.garg@bennett.edu.in
[2] Northsouth University, Bashundhara, Dhaka 1229, Bangladesh
monirujjaman.khan@northsouth.edu

Abstract. Since, plant diseases are clearly visible in leaf so, leaves images can be easily used for detection of the disease. Recent research work shows that several machine learning (ML) and deep learning based methods can be used for the classification of images into various classes. Hence in this paper a comparison has been made between machine learning, proposed convolution neural network (CNN) and pre-trained models for the classification of tomato diseases. However, the proposed CNN based model has also been compressed particle swarm optimization based approach so that model can be deployed on devices having less computation power and storage space. For training the model tomato leaf images have been taken from PlantVillage dataset. In PlantVillage dataset, there are 39 classes for various crop but we have used data related to Tomato crop. In tomato crop dataset, there are nine diseased and 1 healthy class. The best accuracy of model using proposed CNN is 98.4% and 94.9% using k-NN tradional ML method. Pre-trained models gives best accuracy of 93.5% using VGG16. The pre-trained CNN models were compressed using Particle Swarm Optimization technique and a compression of around 60% was obtained on VGG16 model size without loss in accuracy. Similarly, the proposed CNN model has also been compressed by 40% with a drop in accuracy of less than 1%.

Keywords: Convolution neural network · Deep learning · Tomato leaf disease · Machine learning

1 Introduction

Plant disease identification can be very helpful for the farmers and a country's economy by preventing the loss of crops. With introduction of image processing and deep learning methods [1] plant development can be easily monitored to ensure timely treatment of crops which is a neccessity for good growth.

© Springer Nature Switzerland AG 2022
D. Garg et al. (Eds.): IACC 2021, CCIS 1528, pp. 646–659, 2022.
https://doi.org/10.1007/978-3-030-95502-1_49

Several recent research papers explain the usage of CNN and ML-based methods for detecting plant disease [2–8]. Even the diseased part of images is being successfully segmented using CNN models such as SegNet, UNet and FCN [9,10]. The similar research can be applied to medical domain also which may found in [11–13] and its reference.

Rumpf et al. [14] have used sugar beet root leaf images and SVM for detecting 3 type of diseases. Mokhtar et al. [15] have also done binary classification of tomato diseases using SVM to get an accuracy of 02%. Johannes et al. [16] have detected 3 type of wheat diseases using its leaf images and Naive Bayes ML method.

Transfer learning using pre-trained models have also been widely used by researchers for crop disease identificaiton. Mohanty et al. [17] have used pre-trained models namely AlexNet [18] and GoogLeNet [19] for telling the crop name and its disease from its leaf image. Authors have trained the model using PlantVillage dataset [20]. Ferentinos [21] have used VGG and AlexNet for classifying a superset of PlantVillage dataset having 58 classes. Authors report an accuracy of 99.35% on same dataset but very low accuracy on different dataset.

Several researchers have also used CNN design from scratch but accuracy mentioned is not high [22–24]. Wang et al. [22] have used 4 classes of Apple leaf images and trained a CNN of 2 to 10 convolution layers and mentioned best accuracy of 79.3% using 8 convolution layer CNN.

Xu et al. [25] have described a process of light weight CNN construction by distillation process of existing network rather than compressing pre-trained CNN. The distillation process includes parameter compression, network structure acceleration, etc. He et al. [26] have used reinforcement learning for model compression which works without any human intervention and is faster and better than hand crafted features for model compression.

The main contributions of this article can be summarized as below:

- The research describes detection of tomato disease from leaf images using deep learning, transfer learning and machine learning.
- The research also explains process of CNN compression using Particle Swarm Optimization (PSO).
- A multiobjective fitness function was also created for PSO selection process.
- The extensive simulation results have shown the efficacy of proposed methods over existing classification methods.

The rest of article is organized as follows: Sect. 2 provides details of tomato dataset and proposed CNN architecture with 8 hidden layers. Section 3 gives detailed experimental results, after this Sect. 4 explains the process of CNN compression using Particle Swarm Optimization. Finally Sect. 5 provides a brief conclusion to the research findings.

2   Materials and Methods

2.1   Dataset

The dataset of tomato was prepared using leaf images from PlantVillage dataset [27]. The sample images of tomato dataset are shown in Fig. 1. Since the number of training sample vary from 200 to 4000 the images were augmented for classes with less samples and some images were removed from classes with more images to make them uniformly 1400 in all classes. This process was essential to prevent bias for any class. The augmentation was carried out by rotating the images by 90°, 180° or 270° and also flipping the images vertically and horizontally. In addition a random brightness change was also applied on random width of images on augmented images to create more realistic images (refer Fig. 2).

Fig. 1. Sample images of tomato plant diseases, a) Bacterial spot, b) Early blight, c) healthy, d) Late blight, e) Leaf Mold, f) Septoria leaf spot, g) Two-spotted spider mite, h) Target Spot, i) Tomato mosaic virus, j) Yellow Leaf Curl Virus

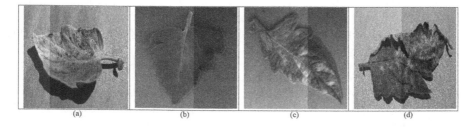

Fig. 2. Applying random brightness change over random width of images for augmentation as in [7]

2.2   Proposed Model

The proposed CNN was comprised of 3 convolution layers with 32, 16 and 8 filters of size 3 × 3. After each convolution layer a max-pooling layer was added of kernel size 2 × 2 to reduce the size of input signal. After these layers a Flatten layer was present and it converted 2-D signal to 1-D. It was followed by a Dense layer of 128 nodes and then an output softmax layer of 10 nodes. The images were resized to 128 × 128 before passing to CNN. The details of proposed model is given in Table 1 and shown diagrammatically in Fig. 3.

Table 1. Proposed CNN architecture.

Layer (type)	Input size	Output size
Conv2d	128 × 128 × 3	126 × 126 × 32
Maxpool	126 × 126 × 32	63 × 63 × 32
Conv2d	63 × 63 × 32	61 × 61 × 16
Maxpool	61 × 61 × 16	30 × 30 × 16
Conv2d	30 × 30 × 16	28 × 28 × 8
Maxpool	28 × 28 × 8	14 × 14 × 8
Flatten	14 × 14 × 8	1568
Dense	1568	128
Dropout	128	128
Dense	128	10

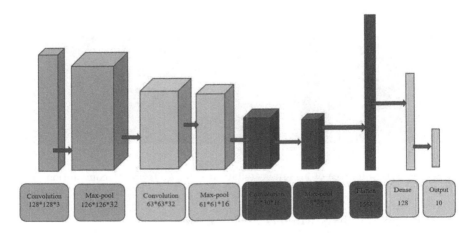

Fig. 3. Pictorial representation of proposed CNN diagram

The hyperparameters used in CNN are detailed in Table 2.

Table 2. Hyper parameters for proposed CNN model.

Hyperparameter	Description
No. of convolution layer	3
No. of max-pool layer	3
Drop out rate	.5
Network weight initialization	Glorot uniform
Activation function	Relu
Learning rate	0.001
Momentum	0.999
Number of epoch	5000
Batch size	64

3   Experimental Results

The experiments were performed on NVIDIA DGX v100 machine. The NVIDIA machine is equipped with 40600 CUDA cores, 5120 tensor cores, 128 GB RAM and 1000 TFLOPS speed. On executing the proposed model on prepared dataset the test accuracy was around 96.8%. After augmenting images as in Fig. 2 the accuracy was enhanced to 98.4%.

The activation images of 1st, 2nd and 3rd convolution layers are shown in Figs. 4, 5 and 6. The figure shows how various features of image such as edges, corners, texture etc. are passed through hidden layers and gets converted into correct output prediction at output layer.

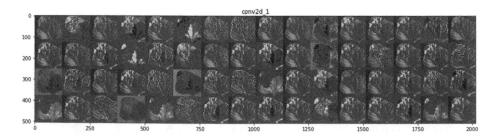

Fig. 4. Activation images of a sample tomato leaf image from 1st convolution layer.

3.1   Pre-trained CNN Models Performance

The 3 pre-trained models used for comparison of performance were chosen as VGG16, InceptionV3, and MobileNet. The comparison of accuracy for three models shows that the best accuracy of 93.5% could be obtained using VGG16 which was less than proposed model as seen in Fig. 7.

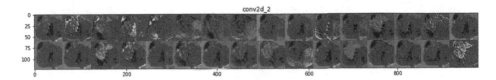

Fig. 5. Activation images of a sample tomato leaf image from 2nd convolution layer

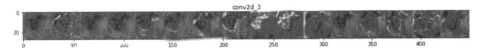

Fig. 6. Activation images of a sample tomato leaf image from 3rd convolution layer.

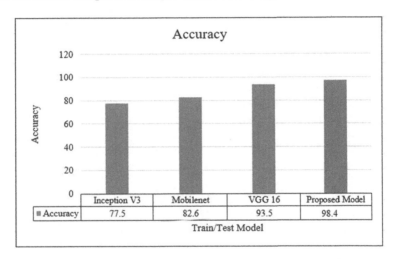

	Inception V3	Mobilenet	VGG 16	Proposed Model
■ Accuracy	77.5	82.6	93.5	98.4

Fig. 7. Activation images of a sample tomato leaf image from 3rd convolution layer.

3.2 Performance of Machine Learning Methods

The ML classifiers used for performance comparison were as below:

- Support Vector Machine (SVM): In this method a hyperplane is found that maximizes the distance between postive and negative samples.
- Decision Tree: These are trees created based on input features using if-then-else decision rules. The more its depth is assumed the more complex rules will be formed to fit train data more accurately.
- Logistic Regression (LR): These are similar to single layer neural networks and learning is done based on gradient descent.
- Naive Bayes: This calculates a probability of class y given a feature vector x by using the probability of each feature vector element given class y.
- k-Nearest Neighbours(k-NN): Input feature vector is decided based on weighted distance of features from k nearest neighbours.

The summary of results of different Machine Learning classifers with different combination of three features: Haralick, Hu-moments and HSV Historgram is given in Table 3.

Table 3. Accuracy comparison with ML models.

Features	Model	True positive	False positive	True negative	False negative	Accuracy (%)	F1-score
Haralick Hu-features HSV LBP	SVM	99	1	621	279	72	0.4142
	Decision Tree	94	6	640	260	73.4	0.4140
	LR	99	1	798	102	89.7	0.6578
	k-NN	100	0	841	59	94.1	0.7722
	Naïve Bayes	1	99	303	597	30.4	0.0028
Haralick Hu-features HSV	SVM	96	4	632	268	72.8	0.4137
	Decision Tree	90	10	661	239	75.1	0.4195
	LR	100	0	797	103	89.7	0.6600
	k-NN	100	0	849	51	**94.9**	0.7968
	Naïve Bayes	1	99	303	597	30.4	0.0028
Haralick Hu-features	SVM	84	16	293	607	37.7	0.2123
	Decision Tree	79	21	176	724	25.5	0.1749
	LR	86	14	267	633	35.3	0.2100
	k-NN	87	13	307	593	39.4	0.2230
	Naïve Bayes	100	0	200	700	30	0.2222
Hu-features HSV	SVM	89	11	593	307	68.2	0.3588
	Decision Tree	43	57	659	241	70.2	0.2239
	LR	98	2	785	115	88.3	0.6261
	k-NN	100	0	837	63	93.7	0.7604
	Naïve Bayes	91	9	303	597	39.4	0.2309
	CNN baed model	100	0	884	16	**98.4**	**0.9259**

The graphical representation of ML classifiers Specificity and is given in Fig. 8. The ROC curve for the ML models is given in Fig. 9.

4 CNN Model Compression

Particle Swarm Optimization (PSO) algorithm was developed by Eberhart and Kennedy in 1995 [28] and is inspired from natural biology which mimics birds flocking.

In PSO process a certain number of initial particle are assigned random position in form of a vector with values 0 and 1. The process of vector creation can be given by Algorithm 1.

Here position vector length n is equal to the number of hidden neurons in a CNN. As algorithm progresses the particles update their position based on their

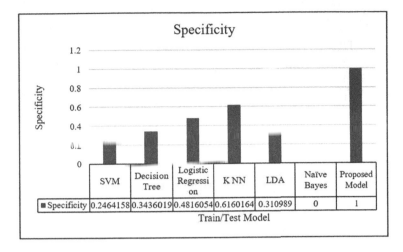

Fig. 8. Comparison of Specificity of different ML classifiers.

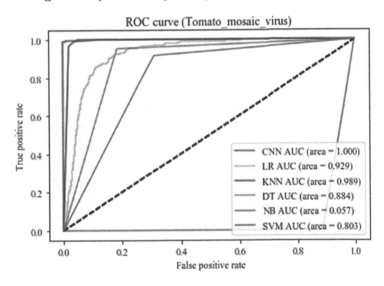

Fig. 9. ROC curves for all ML models with tomato mosaic virus as positive class [7].

Algorithm 1. Generation of particle vector

1: **procedure** INITVECTORS
2:     **for** $i \leftarrow 0$ *to* $n - 1$ **do**
3:         $V[i] = random()\%2$ ▷ random() generates a random positive number

---

velocity (Eq. (1)). The velocity in each iteration is calculated using previous iteration velocity and particle best position global best position (Eq. (2)).

$$x_{l+1}^n = x_l^n + v_{l+1}^n \qquad (1)$$

$$v_{l+1}^n = w_l \times v_l^n + c_1 \times r_1 \times (p_l^n - x_l^n) + c_2 \times r_2 \times (p_l^g - x_l^n) \qquad (2)$$

Here x_l^n represents the position of the nth particle in l^{th} iteration. v_l^n represents particles velocity, p_l^n represents best individual particle position, p_k^g represents best swarm position. c_1, c_2 are cognitive and social parameters. r_1, r_2 are random numbers between 0 and 1. w_l is the inertia weight component. The change in the velocity pictorially is given in Fig. 10. The flow chart of CNN model compression using PSO is given Fig. 11.

Fig. 10. Pictorial representation change in velocity.

Thus starting with trained CNN model PSO was applied on it and based on multiobjective fitness criteria of Specificity and compressed nodes ratio, the models were compressed. The model tries to maximize both the objectives to get best performance and maximum compression. The fitness criteria is given by Eqs. (3) and (4).

$$Maximize(X) = \lambda_1 \times Specificity + \lambda_2 \times \left(\frac{original\ nodes}{compressed\ nodes} \right) \qquad (3)$$

$$\lambda_1 + \lambda_2 = 1 \qquad (4)$$

The equation for Specificity is given in Eq. (5).

$$Specificity = \frac{TN}{TN + FP} \qquad (5)$$

Here TN means true negative and FP means false positive.

Here different combinations of λ_1 and λ_2 were taken such as 0.25 and 0.75 for more emphasis on compression ratio or 0.75 and 0.25 for more emphasis on performance of compressed model.

The comparison of original and final model size and accuracy is given in Table 4.

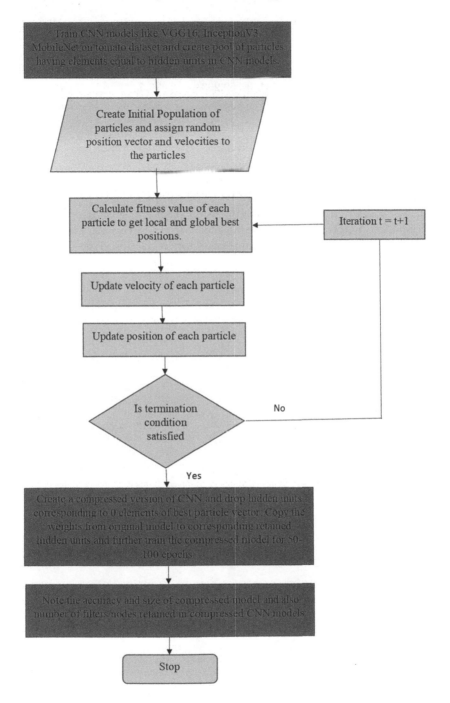

Fig. 11. Pictorial representation of CNN compression using PSO.

Table 4. Comparison of compressed size and model accuracy using PSO.

Model	Original size (KB)	Compressed size (KB)	Original accuracy (%)	Final accuracy (%)
Inception V3	163,734	69,233	77.5	76.4
MobileNet	82,498	33,289	82.6	82.1
VGG16	94,452	37,383	93.5	92.28
Compressed CNN Model	1,696	937	98.4	97.32

The compression was done iteratively for 10 compression steps and specificity at each step was noted. The plot of compression steps and specificity for Inception V3, MobileNet, VGG16 and proposed model is given in Fig. 12. The comparison of hidden units before and after compression for VGG16 is given in Fig. 13.

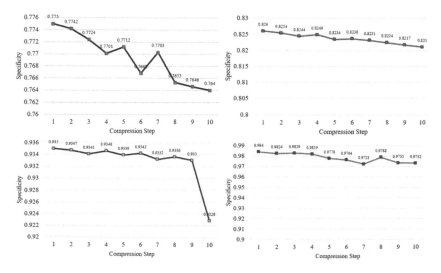

Fig. 12. Comparison of performance with compression steps for InceptionV3, MobileNet, VGG16, CNN.

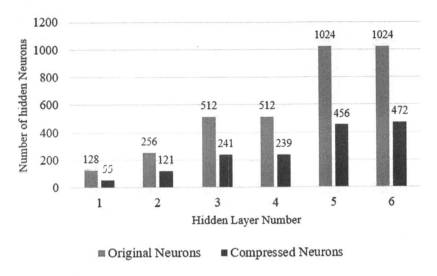

Fig. 13. Comparison of hidden neurons before and after compression for VGG16.

5   Conclusion

The proposed work shows an optimized way of classifying tomato leaf diseases. A comparison of proposed model with traditional ML classifiers and pre-trained models shows the better performance of proposed model. The best accuracy using proposed model is 98.4%. The images were taken from PlantVillage dataset and since there were varying number of images in each class hence they were augmented to make them uniform in all classes. This helped to avoid class bias and enhance performance. The model compression of pre-trained models was also done using Particle Swarm Optimization (PSO) to compress these models and make them ready to be deployed on tiny edge devices. A compression of around 60% could be obtained on VGG16 CNN model.

References

1. Ebrahimi, M.A., Khoshtaghaza, M.H., Minaei, S., Jamshidi, B.: Vision-based pest detection based on SVM classification method. Comput. Electron. Agricult. **137**, 52–58 (2017)
2. Agarwal, M., Singh, A., Arjaria, S., Sinha, A., Gupta, S.: Toled: tomato leaf disease detection using convolution neural network. Procedia Comput. Sci. **167**, 293–301 (2020)
3. Agarwal, M., Gupta, S.K., Biswas, K.K.: Grape disease identification using convolution neural network. In: 2019 23rd International Computer Science and Engineering Conference (ICSEC), pp. 224–229. IEEE (2019)
4. Agarwal, M., Kaliyar, R.K., Singal, G., Gupta, S.K.: Fcnn-lda: a faster convolution neural network model for leaf disease identification on apple's leaf dataset. In: 2019 12th International Conference on Information & Communication Technology and System (ICTS), pp. 246–251. IEEE (2019)

5. Agarwal, M., Sinha, A., Gupta, S.K., Mishra, D., Mishra, R.: Potato crop disease classification using convolutional neural network. In: Somani, A.K., Shekhawat, R.S., Mundra, A., Srivastava, S., Verma, V.K. (eds.) Smart Systems and IoT: Innovations in Computing. SIST, vol. 141, pp. 391–400. Springer, Singapore (2020). https://doi.org/10.1007/978-981-13-8406-6_37

6. Agarwal, M., Bohat, V.K., Ansari, M.D., Sinha, A., Gupta, S.K., Garg, D.: A convolution neural network based approach to detect the disease in corn crop. In: 2019 IEEE 9th International Conference on Advanced Computing (IACC), pp. 176–181. IEEE (2019)

7. Agarwal, M., Gupta, S.K., Biswas, K.K.: Development of efficient CNN model for tomato crop disease identification. Sustain. Comput. Inform. Syst. **28**, 100407 (2020)

8. Agarwal, M., Gupta, S., Biswas, K.K.: A new conv2d model with modified RELU activation function for identification of disease type and severity in cucumber plant. Sustain. Comput. Inform. Syst. **30**, 100473 (2021)

9. Agarwal, M., Gupta, S.K., Biswas, K.K.: A compressed and accelerated SegNet fo plant leaf disease segmentation: a differential evolution based approach. In: Karlapalem, K., Cheng, H., Ramakrishnan, N., Agrawal, R.K., Reddy, P.K., Srivastava, J., Chakraborty, T. (eds.) PAKDD 2021. LNCS (LNAI), vol. 12714, pp. 272–284. Springer, Cham (2021). https://doi.org/10.1007/978-3-030-75768-7_22

10. Agarwal, M., Gupta, S.K., Biswas, K.K.: Plant leaf disease segmentation using compressed UNet architecture. In: Gupta, M., Ramakrishnan, G. (eds.) PAKDD 2021. LNCS (LNAI), vol. 12705, pp. 9–14. Springer, Cham (2021). https://doi.org/10.1007/978-3-030-75015-2_2

11. Agarwal, M., et al.: Wilson disease tissue classification and characterization using seven artificial intelligence models embedded with 3d optimization paradigm on a weak training brain magnetic resonance imaging datasets: a supercomputer application. Med. Biol. Eng. Comput. **59**(3), 511–533 (2021)

12. Agarwal, M., et al.: A novel block imaging technique using nine artificial intelligence models for covid-19 disease classification, characterization and severity measurement in lung computed tomography scans on an italian cohort. J. Med. Syst. **45**(3), 1–30 (2021)

13. Saba, L., et al.: Six artificial intelligence paradigms for tissue characterisation and classification of non-covid-19 pneumonia against covid-19 pneumonia in computed tomography lungs. Int. J. Comput. Assist. Radiol. Surg. **16**(3), 423–434 (2021)

14. Rumpf, T., Mahlein, A.-K., Steiner, U., Oerke, E.-C., Dehne, H.-W., Plümer, L.: Early detection and classification of plant diseases with support vector machines based on hyperspectral reflectance. Comput. Electron. Agricult. **74**(1), 91–99 (2010)

15. Mokhtar, U., Ali, M.A.S., Hassanien, A.E., Hefny, H.: Identifying two of tomatoes leaf viruses using support vector machine. In: Mandal, J.K., Satapathy, S.C., Sanyal, M.K., Sarkar, P.P., Mukhopadhyay, A. (eds.) Information Systems Design and Intelligent Applications. AISC, vol. 339, pp. 771–782. Springer, New Delhi (2015). https://doi.org/10.1007/978-81-322-2250-7_77

16. Johannes, A., et al.: Automatic plant disease diagnosis using mobile capture devices, applied on a wheat use case. Comput. Electron. Agricult. **138**, 200–209 (2017)

17. Mohanty, S.P., Hughes, D.P., Salathé, M.: Using deep learning for image-based plant disease detection. Front. Plant Sci. **7**, 1419 (2016)

18. Krizhevsky, A., Sutskever, I., Hinton, G.E.: Imagenet classification with deep convolutional neural networks. In: Advances in Neural Information Processing Systems, pp. 1097–1105 (2012)
19. Szegedy, C., et al.: Going deeper with convolutions. In: Proceedings of the IEEE Conference on Computer Vision and Pattern Recognition, pp. 1–9 (2015)
20. Hughes, D., Salathé, M., et al.: An open access repository of images on plant health to enable the development of mobile disease diagnostics. arXiv preprint arXiv:1511.08060 (2015)
21. Ferentinos, K.P.: Deep learning models for plant disease detection and diagnosis. Comput. Electron. Agricult. **145**, 311–318 (2018)
22. Wang, G., Sun, Y., Wang, J.: Automatic image-based plant disease severity estimation using deep learning. Comput. Intell. Neurosci. **2017** (2017)
23. Khamparia, A., Singh, A., Luhach, A.K., Pandey, B., Pandey, D.K.: Classification and identification of primitive kharif crops using supervised deep convolutional networks. Sustain. Comput. Informat. Syst. (2019)
24. Gensheng, H., Yang, X., Zhang, Y., Wan, M.: Identification of tea leaf diseases by using an improved deep convolutional neural network. Sustain. Comput. Inform. Syst. **24**, 100353 (2019)
25. Ting-Bing, X., Yang, P., Zhang, X.-Y., Liu, C.-L.: Lightweightnet: toward fast and lightweight convolutional neural networks via architecture distillation. Pattern Recogn. **88**, 272–284 (2019)
26. He, Y., Lin, J., Liu, Z., Wang, H., Li, L.-J., Han, S.: AMC: automl for model compression and acceleration on mobile devices. In: Proceedings of the European Conference on Computer Vision (ECCV), pp. 784–800 (2018)
27. Hughes, D., Salathé, M., et al. An open access repository of images on plant health to enable the development of mobile disease diagnostics. arXiv preprint arXiv:1511.08060 (2015)
28. Eberhart, R., Kennedy, J.: Particle swarm optimization. In: Proceedings of the IEEE International Conference on Neural Networks, vol. 4, pp. 1942–1948 (1995)

Data Breach in Social Networks Using Machine Learning

Monalisa Mahapatra[1], Naman Gupta[1], Riti Kushwaha[2(✉)],
and Gaurav Singal[3]

[1] Business Analytics, Bennett University, Greater Noida, India
[2] Bennett University, Greater Noida, India
[3] Netaji Subhas University of Technology, Delhi, India

Abstract. There is a huge concern over privacy of data and security breaches in the upcoming area pertinent to digital services. There is a phenomenal increase in social media sites so as the increase in the volume of data. Therefore, from the linguistic perspective, to understand and analyze the data has become a complex procedure. In this paper, the investigation is done on the information characteristics which are attributed to data breach messages, first we create a questionnaire to know the basic information about the purpose of using social media applications by various users and their awareness regarding the data breach through these applications and secondly, we tried to find out some meaningful insight out of the data collected to reach to some logical conclusion. A quite different pattern is followed by breach information diffusion in contrast to the conventional news channels where the related posts are subjected to wide attention on social media. The widely shared messages among the tech-savvy groups and the personnel involved in the studies related to security are the key factors. Researchers can mine down the grounded insights to the research questions by analyzing the messages in the field of linguistic and visual perspective over social media. This primary research has been done to analyze people's perception towards digitalization and how the risk of data breach has affected them in using some of the most widely used social media application.

Keywords: Security · Privacy · Social networks · Machine learning · Data breach

1 Introduction

In this fast-growing nation where technology is playing a boom at every sector. The Social media applications are playing a very important role not only in delivering messages but also creating a medium for creation or sharing of ideas, information, and expression in other forms via virtual communities and networks by Udita Joshi [1]. The way technology is advancing in the form of Artificial Intelligence, machine learning, neural networks it is enabling us to complete our tasks in less time with more productivity but with these abilities comes the risk which is slowly coming to surface with due pace of time by Surbhi Gupta [2]. Earlier if any paperwork was to be done people have to do a lot of research, study various theories and then conclude for either making

© Springer Nature Switzerland AG 2022
D. Garg et al. (Eds.): IACC 2021, CCIS 1528, pp. 660–670, 2022.
https://doi.org/10.1007/978-3-030-95502-1_50

a simple presentation or a financial report, everything was noted down on pen and paper. But maintaining everything in the papers was a difficult job for finding any information one may have to go through the entire pile of the whole work which was not only time-consuming but also frustrating and one the record becomes old it was very difficult to even trace it. Whereas technology is faster and more efficient than paper. People have started keeping everything starting from company's information to personal information everything is kept in the cloud system where one can browse anytime anywhere.

With this advancement comes the risk hacking. As the world is moving from traditional pen, paper towards digitalization similarly the risk has also shifted like earlier the paper works were being stolen by people now the data that is being stored have the risk of getting hacked by the hackers. And if for a moment if we keep the hacking part aside for a moment then also now a days the way technology has embedded into our lives it is very difficult to keep any information private, and to add cherry to the cake the social media applications have given the platform where this leak of information is even greater. These apps were created to help us to connect to the world, make new friends, communicate with people, share important information by just sitting at home, share talents and ideas with the rest of the world. But with due course of time some people have made these applications a medium of drawing information about others using them to do illegal activities. To be more specific these have been term as data breach.

Data breach is a fraudulent instance to steel or takeout the information without the prior knowledge or permission of the concerned owner. Whether it is a large organization or a small company, everybody may suffer from data breach. The data stolen may contain confidential information pertinent to trade secrets, customer's data, credit card numbers or matters related to national security. It can cause a serious damage to the reputation of a company due to professed betrayal of trust. This can additionally lead to financial losses should the related records be part of the information stolen. Some of the social media applications such as Facebook, WhatsApp, Instagram are some of the applications where people create their profile to connect with people and these are some of the applications where the risk of Data breach is very high. In this paper, we have created a questionnaire to conduct primary research to gather information regarding the way people use these social media apps and how aware they are with the chance of their information being shared or may be chance of getting public. We have concerned our focus mainly towards the most commonly use application across India that is WhatsApp where every information is private and with recent acquisition how it has affected people thought towards this social media application.

Finally, this paper organization is followed as, Sect. 2 introduces the existing work on similar problems of data breaching in the social networks. Next section introduces about various data breaching methods, process of conduction, current statistics, and data analysis. In Sect. 4, we have presented the results obtained over our own captured dataset showing the data breaches in social networks. In last Sect. 5, discuss the conclusion and future possibilities for this work.

2 Literature Review

With various studies being made on the rising issues of data breaches which are mainly happening through these social media applications. If one studies the paper on "Why managing social media is crucial in the event of a data breach" by Sprinklr [3] one can very well get an idea of how the current engagement of people in social media have such a risk of data breach. It has been noted that negative sentiment among people increases by around 35% whenever there is a data breach and particularly in retail business it increases by 42%. Almost around 75% of the Data Breach occur within the main 4 industries i.e., technology, government, healthcare, and finance. In the paper "Getting to Europe the WhatsApp Way" by RMMS [4], it has been shown how immigrants use these social media applications to know about the place and plan their journey accordingly.

A study made by them on what are the necessary items that can be found on every backpack interestingly apart from food, clothes smart phone was the common item found in everyone's backpack and on digging further it has been observed that WhatsApp was the social media application used for getting information and planning. From a paper on "Need for fulfilment and experiences in social media: A case on Facebook and WhatsApp" by Evangelos Karapanos, Pedro Teixeira, Ruben Gouveia [5] reports on a study of 494 users of WhatsApp and Facebook the findings were that in the case of tool's breach of offline social norms very unsatisfying experiences were found primarily, as well in the case of Facebook content fatigue and exposure to undesirable content. According to the research paper "WhatsApp Doc" by Donnchadh Martin O'Sullivan, Eoin O'Sullivan, Margaret O'Connor, Declan Lyons, John McManus [6] it has been very well reflected how the social media applications have taken an important place not only for making friends or connecting with friends across the world but messaging apps like WhatsApp have emerged as major part in healthcare industry for sharing information regarding patients and for taking major decisions. The broader rise of the smartphone in the broader society has resulted in increasing numbers of healthcare professionals informally introducing this technology to the workplace.

Based on the recent study on "A Social Network Analysis on Study on Data Breach Concerns over Social Media" by Naga Vemprala and Glenn Dietrich [7] it has been observed that there is a wide amount of communication among the groups who are technology focused and security related experts. It is also interesting to know that the users who are not exposed to any kind of data breaches were the ones who reacted to the data breaches more. Not only into these sectors the risk has also affected the politics if one looks at the paper on "Bots and Fake news: Role of WhatsApp in the 2018 Brazilian Presidential Election" by Latifa Abdin [8] it shows the seriousness of the issue of data breach. This paper has highlighted how the hackers highlighted as "cyber-troops" used WhatsApp to disseminate fake news and how this led to a successful misinformation campaign. From all the above articles and research papers one thing is very much evident that the way the use of social media applications has raised over the past few years the risk of the information getting stolen or in simple terms the risk of data breach has increased. And if people do not pay attention to these risks now then the long-term consequences would be very dangerous.

3 Theoretical Background

Let us come to very basic concept of the very important topic that is data breach. To explain it in the simplest way, one can say that Data breach is a fraudulent instance to steel or takeout the information without the prior knowledge or permission of the concerned owner. These data include very sensitive or confidential information like customer data, credit card numbers, trade secrets or matters related to national security.

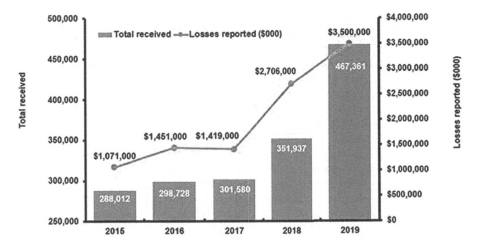

Fig. 1. Increase in data breach over the years

The above Fig. 1 shows how the data breach has increased over the years from 2015 where smart phones and gadgets have just entered the market to 2019 where already these phones have entered to the category of basic needs of everyone. According to the bara graph, the total number of databases have increased twice within just 4 years and if one looks at the losses it has increased to thrice the amount as incurred since 2015. According to a survey conducted by defense grade technology maker Thales, India is said to have the highest incidents of data breaches as compared to the global average. Around 52% of the Indian respondents reported a data breach which was way above the global average of 36% last year (Table 1).

Table 1. Types of data breach

	Definition	Target
Ransomware	As the name implies, the programme acquires access to and locks down access to crucial data in exchange for a price, which is usually paid in bitcoin	Enterprise companies and Businesses
Malware	This is usually referred to as "malicious software," which refers to any application that probes systems in a damaging manner. The "warning" tries to persuade people to download various programmes	Individuals and Businesses
Phishing	Hackers obtain access to sensitive data by sending spoof emails from well-known companies, tricking the recipient into clicking on a link or downloading an infected attachment	Individuals and businesses
Denial of Service (DoS)	A cyber-attack in which the perpetrator attempts to temporarily disable the services of a host connected to the internet to render a machine or network resource unavailable to its intended users	Sites/services hosted on well-known web servers, such as those used by banks

3.1 Breach Methods

Breach methods across industries occurs because of various reasons some of them can be:

- Insider Leak- this occurs when a trusted individual having the full access to confidential information steals the data.
- Payment card Fraud- Using physical skimming devices the credit card details are being stolen.
- Loss or theft- Another mode of loss of data occurs when our laptops, phones get stolen where every crucial information is stored.
- Unintended Disclosure- Sometimes data breach can take place due to negligence or mistakes.

3.2 What Causes Data Breaches?

When a cybercriminal infiltrates a data source and obtains sensitive information, this is referred to as a data breach. They usually do this via remotely gaining access to a computer or network, or by circumventing network protection. Below are the few most common cyber-attacks used in data breaches.

3.3 Recent Data Breaches & Statistics

Here are some of the impactful data breaches of the year 2020.

1. On January 22, 2020, 280 million customer support databases of Microsoft were left endangered on the web.
2. The MGM Resorts also suffered a data breach on February 20, 2020, when the personal information of over 10.6 million hotel guests was disclosed on a hacking site.
3. On 14th April, 2020, the dark web had roughly 500,000 Zoom teleconferencing accounts for sale.
4. On July 20, 2020, Sensitive Data of around 60,000 customers from Ancestry.com were hacked by an unsecured server.
5. On August 20, 2020, Researchers at Comparitech uncovered an unsecured database which contained profiles of users of 235 million Instagram, TikTok, and YouTube which belonged to the Deep Social and defunct social media data broker.
6. On November 5, 2020, hackers released data of Mashable.com's containing 1,852,595 records of staff, users, and subscribers' data.
7. On 10th December 2020, the audio streaming device, Spotify changed their passwords after the detection of data breach.
8. On 18th February 2021, the California Department of Motor Vehicles (DMV) was hit by a ransomware attack through billing contractor, Automatic Funds Transfer Services, following which they alerted drivers of data breach.

Now if one looks at the most widely used social media application Facebook it has been found that around 500 million details of Facebook users were uploaded through a website and made available for hackers. Though the information is several years old but if we look at the recent news in 2018 where a feature was introduced by Facebook where one can search another through their phone numbers following which one of the political firm Cambridge accessed 87 million Facebook user's information without their knowledge or consent, this feature was later disabled by Facebook. Facebook has been struggling with data security issues for years and with the recent Covid pandemic where everything is shifted to a digital mode. The information has become more vulnerable to these hackers. Because people use these social media applications to share important information and ideas. Facebook has not able to solve the issues completely but the recent acquisition of Facebook with one of the most widely use messaging app WhatsApp has raised eyebrows. With this pandemic the concept of work from home has given rise to rapid increase of WhatsApp users, where people have started communicating and taking management decisions, with the above news people have started doubting the safety of the information being shared. This study was done to get a view of the various WhatsApp users across various geographical locations to understand their point view towards these sensitive yet very important topic.

3.4   Data Analysis

This study was conducted to understand the perception of the users of the social media applications and how aware are the people towards the incident of data breach. A Questionnaire was prepared in view of the primary research being conducted across various geographical location in India to get a view from the users of all domains starting from students, business officials to service people to home makers. The survey collected a dataset of 886 users and their viewpoint on various questions based on data breach and usage of social media applications. There was a total of 10 questions which included questions on which social media applications are used more often to, how aware are the users of data leakage by these users to base on the recent acquisition of Facebook with WhatsApp how comfortable the users of WhatsApp with sharing of information after this and their willingness are to shifting their base to other messaging applications like Telegram, Signal or Snapchat. The data collected included mixed responses of users and upon structuring and analysing provided very interesting and insightful information for the same.

The data includes a qualitative approach, so at first the data was converted into quantitative for further analysis. We have converted the categories like gender, occupation to binary classification for easy understanding and research of the dataset. The data was divided into training and testing dataset in the ratio of 70:30. Classification method was used to test the sample dataset. Classification model attempts to draw some conclusion from observed values. There are different types of classifiers, some of them are Naïve Bayes, Decision Tress, Logistic Regression, KNN, Support Vector Machine we have used few of the above methods to predict the accuracy of our model. This dataset based on primary research which indicate people's perception about the shift towards digitalization and how it has affected or changed the way all the work was done. One thing is very clear whether it was pen-paper mode or cloud mode risk is observed at each shift.

4   Results

On studying the dataset, it has been found that Facebook and WhatsApp are the two most common and frequently used Social Media Applications used by around 525 users for Facebook and 365 users for WhatsApp. This shows a clear picture of irrespective of the news of data breach by Facebook people still prefer these applications for various purposes like making new friends, connecting to people, sharing information and ideas (Fig. 2).

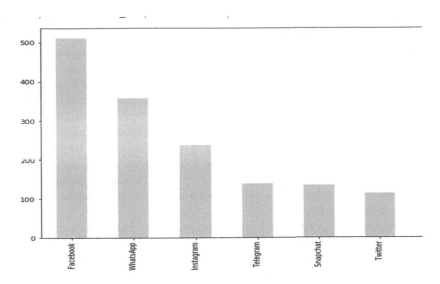

Fig. 2. Social media applications used most frequently

Not only this on digging a little dipper we came across another interesting fact that most users fear that WhatsApp is the social media application which has very high chance of data leakage followed by Instagram and then Facebook (Fig. 3).

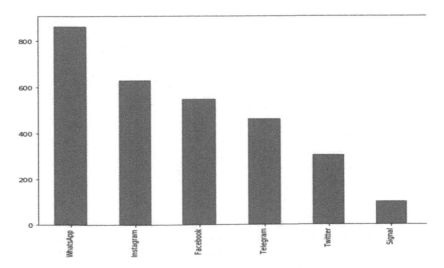

Fig. 3. Top 6 social media applications having a chance of data leakage

Upon working on the codes for classification of this dataset it was found that decision tree was the best model to test for this dataset giving an accuracy of 60%.

Though the model is clearly not the best model but for the initial phase it does provide important information for future analysis and research.

It is observed that Facebook is the social media app where the chances of leakage of personal information is more followed by WhatsApp and what is more interesting is that out of all the fields students are the one who have stated more risk for these social media apps in comparison to other occupations which is very relevant. Social media plays a significant role in every student's life as it is very convenient and easy to not only access information, provide information but also to communicate through social media with people all around the world. But in today's world the way social media applications are taking shapes, directly or say indirectly these have started to control our lives mainly our youth are getting affected by it. In the rush of getting more likes and subscribers today's youth have gone to extremes to fulfil these desires thus making them open to these risks.

With the world's second-largest population and the world's fastest-growing economy, India has a big stake in the AI revolution. According to a report from NASSCOMM, data and Artificial Intelligence could potentially add $450–$500 billion to India's GDP by 2025 and drive India's economic growth. India's 50% population constitutes of youth and interestingly according to the study users between the age group 10–30 does not believe in the fact that India is ready to accept AI in its economy which can be explained by the fact that India is rapidly moving towards digitalization making lives easier but at the same time riskier unless and until there is a safe platform in this digital world shifting to complete automation might be a debate to discuss on (Table 2).

Table 2. Acceptance of AI in india among various age group

Count of AI_GoB2	Column Labels			Grand Total
Row Labels	Maybe	No	Yes	
10–20	128	122	82	332
20–30	137	176	80	393
30–40	18	16	11	45
40–50	28	32	18	78
50 & above	9	7	7	23
Grand Total	320	353	198	871

Total 66.10% of our users includes females rather than males who use WhatsApp in a daily basis and with the Facebook collaborating with WhatsApp has raised eyebrows in sharing personal information or communicating with others as 60% of the users have agreed to shift to Signal for communicating and sharing information. The way cybercrimes are increasing they are attacking large platforms like Facebook, Adobe etc. and being in the top list in the social media Applications these applications are not able to solve these crimes. Until these crimes stop people's data would be vulnerable to these hackers. One way or the other once our information is uploaded and stored in the

cloud storage there is always a chance of data leakage. Here, Table 3 has the list of cyber-attacks that happened in the past years.

Table 3. Cyber Attacks

Database	Date	No. of Affected Users	Description
Police exam database	February 2021	500,000 Indian Police Personnel	Around 500,000 policemen's personal identity information was put up on a database sharing forum for sale
Indian patients test results of covid-19	January 2021	1500 Indian citizens at least	The test results related to covid-19 of thousands of Indian patients were leaked by websites of government
Juspay	January 2021	user accounts of around 35 million	According to Just pay, details related to customer accounts, which included masked card data and card fingerprints of around 35 million customers were accessed by using an unrecycled access key through a server
Big Basket	October 2020	20 million user accounts	Data containing names, email-ids, password hashes, phone numbers, addresses, location, and IP addresses of users were at sell in online cybercrime market
Unacademy	May 2020	22 million user accounts	Email ids, passwords and usernames were at sale at online cybercrime platform

5   Conclusion

For a country like India, it needs more attention towards the capacity as well as capability for the cyber security workforce. Even for the large organizations equipped with top talents and adequate resources dedicated towards cyber security, fall prey to the data breach that cost them millions. Greater challenges are faced by the organizations without such high level of expertise and resources. It needs highly skilled workforce in cyber security to help the nation to address more strongly to the cyber security problems. Every organization needs to realize the relevant threat environments as well as the risks involved pertinent to cyber security and employ the most suitable workforce to do the work. Attention to be given to the contents that are shared on the social media applications. The way digitalization is taking place most of the people mainly the youth are falling in the trap of these fame of getting maximum likes and subscribes that they are not able to realize the information that they are sharing online and how the same can be used to against them.

Due to the data breach faced by Facebook the recent acquisition of Facebook with WhatsApp has made this messaging platform vulnerable to data leakage. Half of the users believed that they should shift to Signal app after the merger of Facebook and WhatsApp, which showcases that data breach has become a matter of concern for each one to such an extent that if an application has a little chance of data breach people are not willing to use that at all. Its high time for these social media applications before building any new future for convenient use of its users it should first focus on securing the data of its users.

References

1. Joshi, U.D., Vanshika, A.P. Singh, T.R. Pahuja, S. Naval, G.S.: Fake Social Media Profile Detection. Machine Learning: Algorithms and Applications by Wiley Publishers (2020)
2. Gupta, S., Singal, G., Garg, D.: Deep reinforcement learning techniques in diversified domains: a survey. Arch. Computat. Methods Eng. **28**(7), 4715–4754 (2021). https://doi.org/10.1007/s11831-021-09552-3
3. Sprinklr. Why managing social media is crucial in the event of a data breach. Weblog. https://blog.sprinklr.com/wpcontent/uploads/securepdfs/2016/03/20151113_WP_EN_Why_Managing_Social_Media_is_Crucial_in_the_Event_of_Data_Breach_V01.pdf
4. Frouws, B., Phillips, M., Hassan, A., Twigt, M.: Getting to Europe the whatsapp way: the use of ict in contemporary mixed migration flows to Europe (June 2016). In: Regional Mixed Migration Secretariat Briefing Paper (2016), https://doi.org/10.2139/ssrn.2862592
5. Evangelos, K., Pedro, T., Ruben, G.: Need fulfillment and experiences on social media: a case on Facebook and WhatsApp. Comput. Human Behav. **55** (Part B), 888–897 (2016). ISSN 0747–5632. https://doi.org/10.1016/j.chb.2015.10.015
6. O'Sullivan, D., O'O'Sullivan, E., O'Connor, M., Declan, L., John M.: Whatsapp doc. BMJ Innov. 3(4) 238–239 (2017)
7. Naga, V., Glenn, D.: A Social Network Analysis (SNA) study on data breach concerns over social media. In: 52nd Hawaii International Conference on System Sciences (2019) https://core.ac.uk/download/pdf/211327978.pdf
8. Abdin, L.: Bots and Fake News: The Role of WhatsApp in the 2018 Brazilian Presidential Election (2019)
9. SELFKEY: All Data Breaches in 2019 – 2021 – An Alarming Timeline. Weblog. https://selfkey.org/data-breaches-in-2019/
10. Juma'h, A.H., Alnsour, Y.: The effect of data breaches on company performance. Int. J. Account. Inf. Manag. **28**(2), 275–301 (2020). https://doi.org/10.1108/IJAIM-01-2019-0006
11. livemint: Data, AI can add $400–500bn to India's GDP by 2025. Weblog. https://www.livemint.com/news/india/data-ai-can-add-450-500-bn-to-india-s-gdp-by-025-nasscom-11597755748693.html

Sentiment Analysis of Customers Review Using Hybrid Approach

Jyoti Budhwar[(✉)] and Sukhdip Singh

Department of Computer Science and Engineering, Deenbandhu Chhotu Ram
University of Science and Technology, Murthal, India
sukhdeepsingh.cse@dcrustm.org

Abstract. Sentiment analysis is utilized for expressing consumer materials such as internet and social media, examination and survey responses, and health material for applications from marketing to customers and medical services. Applications of sentiment analysis to examine Amazon goods are considered. The application of the hybrid technique Naïve Bayes, KNN, and LSTM mechanism are involved in work. Naïve Bayes offered a categorization solution. The data collection would be educated to deliver a greater precision solution utilizing the LSTM-based model. In order to do sentimental analysis, data set customer evaluation was considered. Present work is intended to alleviate the problems faced by earlier research during the analysis of sentiment. The simulation work has integrated a classification mechanism into the LSTM learning model in order to develop a sentiment analysis mechanism to review the Amazon product. The simulation results have concluded that the proposed work is capable to provide a more accurate & reliable solution. Moreover the comparison of three cases has been made for performance analysis where traditional work, naïve integrated approach and proposed work are considered.

Keywords: Sentiment analysis · KNN · LSTM · Accuracy · Precision · F score · Recall value · Naïve Bayes · Performance

1 Introduction

For text mining, product reviews employing feeling analysis are becoming prominent. An experiment in the field of computational linguistics is also being considered. The focus of the present work is on the association between Amazon product reviews [3, 6]. Rating of client products has been taken into account. In addition to Naive Bayes analysis, neighboring mechanism, classic machine-learning techniques are discussed. Deep neural networks together with K Nearest Neighbors were considered by researchers (KNN) [23].

1.1 Natural Language Processing

NLP is one of the 4th Industrial Revolution's most significant technologies and becomes an important area in AI with voice interface and chatbots growing [1]. As the discipline of NLP develops, so does the number of practical applications. It ranges from the very basic to the very sophisticated.

© Springer Nature Switzerland AG 2022
D. Garg et al. (Eds.): IACC 2021, CCIS 1528, pp. 671–685, 2022.
https://doi.org/10.1007/978-3-030-95502-1_51

- Search, spell check, keyword search, finds synonyms.
- Website information like goods, prices, dates, places, persons, or names may be extracted
- Machine translation, voice recognition, personal assistants (i.e. Google translate) [18, 19].

Sentiment Analysis (emotional AI) is an NLP area that seeks to detect and extract opinions from blogs, reviews, social media, news etc. inside a given text [7, 20].

1.2   Sentiment Analysis

Sentiment analysis (emotional analysis) [4] consists of the systematic detection, extraction, measurement, and study of affective states and subjective information via natural language processing. Sentiment analysis for the voice of consumers is widely utilized for marketing, customer services, and clinical medicine, such as reviews and surveys, Internet and social media, and healthcare [5, 21].

1.3   Objective of Sentiment Analysis

The goal and difficulties of feeling analysis may be shown by simple instances [8, 22].

Simple Cases

- It is also used during brand monitoring to consider trends and customer preferences [9, 34].
- Customer support analysis is another case where sentiment analysis is used to know whether the customer is satisfied or not [36, 37].
- Market research to consider the demand and frequency of use of product [32, 33, 35].
- Chris Craft looks better than Limestone, but Limestone portrays navigability and dependability. (Two brand names, two mindsets) [24].
- The film is shocking with many disturbing turns. (Negative word for specific domains used in a positive meaning) [16].
- Their delicious dessert menu should be seen. (The attitudinal word has lately changed polarity in certain areas) [17, 25].
- I adore my cell phone, yet not one of my coworkers will suggest it. (Qualified pleasant feeling, hard to categorize) [28].

1.4   Sentiment Analysis Approach for Prediction

These studies were considered in the present research. Sub-themes known as sentiment analysis are considered [10, 12]. This is sometimes called opinion mining. This was provided as a textual content group. Such a study takes into account people's opinions, assessments, attitudes, and feelings. The application that builds on such a notion has a different nature [26, 27].

Nevertheless, it remains a tough task to discover and monitor websites and extract the information they provide owing to the number of various websites [13]. Every site typically has a significant number of opinions on forum posts and blogs that are not always simple to understand [38, 39].

1.5 Different Types of Sentiment Analysis

To classify polarity in a document, phrase, characteristic, or aspect is a basic goal of sentimental analysis, whether the opinions expressed in a document, sentence, or entity are positive, negative, or neutral [11]. For example, emotional states like pleasure, anger, disdain, sadness, fear, and surprise may be classified as "beyond polarity," which is a more advanced way of classifying emotions [14]. The general investigator, who proposed evaluating textual and psychological patterns separately and examined a person's psychological condition based on his or her speech behavior analysis, is a predecessor of sentimental analysis. Emotional analysis may take numerous forms, such as Aspect Basic sentimental analysis, graduate examination of mental feelings (positive, negative, and neutral) [15].

2 Literature Review

Several articles on product ratings, sentiment analysis, and opinion mining have been published so far. Ronan Collobert [1] et al. utilized the co-evolutionary network. The author proposed a single neural network design and technique of learning for several natural language processing tasks, including language tagging, chunking, and identification of entities, and Semite in role identification. K. Dave [2] has been investigating the extraction of opinions and semantic product review categorization. When acting on individual phrases gathered by online searches, noise, and ambiguity restrict the performance. Maria Soledad Elli [3] did sentiment from considering reviews of customers. They have analyzed results to develop a business model. The author presented that the tool is providing better accuracy. The KNN classification method for multi-class emotional analyses of Twitter data was explored by S. Hota and S. Pathak [4]. Feelings were regarded as 'Emotions.' Opinion mining and this are the same things. Emotions are categorized into many categories in this study. The research and result are that the method suggested works better in all conventional assessment metrics. The opinion mining and sentiment analysis survey was done by B. Liu and L. Zhang [5]. The analysis of sentiments or opinion is the study of the views, evaluations, attitudes, and emotions of individuals, persons, problems, events, subjects, and their characteristics in computing. Callen Rain [6] has extended research work in the area of processing natural language. The neural network has been found famous in the field of sentiment analysis Users of the Amazon website are encouraged to write reviews of the items they buy. R. Socher [7] recommended the use of recursive neural networks to enhance the complexity of tasks such as the recognition of feelings. The purpose of this paper is to utilize both traditional approaches, such as Naive Bayesian, K-nearest, Vector Support and deep learning techniques. Existing supervision learning techniques like the perception algorithm, naive bays, and supporting vector machines are utilized by Xu Yun

[8] and others at Stanford University to estimate the rank of the review. The survey of opinion mining and sentiment analysis was conducted by Ravi Kumar, Ravi Vadlamani [9]: tasks, methods, and applications. The document offers open issues as well as a summary table of 100 61 articles. N. Zainuddin [10] suggested the categorization of hybrid Twitter feelings for 2017.

3 Problem Statement

However, various investigations have been conducted on the subject of sentiment analysis. However, there is limited scope for existing studies. In addition, the performance element is neglected during sentiment analysis. In past studies, the neural network model used takes a lot of time during processing. Several studies offer a solution based on probability leading to an accuracy decrease. Traditional machine learning and analysis of Naive Bayes and K nearest neighborhoods mechanisms must be taken into account. Deep neural networks should be considered together with the existing neural network into consideration (RNN). For the sentiment analysis, there is a need to generate a better answer.

4 Proposed Model

This section has presented the objective of the proposed work along with the methodology used during research.

4.1 Objective of Proposed Work

- Considering existing work related to sentiment analysis
- Defining the issues arising or found in existing research.
- Proposing integration of naive Bayes, KNN, and LSTM approach in order to propose a better solution for sentiment analysis
- Comparing the performance, accuracy of the proposed model with the traditional model.

4.2 Working of Proposed Work

Initially, the dataset of Amazon products is considered for training. Train and test of Amazon dataset are performed using traditional methods to get the error values. After getting the error values and naive classifier is applied in order to find the accuracy by considering the cases of exact difference (ed) and negligible difference (nd). Then a comparison of the accuracy in the case of (ed) and (nd) is made. If Accuracy (ed) is greater than Accuracy of (nd) then the data set is filtered considering ed otherwise dataset is filtered considering nd. Training of filtered dataset is made using LSTM model where epoch, batch size, hidden layer is considered to improve the accuracy. After getting the trained model, the testing module is passed with a dataset of 3000 records to get predictions for 5 classes. KNN classifier is used to classify the result of 5 classes and present the confusion matrix. Finally, the f1score, accuracy, recall value, and precision are calculated using a confusion matrix. These parameters are compared (Fig. 1).

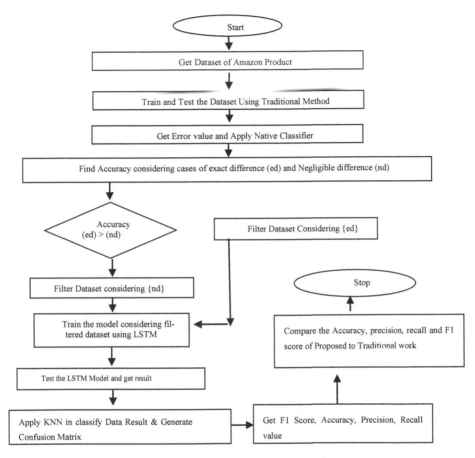

Fig. 1. Flow chart of proposed work

5   Result and Discussion

The simulation is focusing on detecting sentiment from customer reviews regarding Amazon products. During simulation, the data of Amazon cell phone and accessories review has been fetched from jmcauley.ucsd.edu in JSON form in phase 1. This data is converted from JSON to CSV format in order to perform LSTM simulation in phase 2. LSTM classification takes place at phase 3. During classification rating from 1 to 5 has been considered to classify record. Phase 4 is partitioning the dataset for training and testing. Phase 5 and 6 is focusing on the preprocessing of text and converting documents to sequences respectively. In phase 7 creation and Training of the LSTM Network takes place. Finally, phase 8 performs testing over the trained network.

5.1   Accuracy Comparison

Phase 1: Get the Data

a. Get data from

http://jmcauley.ucsd.edu/data/amazon/index_2014.html.

b. Download review of Cell Phones and Accessories

Phase 2: Data Preprocessing

a. Copy JSON record of 10000

https://www.convertcsv.com/json-to-csv.htm.

b. Convert it into CSV
c. Save the csv data for LSTM training and testing

Phase 3: LSTM Based Classification

This section describes how long short-term network text information is classified (LSTM). Obviously, text data is sequential. A text piece is a sequence of words on which you can depend. Use the LSTM neural network to learn and use long-term addictions to classify sequence data. LSTM is an ongoing kind of neural network (RNN) that may learn long short-term dependency between data phases.

Phase 4 Partitioning and Validation Data Set

This step is for the division of training and validation data sets. Data is divided into a training partition & validation and testing holding partition. Specify that the holdout level is 20% then the text information and the labels are retrieved from the partitioned tables. To check that you have correctly imported data, view the training text with a word cloud.

Phase 5 Preprocess Text Data

Create a text data tokenization and preprocessing function. The function preprocess Text specifies these steps at the conclusion of the example:

1. To tokenize the text use tokenized Document.
2. Turn the text into a lower case.
3. Remove punctuation by erasing Punctuation.

Phase 6 Convert Document to Sequences

Use word encoding to transform documents for entry into the LSTM network into numerical index sequences.

The next step is to be padded and trimmed documents, such that the document length is the same. The workout feature allows you to automatically paddle and trim input sequences. But these choices are not appropriate for the word vectors sequences. Instead, sequences should be padded and cut. If the word vector sequences remain and are shortened, the training may improve. Select a length of the target to be padded and truncated documents, then trim documents greater than the target length and connect documents below the target length. The intended duration must be brief for optimum results without the discharge of an excessive amount of data. For an appropriate goal, length sees a histogram of the training document length.

Phase 7 Create and Train LSTM Network

Set the LSTM network architecture. Enter the layer of the input sequence and set the input to 1. Complete a 50 dimensional and equal word embedding layer as an encoding word for inputting network sequence data. Set 80 hidden units and apply the next LSTM layer. Set the output mode to utilize the LSTM layer for problem labeling sequentially. Add a completely connected class number, a softmax layer, and a classification layer.

Specify Training Options

a. Train with solver Adam.
b. Specify a small size of 16.
c. Mix the data every era.
d. Monitoring the progress of training by setting the 'training progress' option.
e. Specify the data validation using the option 'Validation Data'.
f. Delete verbose output by setting the option 'Verbose' to false.

If one is available, train Network utilizes a GPU by default. Otherwise, it utilizes the CPU. Use the option name/value for training Options to specify the execution environment directly. CPU training may take much longer than GPU training. GPU training includes a Parallel Toolbox and the supporting GPU hardware.

Phase 8 Testing Phase

Simulation result for Traditional model.

Here during simulation dataset of 10000 records has been considered for training. And testing has been performed on 3000 records. Where 300 records belong to grade 1, 253 records belong to grade 2, 357 records belong to grade 3, 712 records were from grade 4 while 1378 records where belonging to grade 5. After simulation out of 3000 records, 2575 predication came true while 425 came false (Table 1).

Table 1. Error and accuracy in previous work

True value	2575
False value	425
Total	3000
Accuracy	85.833%
Error	14.167%

Case for Grade 1
If we consider grade 1 then there are 300 cases of grade 1 but during simulation, only 255 out of 300 were traced. And remaining 10, 5, 15, 15 were traced as grades 2, 3, 4, 5 respectively as shown in the following confusion matrix.

Case for Grade 2
If we consider grade 2 then there are 253 cases of grade 2 but during simulation, only 199 out of 253 were traced. And remaining 11, 11, 13, 19 were traced as grades 1, 3, 4, 5 respectively as shown in the following confusion matrix.

Case for Grade 3
If we consider grade 3 then there are 357 cases of grade 3 but during simulation, only 286 out of 357 were traced. And remaining 8, 7, 29, 27 were traced as grades 1, 2, 4, 5 respectively as shown in the following confusion matrix.

Case for Grade 4
If we consider grade 4 then there are 712 cases of grade 4 but during simulation, only 600 out of 712 were traced. And remaining 13, 10, 17, 72 were traced as grades 1, 2, 3, 5 respectively as shown in the following confusion matrix.

Case for Grade 5
If we consider grade 5 then there are 1378 cases of grade 5 but during simulation, 1235 out of 1378 were traced. And remaining 29, 21, 27, 66 were traced as grades 1, 2, 3, 4 respectively as shown in the following confusion matrix (Table 2).

Table 2. Confusion matrix in case of previous work after simulation

	1	2	3	4	5	
1	255	10	5	15	15	**300**
2	11	199	11	13	19	**253**
3	8	7	286	29	27	**357**
4	13	10	17	600	72	**712**
5	29	21	27	66	1235	**1378**
	316	**247**	**346**	**723**	**1368**	**3000**

Simulation Result for Proposed Model
The results of the previous model were obtained to filter the dataset of 10000 using a naïve bayes classifier.

Applying Naive Bayes in Proposed Model
After obtaining the error values, a naive classifier is used to determine the accuracy by taking into account the instances of exact difference (ed) and insignificant difference (nd) (nd). The accuracy in the cases of (ed) and (nd) is then compared. If Accuracy (ed) exceeds Accuracy (nd), the data set is filtered using ed; otherwise, the dataset is filtered using nd. Here during simulation dataset of 10002 records has been considered for training. And testing has been performed on 3000 records.

Applying LSTM Model on Filtered Dataset

425 records have been eliminated considering the naïve classifier. The dataset is of 9577 has been considered for training by the LSTM model. Here batch size is 16, the number of hidden units is 200, and the gradient threshold is 2. This model is considered a fully connected layer along with the softmax layer and classification layer. Where 312 records belong to grade 1, 215 records belong to grade 2, 327 records belong to grade 3, 582 records were from grade 4 while 1564 records where belonging to grade 5. After simulation out of 3000 records, 2607 predication came true while 393 came false (Tables 3 and 4).

Table 3. Errors and accuracy in proposed work

True value	2607
False value	393
Total	3000
Accuracy	86.9%
Error	13.1%

Table 4. Actual grades

	1	2	3	4	5
1	312	0	0	0	0
2	0	215	0	0	0
3	0	0	327	0	0
4	0	0	0	582	0
5	0	0	0	0	1564

Following confusion matrix is presenting that in each grade there is some error.

Case for Grade 1

If we consider grade 1 then there are 312 cases of grade 1 but during simulation, only 270 out of 312 were traced. And remaining 6, 7, 16, 13 were traced as grades 2,3,4,5 respectively as shown in the following confusion matrix.

Case for Grade 2

If we consider grade 2 then there are 215 cases of grade 2 but during simulation, 169 out of 215 were traced. And remaining 3,13,10,20 were traced as grades 1,3,4,5 respectively as shown in the following confusion matrix.

Case for Grade 3

If we consider grade 3 then there are 327 cases of grade 3 but during simulation, only 278 out of 327 were traced. And remaining 9,8,13,19 were traced as grades 1,2,4,5 respectively as shown in the following confusion matrix.

Case for Grade 4

If we consider grade 4 then there are 582 cases of grade 4 but during simulation, only 490 out of 582 were traced. And remaining 13,5,19,55 were traced as grades 1,2,3,5 respectively as shown in the following confusion matrix.

Case for Grade 5

If we consider grade 5 then there are 1564 cases of grade 5 but during simulation, only 1400 out of 1564 were traced. And remaining 31,22,44,67 were traced as grades 1,3,4,5 respectively as shown in the following confusion matrix (Table 5).

Table 5. Confusion matrixes in case of previous work after simulation

	1	2	3	4	5	
1	270	6	7	16	13	**312**
2	3	169	13	10	20	**215**
3	9	8	278	13	19	**327**
4	13	5	19	490	55	**582**
5	31	22	44	67	1400	**1564**
	326	**210**	**361**	**596**	**1507**	

Phase 9

KNN Based Representation of Predication

In the following figure, green markers are presenting true predictions were as red markers are showing false predictions. However true predictions are 86.9% and false prediction is 13.1% but many of the true predictions are overlapped with each other (Fig. 2).

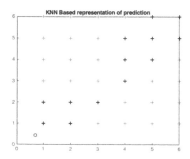

Fig. 2. Graphical presentation of error and accurate data points using KNN

Phase 10
In this Phase Comparative Analysis of Accuracy, Precision and Recall Value has been Made

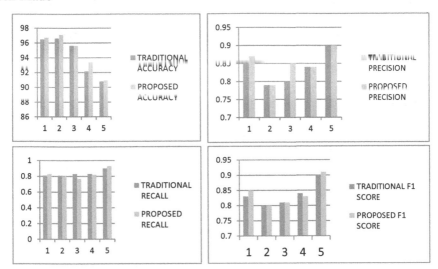

5.2   Performance Comparison

It has been observed that previous research took more time because data is not filtered. The training operation took more time. The proposed work has eliminated the irrelevant records before training operation using the naïve Bayes approach. Moreover, the configuration of the proposed model has also reduced time consumption. The time ratio of traditional, Naïve bayed and Hybrid proposed work is 5:4:3.

The Simulation of Time Consumption in Three Cases has Represented as Follow (Table 6 and Fig. 3)

Table 6. Comparison of time consumption in three cases

Data set	Traditional	Network model with Naïve based filter	Proposed work
1000	0.509837814	0.440136842	0.334695449
2000	1.030794097	0.858116763	0.621696812
3000	1.547334231	1.226298455	0.938384776
4000	2.024383651	1.610470863	1.253386768
5000	2.568361402	2.011340469	1.531965208
6000	3.012016967	2.47053221	1.888877188
7000	3.560913637	2.877825697	2.180116715
8000	4.075732734	3.210164489	2.465036738
9000	4.548824902	3.652236136	2.763942149

(continued)

Table 6. (*continued*)

Data set	Traditional	Network model with Naïve based filter	Proposed work
10000	5.044767836	4.070926777	3.049083499
11000	5.57499612	4.423910578	3.396137228
12000	6.042370331	4.871174826	3.610097421
13000	6.580739094	5.246581873	3.957921825
14000	7.012412293	5.633831212	4.207854981
15000	7.500729383	6.052647162	4.515139093
16000	8.051073584	6.48576407	4.896617524
17000	8.553409875	6.894709821	5.144974468
18000	9.036465609	7.25994748	5.457588716
19000	9.547392558	7.610327802	5.768853314
20000	10.08076758	8.081825985	6.033466858

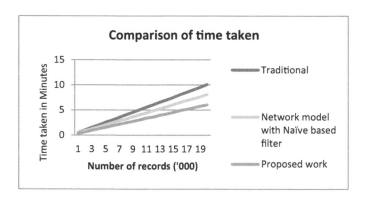

Fig. 3. Comparison of time consumption in three cases

6 Conclusion

Results have concluded that integration of Naïve Bayes, KNN classifier during LSTM based training and testing is capable to provide better accuracy, f-score, precision, and recall values as compared to previous work. The proposed work is found more reliable and flexible as compared to existing researches. Overall accuracy and error in the case of the previous model were 85.833% and 14.167% respectively. But in the case of the proposed model overall accuracy and error in the case of the previous model were 86.9333% and 13.0667% respectively. Comparison of proposed work to previous work concludes that use of hidden layer and classifier makes the training and testing faster and reduces the probability of error during prediction. The classification process supports the LSTM system to predict in less time and more accurate fashion. Moreover, the performance of the proposed work is better because it is taking less time during training. It is concluded that the proposed work is consuming less time as compared to traditional work and naïve based classification work.

7 Scope of Research

This study used Naive Bayes, KNN, and LSTM as a summary. A more flexible and accurate solution is intended to be the result of the research. In upcoming research, the research work could upgrade training and testing procedures. New research may improve the accuracy and reduce the error by introducing advanced classifiers that could be better than Naive Bayes. LSTM model is replaced by a more advanced training model.

References

1. Collobert, R., Weston, J., Bottou, L., Karlen, M., Kavukcuoglu, K., Kuksa, P.: Natural language processing (almost) from scratch. J. Mach. Learn. Res. **12**, 2493–2537 (2011)
2. Dave, K., Lawrence, S., Pennock, D.M.: Mining the peanut gallery: opinion extraction and semantic classification of product reviews. In: Proceedings of the 12th International Conference on World Wide Web, pp. 519–528. ACM (2003)
3. Elli, M.S., Wang, Y.-F.: Amazon reviews, business analytics with sentiment analysis
4. Hota, S., Pathak, S.: KNN classifier based approach for multi-class sentiment analysis of twitter data. In: International Journal of Engineering Technology, SPC, 2018, pp. 1372–1375 (2018)
5. Liu, B., Zhang, L.: A Survey of Opinion Mining and Sentiment Analysis, pp. 415–463. Springer, Boston (2012)
6. Rain, C.: Sentiment analysis in amazon reviews using probabilistic machine learning. Swarthmore College (2013)
7. Socher, R., et al.: Recursive deep models for semantic compositionality over a sentiment treebank. In: Proceedings of the 2013 Conference on Empirical Methods in Natural Language Processing, pp. 1631–1642 (2013)
8. Xu, Y., Wu, X., Wang, Q.: Sentiment analysis of yelps ratings based on text reviews (2015)
9. KumarRaviab, V.: A survey on opinion mining and sentiment analysis: tasks, approaches and applications. Knowl.-Based Syst. **89**, 14–46 (2015)
10. Zainuddin, N., Selamat, A., Ibrahim, R.: Hybrid sentiment classification on twitter aspect-based sentiment analysis. Appl. Intell. **48**(5), 1218–1232 (2017)
11. Asghar, M.Z., Kundi, F.M., Ahmad, S., Khan, A., Khan, F.: T-SAF: twitter sentiment analysis framework using a hybrid classification scheme. Exp. Syst. **35**(1), e12233 (2018)
12. Alsaeedi, A., Zubair, M.: A study on sentiment analysis techniques of twitter data. Int. J. Adv. Comput. Sci. Appl. **10**, 361–374 (2019). https://doi.org/10.14569/IJACSA.2019. 0100248
13. Shathik, A., Karani, K.P.: A Literature Review on Application of Sentiment Analysis Using Machine Learning Techniques, pp. 2581–7000 (2020). https://doi.org/10.5281/zenodo. 3977576
14. Liu, H., Cocea, M.: Fuzzy rule based systems for interpretable sentiment analysis. Int. Conf. Adv. Comput. Intell. **1**(1), 129–136 (2017). https://doi.org/10.1109/ICACI.2017.7974497
15. Abo, M., Shah, N., Balakrishnan, V., Abdelaziz, A.: Sentiment analysis algorithms: evaluation performance of the Arabic and English language. IEEE Expert **1**(1), 1–5 (2018). https://doi.org/10.1109/ICCCEEE.2018.8515844
16. Bansal, A., Gupta, C.L., Muralidhar, A.: A sentimental analysis for youtube data using supervised learning approach. Int. J. Eng. Adv. Technol **8**(5), 1–12 (2019)

17. Alsaeedi, A., Khan, M.: A study on sentiment analysis techniques of twitter data. Int. J. Adv. Comput. Sci. Appl. **10**(1), 361–374 (2019). https://doi.org/10.14569/IJACSA.2019.0100248

18. Sadhasivam, J., Kalivaradhan, R.B.: Sentiment analysis of amazon products using ensemble machine learning algorithm. Int. J. Math. Eng. Manag. Sci. **4**(2), 508–520 (2019). https://doi.org/10.33889/IJMEMS.2019.4.2-041

19. Hasan, A., Moin, S., Karim, A., Shamshirband, D.: Machine learning-based sentimental analysis for twitter accounts. Math. Comput. Appl. **23**(1), 11–32 (2018). https://doi.org/10.3390/mca23010011

20. Sultana, N., Kumar, P., Patra, M., Chandra, S., Alam, S.: Sentiment analysis for product review. Int. J. Soft Comput. **9**(1), 7–28 (2019). https://doi.org/10.21917/ijsc.2019.0266

21. Hassan Raza, M., Faizan, A.H., Mushtaq, A., Akhtar, N.: Scientific text sentiment analysis using machine learning techniques. Int. J. Adv. Comput. Sci. Appl. **10**(12), 157–165 (2019). https://doi.org/10.14569/IJACSA.2019.0101222

22. Valencia, F., Gómez-Espinosa, A., Valdés-Aguirre, B.: Price movement prediction of cryptocurrencies using sentiment analysis and machine learning. Int. Interdiscip. J. Entropy **21**(6), 589 (2019). https://doi.org/10.3390/e21060589

23. Daeli, N.O.F., Adiwijaya, A.: Sentiment analysis on movie reviews using information gain and K-nearest neighbor. J. Data Sci. Appl. **3**(1), 1–7 (2020). https://doi.org/10.34818/jdsa.2020.3.2

24. Kumar, S., Gahalawat, M., Roy, P.P., Dogra, D.P., Kim, B.-G.: Exploring impact of age and gender on sentiment analysis using machine learning. Int. J. Electron. **9**(2), 374 (2020). https://doi.org/10.3390/electronics9020374

25. Shuhidan, S.M., Hamidi, S.R., Kazemian, S., Shuhidan, S.M., Ismail, M.A.: Sentiment analysis for financial news headlines using machine learning algorithm. Int. Conf. Kansei Eng. Emotion Res. **739**(1), 64–72 (2018). https://doi.org/10.1007/978-981-10-8612-0_8

26. Yogi, T.N., Paudel, N.: Comparative analysis of machine learning based classification algorithms for sentiment analysis. Int. J. Innovat. Sci. Eng. Technol. **7**(6), 1–9 (2020)

27. Suryawanshi, R., Rajput, A., Kokale, P., Karve, S.S.: Sentiment analyzer using machine learning. Int. Res. J. Modern. Eng. Technol. Sci. **02**(06), 1–12 (2020)

28. Sentamilselvan, K., Aneri, D., Athithiya, A.C., Kani Kumar, P.: Twitter sentiment analysis using machine learning techniques. Int. J. Eng. Adv. Technol. **9**(3), 1–9 (2020). https://doi.org/10.35940/ijeat.C6281.029320

29. https://mk0ecommercefas531pc.kinstacdn.com/wp-content/uploads/2019/12/sentiment-analysis.png

30. https://miro.medium.com/max/361/0*ga5rNPmVYBsCm-lz

31. https://i.ytimg.com/vi/VXt9SQx5eM0/maxresdefault.jpg

32. Dey, S., Wasif, S., Tonmoy, D.S., Sultana, S., Sarkar, J., Dey, M.: A comparative study of support vector machine and naive Bayes classifier for sentiment analysis on amazon product reviews. In: 2020 International Conference on Contemporary Computing and Applications (IC3A), pp. 217–220 (2020). https://doi.org/10.1109/IC3A48958.2020.233300

33. Inaniya, Y.: Amazon Product review Sentiment Analysis using BERT. Data Science Blogathon (2021)

34. Yadav, N., Kumar, R., Gour, B., Khan, A.U.: Extraction-based text summarization and sentiment analysis of online reviews using hybrid classification method. IN: 2019 Sixteenth International Conference on Wireless and Optical Communication Networks (WOCN), pp. 1–6 (2019). https://doi.org/10.1109/WOCN45266.2019.8995164

35. Guner, L., Coyne, E., Smit, J.: Sentiment Analysis for Amazon.com Reviews. SVM, Naïve Bayes, LSTM (2019)

36. Anas, S.M., Kumari, S.: Opinion mining based fake product review monitoring and removal system. In: 2021 6th International Conference on Inventive Computation Technologies (ICICT), pp. 985–988 (2021). https://doi.org/10.1109/ICICT50816.2021.9358716
37. Hota, S., Pathak, S.: KNN classifier based approach for multi-class sentiment analysis of twitter data. In: International Journal of Engineering Technology, SPC, 2018, pp. 1372–1375 (2018)
38. Hossain, R., Ahamed, F., Zannat, R., Rabbani, M.G.: Comparative sentiment analysis using difference types of machine learning algorithm. In: 2019 8th International Conference System Modeling and Advancement in Research Trends (SMART), pp. 329–333 (2019). https://doi.org/10.1109/SMART46866.2019.9117214
39. Dudhia, D.J., Dave, S.R., Yagnik, S.: Self attentive product recommender – a hybrid approach with machine learning and neural network. Int. Conf. Emerg. Technol. **2020**, 1–4 (2020). https://doi.org/10.1109/INCET49848.2020.9154034

Author Index

Agarwal, Anshuman 82
Agarwal, Mohit 99, 646
Ahmad, Nadeem 148
Alam, Mahtab 305
Anwarul, Shahina 588

Bacha, Vaishnavi 193
Badal, Tapas 82
Bansal, Arnav 82
Bapat, Atharva 410
Bhardwaj, Arpit 294
Bhargavi, Lakshmi Sai 577
Bhowmik, Tanmay 244
Bothera, Abhi 618, 626
Bradshaw, Karen 545
Budhiraja, Ishan 73, 318
Budhwar, Jyoti 671

Carlo, Conti 480
Chakraborty, Susanta 504
Chandna, Swati 633
Chandra, G. Ramesh 193
Chaurasia, Kuldeep 599
Chawla, Yash 214
Chickerur, Satyadhyan 254
Chidaravalli, Sharmila 271
Chodak, Grzegorz 214
Choudhury, Amitava 244

D'Costa, Antonio 123
Deepan, M. 463
Deepanshi 73
Deotale, Anurag 410
Desai, Ankit 399, 410, 577
Deshpande, Saurabh 362
Dewhurst, Richard J. 165
Dhana Satish, A. 11
Dohare, Ravins 148
Dongre, Shital 57
Durga Sindhu, I. 11
Dutt, Varun 348

Fenech, Jake 480

Gandhi, Uttam 626
Ganju, Siddha 377
Garg, Deepak 73, 99, 646
Garg, Lalit 480
Garg, Neha 618, 626
Ghodgaonkar, Aditya 419
Goel, Shivani 294
Gokul Prasad, C. 3
Gopalakrishnan, E. A. 229
Grace Gladys Nancy, B. 25
Gundawar, Sharvari 463
Gupta, Indrajeet 618, 626
Gupta, Lovleen 112
Gupta, Naman 660
Gupta, Suneet Kumar 99, 646

Haritha, D. 25
Hebbi, Chandravva 433
Hussain, Talib 148

Jahna Tejaswi, N. 201
Jain, Sambhav 254
Jain, Srishti 112
Jakovljević, Marina Marjanović 362
James, Katherine 545
Jaswanth, B. 25
Joseph, Rabin 562
Joshi, Brijendra Kumar 519
Jyothish Lal, G. 229

Karthik, S. 3
Karur Mudugal Mathad, Rajashekharaiah 254
Kathpal, Sidharth 377
Khan, Mohammad Monirujjaman 646
Khinvasara, Chaitanya 410
Kiran Kumar, P. 11, 201
Kommanaboina, Balakrishna 419
Kotecha, Ketan 362
Koul, Anirudh 377
Krishnapriya, G. 463
Kumar, Abhinav 148
Kumar, Arvind 294

Kumar, Nitish   463
Kumar, Parteek   419
Kumar, Purushottam   254
Kumari, Suchi   633
Kushwaha, Riti   660

Long, Xiaotian   448
Lu, Jing   279

Mahammood, Vazeer   599
Mahapatra, Monalisa   660
Maiya, Anirudh   433
Mal, Chanchal   57
Malik, Praveen Kumar   318
Malreddy, Sai Venkat Reddy   193
Malviya, Sangeeta   57
Mamatha, H. R.   433
Mary Shanthi Rani, M.   562
Mate, Rishikesh   179
Mate, Yash   492
Mishra, Aditya   254
Mishra, Piyush   39
Mishra, Vipul Kumar   82
Modi, Aakash Jignesh   229
Mohapatra, Puspanjali   39
Mohnot, Arjun   618
Monika Rani, H. G.   133
Muhuri, Samya   244, 504, 633

Naik, Varsha   179
Narla, Jayanth   193
Neeraj   618, 626

Patel, Margi   519
Patil, Nikita   57
Patra, Tapas Kumar   39
Phanindra Kumar, B.   201
Pingale, Shantanu   57
Poonkodi, P.   3
Prajisha, C.   332
Prakash, Vijay   480
Purohit, Saurabh   599
Pushpalatha, K.   133

Rainchwar, Parth   179
Ranade, Aabha   492
Rao, Akash K.   348
Rao, Bharath Raj Mahadeva   271
Rao, Shreyas Suresh   133, 599

Roehe, Rainer   165
Ross, Robert   529

Sabitha, R.   3
Sahasrabudhe, Chirag   179
Sai Kireeti, CH.   11
Samhitha, Kamma   399
Sangeetha, R.   562
Sankhwar, Shweta   148
Sapna, R.   133
Saurabh, Abhishek   254
Shacham-Diamand, Yosi   419
Sharma, Adarsh   57
Sharma, Anshul   480
Shivaprakash, B.   463
Shobana, M.   3
Singal, Gaurav   660
Singh, Amit Kumar   463
Singh, Dilbag   99
Singh, Prithvi   148
Singh, Priyanka   399, 577
Singh, Shashank Sheshar   305
Singh, Sukhdip   671
Sinha, Nishant   294
Soman, K. P.   229
Sowmya, V.   229
Srihitha, L. L.   201
Srivastava, Divya   305
Subham, P.   39
Subramani, R.   463
Surana, Bhavya   419
Swaroop, N.   25

Telge, Saurav   492
Thakkar, Hiren Kumar   399, 577

Uma, B. R.   463
Uniyal, Swati   599
Uttrani, Shashank   348

Vaishnavi, S.   3
Vara Prasad, T. V. L.   25
Vardaan   254
Varshney, Aditya   82
Vasanthi, M. L.   201
Vasudevan, A. R.   332
Venkataramana, D.   463
Verma, Karun   419
Vidya Yasaswini, B.   11
Vinayakumar, R.   229

Vishnoi, Vineet   318
Vohra, Ishita   348

Walambe, Rahee   362
Wang, Chongwen   448
Wang, Duo   448
Wang, Haiyang   165

Wang, Mengyuan   165
Wattamwar, Soham   179

Yadav, Ashima   318
Yash, Prajjwal   463
Yusuf, Mukhtar Opeyemi   305

Zatale, Aishwarya   123
Zheng, Huiru   165

Printed in the United States
by Baker & Taylor Publisher Services